Business Modeling and Data Mining

Dorian Pyle

MORGAN KAUFMANN PUBLISHERS

AN IMPRINT OF ELSEVIER SCIENCE

AMSTERDAM   BOSTON   LONDON   NEW YORK
OXFORD   PARIS   SAN DIEGO   SAN FRANCISCO
SINGAPORE   SYDNEY   TOKYO

Senior Acquisitions Editor	Lothlórien Homet
Publishing Services Manager	Edward Wade
Production Editor	Howard Severson
Editorial Assistant	Corina Derman
Project Editor	Merrill Peterson/Matrix Productions, Inc.
Cover Design	Ross Carron
Cover Image	"Sextant"copyright David Muir/Masterfile
Text Design	Rebecca Evans & Associates
Composition	Top Graphics
Illustration	Dartmouth Publishing, Inc.
Copyeditor	Toni Zuccarini Ackley
Proofreader	Debra Gates
Indexer	Kay Schlembach
Printer	The Maple-Vail Book Manufacturing Group

Designations used by companies to distinguish their products are often claimed as trademarks or registered trademarks. In all instances in which Morgan Kaufmann Publishers is aware of a claim, the product names appear in initial capital or all capital letters. Readers, however, should contact the appropriate companies for more complete information regarding trademarks and registration.

Morgan Kaufmann Publishers
An imprint of Elsevier Science
340 Pine Street, Sixth Floor
San Francisco, CA 94104-3205
www.mkp.com

Library of Congress Control Number: 2002114338

ISBN: 1-55860-653-X

Dedicated:
To Lynda Marjorie and Thomas Ivan Pyle with love and gratitude,
In loving memory of Marjorie Edith Woodward,
For Fuzzy and Zeus, loving and faithful companions,
And always to my beloved Pat.

Contents

Part II Business Modeling

Chapter 4
What Is a Model? 91

Part III Data Mining

■■■ **Chapter 11**

Getting the Initial Model: Basic Practices of Data Mining 361

■■■ **Chapter 12**

Improving the Mined Model 427

Part IV Methodology

▦ ▦ ▦ Chapter 14
Methodology 533

▦ ▦ ▦ MII
Modeling Methodology   545

▦ ▦ ▦ MIII
Mining Methodology   571

Resources   665

Index   673

Preface

Following a seminar presentation, a member of the audience approached me to follow up on a point I had addressed. He explained that he worked in a bank, and also taught a graduate-level data mining course. He asked if I had any advice about how to turn the business description of a problem into a form that could be answered with data mining and data. Indeed, several other people in the same group asked the same question. Since then, I have been asked what is essentially the same question many times and in many places ranging from email discussions to audience questions at academic conferences to business tutorial presentations to individuals engaged in trying to discover how to mine their data. It has become obvious that this is a pressing topic: *How can real world business problems be formulated so that data mining can answer them?* But beyond that is an even more fundamental question: *What problems can data mining usefully address—and how?*

Discovering those areas to which data mining can be applied most effectively, and then translating business problems into a form that can be addressed by data mining and modeling, is very similar to a problem that faces almost everyone studying algebra for the first time—the dreaded *word problems*. How do you turn a statement in words into what is essentially a mathematical formula? In a sense, this book is a long answer to those questions—how to use, where to fit, and how to get the most value out of mining and modeling in strategic and tactical business applications.

What This Book Is About

The core objective of this book is to help the miner or modeler construct and refine mineable models that are useful in business situations. To be sure, there are a lot of different ways of constructing models other than using data mining, and there is a huge variety of different models—more than can be constructed using data mining. However, when data mining is used to solve problems in business situations, a new model is constructed or an existing model is clarified. In this book, you will find a practical, workable, useable approach to getting the best results from mining data, as well as enough theory as is necessary to provide practical, applicable, and useable answers.

Models are an integral part of human life. The models used in data mining are the structures of human knowledge. Whether we realize it or not, all of our knowledge of the world—personal, social, business, scientific, political, emotional, whatever its form—can be structured as a model. We use many tools to change, adjust, or clarify our knowledge—our models of the world. Data mining is just one tool, although an unusual and somewhat unfamiliar one because it is an automated process. These models lie close to the process that we call "thinking," and we are quite unused to the idea that any part of the process of thinking can be automated. Indeed, modern technologies are so challenging to our concepts of what constitutes thinking that they begin to redefine the nature of thought.

However threatening these tools may appear to us at a fundamental level, they are nevertheless extremely useful in an increasingly complex world. Essentially, what all people are trying to accomplish is to improve our directed and intentional control of specific worldly events to achieve ends that are perceived as beneficial. Our underlying assumption is that if we have a better understanding of the nature of and relationship between cause and effect, and can exercise some degree of control over the cause, we can influence the outcome.

This book, then, interweaves two main themes—mining and models. Earlier in this preface I drew an analogy with algebra, which is itself a model. It is a tool that can be used to manipulate symbolic representations in ways that give valid answers. For the unpracticed, it is difficult to translate problems represented in one domain (the word problem) into another domain (the formal symbols of algebra). Fortunately for data mining for business models, all of us start with an intuitive knowledge of the types of models that are discussed in this book, so they are more easily understood than algebraic models. Nonetheless, in order to interweave the two themes of mining and modeling we have to sketch an outline of what these models of knowledge are and how to use them practically.

We don't often look at models as objects in themselves or at how to construct and use them. Yet understanding the range of appropriate models to use in different situations forms the basic "language" that a data miner uses to express the result of mining. But models are not just the result of mining, the "output" as it were. Very often, the miner has to construct a model of a business situation before mining begins. The premining model is used to define where uncertainties are in a situation, to determine where mining can offer the most value, and to discover what data needs to be appropriately mined to discover an answer. Other premodels may define how the data needs to be enhanced or enriched, or they may help determine what features can be usefully extracted. In fact, mining takes place in a realm almost entirely populated by various types of models.

Because models are so important to miners, and to the process of mining for answers to business situations, this book takes both a general look at what models are and how we use them to describe the world, and a more detailed look at particular models that are important in mining.

Data mining and modeling are general-purpose techniques that can be applied to a wide range of problems. The techniques described here can be, and indeed have been, applied across a very broad domain; however, where data mining is principally being applied today is in discovering business opportunities and solving business problems. Because of the current interest in discovering opportunities and solving business problems, the examples used in this book are drawn mainly from the world of business. The choice of business-focused examples is deliberate, although the methods and techniques themselves are just as applicable to, say, bioinformatics or industrial automation. Although the examples from those areas are not so plentiful, you should still find much that is useful, valuable, and interesting.

Data mining is currently used in business as a tactical tool. Clearly it has much value to offer at a tactical level; however, the core business processes take place at a strategic level, and it is the strategic use of data mining that promises the greatest return for a company. Therefore, after setting the framework for mining and for using models, the book looks at using mining both for and within models at all levels within an enterprise, from tactical on up through to the core strategic levels.

So far I have discussed what the book is about. To provide a different perspective, it will help to draw a contrast with what the book is not about. Many books about data mining focus on the details of algorithms and how to manipulate them and the data to some advantage. You will find very little here about algorithms. The topic is covered briefly as different types of models predispose the miner to use different tools. Books that primarily discuss algorithms assume that you already understand the framework in which the problem exists. They also assume that you know how the data relates to the problem at hand, how the data should be manipulated to produce the desired outcome, why the data is thought to address the problem, how the mined model fits into the business environment, and so on. Those are the very assumptions that this book does not make. In fact, it is those specific problems that the book addresses. It addresses directly how to approach, how to think about, and how to structure the surrounding issues to achieve the best results from your mining efforts.

This book covers all of the topics of concern to a modeler and a miner. It covers the methodologies of modeling business situations, as well as the methodologies for mining data, and ties the two together. But that is not enough in itself to equip a modeler and miner in a real world situation, so the book also covers the practical needs of how to identify problems, how to get grassroots and management support for projects, how to identify and quantify business benefits for a project, how to select the right tools to achieve the benefits, and how to construct and refine useful models in every step of the modeling and mining process—except for specific business knowledge in a specific situation. For that, you the reader will have to apply the techniques covered here to discover and uncover what you need in your own specific situation.

Who This Book Is For

If you are computer savvy and work with data to make informed decisions, this book is for you. It provides a framework in which to structure your efforts, and to understand how and where to apply them. It explains how to use models to rationally frame a decision, and when and where mining is the appropriate tool to provide information pertaining to the decision. Although there is much in this book that will help any data-based decision making (perhaps even any sort of decision making!), in truth the assumption of who the book is primarily aimed at is more tightly drawn. I offer the following brief character sketches and scenarios to help clarify who will benefit from reading this book:

- "Anne" works with data every day, supplying other departments with requested data and data summaries. Her boss read some articles about data mining and told her to find out more about it, and ultimately to build models that will help the departments that they supply with data. She knows nothing about data mining and just as much about modeling. *This book is for her.*

- "Barry" is a business analyst. He has worked with the newly created data warehouse—a work in progress more than a completed venture—and has generated some reports. He knows about modeling business situations and something about generating business reports from data. He wants to go beyond the simple statistical reports that he has been using and has heard of data mining; however, what he has learned so far is that 1) data mining has business application and 2) data mining uses several sophisticated algorithms. Barry is looking to discover how the application of algorithms to data can be used practically to solve business problems. *This book is for him.*

- "Catherine" is a financial analyst for her company. Her MBA included several courses in statistics, and she feels very comfortable with the statistical interpretation of her data. As a senior analyst, she has been called in to support the management team in determining the strategic direction for the company. It is clear to her that more is needed than simply providing detailed financial reports, even if they do include several "what if" scenarios. There is plenty of data available, and as the most statistically aware member of the management team's advisory group, she is expected to use this data to inform and enlighten the situation. Although she feels at home with her financial data, she has not worked with non-financial data in setting up and solving business problems. *This book is for her.*

- "David," a senior middle manager, has been espousing the potential business advantages of Customer Relationship Management in his organization. Senior management has asked David to show them how the company's performance can be improved by adopting such a model, the potential pitfalls and difficulties, and how they can incorporate what they already know into this new approach. *This book is for him.*

- "Elizabeth" has been responsible for implementing the company's data warehouse. After much effort, struggle, and disruption, the project to establish at least the beginnings of a useful warehouse is nearing completion. In addition to the warehouse itself, an online analytical processing (OLAP) tool was proposed as the primary means to access the warehouse. Various managers have expressed surprise to Elizabeth that after the huge investment in time, effort, and money, the business intelligence delivered from the project does not seem to meet their expectations. She has been asked to investigate how to improve the creation and generation of business intelligence from this corporate data repository. *This book is for her.*

- "Fred" is a data miner and analyst, having completed several courses in data mining that taught him all about various algorithms and how to apply them to data. This complemented his existing knowledge of statistical analysis, and after the courses, he felt well equipped to tackle problems. Several managers, keen to see what the new tools could deliver, pressed their data on Fred to see what insights he could provide. So far the results, although Fred has been pleased with them technically, have not impressed his customers, the managers. Fred has been asked to determine whether the value of the business intelligence delivered can be improved. *This book is for him.*

- "Gillian" graduated with a degree in sociology before joining her company. Although not working in that field, she learned much about creating and interpreting models of situations, looking at interventions, and evaluating results. As a manager, she feels that these tools and techniques must be applicable to improving the efficiency, organization, and satisfaction of her business operation. However, defining the most appropriate problems and using the data that she has available as well, is difficult. Somehow, her attempts to firmly grasp the problems she sees and produce convincing results to present to other managers have produced less tangible results than expected. Gillian is looking for some method to define the business problems she sees and ways to deliver improvements. *This book is for her.*

■ "Harry" understands both quantitative and qualitative modeling. He has identified a wealth of business problems to address—too many in fact. The number of options open to him are too many to come to grips with, and those he has addressed have had unexpected consequences. He needs some way of organizing and evaluating these problems and dealing with them in a satisfactory way. *This book is for him.*

■ "Inga" has been working with data mining for some time, mainly for the marketing department. So far, her assignments have consisted of an endless round of customer profiling and market segmentation for the company's solicitation, stimulation, and retention programs. She knows that the power of the tools she is using can be used to better advantage for the company, and has convinced her manager to give her the opportunity to show what can be done. However, finding the best place to start is proving more difficult than she expected. *This book is for her.*

All of the people and scenarios represented are based on real people and situations I encountered in modeling and mining engagements. These people face a number of different problems, but they all have something in common: They all are being asked to set up (or discover) business opportunities and problems and propose effective solutions, justified by data. Some have more familiarity with parts of the process than others, but all of them are being asked to expand their view of the situation to encompass areas that they have not looked at before.

They all face one basic problem: how to discover the best course of action. Their problem is to explore the situation and circumstances so that the tools and techniques can be best applied to the data to derive results that can be used to improve the situation. The components of this problem are:

1. Their present insight, understanding, and knowledge
2. The situation and circumstances
3. Tools to evaluate the situation and circumstances
4. Data that might be relevant
5. Tools to evaluate this data
6. Techniques of applying the tools
7. How to discover the right problem

Of course, until the right problem has been discovered (7), the first six parts cannot be used appropriately. This book provides the framework and guidance to tie all of these parts together into a coherent whole. In this book, that process is called *modeling*.

For better or worse, the current state of the technology has made a division of labor between the discoverers of information and the decision makers. A growing number of people in business organizations, either internally or externally, have the task of applying data mining techniques to data, the results of which are going to be used by decision makers who do not themselves either mine or model. It is in part this division that has placed data mining in the tactical realm rather than the strategic. It is, for example, fairly easy for a marketing manager to delegate the discovery of a new market segment to the "data mining group" or the "quantitative analysis group." It is more difficult for that same marketing manager to see that data mining has any role in discovering new products or totally new directions that the company should pursue. Again, corporate accountants may well consider that data mining can detect fraudulent transactions, but find it hard to see a role for mining in the corporate allocation of resources or the structuring of personnel policies. Indeed, unless the miner is directly involved in the managerial chain, it is very difficult for the miner to formulate strategic problems in a way that allows mining to add insight. But both mining and modeling have an integral and important role to play at all levels, including that of core corporate strategy.

In order to make that leap from the tactical to the strategic, the miner and modeler, whether employee or contractor, has to act in the role of consultant. It is for this growing group of internal or external "consultants" that the book is primarily written. It will provide you with the framework to translate the problem as expressed by the problem holder into a structure that mining or modeling can address to return the desired results. Naturally, there is also much here for the computer and data savvy manager, because the frameworks described here ultimately can be used and implemented by corporate management.

How This Book Is Structured

Describing how to begin the modeling process requires weaving understanding out of several threads. Looking at a pattern in cloth requires looking at all of the threads in the cloth as a whole. However, the cloth itself has to be woven one thread at a time; so too with the explanation of mining for models. Rather than a single thread of explanation, multiple threads have to be woven together to create the final pattern. So what then are these threads—the themes—to be woven together?

Surprisingly, one of the threads is *understanding what we already know*. What we bring in the form of existing knowledge and insight, prejudice, bias, desires, hopes, fears, aspirations, and so on affect very directly what we see. To an enormous extent, what we already know determines what we can know. In fact, this is such an important, although not immediately intuitive, thread, that the opening sections take some pains to at least introduce the area in more detail.

Another thread is *the process of solving problems*. As used here, the term *problem* is meant only to convey the difficulty in finding an appropriate course, or courses, of potential action. In other words, the problem is to discover what we could do to achieve particular desired ends. In this sense, the term *problem* also covers business opportunity discovery, as in "The problem is to find the best opportunity to pursue." As we will see, there is never only one course of action possible, and the other explanatory threads woven into the fabric attempt to discover which course of action should be preferred. Although it may seem that discovering the courses of action available is trivial, in practice it can sometimes be extremely difficult.

Another thread involves *characterizing a situation* in terms of our feelings about what matters and how things work together. A more formal description of this is qualitative modeling, but the essence is simpler than the formidable name seems to imply. What we intuit, think, feel, and emote are very important in dealing with business situations. How often is something done because it is the president's pet project? How often is a project ignored because it simply feels wrong, or because "That's not the way we do things here?" Or again, the "chiefs" often miss what is intuitively obvious to the "Indians." Simply ranking potential solutions and crunching numbers to find solutions doesn't always work—perhaps it never works. The tapestry of modeling needs a place to rationally incorporate this thread. It is along this thread that the model will integrate and evaluate this "soft" information.

Of course, *data mining* has to have thread of its own. Data mining, however, is simply a recent extension of quantitative modeling tools, mainly mathematical and statistical tools. Much, although by no means all, of what is introduced along this thread is applicable to quantitative methods in general. However, data mining has its own particular techniques that are different from other quantitative methods. But whatever quantitative methods are used, this is only a thread in the tapestry. It has to be incorporated with the other threads on an equal footing. In many business modeling situations, quantitative data may not be available or needed; however, this book looks at those places where quantitative data is available and usefully included. Thus, the incorporation of data in a quantitative way is a result of the focus of this book, not actually a requirement in all cases.

These threads are present to a greater or lesser degree throughout every part of the book. For ease of explanation, some threads move more to the foreground from time to time than other threads. However, this change of focus is only for ease of explanation. Just as a cloth is made from all of its threads, so too is the explanation of mining and modeling. No one is more important than another, and all are required to complete the pattern.

These threads are, of course, multiple themes present throughout the book—a sort of intertwining of the narrative explanations of the different themes. However, explanations of how things work are hard to put into practice. A final thread is *practical application,* explaining how you can actually build appropriate models and mine specific data to inform these models. You need instructions to be as specific as possible. When the groundwork is laid—in other words, when the general shape of the cloth is apparent—this thread springs to prominence and reveals the things that you should be thinking about, how to identify who you need to talk to, what questions you should ask, and how to ask those questions. It also tells you how to clarify concepts and impressions, identify tools for creating maps of a situation, interpret and present those maps, and interactively improve the maps. Of course, this thread also discusses how to find data, what to do with it, how to model it, and so on, so this thread deals with what to do, but its details have to wait until the groundwork of "why" is laid.

This book draws a clear distinction between the miner and the modeler. In this book, the *modeler* is always concerned with business issues—with structuring the business problem or opportunity, with the business processes, with the business issues of data, with the application of the model to the appropriate business process, with connecting to the stakeholders, with deriving business value, and with return on the resources invested. After the business framework has been discovered, the *miner* is concerned with mining data—with data quality, tool selection, appropriate technique, relationship discovery, levels of confidence, and model clarity. As depicted here, these are two separate roles, and although there is some crossover between them, for the purposes of explanation and discussion they are separated as much as possible. Nonetheless, it's most likely that in many projects the same person will fill both roles. However, the issues, concerns, and activities are different for each role, and even if embodied in the same person, understanding separation of roles will help you accomplish your project.

Part I looks at the forest across its broadest sweep. It provides what may seem like general, introductory material, and indeed it is. As a result of reading this part, neither miner nor modeler will generate a list of actions, or even learn any particular techniques for mining or modeling. So why is it here? In addition to introducing the landscape of modeling and mining, it provides an environment, or approach, that a modeler *must* keep in mind, or risk being tricked and trapped. A modeler is a detective seeking clues, avoiding false assumptions, ignoring the unimportant, and finding the thread of explanation. For a detective, whether fictional or real, the application of logic seldom leads to such simple insights as "Colonel Mustard in the library with a dagger." For the modeler, too, the path to discovery is seldom clearly signposted, nor is it obvious.

Part I shows what a modeler should be thinking about to build successful models. It sets the stage for the more detailed exploration that follows. Included here is an introduction discussing what it means to make a model. Here, too, is a look at the way the model represents the real world, and ways in which models interact with their environment. Also in this part is a high-level introduction to the apparently new activity of data mining. It turns out that data mining is an extension of a human mental activity that has existed for as long as there have been humans. In a sense, data mining may seem to infringe on an activity that has previously been regarded as essentially human, but as we will see, although it extends our reach, it is still entirely up to us to grasp. Part I ends with a brief introduction to framing problems in ways useful to the techniques of modeling and mining. Taken together, this is an intentionally brief introduction that merely skims the surface of what are very deep waters. However, it provides a necessary introduction to, and framework for, understanding the material that follows.

Part II provides a comprehensive look at how to model a business situation. The essence of business modeling is to create a structure that, at lowest cost and with lowest risk, returns the most advantageous gains and engenders enthusiastic support from all the stakeholders. Achieving the design to accomplish exactly this is the essence of Part II.

Part III presents a detailed look at mining data. Data mining, in a business context, is the art of finding, assembling, and preparing data and then applying tools and techniques to that data so that it reveals the insights and relationships necessary to accomplish the goals of the business model as well as the data and business conditions permit.

As comprehensive and useful as the explanations, illustrations, and examples in Parts I through III are, it's Part IV that is a crucial part of the book. Part IV provides two complementary and comprehensive methodologies that will take any modeler and miner step-by-step through all of the stages of creating business models and mining data.

The methodology developed in this book is comprehensive in that it will never leave you wondering what to do next at any stage. From the project start until completion, the methodology presents a sequence of detailed steps for any modeler and miner to follow.

Special Features

The comprehensive Catalyst modeling and mining methodologies developed throughout this book were conceived as a hypertext document. What you, as modeler and miner, need to do at any particular stage depends on what you have discovered up to that point. No two projects are identical, and the problems, options, and situations that you discover will determine what you need to do next. Thus, your exact path through the actions, choices, tests, and techniques will be different for each project. The methodologies are intended as interactive documents, something that you will use as a guide to get insight and advice appropriate to whatever modeling or mining situation you find yourself in—and they refer back to the appropriate sections of this book for greater detail. An interactive version of the methodologies is available for download from the author's Web site *(www.modelandmine.com)*. In addition, the Web site contains a great deal of other resource material to support this book including data sets, worked examples, demonstrations, and tools, many of which are discussed in the book.

A Note on the Use of Terminology

Use of the term "data" is interesting. Etymologically one use of the term "data" is as the plural form of "datum"—both originally from Latin roots. The terms "datum" and "data" (as the plural of datum) were first used in this context in English in 1646 (according to the Oxford English Dictionary).

Historically (rather than etymologically) these terms were used rather loosely at first, and later grew in use with the increase in data collection for the body of knowledge then known as "Natural Philosophy" which later has become known today as the (mainly) physical sciences. Within the academic areas of the physical sciences, which for much of its history had—by today's standards—very little data, the use of "datum" as singular and "data" as a plural construction, has continued. Thus scientists tend to use the terminology "data are . . ."

In 1899, with the embryonic stirrings of the areas of endeavor that have become known collectively as "data processing," the term "data" was first used as a collective noun, thus plural form with a singular construction. Subsequently, in all of the areas of expertise that have roots in the disciplines that come from data processing rather than from Natural Philosophy, "data" is used in its plural form with a singular construction. This has been the accepted usage in these areas for over a century. Thus computer scientists tend to use the terminology "data is . . ."

Data mining grew very largely, although by no means exclusively, from data processing roots and accepted usage of the term "data" is as a collective noun (thus a plural form with a singular construction). Thus the "correct" usage for this term is a matter of which community the user comes from.

The author during professional education and training grew up with the usage that "data is," and it is that grammatical construction that is used in all of the author's writings, including this book.

Acknowledgements

I have to thank my clients, anonymous though they remain in this book, for allowing me the opportunity to both teach and, most especially, learn while working with them on their business modeling and data mining projects. It is entirely from the experience of working on a wide array of projects, in many different business areas and industries, that such knowledge as is described in this book is pulled together.

To my dearly beloved wife Pat, who has worked on this book and is much responsible for clarifying many rather murky parts of the original manuscript, and who is also the Webmaster for the Web site that supports this book, I simply cannot express my gratitude sufficiently. This has turned out to be as much her project as mine.

My friends and colleagues Tom Breur, Marcelo Ferreyra, Elena Irina Neaga, and Ralphe Wiggins read the manuscript and made useful suggestions that improved the final book. And I have to particularly thank my editors at Morgan Kaufmann, Dianne Cerra, who through business circumstances fortunate for her was not able to see the manuscript through to publication as its editor, and Lothlórien Homet, who picked up the project in the middle. My thanks for your patience and help in bringing this book, eventually, into being.

Part I
A Map of the Territory

This book is in part a detailed map of how to construct models of business situations in general, although it focuses on those particular business models that can usefully be explored, informed, clarified, and applied using the computationally intensive analytic techniques known collectively as data mining. Discovering opportunities or solving problems is the usual rationale for modeling a business situation; however, none of the components of the situation exist in a vacuum—they all carry a considerable load of baggage with them.

It is quite possible to dive straight into detailed descriptions of the tools and techniques for developing, exploring, outlining, clarifying, and constructing models of business situations without preamble. It's also possible to get straight down to the "brass tacks" of data mining without looking at any of the surrounding issues or caveats. However, doing so ignores an enormous amount of potentially useful knowledge. Immediately looking at tools and techniques leaves out entirely any idea of the general sense of what it means to be immersed in the live situation: what sort of thoughts and approaches are generally worthwhile; what assumptions might lurk unnoticed until too late; what kind of thought process the modeler or miner may need to follow, explore, or exercise with caution. In other words, what diving into techniques and tools misses is a look at the broader sweep of the actual process of modeling business situations, mining data to clarify the models, and carrying the inferences from the clarified models back into a practical and applicable response to the business problem that produced the effort and activity in the first place. This first part of the book takes a broad look at what it means to model a business situation and what it means to mine data.

If this first part of the book succeeds in its intent, the reader will not come away knowing what to do to model and mine business situations, but rather what to think about, what to beware of, and how to approach the process of modeling a business situation and mining data. The other three parts fill in the details—the methods and methodology needed to model and mine in a business setting. Part I provides the context within which modeling and mining take place. This is the view of the forest, whereas later parts are concerned with the metaphorical trees.

Chapter 1
The World, Knowledge, and Models

Humans have a driving passion to control the world, and indeed, we do understand and control it in ways far beyond the abilities of any other animal. Not only do we understand how to affect the flow of worldly events to produce desired outcomes, but also we can create representations of the world, allowing us to understand and manipulate worldly events in ways that effect control. Furthermore, humans possess a perhaps unique ability to detect patterns, both simple and complex, that occur in the natural flow and change of events. The patterns come in a variety of types, and by symbolizing those patterns and the interactions between them, we can represent the natural systems of the world and produce systems of our own to interact with, affect, and influence the undirected course of nature.

There are many patterns in nature. Some are repetitive: the sun comes up every day and after awhile goes down again on the other side of the sky. Sometimes we see a pattern in change: the day is not the same length, but gets longer and shorter as the seasons roll around. Some patterns are not repetitive but are recognizable as similar to previous examples of the same pattern: thunderstorms happen from time to time but generally have varying occurrences of cloud, wind, rain, thunder, and lightning. Patterns in human behavior, to some extent at least, can help predict how people will react to certain events. Patterns occur in social activity, in animal behavior, in the physics and chemistry of the world, in our mental and emotional life, in fact in every aspect of the world that humans perceive. Symbolizing these patterns with words and numbers enables us to describe these patterns and their behavior as symbolic objects. Associating these object symbols with each other in various ways represents our understanding of the behavior of the world.

It is the structures of these interlocking symbols representing worldly patterns that are called *models*. These symbolic models are one focus of this book, because understanding symbolic relationships allows controlling behavior to be extended from the model to the world; however, having the ability to control leads to the need (and the ability) to decide what actions to take to influence the otherwise uncontrolled flow of events. So extracting appropriate symbols, and understanding their relationships to each other and the world, are intimately intertwined with our ability to make decisions.

Much of the effort of humans through the course of history has been devoted to discovering useable patterns to construct various types of useful models. Data mining is simply the latest in a long line of tools for detecting meaningful patterns and, ultimately, improving control of the world. On a fundamental level, it is no more, nor less, than the automated search for patterns in data sets.

To be useful, discovered patterns are assembled into integrated structures that thereby embrace our knowledge of the world. Data miners and modelers work every day with knowledge structures. They are built from and modified by the events, objects, and features that are their fundamental connection to the real world. New knowledge and insight changes the structure of existing models—that is the whole purpose of mining and modeling. So understanding how such knowledge structures are created, and understanding their properties and how and why they resist change, embrace change, or at least deal with change, are also fundamental to mining for models. This chapter introduces all of these important issues. The introduction is necessarily brief, but the ideas presented provide part of the underlying foundation on which all else is built.

1.1 **The Nature of the World**

The world we experience is an artificial creation. It is manufactured inside our heads, and much of what we experience results from our existing knowledge or experiences. Yet there is an undeniable impression that the world is actually "out there" and that it has a continuing reality that is quite independent of our sensory impressions. Nonetheless, and quite in spite of the "out thereness" of the impression of reality, it is still a construct of our minds—even if the construct is built from commonly experienced sensory events.

Take a very simple example, a rainbow. It is an indubitably real phenomenon that most humans experience as quite independent of our impression of it—unless we are blind, in which case the rainbow has a very different form of reality. In the case of a seen rainbow, we experience the phenomenon as a real object of the physical world. A blind person experiences the same rainbow as an indirectly expressed artifact, a sort of socially created object that may exist as a phenomenon, but relies for reality on the veracity of other speakers. Nonphysical objects, such as the local city government or the size of the national debt, also cross our perception. However real such nonphysical objects may be, and however directly they affect our lives, they are more obviously constructs. To understand either local city government or the national debt as constructed objects requires us to be cognizant of the entire cultural, financial, political, and social framework within which such objects have meaningful existence. Regardless of the phenomenon experienced, all we really have is a knowledge of the constructs applied to incoming sense impressions that enable us to make sense of the world.

These may seem very deep and even somewhat recherché philosophical points. Why is this important to data miners and modelers? In fact, is it important in any practical sense at all? The fact is that all models are constructed from the events and objects that are introduced here. Ultimately, all of modeling and data creation are founded on the issues raised in the following discussion because they form the foundation of our perception and understanding of the world. Thus, all of the types of models that data mining deals with—symbolic models—are created from and modified by these elements.

The world is a place of infinite complexity and wonder, so much so that it defies human comprehension. The best that we can do is to extract and describe simplifications, organizing and sorting sense impressions so habitually that they seem mundane and ordinary. Indeed, without such simplification, we wouldn't be able to function at all. Some of the simplifications we describe as objects—trees and flowers, breakfast and blue, love and speed. Other simplifications indicate the ways in which the objects relate to each other, such as acceleration and attraction, war and malignity.

However, the world is not in its total and unimaginable reality limited by our everyday conceptions. Pursuing inquiry at the limits of everyday experience reveals new effects and phenomena. Discovering these new objects and interrelations leads to all kinds of changes in our relationship with the world. Eyeglasses and lasers, automobiles and nanotechnology, chemistry and the human genome project, beer and burgers. All of these objects, and a vast array more, were developed by exploring beyond the edges of everyday experience: it is the objective of data mining to facilitate the continuing exploration a little further. This book, however, focuses its attention on the realm of business.

Business is an enormous and interlocking knowledge structure, itself of enormous complexity. It exists as a realm in itself, although tightly coupled to every other facet of human life and experience. It is a world of customers, development, marketing, inventory, complaints, profit, returns, and many other specialized events, objects, and relationships. In order to discuss the use of data mining and modeling productively in a business setting, it is important to define explicitly much of the assumed knowledge that we normally take for granted. So although much of the discussion in this section may seem obvious, it lays important groundwork for what follows in later sections and chapters. It may also lead you to think about the everyday minutiae and events of life from a slightly different perspective. It is an introduction to the perspective needed for successful mining and modeling—covering events, objects, perception, data, and structures—for these are the foundation on which knowledge is built.

1.1.1   Events

An event seems to be very straightforward: Something happens. However, as simple as the beginning is, a lot follows. Events happen in the world all the time, and every one is in some sense observed. A human may not observe it, but it is nonetheless observed by the universe as a whole. If a rock falls on the far side of the moon there is, at least at the time of this writing, no human observing such an event. In falling, however, the rock must at some point strike other rocks. Those rocks are affected in some way. Perhaps a few molecules of the surface are knocked off, or the center of gravity of the moon moves infinitesimally. Whatever happens, things are not the same afterward as before, although, for falling moon rocks, the difference is minute and almost certainly undetectable by humans. But this hypothetical event, if it happens, leaves a permanent trace of its occurrence. That is the definition of an *event*—a change in the state of the universe. The change may be infinitesimally small, but every event has its effect. Indeed, some scientists estimate that changing the position of a single electron (a very small mass) by its own diameter (an incredibly minute distance) at the farthest reaches of the observable universe (an incredibly large distance) would change the ultimate trajectory of the break of a rack of billiard balls! That is to say that this miniscule change in the state of the universe is enough so that as the billiard balls bounce around, recoiling from the cushions and from each other, at some point the miniscule change makes the path of the balls different from what it would be without the change. If true, this remarkable effect shows how everything in the universe is connected quite intimately.

Both the rock on the moon and the billiard balls illustrate a problem in discussing events: it is impossible to discuss or define an event without reference to something else. Things only happen when they change their relationship to other things. This means that every event can be expressed only relative to some surrounding framework. Very often, the framework is implicit or assumed. The rock on the moon fell, but the falling is taken to be relative to the center of the moon. In just the same way, all events are relative.

The relativity of events within their framework can be very important in both models and data mining. In reporting any event, there comes with it a whole baggage of assumptions. Many business events are represented as transactions—goods are exchanged for value received. But these transactions are carried on within an enormous cultural framework that gives the transactions validity. So ingrained is this cultural framework that it, and its concomitant assumptions, may be almost invisible to our conscious mind. Yet in many models and mining applications, awareness of the surrounding framework is important. Just as in any other sphere, events may cause culture shock if the assumed framework does not match reality. As discussed in just a moment, this framework of "knowledge" is so powerful that it can define what we see. More importantly, it can actually prevent us from seeing other real events.

1.1.2 Objects

If an event is something happening, an *object* is a thing to which the something happens. In the moon rock example, falling is the event and a rock is the object. Simple and straightforward, but as with events, there are complexities involved with objects, too.

Any object consists of some intuitive definition. There is some minimum set of ideas, feelings, associations, or features about a rock without which a rock is no longer defined. For instance, there is a particular range of hardness associated with a rock. Within the normal range of everyday conditions, rocks have an essential set of properties that establishes them as either rocks or not rocks. The true state of the world, however, is not so easily determined. Some rocks are so soft they are fluids that flow. Now our rock definition needs modifying either to include lava or to decide that lava is some other sort of object. Or again, rock is denser than water, and clearly it will always sink in water. Except for pumice! Pumice is a sort of cooled, frothy lava that has so many gas bubbles trapped inside its structure that it floats. Is pumice a rock? Is it some other sort of object? Really, the definition of rock as including or excluding lava and pumice depends on the frame of reference—and on the needs of the occasion.

Once again, this can seem like a purely philosophical point, but it has important practical consequences. Fortunately, in looking at just the practical consequences for both mining and modeling, the importance of the philosophical debate can be largely set aside without requiring the point to be settled. Whatever it is that any particular simplification of real world phenomena encompasses, it can be regarded as a collection of features. These features form an appreciable matrix—a summation of impressions—that can be taken to indicate the presence of the specified object. For mining and modeling, the state of the features are taken as the defining characteristics of an object without any need to further consider the "true" underlying nature of the object itself. It makes little difference then, whether pumice is "really" rock or not. If, for some particular purpose it is convenient or useful to class pumice as rock, so be it. If, on the other hand, it is convenient to define it otherwise, that too is just fine. Its "real and essential nature" can then be left to philosophical inquiry, not the realm of mining and modeling discussed here.

Nonetheless, defining objects can seem important. In structuring one business model it took over two weeks of hard work just to approach a definition of a customer. The difficulty was quite simply that the framework being used initially was very rigid, yet many of those involved wanted to arrive at a fundamental understanding of the "real" definition of a customer. (Such frameworks, as will be discussed shortly, can be remarkably restrictive about what they allow to be "seen.") Adding flexibility to the framework to allow for several definitions of "customer" took considerable effort.

1.1.3 Perception

Perception is regulated and enforced by the mental models of reality that we have created. The terms *regulated* and *enforced* may seem overly restrictive, but they are completely warranted. Such models actually create our perceived reality and determine what we can understand. Is it really as restrictive to our understanding as presented here? Surely, if the facts are presented, we can see the obvious.

In April 1986, during the early morning in a power plant not far from the major metropolitan area of Kiev, the plant engineers in the Unit 4 reactor in the Chernobyl power plant were running a test. During this test, as all the world now knows, things began to go disastrously wrong. Even as the nuclear reaction was getting totally out of hand, although the disaster had not actually occurred, the engineers "knowing" what was happening continued with the test. They "knew" that the reactor was completely safe, that the core couldn't melt, and that it was quite impossible for it to blow up. What they "knew" was actually completely wrong. Eventually, the reactor core melted and the core did blow up. However, even with the full scale of the disaster laid out before them, the engineers still "knew" that this could not possibly happen. They "knew" that the design of the reactor was such that even if a meltdown occurred, it was impossible for the core to blow up.

The engineers in the control room looked at the reactor instrumentation. The reactor building and the fire that resulted from the meltdown were not in their direct view from the control room. However, it eventually became obvious to them from their instrumentation that something was wrong with the reactor. But they "knew" that it couldn't possibly have blown up. They looked outside to see what had happened. Thick on the ground was a layer of black graphite from the reactor core—all of it fearsomely radioactive. Dyatlov, the engineer who saw the black graphite on the ground, could not accept that what he saw was graphite from the reactor because he knew that for it to be core graphite was impossible. This same engineer also had looked into the turbine room where he saw the glowing chunks of fuel and graphite. Although his eyes registered their physical presence, he couldn't actually see them for what they were. Even in this deadly situation, what he knew to be true prevented him from seeing what was actually there. It was literally inconceivable to him that what he looked at was what it actually was. Because their knowledge of what was true prevented them from seeing, even Amokov, the chief engineer on the shift, continued to assure everyone that the reactor was safe.

Perception is very much regulated and enforced by the existing knowledge that frames any situation. Such is the power of these frameworks that humans have to work very hard indeed to escape from the constraints of perception. Inability to escape from the constraints of preconceptions brought the world a monumental nuclear disaster, and doomed the engineers. The problem is all the more difficult as such frameworks are established because they work and are, in fact, indispensable for functioning in everyday life. It is nevertheless sometimes necessary to make a concerted effort to become consciously aware of the constraints imposed by our perceptual framework. Doing so literally allows a new view of reality. People with one perceptual frame literally see the world differently than people having a different perceptual frame.

As much as this is true in nuclear engineering, so too is it true in all aspects of life, most particularly in business. Viewing business from a different perceptual framework totally changes observations. More than that, it changes what *can* be seen, that is, what it is possible to see. In the days when all stores employed people who waited on their customers from behind a counter, it was almost impossible to see that placing all of the stock on shelves and letting customers help themselves could work. Until presented as a fait accompli, it was regarded as both ridiculous and impossible, and in any case, not something that any customer would want. But when tried, it worked—and in working it forced a change in the perceptual framework so that almost anyone from a western country regards such a system as usual and obvious. But it took the inventor of the method much courage to try to fly in the face of accepted wisdom. Contrary to the old saw "It ain't what you know that hurts you, it's what you know that ain't so," the truth is that it might be both!

Perception is the way that we view the world, whatever its limitations. Perceptions are built out of events that happen to the features of objects and are given meaning by reference to a framework of existing knowledge. The internal recording of these phenomena create and adjust the internal perceptual framework so that what we know constantly changes, and constantly changes what we can know.

1.1.4   Data

Data starts simply, with the recording of events or states of features of objects; however, not all of the events in the universe can be recorded, so some selectivity has to be applied. Data records what the current knowledge framework defines as useful or potentially meaningful events. The selection of events to record is an absolutely unavoidable process but, of a necessity, more is missed than is kept. So data does not represent the record of undifferentiated events that represent the world; recorded data is filtered through perceptions of what constitutes reality. Again, this seems to be purely a philosophical issue, but it does have practical consequences.

It may appear that a governmental or corporate entity records data about everything in sight. Perhaps (at least as a goal) it tries to. But recall that, even if there were no other constraint, what in reality is in sight depends entirely upon the viewer's frame of reference. There are also, of course, practical constraints on recording data. Limitations on time, available effort, and quantity of recording media require restricting what is collected generally to what is considered "useful." In this context, useful usually means that it is in accord with advancing the aims of the current framework model.

None of these strictures on collecting and storing data imply that there is anything wrong, bad, or inadequate about the imposed selectivity. However, miners and modelers must be, and must remain, cognizant that the data to be mined or modeled is inextricably intertwined with the framework in place when it was collected. Business has many such framework models—such as the customer relationship management (CRM) model, the Manufacturing Efficiency model, and the Product Management model—that each views the world differently. Each of these models views different features, events, and objects of the (business) world as important, and thus leads to different features and events being rated as important and meaningful. In fact, what each model sees as features and events varies from model to model.

Data collected under one view of the world will usually tend to support that view of the world (or framework model). If the framework model changes, data previously collected will unavoidably continue to contain traces of the model under which it was collected.

1.1.5   Structures

If we only internally recorded events about features of objects as mental objects, there would be no data for mining and no models in the sense used in this book. But there is more, and it is on this foundation that all of our modern accomplishments are built. Our ability to externally record information resulted in the accumulation of knowledge on a broader societal scale, far beyond that accumulated by one person. At first, the key data storage device was oral tradition. It worked very well, as the stories of the *Iliad* and the *Odyssey* tell us. These oral remembrances of what have turned out to be real events were carried for perhaps centuries before they were recorded in the next form of information capture—writing.

The technologies of storing information—language and writing—helped to create "permanent" knowledge structures. This phenomenon, known as the *time binding* of information, means that people confronting problems did not have to learn how to solve the problem from scratch on an individual basis. Instead, they could draw on accumulated knowledge. It also means that continuous social structures could be perpetuated with the creation of a continuing common and shared framework of knowledge that we call *culture*.

Remember, data starts as the simple recording of events of features of objects. On this foundation, vast structures are built. Culture is one such structure, but all our scientific endeavor, art, politics, ethics, medicine, trade, industry, commerce, and more share that foundation. Such structures can be strenuously self-perpetuating. Indeed, people wage war and die over ideological issues based only on their conflicting knowledge frameworks.

These larger issues are important to data miners and to modelers, even though it is highly unlikely that they will be involved in any attempt at wholesale re-engineering of a major cultural framework. These cultural frameworks exist at all levels, however, from the individual, embracing only a single person, through the frameworks of marriage, friendship, clubs, companies, states, nations, and on and on. Working within a corporate culture—understanding what can and can't be achieved, understanding what the structure defines as success, and understanding where change can best be effected—these important issues and many more are resolved by understanding the structure and the constraints it implies. Successful mining and modeling occur only when those involved understand the structure that exists and within which they work. To some extent, whether great or small, mining or modeling success depends absolutely in changing, modifying, or clarifying the existing structure.

Structures are very important knowledge frameworks, but they are static representations of the inter-relationships among objects. The pinnacle of such structures is a dynamic system. In a system, all of the component parts discussed here—events, objects, features, and so on—have a dynamic and ever-changing relationship. Essentially, systems describe how structures maintain, modify, and adapt to internal and external changes over time. So important are these structures that they are introduced in the next section and examined in more detail in the next chapter.

1.2 Systems

Systems are knowledge structures that explicate the modes of interaction between their components as events occur. We commonly speak of systems as if they are objective things in themselves that exist in the world; however, as discussed in the previous section, systems only represent our abstraction or simplification of how the world works. It should by now be apparent that this is not only a philosophical point without application to the real world. A system is a structure and just as subject to revision as any other structure, thus any system imposes itself on the world and enforces its own particular world-view. The systems of the world itself, if there are such things, do not change. Our explanations (knowledge structures) of the systems can and do change.

Consider an example from the realm of what used to be called natural philosophy and is now known as science: combustion. Aristotelian physics was based on a knowledge framework that included four fundamental elements: earth, air, fire, and water. These four components, and combinations of them, constituted everything that existed. Fire was simply a basic element that needed no further explanation. Around 1723, Georg Stahl, drawing on the ideas of his teacher, developed a different knowledge structure. Very briefly, he proposed that bodies were composed not of the four Aristotelian elements, but of a greater number of "principles." (Drawn from the Latin, *principle* means "primary component," or "basic and indivisible ingredient," something in meaning like the modern *element*.) The idea was that out of these blended principles came the full range of worldly substances, something like the modern meaning of compounds. One of these principles that composes every body, according to Stahl, was the inflammability principle, or phlogiston. It acted something like a fluid and could be passed from body to body, thus transferring heat and other effects. With this explanatory system in place, for the first time phenomena such as respiration could be explained. This framework, in other words, allowed a new view of the universe, revealing that there was something about respiration that needed to be explained. With Aristotelian physics, there was no problem with respiration. This is not to say that Aristotelian physics thought that it had explained respiration; it simply was blind to the "fact" that any explanation was needed. But neither Aristotle's nor Stahl's views changed the way the world works; they only changed what could be seen. (We will return to this example later to see how knowledge structures react and change when confronted with such a shift of perspective.)

Business, too, has such parallel issues. The automobile manufacturing industry in the 1960s used a manufacturing efficiency framework, which defined industry observations and their subsequent reactions. It focused on manufacturing products (cars) as efficiently as possible—long lead times for orders, long assembly line tooling setup, long runs to amortize the cost of setup over as many units as possible. Corporate accounting reflected this framework and measured efficiency in terms of production. Corporate profits and bonuses all reflected the level of activity in the production plants. This model required top-down management with little initiative and less flexibility at lower echelons in the organization. It worked—that is, it achieved the ends purposed and permitted by the framework model. It presaged an era of low-cost automobiles for the American public. Until, that is, the Japanese introduced a totally different framework with which to view the world. Their view was so different from the prevailing view that American automobile makers literally couldn't see any problem because their worldview prevented them from understanding what the Japanese model showed them. After blindness came denial. After denial, rejection. Finally, of course, the industry had to adjust to and accept the new rules of the game. ("Rules of the game" is just another way of describing a knowledge structure.)

A recent business knowledge structure is CRM, mentioned earlier. As already mentioned, because systems are used in this book as the predominant modeling method for viewing the world, Chapter 2 looks at the nature of systems in much more detail than this brief introductory description.

1.3 The Structure of Knowledge

Although modelers can accept a commonsense view of the world and its events and features, and this acceptance can provide them with a very workable approach, how modelers view the structure of knowledge is not so easy to accept at face value. Knowledge has a very rich and complex structure, in some ways much like a multilayered onion. The "reality" that the modeler has to work with very much depends on where the project is located within the overlapping layers of the knowledge structure.

The previous section dealt with how humans view the world. That is the view from the inside outward—in other words, how we view the continuing existence of the world from the perspective of our individual personal consciousness. Exploring the structure of knowledge turns this view around and takes a view from the outside inward—in other words, looking at how internal abstractions of external reality are created, used, and modified.

At the core of our personal knowledge structures lies intimate personal knowledge. Wrapped around that is an implicit knowledge of the world (emotions, feelings, hunches), and around that, explicit knowledge (formal instruction, airline schedules). However, we are enmeshed in a vast overlapping web of other layers of knowledge, some interpenetrating and overlapping. At work, we are members of one group with its associated implicit knowledge (customs and mores) and explicit knowledge (hours of work, assigned desk). At leisure, we are members of other groups, sports teams, and clubs, even associations formed by nebulous memberships like "readers of Steven King" or "watchers of *Star Trek*." Each of these has its own implicit and explicit layers of knowledge, assumptions, culture, customs, and modes of behavior and performance. We carry all these layers with us, and what we know influences to a great extent our observations. An aficionado of baseball sees an infinite level of detail and finesse in the game, but perhaps not much in water polo. Why? Knowledge enfolded in the personal knowledge structure provides the framework for understanding—seeing—one, baseball, but no framework of reference for the other, water polo.

As it is for an individual, so too it is for any social organization or structure, specifically corporations. Small groups, say teams in departments, have their own implicit and explicit knowledge structures, including the departments, sectors, divisions, groups, and so on to which they each belong. Villages, towns, counties, states, countries, regions, continents; committees, churches, clubs, organizations, industry confederations, chambers of commerce, and on and on—each of these perceived groupings carries with it implicit and explicit knowledge. They inform the corporate culture, define a way of seeing the world, and provide a frame of reference for what can be seen, and what cannot. All of us move within all of these layers every day, generally seamlessly. Yet modelers must move into, and work within, knowledge structures that are not familiar, that engender assumptions that are not always apparent, and that preclude certain approaches unless the knowledge structures can be changed to accommodate them. As a result, modelers need objective techniques for discovering, working within, explicating, and accommodating these knowledge structures.

1.3.1 The Problem of Knowing

The fundamental problem of knowing is that of *reification,* defined in the *Oxford English Dictionary* as "to convert mentally into a thing"; in other words, to construct a mental representation of an object or typify a mode of relating. Such a definition explains the meaning of the word, but doesn't help us understand how such a process takes place, or its limits, failings, and problems. A miner has to work within existing frameworks of reified knowledge that exist at all levels from intimately personal to globally social. All knowledge is founded on reification. Since reification is fundamental to constructing knowledge, a brief look at how it works and what its limits are will be helpful.

Reification begins with pattern detection in the undifferentiated flow of worldly sense impressions. To pursue how humans detect such patterns is a fascinating study, but would take us far afield from the matter at hand. Regretfully, we must start by simply accepting the premise that our sensory equipment is up to the job. But what happens afterward is worth pursuing.

Essentially, as the undifferentiated worldly events stream past our senses, our pattern detectors determine the presence, partial presence, or absence of certain fundamental, wired-in patterns. These first-order patterns are presented to second-order pattern detectors that try to find patterns of patterns. How might this work?

Take a very simple example. Suppose that there are a number of visually presented patterns such as those shown in Figure 1.1. The patterns shown there are immediately seen to consist of lines made up of curves and straight sections. This "immediately seen" suggests a pattern detector at work. Suppose, simply for the sake of this example, that the wired-in detectors of the visual cortex are capable of detecting the patterns "curve" and "straight line." (This is not so far from the way things are believed to work, but is a tremendous oversimplification.) So curves and straight lines jump out immediately, but what else is there in common about these patterns?

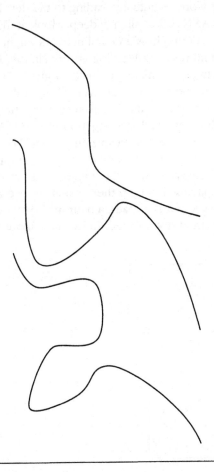

Figure 1.1   Three curves.

Figure 1.2 shows the wiggly lines laid over each other on a common frame. Now it is apparent that all of the lines start and finish at the same point, and all pass through the same point near the middle of the frame. Thus, the lines appear to have something in common, meaning that there is some regularity or pattern that emerges from the wired-in regularities, but it is not detected by the wired-in regularity detectors. The observation that all the lines have a common starting point is a second-order feature. So there is some mechanism that discovers patterns that are built out of the patterns detected by the wired-in detectors.

Our heads are filled with a vast amount of enormously complex equipment. The active equipment for discovering patterns seems to be a vast and intricate network of neurons. These are the neural networks that form our brains. In-depth investigation has revealed some information about how neural networks might work, eventually leading to the development of artificial neural networks (ANNs). So a slightly deeper look at the mechanism of reification involves considering how a neural network might learn a pattern.

The essence of neural network learning is very simple. In one method, given a pattern, the network estimates (predicts or guesses) the form of the pattern. It will very likely be wrong. However, telling it that it is wrong, as well as where and by how much, allows it to revise its estimate for the next time. This is the "traditional" back-propagation method. Another way of learning is to use what is called a self-organizing map (SOM), which very usefully discovers inherent patterns on its own. In this example, imagine that sensors cover the surface over which the wiggly lines are drawn, each attached to a neuron. In laying a line on the sensing surface (or projecting it onto the retina at the back of an eyeball), a neuron "fires" if covered by part of the line and doesn't fire if not covered. In learning about these particular

Figure 1.2   Three curves in a common plane.

lines, the sensors at the beginning, middle, and end positions of the lines will always fire. So the network learns that lines of this type always have at least these three features in common—start, middle, and end points.

Assume that there are lines of other classes. These lines do not begin or end in the same place, nor do they cross the middle. Such lines are classified as different from the first set of lines shown—the network features that define the first class of line are not fired, so they do not correspond to the learned class. Such lines may belong to some other class.

Now what happens when a line turns up that nearly but not quite matches the learned class? Perhaps it begins and ends in the correct places, but only passes close to the recognized middle position. How is this classified? Remarkably, the network will recognize that it is almost the same as the learned class and will report it as such. This feature of a network is truly remarkable. It means that in finding a classification for some new and previously unseen object, the network is attracted to the nearest learned example and will return that as a classification rather than simply saying "unknown object here." The network abstracts some defining characteristics of the object from the examples already presented to it, and recognizes objects that are merely similar.

Neural networks, then, have the ability to organize themselves based on examples presented so that they learn the defining features of patterns. This is an enormously powerful ability. By considerably extending this ability, we reify the world. We can learn to distinguish a Vermeer from a Rembrandt. We can learn to see the intricacies of baseball. We learn to recognize letters and numbers, truth and beauty, happiness and angst. This works because as each new feature detector learns to recognize some feature of the world, that feature itself becomes available to feed back into the mix. The vast and unimaginable complexity of the brain allows us to learn and perceive. By learning new patterns we can see more regularity, order, and pattern, which, in a never-ending spiral, allow us to see and understand yet more. In this sense, the more you know, the more you can know.

1.3.2   Paradigms, Archetypes, Patterns, and Knowing

Reification allows the construction of an enormously rich internal representation of knowledge. An unimaginably vast blending of feature recognition leads to the sensation of knowing and understanding. The core knowledge that we possess is the ability to extract, simultaneously, countless numbers of features from the world's incoming, undifferentiated sensory input. But all of these features are extracted either from wired-in detectors that we are born with or feature detectors that we have trained from all of our life experience to date. This vast, unconscious framework of interpreting feature extractors determines all we can see of the world. It forms for each individual the fundamental enabling mechanism for understanding the world—it is our personal world paradigm.

This paradigm is the overarching rule set by which we recognize, judge, and understand the world. It is, however, built only from our life experience and does not truly reflect the world. It only reflects and informs us about what we have discovered, found useful, and been exposed to over time. Most of the time, we are not only unconscious of our personal paradigm, but we regard it, again unconsciously, as *the* way to view the world; that is, the only, natural, and unarguable view that it is reasonable to take. It is, in a most literal sense, our point of view.

However, all paradigms are flawed. They do not represent the whole of reality (whatever that might be), only a point of view. A major problem is that although they enable us to understand, they also limit our ability to understand.

One of the complex behaviors humans learn is how to read. Reading requires the recognition of letters, which we can quite easily manage. Patterns in letters form words, and those too we easily manage to learn. Take a moment to examine the following sequence of letters:

A E F H I K L M N T

Or try:

A B E G H J K O T U

What is the next letter in each sequence?

Pause to think about it for a few moments. While doing so, think about how your thinking moves as you seek to answer the question. The point is not so much to discover the (an?) answer, but to become aware of how you look for the patterns here.

Or try another.

What is half of thirteen?

Pause here. Take out a piece of paper and write out your answer or answers. As you do so, think about your thought processes. Try to feel the enabling paradigm at work, and see if you feel any restriction or discomfort.

There are any number of puzzles similar to these, and you may well be familiar with them. For many people, pushing against their paradigms in these small ways can be a pleasurable experience. However, wholesale change of our paradigms is very painful, traumatic, and threatening to our personal integrity, so we tend to be very conservative and resist change strenuously. No such massive change is needed here, but we have not moved far from the needs of the miner and modeler. A modeler works with other people's views of the world, and may need to modify or change them. Modelers need to be aware of their internal paradigms, too, particularly where they are restrictive and prevent seeing. And of course, the purpose of these puzzles is to make you aware of your internal paradigms.

For the letters, what was the next letter in the sequence? How did you go about discovering it? The next letter in the sequence is V in each case. Why? Does it help to know that it is V? Does it help to know that it isn't W? And what about the half of thirteen puzzle? How many answers do you have? In fact, there are probably hundreds of different correct, non-trick answers to this question; ten different valid answers are given later in this section (as is the reasoning behind the letter sequence). Does knowing this change your viewpoint of the problem? Why? Perhaps more to the point, how? Given this additional information, go back and review your answers again. Does it change your thinking? If so, how? Perhaps more to the point, why?

In these exercises you are (unless you know the answers beforehand) pushing at the paradigms that enable and constrain your view of the world. Try this story.

Once upon a time there lived a once rich king who had a beautiful daughter, but being beset by a wicked wizard who lived at the end of the earth, had lost all his fortune. His daughter was in love with a handsome prince from a distant kingdom. The prince was famed far and wide for his complete honesty. The wicked wizard had evil designs on the beautiful princess. One day, while she was walking in the garden with her father and the handsome prince, the wicked wizard appeared before them. "Greetings, king," said the wizard. "I have come to make you a bargain. Give me your daughter's hand in marriage and I will make you a wealthy man. Deny me, and I will cast an evil spell on you and turn you into a toad!" Somewhat taken aback, the king turned to his daughter and asked if she would consent to the match. "Oh, no," wailed the princess, "what a fearsome fate. I love the Honest Prince, but I love my father too. What shall I do?" "Well, look," said the wizard, "let's leave it to chance. I'll just turn this tree into gold, which will give you much wealth, and in return I will take one white pebble and one black pebble from the path, and I will put them into this velvet bag. The princess will draw out one of the pebbles. If she draws out the black pebble, she will be mine. If she draws the white pebble, she will be free to marry the prince and you can keep the golden tree. The Honest Prince will be the judge." Well, better a bad choice than no choice, so the princess agreed. But as the wizard slipped the pebbles into the bag, she noticed that both were black! Fortunately, the princess was sharp of wit as well as beautiful, and she drew a pebble in such a way as to foil the wicked wizard. That done, he disappeared in a tower of rage and a puff of smoke, she married the prince, and they all lived happily ever after. But what did she do?

While you are thinking about fairy tales, Bruno Bettleheim, in his book *The Uses of Enchantment* uses a markedly Freudian approach to show how fairy tales might reify abstract experiences of life and, in the characters, personify fundamental commonalities of human experience—at least, using a Freudian framework. What is more, he shows how they are still relevant to our lives today. These are archetypal figures that encapsulate our feelings, thoughts and emotions about central figures and events in human life. Whether this approach is valid (and it has been disputed) it is not only in fairy tales that archetypes exist. All stereotypes—the courteous Englishman, the precise German, the obnoxious American tourist, the pushy used car salesman, the mountains of the Moon, justice, the legal system, the attorney, the doctor, and so many more—are all equally archetypes. So too are such things as food, transportation, my route home, how to fly a kite, a romantic novel, customers, profit, investment, and satisfaction. Such archetypes are fascinating constructs because many of them are of nonexistent entities and can even be about things of which we have no direct experience. Nonetheless, our paradigms are populated by such archetypes.

So what are the solutions to the problems posed earlier? The first string of letters is an alphabetic ordering composed only of letters that can be created with straight lines. Why was it hard to see that? Perhaps because our framework makes it difficult to view letters as figures in themselves. The second string is made from an alphabetic ordering of the first straight line letter, followed by the next letter requiring curved lines, then the next requiring straight lines, and so on. The half of thirteen problem is more easily illustrated than described; it is shown in Figure 1.3. The princess, however, did not focus on the pebble to be drawn, but on the one left in the bag. How does this help? Perhaps you would like to pause here and see if this clue helps. If not, the answer is at the end of the chapter.

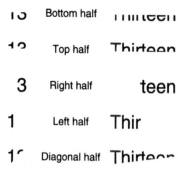

13	Bottom half	Thirteen
13	Top half	Thirteen
3	Right half	teen
1	Left half	Thir
13	Diagonal half	Thirteen

Figure 1.3 Ten interpretations of half of thirteen.

1.3.3 Frameworks for Representing Knowledge

Reification, as discussed, in some sense creates the objects of knowledge. It is a process of converting simplifications of event sequences or impressions into mental objects. However, it is not such objects themselves that form knowledge. After all, objects do nothing—they are essentially inert simplifications—whereas knowledge is clearly dynamic. For the purposes of mining and modeling, very fortunately, it is not directly important how the human brain stores and manipulates its reifications. What is important is to look at a general way of describing and using knowledge. It is within such frameworks that miners and modelers work.

The mental objects that result from reification are of two fundamental types. One of these is the *archetypal abstraction,* a representation of a worldly simplification. Examples were mentioned in the last section. The other fundamental type is the *archetypal interaction,* a representation of how worldly events interact. Add heat to water and it boils. This expresses how two objects, heat and water, interact. Heat is not an object of the real world, of course, only a mental simplification for whatever it is in the real world that goes on when water is boiled. Water is probably not a real-world object either—at a different level of simplification it is a molecule composed of two atoms. All that is important about reified objects is that they allow manipulation and control at the required level of simplification. In order to make a cup of coffee, who cares about molecular structure? The point is that models of knowledge incorporate with the reified objects various rules about permitted interactions with other objects, and the number of interactions is limited.

Far more complexity is required for a fully adumbrated knowledge representation, but miners and modelers do not need to fully adumbrate a knowledge model. As with much else in life, simpler is better. Knowledge structures can be usefully represented as a network of interconnected reified abstractions. Such representations are enormously powerful for illustrating and exploring the structure of how a problem or situation is seen. The representational systems discussed in later chapters add power to such a structure because it can be represented on a computer and dynamically explored. Very often, exploring such representational structures can produce remarkable surprises. For now, it is enough to know that knowledge structures can be represented as a network of interconnections among objects and the interactions that define the connections.

1.3.4 Personal Knowledge

Personal knowledge is one of two types of knowledge that particularly concern miners and modelers. It forms a complex and interlocking mesh that sits at the core of who we are as individuals. For convenience, personal knowledge can be viewed as consisting of two types. The first type comprises the intimate, personal, private, self-identifying knowledge that defines "me." There is enormous depth to this knowledge, including such things as *proprioceptive impression*—the intimate knowledge of the position and state of our bodies— to our instincts and basic motivators. Fortunately, such knowledge is either not directly important to data mining and modeling or is of a type that we, simply being human, understand intuitively. Some of this knowledge, for instance, is communicated as what we call *body language*. It is very fortunate that it is not necessary to delve deeply into this realm because it is a vast territory including such subject areas as psychology and physiology.

The second type of personal knowledge important to miners and modelers can be characterized as the framework of assumptions, prejudices, biases, opinions, and the like that we all carry with us and that is built largely from social and cultural interaction. The assumptions, biases, prejudices, and opinions that each of the participants brings can greatly influence how mining and modeling go forward and whether the result "works." Chapter 6 looks at various methods that are useful in outlining important personal knowledge that can impact on mining and modeling projects.

1.3.5   Social Knowledge

All groups of people, large or small, carry frameworks of social knowledge. Everyone belongs to many social groups, and there is some particular feeling that defines what it is like to be "in" the group, what methods of behavior and performance are expected within the group, and what defines the inside/outside boundary of the group. This holds true regardless of the size of the group, even down to two participants. When couples commit to each other and live together, whatever the legal status of the relationship, there is a sense of the way that the relationship works. This applies just as much for a corporate structure. For a modeler, it is within the corporate social knowledge structure that the modeler has to produce a model that is acceptable.

There is much more to say about how to discover and ensure that the project is set up so that it fits within the various constraints of the corporate frameworks, but these are looked at in later chapters. The purpose here is only to introduce the issues so that when an approach is discussed later, it will be easier to see where the pieces fit and why.

1.3.6   Other Types of Knowledge

There are many other ways of usefully characterizing knowledge. Tacit and explicit, for example, where *tacit* comprises thoughts, feeling, emotions, biases and so on, and *explicit* is composed of documents, images, presentations, and other external representations. A modeler will generally be working with explicit knowledge models; however, it is often the case that models will be judged by tacit criteria. Thus, a modeler may well have to elicit and explicate both types of knowledge to create a successful model.

Another type of knowledge, *recipe knowledge,* involves knowing a procedure for accomplishing something without understanding the underlying structures. Car breaks down, call AAA, tow to dealer, and book a service. This is a recipe of things that work to fix a broken car, although the recipe requires no knowledge of the repair process, and little of cars. The problem with recipe knowledge is that there is no underlying understanding of the systemic relationships, so that if the recipe fails, it provides no help for extending the solution beyond the recipe; for example, what to do if the car dealer were to say: "Sorry, we have no idea how to fix it."

Functional knowledge delves slightly deeper than recipe: The mechanic who fixes your car may have this level of understanding of your car. At this level, the mechanic has a detailed understanding of your car as a system, but only as a functioning entity within a larger system—that of automotive repair. It requires no more than a knowledge of how to identify broken subsystems, how to order new ones, and how to replace the old with the new. It is an extension of recipe knowledge in that it includes knowledge of the function of each recipe so that appropriate recipes can be selected and used. Such a level enables the mechanic to fix your car, so long as the system functions to provide spare parts and tools. However, if your car is, say, a genuine antique for which no parts are available, making new parts may be beyond the level of knowledge available.

Practical knowledge is similar to functional knowledge, but it embraces that realm of what is called "common sense." But common sense is not actually common at all; rather, what comprises common sense depends on the cultural milieu. It provides that level of knowledge that allows easy functioning in daily life. Common sense informs you that you need to change the oil in your car's engine, or you can expect early failure.

Theoretical knowledge provides a multi-layer deep knowledge of relationships and object discrimination that allows for control of worldly events that get considerably away from daily experience. Such theoretical understanding might include knowledge of metallurgy, physics, metalworking, and so on, that allow fabrication of parts for repairing an automobile, including building it from scratch out of iron ore. However, no such knowledge is ever complete because even given a sufficiently large amount of hydrogen gas, we have no practical knowledge of how to construct an automobile from it. Theoretical knowledge indicates that the course to pursue would be to construct a class of star that turns into a supernova. Such stars cook hydrogen into all of the other elements, including iron. They blow up with a stupendous bang and blow all of the raw elements into space. A second-generation star, such as the sun, made from supernova ash may then develop a system of planets, one possibly like the Earth, that have iron as partial constituents. But knowing that gives no indication of how to go about doing it!

All of these apparently different types of knowledge are, in fact, not really different types of knowledge. They are just different models of knowledge. Part II of this book examines in some detail what models are and how the different types can be used by the modeler.

1.4 Changing Knowledge Structures

All of a business modeler's work is done within the framework of a model structure. To some degree, that work is aimed at changing or clarifying some part of the structure. But knowledge structures change in nonlinear, and in fact discontinuous, ways. In practice, this means that a small increase in knowledge or a small adjustment may make no difference—or it may bring the whole existing edifice crashing down! Small causes do not necessarily have small effects, nor large causes large effects. This chapter previously cited the example of Aristotle's earth, air, fire, and water quadrichotomy being replaced by phlogiston. This change precipitated a total realignment in a model of the world that had lasted nearly 2000 years. Shortly thereafter, the crashing change continued as phlogiston was replaced by the idea of oxygen.

We live in a time when crashing and realignment of knowledge structures seems almost commonplace. All kinds of models—social, structural, scientific, cultural, agricultural—have undergone more dramatic change and realignment in the last hundred years or so than in the whole of previous human history. Pundits frequently discuss how to characterize the time in which we live: the atomic age, the computer age, and so on. Each of these candidate "ages" lasts for a briefer and briefer period before the next major characterization appears. It may well be that historians will look back at this time in human history as the time of massive knowledge structural realignment in all areas of endeavor.

Data miners and modelers set out to deliberately change and realign knowledge structures. These are generally corporate knowledge structures, and so far the goals at each stage seem modest. In general, data mining has been used so far only to gain a small tactical advantage. But as the power, performance, and reach of what can be accomplished with mining and modeling are realized, that is changing. Thus, miners, and even more importantly modelers, need to be aware of how to make optimal changes that cause the least disruption and can be implemented with minimal effort and cost. Also, modelers need to be aware of how to implement, monitor, and ensure the performance of the changes so that the process is controlled. The next few sections describe in detail the types of models that modelers work with and the characteristics of how the models are changed.

1.4.1 Symbols and Symbolic Knowledge

All of the models described here are founded on symbolic knowledge. But what is symbolic knowledge, what are symbols, and how do they all relate to one another?

A *symbol* is a regularity in one frame of reference that represents a regularity in another frame of reference. The regularity may be an object, a relationship, or something else, but for now consider only the first two, an object or a relationship. A structure of such symbols forms a symbolic model of the phenomena that it represents. The symbolic structure par excellence is language, which uses characteristic sounds, or characteristic visual representations of sounds, to represent a vast variety of objects and relationships that exist in human experience of the real world. The key point here is that there is some correspondence between the symbol and the object or relationship. This correspondence allows the objects and their relationships to be referred to, and the symbols manipulated, in accordance with rules—in this case grammar. Such manipulation produces describable results that mimic, to some degree, the observed results in the world. This complex concept comes down to no more than that rules of language allow words to be manipulated in ways that generally accord with what we experience. Thus, by using language we can express insights about the world that do, to some degree at least, turn out to represent the world. That is exactly what is going on in this book: the transference of descriptions of objects and relationships in language that the reader can interpret, or map back to, the phenomena of the experiential world.

There is an amazing ability that humans have, perhaps uniquely among all known animals, to intuitively create the mental links that connect symbols to phenomena and phenomena to symbols. If this ability is not actually unique, it is certainly developed to a level not approached by any other known creature. Yet, it is so transparent to us that we are almost totally unaware of the mapping. A car, a desk, and a computer all look exactly like they exist in the real world—it cognitively feels as if it is these abstractions that are real—but perceptually the abstractions are more real than the causal phenomena themselves. Despite the earlier discussion of archetypal patterns and self-learning neural networks, there is a deep mystery here as to the nature and workings of this mechanism. Here is at least one of the facets of the glistening diamond that is intentional human consciousness, and it is one of the facets that presents a barrier to duplicating the full range of human abilities. A modeler needs to be aware of this interface because currently, only a human can translate worldly, experiential phenomena into symbolic representation, and then translate such representation back into anticipated experiential phenomena. When translated, computers can manipulate such symbols. Within limits, computers can translate symbols from one domain of representation into another domain of representation. They can turn numbers into pictures, for instance. But at the interface between the phenomenal world and the symbolic world stands human understanding alone.

Symbolic knowledge, then, is an abstract representation in symbols of objects and relationships that are perceived in some other frame of reference. It includes a set of rules for manipulating the symbols so that the relationships between the symbols are more or less constrained to behave in ways that analogously mimic the behavior of the perceived object in the other frame of reference. Thus, for instance, in the symbolic knowledge representation system of language, the rules of grammar constrain the relationships between words (symbols of things in the perceptual world) to correspond more or less to the perceived relationships between the perceived objects. In general, these constraints mean that grammatical sentences make sense in terms of the perceptual world—but not always. The correspondence is not perfect, and perfectly grammatical sentences can still yield constructions that break down when applied to the real world, for instance: angry lilies sleep furiously.

1.4.2 Knowledge as a Network

Language is the foundational symbolic model. In a sense, all of the models that follow later in the book are expressions in a specialized language or represent some specialized grammar, or both. One of the types of model discussed later is the narrative model, which is based on language. However, for representational and manipulative purposes, language is difficult to work with as a generic representational schema for a structure of knowledge. It is one of the richest, if not the richest, form of modeling available, but it is this very richness that makes it difficult to use as a representational structure. It is much easier to work with a representation described as a network.

Networks recognize objects and their interrelationships. Diagrammatically, these are represented as points and lines joining the points, respectively, illustrating a knowledge schema. Figure 1.4 shows a very simple part-kind-relation (PKR) knowledge network. It can be interpreted as showing that a "complainer" and a "purchaser" are both a kind of "customer." A "product" has a relationship of type 1 with "quality" and a "customer" has a relationship of type 2 with a "product." A "customer" is part of a "market." The actual nature and type of relationships shown need to be described and defined, but aren't shown here for simplicity. Various inferences are possible,

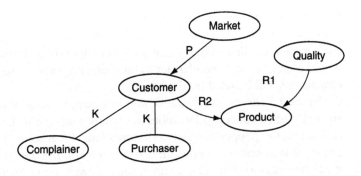

Figure 1.4   Elementary PKR diagram.

even from this simple network diagram, such as that "quality" has some relationship with "customer." Various questions arise, too, such as whether a "customer" being part of a "market" means that "quality" also has a relationship with "market."

PKR networks have a place in advanced data mining applications where data mining is used to extract knowledge schema. Here the network is used in a purely illustrative way, and this book will not discuss computational cognition and automated knowledge schema extraction. The point of this illustration is that a PKR forms a multithreaded network of interactions of various types. Further, such networks can be created within computer systems and manipulated as symbolic representations of knowledge structures. The real-world knowledge structures that a modeler must work with are vastly more complex than any that can be shown here, or even any that can be represented within any modern computer system. Nonetheless, even the simplified knowledge networks that we can create show a surprising correspondence with the way that real-world knowledge structures seem to behave. Particularly of interest to both the miner and the modeler are the insights to be gained into the way knowledge structures behave when modified, changed, or adjusted.

1.4.3   Changing Evidence, Changing Conclusions

Both mining and modeling essentially refine, change, or alter knowledge structures. But entire knowledge structures do not change in simple or straightforward ways as their components change. Earlier in this chapter, when self-organizing maps (a type of neural network) were mentioned, the convergence phenomenon of networks was also mentioned. What this does is to remember a pattern and "pull" other similar patterns into the common matrix that it sets up. Concepts can be imagined as populating a three-dimensional surface with depressions in the surface, each depression corresponding to a learned concept. Actually, the surface must exist in far more than three dimensions, but it is almost impossible to imagine what that would look like, and even harder to illustrate! For ease of description, three dimensions will be used here.

Figure 1.5 shows an illustrative concept map, with the low points representing learned concepts. The more frequently some particular concept is encountered, the deeper the surface indentation. When some new impression arrives, it is positioned on the surface at some appropriate spot, from where it can be imagined that, like a ball, it rolls "down" to the lowest level. Every point on the surface has some "gradient" sloping in the direction toward the nearest low point. As new impressions arrive, the surface adjusts accordingly, but because the low points attract newcomers, this surface has certain characteristics. These characteristics describe how the concepts behave and change in relation to each other as the nature of the concept structures changes.

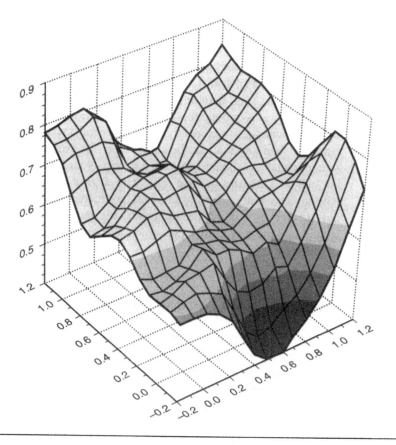

Figure 1.5   Illustrative concept map.

1.4.4 Aggregation and Catastrophe in Knowledge Structures

One characteristic of the surface is that wherever a depression begins to be formed, it begins a reinforcing cycle that tends to attract other points and so deepens the point further. Remembering that this is a map of a symbolic model of knowledge, what does this mean? It means that whatever concept arrives first tends to be regarded as the archetype against which others are measured. It also means that the first thing to be learned tends to be remembered as "true," even in the face of conflicting evidence. It also means that changing the surface in this area is difficult, so learning new concepts that are similar in many respects but different in others is difficult. Roughly speaking, this corresponds to various traits in human learning, such as anchoring. (For information on anchoring and other learning and perceptual phenomena see further reading recommendations in the Resources Section.)

Note that it is impossible for any one part of the surface to be changed without changing all of the other parts of the surface. Minor fluctuations will make little difference even though the whole fabric changes slightly; the general contour of the surface remains unchanged if some depression moves slightly, or rises or lowers slightly. But at some point, a small change will suddenly make an indentation disappear or a new one appear, and this cascades over the whole surface. This makes knowledge structures very resilient—and also very resistant to change. But when they do change, the change is likely to be large and sudden, even though the rearranging change is small. This is like the proverbial straw that breaks the camel's back.

Although the simplified descriptions here are metaphors and models of models, it is important for modelers to be aware that these simple models represent real-world phenomena. In Section 4.2.4, we will examine system models, a class of symbolic knowledge structures, in far more detail. System models map a restricted range of objects and interactions. But just as the more general mappings exhibit complex behavior under change, so too do system models. These models are particularly valuable to the modeler because they can be used to model business structures, as well as many other systems. The point is that complex business systems may resist change to a remarkable degree—and then suddenly and unexpectedly change, perhaps enormously and in unexpected ways. Unexpected, that is, unless pains have been taken to understand the nature of the structure that is being changed.

1.5 Summary

This whistle-stop tour of concepts has traversed a vast territory, much of it little explored by anyone; even where it has been explored, it is not well understood. It is in this uncertain territory that the modeler and the data miner stake out their own small claims and ply their tools. Yet, for all the discussion here, and the description of a model earlier, what, fundamentally, is a model?

Models, one of the principal topics of this book, are where rubber meets the road for the business modeler and for the data miner seeking to use data to characterize relationships in a business model.

Model relationships, sometimes even model objects, are what the miner is looking for, or at least, models are in part built from what the miner discovers while mining. Models come in a bewildering variety of types ranging far beyond just symbolic models. Fashion models, dressmaker's models, aircraft models, ship models, data models, power grid models, mathematical models, logical models, geographic models, cosmological models—the variety is almost endless. Yet as models, they all have certain features in common. The essence of a model is that it forms some idealized representation of a real-world object. Being idealized, it strips away much of the complexity attached to the real object or situation, presenting features of the real-world situation in some more convenient, comprehensible, useful, or useable form. It is crucial to understand exactly what purpose a model serves so that the produced model is not oversimplified or simplified in the wrong direction. It is fine to cast a reduced scale steel or heavy plastic model of an aircraft if it is to be tested in a wind tunnel; it is useless to do so if it is intended as a radio-controlled flying model. Any model, necessarily a simplification, must contain all of the necessary features of interest to the user and be complete enough to model the phenomena of interest accurately enough to be of use. It is very important for a miner to establish what is to be left out, what is to be kept in, and what is to be revealed in any model.

Symbolic models come in a wide variety of types, although data miners today typically work only with inferential or predictive models. Nonetheless, the range of symbolic model types covers a very broad spectrum. More and more, different types of models are being constructed using data mining, so a miner needs not only to know what environment a model is to work in, but also to clearly establish what type of model is needed. Just where do descriptive, interpretive, explanatory, predictive, or prescriptive models fit? How do they differ? What about active and passive models? What is the difference between, and appropriate use of, qualitative and quantitative models? In any case, how is a miner to know which to use when? There are, of course, answers to all of these questions. Those relevant to data mining for business models are explored in Chapter 4. As data mining becomes more capable and sophisticated, the miner needs to be aware of these issues, to understand the implications of different models, and to know which are the appropriate tools and techniques to produce them. The answer to the question of what constitutes a model has to be made operationally. It is quite impossible to say what anything is "really." As this chapter has attempted to show, reality is a relative concept, despite the out-thereness of our sensory experience of the world. For instance, given that a car accelerates from point "A" to point "B," what "really" happens?

Who can say? There is some quantum mechanical wave function corresponding probabilistically to the car, and another, or many others, superpositionally, corresponding to the state of the world that interact in some fantastically complex manner. There is, at a wholly different level of abstraction, a mechanical interaction with the surface of the planet. Or again, there are ecological effects, economic effects, chemical and metallurgical effects, nuclear and atomic effects, sociological, cultural, and even semiotic effects. And the list can go on and on, depending only on what the appropriate frame of reference is for providing an answer. But what "really" happens can be described to human understanding only by stripping away almost all of the things that happen and leaving some poor, threadbare simulacrum of the original richness of reality. All that can be said for what "really" happens is that everything in the whole of the universe interacts in ways beyond understanding. In spite of that, models of reality do empirically work, and are useable, useful abstractions of what happens. Somehow or other, humans have evolved equipment that allows them not only to abstract selected features from the world, but also to connect one level of abstraction to another, and then use the second level that is more easily manipulated to influence the world to selected ends.

The key to using models most effectively lies in the way they are defined. For practical application, this must be a purely operational definition. Although some of this chapter's material may seem at this stage somewhat theoretical and academic, every single point raised here was introduced because it has important consequences for modeling and for mining data to build or improve models. It is an operational definition that theoretical models map onto the world. The question always must be: "What do you want to do with it?" No model is made, and no data mining is carried out, in a vacuum. The rest of the book looks at the practical aspects of building useful models.

1.6 **Supplemental Material**

The princess noted that the wicked wizard had put two black pebbles into the bag. Her problem was that if she drew out a black pebble, the wizard could claim her. She could not avoid drawing a black pebble; however, having drawn a black pebble she "accidentally" dropped it onto the path where it was immediately lost among the black and white pebbles already there. So doing, she said "Oh dear, how clumsy of me. Never mind, we can always see what color pebble I drew by looking at the pebble still in the bag. Obviously I drew one of the other color!"

In the credit where credit is due department, the essential insight in this story was inspired by one of Edward de Bono's books on lateral thinking. This series of books provides an excellent introduction to ways of thinking "outside" the constraints of our mental models, or as business managers often call it, "thinking outside of the box."

Chapter 2
Translating Experience

Experience is a great teacher—it's a well-known aphorism. In fact, our experience of the world—our sense impressions—is our only teacher. Inside our heads we connect those impressions into *meaningful* experiences, not simply undifferentiated impression streams. From the otherwise dizzying wash of continuously streaming experience some regularities pop out that we grab onto and label. When assembled, and to some extent stabilized, the labeled experiences form a meaningful (to us as individuals) distillation of events, and also form the mental structures that we use to view and interpret the world, and to which the continuity of experience constantly adds and changes. This structure is, for each of us individually, our worldview. It is this structure that forms and informs, and to some extent actually is, our idea of what the world is and what it's all about.

Ideas about the world don't remain fixed, at least not for long. As situations and circumstances change, so do our ideas about the world and about the situations that occur. Ideas are our mental furniture. With many experiences in mind, even secondhand ones that come from studying the experiences of others through reading or formal study, our minds are well furnished and allow us to recognize and appropriately respond to many and various situations. When less experienced, and thus with less mental furniture, we recognize fewer situations and are unaware of appropriate actions. But in every case, novel situations require a rearrangement of our mental furniture to encompass and incorporate the new situation. New situations demand new ideas—new thinking.

Today the world seems to be changing faster than ever, particularly the business world. The rapid pace of change demands a constant rearranging of our ideas and a constant search for new ideas—new relationships, new ways of looking at the world, new strategies. But we are a tool-creating and tool-using species, and our tools are not simply those that manipulate the physical world. Some of the tools that expand creativity or discover new ideas are purely mental—tricks or methods that help us organize our thoughts and so "think better." Other tools, however, are external to us. This chapter looks at how the external tools of data mining and systems thinking are intimately linked with, and are external extensions of, our ability to discover and explore new ideas, and how it is that strategies, or strategic thinking at least, is a tool to implement our ideas, hopes, and desires in the world. These are crucial issues to a business modeler because it is the experience of business that has to be translated into a model (the model represents some business "system"), and ultimately the model has to be used to devise, support, or otherwise enable corporate strategic action, be it large or small.

2.1 Mining and Ideas

What is data mining—not as a definition, but as an activity? Obviously it has something to do with data because the word *data* is in the label—but so too is the word *mining,* and until recently that word was used pretty much exclusively to indicate the recovery of valuable physical substances through excavation. By analogical extension, data mining might then be described as the recovery of something valuable from data. But what might the "something" be? Obviously not a substance, because data is a nonmaterial object, even though the medium embodying the data is physical. Perhaps the place to start is by looking at some widely accepted definitions of data mining.

There are quite a lot of definitions of data mining. For example: "[Data mining] is the nontrivial process of identifying valid, novel, potentially useful, and ultimately understandable patterns in data." Or another: "Data mining is the search for valuable information in large volumes of data." Or one more: "Data mining . . . is the exploration and analysis, by automatic or semi-automatic means, of large quantities of data in order to discover meaningful patterns or rules."

Throughout this book, we will look at the automated search for patterns, novel and interesting interactions, and hidden relationships. However, this is really only a description of something that humans have been doing without automated assistance for as long as there have been humans: trying to develop ideas.

How do we generate ideas? Consider this extract from *How to Get Ideas* by Jack Foster:

> The creative act . . . uncovers, selects, reshuffles, combines, synthesizes already existing facts, ideas, faculties, skills. "Feats of association," "unexpected likenesses," "new wholes," "shake together," then "select among," "new juxtapositions," "bisociations"—however they phrase it, they're all saying pretty much what James Webb Young said:
>
> "A new idea is nothing more or less than a new combination of old elements."

Mr. Foster is talking about what an idea is and how to be creative. He could just as well have said that a creative idea is the discovery of an unexpected regularity, which is one way the activity of data mining is described in many data mining texts today. But keep in mind that in essence, there is *no* difference between discovering a creative idea and the desired results from data mining. Of course, the creative idea data set is in the human head, whereas the data mining data set is on a computer. But in the grand scheme of things, that is a trivial difference because the data in the head didn't start there—it started in the world, just as computer data does.

Mind you, there isn't any data mining tool that is going to put human creativity out of business just yet! The computer, with an appropriate program, may discover associations, patterns, regularities, and interactions in data, but it takes a human to recognize them, to determine their worth, to decide if or how to use them, and to implement them in the real world. So computers aren't going to outdo humans just yet, but they do begin to extend our mental reach, as all human tools do in differing spheres.

Without question, data mining is the search for ideas. The importance here for any miner is not the mining, but the discovery of the idea—hopefully a novel idea, a new insight. Very often, the structured searching and design needed to establish the mining project (of the sort discussed in this book) will turn up new ideas or insights even without the application of automated tools. Data mining for business models should be done inside a structure that is carefully designed to reveal hidden assumptions, uncover needs, determine problems, discover data, establish costs, and in general explore the whole domain of the problem. Such intense and focused structured attention directed at realizing an opportunity, solving a problem, or discovering a relationship can itself pay dividends, even without automated tools. Remember that the most difficult part of finding a solution is accurately finding and stating the problem.

2.1.1 Taking Data Apart

Data mining is not a new activity, although the activity now has a new name. The term *data mining* has been used since perhaps the 1930s in a different sense than used in this book, or in most modern books on the topic. The modern usage, which means something like "the automation-assisted exploration of data sets for the discovery of commercially relevant, usable, applicable, and viable insights" dates back to 1995. The original activity before that time was not graced by any particular label and was simply known descriptively as *data analysis*. The word *analysis* means to take apart or to disassemble into component parts. The act of simply recording data is actually a sort of disassembly of the world into component parts that are its measured features. It is necessary first to separate (and to define separation criteria for) some selected phenomenon from all other worldly phenomena. Then a decision is needed about exactly what range of symbols should be used to capture the selected measurements. The symbols selected are usually, although by no means invariably, from a set of symbols defined to follow certain rules. That set we call *numbers*. Therefore, analytic disassembly leads to a method of examining data based on the quantities measured, and thus is called *quantitative analysis*. So quantitative analysis is no more than an examination of measurements of features of the world in an attempt to understand what the measurements reveal about the features, and thus about the world.

One problem with such quantitative analytic methods is that, intuitively, they often seem not to match our experience of the world. Humans apprehend the world in a qualitative way, and any quantitative appearance of the world comes only as a result of applying concentrated and directed attention. It seems, at least at first blush, that the qualitative and quantitative natures of the world express different facets of a common experience; however, this is not really so.

Our primary intuitive experience of the world is qualitative. In whatever follows, it is important to remember that it is the qualitative experience that comes first; the secondary quantitative explanation is trying to explain the primary qualitative experience. Quantitative analysis is only a specialized form of language for expressing some particular ideas about the qualitative experience of the world. Translating the quality of an experience into a language of quantities does not change the essential nature of the experience, nor is one form of expression inherently any better than the other.

However, an algebraic expression does seem to be in some way inherently different from, say, a written contact report, and of course it is. The algebraic expression is a symbolic expression of objects and their relationships, but the symbols used have specifically restricted meanings. Restricting the meanings makes it much easier to specify rules for manipulating the symbols. The permitted behavior and properties of such quantitative symbols can be clearly demarked. Trying to clearly demark exactly and completely what is indicated by an intuitively understandable qualitative symbol is very difficult indeed.

For instance, in trying to forecast future sales, a quantitative analyst (of which a data miner is one) essentially says: "Ignoring all of the things actually happening in the world, and focusing entirely and exclusively on the measurements of the features at hand, then the predicted sales value is the number x." The number x is simply a symbol produced by a sophisticated application of a set of rules. To use it, we may assume that it represents some number of dollars. We may also assume that it has some degree of uncertainty and so will be x plus or minus some other amount, say y. But even then, does this number $x \pm y$ really represent sales? Sales represent more than just a dollar figure. Consider the sales for the organization that you work for—what does a sales forecast mean to you? Optimistic sales projections represent hopes for the future, anticipated future salary, vacations, health care, pay increases, continued employment, and a whole host of other qualitative feelings. If sales projections are bad, it may mean reduced income, finding alternative employment, or dissolution of the company, all of which produce a host of associated qualitative feelings.

Projecting sales figures is a fairly common corporate activity, and the example introduces little that is not straightforward. The significance here is that the miner needs only to find an appropriate symbol or symbols—in this example, the numbers representing projected sales with levels of confidence and applicability. The modeler, on the other hand, absolutely must be cognizant of the qualitative framework into which the quantitative projection has to fit. Whereas the miner works with a quantitative representation of the world, the modeler has to include relevant qualitative experience in any successful model.

So it is that data modeling works with qualitative symbols. It also works with data that is essentially analytic in nature because the act of defining features, measuring states of nature, and recording those measurements is an inherently analytic activity. Throughout all of data mining (not to mention any other quantitative analytic method), it is crucial to keep in mind that the qualitative experience of the world is primary, and that data mining, in trying to explain and inform that experience, cannot supercede it. It is no good attempting the defense "the numbers don't lie" if the result is at variance with the qualitative experience. Of course the numbers lie. All numbers lie! If in no other way, they lie by omission. No numerical representation can ever express the full richness of the experienced qualitative phenomena that they represent. However, so long as they are carefully checked back against the real world, the insights revealed by quantitative analysis can be extraordinarily powerful.

2.1.2 Data and Abstraction

Turning qualitative experience into a quantitative description seems to come fairly naturally under the right circumstances. It's done through a process called *abstraction,* which is a mechanism for turning observations into numbers. As apparently natural and easy as the process seems, it doesn't just happen—it is a human process, not something that occurs separately from our doing of it. Abstracting quantitative descriptions requires rules and symbols. Miners and modelers have to work with data abstractions at a wide variety of levels. As an easy example, consider the number system.

It starts with a series of symbols (0, 1, 2, . . . 8, 9) and a set of rules that assigns each symbol to a quantity of real world objects. Thus the idea of quantity is abstracted (or separated) from the worldly objects themselves.

"Two apples" has the same degree of twoness as "two trees." However, the number system has to go much further than from 0 to 9. Another set of rules describes how to build composite symbols from the simpler symbols. There is no need to explore the details, but, for example, the symbols "1" and "0" can be used to create the composite symbols 10 or 100 or 1000 or 1010 and so on. The composite symbol "100" can be used similarly to a single symbol, say "7," except that its precise indication is different. Rules of the number system indicate differing properties for "7" and "100," but the nature of the single symbol and the composite symbol are identical—they both indicate a similar abstraction about objects in the world. But in order to be useful, of course, these quantities have to be qualified. The real world application of this abstraction differs significantly depending on whether it is, say, "apples," or "trees" or "unit sales in October."

Symbols do not have to be abstracted as numbers, of course. Data miners frequently work with data that is abstracted to non-numerical symbols such as categorical labels—"blue" or "green," for instance. Once again, however, the measurement "blue" needs to be qualified before use. There has to be a blue something—a blue light, a blue car. Although the nature of the rules for using and manipulating categorical labels is different from the rules for numerical labels, there are still rules.

Notice that the process of abstraction is very similar to the reification process discussed in Chapter 1. The end result differs, however. Abstraction produces externalized symbols and rules for manipulating those symbols. Reification results in identification of conceptual objects and relationships, the behavior of which can then be represented through abstracted symbols and rules. Very largely, a data miner works with abstraction and reification without questioning the process or method that created the results. The rules for manipulation are important to a miner, as is the form of the data, but not particularly the process of getting there. The modeler, on the other hand, needs to be very aware of the processes of reification and abstraction because they are what inform the relevance and utility of the model.

Although miners and modelers work with numbers, the number system is only a convenient example. The English language provides another example. In common language, all of the words used are composite symbols (composed, of course, of letters). In English, nouns tend to represent concrete abstractions of objects (boy, airplane), verbs express relations between objects (run, fly), and adjectives and adverbs add qualities to nouns and verbs, respectively (brown, quickly). Recall from Chapter 1 that language provides the foundational form for symbolic models. All other abstractions can, therefore, be regarded as extended, restricted, or special-purpose languages comprising restricted sets of symbols and rules. The symbols and rules are abstracted from the world, but to some degree, all of the languages have to possess symbols for objects and relationships similar to nouns and verbs. To be useful, all of the symbols have to be arranged in patterns, and patterns are very important.

2.1.3 Recognizing Patterns

Patterns, at least as far as a modeler is concerned, are regularities in the world that represent an abstraction. Actually, at least as far as discovering abstractions goes, the last statement seems to be backwards. The worldly events come first, leading to the discovery of the abstractions. This point brings up two issues in recognizing patterns: recognizing a new pattern and recognizing an existing pattern.

The latter is easier to address first because some form of template exists to compare to worldly events. In other words, the pattern already has been discovered and the question is how similar some event pattern is to the pattern template. If some worldly event pattern is close enough to the pattern template, the pattern is recognized. Of course, what constitutes "close enough" and how "close" is to be measured need to be established, but as far as the principle of recognizing an existing pattern goes, those seem to be only details.

Recognizing a new pattern is harder. Initially discovering patterns requires looking at repeated instances of some related worldly event or events. For a data miner, this is captured in the form of data, although a modeler may find that the data is in the form of narrative description rather than a computerized data representation. In principle, looking at the repeated instances represented, the modeler or miner must decide what about the experiences remains constant from one to the next. In principle, it is those constancies that become the defining characteristics for the template. The difficulty in practice is that none of the experiences are likely to be identical with one another. It is quite common in the real world that a repeated experience—commuting to work, say—has many features that are common from day to day, but that never repeat exactly. The details always are different. Recognizing what is common and what is irrelevant detail is not always easy. This, of course, is in a sense once again the reification problem described in Chapter 1.

Recognizing patterns, then, requires either discovering template constancies that remain common across repetitions of events, or matching event relationships to existing, already discovered templates. Of course, the template forms a definition of a feature or object recognized in the world.

There are many ways of discovering patterns in the symbolic representations of data sets, and this is essentially the entire topic of Part III. Several different types of relationships in data describe useful patterns, and the relationship patterns are similar regardless of the type of data in which they are discovered. (For instance, one relationship pattern is "logarithmic," in which the logarithm of one set of measurements has a clear relationship with another set of measurements. Such a relationship is common in many numerical data sets.) However, what the data actually measures determines some very important qualities about what the patterns describe. Thus the underlying significance of any type of pattern can be determined only by considering what the data measures. One such pattern description, and one that is of great importance to the modeler, is the difference between static and dynamic relationship patterns.

2.1.4 Static Patterns

Patterns can be described in a wide variety of useful ways. One way is to look for the relationships between objects. Objects have features, and features can be measured. As already discussed, sets of measurements are taken to represent the object. Static patterns occur with object features when other features of the same, or related, objects change their value. These sorts of patterns are called *static patterns* because essentially the measurements are about the static or unchanging features. They are static in the sense that between the features there is (or is expected to be) a relationship that, however complex, remains constant. This is perhaps easier to illustrate with a simple example than it is to define.

Consider the highly simplified manufacturing and sales cycle for the "Simple Company" shown in Figure 2.1. *Raw materials* flow in from the outside world and accumulate as the stock of *supplies* available for *labor* to manufacture into a stock of *finished goods,* which eventually are sent to customers

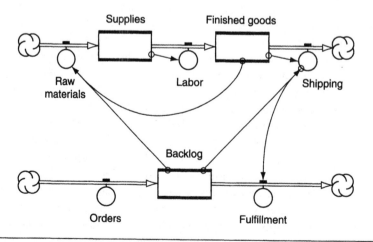

Figure 2.1 System representation of the Simple Company.

by *shipping*. Separately, sales *orders* flow into a stock called *backlog* and are filled by *fulfillment*. The pipes illustrate this flow from clouds to boxes (or boxes to clouds). The clouds represent the world at large—essentially an infinite source or sink for drawing a flow from or for the flow to return to. The circles under the pipes represent flow regulators, and the boxes are accumulators that accumulate a stock of whatever flows into them if more flows in than out.

The Simple Company is arranged so that at the end of every period the backlog situation is evaluated. If the backlog is larger than the amount of finished goods, the company orders sufficient raw materials to build products to cover the difference. Labor always makes as many products as it can from the supplies on hand. Shipping either sends out enough products to cover the backlog or, if the backlog is larger than the finished goods inventory, it ships the entire inventory. Orders come into the backlog as a random quantity between two and eight, and fulfillment is exactly the same number as products shipped (i.e., each unit shipped fills one order).

In order to implement these decisions, information about the state of the system has to be transmitted from place to place. The lines starting with small circles and ending in arrowheads indicate where specific information originates and where it travels. In addition to information being transmitted, it has to be molded by the relationship between the two ends. The number 12 that appears in the random function is a seed for the random series over the range of two through eight. Figure 2.2 shows the relationships from Figure 2.1 in

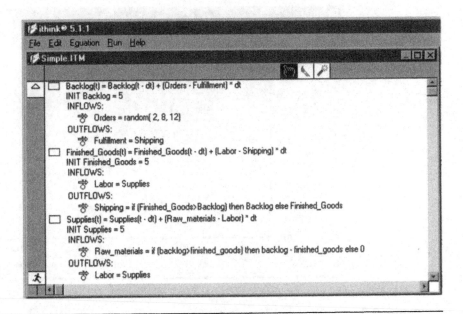

Figure 2.2   Logical structure describing system diagram in Figure 2.1.

mathematical and logical terms. (It may be worth pausing at this point to consider what is going on inside the Simple Company and to try to imagine what will happen when orders turn up.)

Note that this cycle includes two types of entities: stocks that accumulate and diminish, and flows that increase or diminish stocks, depending on whether they are inflows or outflows. These stocks are objects, and it is quite easy to make measurements about them. At the end of every period there is some stock of supplies, finished goods, and backlog on hand. Capturing these measurements at periodic intervals provides a snapshot of the state of the company at any particular time. Considered together, these snapshots form a picture of the ebb and flow of the internal workings of the business of Simple Company. Figure 2.3 shows graphically how the quantities on hand vary. (All of the figures and graphs come from a computerized simulation of the stocks, flows, information links, and relationships.)

Clearly, this method of controlling the business leaves a lot to be desired. However, these snapshots of the stocks on hand reveal the statics (as opposed to the dynamics) of the company structure. It shows the measured features of the objects—in this case, the levels of various stocks—but nothing about how the various levels interrelate. The relationships that link the various stock levels have to be inferred. In this static view of the relationships, given any stock level, it is possible to predict other stock levels and to infer relationships among the stock levels that produce the predicted levels. It

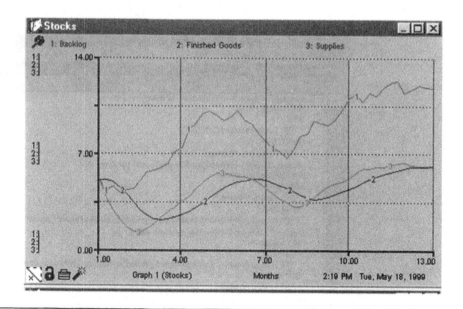

Figure 2.3   Simulated stock levels for the Simple Company.

should be noted, however, that discovering these relationships is not easy, even in this simple example, and although it helps with predicting levels of stocks, it doesn't explain what is happening inside the system that determines the stock levels. For instance, if it is a company objective to reduce the average level of backlog, it is hard to determine exactly what should be done just from the static data.

2.1.5 Dynamic Patterns

The dynamic parts of the Simple Company are clearly the flows. Even the words *stocks* and *flows* indicate that one is static and the other dynamic. Figure 2.4 illustrates the states of the flows. A glance at this figure shows that essentially the various flows are all averages that follow and smooth one leading flow—that of orders. So orders seem to drive the process. Raw materials follow orders, labor follows raw materials, and shipping follows labor. Each succeeding flow seems to be not only a later, but also a smoother version of the earlier flow. Because the Simple Company simulation is set up this way, discovering the situation is not surprising. (However, note that the static view of the stocks did not reveal this simple dynamic situation.)

Clearly, modeling these dynamic patterns reveals the Simple Company in a totally different light than any analysis of static patterns alone. It may seem

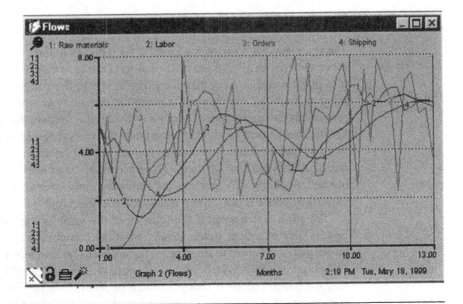

Figure 2.4   Simulated system flows for the Simple Company.

that the dynamic patterns give a clearer picture of what is going on inside the Simple Company; however, they do not reveal that the company is always behind in getting products shipped (i.e., the ongoing high level of backlog). The static model does show that.

To the miner applying tools to characterize relationships, the difference between static and dynamic pattern extraction may not be important. For a modeler, however, the difference can be crucial. Further, as a practical matter, companies generally have captured and recorded information about stocks, and it is only recently that flow information has been gathered. In other words, companies have focused on capturing static relationship information, not dynamic relationship information. (Think of how many companies actually undertake "stocktaking" from time to time—but "flowtaking"?)

There is an important point here: Given an initial static state, the dynamic information is sufficient to re-create the levels of all the stocks at any desired point in time. However, given the static information and the sequence of snapshots, it is not always possible to infer what flows occurred between snapshots. Dynamic patterns capture more information than static patterns, but miners and modelers frequently are able to access only static information. Although the illustration makes clear how important the difference is, those collecting the information in the first place do not always appreciate it. (Looking ahead, Chapter 7 contains more detailed and practical information about business processes.)

2.1.6 Novelty, Utility, Insight, and Interest

There are several reasons for looking for patterns in data and for modeling those patterns in a business environment. One is to clarify the performance of a process within a company, a division within the company, or the company as a whole. Another is to determine the areas in which there are opportunities for improvement and the type of improvement that's appropriate. Yet another reason is to determine what the emerging problems of control are that may frustrate, prevent, or hinder implementation of the corporate plans and how to obviate them. There are many other useful areas that mining and modeling may address, but clarifying these issues is paramount. The expected insight is not, "Keep doing more of the same!"

The truth is that even if doing more of the same is a good, or even the best, course of action, pragmatically what the company wants is something additional or different to do. The real question to be answered is usually not, "What can or should we be doing to improve performance?" but "What *else that we haven't already thought of* can or should we be doing to improve performance?" Even if not explicitly stated, what the client wants is a result that is novel, useful, insightful, and interesting.

Finding something novel through mining and modeling is usually easy; however, novelty isn't enough because the easily found novelty is usually trivial and often not practically applicable. In any case, novelty is in the mind of the beholder, to mangle a well-known aphorism. If a miner's discovery—whatever it is—was known before modeling, it's not novel. If the discovery was previously unknown, however obvious it is, it is novel. This makes objective measurement of novelty difficult and makes any such measurement even more difficult to use. Nonetheless, novelty is one of the pragmatic objectives that ideally needs to be met.

Utility is equally difficult to determine. Some insight, idea, or model may well be highly useful in theory, but is never applied for any number of reasons. Is such a discovery useful or not? Because the practical application of a discovery is required to actually determine utility, the actual utility of a discovery cannot be known ahead of time, although again, pragmatism suggests that any discovery should be assessed for its anticipated utility.

Insight and interest, surprisingly, are susceptible to estimation. Interest, to some extent, can be suggested by how surprising a discovery is. "Surprisingness" is related to a discovery's improbability—the inverse of its probability. That is to say that the less probable an insight is, the more surprising it is. Discovering confirmed relationships, events, or interactions in a data set that have a lower probability than others indicates that those with the lower probability are potentially the more interesting. The degree of insight that such a discovery offers is related to how much of the model framework is affected by the relationship, event, or interaction: the greater the effect, potentially the more insight provided.

Discoveries that are insightful and interesting carry more information (in a technical as well as a colloquial sense) than those that do not. This suggests that it may be possible, in principle, to make measures about discoveries that are at least indicative of their level of interest and insightfulness. Practical applications for discovering and presenting measures of insight and interest are discussed in Part III. Information theory offers an underpinning explanation for how to make measures; an introductory discussion of information theory (for anyone who wishes to pursue the subject further) is included in Chapter 11 of the book *Data Preparation for Data Mining*.

2.1.7   Mining and Pattern Seeking

The purpose of pattern seeking is to use the discovered pattern to influence the course of worldly events. Control is applied when a recurring pattern is recognized, and at the same time some other identified pattern of activities is applied that will produce, or at least tends to produce, desired results. For example, the Simple Company problem might be: "Customers are complaining about how long it's taking us to ship their orders. What should we do to fix the problem?" What they are looking for is some reorganization of the event structure to deal with this problem, that is, a change in the current pattern of operations.

Solving the Simple Company's problems is trivial, but in the real world similar problems may be exceedingly hard to address. It is often not obvious, for reasons to be discussed next, why the problem is occurring, let alone how to modify the structure to introduce a pattern that improves the situation. If data is available, as is often the case, data mining provides a tool for discovering patterns in data. The discovery of such patterns is, as discussed throughout this section, no more than the discovery of ideas or inspiration. But even determining what data is appropriate to mine, and what can be discovered, requires a model of the situation. Data mining is not just the search for patterns. Patterns have to be placed in perspective within a model. Indeed, a model is needed before mining to determine how the mining should proceed, what data should be mined and how it should be mined. The patterns discovered, and their applicability to the situation at hand, depend very much on whether the data to be mined is of static or dynamic relationships, as well as many other factors discussed throughout the book. But in order to generate any mined insights, the mining must be informed by models, many of which have to be constructed before mining begins. Models have not yet been introduced in any detail. There are many types of models, but one of singular importance in data mining, and the one that a modeler most works with when mining, is the system model.

2.2 Systems of the World

Translating experience makes special use of systems. Many worldly objects are actually systems, and all systems seem to possess special features. "Seem to" because, of course, systems are only an internal summary of sense impressions. Nonetheless, systems seem to be "out there," so they are projected to have an apparent independent existence that is separate from our appreciation of them. Plants and animals are systems, as are components of plants and animals; however, a medical student examining the nervous system sees the system as an objective object, a component of the animal examined, also an objective object. More importantly for this book, businesses and companies are systems, too. It means something to be a part of—or not to be part of—a company. Companies have component systems, too. Employees are either in marketing or not in marketing, for instance. So systems form a large part of how we reify the world, especially the dynamic and interactive event patterns. A modeler has to pay particular attention to systems—in the context of this book, mainly the systems of businesses and corporations. They are an important part of translating experience. (Looking ahead, Chapter 6 is largely devoted to looking at systems, systems thinking, and business systems in some detail.)

Systems do not actually exist in the world. They are abstractions, albeit extremely powerful and useful abstractions, and it is often our intuitive experience that systems are as real as many other objects and have an "out-there" reality. Many systems allow an intuitive boundary to be drawn around a collection of objects and relationships. What makes such a collection of objects a system is usually that the internal interactions remain consistent over a wide range of external changes in the environment. Thus, the Simple Company represents a system that retains its integrity as a recognizable system and responds to outside events without losing that integrity. Under certain conditions, such as an extended period of no orders for the Simple Company, the system can no longer retain its integrity, and the system changes or disappears. Although systems are discussed here and elsewhere as if they are "real" complex objects of the world, it sometimes becomes important to remember that they are only abstractions of reality, particularly when the boundary is breached, moved, or is inappropriately placed.

But systems themselves come in quite a few varieties, such as systems of philosophy, physical systems, electrical systems, and so on. In mining and business modeling, there is one particular type of system that is of interest—the dynamical system—although it comes in many forms. Although data mining and modeling are widely used in physical, chemical, biochemical, and many other fields, the dynamical systems discussed throughout this book will be restricted mainly to those social phenomena known as companies. Even so, dynamical systems of companies share characteristics with other dynamical systems, and as far as data mining and modeling of such systems are concerned, one shared issue is of particular interest—what is technically called *open* and *closed form solutions*.

2.2.1   Open and Closed Form Systems and Solutions

The most common type of dynamical systems, or at least the most common type studied, is what is called *differentiable systems*. All this means is that the different feature measurements in the system are related to each other so that as the values of features change, they all change together in smooth or continuous ways. The mathematical equations that describe the relationships among features can be written in the form of differential equations (thus the name differentiable systems). These differential equations represent the dynamics, or flows, of a system. For such systems, given a starting value for all the features using these differential equations, the system can be run forward (or backward) and the state of the system at any point can always be known. (This, incidentally, is exactly the system model that gave us what is known as the Newtonian model of the universe—everything coupled like a clockwork machine.)

Now this amounts to no more than saying that given the state of the stocks in a system and knowing the relations of the flows, the future behavior of the system can be known. This is the concept that was introduced in the previous section for the Simple Company. To be sure, a technical caveat is needed: Sometimes a system has to be described in terms of discrete steps forward or backward rather than as a continuous movement. Such discrete steps mean that difference equations are used rather than differential equations, but that is simply a technical point, and the end result is much the same.

All this is by way of preamble to looking at the difference between closed and open form systems. In systems where it is possible to run forward or backward as described, it is sometimes tedious and unnecessary to do so. The computation is excessive, and it may be possible to derive another set of equations such that plugging in values for the feature states, and given a displacement into the future or past, out pops all of the feature measurements that will be found at that other, displaced time. For such systems, it is not necessary to actually run the system to discover what its state will be under other conditions. Such a solution is called a *closed form solution,* and such systems can be called *closed form systems.* In making a sales forecast, for instance, it may be that some formula is discovered or invented that allows some set of measurements of the current position to be plugged in, plus some specific distance in time in the future, and the output is a forecast value. This is a closed form system because forecasting next year's sales, say, does not require predicting next month's forecast and then using that forecast to forecast the following month's, and so on. The final forecast can be reached in one step. Obviously, a miner often may be required to look for the relationships that define some closed form system or subsystem like sales forecasting.

Open form systems, on the other hand, have relationships that preclude the possibility of any such shortcut. The only way to get from one state to a discovery of some other state is to grind through all of the intermediate steps. The only way to discover the behavior of open form systems is a method of modeling called *simulation.* For instance, the weather is an open form system, and the only even marginally successful way to predict the weather is through the use of simulations. Much anguish has been caused by using closed form approximations to try to discover predictions for open form systems! This may well be because, although the vast majority of systems are actually open form systems, most of the systems investigated by physics are assumed to have closed form solutions. Although this assumption is changing very rapidly, it may be ingrained in the popular imagination; the miner must beware of this assumption.

(This, not so incidentally, is one great advantage of using a systems simulation software package for setting up mining problems. It can run a simulation of the system to explore assumptions, determine sensitivities, provide insights, validate and verify assumptions, clarify the problem statement, and much more that is of enormous use to both miner and modeler.)

2.2.2 The Nature of Systems

All dynamical systems seem to have key features in common. They all have an "inside" and an "outside." Inputs come into the system from the outside, are processed by the system, and then outputs are returned to the outside. This continuous flow requires "energy" that the system extracts from the flow. This energy is used for the internal maintenance of the system structure so that the system retains its integrity despite external changes in conditions. The energy is used up in system maintenance and has to be constantly replaced. The internal relationships between objects that make up the system are highly interrelated and often complex and nonlinear. This means that system behaviors are complex.

These key features may seem simple, but from them flow an enormous complexity of behavior. For instance, all systems will "struggle" to maintain their integrity. After all, if the system was not constructed such that it did so, it would quickly dissipate and disappear as a system. Built into any system is some structure that will resist change and try to maintain the status quo— a sort of inertia mechanism. However, systems are constructed to resist changes from the outside. Internal changes, even small ones, can lead to wholly unexpected consequences and to completely unexpected changes in system behavior. For miners and modelers, this has a double effect. First, when mining to discover relationships within a system, modeling stocks alone is not sufficient to understand the nature of the system. Mining needs to examine most particularly the dynamic flows. Modelers need to take as broad a view as possible to gain understanding. It is important to construct a model of a system before mining so that the mining is put into perspective. Second, when trying to change the nature of a system, if the change is attempted from outside, the system will resist—maybe strenuously.

2.2.3 Coupling and Feedback

The linkages between objects in a system are not straightforward. The exact nature of the relationship between any two objects may well depend on the state of the rest of the system—and the state of the rest of the system will, to some extent, depend on the relationship between the objects in question.

This circular relationship makes understanding the inner working of any, even mildly complex, system very difficult. Nonetheless, in order to discuss the nature of parts of a system, it is necessary to talk about them as if they were separate from the rest of the system. Despite discussing them in this way, it is crucial to understand that everything within a system is interrelated.

Objects in a system are coupled to each other. The coupling measurement ranges from uncoupled (where the objects have no direct effect on each other and are essentially disconnected) to tightly coupled (when changes in one object immediately and unavoidably produces changes in the other). This is similar to the statistical idea of correlation except that correlation only considers the effect of the objects on each other, not the full range of systemic effects. Coupling considers how objects affect each other under the total set of conditions prevailing in the system. Thus, sales may be coupled to the level of the incentive program in place. They will also be correlated with each other. However, if the shipping department goes on strike, sales will inevitably fall as people turn elsewhere to get what they need. This implies that the strike event is coupled with sales events even though the relationship may be difficult to express as a correlation. The idea of coupling is that effects in one part of the system influence the behavior of the whole system, and that no part is immune.

Coupling generally, although not always, manifests its effects on the flows of the system, which in turn affect the stocks and stock levels. But systems also manifest a level of behavior that is directly related to the flows and stocks, yet is separate from it. This is the level of information flow inside the system. Information about what is happening in one part of the system flows through the system to affect all of the events, flows, and stocks. This is often described as *feedback* (or *feedforward* as appropriate) and refers to information about the behavior of some downstream part of the system being fed back to an upstream part to modify system behavior. The Simple Company system, previously illustrated in Figure 2.1, has exactly such feedback when information about the level of the stock of finished goods and the stock of backlog feed back to influence the flow of raw materials into the system. (More finished goods produce less flow of raw materials.) Feedforward can be illustrated by the level of the stock of supplies feeding forward to affect the amount of labor applied. (More supplies mean more labor.)

The effect of feedback (or feedforward) varies greatly. Sometimes it increases a flow, sometimes it decreases it, and sometimes, as in the Simple Company example, the exact effect is not so easily characterized. The effect of backlog, for example, is nonlinear and dependent on the level of finished goods. So the traditional characterization of feedback and feedforward as positive or negative is not always appropriate. A more appropriate characterization is to consider the information flow within a system as either a stabilizing or a destabilizing effect. It may well be that a system that is stable over one range of behaviors can be driven into a state where the information flow begins destabilizing the system. But systems are intricate, and often the destabilizing information drives the system into some other stable state. Of course, the levels of stocks and flow rates may all be different, and the system may be behaving totally differently than before, but systems often have many stable states. On the other hand, it may simply destabilize and self-destruct.

Coupling, feedback or feedforward, and the relationships that exist inside systems are difficult concepts to grasp and understand, and even more difficult to keep track of. Tools that help with doing this are called *systems thinking* tools.

2.2.4 Systems Thinking

Successful modeling, and the data mining that accompanies it, require the use of systems thinking. This involves being aware of the system framework in which the model is being constructed or the problem that is being solved. It requires dismissing the concepts of cause and effect because, from a systems thinking perspective, the only answer to "what caused this effect" is "everything!" Likewise, the answer to "what effect will this cause have," is, similarly, "everything!" The questions to be asked instead help to identify the stocks, flows, and information paths. A systems thinker looks for the patterns that knit together the events that happen without asking which are causes and which are effects. A systems thinker looks for explanations and relationships. There are two characteristics of systems thinking: de-centered association and operational interaction.

2.2.4.1 De-centered Association

Putting some object at the center of attention so that it "radiates" other associations about the central object is *centered association*. For example, consider a company's sales. What is it that produces sales for any company? Pause a moment, take a piece of paper, and write down what you think produces sales for a company.

If you completed this exercise, you probably ended up with a list—most likely a recitation of causes (or factors) that you feel produce sales. That is to say, you believe they are causally linked. If one of the items on the list, for example, is product quality, what you intend to indicate is that as product quality increases, so too do sales. Perhaps your list included some of the motivating factors shown in Figure 2.5.

In Figure 2.5, sales resides at the center and radiates the "driving factors" list around the outside. But does this work? Think about, say, product quality. If the quality of a product is high, and is known to be high by prospective

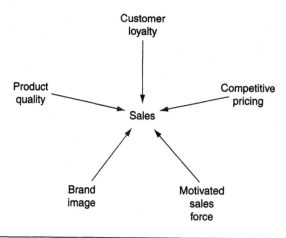

Figure 2.5 Factors promoting sales.

purchasers, they may be motivated to buy it rather than a product of lesser quality. On the other hand, it is only by achieving reasonable sales (among other things) that the company can create products of high quality. So this link is at least a two-way link. The same principle applies to all the other factors that "drive" sales. Solid sales performance leads to a highly motivated sales force just as much as the high sales force motivation itself increases sales. These are all self-reinforcing loops. In fact, they are much more than that.

In the previous paragraph, note the statement ". . . achieving reasonable sales (among other things) . . .". The "among other things" part of the statement means that there are a lot of other factors (in fact, interrelated loops) that affect sales, and that sales affects. This is exactly what a system is—all of the parts are interrelated. No one factor can be put at the center. Everything is very highly and inextricably interrelated—perhaps the figure might be redrawn more as shown in Figure 2.6. Here everything is linked to everything else, as well as to other objects not shown here.

The key point is that the focus in systems thinking is on the fact that system behaviors are generated by the system as a whole, and it is not possible to isolate any one causal factor. System associations don't work in only one direction, nor (usually) only between one object and another. So what's needed here is some way of thinking about the relationships, other than as discrete objects or influences affecting a central object—If everything affects everything else more or less, there is no "center." Thinking, and making associations in terms of mutual interconnections (no one of which forms the central focus), is called *de-centered association*—an important skill for the modeler to develop.

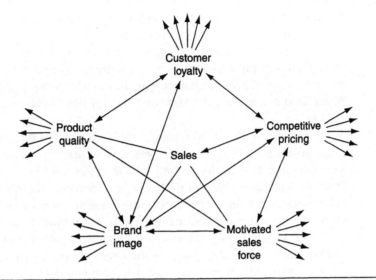

Figure 2.6   Interconnected influences promoting sales.

2.2.4.2   Operational Interaction

Operational interactions form the core processes of a system; they are the flows. How does this change thinking about sales? Because it is the flows—the operational interactions—that are important, the question to ask is not "what causes sales" (because the only answer is the system as a whole), but "what are the relationships that generate sales." At least in this example, the answer to that is the sales force. From there you might want to go on to ask what are the relationships that empower the sales force, and so on, but at this point it should be clear that asking questions with an operational perspective leads to outlining the system that supports the whole.

Further discussion of this topic is included in Chapter 4, and practical, hands-on methods for discovering and constructing appropriate model frameworks, including system models, are provided in Chapter 6. But for now, the quick tour continues by looking at how the results of the modeling effort are used to make better decisions.

2.3   **Strategies and Tactics**

The Simple Company has an opportunity to make a bid to provide Simple products to a client. The sales representative involved tells the sales manager that it is a sealed bidding process. What should the Simple Company do?

What do they need to know to decide what to do? What are the risks and benefits, and how can they be controlled?

Some of Simple Company's products have been waning in popularity. Product development has developed some really neat new products, but marketing is well aware that almost all new products flop in the marketplace. What should marketing do, and what do they need to know to decide what to do?

At the Simple Company's plant, manufacturing has difficulty in meeting peak product demand. The vice president of manufacturing reports to the president that it seems likely the problem is due to old equipment and that it needs replacing. This will probably be expensive—both in terms of outright purchase as well as production disruption and training. What should the president do, and what does he need to know in order to decide?

These are business problems, albeit highly simplified ones, that business managers face every day. Some of the decisions are informed by corporate policies, whereas others have to be met fresh and decided from the ground up. Some corporate policies are quite necessary because, as a practical matter, it is quite impossible to make every decision from scratch every time. (Which leads to yet another decision—what are appropriate corporate policies, and how often should they be revised?) These corporate policies are, in fact, rules for making routine decisions. In one form, that is exactly what a strategy is—a preset decision procedure. It is not a ready-made decision, but a framework of "If this happens, then do that" rules.

2.3.1   Strategic versus Tactical Decisions and Actions

The difference between strategies and tactics is somewhat blurred, even in military circles, where the terms were devised. A commonly accepted difference is that *strategies* represent sets of available activities that are possible in some particular set of circumstances, each of which leads to a different potential outcome; *tactics,* on the other hand, usually indicate concrete actions that actually put some strategy into effect by attempting to influence worldly events. Games are often used to illustrate the point, and chess is a good example.

The game of chess doesn't start with strategies and tactics. Separate from those are both higher-level features (the object of the game, which is to place the opponent's king in checkmate) and lower-level features (the rules of the game). The rules include such criteria as the size and layout of the board, permitted moves for the pieces, and so on. Strategies exist, at least for chess, in the space between the objective and the rules. For instance, one general strategy is to control the center of the board. Another is to use your knights early. Other strategies that a player develops as play progresses attempt to induce the opponent to enter positions of weakness so that the player can gain an advantage. However, deciding to adopt particular strategies, say using knights early, doesn't in itself achieve much. Tactics are needed—choosing either the king's knight or the queen's knight, selecting a legal move, and physically moving the selected knight to its destination square.

Essentially, strategies represent options available together with associated payoffs—potential advantages, or disadvantages that may be had by implementing the strategy. Tactics, although several may be available to implement any particular strategy, essentially are sets of rules for putting a strategy into practice.

So, given a problem and a context (the situation that exists, including all relevant factors bearing on the circumstances of the problem), strategies are the options available to attempt to change the undifferentiated course of worldly events. In a sense, such strategies, as well as the tactics, are simply rules describing possibilities, outcomes, and actions needed to achieve those outcomes. The problem in both business and chess is to decide which rules are available and then which to choose—in other words, how to choose strategies and how to implement them with tactics.

2.3.2   Dealing with Problems

A major practical use of experience is to use it to solve problems. This means no more than determining how to intervene in a situation that presages a less than satisfactory outcome and convert the situation into one with a more desired outcome. This is the crux of the whole mining and modeling endeavor, at least as far as business modeling and mining are concerned: discovering new or better ways to influence events, to some extent discovering new strategies, and calibrating (estimating risk, resources, and likely result) selected strategies. Here is where "the rubber meets the road."

Just as with chess, business problems consist of multiple levels or layers of possible objectives, strategies, and tactics. At the top is the objective, which may well be "maximize shareholder value." Whatever it is, it is the primary objective that informs all that the company does. The corporate objective(s) is not optional! However, at any subsequent level, there are always options, and it is choosing among them that is the crux of dealing with problems.

The three components in any problem are:

1. The set of strategies available.
2. For each strategy there is a set of possible outcomes, each with some associated probability that it will happen.
3. The ultimate "value" of each of the possible outcomes.

The basic idea is to set out in some organized way all of the options and payoffs, along with the associated probability that any payoff will result, and from that generate a table, graph, or other representation of the expected values for each set of options. Throw in some adjustments for the amount of risk the decision maker is willing to accept and the choice can be made. All well and good—in theory. But much of the needed information is very likely to be unknown, even unknowable. Other information might be known in principle, but difficult to obtain in practice. Or perhaps all of the strategies (options) available are not clear. What do you do then?

2.3.3 Types of Uncertainty

There are at least three types of uncertainty in dealing with problems: strategic uncertainty, outcome uncertainty, and world state uncertainty.

Strategic uncertainty describes a situation in which all of the strategies available are not clear. For instance, in the second of the Simple Company problems outlined previously, the product launch problem, there are apparently an almost infinite number of options. The company might, for instance, launch a full-scale product release immediately or test market it in a number of possible areas, or conduct market research using internal sources or an outside consultant, or any of a vast array of other options.

Outcome uncertainty is the uncertainty of knowing the likelihood of any particular outcome, even when all of the relevant conditions are known. This is the uncertainty, for instance, that is associated with knowing the outcome of flipping a coin, even when it is quite certain that the coin is a fair one. For the Simple Company, this again could be the product launch problem. Given that most products fail in the marketplace (say, for example, the risk is 80% fail, 20% succeed), this is the equivalent of flipping a coin that comes up heads 20% of the time and tails 80% of the time. Even having done market research, the best that it can get to is the 80/20 outcome risk. Having reduced the strategic uncertainty to a minimum, outcome uncertainty is an 80%/20% gamble.

World state uncertainty is the uncertainty associated with being unsure of the state of the world. This uncertainty is associated with being unsure that the coin is fair in the first place. If it were fair, you might rationally expect a 50/50 outcome on any one flip. If it were not fair, some other ratio of outcome would apply, but what that outcome ratio is remains unknown when you are uncertain of the world state. For the Simple Company's product launch plans, the world state uncertainty is knowing whether the real chances for their product in this market, with this economy, and under these inflationary conditions, and given what the competition will do, and so on, really is 80/20, or some other ratio.

When making decisions, strategic uncertainty needs to be circumscribed—the possible options need to be narrowed in some rational manner. The other two types of uncertainty need to be estimated and, if possible, reduced.

2.3.4 Costs of Reducing Uncertainty

It is always possible to reduce at least outcome and world state uncertainty. But, as with everything else in life, nothing comes without a cost. The universal law of "There Ain't No Such Thing as a Free Lunch," or TANSTAAFL, reigns supreme. In some cases, the cost is in dollars and in time—it is usually possible to buy more data or research to reduce the level of uncertainty. In other cases, it is possible to use statistical techniques, such as likelihood estimates, to at least quantify the uncertainties. There are other techniques that also can reduce the amount of variability in distributions, and that, too, reduces the levels of uncertainty. These also extract costs, perhaps in computational time and expertise. Sometimes it is possible to discover patterns that allow for reducing the level of uncertainty over time. Although all of these are possible, it is always a question of how much you have to pay to get what you need.

Another way of reducing uncertainty is to "move the goalposts". If the strategies can be enumerated and the outcomes estimated, each of them represents a possible potential profit or loss. Game theory calls these *payoffs,* and by using this theory it is sometimes possible to adjust how often each of the strategies is used in a way that optimizes the payoffs better than using any single strategy.

2.3.5 Deciding with Constrained Options

Almost always, a company has limited resources at its disposal for the available options that it could pursue with less limited resources. So the actual options that can be pursued are constrained by the resources available. Yet corporate management obviously wants to make the best use of the resources at its disposal. This is a very common problem, and there are some quite well known ways of setting up and solving such problems. Most MBA students will be very familiar with the techniques of linear, and maybe nonlinear, programming.

Even though the techniques are now well known, setting up the problems to arrive at accurate solutions assumes that the input parameters are also well known, or at least well defined. In the real world, that is not always true.

2.4 **Summary**

Translating experience isn't exactly straightforward. In fact it's downright paradoxical that at the same time it's so easy and so hard. It is easy because to a great extent it is a simple, intuitive process that happens without our noticing or paying attention to it. We are simply unaware that our experience of the world consists of sense impressions; we experience the world as an "out-there" independent reality made up of objects, some of which are dynamic and reactive systems, but objects nonetheless. On the other hand, because an intuitive impression of the world is so immediately present, it takes conscious and concerted effort to get beyond the world intuitively perceived. This is what makes translating experience hard. What is it that our experience is translated into—at least as discussed in this chapter?

Experience, for business purposes at least, has to be translated into an external representation. Implicit assumptions about relevant objects and systems need to be put into an externalized form so that the features and relationships that seem relevant and important can be examined, discussed, manipulated, experimented with, validated—basically, so that they can be used. It is the modeler's job to create or—if not actually starting from scratch—to define the features and details of these externalized representations. The purpose for all this activity is essentially to get some better idea of what to do. To get ideas (where this chapter started) is not easy or straightforward, and good ideas—that is, effective reassessments of object relationships in the real world—are at a premium.

Although systems representation is by no means the only way of translating experience into an externalization, it is by far the most common method that a business modeler uses. Very often, the externalized representations are not explicitly represented as a systems model, that is, the representations are not necessarily created using techniques explicitly known as systems thinking. Nonetheless, almost all representations of business situations (in other words, models of some part of the business situation) do recognize, at least implicitly, that they are both systems in themselves and part of some larger system. A sales forecast, for example, recognizes that there are interacting effects that affect the final forecast figure—in other words, a system. That forecast is based on assumptions about how the rest of the corporate enterprise performs, and assumptions about the rest of the world such as the economy and the business climate. Explicitly using systems thinking is not, by any means, the only way to build a useful representation of such business systems. It is, however, an enormously powerful and useful way, and one that works to generate sufficiently complete and adequate models to be usefully understood and applied, with many of the assumptions revealed. So useful and powerful is this method of thinking that all modelers will find it very worthwhile to master the techniques of system thinking, briefly though they were sketched here.

Ultimately, for what purpose is all this activity—the search for ideas, the construction of external models of business systems? Why the effort, and indeed, why the concern for modeling whether or not supported by mining? The purpose has to be to apply the insights discovered to gain some benefit. But benefit comes only by applying the insights, in other words, by acting to change the prevailing state of affairs so that the desired perceived benefit is more likely to come about. This is where strategy enters the picture.

Models and strategies have little to do with a business' objectives. If an executive decides to maximize shareholder value, as some say the proper concern of a company ought to be, so be it. Models, at least business models, have little to do with informing desires. What we desire to achieve, whether personally, in business, or as a corporate entity, is an emotionally determined decision. However, once determined, these objectives can be achieved, if at all, only through the use of strategies—alternative choices for deploying the resources available with the intent of gaining the objective. Strategies do fall into the modeler's province. An important purpose for some models is to evaluate the cost, risk, and probability of success for each of the possible strategies. This is part of the role of scenario evaluation—playing with "what-if."

The whole purpose for modeling and mining in a business setting is to discover new and effective ideas about the business-relevant systems of the world, and finding the best strategies to improve a company's lot. The core concepts on generating ideas introduced in this chapter will be the miner/modeler's bread and butter.

Chapter 3

Modeling and Mining: Putting It Together

This chapter introduces the issues in the area where mining and modeling merge. Modeling is a continuous process throughout all of mining. First, a framework model has to be discovered to frame the problem. As mining progresses, the framework model will be revised, and several different types of models are needed for understanding and using what is discovered in the data. Although models inform the direction and progress of mining, mining is the activity that clarifies and gives substance to the models. Models define areas of inquiry; mining reduces the uncertainty about, and explicates the relationships that exist in, important areas that the model identifies. Mining, in other words, clarifies the guesswork, hunches, and assumptions that initially established the framework for the problem. In short, mining reduces uncertainty.

All mining and modeling activities pursue one goal: to deal with some identified problem. (Recall that it may also be to deal with opportunity discovery; however, to avoid continued repetition, the term *problem* is used from here on in this book. Simply recall that the problem may be to identify or quantify characteristics of a suitable opportunity.) If conducted at a strategic level, mining and modeling can explore and clarify an entire problem area. The problem, or problem area, is addressed by making a decision that is informed by the results of mining and framed by modeling.

In colloquial speech, the word *hypothesis* often is used to indicate a hunch that doesn't seem to be rigorously founded on data, but nonetheless feels intuitively correct. Usually, local or personal experience and anecdotal evidence support the hypothesis proposed, but the colloquial use expresses a qualitative expression of confidence, rather than a quantitative one. Data mining seeks to understand what data offers in the sense of generating hypotheses about the data; however, data mining not only proposes hypotheses about data, but also makes possible rational estimates of the reliability of the hypotheses, and under what range of worldly circumstances they are likely to hold up. It is these hypotheses that clarify and inform the proposed interactions in any model. In other words, these are hypotheses about how the model works and not only can be developed by examining data, but also can be checked and confirmed.

Many types of models are used to represent business situations, including the system model, the game theory model, and the linear (or nonlinear) programming model (each mentioned briefly in the last chapter), and many model types yet to be introduced. But whatever type of model (or models) are used to represent a situation, all of them need to have the assumptions on which they are built, and the estimates from which their conclusions are drawn, estimated as accurately as possible. That is the work of data mining.

The first chapter cruised over the territory of how we perceive the world, why it is important to a miner and modeler, and how symbolic models allow us to understand and manipulate the world. The second chapter introduced data mining as a sort of idea finder that is only an extension of a human mental activity. Chapter 2 also introduced the idea of systems and systems thinking, and how these two concepts blend to produce strategies and tactics for attempting control of some part of the world. This chapter, the last of the introductory chapters, introduces the final concepts needed in mining for models. Here we look at the background to discovering mineable problems within the framework model; briefly explore the nature of, and problems with, raw data; and examine what theories are from the miner's perspective. This chapter also introduces the types of findings that must result from the mining and modeling to provide the support for making effective decisions.

3.1 **Problems**

Although there are a huge variety of possible problems, fortunately the data miner has to deal with only a very limited range and type of them. Furthermore, by focusing on business problems that can be solved by data mining, the types of problems to be considered are even more restricted. Problems are always related to the inability to control a situation. In business problems of the sort that data mining addresses, the answers generated are almost always in response to questions about how best to deploy resources under the prevailing circumstances to generate desired results. Chapter 2 ended with a discussion of strategies. The answers data mining produces are, for business problems, usually in the form of tactics or strategy evaluations. Or, perhaps more accurately, the models created to inform the mining usually turn the answers produced by data mining into business-applicable strategies or tactics.

A miner is invariably presented with a data mining task in a form very different from that of a clear-cut problem. Sometimes the task is even in the form of: "Here's some data. Build a model and tell us what we need to know." Whatever else a data miner may be, the miner always is a consultant—not necessarily an outside-the-company consultant, but someone who comes to the problem as an outsider. This is true even if the problem owner and the data miner are the same person. If the mining is to be done within a company with more than one employee, time and resources have to be recruited for the project, support promoted, outlines agreed upon, and implementation planned. In short, it has to be a corporate effort and thereby draw on corporate resources. The miner has to work within the framework and discover the real problem to be solved, in what terms it has to be delivered, what needs and constituencies it has to satisfy, what constraints are imposed by all of the restrictions discussed so far, and generally how to meet corporate expectations, if possible. But perhaps the miner's major task is to manage the expectations within the rest of the organization. In short, there are a lot of problems with problems!

As always, there are guidelines for a methodical approach to discovering the real nature of the task, revealing hidden assumptions, and meeting all of the other difficulties along the way. These are examined in more detail in Chapter 5. If you have the benefit of being inside a company, or if you are managing a mining project and can, to some extent, ameliorate some of the difficulties of an outside consultant, so much the better. There will nonetheless still be a whole raft of problems that have to be met head on and addressed regardless of your position inside or outside the organization.

3.1.1 Recognizing Problems

What is there to say about recognizing problems? Surely everyone recognizes a problem if it walks up and bites them, don't they? Well, yes, but that's just the problem. The problems approached by mining and modeling almost certainly won't walk up and bite. Usually, they are someone else's problems, and they may not articulate them as problems per sé. In truth, more than one data mining project has started with a business manager saying, in effect, "Take my data and tell me useful and interesting things about it that I don't know!" Well, the data miner has a problem all right—to discover what the business manager thinks is interesting and useful to know and why those things are interesting and useful to that manager. It may well be, and in fact, is very often the case, that the manager may have some general feeling of dissatisfaction, or perhaps some general sense that things could be improved somehow, but has not actually articulated the feeling or nailed down why it seems that way. Equally often, the manager is aware of a problem's symptoms and requests a fix to make the symptoms disappear; however, without being aware of the underlying reasons for the symptoms' appearance in the first place, discovering a permanent solution can be very hard. So recognizing the right problem that the miner and modeler need to work on is not always straightforward. It is very often (in practice, almost always) not the "problem" initially presented.

Any significant data mining and modeling project requires considerable interaction between the manager and the modeler, and later the miner, as they establish the framework for the problem and decide the exact nature of what needs to be discovered or clarified. Later, if the modeler continues to work with the problem holders toward a solution, they need to interact even more as they evaluate and decide on the options (strategies). Chapter 6 provides an array of practical techniques that the modeler and miner can use in working with the problem holders to clarify objectives. But the first order of business must be to obtain a useable description of the problem.

3.1.2   Describing Problems

To describe a problem effectively, miners and modelers need to grasp the metaphorical territory that encompasses the problem, that is, to create a map that illustrates the manager's existing understanding of the situation. (The term *manager* may, of course, encompass a group of people and is used here for convenience. The reference is intended to encompass everyone who is involved in trying to define and solve the problem from the company's perspective.) The best way to create such a map is to do so in an interactive, intuitive, and iterative way. Interactive in that all of the parties involved participate. Intuitive in that all of the parties can understand the map without needing any lengthy introduction to the meaning of the techniques used. Iterative in that it is easy to continually refine and update the map from session to session.

Why create such a map? It may well be, and very usually is, that in many areas the scenario and the problem are not clear or well understood. It may well be that different parties think that some part of the map should work one way, and other parties think that it should work another. Actually, what is at issue is that different people think that different features and relationships are important—necessary even—to explain how some part of the situation "works." And when the map fails to encompass differing beliefs, conflicting explanations arise. To help alleviate such conflicts, any mapping technique must be able to deal with ambiguity and multiple alternatives. In fact, creating such a map often serves to increase the apparent number of problems and decrease the apparent consensus understanding of the situation. Good! Great, in fact. Only when it is clear that there is something to fix will the group be motivated to actually discover the problem, develop a solution, and fix the problem.

Chapter 6 provides practical techniques for creating a situational map from conversation, from discussion, or from documentary sources that describe the situation. They are drawn together here under the general description of cognitive mapping, in that the end result is a map of the cognitive "landscape" of the problem area. Creating this cognitive map is frequently very revealing to those involved and generates a sense of interest and involvement. Practicing the techniques given here, and expanding on them using the resources available on the author's Web site *(www.modelandmine.com)* and from other sources, will repay the miner and modeler enormously.

3.1.3 Structuring Problems

Often the final expression of a cognitive map is a system diagram. (Chapter 2 introduced the concept of system diagramming; Chapter 6 provides details.) It is not always easy to progress from cognitive map to system diagram because most of the ambiguity and conflict have to be resolved before the system structures can be diagrammed. Attempting that transference may reveal the very problem areas for which smaller scale submodels have to be constructed and data mined. Even given that the system diagram is created and the appropriate strategic (or tactical) problems for mining are identified, that still leaves the actual mining problem to be structured.

Structuring problems requires identifying the inputs (the data being used for mining, assumptions, and so on) and outputs (strategic options, probabilities, relationships, and so on), and formulating the whole thing in a way that can actually be mined or modeled. What are the inputs? What outputs are needed? What data is needed? Does the data make sense? All these and more questions need to be addressed. The issues raised in Chapter 1 are always present—what is the assumed knowledge structure? In addition, the problem will have some internal dynamic of its own. Sometimes the problem requires a single solution; sometimes it requires a sequence of steps to complete. Some problems have optimal solutions if all of the necessary information can be developed. On the other hand, some problems have no optimal solution, even in principal. All of these issues contribute to the structure of the problem. But the biggest difficulty in adequately structuring a problem for solution is discovering all of the relevant factors, including those infamous hidden assumptions.

3.1.4 Hidden Assumptions

"Oh, I assumed that if we knew what people wanted in their cars, it would help us sell more cars. How does this help?"

"But I thought it was obvious that we would get a mailing list!"

"It just seemed reasonable that if we discovered the people who responded to our mailing that these would be the same people who would be willing to contribute money to our cause. Why didn't it work?"

"But if you can predict the waste, I thought that you would easily be able to say what caused it—and how to stop it!"

"I was sure that if we had a profile of the customer, it would allow us to improve the catalog. That's why I asked you to make the profile in the first place. Now that you've given it to me, how am I meant to use it to get more business?"

Experienced data miners will no doubt recognize at least some of these statements. All of them resulted after what was *technically* a successful mining of data. The answer requested was indeed produced—it's just that the wrong answer was requested! This is very much a case of "be careful what you ask for, you just may get it." It might seem reasonable to say, "Yes, but surely it is up to the problem holders and owners to specify the question that they need answered. If they ask to have the wrong problem solved, what can I do about it? Isn't it up to me as the miner and modeler to answer the question they ask?"

Of course, the question asked does have to be answered. However, it is equally important to the success of a modeling/mining project that the *needed* answers be found—not just the answers requested. For that to happen, it is up to the modeler to try hard to discover what the assumptions are before mining starts. The worst sorts of assumptions to deal with are hidden assumptions, because they are almost invisible. Even the problem holders and owners may not be conscious of their own assumptions—until the results come in. The modeler may not share the background framework of assumptions that are in place, and so needs to pay particular attention to this area before beginning.

Once again, there are techniques for revealing hidden assumptions. Working through the system structure in the form of a cognitive map is one such technique. Locating the model in the appropriate decision map level (see Section 5.3) is another. Another is to work through in detail how the produced strategic or tactical solution will be applied; how long it is expected to be effective; who is going to apply it; what levels of knowledge; expertise, or training are needed to use it; and so on. Chapter 8 in part looks at some of these issues.

However it is done, the miner needs to have a clear problem statement to begin mining. With luck and hard work, the problem that the miner works on will be relevant and not beset by hidden assumptions. From that point, it's time to look at the data available.

3.2   **Data about the World**

As far as the miner and modeler are concerned, the world is made of data, which is no more than a reflection of qualitative and quantitative impressions in a recorded and stored form. Capturing those qualitative and quantitative impressions uses a technique called *measurement*. When so named, it sounds very exact and somewhat forbidding, although it is no more than a simple process. Measurement involves comparing some defined worldly phenomena against some set of internal or external standards, and noting the compared differences or similarities.

Collecting these measurements, and organizing them in some manner, produces the raw stuff of data mining—data.

3.2.1   The Nature of Data

Data is very fickle stuff. At best, it is but a pale reflection of reality. At anything less than the best, it seems intent on leading the unwary astray. Invariably, the data that a data miner has to use seems particularly well constructed to promote frustration. The problems begin with the fact that the data for mining was often collected without any thought that it might ever actually be analyzed for some purpose. It just seemed like a good idea at the time! If some future analysis was envisioned, it almost certainly was not the actual problem currently presented to the miners and modelers.

In an ideal world, the miner could design and orchestrate the collection of data for mining. The measured features would be pertinent to the problem. The granularity of the measurements would allow a suitably precise answer to be formulated. There would be no missing and empty fields. The data would be collected consistently. Adequate redundancy would be built in. The data would be validated to ensure that it really represented the measured phenomena. And fairy godmothers really would flit about doing good deeds!

There is a real shortage of fairy godmothers when it comes to collecting data. In fact, it seems more like the ugly sisters have a hand in every pie. Real world data sets are brimming with faults, failings, inadequacies, noise, dirt, and pollution. But a data miner is constrained to work with the real data that happens to be at hand and simply has to make the best of it.

3.2.2   Measurement and Description

The problem with data starts with measuring features of the world. In spite of the "out-thereness" of the apparent world mentioned in Chapters 1 and 2, measurements are invariably and unavoidably contaminated by the worldview of the measurer. Measurement is no more than determining and reporting (even if only in your head) the quantity or quality of some experience. Because what you know affects what you see, the contamination is unavoidable.

As an emotionally intuitive example, suppose that three human males are communicating their experience of encountering one particular human female. Consider three possible reports of measurement taken during their observations of the interaction:

> Measurement report 1: "Man, she was a stunning blonde! Knocked my eyes out. Blue eyes, and what a figure! A fabulous, gorgeous looker!"
>
> Measurement report 2: "Her taste was exquisite. Her selections showed such a finesse of discrimination that I was amazed."
>
> Measurement report 3: "Her erudition was impressive. Clearly she has one of the finest minds in the area today. Her level of education, insight, and understanding is simply without parallel in my experience."

Clearly, the female in question impressed all the men. Can you imagine the characteristics of each of the three men who made these reports? Each of these descriptions does indeed tell something about the female in question—but it tells at least equally as much, if not more, about the interests, taste, worldview, and motivations of the man making each report. You might hazard guesses as to the age, occupation, social status, and so on of the men involved, simply by the measurements (or "facts") they report. In other words, given "just the facts," you may conclude as much, perhaps more, about the reporter of the data than about the subject reported.

So it is for *all* data collected. It may not be so intuitively obvious in many cases, but data is always collected for a purpose, and the collected data is filtered by assumptions, perceptions, interests, and motivations. As ever, what is already known defines what is believed to be important to measure about the world. It is unavoidable, and the miner and modeler simply have to use the data at hand—at least to start. But the fact that the "objective" data is not simply an unbiased representation of the world may not be immediately apparent to the manager involved. After all, many managers are used to making decisions based "just on the facts"; however, each of the three reports above report only the facts, too. All facts unavoidably carry traces of the prevailing framework model, conscious or unconscious, that defined that these were the important facts. But even then, and with the best will in the world, capturing all the facts is impossible. The world is far too complex a place for comprehensive measurements to be made, even when restricted by a framework model. Everything collected has to be simplified, and that too can cause problems.

3.2.3 Error and Confidence

One evening as you are strolling home, you find yourself wandering into the joke about the drunk who is looking for his keys under a lamppost. (He dropped the keys elsewhere, but is looking under the lamppost because the light is better.) You help him out a little. He mumbles something about having been to the doctor that day, and the doctor told him that he was exactly six feet tall—and he wishes that some of those six feet would get out of his way so that the two that carried him there could get on with carrying him home! Finally, he starts on his way home. By chance, you notice as he leaves that the lamppost is labeled as 12 feet tall. You also notice that the top of the drunk's head is exactly 6 feet from the lamppost and that he casts a shadow on the ground. How long a shadow does he cast?

This seems like a fairly simple problem of exactly the sort that no doubt annoyed in school. You can probably whip up a quick diagram of the sort shown in Figure 3.1, which lays out the relationships just mentioned. It would seem from the simple diagram that the shadow must be exactly 6 feet long. All well and good, but . . . in order to solve the problem, you made a number of simplifying assumptions. Of course, they had to be made in order to solve the problem, but it's best to review some of them. One assumption is that the drunk was standing up! He might have been lying on the ground, or crawling home on hands and knees—after all, he was drunk enough to look for keys where there was light, not where he lost them. Then again, another assumption is that the ground is completely level and flat. Another is that the light bulb on the lamppost is exactly at the top. And that the lamppost is vertical. And that the light casting the shadow was from the light on the lamppost and not from, say, the moon. And that the 6-foot height, even if the drunk was standing up, was measured by the doctor with the drunk wearing the same footwear as he is currently wearing. And that his hair, or hat if any, didn't affect the casting of the shadow. Any number of other assumptions could be added here. In fact, there are so many assumptions that the whole idea of determining the length of the shadow becomes rather problematic. If any of the assumptions made do not, in fact, apply to the situation, the length of the shadow may be something completely different from what you expected.

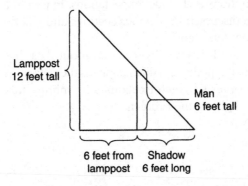

Figure 3.1 Length of shadow.

But the problems do not end there, either. What, for instance, does it mean to say that the drunk's head was "exactly 6 feet from the lamppost?" That is an impossibility all by itself! If his head was 6 feet from some particular point on the lamppost, it must have been some other distance from other points on the selfsame lamppost. In fact, this whole problem can be picked apart until there is so much uncertainty that you will easily sympathize with the poor fellow's predicament in the first place. Look for answers where the light shines!

The point is that all data is just as subject to caveats and uncertainties as the data in this problem. All data represent a very simplified view of a very complex world. We simply do the best we can, and much of the time, the best is good enough. But any data set has just as many built-in possible sources of error, and just as many assumptions, as these few measurements for determining the length of a shadow. In data mining it is important, sometimes critically important, not only to uncover and state the assumptions made, but also to understand the possible and likely sources and nature of the errors, and to assess the level of confidence of any insight, prediction, or relationship. Fortunately, there are ways of doing exactly that—but only once the assumptions are uncovered.

3.3 Hypotheses: Explaining Data

Data is always approached with some hypothesis (in the colloquial sense already mentioned) that may explain it. There should also be a hypothesis to explain why this particular data is thought to address the problem for which it is to be mined. However, there is more to hypotheses than explaining the data. There is also always some underlying explanation for why data mining is thought to be able to answer the question at hand. It is important to understand this reasoning because it is embedded with a weighty baggage of underlying assumptions, hopes, expectations, and fears. If these are not clearly explicated, the project can easily founder on the uncharted rocks of unjustified assumptions and unmet expectations. In part, this last hypothesis has already been discussed in previous sections and will be visited again in more detail in Chapters 5 and 6.

This section introduces two hypotheses about data that turn up in data mining: the internal hypothesis, which explains the data in its own terms, and the external hypothesis, which explains why mining this particular data should help shed light on the problem.

3.3.1 Data Structures

Every data set has some structure. Even a data set that includes completely random data has a pattern—it's just completely random! (Although a completely random data set is of no value for mining.) But if the data set is not completely random, then there is some nonrandom pattern enfolded within it. This pattern, whatever it may be and however it may be characterized, enfolds the useful information that may be mined.

Structure comes in different forms. Some types of structure are intentionally and deliberately established externally to the data. For instance, recording sales to the nearest penny is a deliberate choice. Recording the sale total and items included in the sale is also a deliberate choice. These choices form a sort of scaffolding that support the actual values. With the choices made, the data stored must conform to them, and thus it is structured in at least this way. These choices, a careful reader will immediately realize, are where part of the worldview of whomever or whatever organization made the decisions is imposed on the data. Such structures as this are fairly self evident, but worth close study.

Other structures also are deliberately imposed on the data but constrain relations between the values that the data takes. An easy example is the imposition of business rules on data. If such structures exist, and they almost always do, they too deserve close scrutiny.

Then there are the patterns in the data that reflect various states of the world, at least as modified through the other structures imposed on the data. It is usually, but by no means always, these structures that carry what is expected to be the information that is mined. In these patterns of the world, submerged and distorted by the selection and measuring process, lies the hope of clarifying and improving the model created to solve the problem. It is the miner's task to unwind this Gordian Knot, unweave the tangled skein, and lay out the threads of understanding and clarity of explanation.

3.3.2 Interaction and Relationship

Measured objects interact in some way in the real world. Of course, it is always possible that the interaction turns out to be that the objects are, to all intents and purposes, disconnected from each other. For instance, the length of the grass near your house has almost no effect on what you had for breakfast. However, in data sets for modeling, and more particularly those for mining, it is always assumed (with or without justification) that the data on hand does have some meaningful interaction or relationship enfolded within it. For the rest of this discussion, indeed, throughout the rest of the book, we too will make this assumption. This is the last time that the point will be emphasized, so it is worth noting that it is indeed an assumption. It is one of the assumptions that needs to be both stated and justified logically during the course of modeling.

Justifying an interaction may seem unnecessary. There are, nonetheless, many cases in which totally unjustified associations are assumed. Being unjustified does not make them wrong necessarily, but because there is no interactive explanation connecting the parts of the system to which they belong (what is called outside the systems thinking arena a *causal explanation*), no confidence of any level can be justified in any conclusion drawn. It is quite possible, for example, to get predictions of stock movements based on the level of the Yangtze River, or whether a team from the NFC or AFC wins the Super Bowl, or the position of the planets. Indeed, there is some association between the two sets of measurements. There is also a relationship between the length of the grass near your house and what you have for breakfast. At least for a while, those associations may appear to hold useable information for determining something about the state of one from the state of the other. But what isn't apparent is any explanation that connects the two sets of measurements together into a systemic relationship. Without such a systemic explanation, no level of confidence is justified that the connection is anything more than coincidence. Thus, it is in part the modeler's job to discover just such a systemic connection that can, at least in principle, be justified in any data sets to be mined.

Given such a justification, interactions appear in a variety of types and styles that can be characterized in a number of ways. Each of the methods offers a different perspective about the data, and each of the methods characterizes the interactions in a different way. Moreover, some of the methods will discover associations and interactions that other methods will not notice at all. So how is the appropriate method of characterizing the enfolded relationship to be discovered? Should we just try them all?

The answers to these two questions are determined by the hypothesis about the data that is brought to mining by the modeler. This is one reason that the model has to be constructed before mining the data. The hypothesis presupposes, with justifiable reason, that some particular method of characterizing the relationship will best reveal what is enfolded in the data set. Some methods will, when compared to the needs of the model, produce descriptions of the interaction that are inappropriate, even unuseable. So selecting the actual method appropriate for characterizing data is a judgement call, informed by the model (or submodel) developed before mining begins. This is one good reason that attempting to start the mining process with data ("Here's some data, tell me what I need to know!") yields little benefit.

3.3.3 Hypothesis and Explanation

Why are you reading this book? Pause here a moment and think quickly of a brief statement that answers the question.

What was your answer? Actually, the answer is not the main point. The question posed probably induced you to provide an explanation. Whatever it was, it almost certainly started with the equivalent of one of two expressions: It was either a "because" explanation or an "in order to" explanation. What we regard as an explanation almost always falls into one of these two forms. This is just as true for business problems as it is for personal questions.

"Because" explanations provide a scenario that explains the reasons, motivations, driving factors, or what we see as causes for the situation to be explained. "I am reading the book because my job requires it." ". . . because it looked interesting." ". . . because I have insomnia." These "because" explanations present the array of circumstances that existed to provide a motivation for reading the book. Such "because" explanations tend to be closed, that is, they explain a set of circumstances that existed leading to the action or event explained. (What non-systems thinkers may term a *causal explanation*.)

"In order to" explanations tend to be open and deal with means and ends. "I am reading this book in order to learn data mining" ". . . in order to capture more customers" ". . . in order to make my fortune on the stock market." (If you succeed in the latter, the author would appreciate a note as to the method!) These open explanations deal with how the present circumstances are intended to influence future events. "Because" explanations say, "the world exerted its influence such that the present circumstances came about." "In order to" explanations say, "the present events are intended to modify the world in thus-and-so ways."

Data mining and modeling can create either type of explanation of data. However, both explanations are not equally useful, depending, of course, on the need. That need is informed by the model, which is informed by the problem, and the problem is attacked only through a decision.

3.4 **Making Decisions**

The Maltese Falcon is in your possession! (This is an extremely valuable, solid gold statue that motivated the plot in Dashiel Hammet's novel, and Humphrey Bogart's film of the same name.) You have called Casper Guttman—the Fat Man—and he is willing to pay you handsomely with a very large number of large denomination bills. Hooray! But wait! Guttman is not a man known to be particularly trustworthy. He has asked you to his hotel room to deliver the statue where, he has assured you, he will give you the money. But you know that if you turn up with the Falcon, he is very likely to knock you on the head and disappear with both the Falcon and the cash. So you propose an alternative plan. You will leave the Falcon in a combination locker in the San Francisco airport, and he will leave the cash in a combination locker in the Los Angeles airport. You will then call each other and give each other the combinations to the lockers. Each will then go to the appropriate place. You will get what you want without any danger to you, and he will get what he wants.

Just as you are about to deposit the Falcon at the San Francisco airport, a thought occurs: What if he doesn't leave the cash? If you leave the Falcon, then he gets the Falcon and he gets to keep the cash. You get nothing. On the other hand, you could keep the Falcon, call him as if nothing had changed in your plan, and then you get to keep both the cash and the Falcon! However, what you would really prefer is for the exchange to go ahead as planned—and you know that Guttman would like that, too. If, as your final choice, neither of you leaves anything in the lockers, the whole exercise is completely futile because neither of you gets anything that you want. So what do you do?

This problem is a formulation of what is known as *The Prisoner's Dilemma*. Should you cooperate with each other, or should you defect? Most considerations of the Prisoner's Dilemma lead into a discussion of how game theory can be used to look at the options and determine payoff strategies. However, there is more to this problem, in fact to any problem, than a payoff matrix. How could this problem that you face possibly be addressed?

3.4.1 Frameworks for Decision: Representing Choices

Separate from, but including the various strategies devised by statistical decision theory, game theory, or any other theory, there are essentially five ways of dealing with problems. These are simply the five options available in everyday life.

First, ignore it. You could have done that it in the first place when you discovered the Falcon. "Oh ho," you say, "that's the Maltese Falcon! Well good for it. Nothing to do with me. I'm off to lunch." So you leave the Falcon for someone else. But that, you will say, doesn't deal with the problem as presented. Fine. So having actually gone as far as contacting Guttman, you simply drop the Falcon into the waste basket, and walk out of the plot. What Guttman does, or does not do, no longer concerns you. What happens to the Falcon no longer concerns you. Just ignore the problem, and it disappears! (Maybe.)

Second, absolve the problem (i.e., pass the buck). Hand the Falcon over to the Lost and Found. Call the police. Call Sam Spade and dump the thing on him. Anything, in fact, that removes the problem from your purview. This deals with the problem as far as you are concerned.

Third, the problem dissolves. When values encompassed in the problem situation change, either through internal action or outside change, it totally eclipses the original problem valuation. So Guttman has offered you (say) a million dollars. But on the way to the San Francisco airport, you stop to buy a lottery ticket. After all, you feel that this is your lucky day. And it is! You win the lottery—say $100 million. The problem dissolves. Guttman's million and the situation remain the same, but your valuation of it changes. "Hey," you say, "another million might be nice, but the tax man will only get it anyway. Who cares!"

Fourth, resolve the problem. This modifies the situation, removing it as a problem. The problem is the chance of defection by Guttman. (Of course, his problem is the chance of defection by you, but you are not concerned about that, and in any case, what you really want is for him to have the Falcon, and you to have the money.) If you remove the chance of his defection, the problem is resolved. Get Guttman to put the cash in escrow somewhere, with you as the only person authorized to withdraw it. (He might also then want you to put the Falcon in a safety deposit box and authorize Guttman exclusively to remove it.) You get receipts and attestations. Now you can both see that the goods are what and where you say they are before the transaction is made. Neither of you can renege. Problem resolved.

Fifth, solve the problem. This is where the discussion of game theory enters the picture. Solving a problem means dealing with it on its own terms. Decide on your best payoffs, chances, and so on. Here you have to accept the situation, the rules and limitations, and determine, given the situation as it is, on some best course of action. (At this point, in order to discover how to best deal with Casper Guttman and exchange the Maltese Falcon by using game theory to help decide what to do, you're going to have to pick up a book on game theory and several on the Prisoner's Dilemma. The problem is not straightforward! See pointers in the Resources section.)

Of the five basic ways of dealing with a problem, solving it may not be the best choice. Solving a problem means playing by the rules that the problem establishes. The alternatives allow for far more creativity, reaching outside the problem's framework and finding some way of changing the rules. Developing strategies for ignoring, absolving, dissolving, or resolving the problem are often no more difficult than developing a strategy for solving it—and sometimes it's easier. However, the only formal approaches for dealing with problems seem to fall exclusively into the area of solving problems. Two popular approaches are game theory (more properly the Theory of Games of Strategy) and linear programming.

Both of these approaches have been mentioned already, and will be mentioned again in this book. However interesting and useful they are in their own right, and in solving some types of problems, this book touches on them only lightly. The reason for introducing them at all is because both modeling and data mining may be used to assist in setting up problems for solution using one of these techniques. So although there is no opportunity here to discuss them in any depth, an introduction is useful.

This book takes it for granted in Parts II through IV that the problem has to be solved and that data mining is to be employed. However, as a business modeler you should look explicitly at the alternatives to solving the problem. One of the other four approaches may well be a better alternative than accepting the problem at face value.

3.4.2 **Playing Games**

The Maltese Falcon dilemma has already presented one of the types of problems that can be solved using game theory. "But," you may quite properly ask, "what about the Maltese Falcon is a game?" Well, nothing actually. The theory takes its name from the study of certain kinds of games, and sees what abstractions from those games may be more broadly applicable to problems and decisions in other domains. Sometimes it can be very useful.

The key point that allows some problems to be solved using game theory is that there must be more than one "player," and the "winning" of the game requires there to be a "loser." In other words, there must be some conflict of interest.

Essentially, the idea is to work out various moves that each player can make within the confines of the rules of the game. These optional actions are labeled *strategies* (a word used in several different contexts in this book). Various strategies are available to each player, but are perhaps different for each player. For each strategy there is some outcome, in game theory called a *payoff*, that makes it possible to lay out in some formal way—say, in a table—all of the possible combinations of strategies for each player and the payoffs that eventuate if an opponent uses a responding strategy. With this combination of all initiating and responding strategies and their associated payoffs, it sometimes becomes possible to discover some optimal strategy or strategies. The Prisoner's Dilemma is one case in which there is no one optimal action under all circumstances.

Game theory is not simple or straightforward, and where it is applicable it can reveal some remarkable insights. One problem for applying game theory to real-world problems is that the strategies, and particularly the payoff values, are not always clear. The world is a place full of FUD (fear, uncertainty, and doubt), which can preclude setting up the problem clearly. That, of course, is where data mining and modeling can sometimes contribute—not in the solution of the games, but in identifying strategies and their payoffs.

3.4.3 **Linear Programming**

The Battle of Britain raged over southern England during the early years of the Second World War. The weather was beautiful. In fact, it was one of the finest summers in England in living memory. On those beautiful summer afternoons, the author's grandparents went for country picnics on the South Downs, an area of England southeast of London. While they ate their picnic lunch, sometimes within the walls of a Roman fort built nearly 2000 years before, vapor contrails crossed the clear blue summer sky as killing machines fought for supremacy. Fighters of the Royal Air Force faced the Luftwaffe in that deadly duel. The contrails were those of Messerschmitt and Spitfire, Dornier and Hurricane.

The Luftwaffe were based in the fields of northern France and had to cross the English Channel to reach Britain, but in spite of the good weather and watchers on the coast, there was never enough warning of the appearance of these enemy aircraft. But the British had a secret weapon—a radio detection and ranging system later called *radar,* developed by people called "back room boffins." However, the secret weapon alone was not enough. It was wonderful for detecting and ranging the incoming enemy aircraft, but what was the Air Force to do with this information to best use it? The operational squadrons were a very scarce resource, because of a desperate shortage of trained pilots. The boffins were asked what they could do to help flight operations.

A small group of boffins was diverted to the task, and they worked for "Radar (Operations) Research." Later the name was abbreviated to Operations (or sometimes Operational) Research, as it remains to this day. What started as a search for techniques to best use the very constrained resources of the Royal Air Force to hold off the enemy turned into a battery of techniques useful in many other real-world problems. One of the key techniques developed for planning the best use of scarce resources was linear programming. It was this tool, coupled with input from radar stations, that formed an indispensable and crucial strategic advantage in winning the Battle of Britain. By one estimate, radar doubled the effectiveness of the Royal Air Force, and Operations Research doubled it again!

Modeling and data mining today can play the same part in setting up problems for operations research-type solutions as it does for game theory problems. The more accurate the inputs to any system, the more accurate the outcomes. This, of course, is no more than the reverse of the well-known aphorism GIGO (garbage in, garbage out.)

3.5 **Deciding**

After all has been said and done, the whole purpose behind all of modeling and mining is to decide what to do. If the effort did nothing to help decide what to do, it would quickly be abandoned for something more useful. But it is useful, and the modeler/miner's whole purpose is to provide some basis for deciding what to do. That, however, isn't straightforward.

In any situation, there are a number of ways of deciding. For instance, what should we do? Or, alternatively, what could we do? Or again, what would be best to do? These questions call for different frameworks for deciding, frameworks that the modeler has to accommodate if the advice given is to be useful and relevant.

3.5.1 Normative Decisions: What Should We Do?

One possible way to decide what should be done is to appeal to some framework, or code of conduct, that prescribes and proscribes particular actions and courses of action under particular circumstances. The law is an example of such a code of conduct. A smaller scale example might be something like the rule of thumb that says, "If you want to get good grades, you will have to study hard." Such frameworks of rules are called *normative* in that they provide direction as to what should be done; however, they are only as binding as anyone chooses them to be. That is to say that accepting the validity or relevance of such sets of rules is optional, and anyone who chooses not to accept them isn't bound by them—at least insofar as deciding is concerned.

There is a normative framework for deciding what should be done that is often appealed to as if it were a law of nature. This framework, which is well grounded in observations of the way of the world as it actually appears, is the normative framework that a modeler almost invariably seems to be working in, although it is regarded as optional by most, if not all, of the people with whom a modeler works. That is the *normative theory of probability*. For a modeler, it is very important to understand that probability theory is regarded as optional, even by those who pay it apparent lip service. Humans often do not reason probabilistically—and don't accept probabilistic reasoning even when clearly presented. This fact is so important that what it means in practice needs to be looked at more closely.

3.5.1.1 Hot Hands, Cold Logic

Basketball fans and commentators are particularly fond of something called the "hot hand." The idea is that players have "streaks" of outstanding performance periods. Specifically, a player is more likely to shoot the ball into the basket after a couple of consecutive successful shots. So, such players with the hot hand are called *streak shooters*.

Basketball, like many other popularly followed sports, is a sport of statistics. The sport is described at least as much quantitatively as it is qualitatively. This is a clear case where quantitative appreciation is a part of the qualitative pleasure of the fan. The statistical measurements, then, are available to be analyzed, modeled, and even mined. So the hot hand phenomenon is one that attracted the attention of statisticians and analysts who were able to examine it with the tools of probability theory.

Let's suppose that some particular player made, over the course of some long period, 50% of his shots. This, not by coincidence, means that the player's chance of making a shot should be exactly the same as the chance of a flipped fair coin coming up heads. So here is an opportunity to try an experiment. Take a fair coin and toss it for a while—say the number of times a player shoots in a season. Call the heads "made shots" and the tails "missed shots." What does it look like?

Actually, the pattern of heads and tails resulting from such a fair tossing of a fair coin is, unless you are already familiar with it, not what most people would call random. There appears to be too many runs of heads or tails together. For instance, one such sequence (and not one especially selected to illustrate the point) produced:

HHHTHHHHTTHHTTHTHTTTHHHHHHTTHHTHTHHTHHHTTHHHTTHHT

It turns out that in this run of 48 flips of a real coin, one presumed to be "fair" in the sense that it has no particular bias to come up either heads or tails, there were 29 heads (60%) and 19 tails (40%). This is not what is intuitively expected, perhaps, but it is in line—or at least, it is not out of line—with what statistical considerations would say should be expected. If instead of flips of a coin this series represented 48 consecutive attempts to make a shot by a basketball player, it might be taken to confirm the hot hand idea.

Now, a real player's skill is an important factor in the proportion of shots made. It may well be that a good player makes more shots than misses. This, however, doesn't affect the statistical reasoning. After considerable statistical examination, there is no statistical evidence of the hot hand phenomenon. That is to say, considering the overall ability of a player to make shots (sometimes statistically called the "base rate"), no significant fluctuation from a random series with that base rate can be found.

So what does all this mean? If you accept that the theory of probability is a valid description of the world, then you "should" accept that the hot hand phenomenon doesn't exist—"should" in the sense that this is a framework of reasoning that prescribes for those phenomena within its domain what you have to accept if indeed you accept the framework as valid. If indeed this framework is valid, and the reasoning is valid, then it has consequences for what actions "should" be taken in the real world. It is no use passing the ball to a player with a hot hand simply because the player has a hot hand. Such a strategy will result in a poorer team score than passing the ball to the best scoring player in a position to shoot the ball.

What of the result in the real world? Well, as reported in *How We Know What Isn't So: The Fallibility of Human Reason in Everyday Life* (T. Gliovich,

1991, The Free Press), Red Auerbach of the Boston Celtics responded to this information with, "Who is this guy? So he makes a study. I couldn't care less." Bobby Knight, formerly of the Indiana Hoosiers, responded that, ". . . there are so many variables involved in shooting basketball that this paper really doesn't mean anything."

Clearly, these responses indicate that probability theory is not universally accepted as normative. Now, this can be interpreted as another instance in which what you know determines and enforces what you can know. The problems are that mining is entirely based on models grounded in probability theory; the modeler has to explain the results; and when deciding what "should" be done, it's important to discover what normative model holds sway. If necessary, the modeler needs to be prepared to lay the groundwork that supports the conclusions, particularly if they fly in the face of accepted intuition.

3.5.1.2 Hot Logic, Cold Markets

A marketing manager wants to launch a new product. History indicates (for the sake of this example) that most new products are launched into unreceptive markets. In fact, judging from history, the marketing manager already knows that products of this type have a 10% chance of success. Put another way, 9 product launches in 10 result in an unprofitable outcome. Wanting to improve the odds of a success, the manager calls on you as a modeler for advice.

You suggest that test marketing the product would produce the data needed to better determine the chance that the product will be successful. The marketing department, being familiar with this concept, proceeds with the test. The marketing manager then returns with the test results to ask your advice.

You create a model based on the results of the test marketing. After extensive testing and calibration of the model, it turns out that for products of this type, when the product turns out to be successful, the model predicts success 90% of the time. However, it also turns out that for those product launches that aren't successful, the model still predicts success 20% of the time. Another way of describing the results of the market test model is that it has a hit rate of 90% and a false alarm rate of 20%.

It turns out that in this case, the market test model clearly points to a market success for the product. Given this information, what would you advise is the actual chance of success? Or, what will you tell the marketing manager?

The marketing manager, looking at the test marketing model results, says, "Looks like the chance of success is 90%! Great work—lets get the product launched." Do you agree? What, at this point, do you think the chance of a successful product is if not 90%? If you don't think it's 90%, do you think it's more or less than 50%?

Let's suppose that there are 100 products of this type, and that these percentages apply exactly to them all. That means that we know for sure that of the 100 products, 10 of them succeeded and 90 failed in the marketplace. Of the 90 failed products, 20% of them, or 18 products, would be, according to this model, falsely predicted to be successful. Of the 10 successful products, 9 of them would be predicted as successes, one of them would be predicted to fail. So the numbers of products in each category look like this:

1: Failed in the market; predicted as a success: $90 \times 20\% = 18$

2: Failed in the market; predicted as a failure $90 \times 80\% = 72$

3: Succeeded in the market; predicted as a success $10 \times 90\% = 9$

4: Succeeded in the market; predicted as a failure $10 \times 10\% = 1$

This product is predicted as a success, so it must fall into either group 1 or group 3 because they are the only groups where the model indicates success. Groups 1 and 3 total 27 products, and out of these 27 products only 9 are in Group 3, where the product was both predicted to be successful and actually was successful. So the actual probability of success has to be 9 chances in 27, or 9/27, or about 33%.

Is this in line with your intuition as a modeler? If not, what went astray? This kind of reasoning is very important to every modeler presenting results to support decision making in a business situation. Many business models predict outcomes. Very often, some value is ascribed to the outcome of a predictive model, often called the "expected value" of the choice modeled. If this product is separately predicted, for instance, to create $1 million in profit, if it is indeed successful, and the 90% success rate were used, the expected value assigned would be $90\% \times \$1,000,000 = \$900,000$. Given this expected outcome, the marketing manager might feel quite justified in spending $300,000 to roll out the product.

However, the true situation is very different, in that the expected value of the outcome in this case is more nearly $33\% \times \$1,000,000 = \$330,000$. Spending almost the whole of the expected value of the profit to roll out the product should give any marketing manager pause.

3.5.2 Finding Possibilities: What Could We Do?

Decisions are motivated by problems, which in turn are motivated by a perceived need for change. Or in other words, as already discussed elsewhere in this overview part of the book, decisions are called for to select among options when it seems that there is a need to change the course of events to bias those events toward a more beneficial outcome. In this sense, decision making is about managing, or even promoting, change. Yet all changes in the world are not the same. That's pretty obvious. But what is not so immediately obvious is that not all changes are of the same type, and selecting options very much depends on the type of change desired.

3.5.2.1 *Plus ça change, plus c'est la meme chose*

Change without change is such a well-recognized phenomenon that it is encapsulated in many common aphorisms. The French expression translates into colloquial English as, "the more things change, the more they stay the same." So well known is this expression that it is almost as well known to many native English speakers in the original French as it is in its English translation. A similar aphorism with much the same intent is "rearranging the deck chairs on the *Titanic,*" which recognizes that some changes in details make no real difference to the situation.

In contrast, some changes do bring about a change in the immediate situation, but have an effect that is the absolute opposite of that intended, so that although the situation as a whole hasn't really changed in its total structure, the role of the players is reversed. In *The March of Folly,* Barbara Tuchman looks at several historical situations where exactly this sort of reversing of the situation happens. This appears a very direct case of "the more things change . . ." The reversal of circumstances does indeed represent a change, perhaps a seemingly significant one, yet from a different perspective it's hard to say what about the overall situation is really different.

What is it about these changes that leave something essential about a situation unchanged? Are there other types of change? Looking again at aphorisms for a clue, major sorts of change are often discovered by "thinking outside the box." But what sort of a box is it that this intuition captures? And what is outside anyway?

Discovering some sort of answer to these questions needs at least an outline sketch of a theory of change. More than that, though, any theory of change, even an outline sketch, needs to deal not only with change, but also with persistence. After all, when it's deck chairs that are being arranged, the insight is that something persists despite the change. Persistence needs to be explained every bit as much as change. These two phenomena are so intimately related that they are but facets of the same thing.

3.5.3 A Sketch Theory of Persistence and Change

Many of the complex phenomena of the world appear to us to be related as systems—combinations of objects, events, and circumstances that are closely interconnected and interrelated with each other, and which somehow seem to interact and react to and with the world as a whole. One of the most important features of a system, as previously noted in the section introducing them earlier, is that it has a boundary—an "inside" and an "outside." Thus, whatever else it may be, a system is a group of objects, relationships, and so on, tied together and contained within the boundary.

The night was dark, and the time was late as a young man wrote furiously, for at dawn he faced death. It was 1832, and the young Evariste Galois, just 20 years old, was fated to fight a duel. In the morning he fought his duel, and was mortally wounded and left to die. Yet, his furious scribblings from the night before (he many times frantically wrote "I have not time, I have not time" on his notes) founded a branch of mathematics that has, and will continue to have, an important impact on our understanding of the world long into the future. His 60 hastily written pages serve as the foundation of group theory. One of the points that this theory encompasses is the way that the content of groups can change.

3.5.3.1   Systems as Groups

Some, but by no means all, systems recognizable in the world are groups in the sense proposed by group theory. So not all systems are groups (in this sense), although many systems are built from component systems that are groups in the group theoretical sense. (So as not to become unnecessarily repetitive, in this section the term *groups* is used to indicate a group within the framework of group theory.) In sketching a theory of persistence and change, these systems that are groups are very important.

The first important property of a group is that it has members. It's not important that the members are alike in any way except that they must all share some common membership characteristic. Also, in order to be a group, any members must be able to be combined such that any combination is also a member of the group. So, to take a very simple example, numbers form a group. Combining numbers (say with addition or multiplication) produces a result that is just another number—a member of the group.

Another property of the way that group members combine is that the order of combinations mustn't affect the outcome. For instance, in order to go from point to point in Manhattan (where most of the streets are laid out in a regular grid), it matters not how you combine the directions, "go north one block, go north one block, go east one block, go east one block." You could go N,N,E,E, or N,E,N,E, or E,N,N,E, and so on, but whatever combination you choose, starting from a specific location, you end up in the same place.

Another important property of a group is the presence of an *identity member*—a member of the group such that a combination of any other member with the identity member gives the other member as a result. For numbers, when the combination operation is addition, the identity member is zero—any number plus zero gives the original number. For multiplication as the combination operation, the identity member is one—a number multiplied by one gives the original number. For moves in Manhattan, the identity member is "stand still." For a group that comprised the barks of my dog, the identity member would be silence.

The final property of groups that needs to be looked at here is that every member has a reciprocal member, such that if the member and reciprocal member are combined, out comes the identity member. For moves in Manhattan, the reciprocal member for "go east one block" is "go west one block." Combine them and the result is identical with "stand still." For dog barks, an exact recording of the bark, inverted and combined with the original, would give silence. (However unlikely this may seem, it is the principle of noise cancellation, and is used in microphones in noisy situations [like aircraft], and in noise-reduction headphones for portable cassette and CD players.)

For worldly systems that are groups, manipulating the group components is very much like the metaphorical rearrangement of the deck chairs on the *Titanic*. This is the "what goes around, comes around" type of change. The components of the system change their rearrangement, but nothing has extended beyond the system to disturb the world further afield.

3.5.3.2　Deck Chairs in Business

There are many times when organizational structures rearrange their components without changing anything apparently meaningful outside the system. The very phrase "business as usual" applied to Washington, D.C., (that is, the U.S. government) carries exactly this connotation. It appears very convincing to many outside observers that the more things change in Washington, the more they do stay the same.

In a business situation, this is exactly the situation that applies when one company competes with another on its own terms. For many years, Pepsi and Coca-Cola were rivals. Pepsi spent many long, hard hours scrutinizing Coke in the marketplace and concluded that the trademark hourglass shape of the Coke bottle gave Coke its competitive advantage. Given that assessment of the situation, which with hindsight seems completely accurate, Pepsi went all out to attempt to overcome Coke's advantage. Pepsi poured millions of dollars and many years into the effort. In 1958, Pepsi introduced the "swirl" bottle, which remained the standard packaging for 20 years. Yet, with hindsight, this was an effort in futility. Rearranging the deck chairs indeed.

3.5.3.3　Getting out of the Box

"Thinking out of the box" is an aphorism, but one that truly recognizes the underlying nature of what needs to be done. It turns out that it's not exactly a box, but the boundary of a system that needs to be crossed. The aphorism refers to discovering a change that is not within a group-theoretic type change. What is sought is a change that is external to the group system and that has impact on the internal workings and relationships of the system. In this, too, there is some underpinning theory from mathematics that is usefully included in the sketch theory being discussed. It is called, rather forbiddingly, The Theory of Logical Types, and was developed by Alfred North Whitehead and Bertrand Russell in their monumental, but doomed to fail, effort to put mathematics on a firm logical footing with the *Principia Mathematica*.

The Theory of Logical Types also deals with collections of things, although it usually uses a slightly different terminology from group theory. Here the group is called a *class,* and classes have members, but many essentials of the two theories are the same. Both can be applied to the components of systems that meet the necessary criteria. Indeed, it does turn out that they are often coterminous. One of the fundamental requirements (called an *axiom*) of this theory is that anything that covers all of the class (group or system) must not be part of the system. As an example, all of the customers of a company are a class, but the class of all customers is not itself a customer. Or, again, executives of a company are a class, but the class is not an executive of the company.

Said this way, it seems fairly intuitively obvious, but it hasn't always been so. More to the point, when analyzing complex systems that form hierarchies of classes, it's not always easy to keep these things straight.

Getting out of the box is stepping out of the system of endless "what goes around comes around," and changing the system from the outside. This requires moving to a meta level, getting to a higher dimension, or looking in from the outside. It involves not playing by the existing rules of the game. For instance, Chapter 1 pointed out that the foundational modeling tool is language. We can describe almost anything with language—except language. To do that we have to invent another language, a meta language, especially for talking about language.

Or again, we are aware of changes in the world: the temperature and pressure of the atmosphere, for instance. Those changes can be described easily—it's 10 degrees warmer now than it was 12 hours ago. But it requires another level of discussion to talk about the changes in the changes—global warming, for instance. It would be another level again to talk about the changes in the changes of the changes. This can go on forever, although perhaps not meaningfully.

3.5.3.4 Pepsi out of the Box

John Scully, in his autobiography *Odyssey,* described how he rethought the situation with Coke. He realized that the Coke bottle had almost become the product and that meeting it on its own terms wasn't going to succeed. After struggling with the problem, he asked himself a question that started to move his thinking out of the box, "How should problems like this be approached?"

The key meta insight, the one that changed the group theoretic "going around and coming around," was when he saw the need to "shift the ground rules," which is what he says on page 21 of his book. At this point, he pulled back and asked what the customer really wanted.

From there he set up a study. He offered a group of research customers special discounts for purchasing Pepsi in return for detailed information about their consumption habits at home—and discovered something startling. No matter how much Pepsi the test customers hauled home, they consumed it all!

This was the first discovery of the now well-known fact that however much snack food people buy, they consume it all. But it did change the entire nature of Pepsi's marketing strategy. Scully realized that the way to compete was to use larger and more varied packaging that would simply get more Pepsi into people's homes. That strategy really did change the rules— and change the system. This was what is called a *disruptive change,* in that the result was to drive the famous hourglass bottle into extinction in the United States. (Although it is making a sort of postmortem guest appearance lately, the hourglass Coke bottle certainly no longer defines the product, as it did for more than 20 years.) Pepsi dramatically expanded its market share on John Scully's insights, and has kept it ever since.

3.5.3.5   Modeling out of the Box

This section looks at what we could do. Most of the section has laid the groundwork with a sketch outline of a theory of persistence and change. Although it is only a sketch, it points the way to much deeper issues. For instance, it points to the idea that a mathematically based and rigorous general theory of persistence and change might be possible. But not only that, it points to limitations in the reach of business modeling, at least for the present.

Change has been studied for thousands of years. One of the oldest written documents that has come down to us today deals exclusively with change—the *I Ching*. This is an ancient Chinese book that presents a qualitative theory of change, and qualitative metaphors for understanding it. Today, we prefer our theories and metaphors to have a quantitative foundation and (ideally) a qualitative interpretation. Perhaps group theory and the theory of logical types, as applied to systems theory, presages a more firmly grounded and comprehensive theory of change: one that has metaphors that we can apply directly to manipulating the world. But if we succeed in this, it's what we today call creativity, and we don't yet know how to bottle that! The best that can be said realistically is that perhaps these are pointers that one day, some part of what is an exclusively human capability will be automated. But if we do get there, it will be a long time coming.

Business models are, perforce, of business systems. There are no tools, at least at present, for creating meta models. Perhaps a more rigorous theory of persistence and change will lead there eventually, but business modeling is pretty much limited to in-the-box modeling at the moment. Not that such models aren't useful—sometimes enormously so. But business modeling, even supported by data mining, is not yet ready to reach outside the box. This is not to say that a modeler will not be expected to take part in the analysis and discussions of deciding what can be done. But what can be done with to-day's technologies pushes beyond the present limits of business modeling.

3.6 **Summary**

Socrates is pretty much responsible for getting the ball rolling on this one, as with so much else in our lives. One day in the agora (the marketplace), Socrates was standing around with some acquaintances, annoying them as usual (which is why they forcefully persuaded him to drink hemlock in the end). He had a rather uncomfortable knack of asking questions of experts that ended up with them realizing that they didn't know what they were talking about. Callicles, no friend of Socrates, was seen coming into the area and Socrates called him over.

"Leave me alone!" he retorted. "We've had quite enough of your nonsense here—why can't you just shut up and leave us in peace."

"But please, Callicles," replied Socrates gently, putting his arm round Callicles' shoulder, "we are engaged here in an endeavor of some importance. We are trying to discover what course of life is best."

And we have been trying to find out ever since.

What is best to do very much depends on the objective. If the object is more profit, the best things to do might be very different than if the object is to attract more customers, or reduce churn, or raise the stock price, or produce a better product, or any of a host of business objectives. John Scully's objectives were several—more market share and more profit, among others. Whether in or out of the box thinking is needed, understanding the objective is paramount in determining and selecting the best course of action from those possible and available. With objectives set, business models can help evaluate possible outcomes and support choices between options. But this requires understanding the frame that surrounds the problem. This is a crucial issue that is taken up in the next chapter, the first chapter of Part II, which develops the detail of business modeling.

Part II
Business Modeling

Models are utterly crucial to all areas of life, especially business. Every day business managers at all levels take actions to change the behavior of the business in ways intended to benefit both business and manager. Yet many models are empirical and experiential—not the sort that a business modeler can work with. A business modeler has to create models that capture insights into the way the world really works, identify and satisfy all of the conflicting requirements of the various stakeholders, create usable models that make sense, fit the model into existing business processes, justify the model based on the data available, and deliver on time and under budget. The on time, under budget requirement lies in the arena of project management, not discussed here. All else that a business modeler needs is wrapped into Part II.

Take note that models are designed backwards and built forwards. What this means is that everything has to be considered prior to building, particularly deployment issues that come at the end of building (and at the end of this part of the book). As noted in the instructions for any complex device, "Before assembly, please read all the instructions!" Also keep also in mind the adage, "Measure twice, cut once."

A note about the references to the methodology. Part II describes how to discover, specify and create business models for later mining. There are many references in Part II that point to the place in the methodology that deals with the topic being discussed. References to the methodology look like this: (MII:AB.1) MII: points to the methodology associated with Part II. (There is no MI as Part I has no methodology associated with it.) Thus the reference (MII.AB.1) points to the methodology for Part II, Action Box 1. The methodology will be found in Part IV following Chapter 14, that fully explains how the methodology is constructed and how to use it.

Chapter 4
What Is a Model?

It is impossible for any of us to function in our personal lives, let alone in business, without models. Almost every conscious act that any of us ever takes is predicated on a model of some sort. For instance, if you are stopped at a turnpike tollbooth in the United States and the toll collector hands you a Canadian quarter in your change, you would probably hand it back. Why? The easy answer is that a Canadian quarter is useless as currency in most of the United States, so you don't want it. But that answer begs the question, how did you recognize that you didn't want it? The answer, of course, is that you have a mental representation, or "model" of what a U.S. quarter looks like, and the Canadian quarter doesn't fit that model. Moreover, other related models about how the financial and economic systems of the United States work tell you that Canadian quarters don't work in those related models. These models function as our mental representations of the world, and they are dynamic and flexible. For instance, the U.S. Mint has introduced quarters of several different designs commemorating the states of the Union. Our mental models of quarters, therefore, need to be constantly adjusted to allow for these changes.

Models live in a world dominated by data, information, and knowledge. As far as businesses are concerned, this is a world of business information (BI) and knowledge management (KM). Now it's quite true that the results of modeling and mining do indeed reside in these specialties, but note that it's the results that live there, not the modeling or mining activities themselves. It is also true that BI and KM researchers identify far more components than data, information, and knowledge in systemic descriptions of their areas—they also include important attributes such as understanding, intent, and insight. However, for the purpose of looking at models, it is enough to consider only three concepts: data, information, and knowledge. It is these concepts that need to be clearly explicated in terms of what they mean to the model—and the modeler.

Understanding the power and utility of models requires coming to grips with the structures of data, information, and knowledge. Following a brief introduction to these topics, the chapter looks at models (and their relationships with data, information, and knowledge) and characterizes them along five dimensions: inferential/predictive, associative/systemic, static/dynamic, qualitative/quantitative, and comparative/interactive. These dimensions provide a framework for understanding how models work. Finally, the chapter examines the process of modeling as the modeler views it, and ends with a look at the difference between a comprehensive statistical description of the data and the creation of a data-based model description of the world.

4.1   Introduction to Data, Information, and Knowledge

All models are based on data. All data originates in the world. Mental models are based on data that reaches us through our senses. However, the models dealt with in this book are based on data that is collected and stored in a format that is external to our individual mental representation. In creating models that are formed from such externally stored data it's important to explicitly consider the process that turns data into information and information into knowledge because this is, in part, the process that the modeler has to practice as a technique—one of the most basic processes of modeling. Because it is so fundamental, it's important to pin down exactly what happens, what goes in, how it's changed, and what comes out, throughout the transformation at each stage.

4.1.1   Data

From a philosophical perspective, the observed and the observer are inextricably intertwined. Thus, again philosophically speaking, there are no such things as "objective facts." This is important to realize because all such so-called objective facts carry an enormous amount of associated, but often unnoticed, baggage. No fact exists without its associated context. Data, however, is often described as collected objective observations (or facts) about the world. Often, a discussion focusing on what makes data data, as opposed to anything else, rests on the putative objectivity of the facts. Although this may not be the best characterization of data, it is as good a place as any to start.

Consider a simple "objective" measurement of the outside temperature. Any reader of this book could almost certainly make such a measurement practically without thinking about it, and in such a way that observers would probably agree was "objective." However, in order to make any such measurement, a vast array of assumptions come into play. For instance, we have to agree that "outside temperature" is energy measured as the average velocity of air molecules in such a manner as, ideally, to be uninfluenced by the direct radiation of any heat-radiating body (like the sun). We also have to agree to the use of a particular scale and an acceptable degree of accuracy. Never mind that the terms "average," "velocity," "air," and so on all carry cognitive connotations—the task of temperature measurement is one that has a widely and commonly accepted operational construction.

In a business setting, the operational definitions associated with the apparently "objective" measurement of, say, customer behavior, may be far more difficult. Even in making such well understood business observations as measuring return on investment (ROI), defining exactly what comprised the investment and exactly what comprised the return can lead to significant problems. It is not uncommon for discussions of ROI for a project, for instance, to debate and adjust the presented results. If such results can be debated, let alone adjusted, there is clearly not an objective "fact" in ROI. The key point here is that although data is often described as "a collection of objective measurements," even such "objective" observations include assumptions of and about the observer.

The observer doesn't even have to be a human being. When the observer is some mechanical device, such as a point of sale (POS) scanner, the observed facts still carry conceptual baggage. It is simply that the surrounding assumptions were in full play at "design time," when the system was designed to collect particular facts. The machine, of course, makes no interpretation of the facts that it records, but the recorded information is no less ambiguous even though it was collected using an automated method.

Data, nonetheless, is formed from observations of the world. When such observations are collected, they are indeed data. However, data is not a collection of "objective" facts (as is often stated or implied), but the collected assortment that is uninterpreted in any way. Data is simply a collection of symbols representing that particular events occurred within particular contexts. The event symbols characterize the extension, duration, quality, quantity, and so on of the event. However, it is its wholly uninterpreted nature that makes the collection data, and nothing more.

4.1.2   Information

Information forms much of the background to today's world. We are perhaps the most information aware—not to mention the most information awash—people in history. This surfeit of information is itself a problem. But just what is "information"?

To say that information is interpreted data, or data "endowed with meaning and purpose" in Peter Drucker's famous expression, somewhat begs the question of the relationship between data and information. Clearly, there is a close connection between the two, but what is it exactly? How do meaning and purpose come to endow data?

Information is bicameral in nature; at the very least, it is always a summary of the data from which it is formed. However, it is not enough to simply summarize data to have information. It is at this point—summarization—that to be considered as information, the summary has to receive its endowment of meaning and purpose. But meaning and purpose are relative terms. Purpose is a quality wholly external to the data providing the information. Purpose is, as beauty, in the mind of the beholder. Or at least, as far as purpose is concerned, it is in the ends or intents of the summarizer of the data. Thus, for data to provide information, the summary of the data must be made in such a way that it addresses the particular ends, or purposes, of the informed.

If information is a summary of data to some purpose, what of meaning? That, too, is in the mind of the beholder. For instance, unless you happen to be a medical doctor, a technical discussion of the latest cancer treatment and its impact on the cellular mass of a tumor—even if the discussion is based on the latest data—would completely pass you by. You simply do not have the necessary mental framework to interpret the information presented, and thus, it has no meaning for you. The meaning of any summary of data is present only to the extent that the informed has the necessary interpretive structures to incorporate the information within an existing knowledge framework. Thus, the same data looked at by different summarizers, each of whom brings different existing knowledge to bear on the summarizing of the data, will produce different information from the same data.

The important point so far is one that is generally crucial for models, and is no less crucial to gleaning information from data—it is that of *context*. For instance, the context within which temperature can be measured is the considerable amount of relevant physical science that bears on the subject. It is this context that gives the data its particular meaning. Similarly, POS data is framed within the context of the business transaction that generates it. Furthermore, the context must be one that the informed recognizes. Thus, information is, at least in part, summarized data placed in a context.

If the informed bring meaning and purpose to the data summary, what of the nature of the summary itself? That is to say, given that meaning and purpose are external requirements that direct the summarization, what is the form of a summarization? Directed by the appropriate context for the summary, data summarization mainly looks at groupings and relationships within the data. It groups likes with likes, segregates and distinguishes similar groupings from dissimilar groupings, and characterizes relationships among all of the groups.

For instance, if it was based on some data, the summary statement "fewer Web shopping carts are abandoned by shoppers with coupons than by those without coupons" is information that can demonstrate every point in this section. What is a "Web shopping cart?" If you have the knowledge to understand the context of this piece of information, it is meaningful—if not, the statement is nonsense. Similarly, you would need to understand that the "coupons" in the summary statement were not the physical objects also associated with the same word but some metaphorical electronic extension of the idea. One of the groups identified is "abandoned Web shopping carts," which segregates it from all other groupings of shopping carts. When all of the abandoned shopping carts are considered as a group, a joint relationship is described between them and two other groups—the group "shoppers with coupons" and the group "shoppers without coupons."

Such a statement, informative as it might be, is hardly a complete summary of the data on which it is based. More objects might be distinguished, relationships might be more completely defined, and limits of confidence, accuracy, and expectation could be included. All of this is possible—and if continued indefinitely, will generate endless details concerning the original data. Indeed, it might be possible to generate more "information" about the data than there was data in the first place! Information, as a summary in context, has to be as succinct as possible while filling the needs set by the requirements of meaning and purpose, but no more so.

In short, information, at least so far, seems to be a summary of data placed in context—and indeed, it is. This is one part of its bicameral nature. There is, however, a powerful, although complex, theory of information known, unsurprisingly, as *information theory*. Although its very technical aspects need not be explored at this juncture, the theory has some crucial points. One of the most fundamental is that information has to be communicated to inform. This means than that the summary just discussed must be passed into, and incorporated in, a contextual framework. However, information theory also points out that any informative communication unavoidably comprises three elements: information, noise, and redundancy. Each of these parts is present to a greater or lesser degree in any informative communication, and they all must be present to at least some degree, however small. "Information," in this information theoretic sense, is that part of the communication that comprises the valid features of the summary—those that do apply to the data. "Noise" implies that, to a greater or lesser extent, some part of the communication expresses conclusions that may seem to be about the data, but are in fact invalid. "Redundancy" implies duplication in that some part of the valid information turns up in the communication in more than one way.

Thus, *information* can be described as a communication of a summary of various similarities, differences, and relationships discovered in data, described within a particular context that includes valid characteristics, erroneous characteristics, and repetition. So, for the purposes of modeling (and mining, too), information is indeed a summary of the data—but one with many caveats, all of which need to be appreciated by the modeler.

4.1.3 **Knowledge**

Knowledge is intimately intertwined with information. In fact, as the discussion of information revealed, information cannot inform without the presence of existing knowledge. This creates a philosophical merry-go-round of the chicken and egg sort. (Actually, the answer to the chicken and egg riddle is simple—the egg came first because dinosaurs laid eggs long before chickens came on the scene.) However, if it takes a modicum of knowledge to recognize information, and it takes some minimum of information to glean a modicum of knowledge, where on earth does this riddle start? Well, the easy answer is that we all are hard wired with start-up knowledge in the configuration of our brains; the hard answer is far beyond the scope of this book! (For some possible pointers, see the Resources section at the end of the book.)

One marked difference between knowledge and information is that information is static in its transmission. (Even if the information changes as the context and data change, a single informing communication itself is constant in its content.) Knowledge, on the other hand, is ever dynamic and changing, dependent for existence on the context in which we find ourselves. Knowledge is, in fact, a process, not a thing at all. Information assails us at all times. It pours past our senses—for the most part ignored—as we extract only recognizable information and incorporate it into what we already know. Thus information changes, in some small or large way, the whole dynamic structure of our knowledge.

Such a description is fine in principle, but for us to wrestle with understanding the nature of knowledge (understanding is something beyond knowledge again, and not covered here) we need a more static concept for knowledge—something to grasp that does not continuously morph into some other shape. For that, a working description of knowledge will suffice.

To get there, first note that knowledge has to be about (or of) something. To have knowledge of something requires being able to describe its role and interactions. Consider, for instance, an orange. What do you know about it? If you were to describe it to someone who knows nothing of oranges, you might describe how it grows, or how it's used, or its economic role, or a set of features by which it could be recognized, or any one of a vast range of possible ways that the orange interacts with the world. The same is true with knowledge of nonmaterial objects like ROI or inflation, or even the description of a customer. In other words, knowledge of the orange is explicated as a set of operational depictions that relate the orange to the world. The key here is that knowledge is explicated as operational depictions. Such an explication is, of course, information, in this case, intended to transfer knowledge from a "knower" to an "unknower."

But so far this is only a recipe for turning knowledge into information. It is not yet a description of knowledge. When you use knowledge, or even when an expert system or robot that encapsulates it uses knowledge, two separate actions are needed. The first is recognition of a particular situation. The second is recognition of a set of operations that it is possible to carry out in the recognized situation. Now, to be sure, much more is needed to take action in the real world than just recognition of a situation and recognition of actions possible in that situation. But here, consideration is limited only to what constitutes knowledge, and that comprises only these two components: context recognition and action selection. (Decision making, for instance, is an extension beyond simply having knowledge, and requires selecting among the various known actions possible in the recognized context.)

Do you know, for instance, how to read a book? If so (and as a reader of this book it is a forgone conclusion that you do), the knowledge of how to do so comprises an enormously complex set of actions including holding the book, opening the book, and turning pages, every bit as much as it includes the recipe for scanning letters, absorbing words, and gleaning understanding from them. The decision to actually read a book, and then to select this particular book, comes from knowledge, but is not itself knowledge. Fortunately, it isn't necessary at this point to explore motivations, decisions, actions, and goals.

Knowledge, then, can be described as a set of operational recipes together with the contexts in which those recipes can become effective—in other words, what it's possible to do, and when it is appropriate to do it, to achieve particular results. The results may not be certain, but the degree of uncertainty—or at least the fact that there is some uncertainty—is included in the level of expectation of the results.

This, then, forms the underlying strata from which models arise:

> *Data:* A collection of unanalyzed observations of worldly events.
>
> *Information:* A summary and communication of the main components and relationships contained within the data and presented within a specific context.
>
> *Knowledge:* An interrelated collection of procedures for acting toward particular results in the world with associated references for when each is applicable along with its range of effectiveness.

Or, somewhat less formally:

> *Data* is what happened;
>
> *Information* is how you know it happened; and
>
> *Knowledge* is what to do about it.

4.2 **An Observer's Guide to Models**

As just discussed, models use a framework that encompasses data, information, and knowledge. In fact, in a sense, models are knowledge. They are intimately connected at one end with data, they to some degree provide interpretation of the data to some purpose, and they end with knowledge. In another sense, models encapsulate the information present in data within some particular framework. However, models have a singular feature in that, under the appropriate circumstances, they can go beyond the constraints of the data from which they are created. But looking at models and their workings requires a method or structure that allows description of their relevant features.

Models can be described in many different ways. However, in business applications, models can usefully be described as falling along the five continua mentioned in the introduction to the chapter. These are:

1. inferential/predictive
2. associative/systemic
3. static/dynamic
4. qualitative/quantitative
5. comparative/interactive

These five continua certainly do not exhaust all of the ways in which models may be classified or described; however, all business models can be usefully described as falling somewhere along these dimensions, and are usefully understood by doing so. Thus, it is worth looking at the dimensions of this descriptive framework in a little more detail.

4.2.1 **Inferential Models**

Inference and prediction are commonly viewed as the raison d'être (reason for existence) of models in business situations. This is not quite true, but it is an understandable misapprehension. The true purpose for models in a business setting, as will be seen later in this, and in the next two chapters, is to capture and encapsulate corporate knowledge. However, because knowledge is itself so intimately connected with selecting outcome-based actions (which can often look like predictions), the confusion is understandable.

Inferential models are also known as explanatory models, and either description is equally appropriate. Being wholly based in data, such models necessarily explain (or explicate inferences about) the data. The problem comes only when trying to apply such inferences or explanations back to the world, for then it's apparent that if the data didn't actually reflect the world, the models won't work well when applied there. However, explanatory or inferential models can be among the simplest, and most useful, kinds of models. They are also among the easiest to understand. Despite the fact that inferential models are intuitively understood in general, a brief look at their inner workings is valuable because to some extent all models can be viewed as inferential.

An inferential model essentially relates objects to each other. The objects have to be represented in the data, and are usually represented as variables—either singly or as groups of variables. This way, an object is represented as a set of values about one or more features of the object in question. Thus the object "customer" may have all kinds of associated features, such as SKU (stock keeping unit) purchased, price, address, name, customer number, order number, date, time, and a host of others. The behavior of a specific customer on a specific occasion is then represented in the data by giving each of the features a specific value according to what was observed to happen in the world.

To take a particularly simple example of an inferential model, you might, in an effort to understand where extra personal poundage is coming from, create a data set that represents four objects. You would need only three variables to make such a representation—weight in pounds, food intake in calories consumed, and daily exercise in calories burned. The data set as a whole represents the behavior of the fourth object—the one with the extra poundage. Keeping regular records over a period of time produces a data set, which is no more than a list of noted values of the features mentioned. As shown in Figure 4.1, examining the data set reveals a relationship between these three variables. Examining such data might allow you to infer that more exercise, for instance, while holding food intake constant, "explains" why weight is diminishing. That is to say that, with food intake constant, you can infer that increasing levels of exercise are associated with reducing levels of weight. Or looked at in a

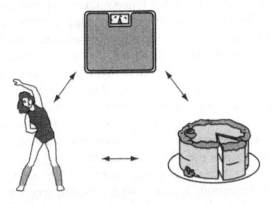

Figure 4.1   Explaining personal poundage.

different way, if asked about the weight loss noticed, an acceptable explanation, based on the data, would be the increase in exercise.

However, any such explanation (or inference) immediately leads to the apparent ability to make a prediction: more exercise leads to (causes) less weight. However, it could, perhaps, also lead to the prediction—one that seems equally justified considering only the data—that less weight somehow causes more exercise. Common sense seems to imply that it is the increase in exercise that produces the decrease in weight; that is to say, the exercise has to come first. This "common sense," however, is external to the data—it is additional knowledge, not part of the data set itself. So even if the data is valid and the associations discovered are "real," predictive use of an inferential model can be quite inappropriate.

This model, in fact, does no more than describe associations and relationships between objects (variables). No valid inference from the data alone is possible other than that certain features seem to be associated together. This is therefore termed an inferential (or explanatory) model because, inherently, there is not necessarily any predictive power in the model, but it does allow the interactions to be inferred. Frequently, such inferences are termed "explanations." (There may in fact be predictive power in such a model, of course, but there is no support for such a conclusion in this sort of model as it stands.)

4.2.2 Predictive Models

At the other end of this continuum lies the predictive model. This also may be an associative model (it could be some other type of model, too) in which care was taken to separate cause and effect. This causal separation is usually made in time, such that associations are made in the temporal direction leading from what came first to what followed. In the previous example, care would have to be taken to note that exercising came before weight loss. When one event follows another in data, we can often infer that one causes another—but by no means is this always the case. For instance, day always follows night, but we do not conclude that night "causes" day in any usual use of the term. The problem here is that it is impossible to determine cause and effect by considering only the internal relationships of a data set alone. The data may provide clues, but predictive models require an explanation of the data that is external to the data in some way and that describes which phenomena are causes and which are effects.

Given such a rationale, and allowing that objects and their interrelationships form an important part of such a model, predictive models all attempt to determine a later outcome of a prior situation. There are many ways of achieving predictive power in models, but the most common rely on using techniques that lie along the associative/systemic dimension discussed next.

4.2.3   Associative Models

Also called a correlational model, an associative model depends on finding the association, or correlation, between the attributes of objects. For example, if asked to describe what affects sales, you might develop a "laundry list" similar to that shown in Figure 4.2. Most frequently, such lists comprise between 5 and 9 (7 ± 2) items, often described as *factors*. Thus, price might be described as a factor affecting sales. An associative model is based on the assumption that to some greater or lesser extent these factors drive sales (if this is a predictive model), or are at least associated with sales (if an inferential model).

In an associative model, it might very well be fully accepted that *gross national product* (GNP) does not directly affect sales, nor does the level of sales of the product or company being modeled have any particular influence on GNP. However, the model proposes that for some reason there is a reliable connection such that they do, in fact, vary together, and that the way that they vary together can be characterized.

To see how this can occur, see Figure 4.3. This figure illustrates a relationship among the presence of rain, the presence of open umbrellas, and the motion of windshield wipers. An associative model will be quite happy to infer that there is a reliable relationship between the presence of open

Figure 4.2   Factors affecting sales.

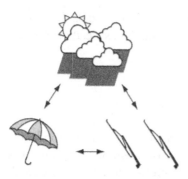

Figure 4.3   Associations among rain, open umbrellas, and windshield wipers.

umbrellas and the motion of windshield wipers, characterize that relationship, and leave it at that. If a causal model isn't needed, that's fine. The model proposes that there is some "hidden" or "latent" variable that may or may not be discovered (in this case, it would be the presence of rain) that would "explain" the connection.

A glance in any business or economics magazine will reveal countless examples of these types of models. Almost everyone has heard of leading indicators for the economy. The idea is that the present values of such leading indicators are associated with the future value (or at least, with other measures of the future value) of the economy. Or again, a company might make a market segmentation model to try to better understand the behavior of the company's customers. The assumption here is that whatever data the company has describing its customers is in some way associated with different group behaviors.

Such associative models can work well, but they have significant drawbacks. Mainly, they incorporate a significant number of unverifiable assumptions. It is not the model incorporating assumptions that is the problem; all models necessarily incorporate assumptions. The problem is that they are not verifiable, at least, not until long after the fact. To consider a specific example, the actual leading indicators in the leading indicators model of the economy have to be revised from time to time. After-the-fact analysis reveals that the actually used leading indicators that need revising were either no longer indicating, no longer leading, or neither indicating nor leading. Also, the model works only if many assumptions hold true, such as sufficient indicators were identified, all of the important indicators were included, the indicators remain relevant, and the range and distribution of data used to build the original model were the same range and distribution used later. Indeed, there are many "ifs" about such a model, and it can only be discovered later if they did indeed hold true.

In truth, associative models can work well. However, formally structured associative models were invented at a time when little computing power was available save pencil, paper, and brainpower. Today the opportunities are broader, and new possibilities have opened up. One of them is the systems model—the other end of the associative/systemic dimension.

4.2.4 Systems Models

Systems models view the world as an interconnected and interrelated mesh of events. A systems model looking at sales would note that, at the very least, although the level of sales did indeed depend on the product's price, so too, at least to some extent, did the product's price depend on its level of sales. To a greater or lesser degree, the same holds true for all of the other inter-actions in a systems model. However, there are two other particularly notable differences between associative and systems models.

First, in an associative or correlational model, all of the correlations are symmetrical. Correlation can be measured in several ways, one of the most common being the Pearson Moment Correlation Coefficient. This correlation coefficient is represented by a number between $+1$ and -1. It can be looked at as two parts, the sign and the number. When the sign is positive, it means that the correlated features change value in the same direction; for example, more calories consumed, more weight gained. A negative correlation means that the associated features move in opposite directions—more exercise, less weight. The number indicates the strength of the association: 1 means they are perfectly associated, so that knowing the value of one completely defines the value of the other, and 0 means that they are perfectly independent of each other, so that whatever is known about one tells nothing of the value of the other. This correlational measure also is symmetrical, which is to say that if the correlation between calorie intake and weight is $+0.6$, then the correlation between weight and calorie intake is also $+0.6$.

Such a symmetrical correlation may seem logical at first glance: the relationship is the same from one to the other as it is from the other to one. However, what of the relationship between, say, GNP and the level of one product's sales? In this case, it is quite logical to suppose that the level of sales is associated with the level of GNP. Perhaps greater GNP associates quite strongly with increased level of sales. From this one might very well expect that GNP is strongly correlated with the sales level for the product. However, although the correlation is symmetrical, one wouldn't really expect that a fluctuation in the level of sales of one product would have much of an im-pact on GNP. Thus, using a correlation-like measure to describe effect, it might be that GNP has an effect on product sales of $+0.6$, whereas sales has an effect on GNP of almost 0.0, that is, no noticeable effect at all. This difference in strength of effect, depending on which direction is considered, is not reflected in measures of correlation. Yet, it is exactly this sort of non-correlational, nonsymmetrical interaction that is important in a systems model. In business, as in life generally, there are an enormous number and variety of important yet nonsymmetrical interactions in which the direction of the effect is crucial to understanding what is occurring.

The second notable difference is that whereas in an associative model it is the associations (correlations) that form the entire structure of the model, a systems model regards the data as an incomplete set of instances describing some larger phenomenon or set of phenomena. A system is an essentially dynamic structure. Although it is possible to look at and measure the states of the features of a system at some instant—a sort of snapshot—such a snapshot is *not* a snapshot of the active features of the system. But it is these active features, the dynamic interactions, that are important. Measurements of water height, flow rates, turbulence, turbidity, mineral content, and so on tell little of the experience of shooting white-water rapids through the Grand Canyon, even if the measurements are taken in that white water. It is the dynamism of the experience that is crucial; no snapshot can capture it.

Thus, although a purely associative model is in and of the data—indeed, the data is all there is for such a model—a systems model is of, but not in, the data. It is a model *about* the data, not a model *of* the data. Indeed, a perfect associative model could, given suitable inputs, re-create the data set from which it was made. However, a systems model is more concerned with accurately modeling the interactions that produced the data, and may well not exactly reproduce the data set. This is because the systems model recognizes that any particular instance of collected data in a data set may not, in fact, be reproduced in the real world—even if conditions nearly identical to the original are used. The world is variable and continuously morphing off to somewhere else. Systems models are not concerned with duplicating any specific set of data, but with representing the generating behavior of the features in the world that gave rise to the unique data set.

To this end, systems models recognize three types of phenomena in the world: stocks, flows, and information exchange. *Stocks* are represented in the world as things that accumulate or diminish. They can be physical accumulations (such as finished goods inventory on hand), arbitrary symbol accumulations (like credit card balance outstanding), or totally nonphysical phenomena (such as level of morale or satisfaction). (Note that, perhaps contrary to intuition, things don't need to be either measurable or measured to be modeled. It is enough that they can be signified and placed in context.)

The second type of phenomenon that systems models look at is *flows,* which give rise to the accumulation or diminution of stocks. Just as a river flows into and accumulates in a reservoir, so too do produced units flow into and accumulate in inventory, and management attention and appropriate reward flow into and accumulate in morale. Most accumulations not only fill, but also empty. In a systems model, too, flows run both into and out of stocks.

However, flows in the world are regulated—some by chance events, as with rainfall, and some by planned interaction and intervention, as with inventory. Systems models recognize these as a third type of phenomenon, *information exchange*. To be sure, in the real world, we often look at a phenomenon, say rainfall, as consisting of both flow and information; that is, 6 inches of rainfall is both a flow of rainfall and the information that it rained 6 inches. In a systems model, the information is represented separately as information exchange.

The key point here is not, from this brief description, to understand and be able to create and use systems models. Rather, it is to differentiate the ends of the associative–systems model dimension. These are the ends of a dimension that is a continuum; models are not classifiable as either one or the other. Very often, in practice, they blend into each other to a greater or lesser extent. Associative models, however nonsystemic they may be, seldom are concerned exclusively with a single data set to the point of scrupulously reproducing the data, nor is a systems model in practice indifferent to reproducing the data on which it was based. The point here is to recognize that there is a continuum, and to recognize its important features.

4.2.5   Static Models

Another useful way of viewing models, another continuum, stretches from static through dynamic characterizations. Once again, this characterization is not exclusive of the other dimensions so that, for instance, an associative, inferential model could be static, dynamic, or somewhere in between. The static/dynamic depiction has two parts. One part refers to the internal structure of the model; the other part refers to the way the model deals with data to which it is exposed.

In its most extreme form, a static model applies to one, and only one, data set. When internally static in form, the model, once created, is fixed. For example, a purely associative model has a form that is fixed by the data set from which it was created. It doesn't matter which metric is chosen to determine how "best" to model the data; in almost every case, the chosen metric provides only one best way to make the model. In fact, for such techniques, if the metric chosen to determine a best fit turns out in some particular case to be ambiguous (there being in that particular case more than one best fit), such techniques can have major, even fatal, problems. In this view, then, there is only one best way to model a data set, and the model, once discovered, is unchanging. Of course, such a model can be applied to other data sets to discover how well it explains that other data set or predicts from it, but the model is unchanged and unaffected by other data.

Even a systems model can have an internal structure that is static. A systems model doesn't have a "best fit to a data set" metric in quite the same way as an associative model. Nonetheless, once the components of the systems model (the stocks, flows, and information exchanges) are all determined, it too can be static in that exposure to additional data has no influence on the internal structure of the systems model itself.

Once created from a data set, the structure of static models is unaffected by any other data. Of course, no such model is assumed to be permanently valid. At some time or change in circumstances, the static model may well be discovered to be ineffective for the purpose for which it was created. Then, a new model is developed and the old one discarded. That's the point—the old model is discarded, not in some way updated. A new data set would be discovered and a new model created, incorporating the changed circumstances. The new static model would be used in place of the old.

In some modeling environments, a cycle of creating static models may be set up specifically to deal with changing conditions. Sometimes this re-creating of static models cycle is represented as dynamic modeling. Although it is a valid way of dealing with changing circumstances, and may work quite as well as a dynamic model in the same circumstances, it is not dynamic modeling.

4.2.6 Dynamic Models

A series of static models does not constitute a dynamic modeling approach because there is no element of incremental learning. The notion of incremental learning introduces a concept that is central to dynamic models, but is not present at all in static models.

Incremental learning has to be embedded in the structure of a dynamic model. The discussion of models so far has covered what models accomplish in various terms. Understanding incremental learning needs another perspective on how a model relates to the data on which it stands. This needed perspective separates information representation from model interpretation.

In some sense, a model is a summary representation of the information enfolded in a data set. The associations discovered or the systems proposed are, in a way, no more than a summary explication of the information that the data set enfolds within it. A model, of course, is a contextual creation because it is, perforce, created for some purpose and to present some meaningful result. So a model is itself a summary statement about the data that is endowed with meaning and purpose. It is a re-expression of at least part of the information that the data holds. That information re-expression is embodied in the structure of the model.

So far in this discussion, there has been no mention of how a model represents the information enfolded in a data set. That is, there has been no discussion of what form or mechanism might be used to actually express the information content of the model. There are quite a number of options, such as mathematical expressions, a data set of parameters with an interpreter, an influence map, a belief network, and many other possibilities. However, in an operational sense, there always have to be two parts of a whole model: the information representation structure and an interpretation mechanism. Even for a noncomputational, correlational model, both parts exist. Mathematical expressions that are correlational equations represent the information summarized from the data. However, interpretation occurs only when the expressions are in some way active, such as when they are manually solved for a particular instance. The equations themselves are only an inert symbolic representation of the data, endowed with meaning and purpose. The same holds true for any model, although it is often a convenient shorthand locution to refer to the mathematical expression, or other symbolic representation, as the model. The hidden assumption in any such shorthand, however, is that there always has to be a bipartite model that additionally includes the active interpretation mechanism.

When discussing a static model, because the parameters are unchangeable after the model has been created, the interpretive actions taken by the interpreter are fixed and there is usually little point in conceptualizing them separately. For static models, then, the parameters representing the information do not change. However, for dynamic models, although the interpretive structure may well remain fixed, the actions that it takes, driven by the parameters that represent the changing information, do change as learning takes place. In this case, these two components of a model—information representation and interpreter—have to be conceptualized separately. Such a separate representation is shown in Figure 4.4. (The interpreter is

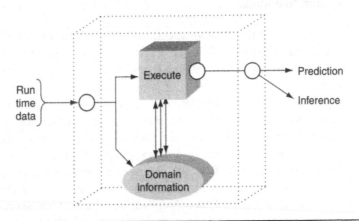

Figure 4.4   Components of a dynamic model.

shown as the "execute" portion of the model because it executes the knowledge structure.)

In practice, models that use this approach usually call the extracted information *domain knowledge,* an unfortunate choice of terms given the present discussion, because it is really information about the domain of enquiry (thus "domain information") that is stored there, not knowledge. This discussion, for consistency, uses the term *domain information,* and that is what is shown in the illustration.

Incremental learning takes place when new information changes what is "known." Clearly, this doesn't happen in a static model, because new information (incorporated in new data) makes no difference to the internal structure of the model in any way. In a dynamic model, new information does make a difference. Indeed, new information is constantly incorporated into the existing domain information. In some sense, the dynamic model continuously "learns" as it goes along. This has several implications. For instance, given that a dynamic model has identical inputs at two separate times, it may well produce different outputs based on those inputs, depending on what it has experienced in the meantime. Or again, perhaps not all of the information is equally valid. Perhaps older information is less relevant than more recent information. How is the older information to be "forgotten"—and how much is to be forgotten?

Although dynamic models raise a number of issues that seem not to be present in static models, the impression actually turns out to be misleading. In any case, workable answers to most of the problems can be found. The issue, really, is to understand the nature of the different modeling techniques and the possibilities and limitations inherent in each, and to be able to recognize and select a model appropriate for any situation.

4.2.7 Qualitative Models

The qualitative/quantitative spectrum has much to do with the type of data from which the model is drawn. Certainly, the vast majority of a data miner's work is based on nonqualitative types of data, usually pretty exclusively numerical and categorical types of data. However, a business modeler will be quite concerned with qualitative models, at least during some stages. Qualitative models are based on summary data, but in this case, it is usually experiential and descriptive. The most common qualitative models are based on narrative, often in the form of text or speech. In business use, qualitative models may be made from the results of a focus group, for instance. However, a management description of a problem situation will also be presented using qualitative data. This only means that the problem situation will be described to the modeler in words. It may be a verbally delivered problem statement, or perhaps one supported by documentation consisting of words and perhaps illustrations. However, it is from the narrative, textual, and diagrammatic presentation that the modeler has to begin to create and structure a model of the business situation or problem. In at least this much, every business modeler has to work with qualitative models.

Indeed, this whole book is itself a narrative, illustrated description about modeling—a sort of description of a model of how to make models. Thus, this book is itself a large and complex qualitative model that attempts to describe and structure business modeling. It is based on qualitative and quantitative experience (the author's) and presents a summarization of those experiences, highlighting the meaningful objects and relationships with the purpose of communicating how to duplicate any desired results to the model's user—you the reader. So, this book is itself a summarization of data, endowed with meaning and purpose, and offered as a communication. It is in every way a model—a qualitative model.

Qualitative models may be built from a vast range of data including images and film, sounds and speech, and narrative and dialogue. However, much of what a business modeler uses can be reduced to text. Most of us have been taught at least rudimentary qualitative modeling techniques, even if only "reading for comprehension" in high school. However, there also exists a wealth of more formalized qualitative modeling techniques, ranging from the somewhat unstructured cognitive mapping up to and including the coding and qualitative networking techniques frequently used in the social sciences. In later chapters, some of these techniques are reviewed in more detail.

In exactly the same way as for any other model, a qualitative model, with meaning and purpose, identifies the relevant objects in, and summarizes from, data, and identifies relations between those objects that are present in the data. Thus, as with any other model, in the end, a qualitative model can be associative, systemic, and so on. It can be used for inference or prediction. It is simply a model, similar in purpose and function to any other model that is based on qualitative data.

4.2.8 Quantitative Models

At the other end of the spectrum from qualitative models lie quantitative models. These models are based on (usually) numerous measurements of recorded observations, so they are based on data that is different from that used for qualitative models. Quantitative measurements have an inherent structure that is not present in qualitative data. Quantities are all recorded against a prespecified scale, usually either numerical or categorical. Collected quantitative data is usually structured as a table, with columns representing the variables and rows as the instances of simultaneously recorded measurement values.

Using structured data, and a structured representation of the data, allows application of various techniques that are not immediately applicable to qualitative data. Those techniques are not reviewed at all in this chapter because they are part of the techniques of data mining, which are covered in Part III. However, qualitative analysis techniques also include a wealth of statistical and summarization techniques, as well as the more recent computer-aided techniques of online analytical processing (OLAP).

Significantly, models variously described as inferential/predictive, associative/systemic, static/dynamic, and comparative/interactive (discussed next) can all be made equally well from either qualitative or quantitative data. However, this quantitative/qualitative distinction represents a continuum, not a dichotomy.

One of the challenges facing data miners is how to incorporate external domain knowledge into quantitative models. This issue, discussed in Chapter 6, can be addressed using several possible approaches. However, managers, practitioners, and experts in some area almost always communicate the domain knowledge that needs incorporating in the form of qualitative statements. As business modeling matures, models comprising a blend of qualitative and quantitative data will clearly become more prevalent.

4.2.9 Comparative Models

These models lie at one end of the comparative/interactive dimension. As the name implies, such models deal with comparisons within the data from which they are made. The implied comparison that the name focuses on is the comparison of instances (or rows or records) in the data set. Whether quantitative or qualitative, data used for constructing models consists of descriptive reports of various cases in which notable events transpired. To be sure, qualitative models may well be built from narrative summaries of source data, and are thus built, perhaps, from information rather than data. But ultimately, lying behind all else, things happened, were noticed, and salient points were noted. In whatever form it arrived, this is data. Noted points associated with a single event are grouped so that the association remains, and such a group of associated noticed events can be described as an *instance*. (No technical definition here—it means no more than "in this instance thus and so happened.")

Each instance represents a unique occurrence, although there may be other instances that are seemingly identical. The identicality would be due to apparently separate instances sharing identical characteristics for all of the noted states. For the purpose of modeling we frequently accept that, even though there is no way of telling such instances apart; they do nevertheless represent different events. The assumption is that there is some unmeasured characteristic—or at least, an unrecorded characteristic—that could, were it known, serve to uniquely identify each instance. Figure 4.5 shows a small table of quantitative information in which several separate instances seem to be identical.

In looking at the figure, discovering that several instances seem identical requires comparing the instances with each other. It is only by making such between-instance comparisons that it is possible to note not only that some of the instances have all their features in common, but also that in other comparisons they have features that differ. It is such between-instance comparisons that form the basis of a comparative model.

Comparative models are less likely to be probability-based than their interpretive cousins. This means that, for instance, the *fact* that "2-1-6" occurred for an outcome of "D" is important. How often it occurred is not. Even if this instance occurs only 1/10,000, or even less, of the time, it does not invalidate the fact that an explanation of this instance is required, because this is a combination of observed circumstances that actually happened. Or again, the fact that "4-9-4" with an outcome of "F" seems to predominate makes it no more significant as far as explaining or comparative modeling is concerned. Comparative models tend to be concerned with which patterns occur and to make less—or even no—use of how often each pattern occurs. Remember to look at the instances that do occur, and explain those by comparing them with others that do (or do not) occur.

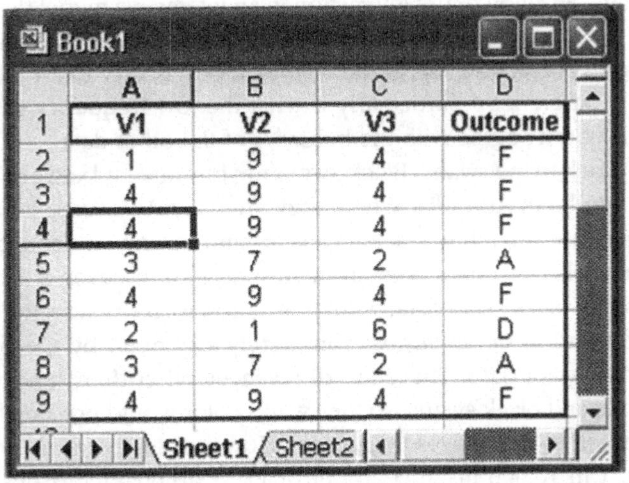

	A	B	C	D
1	V1	V2	V3	Outcome
2	1	9	4	F
3	4	9	4	F
4	4	9	4	F
5	3	7	2	A
6	4	9	4	F
7	2	1	6	D
8	3	7	2	A
9	4	9	4	F

Figure 4.5   Comparing instances for comparative modeling.

There is a famous illustration of a logical point, which essentially conveys that no matter how much evidence there is in support of a position, a single counterexample undermines the position totally. The illustration observes that, when the position states, "all swans are white," finding a million white swans offers no support in the face of finding a single black swan. This is exactly the type of situation that comparative models seek to model. Small though their number may be, the presence of black swans needs explaining. Comparative models are wholly concerned with similarities and differences between instances.

4.2.10 Interactive Models

Whereas comparative models compare individual instances—one against the others—to discover similarities and differences among instances that have actually occurred, interactive models look at the interactions that take place between the measurements as their values change. Thus, interactive models focus on the variables and characterize the changes that take place between the variables. In terms of the table layout used predominantly for quantitative data, comparative models focus on data row by row to make comparisons between the rows, whereas interactive models focus on the data column by column and characterize the interactions between those.

Interactive models are usually probability based, or, to put it another way, they tend to be sensitive to the frequencies with which the different patterns occur. Such models try to find a way of characterizing the behavior of the interactions over the full range represented by the data available. However, characterization of the interaction in an interactive model describes, as closely as possible, a sort of "average" behavior. This means that, for instance, should a state occur 1/10,000 of the time or less, it is very likely to make no noticeable difference—particularly if what the low frequency of occurrence data tells doesn't agree with the behavior of the other data.

Back to the swans. Black swans are few and far between (unless you happen to be in Australia, where they are native). Assume no antipodean data. There are still a few black swans around, mainly in zoos, but precious few. Data collected about northern hemisphere swans, even if it included a minute trace of black swan data, would be almost totally unaffected by it, black swan information being almost completely swamped by the predominance of white swan data. There are differences other than simply color between white and black swans, so the swan's color would presumably be associated with other differences in the data. However, an interactive model would see the 1 in 10,000 instance about black swan characteristics as just so much "noise" and would effectively ignore it in finding an optimum way to characterize the data.

Interactive models are particularly widely used in statistical and data-mined models of quantitative data. However, this again is a continuum, and the modeling methods tend to merge into each other. For instance, the modeler dealing with the swan data might discover the information about differences and prevalence of white and black swans, and choose to segregate the data based on knowledge of the between-record differences. Or perhaps a technique of clustering outliers (instances that are highly dissimilar to the bulk of instances) would reveal the black swan group. This clustering is a form of comparative model.

4.2.11 Summarizing Model Types

Thus far, after laying some groundwork for discussing models, this chapter has looked at various descriptions of models and represented them as useful for describing models in business. Because there is a vast array of other ways of describing models, why, an astute reader might well ask, are the descriptions presented here of particular value? There are indeed many types of models useful in business that are not well encompassed by the descriptive framework discussed in this chapter—for instance, prescriptive or "recipe" models. (Prescriptive models provide a list of instructions for accomplishing some specific objective under a specific set of circumstances.)

Asking why these particular descriptions are selected is indeed a very good question, particularly because this is not represented as a comprehensive listing of model descriptions that are of value in business. However, these descriptions were chosen because they provide a comprehensive enough framework to encompass all of the models that a modeler in a business environment will use while mining data. It is the use of these models when mining data that makes their selection relevant. To this end, the intent here is not to provide a comprehensive descriptive framework for all models that might be used in business, but only those of value to the data miner when building models in a business setting. The particular descriptions introduced in this chapter, and used throughout the rest of the book, serve well to bridge the gap between data (the raw material that the miner will work with) and the business value delivered that is the ultimate goal of the mining/modeling project.

For many business tactical problems addressed by data mining, it often seems that a "canned" solution has already been discovered and that all that has to be done is to "apply the methodology" in order to deliver whatever results are desired. For instance, it may seem that the "cross sell" problem is well understood, especially because many cross sell models are used today. However, closer examination of any individual cross sell problem, together with the data available to solve it, almost always shows a totally different story.

For instance, it appears (in cross sell at least) that what is needed is a predictive model because the business problem seems to require a prediction of what is the "best" next product to offer the customer. Assuming for the moment that it is a predictive model that is needed, and leaving aside the problem of deciding what "best" might mean in any particular case, simply knowing that a predictive model is needed is not enough to specify what a miner needs to accomplish. However, armed with the descriptive tools for models in this chapter, at least some of the questions and problems become evident. For instance, is an associative or a systemic model needed? The limitations and difficulties with each can—when recognized—be discussed, and an appropriate solution for the problem faced by the business manager can be devised. Such a model may well incorporate qualitative information from the business manager, as well as quantitative information available from the data at hand—but again, only if the issue can be seen. Using the model framework described in this chapter, similar issues and questions are raised that help the data miner define the business model in data mining terms.

4.3 Modeling as an Activity

So far, this chapter has described models and provided a useful framework to characterize them. This, however, is not at all the same thing as describing modeling as an activity. Although a modeler uses a framework for describing models just as much as the available data, what actually happens is an activity—modeling. The activity of modeling—the modeler's issues and concerns—is every bit as important as the descriptive framework and the data. The rest of the chapter, in this final section, begins to look at overall considerations involved in making models.

4.3.1 Objectives

Every model is built with some purpose in mind. This would be true even if models were only built "for fun." In that case, having fun would be the purpose. However, almost all business models are built to improve efficiency or profit, reduce costs, or fulfill some other stated objective. But having an objective in mind and clearly articulating it are not one and the same thing. That's one problem. Another key concern is trying to meet arbitrary objectives.

For instance, a business manager may look for a solution that includes a modeling strategy to deal with an underperforming set of customers. However, if that underperforming group is defined as "the least profitable 10% of our customer base," then no model will ever solve the problem. No matter what manipulations, reduced cost of service, or profit increases are produced, the bottom 10% will always exist. Of course, if the modeler knows that the objective is defined in such a way that success requires removing the bottom 10%, the problem can be alleviated right there because, when expressed in these terms, it is obvious that such a thing can't be done. However, remarkably often, key business definitions turn out to be either not defined in any clear way or defined in some arbitrary way that incorporates a "Catch-22" gotcha.

When business objectives are not clearly defined, the modeler is often expected to make operational definitions. As an example, customer attrition is widely considered to be a serious problem, and suitable for management at least partly through modeling and data mining. However, in several attrition model business problems worked on by the author there has been no clear management definition of what constituted customer attrition. (The response of senior business managers in one of the largest international banks in the world is fairly typical: "That is something that we expect you to tell us.") The author confesses surprise that a key metric for a major corporate business problem is left vague, although much discussed as a business metric, but that is the fact. The major problem for the modeler is that, unless defined, it can't be measured (even qualitatively), and if not measured, it can't be managed. (Qualitative "measurements" can be used for items such as morale that can't be measured in a quantitative way very easily or effectively, but are nonetheless observable phenomena.)

A modeler must always work toward a clear and defined objective. Easier said than done! Although management may not have a clear business definition (perhaps not even a clear description) of the objective to be met, they almost always have at least a qualitative expectation about the desired result. Giving the modeler a free hand, as it were, to design and define the objective doesn't allow the modeler to simply define an objective that is easy to model, make the model, declare victory, and leave. Even with no clear definition from management of the problem to solve, whatever measure the modeler devises must meet the (perhaps unspoken) qualitative expectation. Thus, it is always well worth the modeler asking (and then clarifying the answer to the question), "What do you expect to get out of this modeling/datamining project?" Or, "What does success look like?"

4.3.2 Empirical Modeling

Empirical modeling is one pole of yet another possible dimension for describing models. The other end of this continuum consists of theoretical models. However, when creating business models, and particularly when using data mining to do it, it is always empirical models that are created. The term *empirical* implies that the model needs to reflect some phenomena that exist in the world. Such models are built from direct experience of the world (data), rather than being based on aggregated information such as "basic principles." (However, as discussed in a moment, this doesn't mean that theory isn't an important consideration, even when empirically modeling.)

One apparent problem is that there is no apparent "best" way to empirically model any given data set. Now it is quite true that any data mining, or even any statistical algorithm, uses a metric that does define some specific "best" way of modeling a given data set. In fact, it is often the case that minutely changing either the data set or the criteria that defines "best" produces enormous differences in the structure of the model. However, what is intended in talking about the lack of one best way to make an empirical model is not based on the technical criteria of the data analysis method. And here is where theory already raises its head. It is impossible to approach any data set without some theory. For example, even in simply looking at a data set to decide whether the data is reasonable to work with, modelers unavoidably have to have in mind some idea (or theory) of what "reasonable-to-work-with" data looks like. Moreover, it is always possible to explain (or have a theory about) what is going on in a data set, even if it's spurious. (Thus, the supposed relationship between the height of women's hemlines, or the flood height of the Yellow River, or a particular sports team performance and the performance of the U.S. stock market.)

Even applying reasonable constraints to the explanation (and reasonable constraints are themselves based on some theory about what is reasonable), there still remain several to many ways to explain what is happening in any data set. Thus, justifying any particular explanation is always problematic. On the other hand, this multiplicity of competing explanations is actually a strength, not a weakness.

For one thing, with many explanations in play, the complaint that "they can't all be the real explanation" isn't really valid. There can, in fact, be several good explanations, all valid, that explain what is happening in a data set; for instance, a particular customer can have many motivations for choosing a particular product, or for ceasing to be a customer ("attriting" in the latest parlance). It is very likely the case that no one single factor was *the* cause to the exclusion of all others. So it is quite possible that an interlocking set of modes of explanation can be found in any particular data set—even when some of the modes seem to be in conflict with each other. That, too, is the way of the world.

However, even conflicting explanations may be valuable. Such results clearly indicate that the evidence is inconclusive—that is to say, either more or better data is needed. More importantly, having multiple explanations that are all possible contenders as the "best" explanation in any given model means multiple starting points in exploring the territory described by the data. A multiple starting point approach is more likely to discover the path to the "best" model, if indeed one exists, than using one single "best" theory to make the exploration.

So, even though modeling works with empirical models, at least in the areas covered in this book, theory plays an unavoidable and necessary role.

4.3.3 Explaining Data

Much of the work of modeling involves creating and deploying predictive models. Such models are often termed as "explaining" the data, although the method of explanation implied may be rather technical. However, explaining model operation and results in human terms is very often an important objective of a model, even when it seems that an explanation is not what was originally requested. This may be true even when the project specifies only a predictive model. If an explanation is explicitly requested, delivering an understandable one is all the more important.

Explaining data, which is tantamount (at least in expectation) to explaining some worldly phenomenon, has to be done in the simplest terms possible. Explanatory modeling requires providing the simplest possible explanation that meets the need. This inevitably means deciding what can be discarded or ignored. It also means providing either cluster explanations (males over 40 who smoke and drive sports cars) or single variable linear explanations (incidence of churn increases until the 12-month point when it begins to fall slowly). Interactions between variables and nonlinear effects of any complexity range from difficult to impossible to explain in a humanly meaningful way. Even in systems models, the objective is to remove as much complexity as possible, and to characterize the nature of the interactions of stocks, flows, and information links in the simplest possible way. In systems models, individual interactions may be characterized nonlinearly and the total nature of the system may be highly nonlinear, but the primary objective when modeling should be to make each part of the systems representation as understandable as possible. A systems model's objective for explanation must be that the parts can be intuitively understood separately, although the overall system performance may well be, and often is, highly nonintuitive.

Explanatory models are not often, in business anyway, wanted purely for their explanation, but so that some action can be taken (i.e., to support decision making). In this case, modeling explanatory models has more constraints. These decision-support explanatory models are a form of strategic model because they assist in discovering some appropriate strategy in a particular situation. For brevity, in this section, this type of explanatory model is termed a *strategic model*.

In any data set used for strategic modeling, there may well be (and when using data mining, almost invariably is) a wealth of data. However, strategic modeling requires looking at the data in a slightly different way than for other models. Some of the variables will describe events or circumstances in the world that can be manipulated to some greater or lesser degree. For instance, product price is such a variable. It is to some degree within the control of a company, although it is almost certainly subject to many real-world constraints. A marketing department, for instance, may be able to double or halve the price of some product, but a 10-fold increase may be vetoed by senior management, and a price of $0.00 would require more strategic readjustment than the company is willing to embrace. Thus, in this example, product price is a controllable variable within limits. (The limits that are possible may well be outside the range of the data currently available when modeling.)

In addition to the controllable variables, there may well be, and usually are, variables describing concomitant phenomena. This is stuff that happens. It happens at the same time as the outcomes of interest, and at the same time as the controllable variables are deliberately changed, but concomitant variables measure the stuff that happens that is at least outside direct control. So, for example, the interest rate might be such a concomitant variable. There are also indirectly controllable variables: sales, for instance. These are often, although not always, the variables about which strategic decisions need to be made, based in part on the model. Such indirectly controllable variables are not directly amenable to manipulation, but may be affected by variables that are.

All this preamble about strategic models leads to an important point: a strategic model cannot be used for its intended purpose unless it explains the directly controllable, or at least the indirectly controllable, variables. In building an explanatory model, it may well be that some of the concomitant variables produce some technically "best" explanation. Indeed, it may be that the controllable variables do not themselves form any good explanatory model. (This is useful, if not very welcome, information because it means that, at least using the variables available, the phenomenon of interest cannot be affected.) However, if the purpose is to support decision making, modeling must concentrate on what can be controlled. (It is not considered very helpful to say to a vice president of marketing, "Well, I can predict your future sales to some degree, but there is nothing that you can do to affect them with this model!")

4.3.4 Modeling Assumptions

We live in a world of assumptions, and the danger posed by accepting and acting on hidden assumptions is discussed in several places in this book. But modeling carries some assumptions of its own, separate from the assumptions that may be embodied in the model itself. One assumption is that the data is somehow "generated" by the world. For simplicity, in fact, simply to make modeling possible in the first place, some sort of generating mechanisms are assumed to have produced the measured values of the variables. Looking at the actual measured values produces various summary and descriptive estimates, called *statistics,* about the data—mean, variance, and so on. The assumption presumes that whatever mechanism created these statistics, with the particular characteristics peculiar to them, can in fact be adequately summarized by such an assumption. Fortunately for modelers everywhere, it very often can. However, this is only an assumption—no more than that. The actual mechanism responsible for creating any set of data is almost certainly best understood as a very complex, highly interrelated, nonlinear system. It is almost certainly subject to all kinds of external shocks and adjustments, and when modeling, it is well worth giving considerable thought to the actual nature of the "generating mechanism," particularly for the most significant variables.

A key, in fact a crucially important point in some instances, is that the proposed generating mechanism, although it produces data similar to the data actually encountered, may not do more than resemble the actual data except over a limited range. Such an assumption, if not treated very gingerly indeed, can lead to great difficulty in reaching an adequate explanation. Some of these considerations are rather technical, and are explored more fully in Part III on data mining.

4.4 Summary

This chapter provided a framework for examining the nature and structure of models. They come from data, embody information, and provide knowledge. There are many ways of describing models, even when the models being described are limited to business models. However, this chapter provided only a set of descriptions of business models. The descriptive dimensions introduced were chosen specifically because they help to describe and categorize business models in ways that are most easily connected back to the data on which they are to be built. However, whether mining or modeling, the models will ultimately address social and economic phenomena that are of interest to business managers as they attempt to gain and maintain competitive advantage for as long as possible in an ever-shifting landscape.

The modeler will have to provide models that have business value, even when problem definitions are unclear—even to the managers struggling with the problems. It is important that the modeler develops skills and techniques in discovering hidden assumptions and unarticulated expectations, and clarifying the actual objectives. That is the main topic for the next chapter.

Chapter 5
Framing Business Models

Two hikers were strolling along a forest track when, rounding a bend, they suddenly came face to face with a bear. All stood frozen for a moment. Suddenly one of the hikers started flinging off hiking gear furiously, evidently preparing to flee. "What are you doing?" cried the other hiker, "No one can outrun a bear!" "I don't have to outrun the bear," replied the first, "I only have to outrun you!"

So it's an old joke that you've probably heard before. But when you heard it for the first time, perhaps it made you chuckle, even a little. Why? Well, at first the problem seems to be for the hikers to escape the bear. When one of the hikers frames the problem in a different way, the sudden reframing is a surprise, and it changes the whole meaning of the situation. And just as for this old joke, it is the framing of a situation or problem that creates its meaning.

Scenario: You are a data miner working for the marketing department of a large direct marketer. The company has developed a new product and test marketed it successfully enough for management to feel it is worth rolling out into the marketplace. The results of the test marketing are available, and marketing management decides to acquire a list of prospective customers from a database company. Your manager describes the project to you, directing you to work with the prospect list to provide target segments. How do you respond? Is there a framework here? If so, what is it, and how does it impact you? Should it impact you? If so, what do you need to know? What does management need to know? Which issues should be discussed? Pause here a moment and think about who is assuming what, and what has to be done. Jot down your thoughts briefly before continuing.

In this example, there are all kinds of operational issues that are not directly related to the framework, such as why is this data set thought to contain the information necessary to create the profile desired, and in what form is the result of the data mining needed? However, the framework of this example addresses different issues. Framework questions address issues such as: do we want the maximum number of customers or the maximum value per customer? Is this product to be considered alone, or is the impact on our current product sales to this target market to be considered? You may well have thought of many other issues that should, or at least could, have been better addressed deliberately, rather than simply left to the assumptions made. If you made a list of ideas for this scenario, revisit it after reading this chapter to see how your thoughts and appreciation for setting a frame for this problem have changed. You will certainly have some new techniques for framing a problem, even one as apparently simple as this example. (See MII.AB.9)

Frameworks set ground rules. Frameworks also entail assumptions, approaches, and options—choosing some and discarding others. Every problem has to be framed, and every model has to be built within a framework. This chapter is entirely about what goes into creating the framework in which to build a model.

All of the topics visited in framing a problem for modeling are revisited again later in other chapters that deal with modeling. However, the way that the topics are important to the frame is different from the way that they are dealt with when actually creating and manipulating a model. The frame has to come first. As an example, consider risk. This is a single consideration in the frame, and assessing and modeling risk is an integral part of many models. When setting the frame, the problem owner and the problem stakeholders have some idea of the particular risks that concern them. Any model has to include these in the frame—although, of course, the model may later reveal other risks as equally or more important. As you will see, modeling risk—that is estimating risks, comparing them to benchmarks, creating a representation, evaluating constraints, and so on—is a very different perspective on the issue of risk. In the frame, various risks are being introduced into, and established in, the model. When modeling, the risks are being clarified, evaluated, and assessed. Framing the risk part of a problem ensures that the appropriate risks, and the appropriate features of those risks, are present in the model. Modeling risks results in determining how the risks framed actually behave in different situations. As with risk, so it is with framing all the other issues.

A frame is set in much the same way as a photographer frames a picture. A photographer has to decide what to include, what to exclude, what the style and subject matter should be, and what is to be emphasized and de-emphasized within the final picture. Choices of subject matter, lighting, focus, depth of field, and so on all play a very significant part in the final image. These choices, in the hands of a skilled photographer, determine what the final picture communicates. Look at the stunning difference in intent, meaning, drama, type, style, and effect in Figure 5.1. What a difference between "In Glacier National Park" taken by Ansel Adams between 1933 and 1942, and "Wife of WPA Worker, Charleston, West Virginia" taken by Marion Post Wolcott in 1938. Adams celebrated the magnificence of America's natural beauty whereas Wolcott focused on the plight of people during the Depression.

Valley, snow covered mountains in background,
"In Glacier National Park," Montana
Ansel Adams, 1933-1942

Wife of WPA worker,
Charleston, West Virginia
Marion Post Walcott, 1938

Figure 5.1   Contrast in framing.

In exactly the same way, the framing of a model determines what the final model shows and means.

5.1 **Setting a Frame**

How much does framing really matter? Part I mentioned the disaster at Chernobyl, and how the engineers' framework model prevented them literally from seeing what was in front of their faces. Does this really carry over into business situations?

One company had decided to conduct a training session for its managers. The session was intended to foster team building and communication. To participate in the exercises, the managers formed groups. Much fun was had by all until one exercise, based on the Prisoner's Dilemma, was introduced. The Prisoner's Dilemma, briefly described in Part I in the Maltese Falcon scenario, creates a situation in which it is possible to cooperate or defect with differing results. In this case, the cooperation or defection occurred between groups. Each group had opportunities to work with other groups one-on-one. At this opportunity they could cooperate or not cooperate (termed "defecting") with the other team. There were several possible outcomes. If the two groups cooperated, small benefits (in the form of points in the management exercise) accrued to both groups. If one group cooperated when the other defected, the cooperating group lost a point, and the defecting group got more points than if it had cooperated. However, the defecting group did not get as many points as both groups together would have received by cooperating. If both groups defected no points were awarded. The object of the game was to gain as many points as possible.

So, imagine yourself as a member of one of these groups. If the object of the exercise is to get as many points as possible, what do you do? Stop and think a moment. In your own words, define the problem that you face and an approach to deal with that problem. Exactly how will you behave in order to comply with the instruction? Pause here.

What you do depends entirely on how you frame the problem. And frame the problem you must, because in this case there is no default choice. What does "get as many points as possible" mean? You simply have to make a decision. Does it mean your group should get the most points it can? Or does it mean that the global accumulation of points across all groups should be as high as possible? And whatever you decide it means, what do you think the other groups will decide it means? How are you going to frame this problem? And indeed, until you have framed the problem, you can't decide which actions to take—that is, which strategies to adopt.

Just an exercise, you think? This "game" has caused ructions, indeed, near riots, at some management training seminars. The managers involved in this game can become highly emotional because they have made enormous emotional commitments to their chosen frames and positions. In one version, the groups are set up as divisions of a company, and the game involves gaining or losing revenue between divisions. Managers can become deeply involved, emotionally committed, and highly incensed, especially if most groups are cooperating and one is defecting. The defecting group (company division) gains points at the expense of all of the groups (the rest of the company) as a whole. The cooperators see them as traitors. But from the defector's frame of reference, the cooperators are wasting points. They are laughing all the way to the point bank—unless everyone starts defecting.

But this is just how some companies do work, with each division trying to maximize its divisional profit, even if other divisions suffer. Which is right: Should the company work to profit as a whole, or should each division compete against all of the others as if they were totally separate? And what if they are not divisions of one company, but separate companies held and owned in common? There is *no* right or wrong answer. There is only how you frame the problem.

As a modeler you do not have to invent, devise, or select a suitable frame. All you have to do is determine what the problem stakeholders see as the appropriate frame for the problem. Of course, if you have responsibilities other than, or in addition to, being a modeler, you may be responsible for actually devising or selecting a suitable frame. However, the practitioner modeler's first job is to discover the existing frame. More than simply discovering it, however, the modeler's job is to produce an objective representation of the frame in some form—in other words, a map. One good way to discover and map the frame, perhaps the best way, is to talk to people. Chapter 6 contains practical interviewing techniques, but given those techniques, what issues are important in creating the frame? And how are they to be mapped?

5.1.1 Framing the Decision Process

Ultimately, defining the problem results in a decision to do something to change the current circumstances and resolve the problem. At the heart of the decision-making process lies the selection of the best option available under the circumstances. The frame maps all of the issues that go into recognizing the circumstances, the options, and the selection criteria. The rest of this chapter develops all of the components that form the decision-framing process. Figure 5.2 shows a map of the territory. It includes a high level look at the components developed in this chapter, and their relationships to each

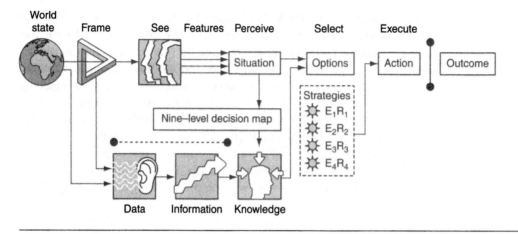

Figure 5.2 Decision framing process.

other and functions within the whole. This is the guide to the territory explored here. (In this explanation of the decision-framing process the *key words* italicized in this explanation match the process map moving from left to right sequentially, or, where necessary, top to bottom. The parenthetical references refer to the chapter sections that expand on the topic.)

The process starts with the *world state* (1.1), as illustrated on the left of the figure. Whatever happens, it happens because of a perceived need for change because of a gap between where we are and where we would like to be.

However, as noted in Part I, we all have a *frame* of preconceived notions, a model of the way the world works that tells us what's important and allows us to interpret the world state. So too do companies, and their framing models of preconceived notions determine what the company *sees* in the world state through business model frames such as CRM (Customer Relationship Management), JIT (Just In Time), and ERP (Enterprise Resource Planning) that inform the managers what *features* of the world state should be noted.

Although the framing model of preconceived notions informs what features are important to see, what is *perceived* (1.1.3) is a *situation* (5.3.1 and 5.4) wherein those features take on specific values.

The frame provides many simplifying assumptions about the situation. The nature of the assumptions, and the level of complexity remaining in the situation, has to be explicated (for modeling) and is mapped into the *nine-level decision map* (5.3.2).

Recall that *knowledge* (4.1.3) [gained from *information* (4.1.2) that is summarized *data* (1.1.4 and 4.1.1)] provides a list of potential actions that could be taken in a recognized situation. This knowledge, informed by the characterization provided by the nine-level decision map, is applied to *select* actions from the *options* (5.5.5) available.

The actions are in the form of *strategies* (5.5.1), each of which has an expected payoff associated with it, and a risk level associated with getting that payoff. (Indicated in the figure by a symbol for the strategy, "E_n" for the expected payoff, and "R_n" for the risk characterization [5.6.1.]).

The *execute* phase actually takes the *action* by implementing all of the necessary steps to change the course of events.

Throughout the entire course of making the decision, the actual *outcome* remains totally unknowable, thus shown barred from the rest of the process. Although it is the purpose of the decision process, only the due course of events will reveal what the outcome is.

For a modeler, understanding every phase of this process is crucial. A successful model incorporates input from every stage of this process, and the modeler needs to clearly understand the assumptions, requirements, and expectations from the stakeholders of every step in this process—even if the stakeholders are not themselves immediately aware of all the issues. If that's the case, it's the modeler's role to develop the needed framing for the decision process with the stakeholders. Helping the modeler perform that role is the purpose of this chapter. (See MII.TB.7)

5.2 Objectives: Getting your Bearings

The first order of business is to define the objectives. In many modeling applications the initial problem statement is made not in terms of the objectives, but in terms of what the problem owner thinks is a desired solution. So you may ask: "What are the objectives for this project?" and get a reply similar to, "To build a predictive model that will indicate who will buy products from our catalog!" Given this objective, off you go to do exactly that. Returning with the model, which improves the response rate by 400%, and expecting success and kudos, you find that your project is counted a failure. Why?

Perhaps the catalog was losing money before the model, and is still losing money in spite of the improvement, so the problem has nothing directly to do with response rate. Perhaps it's more to do with whether the company should be in the catalog business at all. Or maybe it's determining how to find out if the catalog can be profitable. Or perhaps it's finding a different product mix, page layout, customer demography, or any number of things. It may be finding an alternative strategy, or merely different tactics. In this hypothetical example, the objective has nothing to do with making a predictive model to improve response rate—that is just what the need stakeholder who owns the problem thought a solution might be. (Stakeholder types are discussed in the next chapter.)

So, you will have to explore the objectives, and be somewhat skeptical of them, too. Find out how the stated objective will help, or what it will achieve. Ask why this is thought to be an appropriate objective, and what else could be achieved. Ask what a perfect result would look like, and why such a perfect result cannot be accomplished.

From time to time, try to express the objectives as a statement of the form: "The objectives of this model are to be expressed primarily in terms of . . . , and secondarily in terms of . . . ." The expressions in the blanks might be "customers" and "profit", or "returns" and "production failures." It is this "framing in terms" technique that will help identify the primary objectives that frame the model.

Fundamentally, framing is done in terms of what is required of the model. This is a simple extension of how we answer any question. Perhaps someone asks what you want out of your next job. You could answer in terms of salary, time off, job satisfaction, career advancement, or even recreational aspirations. A full and complete answer addressing all possible terms would take forever! Almost certainly the questioner has particular terms of an answer in mind. Perhaps: "In terms of salary, what are you looking for from your next job?" So too it is with discovering the framing terms for a model.

In short, the frame into which a model is placed provides the meaning that it yields. More than that, it actually creates the meaning it yields.

5.3 Problems and Decisions

Models are built only when there is an identified problem. (As a reminder, the "problem" could equally well be to discover an opportunity.) Certainly, a model could be built of a nonproblem situation, but if there's no problem, well, there's no problem, so why bother? And indeed, in practice, no one does bother. It takes time, effort, and resources to build a model, and if no return is expected the resources are better used elsewhere. Practically, in business, models are built only to help deal with problems. The fact that there is a problem implies some level of uncertainty in determining which course of action to pursue. Resolving that uncertainty, and determining a course of action, requires a decision. A decision chooses between alternative courses of action and, in that choice, deliberately selects a specific intervention (or sequence of interventions) in the course of events.

Ultimately, the purpose of modeling, at least in business, is to inform decision making. Clearly, part of the framework requires identifying the type, nature, range, and scope of the decision(s) that the model is intended to address.

Models serve three basic decision making purposes in a specific situation:

1. To clarify risk
2. To determine options
3. To evaluate possible outcomes

So-called "rational" decision making in a specific situation requires these three inputs—available options, possible outcomes, and associated risk. Because these are key inputs into decision making, these are the key outputs required of a model, at least if a rational decision is to be made as a result. However, regardless of the fact that business decisions require these inputs, not all decisions are equal.

5.3.1 Decision Symbols

There are several types of decisions (such as intuitive, reactive, or preferential) that are not of concern here. An intuitive decision, for instance, is exactly what it seems: a decision based on intuitive feelings. Let's say you had a cup of coffee. Why? Well, the real reason is probably because you felt like it. If pressed, you could probably make up a rational sounding explanation, but that is an after-the-fact reason, or a rationalization. The action came first in this example, the reason afterward. Intuitive, reactive, and preferential decisions are not a concern here because they don't address solving problems. (At least, not in the sense that the term *problems* is used here.) Other motivations lie behind them. Although they exert a degree of control over the world, and they do modify the undifferentiated flow of events, these types of decisions are not primarily dealing with rationally solving a problem.

Another class of decisions that are not of concern here are those that don't seem to be made at all. The expression "making a decision" seems to imply some sort of situation analysis before deciding on a course of action. In practice, many decisions seem to simply emerge. This is true for both personal and business decisions. With these types of decisions, it becomes apparent only after the fact that a decision was actually made. Perhaps the action needed was simply assumed into existence. Maybe a sequence of tiny, seemingly inconsequential decisions resulted in a major alteration in events. However it happens, this is a time-based decision process rather than an analysis-based decision process.

Business modeling and data mining support only one particular type of decision making: rational decision making. For a *rational decision,* the reasons come first: the decision is deliberate and follows analytic and (when using modeling to support it) synthetic reasoning. Other types of decisions are relevant, useful, even vital, in business. They are not, however, based on modeling. From here on, whenever the discussion refers to a decision, unless specified otherwise, it is a rational decision that is intended. It is a rational decision in the sense that there is a normative structure of the type introduced in Part I that supports it.

Before describing and typing decisions, we need to choose a way to describe the form of a decision. In this book, decisions are constructed from several simple parts. Figure 5.3 shows the decision components. At the center of the figure is a nexus point that represents the place in the process where all the elements are pulled together, and at which a decision is made. The following describe the parts of a decision:

- *Situations.* On the left, the figure illustrates the current state of the world. This is a summation of all events up to the decision nexus, forever fixed and immutable. (In less refined language, since stuff happens, this is the happened stuff.) Not everything in the world is relevant. Almost certainly the phase of the moon and the current distance to the Andromeda galaxy are wholly unimportant. Relevant happenings form situations that are to be addressed by the decision.

- *Options.* Situations present certain options—different sequences of actions that could be taken in the circumstances prevailing in the current situation. Some options, if selected, will likely preclude others. Some options will require resources that it is undesirable to commit. It might be possible to select several options simultaneously, and in so doing make them interact with each other in complex ways. In any case, each optional sequence of actions will be expected to have a different outcome.

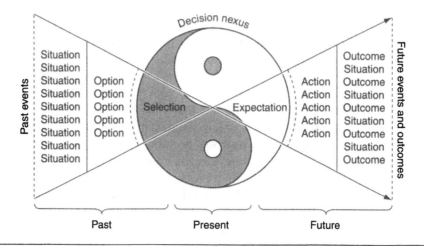

Figure 5.3 The "Nexus" view of decision making.

- *Selection.* In the figure, the central circular symbol and the dotted curves, encompass the actual decision nexus. Making a decision is actually selecting an option and acting on it. What is selected is one of the options. The choice of option is based on the expected outcome for that option compared with the expected outcomes for the other options. Implementing the decision requires acting so as to influence worldly events.

- *Expectations.* Each option has associated expectations about what will result. (There are still expectations from an action even if the action is "do nothing," because this is a deliberate choice to let events proceed specifically unmodified by the decision maker's action. If such a decision had not been made, the decision maker could have acted in a way that did influence the events specified, perhaps inadvertently or as the result of acting on some other decision.) At the time of the decision, it is impossible to know the actual outcome. A selection from the available options is needed based on evaluating expected outcomes.

- *Actions.* With the selection made, actions modify the flow of worldly events. However, the actual results of the decision, made on the basis of *expected* results, may not turn out as anticipated.

- *Outcomes.* In the real world, outcomes are the result of the decision. Outcomes have nothing to do with the making of a decision because they are totally unknowable at the time the decision is made. They are interspersed with the situations that arise in the world that are not results of the decision.

Taken together, these are the components of a decision: situations, options, selection, expectations, actions, and outcomes.

As with any map, this one necessarily distorts the territory it illustrates. Figure 5.4 illustrates another equally valid, but different way of characterizing decision-making. Here it is viewed as a continuous process where situations

Figure 5.4   The continuous view of decision making.

yield options, options require selections, selections (and implicitly, actions) produce outcomes, outcomes produce situations, and so on. Here, the wheel rolls on forever as we continually make and remake the world we live in, interacting and responding continuously. The first map focuses on a single decision, the second on continuing interaction with the world that requires continuous and endless decisions. Even so, in both maps, the basic components are similar. These components are used to build a map of decision types.

5.3.2   Decision Maps

There are a wide variety of decision types. In making a map of various relevant decision types, we have no need for a comprehensive map that covers all types of decisions. What is needed for framing the model is only a map of rationally made decisions. Figure 5.5 illustrates this map.

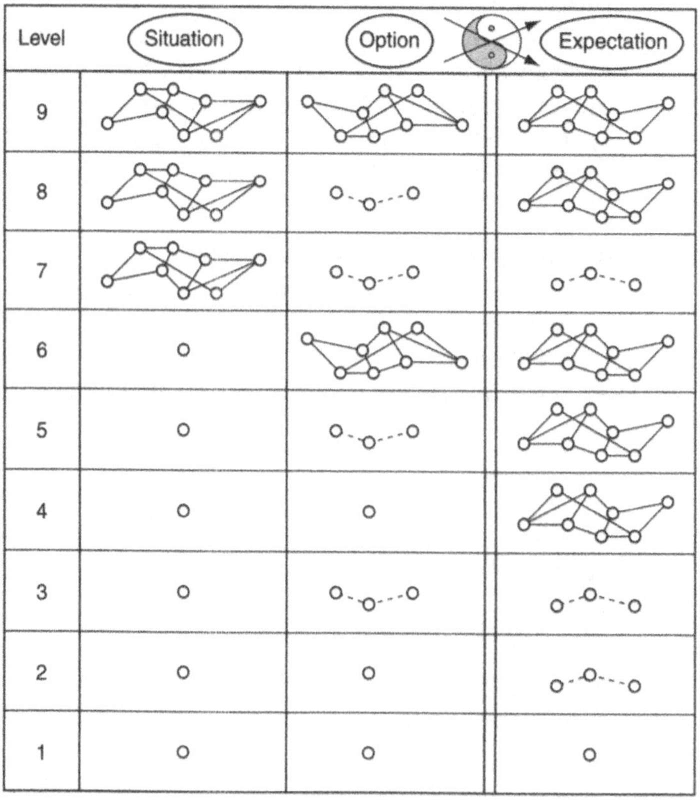

Figure 5.5   Decision Map.

The decision map shows nine levels of decisions. Each of the levels increases in complexity from the bottom, level 1, to the top, level 9. The small circles represent discrete elements of, or issues in, the situation, option, or expectation segments of the problem. A single circle represents a single element or issue. The symbol with three circles joined by dotted lines shows that there are several elements simply related, and that the interrelations are not considered consequential for the model. The symbol with multiple circles joined by solid lines indicates that there are multiple elements, interconnected in possibly complex ways, and that the nature of the interconnections is at least as important as the elements themselves.

> Level 1 shows a single situation that calls for a decision. There is only one option considered viable, and only a single expected outcome of that option is considered relevant.
>
> Level 2 shows a single situation and option, but several separate outcomes are expected, the outcomes being simply connected.
>
> Level 3 shows one situation, several simply connected options, and several simply connected outcomes.
>
> Level 4 shows one situation and one option, but multiple outcomes that interact with each other in complex ways.
>
> Level 5 shows one situation, several simply connected options, and complexly interacting outcomes.
>
> Level 6 shows one situation, several complexly interacting options, and several complexly interacting outcomes
>
> Level 7 shows several complexly interacting situations, several simply connected options, and several simply connected outcomes.
>
> Level 8 shows several complexly interacting situations, several simply connected options, and several complexly interacting outcomes.
>
> Level 9 shows several complexly interacting situations, several complexly interacting options, and several complexly interacting outcomes.

Brief and overly simplified examples of each type of problem are shown in Table 5.1. These are, of course, "toy" problem descriptions, not intended as fully detailed examples. (They are not toy problems—only toy descriptions.) Full and realistic descriptions would need lengthy case studies, and these examples are intended only to give a flavor of the types of problems at each level. The point here is to understand what the problem levels represent, and how they affect framing the model.

Looking at the map, there seem to be several potential entries missing. There are, after all, 3 items in each of 3 columns. There are 27 ways to

TABLE 5.1 Decision Map Examples

Level	Situation	Option	Expectation
1	Segment a potential prospect list.	Predict who will respond to a solicitation.	Score for proclivity to purchase.
2	Retailers are returning goods in excess of acceptable limits. No detectable changes in product quality.	1. Determine reasons for returns. 2. Target program to reduce returns.	If effective: 1. Reduced returns 2. Greater retailer satisfaction 3. Less goods manufactured If ineffective: (other expectations)
3	Losing customers to competition.	1. Media advertising 2. In-store incentives 3. Direct marketing	1. More customers in stores 2. More purchases by customers when in stores 3. Higher value purchases
4	Fraud in branch offices.	Reduce fraud.	Less fraud, higher branch profit, but antifraud efforts will affect morale. Morale affects service level and staff retention. Staff retention affects training levels and staff quality and impacts budget. Profit level and staff turnover both affect levels of fraud and staff turnover.
5	Excessive failure rate in product manufacture.	1. Better operator training 2. New manufacturing machinery	Impacts corporate resources, plant management, personnel planning, and labor relations.
6	Withdrawal of major competitor from market.	A nest of interacting options to do with products, repositioning, marketing, and so on.	A vast array of possible and interacting results.
7	The company uses the CRM model of business. This is a complex web of interacting issues that frames and informs the worldview.	The marketing department wants to explore only the issues in deciding how to build customer portfolios. Other CRM issues, such as the value proposition and risk/reward sharing profile, are not considered relevant in this decision.	Only performance of the separate portfolios is used in evaluating the value of the portfolio. Marketing feels that it does not have sufficient data to warrant investigating portfolio interaction in this decision frame.

continued

TABLE 5.1 Continued

Level	Situation	Option	Expectation
8	As in level 7, the company uses the CRM model of business. This is a complex web of interacting issues that frames and informs the worldview.	Building on the level 7 decision, data on customer portfolio interactions has been collected, and seems to be significant. Marketing needs to determine how to balance the portfolios in light of the new data.	Expected portfolio performance interactions form a significant part of understanding how the marketplace reacts and interacts to the company's CRM approach, and determining how to improve portfolio profiling.
9	Emergence of a new technology. It is the vast web of interacting technological, cultural, and business situations that drives this. For example, suppose room temperature superconductivity was achieved.	There is a vast array of interacting options.	At this level, the possible results are highly interactive. A new technology at this level can be expected to have an enormous impact at many levels of society and technology, all interacting with each other.

combine the 3 entries "single," "multiple," and "complex" in the 3 columns "situation," "option," and "expectation." With 9 present, there seem to be 18 potential combinations missing. Why? Actually, the reasons are straightforward, but not directly related to an explanation of framing a problem, or to using the map. So as not to interrupt the explanation of the map at this point, an explanation of why the "missing" entries are not in fact missing is included in the supplemental material at the end of this chapter.

5.3.3 Setting the Decision Frame

The decision map is a powerful tool for identifying the type of decision to be modeled. Identifying a decision with one of the decision levels on the map shows the modeler many of the issues that need to be dealt with and the assumptions made, albeit unconsciously. Remember that in identifying the problem level on the map, it is not the actual world state that is to be mapped. For any problem, the conditions in the world are enormously complex. The problem's stakeholders will already have made many simplifying assumptions (consciously and unconsciously), and it is the problem as presented to the modeler that is to be located on the map. Even the Level 1 situation shown in Table 5.1 is, in reality, an enormously complex phenomenon; however, for the purposes of decision making, many simplifying assumptions have been made. The example Level 1 problem from Table 5.1 shows that, as the problem is presented to the modeler by the stakeholder experiencing the problem, all situation components have been assumed to be effectively collapsed into a single issue. So too with the options and expectations. Thus, framing the problem in this way by placing it on the decision map reveals clearly many of the assumptions in the decision process. Revealing them means that they are no longer hidden assumptions, and are amenable to questioning and modification. But with the decision located on the map, what next? How does this help?

The map shows a problem broken down into three component pieces: situation, options, and expectations. Each of these components requires separate consideration, and may even require separate models. Each of these components of the overall decision model has separate issues in framing that need to be explored separately. The next three sections explore each separate part—situation, options, and expectations—in more detail.

5.4 Modeling Situations: Connecting the Decision to a Worldview

The *situation* is the current state (at the time of the problem) of what is relevant in the real world. The difficulty here is that our view of the world is determined by whatever model is used to view it (recall Chernobyl). Such a model frames our view of the world. It is very unlikely that a modeler will ever have to construct such a worldview model from scratch. (Constructing and modeling a whole worldview from scratch would be a truly massive undertaking!) Instead, the modeler must simply adopt whatever worldview model the client is currently using, or perhaps one that the client wants to use in the future. This type of model, of course, has been called a *framing model* elsewhere in the book. It is still a framing model here, and in decision making it will be used for framing the situation. How?

A framing model identifies particular aspects of the world as being important and relevant. Perhaps a particular framing model says that "rate of inflation" is important. A situation model must then capture the current value, say "rate of inflation = 3.5%." Thus, when making a decision, the framing model only points out what is important. The situation model is then just a set of values for features that the framework model points to as important. (Imaginary conversation—Framework model: "State of precipitation is important, you know." Situation model: "OK. Not raining today!") Thus, the framing model and the situation model are not quite one and the same. A situation model is a single, particular representation of what the framing model points to as important and relevant.

So far as business modeling is concerned, framing models abound. Such framing models are called *business models,* and each constitutes a particular overarching philosophical approach to business. Just in time (JIT) models point to one set of considerations as important to a business; enterprise resource planning (ERP) models point to another set, not entirely dissimilar in some aspects from JIT. Customer relationship management (CRM) has yet a different set of issues that the model indicates as relevant and important. These business models are large and frequently complex, even though they all simplify the complexity of the world rendering it manageable.

Business decision making starts by using whatever business model the problem owner selects to frame the situation. (The selection, of course, may be entirely unconscious.) The business situation represents the current state of the world as looked at through the prevailing business model so that the problem holder and the modeler look at the world through, say, "CRM colored glasses." What they see is defined by the "color" of the glasses, and that view *is* the business situation. Thus framed, the situation model for the decision is set up.

In almost all business decisions, a modeler will never have to create a framework model. All of the decisions up through Level 6 collapse the complexity of the world to a single issue. That single issue may well be part of a larger business model, but either the stakeholder experiencing the problem has deliberately decided to collapse the complexity to a single issue, or perhaps is unaware of the other connected issues. Even when more than one issue is present in the situation, almost never are all of the issues present in the whole business model involved—just a few selected issues. Remember that a situation model is, even at its most complete, initially only a single instantiation of values in a framework model. Developing a full framework model is strictly outside the needs of the decision. Before the decision is framed, the completed business (framework) model is assumed.

5.5 **Options: Assessing the Possible**

In spite of the prevalence of the use of the term *strategy* in connection with business, it is surprisingly hard to find the term defined, and particularly to find a definition that separates the term *strategy* from *tactics*. Both come from Greek words: *strategy* originally meant "one skilled in the art of generalship," *tactics* meant "to set in order," or "skilled in the art of deploying troops." Or at least, so the *Oxford English Dictionary* relates in slightly greater length.

So far as modeling is concerned, these terms are used in fairly precise ways. The more precise meanings do no violence to the meanings generally inferred in business use, but may not include all that is encompassed by the less defined business uses of these terms.

5.5.1 Strategies

Game theory is a traditional tool in the decision-making arsenal. It also serves as a good starting point for discovering how the term *strategy* is used in modeling. Understanding the intricacies of game theory is not necessary for framing a model, but a very brief introduction to a small piece of the theory will explain how the term is used.

In game theory, there are always at least two players who contend with each other. Further, game theory assumes that there is some advantage to be gained for one or other of the two opponents, and for which the opponents contend. Each player has the option to do particular things that bring the player some level of return, usually called the *payoff*. This payoff is used to keep some sort of score for each player as the game progresses. A *strategy*, in game theory terms, comprises not just a set of actions, but a plan of campaign so completely controlled by the player that no intervention of the opponent, or of nature, can interfere with its complete execution. This does seem like a somewhat tall order! Nonetheless, it can be done, and each player has several strategies that can be played, each resulting in some specific payoff associated with that strategy.

An example will help to explain. Consider the Prisoner's Dilemma mentioned earlier as a management game. How could such a game be represented? Figure 5.6 shows a matrix that contains the payoff amounts for each player using each strategy. The two players shown are "A Team" and "B Team." Each player has two possible strategies: to cooperate with the other player (shown by *C*) or defect (shown by *D*). Note that when it is time to play, each player has total and complete control over this choice. No interference by the other

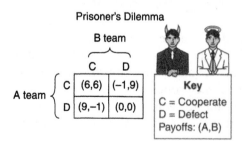

Figure 5.6 Payoff matrix for game theory representation of Prisoner's Dilemma.

player, or by nature, can influence the player's choice to cooperate or to defect. For each player, there is a payoff shown in the matrix. The A Team payoff is shown as the left-hand number in the bracket; the B Team payoff by the right-hand number. As you can see, a negative payoff, or loss, is quite possible. So, for instance, if the A Team defects when the B Team cooperates, A gains 9 points and B loses 1 point. If both cooperate, both gain 6 points.

So much for game theory. Although there is a vast amount more to say on that subject, this is enough to understand the meaning of the strategies on the decision map. For game theory, a strategy is a plan of campaign that is in the control of the player, and that generates a payoff. In modeling, and pressed by the real world, some of the hard edges are left off the strong demand that no intervention can interfere with complete execution, but the rest of the description remains intact. For modeling, *strategies* are plans of action that can reasonably be expected to be completed as intended and that have a payoff. What is a reasonable expectation of completion? Of course, that depends on many factors, but it might mean something like "a better than 98% chance of completion." As modelers, there is no need to get "bent out of shape" about making it precise. If the stakeholders are happy, fine. As a modeler, just be sure to check. Real strategies do not always execute perfectly, but if one doesn't execute at all, it's no strategy!

5.5.2 Tactics

So what of tactics? Consider the Level 1 decision example of a marketing campaign. Assume a prospect database to be segmented into likely segments. We have not discussed the structure of a strategy yet, but assume that informally one strategy may be described as "mail to top 10 percent." This is a strategy because it is a plan of campaign that the company almost certainly can execute, and it has a payoff. When this strategy is executed or put into action, the tactics actually implement the necessary sequence of real-world actions. Tactically, real money would be spent on paper, printing, creative, postage, computer resources to de-dupe the mailing list, and so on. For the selected strategy, these are the tactics: the plan of actions that actually realize the strategy. There is, however, no payoff for implementing each tactic— the payoffs occur only after the tactics are all executed, and the payoffs accrue to the strategy, not to individual tactics.

Strategies and tactics are relative, however. There is no hard, fast, or absolute distinction between the one and the other that can be based on the actions that each specifies. For instance, if a strategy is for the Wobbly Corporation (A Division of the Simple Company) to increase sales efforts for Wobbly Widgets, one tactic for this strategy might well be to run a direct mail campaign. At this level, all of the details of implementation are subsumed into the tactic. It is assumed that, as a tactical matter, this action can be executed as-is without further direction. Further, the payoff would not accrue to the direct mail campaign, but to the strategy, (i.e., that of increased sales efforts for the Wobbly Widget product line). And really, this is the differentiation point in modeling between strategies and tactics. Tactics do not themselves have payoffs, they simply execute strategic decisions. However, tactics may otherwise be indistinguishable from strategies. For convenience, tactics can be designated as partial strategies that have no payoff. (It will turn out that they also lack other components essential to strategies, too. They are still usefully designated as partial strategies in a modeling environment, and more to the point here, can usefully be framed as such.)

5.5.3 Linking Strategy Payoffs

So far as decisions at Levels 1, 2, and 4 are concerned, there is only a single strategy to address. This represents a single option that is to be evaluated. The only decision is about whether or not, or perhaps when, to execute all of the actions required based on a consideration of the anticipated results. (*Anticipated results* are, of course, what the map shows as the *expectation*.) Even at Levels 3, 5, 7, and 8 there is no concern with any interaction between strategies so, at least as far as the payoffs are concerned, each strategy can be evaluated separately. But what does the linkage at Levels 6 and 9 mean? For decisions at these levels, considering the impact of the linkage is defined as a necessary and integral part of the decision-making process. But what is this linkage? What affects what exactly?

When *options* are linked, it indicates that the *payoffs* are significantly interrelated. That is to say that the payoffs are expected to vary depending on which strategies or set of strategies are executed. Suppose two strategies are significantly linked (call them S1 and S2). For convenience, call executing the action sequences in the real world "firing" the strategies. The individual payoffs for S1 and S2 are different if S1 is fired alone, if S2 is fired alone, or if S1 and S2 are fired together.

As an example of such a linkage, suppose strategy S1 is to telemarket to a market segment and strategy S2 is to direct mail the same market segment, as illustrated in the outcome matrix in Figure 5.7. You would rationally expect that the payoffs would be different if you just called, just mailed, or did both together. Given, say, that a customer in the segment can respond only once, calling would get some, mailing would get some, but both together would hit some who had already responded to the other solicitation. Note that if you execute one strategy alone, the payoff for the other has no value, not even 0. An unexecuted strategy has no outcome payoff value. Outcome

Figure 5.7   Outcome matrix when firing multiple strategies with interacting payoffs.

payoffs occur only when strategies are fired. Even for this simple example, it is clear that the payoffs must be linked.

(Take care not to confuse an expectation with an outcome. Decisions are based on expectations. Payoffs of fired strategies accrue the values of outcomes. At decision time, only the expectations are known—the outcomes are unknown and unknowable. However, if the outcomes are expected to be linked, the expectations must reflect the same linkage. The outcome matrix can be constructed only after the event; the expectation matrix is constructed before the event. Figure 5.7 illustrates an outcome matrix; an expectation matrix must reflect any expected linkage.)

5.5.4   Threading Strategies Together

In the discussion of tactics, the Wobbly Corporation wanted to implement a strategy of increasing sales for Wobbly Widgets. The strategies were not related by linking payoffs; they were threaded together in action sequences. The tactics for the sales campaign might include in-store incentives, direct mail, and a Web-based promotion. But, as already discussed, looked at from a different level, these might also be seen as strategies in their own right. Somehow a map of the strategies has to be able to reflect which strategies are potentially fired by (and fire) other strategies.

When *dependencies* are linked, it indicates that strategy *firing order* is significantly interrelated. The payoffs of those strategies higher up the thread roll up the payoffs of those lower down the thread. At the bottom of the thread are the tactics. Having strategies "higher" and "lower" on the threads implies that they can be represented hierarchically.

Figure 5.8 shows the hierarchy for the Wobbly Widgets promotion. At the highest level is the "increase sales for Wobbly Widgets" strategy labeled "$10S_2$". Strategies are numbered uniquely for identification by the first number. For the highest level strategy in this example, that reference number is 10, and although the strategies are laid out in numerical order in this figure, the numerical ordering has no significance. The subscript 2 is significant and indicates the level of a strategy on its thread. Subscript 0 indicates a tactic because it is at the lowest level.

All strategies can be individually fired following a decision to do so, regardless of their place in the hierarchy, and firing flows only down the hierarchy. There is no need to fire a higher level strategy, if one is present, in order to fire a lower one. If $7S_1$ is fired, the diagram indicates that it in turn fires four strategies: $1S_0$, $2S_0$, $3S_0$, and $4S_0$. (In this case, these four are also tactics that connect directly to the real world. This is shown by their level, 0.) If fired, strategy $8S_1$ fires strategies $3S_0$ and $4S_0$. However, if both $7S_1$ and $8S_1$ fire together, $8S_1$ prevents $7S_1$ from firing $1S_0$. Perhaps $1S_0$ prints special store coupons that are not needed if direct mail coupons are available. Looking again at the figure, both $7S_1$ and $8S_1$ fire $3S_0$. Perhaps $3S_0$ is an action, like having coupons designed that is required by either strategy. Of course, if the highest level strategy, $10S_2$, fires, all three strategies lower on their threads fire too, and the firing ripples down the hierarchy.

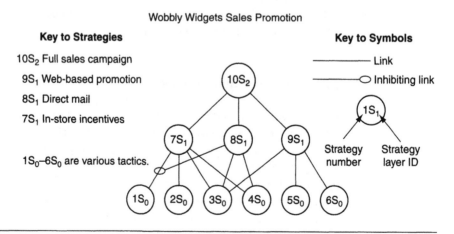

Figure 5.8 Threaded strategies in a hierarchy.

Another useful representation of the threads is depicted in Figure 5.9. This shows the firing strategies along the top and the fired strategies down the side. Tactics are shown in italics and grayed out because they cannot fire other strategies and therefore will always have empty cells. It is not necessary to show tactics on a firing matrix; their inclusion here is only for completeness. A 1 indicates that the strategy numbered on the left of the matrix is fired by the strategy numbered at the top. A bracketed number in a column indicates an inhibition by the column strategy of the bracketed strategy firing the row strategy. In Figure 5.9, for example, firing $8S_1$ inhibits $(7S_1)$ from firing $1S_0$.

5.5.5 Mapping Options as Strategies

Options can only be mapped after the problem has been mapped to an appropriate decision level. If the problem is mapped at Levels 1, 2, and 4, the only remaining options mapping activity is to characterize the option part of the single strategy. Figure 5.10 illustrates this in the top box. The dashed boxes indicate that there is more to a completely specified strategy than just the option part discussed so far.

For a problem that maps to Levels 3, 5, 7, and 8, the situation is only slightly different. The problem holder has defined the problem such that

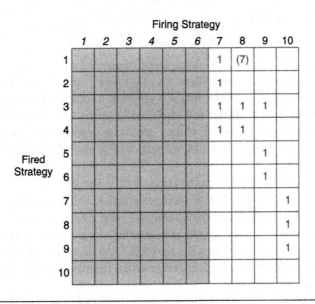

Figure 5.9 Strategy firing matrix.

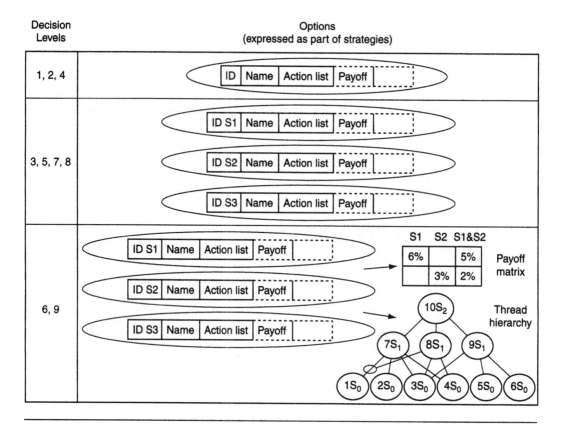

Figure 5.10 Beginning of defining an option as a component in a strategy.

interactions among options are not construed as relevant to the problem. The strategies, although there may be several, are essentially considered independently. A modeler might well want to discuss the actual state of this independence with the stakeholders in terms of both payoff linkage and thread linkage. However, if they are to be considered independently from each other, a list of the option parts of the identified strategies suffices to map them.

For decisions that map to Levels 6 or 9, the strategy descriptions have to additionally map the payoff linkages and thread linkages. Payoff linkages are mapped as payoff matrices similar to the one introduced in Figure 5.7. Thread linkages are mapped as hierarchies, or perhaps firing matrices, of the sort introduced in Figures 5.8 and 5.9. (An example at the end of the chapter eventually pulls all this together when discussion of all of the elements in the map is complete.)

There is a difficulty here. Although the payoff has been discussed in general terms, and a place for it in the strategy has been made in the form of a payoff matrix, there has been no detailed discussion of what this payoff is, nor how to map it. This is because the payoff (as far it can be known at decision time) is intimately linked to the last part of the decision map itself—the expectation. Strategies straddle options and expectations, and before the whole strategy can be mapped we must look at how to map expectations.

5.6 Expectations: Assessing the Future

As the well-known aphorism has it, "Prediction is very difficult, particularly when it has to do with the future!" But all problems have to be faced, and all decisions made, with complete ignorance of what the future actually holds in store. We can, of course, make a guess about what will turn up. Sometimes the guesses are quite good. We also can guess about how interventions that we make will turn out. But at bottom, they are all guesses—although not uninformed guesses. In fact, by looking at what is going on now, and looking at how things have turned out in the past, our guesses about the future are right often enough that we can sometimes build a fairly good picture of the future. The picture we build is often good enough that things do come out as expected. And we have found that it is quite reasonable to give our expectations a concrete expression in terms of probabilities and risks. And it is in terms of these probabilities and risks that we express our expectations of particular outcomes. So in order to put expectations into the frame, we must look at probabilities and risks.

5.6.1 Probably a Risky Business

Probability has a venerable history. It has been earnestly studied over hundreds of years, and still the question of what probability is has yet to be settled. It is certainly not going to be settled here. (Of course, having read this far through the book, it may occur to you that probability is measured to address a problem, and so what it "really" is depends on how the problem is framed. But we will let that discussion pass.) So far as probability needs to be defined here, it will simply measure how likely we believe some event is. (And leave the term *likely* in the same heap as *probability*.)

First, a note that the purpose of this explanation is *not* that you should learn to be able to calculate risk. There is more to modeling risk than is discussed here, and in any case, calculations are what computers are for. When actually modeling risk, data mining is a good tool. The purpose of this explanation is that you should understand why the components discussed are needed in the frame. To explain that requires that you look at a few numbers.

The two traditional ways to determine probability in elementary statistical texts are to:

1. Look at the historical record of similar events and use the ratio of occurrence to nonoccurrence under a set of circumstances.
2. Count the total number of ways an event can come out and declare the probability to be the proportion of each individual occurrence to the total number of possible occurrences.

In any case, a ratio of occurrence to nonoccurrence is the result, and can be expressed conveniently as a percentage. Risk is far more than simply probability of occurrence of some event. Showing what goes into the frame about risk requires a brief discussion of how risk is modeled.

The Wobbly Corporation decides it has $10,000 it can invest to run one, and only one, of three proposed marketing strategies for Wobbly Widgets: an Internet Web-based promotion, direct-mail solicitation, or in-store incentives. Just to make it easy, assume for the moment that the actual probabilities for the outcome of each strategy can be known. And further, being short of cash, the Wobbly Corporation is interested in running only the lowest risk of these campaigns. The outcomes of the campaigns are to be judged by the amount they return. And finally, although the real-world distribution of possible outcomes covers a wide range, the risk is to be judged on only three possible outcomes for each strategy: 1) the most likely profit, 2) break-even, and 3) the most likely loss. (The restriction on only three outcomes is to keep the explanation manageable. Such constraints aren't needed in an actual frame or in a model.)

Figure 5.11 shows the probability of each of the three selected outcomes for each of the three strategies. The standard statistical way to determine risk is to consider how valuable each outcome is and multiply that value by its probability. This gives what is called an *expected value*. Add the expected values together for each strategy, and that is the *expected return* for the strategy. The statistical use of the term *risk* measures how dramatically the expected values differ from each other using a measure called *variance*. This in some way measures how likely you are to get any particular return—more variance, less likely, more risk. The results of these calculations are all shown in the figure.

(The reasoning for equating variance and risk goes something like this: The larger the variance, the more dispersed are the values of the potential outcomes. The greater the dispersal of potential outcomes, the less the confidence in getting any particular outcome. The less confidence in getting any particular outcome, the more the risk of some outcome other than the desired one.)

Figure 5.11 shows, for instance, that for the strategy Web there is a 75% chance of getting $12,000, which gives an *expected value* of 75% × $12,000

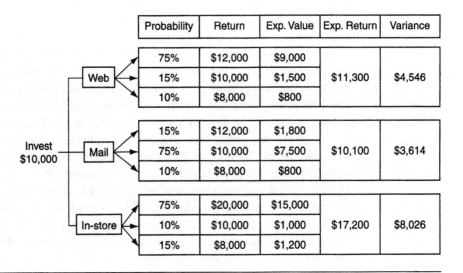

Figure 5.11 Return and risk assessment for three strategies.

= $9,000. The other expected values of $10,000 and $8,000 for this strategy are calculated similarly, and are also shown. Add the expected values for all three outcomes in this strategy and the *expected return* for the strategy is $9,000 + $1,500 + $800 = $11,300. The variance of the three expected values ($9,000, $1,500, and $800) is $4,546 to the nearest dollar.

Looking at all three strategies statistically, the least risky is the strategy Mail, but risky or not, it doesn't look promising. The problem with this method of evaluating risk and return for each strategy is that it doesn't seem to match intuition. Intuitively, the strategy In-store looks as if it might be the one to go with even though it has the highest variance and the highest potential loss. It certainly has the highest potential gain. However, there is still another problem with this way of assessing risk, and that is the selected target.

5.6.2 Risk Selection

Hidden in the original description of the problem is this sentence: "The outcomes of the campaigns are to be judged by the amount they return." This sentence chooses to target one particular risk—return. But these strategies entail other possible targets. Suppose that the risk target had been chosen differently—would that have made any difference to the perceived risk?

Suppose that the target is not return but, say, new customer acquisition. Where is the risk here? Unless the Wobbly marketing department is having a particularly bad day, or is feeling particularly obnoxious, any strategy is going to result in attracting at least some new customers. One strategy may work better than another, but none will actually drive customers away. So there is, we will assume, no actual risk of losing customers. The risk seems to be that we won't get as many as we might have done with a better strategy. In this case, the strategy with the highest variance may well be the one with the best chance of getting the most new customers, and is thus the least risky.

There are two points here. The first is that in the frame for the strategy, it is crucial to specify the risk target or targets. (There could quite easily be more than one.) Wobbly might be interested in evaluating strategies for both the risk of not making a reasonable return and, simultaneously, the risk of not getting the most new customers. So far as modeling them simultaneously goes there is no particular difficulty, so long as they are specified. It is clear that it is meaningless to ask how risky any strategy is unless the terms of the risk to be assessed are specified first.

The second point is that it is clear that some better method of characterizing risk is needed, so that's the next topic.

5.6.3 Satisfying Gains, Regrettable Losses

Risk is clearly not just an expression of the chance of a loss. In the second example above, finding new customers, there is no chance of a loss. The risk is only that the gain won't be as much as it could have been. And in the first example, the strategy that has the greatest chance for a loss (in-store incentives) would intuitively seem to have that loss outweighed somewhat by the size of the potential gain. Obviously, a single measure of the variance of the potentially expected outcomes isn't enough.

The clue to finding a better measure is in discussing the loss-risk and the gain-risk separately. When seeking new customers, the risk is that the most satisfactory result will not eventuate. Clearly, that is a regrettable situation. When seeking return, the most satisfying option is to get the largest return. The most regrettable outcome would be to get the greatest loss. Yet the strategy that offers one also offers the other. In general, the risk here seems to be either that the strategy selected won't be the most satisfying or that it will entail the greatest cause for regret. Clearly, some measure of the potential for satisfaction and regret for each strategy would be very useful.

By way of developing a better risk measure, Figure 5.12 reworks the previous example. The first change is that this figure shows potential gains and potential losses rather than the expected values of the outcomes. Next, there are several additional columns to the right of the calculations. The first three show the expected gain and expected loss restated as potential satisfaction and potential regret. The mean of these is also shown. This mean, of course, is no more than the expected value of the strategy. The assumption here is that the

	Probability	Yield	Exp. Value	Pot. Satisfy	Pot. Regret	Mean Value	Raw Risk	RAVE	Bmark	Bmark Risk	BRAVE
Web	75%	$2,000	$1,500	1,500	200	1,300	0.76	994	20%	—0.33	—437
	15%	$0	$0								
	10%	—$2,000	—$200								
Mail	15%	$2,000	$300	300	200	100	0.2	20	3%	—0.87	—87
	75%	$0	$0								
	10%	—$2,000	—$200								
In-store	75%	$10,000	$7,500	7,500	300	7,200	0.92	6,646	40%	0.25	1,790
	10%	$0	$0								
	15%	—$2,000	—$300								

Figure 5.12 Determining Risk Adjusted Value Expected (RAVE) and Benchmarked RAVE (BRAVE).

amount of potential satisfaction to be derived is in proportion to the gain possible, and the amount of potential regret is in proportion to the loss possible.

The next two columns are titled "Raw Risk" and "RAVE," which is an acronym for Risk Adjusted Value Expected. *Raw risk* is a number determined such that it varies its value between +1 and −1. When it registers +1, it indicates that the strategy offers pure satisfaction. When raw risk is −1, pure regret is indicated. A number in between the two indicates some intermediate balance between satisfaction and regret. The details of the calculation are very straightforward, but not important to the explanation here, so they are included in the supplemental material to this chapter.

Even for a purely satisfactory strategy (raw risk = +1), the actual amount of satisfaction available depends on the expected value of the strategy. However satisfying the strategy, you can't get more value out of it than there is to be had! Adjusting the expected value for the strategy by multiplying it by the raw risk yields the *risk adjusted value expected (RAVE)* for each strategy. Note that if the target had been "captured new customers," every strategy would offer pure satisfaction, so the value of RAVE would equal the expected value for the strategy.

5.6.4 **Benchmarks**

RAVE offers a good indication of risk, but there is one large assumption built in. The examples shown assume that a strategy that returns exactly what is invested in it carries no risk. That is not true in the real world. If the Wobbly Corporation invested $10,000 to get $10,000, they would regard it as a bad

use of their money. In fact, since they could have used it elsewhere to actually earn something, Wobbly's accountants would regard such an investment
with considerable regret. So a zero return is not actually a no-regret situation.
Further, Wobbly's marketing manager might look at the direct mail promotion and regard any return less than 3% as not worth having. Perhaps that
seems to be the industry average return for this kind of promotion. Similarly,
if using a risk target of new customer acquisition, capturing less than some
expected number, say 100 new customers, might also be regarded with regret and as a waste of the investment required to capture it. Perhaps the industry benchmark for new customer acquisition cost is thought to be $100.
So clearly RAVE does not quite yet meet the need for a risk indicator.

The RAVE number needs to be modified to reflect prior expectations
about performance. These prior expectations are the *benchmarks* against
which any performance is to be compared. The right-hand three columns of
Figure 5.12 show this adjustment. Again, the adjustment calculation is not important in this explanation; details are included in the supplemental material
to this chapter. One column shows the benchmark. In this example, it is
shown as a percentage return; however, benchmarks can be anything convenient—interest rates, level of inflation, industry standard performance,
even wishful thinking, although that is to be discouraged!

Benchmarks modify the raw risk measure to give a benchmark-adjusted
risk. For instance, the strategy "mail" has a raw risk of 0.2. Some, but not
much satisfaction to be had here on balance and indeed, the $10,000 invested
produces an expected return of only $100 (shown in the column Mean
Value). Selecting a benchmark for this strategy of 3% (shown in the column
Benchmark) requires at least a $300 return. This benchmark value indicates
that the problem holder, say the marketing manager, regards anything less
than a 3% return on this strategy as regrettable. Given this benchmark, the
raw risk of 0.2 is modified into a benchmark-adjusted risk of -0.87. This
turns a small level of satisfaction into quite a lot of regret. Of course, the expected value of the strategy is small ($100), so the final measure, the
Benchmark Risk Adjusted Value Expected (BRAVE) is also small, but now
negative at -87. Adopting this strategy would cause regret, not satisfaction
as the RAVE had indicated.

Thus, it is important in setting the frame for risk evaluation to discover
what benchmark performance is expected, and exactly what constitutes the
relevant benchmark for the risk targeted. In the end, how much risk is involved in a strategy depends on how BRAVE it is!

5.6.5 Strategic Risk

At last, after looking at how risk is addressed in a model, the actual components that go into the expectations part of a strategy are clear, as are the rea-

sons why they are needed. Figure 5.13 shows the completely assembled strategy that was begun in Figure 5.10. Figure 5.13 adds the final components to complete the strategy. These components are:

- *Probabilities:* Although the example assumed that the actual probabilities could be known, that is not possible. However, risk assessment requires specifying some way of determining the probabilities associated with each outcome. Obviously, these will not be exact, but the better and more justified the estimates, the better will be the risk assessment.
- *Payoff:* Although the payoff was introduced earlier, only when the probabilities for each outcome are determined can the expected payoff be discovered. Although the explanatory examples discussed here used three discrete outcomes for each strategy, numeric models have no problem handling continuous outcomes and continuous probabilities.
- *Targets:* Each strategy can have one or more risk targets. There is no problem modeling multiple risk targets, and although not mentioned in this brief explanation, assessing overall risk for a multi-target strategy is not difficult. Defining a risk target requires determining how the risk for that target is to be measured.
- *Benchmarks:* Every target requires a benchmark. A usual default is that risk is 0 when return equals investment. In almost all cases, that is not true in the real world. To get back no more than what is invested is almost always a regrettable situation. Without adequate benchmarks, risk modeling is usually of small value. (Return and investment are used generically here and are not restricted to money measures. Investment is whatever is put in to get the return; return is whatever the strategy is measured to produce.)

5.7 Final Alignment

Business models are purpose-built structures. They have their own internal purposes, whether it is to predict fraud or model the world economy. But all

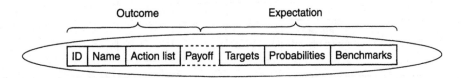

Figure 5.13 Completed strategy spanning outcomes and expectations.

models share external purposes that are part of their frame. Three of the purposes have already been mentioned—to clarify risk, to determine options, and to evaluate outcomes. But that alone is not enough. Every modeler must keep firmly in mind that the three touchstones by which the final results will be judged are novelty, utility, and interest.

Models support decisions in each of three areas. Models help both develop and explore new options. Given the options, they explore the likely outcomes for each so that an informed decision is possible. The risks of each action are then determined—at least as well as they can be known. Finally, options are explored in the situation. Each option is developed as a possible strategy for action for which outcomes and risk are evaluated. But although a modeler has to set a frame around the whole model, and the whole model has to be explored, not all features of the final result will be of equal interest to the problem holder and owner. For simple models, final alignment of the frame may seem obvious. However, using an alignment matrix, such as that shown in Figure 5.14, can help to organize thoughts for more complex models.

Such a matrix can serve as a sort of "sanity check" for the modeler and also serve to help set expectations among those who will be using the model. For each of the column and row junctions, ask how important it is in the overall model. Enter scores in a range, say, of 1—10. When such a matrix is completed with the participation of all involved, normalize it so that the most important box contains a 1 and the least important a 0. Now review the matrix with all parties. Does it make sense? When everyone agrees, it indicates where effort needs to be concentrated, thus providing a frame for the whole project.

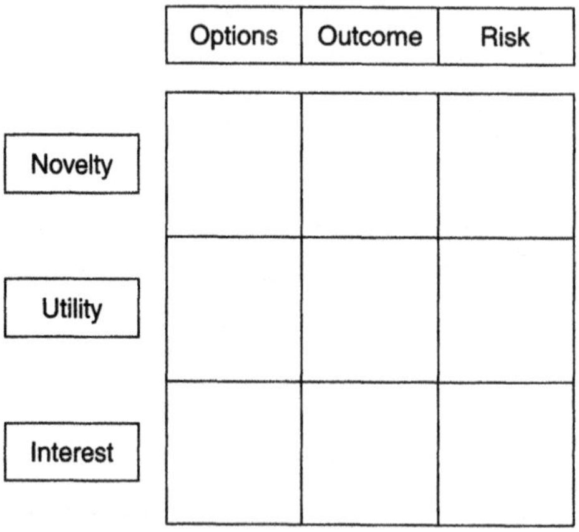

Figure 5.14 Alignment matrix.

These three features of a model—novelty, utility, and interest—are part of the general expectations from modeling. As a modeler be aware of these, and in setting the frame, look for where the novelty is wanted, what is considered useful, and what is interesting. The easiest way to discover this is to ask! Although important, this part is easy—unless it is overlooked.

5.8   Mapping the Problem Frame

This chapter has spent much time looking at one tree in the modeling forest. It is a crucially important tree—that of setting the problem frame—and we have spent a fair amount of time crawling about the branches and even stopping to admire an important leaf or two. It is in truth a crucially important tree, acting as a gatekeeper to exploring the whole forest. However, in such a detailed examination, the overall structure of the tree may have been lost. Now it is time to step back and look again at the whole tree, then to step back still further and look at the place of this tree in the forest.

Mapping a problem using the techniques and tools developed here is quite easy. This chapter has developed a comprehensive map into which any rationally decidable problem can be placed. Fitting the problem into the map is easy, even if getting to understand the map was not. The easiest way to show how to map a problem is to actually map a problem.

Before beginning, note that just because all parts of a map exist, does not mean that they have to be used. If you were to drive from New York to Tampa, a road map of the United States would come in handy. However, on your journey, the part that covers California is not going to get much use. It is there in case you have a sudden change of plan, or need to go there another day. But just because the map covers California does not mean that you have to drive there. So too with the decision mapping techniques developed here. All the parts are in place if needed. That does not mean that they all have to be used. It does, however, allow conscious knowledge of where the decision did not go, which might be just as important as where it did. For instance, just because the map has all the tools necessary to fully frame risk in a model does not mean that the stakeholders necessarily care much about risk, nor that the modeler actually has to model risk. This is a map that only lays out where you can go. There is no compulsion that says you must go! However, as a modeler, you should be aware of the issue and discover the stakeholder's concerns.

Figure 5.15 pulls together the elements for creating the whole map. Here it is easy to see how each piece relates to the whole map. There are two steps in framing the actual mapping process—a prologue and a postlogue—and nine steps in mapping the problem. (The prologue and postlogue are the parts

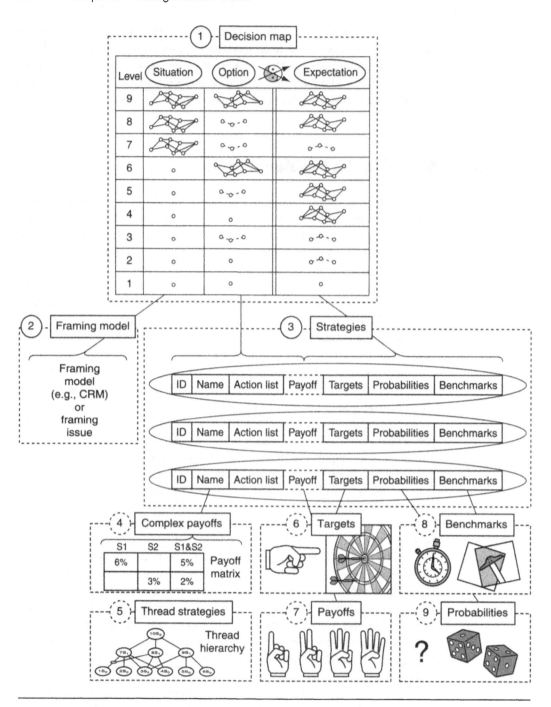

Figure 5.15 Mapping a problem.

referred to in this chapter that come before and after the mapping process proper; they are not shown on the process map.) The items shown numbered 1 through 3 in bold circles are required for every problem; the other six depend on circumstances. For some problems, the steps will be far more complex than others. But the steps remain the same for framing any rationally based decision. Reviewing this map will call to mind all of the issues in each step. The steps are:

> **Prologue:** Find the terms of the problem.
>
> *Step 1:* Locate the decision on the decision map.
>
> *Step 2:* Discover the framing model or issue.
>
> *Step 3:* Build the needed strategies.
>
> *Step 4:* If several interrelated payoffs exist, map the relations.
>
> *Step 5:* If interdependent firing of strategies exist, determine the threads.
>
> *Step 6:* Determine the targets.
>
> *Step 7:* Determine the payoffs.
>
> *Step 8:* If modeling risk, determine the benchmarks.
>
> *Step 9:* If modeling risk, determine the probabilities.
>
> **Postlogue:** Final alignment.

5.8.1 Wobbly Widgets

The Wobbly Corporation has something of a problem with its Widget product line and would clearly like to improve sales if possible. The question, of course, is where it can get the most bang for its buck. Its problems, inasmuch as we know them so far, have been discussed during this chapter. What does an actual map of the problem look like?

Figure 5.16 provides a sort of fill-in-the-blanks map of the problem. The purpose of the map is to make sure that the modeler "has all the bases covered." The top line identifies this as a level 3 problem. The problem is to decide about a single issue (Widget marketing) and has several not strongly connected options. To the right of the options symbol is 0 above 3. The 0 indicates that there are zero linked payoffs. (The company wants to know which of three strategies is the best.) Finally, to the far right, are several simply linked expectations (one for each strategy). Below the strategy symbol to the left is a crossed out payoff matrix. Only one strategy will be fired. Below it is the strategy thread map, not strictly needed because only one strategy will be fired. On the right are the notes outlining the expectations—targets, payoffs, benchmarks, and probabilities for each strategy. Although this is a summary only, there is still a lot of information on the map, and every point has been checked for modeling this problem.

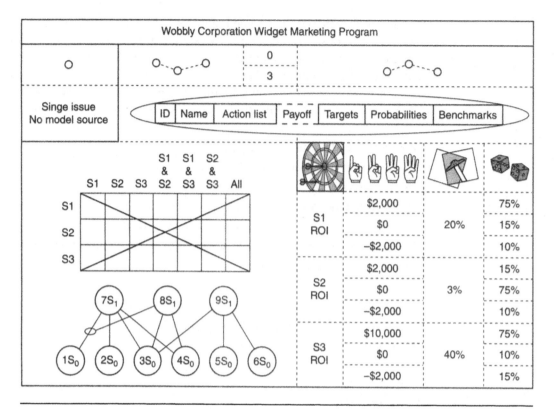

Figure 5.16 Problem Map.

5.8.2 Mapping, Modeling, and Mining

The map developed here has a place for all the elements of rational decision making—but how does a modeler use this map to create models? Where does data mining come into the picture?

Models, as it will turn out later, model business situations, and have their impact by modifying business processes. This chapter provides the information to create a frame around the model so that it will meet the needs of the business, as expressed by the stakeholders. So the content of the chapter contributes to understanding what the model has to provide and also to clarifying many assumptions, hidden or not.

However, data mining is an excellent tool for both discovering and representing relationships. There are many relationships described in this chapter on framing that, so long as data is available to describe them, can be discovered and characterized using data mining techniques. For instance, recall that for strategies, when options are linked, the payoffs are interrelated. Almost always the characterization of the linked interrelationships will not be obvious, but will be discovered in, and can be characterized from, the appropriate data. Indeed, at any of the six levels of the decision map (4 through 9) for which issues are linked in complex ways, if data is available, data mining may the most appropriate way to characterize the relationships.

However, the main application of data mining comes when the problem is framed, and the main question then is to determine exactly what the expected outcomes are for each of the strategies to enable a rational selection among them. Data mining also will be used in assessing the risks continuously rather than using only three levels of outcome as in the example.

In truth, this is only one of several ways of framing a modeling project, and as noted, this is the frame that supports rational decision making. Other ways of framing the model, such as for modifying business processes, appear in later chapters. Nonetheless, using the method developed here works well for models in all business situations.

5.9   Summary

Getting the correct frame around a problem is absolutely essential to creating a useable problem model. And *all* models are built to deal with problems. The key to building a model that addresses the user's need is in discovering what that need really is. That is what framing a problem is about.

This chapter has set out a comprehensive system for discovering and defining all of the necessary elements that go into modeling a rationally made decision. It also has set out guidelines and provided a number of techniques for ensuring that the model will reflect the wishes, interests, and intents of the problem holders and owners. All of the issues and explanations are aimed at keeping the modeler on track, and assisting a modeler in exploring the problem frame with the client.

The remainder of Part II deals with practical techniques for discovering the needed information, and for actually extracting and creating the model defined by the map from that information.

5.10   Explanation of the Decision Map

The decision map includes only 9 entries out of a possible 27. Table 5.2 includes all possible combinations of issues. It is important to remember that the decision map is not intended to represent the true state of the world, but

TABLE 5.2 Decision Map Exception Table

Situation	Option	Expectation	Explanation
Single	Single	Single	Level 1
Single	Single	Multiple	Level 2
Single	Single	Complex	Level 4
Single	Multiple	Single	Reason 2
Single	Multiple	Multiple	Level 3
Single	Multiple	Complex	Level 5
Single	Complex	Single	Reason 2
Single	Complex	Multiple	Reason 2
Single	Complex	Complex	Level 6
Multiple	Single	Single	Reason 1
Multiple	Single	Multiple	Reason 1
Multiple	Single	Complex	Reason 1
Multiple	Multiple	Single	Reason 1
Multiple	Multiple	Multiple	Reason 1
Multiple	Multiple	Complex	Reason 1
Multiple	Complex	Single	Reason 1
Multiple	Complex	Multiple	Reason 1
Multiple	Complex	Complex	Reason 1
Complex	Single	Single	Reason 4
Complex	Single	Multiple	Reason 3
Complex	Single	Complex	Reason 3
Complex	Multiple	Single	Reason 2
Complex	Multiple	Multiple	Level 7
Complex	Multiple	Complex	Level 8
Complex	Complex	Single	Reason 2
Complex	Complex	Multiple	Reason 2
Complex	Complex	Complex	Level 9

Reason 1: Multiple simply interacting issues can be represented separately. Because the interactions between the issues in the situation are not considered important, each issue can safely be considered separately. As Figure 5.5 depicts, when the interactions between the situation issues are unimportant, the option issues, however complex within themselves, are separate for each situation issue. So these individual situation issues can be represented as separate single-issue decisions, and can be individually represented by levels 1 through 6.

Reason 2: Expectations are attached to options and, thus, the way in which the expectations interact can never be less complex than the way the options interact. It is, however, possible for more complex expectation interactions to be important in the decision—see levels 2, 4, and 5.

Reason 3: Where a single option is to be considered, the decision can be represented using the equivalent representation of collapsing the situation to a single issue (i.e., levels 1, 2, or 4).

to represent the parameters of a decision as presented for determination. A very complex world situation might be simplified so that the decision is to be made about only a single issue.

For example, the whole problem: "Should I have lunch now?" is enormously complex. The issues in the situation are staggeringly diverse ranging from the world food situation to complex biochemical issues, not to mention all of the social and cultural implications. If the world situation is to be represented, the options are equally vast ranging in scale and scope, as are the expectations. Yet normally, this is far more usefully represented as a problem requiring level 1 representation.

Regardless of the true complexity of the actual world situation, in using this map, the modeler has to locate the problem as presented, not the problem as it exists in the real world. Without this simplification, all problems are level 9 problems, and are simply intractable. Simplification makes them tractable.

The table uses words to represent the symbols used in the decision map in the chapter. *Single* refers to a single issue, *multiple* to a simply connected set of issues where the interconnections are considered unimportant, and *complex* to multiple issues where the interconnections are to be considered. The columns correspond to the same columns shown in the map, situation, option, and expectation. The additional column *explanation* contains an explanation for the entry. If the entry occurs in the decision map its level is indicated. If it is not included for some reason, a reason number is shown. The reasons corresponding to the reason numbers are given below the table.

5.11   **Risk Calculations**

The risk discussion in the main body of this chapter skipped over the calculations necessary to determine the risk adjusted value expected (RAVE) and benchmarked RAVE (BRAVE) values. The examples shown here extend the discussion in the chapter by showing how to determine the actual RAVE and BRAVE values.

5.11.1   **Raw Risk**

Figure 5.17 shows the Web calculations from Figure 5.12. The raw risk value is determined using the formula shown in the figure:

Risk

Probability	Yield	Exp. value	Pot. satisfy	Pot. regret	Mean value	Raw risk	RAVE	Bmark	Bmark risk	BRAVE
75%	$2,000	$1,500								
15%	$0	$0	1,500	200	1,300	0.76	994	20%	—0.33	—437
10%	—$2,000	—$200								

$$\left[\frac{2 \times \text{Pot. satisfaction}}{\text{Satisfy to regret range}}\right] - 1 \qquad\qquad \left[\frac{2 \times \text{RAVE}}{\text{RAVE + B mark offset}}\right] - 1$$

$$\left[\frac{2 \times 1{,}500}{1{,}500 - (-200)}\right] - 1 \qquad\qquad \left[\frac{2 \times 994}{994 + 2{,}000}\right] - 1$$

$$\frac{3{,}000}{1{,}700} - 1 = 0.76 \qquad\qquad \frac{1{,}988}{2{,}994} - 1 = -0.33$$

Figure 5.17   Determining adjusted risk values.

$$((2 \times \text{Potential\_Satisfaction}) / \text{Satisfy to Regret Range}) - 1$$

As the figure illustrates, this turns into an estimate of 0.76 in this case. The calculations are simple, but the implication of this figure is that there is 76% more potential for satisfaction than there is for regret so long as breaking even is the goal.

5.11.2 Biasing the Expectation: BRAVE

The difficulty is, as explained in the main body of the chapter, expectation that the investment will be returned intact, but without gain, is not considered to be a beneficial risk. After all, the money could have been held in cash, and without any risk at all the same dollar value comes out at the end as went in at the beginning. Some return—that is, some increase—is required for the investment to be worthwhile. Chapter 6, Section 6.4.3 discusses the present value of a future potential gain, but the essence of the discussion is that having the same number of dollars (or whatever currency works for the reader) tomorrow as are in hand today is a *loss* of value. So, to stay in the same place as far as investment goes requires at least that the number of dollars (or whatever) increases by some amount. The amount of increase required to at least break even is called here the *benchmark amount*. This is the ratio that BRAVE represents. Given the base rate expectation for a risk-free (or at least relatively so) return, how does the expected return from this investment compare?

The calculation is simple, the implication is not, but it is at least fully justifiable.

Both of these calculations are "normalized" between values of ±1 by dividing twice the actual value by the range (offset by the minimum value), which results in a value between 0 and 2, and subtracting 1 from the result. Thus, the final normalized and scaled value has to be in the range of −1 to +1 (or total regret to total satisfaction).

Chapter 6
Getting the Right Model

This is a chapter full of art rather than science, for discovering the right model is without doubt an art. It is art at least in part because there is no one "right way" to discover the right model—although there is always a right model to be discovered. Only one rule exists for discovery: practice. All else consists of rules of thumb and helpful hints.

Nonetheless, despite the lack of some formal procedure for model discovery, there is still a necessary progression of activities. At first the modeler personally and interactively explores the territory to be modeled. Sometimes this may be quite cursory, as when a business manager requests a tactical model based on a preconceived notion of the problem that needs to be solved (e.g., "Build a customer segmentation model for me!"). Sometimes exploring the territory to be modeled may turn out to be the most significant and time- and skill-consuming part of the whole discovery effort, as when the modeler assists a senior management team facing a serious strategic challenge under novel circumstances. Regardless of the level of difficulty of the model discovery challenge, some common threads that the modeler needs to know apply to all discovery situations, and it is with these that the chapter starts.

Next, when the modeler has some idea of the business situation, it is important to map it as an objective statement. To be sure, mapping may turn out to be part of the discovery process, but for the sake of illustration, it is tackled in this chapter as a relatively separate issue. The separation is artificial at least inasmuch as discovery is really a participatory process with the modeler and, to a greater or lesser extent, all of the stakeholders. It is very important that the modeler's map of the proposed model space be both available and intuitively accessible to everyone who is interested. Creating the map dynamically with members of the management team, incorporating their feedback and insights, may well be a crucial element in the discovery process.

A third stage of discovery, one that is not always needed but sometimes turns out to be crucial, is the creation of a simulation of the map that allows a dynamic and interactive exploration of the map's limitations, sensitivities, and implications. Such a simulation model allows a lot of assumptions to be checked, and a lot of false starts to be avoided, before the final model is built.

These three stages are the steps that any modeler has to take during model discovery. However, this is art, not science. There are many routes that lead to the same destination, and so long as the route taken fills the need for the modeler, and is easily accessible, comprehensible, and useable by everyone involved, then that route can be counted a successful one. If you are an experienced modeler, and are familiar with software tools and techniques for model discovery, this chapter is not intended to persuade you to take some alternative route. However, if you are not familiar with the discovery process and are not aware of suitable tools and techniques for all stages, this chapter lays out a path and describes tools and techniques that the author has found useful and helpful.

For ease of explanation and illustration, and so as not to be unnecessarily repetitive, the chapter proceeds from stage to stage along one set course as if this were the only path to follow. Such description saves having to hedge at every technique introduced or tool used, with caveats and notations that each is optional or something the reader might want to consider. The purpose is to provide a path for the novice to follow, not to attempt to stipulate that this is the path for all to follow. Despite this plan, and although the suggested path here provides a valid approach, sometimes additional tools or techniques are useful. It's impossible to be universally comprehensive, and there are other tools and techniques not referred to in this book. The tools and techniques suggested in the main course of the chapter won't necessarily be intuitive or easy to use for all readers. Use whatever tools and techniques that are most comfortable and familiar to you and that have worked for you. Those described here should be regarded only as suggestions. But while the tools suggested are optional, this is a path that you will have to take in discovering the right model for your situation.

6.1 Interactive Exploration of the Territory

Approaching a complex situation is never easy, and most business situations are nothing if not complex. The first task faced by any modeler is to understand enough about the business situation to be able to ask intelligent questions. To a great extent, that is what setting the problem frame (Chapter 5) is all about. Framing a problem, and understanding the framework within which any solution has to be discovered, is the activity that is designed to ensure that all of the important issues are addressed, that assumptions about the situation are at least revealed, and that issues to be excluded are at least knowingly excluded for a reason.

That having been said, it still leaves the modeler short of the practical means for actually creating the framework. In other words, it's fine in theory to describe what goes into the framework, but who to talk to and what to say is the practical problem.

Actually, the situation isn't fearsomely difficult. All humans are equipped for social interaction—it's part of our built-in capabilities. Interactively exploring the area that needs to be modeled requires no more than the skills of basic communication, somewhat sharpened and focused toward the needs of the modeler. But before this crucial interaction can begin, it is just as important to identify the players—the stakeholders—and their needs and motivations.

6.1.1   Stakeholders

(See MII.AB.8, MII.TB.1) One big question the modeler needs to answer is who to talk to. The general answer is: everyone who needs to be involved. More specifically, there are five groups of people, or *stakeholders,* who need to be involved in any modeling project:

1. Need stakeholders
2. Money stakeholders
3. Decision stakeholders
4. Beneficiary stakeholders
5. Kudos stakeholders

Often, some people fall into more than one group, and the number of stakeholders in each group varies widely. However, for any modeling project, the people who form these stakeholder groups are the people who have to support the project.

6.1.1.1   Need Stakeholders

The need stakeholders are those who actually experience the business problem on a day-to-day basis. Very often, they have developed intuitive or reasoned ideas about what causes the problem, what the solution is, and how it should be applied. This can be very difficult for the modeler. Need stakeholders are very often too close to the problem to see it in a wider perspective. They are quite likely to express the requirements not in terms of the problem, but instead in terms of the desired solution.

However, their perspective is very important. Needs that are driven from a tactical level have to be treated warily. If a manager is compensated by the number of calls per hour his team makes, for example, the model required by this stakeholder has to increase the number of calls per hour, even if each call has a negative impact elsewhere. In one situation, this was almost exactly the case. Investigation of the problem and solution spaces revealed that each phone call that achieved its apparent purpose did, in fact, cost the company money. The management team acknowledged this problem as a true description of the situation. Yet, none of the management team knew how to change the situation—specifically, how to change management's measured objectives—and the need stakeholder still remained motivated by the incentive program to increase the closure rate per phone call. Ultimately, the deployed model helped to increase the number of calls per hour—so that the need stakeholding manager was satisfied, and so were the telemarketing team members who were compensated based on closure rate.

Whether this solution made sense from a management perspective is hard to determine. The company in which this solution was deployed is a complex system, and without modeling all of the relevant interactions, it is impossible to fully assess the total effect of increasing the closure rate per call on the company. Clearly the management team, although they weren't able to (or at least didn't) articulate their reasoning, felt that improving the closure rate was, overall, beneficial to the corporation.

Tactical-level need stakeholders are often resistant to change. Generally, what they really want is a faster or more efficient way to do more of the same. Changing or replacing a system takes time, effort, and resources that almost certainly will detract from meeting existing short-term goals—and the perceived need may well be to improve performance against those selfsame short-term goals.

This is not intended as a negative view of tactical-level need stakeholders. They are frequently highly capable and dedicated managers who are well aware of the larger implications of the perceived need, and who will often be the first in line to champion a larger scale approach to a problem than their own need demands. However, a modeler is well advised to take a somewhat skeptical approach to the need, at least as initially expressed, since there may be a larger problem to explore. Furthermore, the need may be expressed as an expected solution, not as a description of the problem. Whether it is the larger or the more restricted version of the problem that is modeled in the end, the exploration should at least acknowledge that a larger area to explore may well exist than that expressed by the needs stakeholder.

6.1.1.2 Money Stakeholders

These stakeholders hold the purse strings—they will commit the resources that allow the project to move forward. The business case document written to support modeling (see Section 6.4) is largely addressed to the money stakeholders, and it has to be expressed in terms that appeal to them. Although the money stakeholder could equally well be titled the "resource stakeholder," the fact is that money talks, and these stakeholders listen to that language, thus their title.

However, these stakeholders are interested in more than just the cost of the project and the anticipated benefits. Recall that every problem is only an expression that change is needed, and thus any model is only a catalyst to that change. Almost certainly, capturing the data and constructing the model is the smallest part of the money stakeholder's purview. Any change requires modifying the behavior of an organization, and that takes time and resources, too. Even investigative modeling is likely to be recommended only if the whole project is potentially valuable. The money stakeholder, as a money stakeholder, is only a "gatekeeper" for the project. It is usually not possible for this stakeholder to say yes to a project—that is the purview of the decision stakeholder—but they can easily say no if the numbers aren't convincing.

6.1.1.3 Decision Stakeholders

Decision stakeholders make the decision of whether to execute the project. This is another person or group that the modeling business case has to address directly. But the identity of the decision maker isn't always obvious. It is invariably one person who ultimately makes a decision, but often that person is not directly involved with the modeler, relying instead on input from the people who have spoken with the modeler. Sometimes the modeler interacts with a team and with the team members individually. This again makes it difficult to identify the decision stakeholder. Teams and committees don't make decisions. At best, they reach a consensus as to the recommendation they are going to make. This may make it very difficult to understand the decision stakeholder's needs.

The clearest way to identify the decision stakeholder is to determine whose budget is going to be tapped to pay for the modeling and mining. However, even this isn't infallible. The author is engaged on several projects where several different managers all contribute a little from their budgets to a common "pot," and all benefit from the modeling and mining that results.

However, whether there are one or many decision stakeholders, it is important to understand their needs, motivations, and expectations.

6.1.1.4 Beneficiary Stakeholders

This is a crucially important group to include at all stages of the modeling project. These are the people in the corporation who will get the "benefit" of the results of modeling—the folk who will be directly affected.

All companies are social organizations and are also complex systems. The organization and its social structures have to change whenever an organization changes its behavior. It is crucial to the success of any project that it receives both management support and grass roots support. The beneficiaries in this description are the grass roots whose support is so crucial.

Beneficiary stakeholders, all by themselves, have the ability to promote the success or bring about the failure of many, if not most, modeling projects. As an example, one company implemented a project using two separate groups totally distinct from each other. In one group, the team of beneficiary stakeholders was compensated for individual performance. This promoted a sense among them that the better they performed against their neighbors, the better off they were. There was no sense of group cooperation. Although this group was involved as much as possible in all of the promotional material and events designed to engender support for the project, none of it altered their sense that they were involved as individuals competing with each other.

In contrast, the second group, following the project's recommendations, reformed into teams. Each team member was compensated for team performance. Even without the model implemented, the teams in this group already had the more experienced members coaching the less experienced members and organizing the work internally to increase team performance.

The modeling project provided both groups with greater insight, and produced options that were designed to be most valuable to the company, and at the same time tailored to best meet customers' needs. However, the modeled system required multiple steps for completion. The original, premodeling process had been designed with the assumption that an individual would complete a transaction in one step. Thus, in the first group, individual performance was judged on whether one person completed the entire transaction. The first group, which had resisted forming teams, performed at 80% of their previous level after six months, and the project was abandoned. In fact, the group manager expressed the opinion that, "This data mining isn't all it's cracked up to be. Experience is what counts, that's all."

The second group's experience was totally different. After one month, the second group was already performing at 120% of its previous level, and after six months at over 200%. They also suggested further changes and improvements in the work process, and requested additional modeling.

The point is that success is in implementation, not just in modeling. Without the support, involvement, and input of the beneficiary stakeholders, implementation won't happen.

6.1.1.5 Kudos Stakeholders

These stakeholders are often the people who have "sold" the project internally. Credit for a success will accrue to them—but more importantly, so will the negative impact of a less than successful project.

It's very important to understand from the kudos stakeholder what it is that constitutes success, and how the ultimate result of the project will be judged. Understanding the judgment criteria usually will not affect the modeling very much, and the mining hardly at all, but it is crucial for correctly setting the frame for the problem (see Chapter 5).

Very often, these stakeholders will impact the success of the project as they are the senior management sponsors who will "go to bat" for the project when the chips are down. Such champions inevitably, and by their very commitment to support the project, will get the blame if the project goes awry (although it is part of life that any actual kudos for the project may be taken elsewhere, probably further up the management chain). Nonetheless, these stakeholders do feel a personal sense of involvement with, and responsibility for, the success of the project, even if they are not otherwise directly involved.

6.1.2 Talking and Listening

(See MII:DB.2, MII:TB.2) Once the stakeholders are identified, meeting with them to determine their needs is the next step. It's really important to speak with the problem stakeholders with a specific intent and purpose. That is to say, for every meeting, discussion, or conversation, either with individuals or groups, it's important to be able to answer the questions, "What do I want to get out of this session?" and "What's my bottom line here?" The idea isn't to focus self-centeredly on this topic to the exclusion of listening. On the contrary, the point is to have a touchstone during a session against which to gauge progress, and to avoid having the session wander aimlessly. It's a part of the old truism that time is valuable—both the modeler's and that of whoever else is in the session.

Sessions may be formal or informal, and the modeler or someone else can set the agenda. However, the modeler should always have a focused objective, undeclared or not. If the modeler has arranged the session, it's always a good idea to schedule a fixed time for all participants. It makes it much easier to coordinate calendars! With that in place, it is now the modeler's job to play the detective.

6.1.2.1 Initial Questions

In any situation, start by getting the situation discussed openly and by having all of the participants talk about the issues in broad terms. Doing this means asking broad questions such as, "What are the general objectives for the project?" or "What do you see as the major problems in this situation?" In these initial questions, it is important not to make assumptions. The modeler may well approach any of the business problems from a totally different perspective than the problem holders and owners, and any assumptions that the modeler makes about the "obvious" objectives or major problems may well not be of particular concern to business managers who understand how to address those "obvious" issues. Thus, the modeler must keep an open mind, assume as little as possible, and draw out the other participants about the issues that they see as important.

During this initial session—and, indeed, throughout the entire interview process—it's important to be a mirror: "What I'm hearing you say is, . . .". Reflect back whatever points or understanding are appropriate. When mirroring, even if the modeler has reflected back an identical wording or statement, the reaction to it is often something like, "Well, that's not quite what I meant, it's more like . . .". At this stage it's crucial to simply accept whatever is offered, and to offer no commentary. The whole point is to try to explore the situation in as broad terms as possible. If there is discrepancy, confusion, or outright conflict in the way the situation is explained or viewed by the participants, that's fine at this stage. It's just important to get as broad a view as possible of the territory and issues involved.

Also, note where the team draws its boundaries. "Well, I'm not so sure that that's important here," or "That doesn't seem relevant at the moment," are both indications of boundaries and assumptions that may need to be explicated later, and possibly explored. But whatever and wherever they are, they need to be noted since they will form an important part of the way the problem or issue is framed. If in doubt, the old standby "Who, What, When, Where, Why, and How" is a good place to start exploring.

6.1.2.2 Getting a Helping Hand

Clearly, as a modeler, unless you happen to be a subject matter expert about the situation at hand, and very often even then, you need help in understanding the ramifications of the situation. That's good, and the best way to get the needed help is to ask for it. Some requests can be quite direct, such as "Can you help me understand this please?" But one particularly useful question that bears repeating from time to time (albeit in slightly altered form) is "What should I be asking you now?" Or, "If you were in my position, what would you be asking about at this point?"

Asking participants to change their perspective and look from the outside of the situation inward is often useful. During exploration it's very helpful, especially when a knotty issue arises, to pass the ball back and wait for suggestions about resolving or solving it. Very often this technique stimulates a lot of insight and thought about the issues. The point during all early discussions is not to try to solve problems, but to explore issues, and this leads to the need to ask open-ended questions.

Essentially, open-ended questions are questions that cannot logically be answered with a "yes" or "no" answer. "Do you want to address how to resolve the labor issue?" is a closed question. If the answer is "no," it at best indicates a limit to the area of the discussion, but leaves no clue as to underlying assumptions or issues. A better approach would be the open-ended question, "What direction should we take about resolving the labor issue?" Whatever the actual response, it is far more likely that this question will deliver usable and useful information; even if it is about the same limits to the area of discussion as the previously closed question, the answer will still most likely carry more information about assumptions as to why this is not an issue to consider. The object, of course, is to get the assumptions out in the open where they can be examined.

6.1.2.3   Answers and Opinions

The modeler's role may be blurred at first, even ambiguous. After all, the modeler is there to help the team (and although the term *team* is used, it could consist of just one person). Thus, willy-nilly, the modeler is in the role of "problem solver" or "expert." Now the modeler is part of the team as an expert—but the expertise is in modeling, not necessarily in the subject matter at hand. To a great degree, the modeler must act as a facilitator, because the modeler's role is to help the team come to a conclusion or a resolution, or to find a solution as appropriate, through modeling—not through any essential insight or experience into the problem domain that the modeler brings to the table. The modeler—as a modeler—should reserve opinions about the situation, even insight or expertise that seems useful and relevant, until a clear change of roles from modeler to some other role is possible.

For example, the author usually uses a laptop computer and notepad during exploratory sessions. In order to signal a change of roles, it is important to give both visual and verbal clues that roles are changing. For one thing, it is very difficult to effectively listen to the needs and issues of the team while at the same time focusing internally on offering cogent and apposite opinions—and as a modeler, listening is paramount. Thus, moving the computer away, putting your pen or pencil down, changing position, and verbally indicating the changed role (Well, since you ask my opinion of . . .") give important clues to the changed role from modeler to expert. However, as a modeler, you are there only to interact, listen, and facilitate the exploration process.

6.1.2.4   Purposes

One of the modeler's crucial objectives is to understand the true, underlying, or real purpose for the whole project. The "build a customer segmentation model" statement mentioned at the beginning of this chapter does not really describe the purpose of the project. Of course, the immediate purpose is to build a segmentation model, but what is the intermediate purpose of the project? The intermediate purpose might be a customer segmentation for sales (who to sell which product to), marketing (who to ask which features are important), accounts receivable (who will and who won't pay), or something else. On the other hand, ultimate purposes, such as "to yield the maximum contribution to corporate value for the minimum resource investment," are usually too large a goal to immediately affect modeling.

It's not always easy to discover the intermediate purpose. The problem stakeholders may find it difficult to articulate an answer that is useful to a modeler when directly asked about the purpose of a project. But the stakeholders will always have an expectation of what success looks like, and will almost always be able to articulate that clearly enough. Useful questions in this area elicit this expectation of success, and a straightforward, "What will the outcome be when this project is successful?" often works to discover the important purposes. However, more detailed questions in the same vein help, too. Questions such as "What will you be doing differently when the project is successful?" or "What will you know on the completion of a successful project that you don't know now?" are very useful in discovering the important purposes of the project. Building concrete objectives for the project is much easier with answers to such questions.

Another technique useful for understanding the purposes of the model, and its place in the overall corporate strategy, is to create a goal map. This helps to focus the discussion and align the goals and objectives that the model needs to address. Creating such a map is covered later in this chapter in Section 6.4.2 on creating the business case, and a map is illustrated in Figure 6.15, so it is not further mentioned here.

6.1.2.5 What If You Get What You Asked For?

Unfortunately, the results of modeling are often never deployed. Sometimes there are indeed good and valid reasons for such nondeployment. It's always possible that the business objectives were reached sometime during the modeling effort, or perhaps the objectives changed before deployment could begin. Sometimes the reasons are unfortunate for all concerned, and it turns out that no plan for deployment was ever made, having been postponed until the model was complete—and ending up indefinitely postponed. But sometimes projects fail for lack of complete exploration early in the process. Perhaps no one seriously considered what they would do if they actually got what they requested.

Imagine a project that calls for ranking a data set of prospective customers, so that the most likely to respond person has the highest score, and the least likely to respond has the lowest score. When asked about success, stakeholders may envision simply contacting the most likely candidates, thus increasing the conversion rate, and bringing in more customers at a lower cost of acquisition. What could be the metaphorical fly in this ointment?

Well, perhaps the pool of prospects is small enough, and the cost of contact is low enough that all of the prospective customers are going to be contacted in any case. What, then, does the score affect? In this case, not much overall—so what is the purpose in implementing such a program? Or, suppose that the program is to be implemented through telemarketing. There are plenty of prospects available, and it seems like a really great idea to increase the conversion rate. But . . . ! Very often, telemarketers are compensated on the number of calls per hour converted to orders. Programs are budgeted at particular costs, and providing a model that doubles or triples the conversion rate enormously impacts the cost of the program. If bonuses are paid for high conversion rates, deploying the model might indeed raise the conversion rate, but instead of lowering the cost of acquisition, it might actually raise it because of the additional bonuses that then have to be paid. And both of these scenarios have happened in practice . . . more than once.

The point is to consider the overall effect the project may have. In other words, what if you do get what you asked for? Will it make a difference? If so, where and to whom will it make the difference and what else will be affected?

6.1.2.6 Expectations

Expectation management is a two-way street. In a way, much of Part II is about managing expectations. Discovering appropriate frames of reference for the problem, creating a map of the problem, discovering assumptions, determining the role of risk, and so on, are all techniques designed to, in part, align modeler and client/stakeholder expectations. It's equally important to be clear about the timeframe needed for the project, and particularly about the quality, performance, and effective life of any model, as well as the effort needed to deploy and maintain the deployed model.

Expectations, as the previous section points out, have to be discovered, if only so that the appropriate goals can be set. But as mentioned before, expectation is a two-way street. What are *your* expectations for the project? What resources do you expect to have? What resources do you expect to need? How do you expect to access the data? What tools do you expect to be made available? What tools do you expect to need? Which parts of the project do you expect to do yourself? What parts of the project do you expect to assign to others? What skills do you expect to need? How long do you expect the project to take? What form will the deliverables take? And so on.

Expectations are closely allied to assumptions, and the unarticulated, unstated expectations are so close to hidden assumptions that they will serve as indistinguishable "potholes" along the road to success. Use these same framing techniques for yourself as a modeler—what do you expect success of the project to look like for you personally? And if you achieve it, what then?

6.1.2.7 What? So What? Now What?

Three key questions encapsulate most of what is in this section:

- *What?:* What is the situation, what's wanted, what's going on, what's expected? The question at this stage reminds a modeler to focus on understanding the basic issues, the context, and the situation.
- *So What?:* For each of the "whats," why do they matter? What impact does each have on the business situation, on the modeling requirements, on the modeling project, and on the modeler? This stage reminds the modeler to focus on understanding the relationship between the basic "what" issues and solving the business problem, creating the model, and deploying the solution.
- *Now What?:* What actually needs to be done next as a result of each of the "so whats"? This stage reminds the modeler to concentrate on the practical needs of getting the necessary data and creating a model in the form needed that serves the needs of all stakeholders, that addresses the business problem, and that can be deployed.

These three questions, and what they imply, provide goals for each stage of the interview and discovery process. Although important, getting answers to these questions does not complete the exploratory process. Modeling the business situation is a key technique to gaining a more thorough understanding of the project.

6.2 Modeling the Business Situation Using Metaphors

(See MII:AB.13, MII:TB.8) Models do not reflect reality, only perceptions of reality. This is an important concept because it means that models are symbolic representations of perceptions of events as filtered through a (or several) human mind(s). Not only is what is "really" happening impossible to grasp, but it also isn't of any value to attempt to describe it—at least, not to a modeler.

Models are designed to strip away the complexity that is inherent in the real world and to represent some important features that humans can appreciate, react to, and use to influence the course of events. What is important in any situation has to depend entirely on the aims of the people involved, as well as the context and situation in which they find themselves. All this has been covered earlier, and need not be explained again here. However, a business modeler has to create models to address the purposes and expectations of the stakeholders in terms familiar to them. Frequently, people who do in fact agree on the broad outlines of "the way things work" not only do not agree in detail, but also describe their appreciation of what is going on in different terms from each other.

All descriptions are metaphors, likening one set of experiences to another, more familiar, set in another domain. The roots of all our metaphors convert experiences into analogous (to some degree) depictions that reflect our immediate physical sense impressions of the world that arise by virtue of the fact that our minds inhabit human bodies. Do you grasp what I am saying? No, of course not—at least, not physically. It's a metaphor that analogizes our ability to hold physical objects in our grasp to our metaphorical mental ability to "grasp" (a physical action) "ideas" (a totally nonphysical and ephemeral structure). The use of such metaphors extends our understanding of the world in practical ways that allow us to use that understanding to influence outcomes. It isn't regarded as nonsense, for instance, to extend the metaphor and talk about the shape of an idea, its texture, its size, and so on.

Business modeling requires the use of several metaphorical structures; however, not all are equally appropriate in all circumstances. Some metaphors deliver insights that are absent from other metaphors. The large-scale metaphor "business is like war" implies "running a company is like running a military campaign." However, totally different metaphors such as "business is like dancing" or "a company is like a tree" imply a totally different set of implications. In fact, business is like business, not like war, dancing, or trees, yet the metaphors enable insights and approaches that may contribute value.

Modeling business situations requires the use of metaphors that illuminate business processes; for example, *objects* are used as the fundamental metaphor to analogize some features of the business. The implication is that such objects have a fixed set of attributes associated with them, that the values of those attributes may vary, and that the variance in attribute value is in some way, and to a greater or lesser degree, associated with the variance in features of other objects. Essentially, the modeler needs to meet two objectives here: 1) identify the objects, and 2) identify the important relationships.

Several different metaphorical structures for explicating models are suggested in this chapter. Not only is there no "right" way to construct a model, there equally is no "right" metaphor. The following suggestions often have usefully turned out to represent important features in ways that led to effective interventions. These are useful, not comprehensive, and they can help structure thinking about model creation. However, different metaphors lead to different insights, and wholly novel metaphors let us see facets of the world, and connections, that were hitherto not even considered.

One very useful technique in finding alternative, novel, or unfamiliar metaphors to use that the author suggests in seminars and workshops is to find a magazine in a field that you have never heard or thought about, and at first blush seems totally irrelevant to your field. Buy a copy. Read through the magazine. However, don't just read it—read it with the assumption that it contains at least one, and maybe many, useful approaches to problems, issues, and situations that are directly relevant to you. Your job is to find them. Imagine that you are required to explain what the concept discovered is, and that you have to explain exactly why this idea is applicable and relevant. This is wonderful thinking practice, and can vastly extend your flexibility in discovering new analogies and seeing new aspects of situations. (The author has never come across a nonfiction magazine, however obscure, that when used in this way didn't reveal at least one insight. The problems that we all face seem to be common. Only our expression of them, and our way of dealing with them, varies.)

The objective of this section is to sketch a variety of metaphors for modeling business processes in just enough detail to let the reader determine whether the metaphor is appealing. Choose one that feels right, or choose some other metaphorical representation if that feels more comfortable. But always remember that there is no "right" way to represent the world, and that what feels comfortable and intuitive to you may not feel so to other people with whom you have to work and communicate. Whatever representation for the model you choose to use, it has to feel intuitive and comfortable to the stakeholders too, not just to the modeler. As a modeler, you are going to be using your metaphorical representation for yourself, in one-on-one discussions with stakeholders, and in open discussions with groups of stakeholders, so they have to be comfortable, familiar, meaningful, and intuitive to the entire stakeholder group. Thus it is important to work with all stakeholders to make sure from their input that the metaphor works for all. The only constraints on these metaphors for modeling are that they need to lead to discovery of relationships requiring characterization, and point to what data is needed to actually characterize the relationship.

6.2.1 The Systems Metaphor

It is persuasive to regard the world as consisting of many systems (see Part I of this book). The enormous depth of the systems metaphor can only be skimmed over here, but this should be enough not only to give a flavor of what systems entail, but also to explain how to apply the elements of systems thinking in the construction of models.

One key idea that lies at the core of systems is *feedback,* which is no more than interaction between processes. Essentially, the effect on an object reaches back to modify its cause to some greater or lesser extent. Thus, it might be supposed that raising the price of a product ultimately leads to lowering it. Perhaps raising the price reduces the number of customers purchasing the product, which produces a tendency to lower the price so as to increase the number of customers. This is negative feedback, in the sense that the effect tends to produce results that negate the change. Positive feedback might occur if the price increase produced increased profit, and the desire for even further profit promoted another price increase. Negative feedback tends to stabilize systems, whereas positive feedback tends to destabilize them. After all, price and profit cannot be indefinitely increased. Figure 6.1 shows these two possible relationships in a simple systems diagram. The central "+" shows a reinforcing loop, the central "−" a negating loop. The smaller "+" by the rectangles "profit" and "price" indicate that higher price means more profit, and more profit means higher price. Similarly, the smaller negative signs indicate that higher price leads to fewer customers, and less customers leads to higher price. (Remember, the "−" sign means that the cause and effect move in opposite directions.)

Another key idea is that everything interacts with everything else to some degree. It is necessary to simplify the infinite degree of interactivity when making an actual system representation, but all of the interactions between system components have to be considered, even if, in the end, they are not all represented. All system components may potentially interact with each other with either positive or negative feedback.

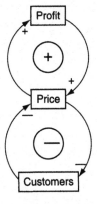

Figure 6.1   Simple systems diagram.

6.2.1.1 Balance, Cause, and Effect

Most systems do not fly apart or collapse. There are, of course, many systems in which those things happen, but by virtue of the fact that they do, they don't form sustainable systems. They may be systems, albeit unstable and temporary ones, but the systems that mainly interest the business modeler are stable systems. By their very nature, these have feedback loops that tend to perpetuate the system. For instance, as Figure 6.2 shows, more orders increase backlog, but increased backlog reduces the orders. Similarly, increasing backlog increases production, but increased production reduces backlog. Otherwise undisturbed, and depending on the exact nature of the relationship among the components, this simple system will reach a balance at some point.

However, what affects which components in a system is not always clear. The simple systems described so far have been described logically—but all systems transcend logic. For instance, it is a logical statement that more backlog leads to more production. (It may be wrong—that is, not a factual description of the world—but determining that the relationship is faithful to observation is an issue separate from logic.) It is also a logical statement that more production leads to less backlog. But these statements cannot be logically combined, that is,

> Statement A: The higher the level of backlog, the higher the level of production.
>
> Statement B: The higher the level of production, the lower the level of backlog.
>
> Therefore: The higher the level of backlog, the lower the level of backlog!

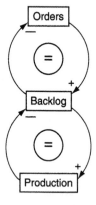

Figure 6.2 System feedback loops.

Logic doesn't recognize time, and time is a crucial element in all systems. So the relationship between components in a system has to include what might be called a *propagation delay*—how long relative to other changes does it take for the effects to propagate through their related connections. And accounting for the effects of time can have surprising consequences.

Suppose you work in a warehouse and take a coffee break at random times during the day. During a coffee break, you wander out onto the loading dock and watch the next delivery truck arrive, deliver goods, and leave the dock. It turns out, after several months of watching, that 75% of the trucks you see are from Zoomalong Logistical Services and 25% are from Acme Trucking and Storage. One day, you are in a management meeting and the discussion turns to delivery services. Commenting that the company seems to have quite a reliance on Zoomalong, you are then surprised to discover that this isn't the case. In fact, the company receives exactly 50% of its deliveries from each of the two companies. Given that your coffee break observations are accurate, how can these two apparent facts be reconciled? The clue is in the effect of time.

Relationships and reaction time are the two crucial elements in systems. Unfortunately, the traditional ideas of cause and effect simply don't serve to describe relationships in any system. Which parts of the system cause what effects? The answers in the simple, two-part systems sketched so far have to be that either element causes the other, or both cause each other. Both seem to be causes as well as effects. The problem is not just that, in system terms, causal explanations do not make sense, it is really that they aren't helpful in explaining what's happening. A causal explanation requires stopping time and breaking apart the relationship loop. The rules of cause and effect inside systems change from their everyday form, as illustrated in Table 6.1.

TABLE 6.1 Comparison of Traditional and System Causal Interactions

Traditional	Systems
Cause and effect are separate with the cause preceding the effect.	Cause and effect are inseparably intertwined with each other and they are linked, not precedent and antecedent to each other.
Effects follow their causes directly in time and nearby in space.	Effects may follow their causes at any time and in places remote from their origination.
Effects are proportional to their causes.	Effects may be out of all proportion to the apparent cause.
Causes that occur more than once produce similar effects for each occurrence.	The effect of any cause is not constant and depends on the state of the system.

But what was the cause of the odd observations of the prevalence of Zoomalong trucks at the loading dock? In fact, time is the key component of the explanation. The delivery trucks only arrived when scheduled. The Zoomalong trucks arrived every hour at a quarter to the hour; Acme trucks arrived every hour on the hour. Thus, for 45 minutes every hour, the next truck due was a Zoomalong truck. For 15 minutes every hour, the next truck due to arrive was an Acme truck. That means for 45 of every 60 minutes, or 75% of the time, Zoomalong would be the next truck seen. If you appeared on the loading dock at random times and waited until you saw the next truck, 75% of the time it would be Zoomalong. Yet, the proportion of Acme and Zoomalong trucks arriving every hour is indeed 50/50. It is very easy to take a random sample of measurements that reveal only a part of a system's performance and erroneously generalize it into a representation of how the whole system performs.

Notice that the crucial point in characterizing system behavior is the relationships among components. Because these relationships are important, it is equally vital to characterize them with the greatest possible fidelity. Where the system describes important business behaviors, and data is available, data mining is an excellent tool for characterizing these relationships. When data isn't available for important relationships, the system description points out what data should be collected, and exactly how important the relationship is in understanding actual system behavior.

Another important feature of systems, alluded to earlier in this discussion, is that systems unaffected by outside disturbances tend, by virtue of their relationships, to settle into stable states. These stable states can be regarded as "attracting" the system to settle in those states, and such states are therefore known as *attractors*. Systems can have more than one attractor—in fact, they can have a very large number of them. After systems get into an attractor, they tend to stay in that state and to resist outside changes. However, it's quite possible that once enough change is applied to the system, it will suddenly change to another attractor.

Figure 6.3 illustrates how corporations learn from their behaviors in the world. The explanation of this two-loop system can begin with the box indicating the "difference between where the company is and where it wants to be." The company recognizes these differences as problems, which lead to "decisions" to make changes. The decisions, when executed, lead to "actions in the world," which in turn lead to "experience and results of actions" in the world, which changes the circumstances of the company—and off around the loop again. However, learning is embedded in the company in the form of business practices that, after a delay (shown by the clock) change "established business processes" that also effect what "decisions" a company can and will take. (This corporate learning system is reminiscent of the dynamic model described in Section 4.2.6.)

The key points in any system representation for the business modeler are:

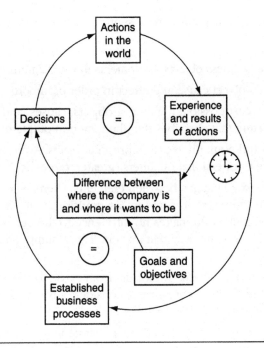

Figure 6.3   Learning behavior of corporations.

- A system is an entity that maintains itself over time through the interaction of its component parts.
- The behavior of the system depends on the relationships among the parts, not on the nature of the parts themselves.
- What systems have in common, despite their many different functions and purposes, is that they can all be understood by using a common set of principles.
- Systems are built from smaller systems, and themselves form parts of larger systems.
- The behavior of a system emerges from the interaction of all the parts according to their relationships, which is to say that none of the individual parts, or the separate relationships among the parts, has the properties that the system demonstrates.
- Understanding how each of the component parts of a system works does not help explain how the system works, but it does allow system representations to be constructed that better mirror observation.
- Each part of a system influences the whole system, although not necessarily in simple ways, nor is the scale of the influence on the system necessarily proportional to the scale of change in a part.

In creating a system diagram to represent a situation, try the following:

- Identify the business objects as elements in the diagram.
- Include each object cause and effect in order of importance.
- Include the least possible number of objects, causes, and effects that result in a system that describes the phenomenon of interest.
- Use nouns and noun phrases to represent objects. Avoid the use of verbs and relative or directional qualifiers (greater, more, decrease, etc.).
- Identify the key linkages between elements. (Remember, any elements that aren't linked represent an assumption that the linkage that exists in the real world makes no difference to the behavior of the non-linked elements in any way that matters. This assumption is subject to review.)
- Use arrows to point loop connectors from cause to effect. (When thinking about this "causal" connection, consider only one link at a time and assume that the rest of the system is frozen.)
- If a change in one element leads to a change in a connected element in the same direction, indicate the relationship with a "+."
- If a change in one element leads to a change in a connected element in the opposite direction, indicate the relationship with a "−."
- Indicate the character of each system loop. A positive reinforcing loop is shown by a "+" in a circle near the center of the loop; a negatively reinforcing loop is shown by a "−" in a circle near the center of the loop. A balanced loop (that will, if undisturbed, approach an attractor) is shown by an "=" in a circle near the center of the loop.
- Indicate where time delays are important.
- When the system diagram is complete, look at it in total and make sure that it seems to make sense.

System diagrams are one way to represent a business situation and are quite intuitive; however, system diagrams aren't the only way to represent systemic structures. Other ways include influence diagrams and systems models; these two alternative representations are also available as software that can be used to extend the passive diagrammatic representation into a dynamic simulation. The remainder of this section looks at a couple of tools, each of which uses a different approach to systems representation. This section, however, hardly scratches the surface of the wealth of information and the depth and richness available in systems thinking, systems representation, and systems modeling. (For some pointers on where to find additional information, see the "Resources" section at the end of the book.)

6.2.1.2 Influence Diagrams

Naturally, all of the relationships in a system can be expressed as influences, and one way of describing systems is by using an *influence diagram* such as the one shown in Figure 6.4, produced using a tool called Analytica. The meaning of influence diagrams is fairly self-evident, which is one of their strengths. The symbols used in this system are shown in Figure 6.5. The rectangle shows the features that are in immediate control (in this example, product price). The hexagons represent the outputs from the system—the objects that are to be ultimately influenced, if possible. Ovals, which aren't

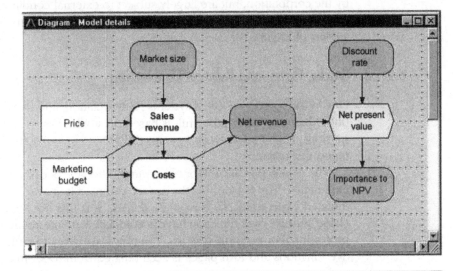

Figure 6.4 Influence diagram.

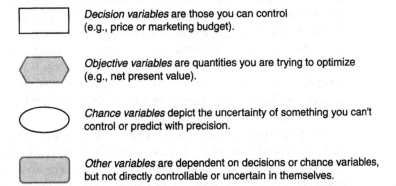

Decision variables are those you can control (e.g., price or marketing budget).

Objective variables are quantities you are trying to optimize (e.g., net present value).

Chance variables depict the uncertainty of something you can't control or predict with precision.

Other variables are dependent on decisions or chance variables, but not directly controllable or uncertain in themselves.

Figure 6.5 Influence diagram symbols.

used in the simple influence diagram shown in Figure 6.4, are used to indicate variables and factors that are part of the external environment, but are not amenable to being influenced by the system. Round-cornered rectangles are used to depict features of objects that are only indirectly controllable, usually through the indirect manipulation of controllable variables.

In Figure 6.4, for instance, "price" and "marketing budget" are, to all intents and purposes, directly controlled by corporate decision. (This is, of course, an oversimplification—an assumption—since all corporate decisions and circumstances are influenced by external events. Identifying assumptions and questioning them is always an important part of model construction.) "Sales revenue," "costs," "market size," and so on are indirectly influenceable by the corporation, but are largely subject to external conditions rather than corporate control. "Net present value" is chosen as the variable that is the subject of inquiry.

6.2.1.3 Stocks, Flows, and Relation Connections

One founding conception of systems representation, and one that has turned out to be remarkably powerful, is based on stocks, flows, and relation connections. High Performance Systems (HPS) has created software that implements this concept.

The reason that the author can write this book is because of accumulated experience. The reason that the reader can read it is also because of accumulated experience. To a separate degree, it is this book you, the reader, chose because over time you have accumulated an interest in the subject for professional or personal reasons. The physical energy to perform the cognitive functions and turn pages is accumulated from food. In all these cases, and a vast number more, these accumulations lead to stocks—of experience, knowledge, interest, and energy.

The accumulations or stocks are one of the foundation concepts of this systems representation. Notice that the accumulated stocks don't have to be physical accumulations, and that in these examples, most of them are not. Morale and interest can accumulate just as much as manufactured units and cash, and equally can diminish, too. Of course, although these stocks only metaphorically accumulate and diminish, the question is how that happens. Imagine the accumulator of any stock as a kind of tank. Into this tank flows experience, knowledge, interest, energy, or whatever, where they accumulate; similarly they can flow out and so diminish.

Characterizing the performance of a system requires associating numbers and qualities with the objects in the system, and explicating exactly how the relationship affects the values of stocks and flows. Figure 6.6 shows an illustration of a collection of system objects that HPS designates a "main chain," which in this case outlines the customer lifecycle. In this figure, the rectan-

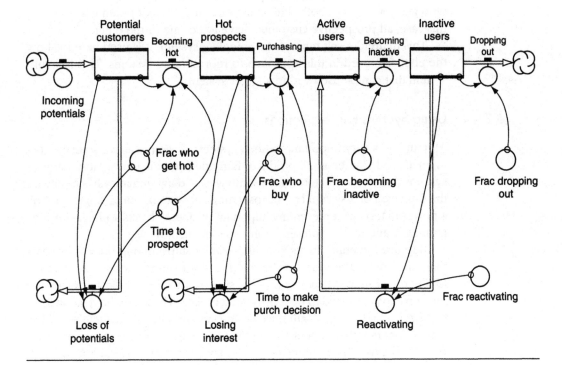

Figure 6.6 Stocks, flows, and connections.

gles represent accumulators (tanks) which the stocks flow into and then out of by way of "pipes." The pipes are generally unidirectional, so the stock can flow only in one direction, although sometimes flows can go both in and out in the same pipe. At left is a tank labeled "potential customers." A pipe connects into it, which contains a "faucet" that controls the flow and is labeled "incoming potentials." Two pipes flow out ("loss of potentials" and "becoming hot"), which indicate the ways that potential customers migrate to other states. Obviously, there is some rate at which potential customers arrive which depends on many factors, including the company's sales and marketing efforts. However, the "cloud" shown on the extreme left specifies the assumption that, although customers do flow into this system from the world, all effects that produce this arrival of customers are not relevant to this system. Thus, this system considers only the customer cycle, *given* that customers do arrive at some particular rate.

The outflow of potential customers through loss also shows the assumption that whatever happens to them after they disappear is of no relevance to this system, thus, the outflow to a cloud. The circles in this figure represent information, which is a vital part of the diagram. The circle labeled "frac who get hot" links to both "becoming hot" and "loss of potentials" since, in this case, all prospective customers have to do one or the other.

This figure doesn't represent a complete system; it is used here to show the elements used in this approach to representing systems. This is a subsystem that can be used within a larger system.

6.2.1.4   Using Systems Representations

Although it is very important to keep systems as simple as possible, modeling real-world systems still produces fairly detailed diagrams. Most software systems representation tools have some way of diagrammatically simplifying the full detail of a system by encapsulating subsystems into a single symbol: a powerful tool for representing important business objects and relationships intuitively and making presentation and explanation easy.

Because the entire focus is on the relationships among objects, systems diagrams focus attention on the need to understand these relationships. Chapter 7, Section 7.1, points out that systems diagrams indicate exactly the relationships that need to be represented in data. These are the relationships that have a high level of influence on the system outcomes of interest. It becomes apparent that understanding the exact nature of some relationships is very important in determining system behavior. In these cases, it isn't enough to rely on assumptions, or even intuitions, of the nature of the relationship. Demonstrating that a small change in the exact characterization of a relationship has a potentially large impact on system performance goes a long way toward creating a persuasive case that data needs to be collected that actually allows the relationship to be accurately characterized. This helps to explain why just mining data ("take my data and tell me interesting and useful insights!") is so difficult and often unsatisfactory—there is no model that helps to explicate the relationships and areas of interest.

A great advantage of an automated systems representation is that the tools allow the whole system to be simulated, and its performance explored. Not only is this a lot of fun, but it also provides direct experiential evidence of whether the imagined system does, in fact, work as expected. Very often, it turns out that the system as imagined not only does not duplicate the performance that the world produces, but it also as a whole does not produce the results that its imaginers expected. Such simulations can be used as wonderful tools to adjust preconceived notions of the way things work, and to allow understanding of a business situation to be adjusted to better reflect the performance of the world. Very often, they show where business-crucial information about the world is simply not being collected.

Systems, useful and powerful as they are, are not the only metaphors useful in constructing business models. The remainder of this section looks not at alternatives, since all of the following metaphors can be used to produce systems representations, but additional ways of imagining business issues for modeling.

6.2.2 Physical System Metaphors

Our immediate impressions of the world are that it exists as a separate entity from our "selves" and that it is a primarily physical place. For instance, the term *objects* used in the expression *business objects* is derived analogously from our experience of physical objects such as trees, doors, houses, and cars. All such physical objects have physical properties of various kinds: hardness, color, density, and so on. Physical objects also incorporate our notion of change: some objects are changed, and some participate in change but are themselves unchanged. A door changes color when painted, and the paint changes state when applied, for instance; however, opening the door may change its state, but it does not change the door itself.

Extending our immediate appreciation of the world by using metaphorical constructs allows us to use all of the associations that accompany the metaphor. Opening a door provides access to the space across the portal, and the meaning of "opening the door to business" is metaphorically intuitively grasped. However, the metaphor is accompanied by many connotations that may be useful. For instance, doors can be closed, and so can the opportunity. Doors can be easily accessible or not, and so can the opportunity to do business. Doors can be constructed where there are now only walls, and new business opportunities may be constructed in the "walls" of a company. Such metaphors can be almost indefinitely extended, and often very usefully and creatively, although it is always possible to extend a metaphor beyond its ability to assist insight.

In constructing business models using physical analogs as inspiration, and as thought and imagination support tools, it is useful to somewhat circumscribe the metaphors and concentrate on generalized physical models. The most useful physical analogs are those describing fixed properties, such as density, weight, and so on, and variable energetic concepts, such as pressure, flow, work, and power. Imagining business situations analogously in such terms can be very useful in structuring them and pointing to useful relationships and data that are needed to model them. However, remember that this metaphor is not suggested because it is in any way "better" than some other metaphor that could be just as fruitful. (Perhaps biological systems with cell membranes or chemical reactions and biological energy transport systems would be more intuitive and appropriate, depending on the circumstances.) The metaphor of the physical world is suggested only because it represents a common experience of the world shared by, and intuitive to, most people. (If they are understood by the modeler and stakeholders, biological cells using ATP for energy transport, the Golgi apparatus, the Krebs cycle, and so on, can be enormously useful as metaphors for business. But they are generally not well enough known and understood, and therefore simply do not, in general, have the connotational richness to work well as business metaphors.)

6.2.2.1 Variables

A vast number of physical variables are measured by the scientific community, and some are useful in modeling business situations—specifically, what things change, why things change, and what is needed to bring about particular changes. Change is of primary concern, so the variables chosen are those that bear on the what, why, and how of change.

Variables in physical models are not so much about things that do change as about things that can change. Changes of state require energy, so most variables measure results from expending energy. Useful variables in business modeling include measures (listed alphabetically) of:

- *Energy:* The capacity to do an amount of work. Heat is an energy form able (among other things) to raise the temperature of water. Energy is usually measured in specific quantities, so one calorie is the heat required to raise one gram of water through one degree Centigrade. Analogously, "marketing budget" is the energy form able (among other things) to raise the likelihood that entities in the market will become prospects. One customer acquisition unit might be the amount of resources required to convert one prospect into one initial-purchase customer.

- *Flow:* The amount of motion produced by expending energy measured as the total distance moved by all the objects affected. Thus, two cups, each moved one inch, results in two cup-inches. Physically, this results in measurements of quantity in time, say gallons per second. Analogously, two prospects moved to make an initial purchase each day results in two prospect conversions per day.

- *Power:* The rate at which work is performed, or the rate at which energy is converted. An automobile engine converts chemical energy (gasoline) into mechanical energy (acceleration). The power of an engine is measured in kilowatts (typically in Europe) or horsepower (typically in the United States). Note that an engine has a maximum rate at which it can make the conversion, and a rate at which it is most efficient. Companies can be regarded as converting energy in the form of various resources—

human, financial, and physical—into other forms of energy, such as customers, profits, pollution, and so on.

- *Pressure:* The amount of work that must be done to move an object from one place to another. Pressure is usually discussed in terms of a pressure difference. Pressure is required to move water through a garden hose—the higher the pressure, the more water is moved. Actually, the water flows from higher pressure to lower pressure so that from the tap to the outlet, there is a pressure drop, and it is the difference that determines how much water will flow. Dollars flow through corporate "pipes" from places of high pressure to places of low pressure. Or again, we metaphorically speak of applying pressure in companies to bring about some desired change.

- *Work:* The amount of energy expended in a specific time. A 100-watt lightbulb consumes 100 watts of energy, and when switched on for an hour, it consumes an amount of energy described as 100 watt/hours. However, most notable here is that only about 5% of the work goes into producing the desired output (light), with 95% of the work being wasted in producing unnecessary, even unwanted, side effects—mainly, in this case, heat. One measure of work in business is person-days—the number of people working at a task multiplied by the number of days they worked. Note that here, too, only some of the work will produce the desired outcome with the rest producing side effects.

Also called variables (and taking some liberties with the physical equivalents, as before), but usually having fixed values in any particular object, are:

- *Friction:* The amount of work required to overcome the energy dissipation of an object. Newton pointed out that without friction, and without external forces acting on it, an object set in motion would continue in uniform motion indefinitely. In fact, any moving body does work (expends energy) in overcoming friction, and so eventually comes to rest relative to the body with which it is frictively interacting. Many business processes experience friction. Expense claim reporting, say, or inventory control processes not only take effort (energy) to set up, but once up and running require a constant input of effort (energy) to maintain. Left to themselves, such systems "run down." Similarly, it takes energy to maintain staff levels, both in head count and training levels. "Natural attrition" is one human resource equivalent of friction.

- *Inertia:* The amount of energy required to produce a given change. Water, for instance, has a thermal inertia and, compared to other substances, requires more or less input of heat energy to produce a one-degree change in temperature. Physical bodies, such as different cars, accelerate at different rates with an identical input of energy if they have different inertia. They also must dissipate the "absorbed" energy when braking through friction between pads, rotors, and ultimately, tires and road surface when stopping. Business processes and organizations sometimes certainly seem to have inertia, and march on long after all need for them is passed and require great effort to halt or change. Some products, such as the VW Beetle, seem to have inertia. (Production of the Beetle rolled on much unchanged for over 50 years, and even when forcibly stopped, burst out again in a new incarnation!)

- *Mass:* $e = mc^2$ expresses the now famous Einsteinian insight that the amount of energy locked up in a physical object is equivalent to its mass multiplied by the square of the speed of light. Under gravitational acceleration, mass gives an object the attribute of weight, and it's measured in the same terms—pounds, grams, and so on. Under weightless conditions, an object has the same mass, but no weight. Mass can be converted to energy (as in nuclear reactors, as well as nuclear and thermonuclear bombs). Energy also can be converted to mass, although in the physical world so much energy is needed to produce even a minute amount of mass that it's hardly ever noticeable. In business terms, the conversion may produce more noticeable results. Inertia is proportional to mass—the more the mass, the higher the inertia. (There's an example of this in the next section.)

There are many other physical measures that can be used to think about and structure business situations, and as a modeler you may develop more of your own. The only important features these metaphors need to have is that they are intuitively understood by your business constituency (particularly the stakeholders), that they are perceived as relevant ways to describe a business situation, and that they prompt and promote useful and fruitful insights into describing the business situation. Almost invariably, when appropriately defined for the business context, they will immediately point to what data is needed to describe the situation. It is even more useful if they also point to intuitively evident ways to actually capture any data needed, or to format and code existing data so that it describes the behavior of the variables of interest.

However, not all variables are used in the same way. Even the same variables can be used in different ways. In trying to formulate a physical analogy to depict business systems, it's important to also consider how the variables are used in the framework.

It's useful to think about variables in three ways, called here across, through, and against variables. These are discussed in the next three sections. Briefly, *across* variables deal with pressure where force has to be applied across (or to) a situation to engender motion. *Through* variables measure the motion that results from the pressure of the across variables. *Against* variables measure resistance to motion, and unintended effects that are more or less unavoidable. Across, through, and against variables correspond respectively to pressure, flow, and friction.

6.2.2.2   Across Variables

As a simple illustration of across variables, consider using a physical analogy in a situation requiring a model of new product development. Perhaps the initial sketch might be something like that shown in Figure 6.7. Product development is represented by the cylindrical mass. As a new product is developed, the mass has to be moved from left to right—the farther to the right the mass appears, the closer you are to completing product development, or perhaps to introducing more products. Moving the mass requires a force, but movement of any mass requires overcoming inertia and friction; only the energy left after overcoming these other effects goes into producing the desired motion.

This analogy, when translated into a model of new product development, raises several questions. For example, what constitutes the force applied across the mass? Certainly, managerial direction as well as corporate strategic goals apply force to new product development, but so too do availability of resources, degree of urgency, market conditions, and so on. Is there data available about these entities, and if not, can it be generated? Also, what of the other variables? What constitutes inertia? Perhaps it is characterized by existing product development commitments, scheduling practices, lack of necessary skills, communication delays, poor morale, and a host of other possibilities. Friction, recall, is the unavoidable conversion of energy into unwanted, but unavoidable, side effects. Whereas inertia represents circumstances that can be changed with continued application of pressure, frictional losses are inherent and, although they may be reduced, they can never be

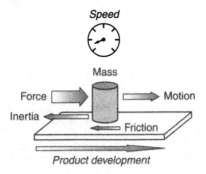

Figure 6.7   "Across" variables.

eliminated. Frictional losses might include meetings, management reviews, vacation, training commitments, recruiting new team members, restructuring, sick days, administrative requirements, and so on. The final result after all these losses is motion toward the goal.

However, as Figure 6.8 shows, the analogy suggests that more massive teams, for the same energy input, have more inertia and friction to overcome, and achieve less speed for the same input of energy. Figure 6.8a shows the same situation as in Figure 6.7. In Figure 6.8b, some time has passed, no force is shown being applied, but inertia continues motion forward and the development has gone much farther than shown in Figures 6.8c and 6.8d. Note that the increase in mass can be modeled too, since building the product development team, or extending it, requires an input of energy in the form of, perhaps, staff, training, expertise, and so on, thus converting energy to mass rather than motion.

Whether this is a valid and useful analogy for any specific instance is not the point here. The point is that constructing such a physical analog and then matching it to the business situation forms a framework for determining what

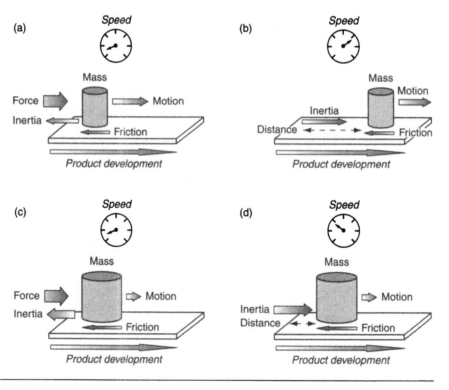

Figure 6.8 Effects of mass on motion.

relationships are important and what data is needed to describe the situation. We use these analogies in our everyday approach to life and to business problems, although rather more casually perhaps. This example might be no more than an extension—very considerably—of the metaphorical question, "What does it take to get the product development team up to speed?"

6.2.2.3 Through Variables

One metaphor used a great deal in business is the chain metaphor: chains of command, responsibility, and supply are often mentioned. Another is the value chain, which can become a very complex representation. As an example, consider the value chain for oil depicted in Figure 6.9.

The value chain shown here comprises six stages:

- *Acquire:* The point in the value chain when whatever is to pass through the value chain is actually acquired. In this example, illustrated by an oil platform, the raw material of crude oil is transformed from not being available at all to having been actually acquired.
- *Manage:* Managing the raw material adds a great deal of value since, in this example, oil that remains at the wellhead is only of potential use, and thus of potential value. Managing the raw material in this case is illustrated with a pump that transports the oil from its source to some other location. In this example, the destination shown is a refinery.
- *Transform:* Raw materials have to be transformed from their raw state into a processed state. In this example, an oil refinery transforms oil into many other things, including oil, gas, gasoline, foodstuffs, plastic, paint, pharmaceuticals, and a huge host of other outputs.
- *Assemble:* Although the transformed materials are considerably more valuable than when raw, it is yet more valuable when the transformed materials are assembled. Oil is assembled into almost every modern product today and is an utterly indispensable part of all modern technology, at least as this is being written. It is included in houses, cars, medical equipment, computers,

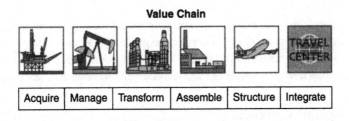

Figure 6.9   Value chain for oil.

and clothes, and has become a completely ubiquitous material of daily life, without which civilization would not exist as we know it.

- *Structure:* As important as assembly is, the next step on the value chain is to create structures that use the assembled products. In this example, the aircraft, which is largely made of oil-derived materials and is powered by oil-derived materials, is part of a structure that is, in this example, an airline. The author, personally, could make no use at all of such an assembled product as a major commercial aircraft without the structure of the airline—couldn't afford to buy it, service it, or learn to fly it—but the structure makes it valuable from time to time.

- *Integrate:* The final step in this value chain is integration of structures, in this case, illustrated by a travel agency. The value offered is potential access to all the airlines (and passenger ships, hotels, rental cars, airports, and so on) that exist.

This is just a brief view of a long value chain, and many different corporate entities span most of it, each adding value to the incoming component through their business processes. However, the point here is that the chain metaphor—one of linked processes—can often be more appropriately modeled by the dynamic idea of a value stream, rather than the static representation of a chain.

There are two completely different ways (at least) to model this value chain. Note that when the resource is initially acquired, it has the potential to be used. At every step in the value chain, the corporate entity involved in that link extracts value from the flow of the resource, and then lets the resource flow on downstream. In this metaphor, the flow travels from high potential to low, just as a stream flows from source to sink, from spring to ocean, and can be used to generate electricity and irrigate fields along the way. Here, the metaphor calls for corporations to create the "dams," "generators," and "farms" that can capture the value of the flow.

On the other hand, the resource requires transformation at every stage, so perhaps it is a question of adding energy to the flow so that the stream is pumped uphill. Now the metaphor calls not for extracting value from the flow, but for adding value to the flow. Which is "correct"? Neither is correct. Whether either is of any value, or whether the metaphor of the value chain itself has any utility, depends entirely on whether it leads to any useful insight. Perhaps it's more like "stone soup" where someone brings a pot of water and a stone. Others turn up with this and that to add to the pot and eventually it turns into soup, so that a large number of inconsequential additions add up to a valuable result.

6.2.2.4 Against Variables

We generally use two metaphors for time. One metaphor can be characterized as the ever-rolling stream, and has two scenarios. In one scenario, we are carried past the scenery. The other scenario places "me" as a static point, a "rock in the stream of time." Here, the sweep of events flows past, and washes against "me." The essential idea is that the business is buffeted and pressed by the slings and arrows of outrageous fortune.

However, a second metaphor also can be useful. Imagine a flowing stream in which a vortex curls lazily. Around and around it whirls, self-sustaining and self-perpetuating, yet ever changing. Although the vortex is an object, it is never composed of the same water for two instants together. Always new water flows through it, yet the self-organized vortex remains.

People and companies both are like these vortices. For people, food and oxygen pour in, energy is extracted, material is incorporated into our bodies, other material is sloughed off as waste—never are we physically the same for two instants. Yet some essential spark endures such that, although totally physically different after some years, still we are "the same." So, too, experiences pour through us in an ever-novel panorama, yet our sense of identity endures despite the changes wrought by time and experience.

Companies also change. Not only do the people change, but business processes change, skills change, and markets change. For any company that has lasted a century, almost every conceivable thing about it has changed—yet we recognize it as the "same" company. What are the important flows: people, skills, material, knowledge? What are the interacting elements that maintain the company when all of its parts are changing? Identifying the components of these metaphors produces some very interesting modeling possibilities.

All metaphors are potentially useful for creating models. Metaphors are how we humans comprehend the world, how we digest experience, how we grasp the meaning of events. Modelers need a wealth of metaphors at their fingertips, but more than most, modelers need to sharpen and refine their metaphors to a level of detail that allows data stream characterization. Metaphor is an intuitive and powerful representation tool, but the results of the metaphorical exploration have to be represented in a way that is intuitive to, or at least easily explained to and grasped by, the stakeholders. The next section addresses these needs.

6.3   **Exploration Tools**

One-on-one exploration of problems is very useful and frequently productive. On other occasions, group sessions are necessary, especially with multiple stakeholders simultaneously contributing. A very useful skill for a modeler to develop is a set of exploration tools that can be used individually and with groups, and for presenting interim results. Many of these tools, such as the interview techniques described at the beginning of this chapter and the metaphorical representation tools just discussed, can be used for exploration.

These tools, however, may not be easily used as aids during the exploration process. The tools discussed in this section, although not exclusively exploration tools, work well in this role.

6.3.1 Mind Maps

(See MII:TB.11) Maps show features and objects of interest, not the whole territory. They attempt to present visually an individual or group understanding of a situation. Such maps may or may not match reality very closely, but matching reality is not the issue; matching the mental image is the primary objective. Of course, this is only a step on the path toward finding a map that more closely matches the situation of interest in a way that fits the world. It is perhaps a step toward a system diagram, or some other metaphorical representation, but that is not where to start.

An easy way to begin is with the techniques of *mind mapping*—a quick way to sketch mental maps that are very simple and easy to create, yet which communicate a huge amount of information very succinctly. They are useful for many applications, and especially for describing situations.

Mind maps are conceived as a visual expression, so they are very good at capturing nonlinear descriptions (not nonlinear in the mathematical sense, but to contrast with the linear type of note taking that results, say, from a bulleted list or sequentially taken notes). Figures 6.10 and 6.11 show two of the wonderful mind maps from *Mapping Inner Space* by Nancy Margulies. They need no explanation and are entirely obvious in what they have to say—and that is the whole point. To explain these concepts here would require many lines of text, and still the concepts would not be able to be absorbed as quickly and intuitively as with a mind map.

Ms. Margulies' maps are wonderfully visual, and with her quick sketches her maps are a joy to see. Her book has a lot of helpful tips to aid the novice mind mapper use illustrations, but the author has to admit that his mind maps are far more text-based, and less graphical, even when done by hand. They are, nonetheless, still far quicker to produce, more intuitive to interpret, and get a lot more information down more quickly and in more compact form than text-based notes. They also inherently point to relationships and connections in a way that other types of note taking do not.

However, mind maps are not limited to hand-drawn sketches. Various mind mapping software products are available, such as Visual Mind, which was used to create Figure 6.12 on p. 198. This figure shows a very small part of the mind map for this chapter (and is available for download; see the "Resources" section at the end of the book). This mind mapping software is a real boon to anyone who uses a computer more than paper and

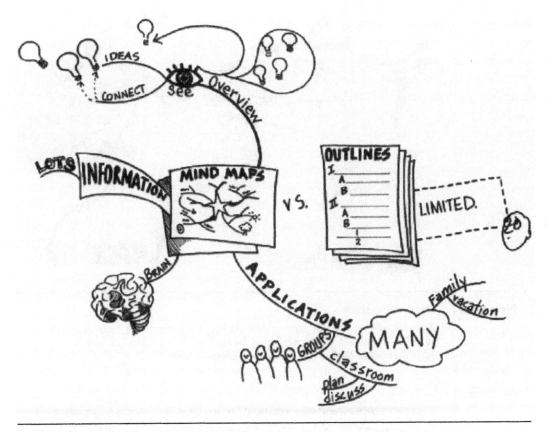

Figure 6.10 Mind map uses.

(From *Mapping Inner Space: Learning and Teaching Mind Mapping* by Nancy Margulies. © 1991.
Permission to publish granted by Zephyr Press, P.O. Box 66006, Tucson, AZ 85728-6006. (800) 232-2187.
www.zephyrpress.com)

pencil. An additional benefit is that with a projector connected to a laptop, these tools can be immediately used in a group setting to quickly sketch situations. The maps are "public" property, so they can help a group come to a consensus.

6.3.2 Cognitive Maps

(See MII:TB.11) It's a short, but significant, step from mind maps to cognitive maps. A cognitive map is similar in many respects to a system diagram. Rather than depicting the associations that are easy and intuitive in mind maps, cognitive maps have to identify objects, features of objects, and significant

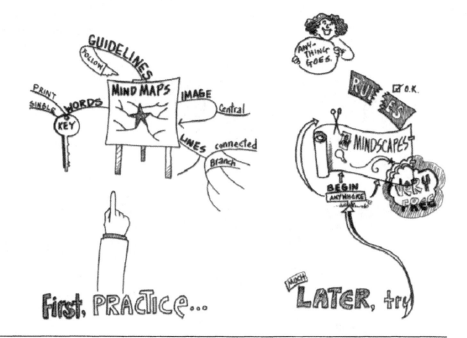

Figure 6.11 Mind map guidelines.

(From *Mapping Inner Space: Learning and Teaching Mind Mapping* by Nancy Margulies.
© 1991. Permission to publish granted by Zephyr Press, P.O. Box 66006, Tucson,
AZ 85728-6006. (800) 232-2187. *www.zephyrpress.com*)

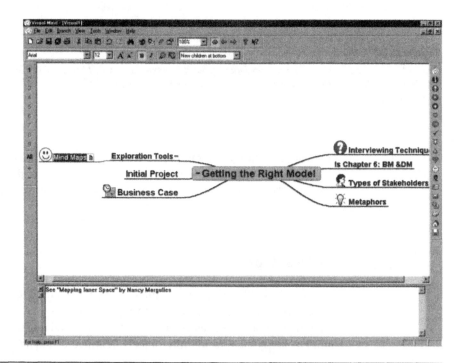

Figure 6.12 Mind map using Visual Mind.

interconnections between them. Cognitive map objects have two important characteristics:

- The objects exist only inasmuch as we interact with them. (It's important to note that all objects are a result of our projections onto the world. Perhaps they should be called "subjects" as they are subjective, not objective. It's important to remember this since the discussion sometimes turns to what is "really" going on in the world rather than what's really going on in our heads. The choice of objects is a *very* subjective business. Something is indeed going on in the world, but all we are aware of is what happens in our heads when the something happens in the world—and we're free to draw the lines where we may.)
- Properties of objects exist only inasmuch as the objects interact with the world. The properties are in the interactions, not in the objects. That is to say, the interactions that we call "properties" are only elicited behaviors or operational depictions that occur when we observe and interpret objects relating to each other.

Consider, for instance, that the "hardness" of a physical object is apparent only when the object is required to operate in the world where the property of hardness forms a relevant part of the way that we observe and describe what happens. The same is true with properties such as "customer loyalty."

Figure 6.13 shows a small cognitive map created with a tool called Inspiration. This map is based on an article in *Harvard Business Review* titled "The Buzz on Buzz" by Renée Dye (November/December 2000 issue). For the sake of visibility in the figure, the map is not a complete representation. Cognitive maps can become quite extensive, and one of Inspiration's strengths is that its "canvas" is quite large, which allows creation of big, complex maps.

6.3.3 Cognitive Models

(See MII:TB.12) A cognitive model takes a step further from a cognitive map, in that its distinguishing feature is in the specification of the relationships. A *cognitive map* indicates that an important relationship exists, and the general direction of its influence. A *cognitive model* precisely characterizes the indicated relationships, which requires determining units of measure for the objects, ranges of values, the "shape" of the relationship, and the strength of the interaction. With data available, of course, this is where data mining comes strongly into the picture, since data mining is an extremely powerful tool for characterizing all of the features of a relationship, whether the measured values are numerical or categorical, and whether the relationship is linear or highly nonlinear.

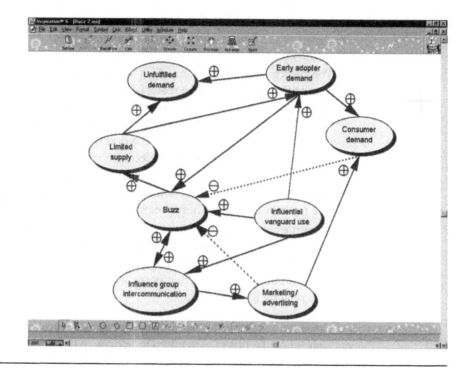

Figure 6.13   Cognitive map using Inspiration.

It isn't necessary for a cognitive model to be automated. Representing the relationships by, say, differential equations or difference equations, together with confidence bands and a representation of the distribution of errors across the range of interaction, provides a cognitive model just as much as an automated version does. However, if the model isn't automated, the next step in understanding and verifying the nature of the system is impossible. It is also, in practice, enormously easier to point and click or drag and drop to create the models because the very essence of systems is that they are dynamic and interactive. A nondynamic cognitive model can be very informative and provide much insight, but it misses a vital element of a system—that it does something other than just sit there!

6.3.3.1   Simulation

(See MII:TB.13) Running a system through its paces is fun. It's where the unexpected happens, and what happens is often counterintuitive. Humans are notoriously bad at guessing what even slightly nonlinear systems are going to do, and do even worse with highly complex, interacting systems—even when all of the interactions are linear. We're pretty hopeless at guessing what complex, nonlinear systems are going to do. But it turns out that we are smart enough to make devices that can do the guessing for us—simulators. These allow all of the objects and all of the relationships and their details, specified as best we can, to be plugged in, and then the simulator behaves as it will while we watch.

To run a cognitive model as a simulation, simply plug in actual values for some of the system's variable values. After a while, the system will settle down, or not, as the case may be. When running, adjustments can be made to the values of some of the variables and the results on system performance immediately begin to show.

6.3.3.2   Calibrating Cognitive Models

(See MII:AB.12) Of course, perhaps the system doesn't settle down after a while. Perhaps it collapses into quiescence, or perhaps it "blows up" with all of the values shooting off into the stratosphere. That's fine. If the system is a brand new design, it simply means that more design is needed, probably more feedback loops. There's a different problem if the system is intended to reproduce some existing real world system and it collapses where the real world system doesn't, or appears not to!

Simulation time almost always ticks by far faster than real time. Hours, weeks, or months of simulated time may pass in seconds of elapsed time. This isn't always the case. Modern aircraft are designed in parts. Often the parts are simulated for their behavior. When simulating an aircraft wing flying, it may take hours to simulate a few seconds of flight. However, the insights gained into what's actually going on make such simulations extremely valuable. But for business simulations the point is to try simulating things that are unwise to try in practice until better understood, so faster than real time is pretty much the rule. When simulated time is flowing by so fast, a collapse may happen that takes a long time, possibly years. So it's possible that the real world situation is indeed disintegrating, but slowly, more like coming to a slow boil. In the real world, the disaster may never happen because the impending problem is noticed and fixed first. Still, that's not always the case, because unintended wars still happen, and so do corporate collapses, investment bubbles, environmental disasters, and many other business system failures.

However, cognitive models can be very usefully calibrated against what really happens in the world, if data is available. If a cognitive model "works," it should describe in its limited terms the system in the world of which it is an abstraction. With data, the simulation can be set so that its starting state matches some specific time in the past. From there the simulation can evolve for a while over a period for which there is data. It may, or may not, follow the course that real events took. It can't be expected that a system model, even one that accurately represents the system of interest, will duplicate the path of events that the world actually took. The problem is one of constraints.

How many ways are there to get from New York to San Francisco, London to Rome, Mogadishu to Timbuktu? So many that it's effectively impossible to put any upper bound on the number. But how many shortest ways are there? Well, several—shortest in time, shortest by distance, shortest practicable distance, and so on. No matter how many shortest routes there are, however, it's vastly less than the number of possible routes.

Constraints work in two places in system simulations. First, the system itself has broader constraints than the past performance of the world. The world has already followed its path from start to finish, and this single example of all the possible paths that it might have taken is fixed—the simulation isn't. Second, it's possible that there are several systems—perhaps an infinite number, similar to the number of routes between two points—that are all different from each other, yet all represent a valid explanation for the data. The paths that such systems take may not be similar to the path taken by the world, or to the paths taken by other valid models.

This is one reason that the system must be constrained to be the simplest possible model. It's rather like constraining the route between two points to be the shortest. It doesn't squeeze all the ambiguity out, but it tightens the limits on what's possible.

Calibrating the model ideally requires matching the system performance back to the world's performance and having them agree. This isn't really a very likely outcome in practice. However, since the world is constrained (to the path that it has already traveled), it's the system model that is less constrained. In multiple runs of the model (which will be different on each occasion if the relationships have confidence limits built in), it's probable that the path taken by the world won't be exactly duplicated, but it should lie inside the extremes of the model. Sometimes—surprisingly often—the concordance between world and data can be really good, which is a hopeful sign. A valid system model will always include the performance that the world actually exhibited.

6.3.3.3 Knobs, Dials, Levers, and Switches

(See MII:AB.12) Recall that knowledge (at least as used in this book) is a connection between inputs and outputs. The inputs are filters that recognize sets of relevant features, and every set of such features associates with a set of available actions and outcomes associated with the actions. The set of input features form context and event significance (that something happened and what it means). The actions are options that can be selected, and each has an associated outcome together with an associated degree of certainty.

For instance, if the event is "my best programmer just resigned," what it means depends on a vast number of factors, including whether there is a project running, whether the company is growing or shrinking, whether the department is being increased or reduced, and any number of other contextual or situational clues. Available actions include "do nothing" (always a valid option), hire externally, hire internally, promote internally, borrow from another department, hire a consultant, and so on. Each of these actions has a different potential outcome.

As noted earlier, managers have to manage: practicing the art of recognizing situations and taking appropriate actions that are effective. The manager's core responsibility is to make appropriate selections because managerial performance is judged almost entirely by selection appropriateness. The ideal information that a manager wants presents clues to recognizing situations unambiguously. This is exactly what an aircraft cockpit does for a pilot. Pilots have various dials (and other, mainly visual, indicators) that present relevant information that represents the situation, and alarms that present alerts that action is needed, like stall warnings, low fuel warnings, and so on. The pilot takes action by moving levers, knobs, and switches, which, being part of a system, have larger effects elsewhere. Moving a few levers 12 to 18 inches, for instance, produces a change of several thousands of pounds of thrust from the engines.

As Figure 6.14 shows, systems simulations can be fitted with visualizations of control panels, which provide images of knobs, dials, levers, and

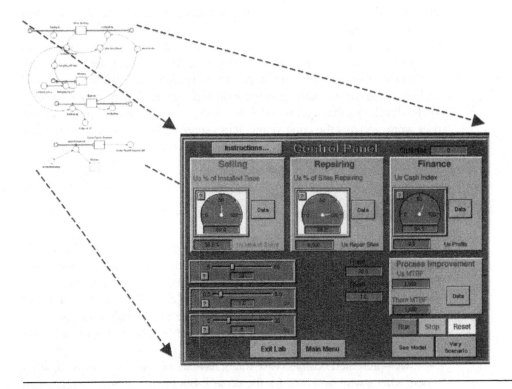

Figure 6.14   System simulation control panel.

switches that show the state of the business situation simulation. (One of the dials, for instance, at top right shows the state of corporate finances.) Such a control panel could be used to provide a synopsis of an actual business situation, but here serves to explore the complexities of business situations without the danger to the company that real world experimentation poses.

The modeler must beware that by the time the system simulation is constructed and important relationships are being sought for mining, very often a manager's favorite knobs, switches, and levers turn out to be connected to nothing that makes any difference to the system. The problem is sympathetic association—I do "this" and "that" happens. If "that" was going to happen anyway, my doing "this" may have been irrelevant. Nonetheless, the manager has the distinct impression that doing "this" does produce an effect of "that," even though there is, in fact, no causal connection. Very often, the author has been hard pressed to explain why a management team's controls don't make much, if any, difference to the model performance. It's a difficult issue, and one that has to be approached diplomatically.

Nonetheless, creating a system simulation based on management understanding can be incredibly useful. Many of the crucial relationships in the simulation may well be based on no data at all, only on assumptions and intuition. (Intuition is right remarkably often.) This immediately points at where data is needed to make more effective management decisions. It also points at which relationships are important to characterize. More than that, it serves as a powerful check on model performance. Finding explanatory models is no more, in system terms, than characterizing parts of the system. If the simulation has been working and stops, it is very likely that this is a quick and early warning that something in the world has changed. It provides immediate feedback to a manager that the decisions are no longer as appropriate as they were, and that the context and alarm sensors may be missing something important. (For more detail on management levers, see Section 7.1.3.2.)

6.4 **The Business Case**

(See MII:AB.5, MII:TB.4) How do you as a modeler, or as part of a modeling/mining group, get support for a project? Although the stakeholders may be the ones who most often will be garnering support, the modeling (or analytics) team may be expected, as part of their charter, to propose areas of exploration. They are certainly going to be asked to provide justification for the required resources for any even slightly sizable project. Preparing a business case is the place to start.

A well-presented business case might have to include details of who, what, when, where, why, and how for the project. But the focus, and the reason for existence of the business case, is entirely concerned with only one of these: why is this project to be undertaken? The business case explains in management terms—and note the phrase "in management terms"—why, and how much, the project will contribute to the business. The essential job of the business case is to quantify the return expected for the invested resources. To be sure, it will have to identify the resources, how they will be used, and why this use is expected to have the effects proposed, but its essential job is to convincingly portray to the business managers involved that the impact resulting from the resources used is worth having, and is a good use of the resources available. Remember that any project in any company, including business modeling and data mining projects, compete for the company's limited resources. Business managers will commit resources only to projects that offer good value. That comes down to numbers, and wherever possible, to dollars (or whatever currency is appropriate). Since many business modelers and data miners may not be familiar with preparing a business case, this section includes a few tips.

6.4.1 What Is a Business Case?

Very simply, a business case is the material that is presented to decision makers to persuade them that the idea proposed should be pursued. Although it is prepared for, aimed, and directed at this specific constituency, it has to appeal to a broader audience, too. It naturally has to appeal to the stakeholders discussed in Section 6.1.1.

In order to gain support and be successful, the project must engage senior management and executives from the very beginning. The project objective includes far more than just creating a business model and mining data to characterize the model. The ultimate objective is to change corporate behavior in some way, or perhaps (although even more difficult to justify, but just as important to corporate performance) the objective is to derive insight that prevents the corporation from taking an action that is being contemplated. Whatever the purposes of the project, there will come a time when the project's success depends entirely on the company changing its behavior in the face of corporate inertia. (Inertia, remember, doesn't mean reluctance to move; the corporation may be moving and moving swiftly. Changing the direction of corporate "charge forward" is just as tough. Imagine the corporation as a head-down charging rhino where the inertia is all moving in one direction. Changing the direction of charge is tough!) At this point, the "energy" input to apply sufficient "pressure" comes only from a senior management champion. Only senior management commitment counts when political and budgetary battles have to be fought.

The plan has to appeal to the beneficiary stakeholders. Although they may not be involved during the plan's formal presentation to management, if the impact is large enough, it will form the basis of what the rumor mill has to say about the project. In a long or large project, the beneficiary stakeholders have to be kept involved with bulletins, updates, or newsletters, and must be encouraged to provide feedback to the project. All parties need to be involved and so feel a sense of ownership. However, it's the business plan that very largely sets the initial tone for the project, and if it sets an inappropriate tone at the start, overcoming such perceptions later ranges from very, very difficult to impossible.

Chapter 5, in looking at one way of assessing risk, discusses the need for benchmarks of performance. (See Section 5.6). No improvement or change stands alone, but exists only in comparison to some existing baseline. The business plan has to explicitly include the baseline benchmark, for without it there is no way to measure the improvement or increased return from the project. The project has to promise in some way to do things better—but better than what? Whatever it is that is to be the standard of judgment has to be included.

Changing corporate behaviors is not easy. There are several barriers to change that are common in most organizations. The business plan has to address how the barriers are to be overcome. These barriers are the "friction" that impede "movement" toward the goal. The most significant include:

- *Inflexibility:* Success requires the corporate organization that has to embrace the changed practices, policies, and procedures to have the infrastructure in place to manage the change that the project requires. The business plan has to address the needed basic management issues.
- *Lack of management support:* Without a senior management champion, when the going gets tough who fights for it? No one. It's essential to engage senior management, and in doing so the manager(s) who must be engaged is in the crucial stakeholder group mentioned earlier as the kudos stakeholder(s).
- *Limited resources:* All companies have limited resources, but any project requires either getting additional resources or redirecting already committed resources to the project. If the project is to be a success, it has to successfully present the case that it represents a better use of the required resources than any alternative use, including the use they are being put to at present.
- *NIH:* This is the famous "not invented here" syndrome. People don't readily embrace changes that come unbidden from the outside. Many of the suggestions here are intended to help engender the feeling that the project, and its results, were in fact "invented here" and to engage all participants with a sense of ownership and a vested interest in the successful outcome of the project.

- *Technology issues:* If the technical solution won't scale, or if the technology isn't sufficiently robust, the solution won't deliver its projected value. It's very important to address the technology issues and make the case for scale and robustness just as much as it is to determine what technologies and support are needed.

6.4.2 Aligning the Business Case with Corporate Needs

The business case has to be aligned with the needs of the business. The business case itself not only has to present a plan that is aligned with the business, but also it has to explicitly show how it aligns on at least two dimensions. It can also usefully include explicit references to alignment on several other dimensions. The two dimensions that must be included are:

- *Business goals:* The project needs to be aligned with business goals because positioning and demonstrating that the project is closely aligned with business goals provides a compelling reason to complete it. Again, as in other areas, a visual map of the situation is an effective tool for demonstrating that the project is aligned with business objectives. Figure 6.15 shows a goal map with six goal levels. (See MII:TB.5) For illustrative purposes, this map is more generic, and less complete, than a full business case goal map. The top-level goal represents one, or more, major corporate objectives that the project is designed to support. Such high-level goals are usually at too high a level to usefully model. Each lower level until level 4 shows goals that are more detailed than the goal above until, in this example, the subgoals at level 4 provide a description of *process variables* that can be measured and captured. (For more on discovering process variables, see Chapter 7.) These process variables describe the business process, and will generate the data that will be mined; they are also the measures that will be used to describe the states and interactions to be modeled. The fifth level describes "this" project, and clearly shows exactly which business goals it supports. The sixth level shows the corporate and other resources that are needed to support completion of the project.
- *Timetable:* (See MII:DB.2) It's crucially important to set realistic time objectives, not aggressive ones. Remember the aphorism "It takes longer than it takes, and it costs more than it costs." This aphorism holds even when you have allowed for its effects. Include in the project plan contingencies to handle the inherent risks in the timetable.

Including a discussion of how the business case aligns on these two criteria is absolutely essential. However, there are many corporate goals that are

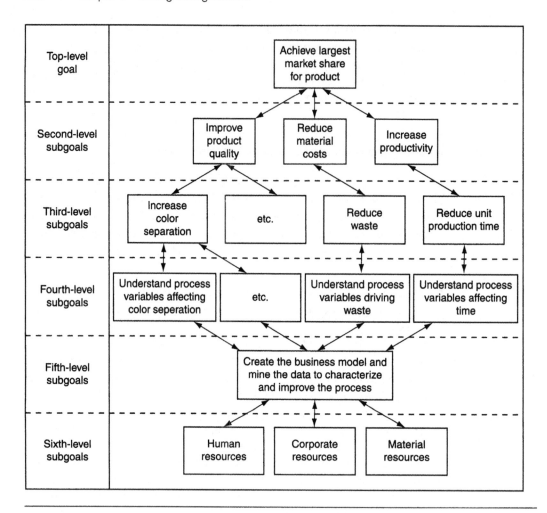

Figure 6.15 Goal map.

almost never stated, and so can be characterized as "hidden" criteria. Just as hidden assumptions are like rocks hiding in the shallows of a rough sea waiting to catch the unwary, so too can these hidden business criteria leap out to bite. The hidden criteria to at least consider, and also to explicitly address if possible in the business case, include:

- *Corporate culture:* All corporations have a culture, and very powerful it is, too. To avoid the strife of "That's not the way we do things around here," make sure that the plan does align with corporate culture. Recruiting the support of the beneficiary stakeholders is an important part of aligning with corporate culture. The business case (keeping in mind the earlier comment that this business case will set the tone and expectations of everyone involved in or touched by the project) should include specific descriptions of exactly how it aligns with corporate culture, and what methods will be used to keep it so aligned.

- *Corporate investments:* Companies budget their resources. The budget reflects an often unstated investment strategy. Projects that align with the corporate investment strategy will certainly find more budget and support than those that are aligned only with its minor goals. To discover the investment strategy, don't look at where the corporation makes its largest investments such as payroll, because those are often mandatory. Look at the types of investments that the company makes with its discretionary spending. Training? Research and development? Process improvement? And what types of training, R&D, process improvement, and so on. Align the project to support the corporate resource investment goals, and show in the business case that it is so.

- *Process capabilities:* All companies have business processes. What level of process change does the project require? Does the company actually manage process change at the level required? Note that some business processes, and their subprocesses, are actively created, managed, and maintained by a company, whereas others spontaneously emerge and perpetuate themselves unmanaged. A corporation's ability to change, and to absorb changes thrust upon it, depends very largely on the capability and flexibility of the company to manage and reorganize its work processes. Indeed, unmanaged processes are sometimes not even officially "seen" by a corporate organization, let alone managed. However, the ability to effect change depends entirely on the corporation's ability to exert control and in order to change its work processes to adapt to changed situations. Thus, aligning the project with achievable process capabilities, and change-capable process capabilities at that, is essential. Showing that this is so may be a crucial part of the business case. It answers a good part of the question, "Well, how are we going to do it anyway?"

6.4.3 Preparing the Business Case

A business case is intended to convince someone to make a decision. Decisions aren't made in vacuums, but are made relative to alternative choices. The business case intends to unambiguously present one of the alternatives as the course to adopt, and intends to persuade the manager that the facts and circumstances justify the course recommended. But managers choose between alternatives, and if in presenting the business case no alternatives are mentioned, the manager will, through questioning, frame the discussion of alternatives. Whoever prepares the business case should not only be fully prepared to discuss alternatives, but also should actively introduce and discuss how the presented case compares to various alternatives. This allows the presenter to frame the choices and discuss the relevant alternatives so that the business case is presented in its most favorable light.

The business case for a large project will present several to many different issues that require management decisions. It's important to present each alternative separately so that the issues for each decision are clear and not intertwined with the issues for other decisions. Every issue that can be separately presented, discussed, and considered should be.

Discussion of alternatives will almost always be most effective when the discussion is in terms of money. However, note that money that has already been spent, whether that spending might have been relevant to the project or not, is no longer relevant. Past spending is of no consequence whatever in presenting the business case. In accounting terms, these previous expenditures are called "sunk costs." All that is important is how to move forward from where you are, with what you have, to get to the best result. Remember, in presenting the future value to be derived from implementing the project, managers discount the future value of money. That is to say, a potential dollar tomorrow is not worth the same as a dollar today, and the further into the future the projection goes, the less value the future dollar is accorded today. To see how this works, start with the formula for determining how much a present value will grow into at a future time if invested at some rate of interest:

$$FV = PV(1 + i)^n$$

which can be translated as future value *(FV)* is equal to 1 plus the interest rate *(i)*, multiplying the result together the same number of times as there are time periods *(n)* and multiplying the result of that by the present value *(PV)*. Thus, the future value of $1,000,000 at a 3% per year interest rate after 5 one-year periods is:

$$FV = 1,000,000(1 + 0.03)^5 = 1,000,000(1.03)^5 =$$
$$1,000,000 \times 1.159274074 = \$1,159,274.07$$

The present value of a future amount can be calculated by transposing the previous formula into:

$$PV = FV/(1 + i)^n$$

so that the present value of $1,000,000, to be gained over 5 years at 3% interest, is:

$$PV = 1,000,000/(1 + 0.03)^5 = 1,000,000/(1.03)^5 =$$
$$1,000,000/1.159274074 = \$862,608.78$$

Thus, the present value of a future amount is not the future amount, but a discounted amount. When the business case and the expected return are discussed, it is the discounted amount that is important to the manager.

Is this important? Yes! It shows that the business issues have been considered, not just the technical, managerial, and deployment issues, and the business case has to be designed to support only the business decision, and must reflect business values and support business judgments.

Numbers are crucial, and a business manager will make much, if not most, of the decision based on the numbers. The numbers on the table will do most of your talking for you—but only if you can demonstrate that they are valid business numbers, and that the business case is presented in business terms. However, there are any number of factors that simply cannot be quantified, such as the effect on customer satisfaction or corporate morale. These are qualitative factors that also need to be weighed in the decision process.

6.4.4 Return on Investment (ROI)

(See MII:AB.7) As far as presenting the business case goes, numbers come first, which is fine—but how are those numbers to be developed? The simple answer is that the most important number in the business case is the estimated return on investment (ROI). In any analysis that leads to an ROI calculation, two separate investments (costs) and two separate returns (gains) have to be quantified.

Investments:

- *One-time investments:* These are the investments that need to be made to complete the project, but once made will not require further investment. An example of a one-time investment would be the purchase of software, training, or resources (like this book!) that are needed to complete the project. These are also known as *nonrecurring costs.*
- *Ongoing investments:* These are investments that will continue to be needed over the life of the project, even when the model has been deployed. An example of ongoing investments would be monitoring the model to ensure performance, continuing training of new users, or additional and continually needed resources for the deployed project. These are also known as *recurring costs.*

Returns:

- *Tangible returns:* Essentially, these are all the quantifiable returns that can be expressed in financial terms. These are also called *tangible benefits.*

- *Intangible returns:* In a nutshell, intangible returns are all of the (usually) qualitative benefits, such as improved customer satisfaction or increased morale, that cannot immediately be quantified. (Nonetheless, these are returns that are expected to have a positive impact on the financial return.) These are also called *intangible benefits.*

Describing the returns and investments considered in an ROI analysis is fairly straightforward. However, there are many roads that can be traveled to reach a justification of an estimated project ROI. Here is a very brief look at several of the most popular, listed alphabetically. There is no space here to describe these analysis methods in any detail. Whole books have been written about the intricacies of each of them, but not much detail is needed by the modeler (or miner) who wishes only to make a business case. Glean the principles that underlie each method, and use the one that seems appropriate and suitable with some degree of confidence. (There is a very brief pointer to further reading on these topics in the Resources section, but any detailed knowledge requires a study of business practices that is almost certainly not needed to make the business case. If the project becomes large enough that it needs a business plan rather than a business case, look for an MBA!)

- *Breakeven analysis:* The idea of breakeven analysis is simple. The project has a return over time. Some of the costs are fixed and some are ongoing. The ongoing costs may change over time, but nonetheless, they constantly reduce the return from the project. The fixed costs, on the other hand, are eventually covered so long as the return is greater than the ongoing investments. At some point, the net return will equal the fixed investment needed to get it. That is the breakeven point. From this time on, the return accrues to profit. Breakeven analysis presents a justification for determining exactly when the project will break even.

- *Cost/Benefit analysis:* This analysis associates a specific benefit with each specific cost. One major problem with this type of analysis is that it can lead to trying to justify cost saving as a benefit. This can translate (much to the author's surprise on one occasion) as the following query from an executive: "Fine, what's the headcount reduction, and who do you recommend?" Unless you are an MBA, or someone skilled in management in such areas, represent the costs as costs and the benefits as benefits, and steer away from cost savings/reductions.

- *Investment opportunity analysis:* Recall that the business has an investment policy, whether it is made explicit or not. Any company wants to make the best use of its resources by investing them in the opportunities that promise the highest return. ROI can always be expressed as an interest rate earned on the money invested. Investment opportunity analysis compares the projected return from various opportunities. However, it's not just the level of return that's important; consider also how to compare the scale of the opportunity and the risk of the investment. Remember that companies want to have as much as possible of their resources invested in profitable opportunities. Small, low-resource requiring ventures, even if they offer a low-risk/high-return opportunity, still leave the manager with the problem of choosing where to best invest the bulk of a company's resources in value-generating projects. Thus, the scale of the investment opportunity also has to fit with corporate investment needs.

- *Pareto analysis:* The Pareto principle, often called the "80/20 rule," says that a few of the causes are responsible for most of the effects. Restating this principle, most of the effect can be had by addressing only a few of the causes. Pareto analysis in a business case ranks business processes by their effects, showing (if the principle holds, which it usually does) the project's impact on corporate performance by improving one, or a few, of the identified processes. The intent is to show first that a few processes have most of the total impact demonstrated, and then that addressing only those few processes will have a large impact on corporate performance.

- *Sensitivity analysis:* The idea of sensitivity analysis is to show that there are points in the business processes of a company where small influences can make large differences. For instance, such an analysis might show that price/performance is extremely sensitive to package size (which, in fact, turns out to be the case for many consumer products). The sensitivity analysis might show that different size/quantity packages should be tailored to different demographic groups for a significant increase in performance. Thus, the analysis would show the sensitivity of the market to these relatively small changes.

- *Trend analysis:* The data miner should have a strong edge in presenting trend analyses—after all, this is exactly where a principal strength of mining tools lies. Trends express relationships and use them to make projections. Forecasts are trend analyses, as would be a projection of increased training costs with increased staff, new product acceptance rates, where a product is on its "S" curve of adoption, and so on. Trends are almost uniformly presented graphically and (needless to say for a data miner) should have all of the normal caveats associated with such projections. (If you are dipping into this book and have not come across these caveats, see anywhere in Part III, for instance, or the earlier chapters of Part II.)

6.4.5 Assembling and Presenting the Business Case

(See MII:DB.4, MII:DB.5) The business case, recall, is defined here as the material that is presented to decision makers to persuade them that the idea proposed should be pursued. The material should include at least a written report and an in-person presentation. The report should comprise seven sections: the management summary and six subsequent sections. The management summary should itself be broken into six sections, one section summarizing the content of each of the main sections of the business case. Here is a brief look at each section, and what goes into it:

- *Management Summary:* **This must be short.** No more than two sides of a single piece of paper, and one side only is better. Put in the minimum possible amount that describes the main conclusion of each section. The object of this is to have the manager read it, and no manager wants to read a novel. In spite of the space requirement, use graphs and tables to make the point where possible. It is very likely that this is the only part of the business case that will be read, and it is on the basis of the summary that the case must be made, and that the decision will be made. This summary needs to have six headings, one corresponding to each section in the rest of the report. The other sections contain support material that may be referred to during the presentation, and possibly referred to by the manager later, but the chance that the whole business case will be read and digested in detail is very small. Therefore, polish the management summary.

- *The Opportunity:* Title it thus, although this section addresses what is called elsewhere in this book the business problem. In management terms, however, it is an opportunity to profitably and effectively invest resources. Describe the opportunity in these terms, why it exists, and the potential return inherent in the opportunity.

- *Current Situation:* What is the situation that exists in the company at the moment? Why is this situation not going to capture the potential value? What is the background that puts the organization in a position to act now?

- *Alternatives:* What else could the company do in this situation? (Be sure to address the issue of doing nothing different.) This is where much of the analysis will be presented.

- *The Solution:* What do you propose to do? Why this choice? What is the anticipated result? Why does this fit with the corporate objectives? Include a description of the metrics by which the results can be measured and what they mean to corporate performance.

- *Resources:* This is the one section that will certainly be scrutinized apart from the management summary. Here is where the financial analysis goes.

- *Proposed Action:* This outlines the timetable, how the resources will be used, what deliverables can be expected, and when.

This is a brief description of what goes into the business case. Keep the whole thing as short as possible, but cover all of the main points. A business case document must be complete, but it shouldn't try to be comprehensive. The idea is for the business case to be convincing. It needs to indicate what will be done, why, when, what the result is expected to be, and how you propose to measure it. It doesn't have to contain a detailed project plan, nor outline all of the individual steps needed, nor identify all of the tools, technologies, techniques, and training needed. These are usually not relevant to the business manager who will make the decision, although they are very relevant to the modeler. But this document is not for the modeler, or the data miner—it's for the business manager. So focus and concentrate on business management needs, not on technical needs.

6.5   **The Reality: "What Can You Do with My Data?"**

(See MII:DB.1) The purpose of using data mining in business modeling is to apply it as a tool that will support informed decision making and the tactical deployment of solutions in a company. Almost all of Part II of this book is focused on discovering the necessary features of a problem. Data mining and business modeling are not solutions in search of problems—the problem always has to come first. But this is not the way that many initial data mining projects happen. One purpose of this book is to show that data mining supports business modeling as a way to solve problems.

Frequently, however, the cart comes before the horse. A manager somewhere in a company has heard of the possibilities of data mining and wants to discover if it has any value. A decision is made, someone with data mining expertise is located, and the corporate database—collected at enormous expense—is made available. The question is, "What problems can you solve with my data?"

The modeler's problem, then, is to develop a project based on this data. Frequently, the manager involved has a degree of exposure in the success of the project as a kudos stakeholder. The manager has "sold" the idea that data mining has something to offer, found budget and resources, organized access to data (which may or may not be useful), secured a degree of internal commitment and support—and now has to deliver some results. As a needs stakeholder, the manager needs a successful data mining project, but usually does not have an identified, specific business problem for the mining to address.

This book highly recommends discovering the problem first. Data mining and business modeling are tools just like any other tools. No company buys tools first and decides what to do with them afterward. Would you purchase a really high quality sewing machine with the finest specifications simply because it was available? Only if you had a desire to sew something—and even then, a fine sailmaking sewing machine is not ideal for making clothes. Can you imagine a company (in its right mind anyway) purchasing tools first and then deciding what corporate activities to undertake? Even when geologically mining, companies don't dig first and see what has come up afterward. Inviting a mining company to "come and mine my backyard to see if there is anything of value there" won't work. Even if there is oil in your backyard, a diamond or gold mining company won't be interested. And in any case, the question is whether the oil is present in economic quantities. Analogously, so it is with data mining. It isn't appropriate to mine first and see what is discovered afterwards—in spite of the fact that very often this is exactly what is requested in practice.

However, it is valid to ask what types of tasks particular tools can undertake, and what they are particularly useful for before actually committing time and resources to purchasing some and learning to use them. The biggest problem still comes when the data comes first. And all too often the data does come first and *that* is the business problem the modeler must face. Since this is a common business situation confronted by data mining-based business modelers, the author would be remiss not to at least discuss how to deal with such a situation.

6.5.1 Hunting for a Problem

The "What can you do with my data?" question leads to a problem hunt. Until a problem is identified, there isn't anything that data mining or modeling the "business situation" can achieve, because there isn't a business situation. Remember that data mining is useful only when the business situation contains relationships that are described by data. So, if the data comes first, the question to discover is why this particular data was collected. What business situation(s) was it originally intended to describe? What business problems existed that created an apparent "need to know"? Were those problems solved?

6.5.2 Problem Opportunity: The Corporate Value Chain

(See MII:AB.4, MII:TB.3) The place that any search for problems has to begin is with the company's value chain. Corporate value chains are immensely complex in detail, but in principle simple. All companies face one fundamental problem: to have the right product in the right place at the right time, in the right quantity and for the right price. All of a company's core business processes focus on this multi-part objective. The subobjectives form a system, that the author calls the P³TQ (Product, Place, Price, Time, Quantity) system. This system is illustrated in Figure 6.16. These key components mutually interact. Which is the right product, for instance, depends very much on the customer. No doubt who the customer is also depends on time and place, and so on. The tools that any company can deploy to understand and manage the intricacies and vagaries of its unique P³TQ system are data, forecasting, and resource deployment. Crucial relationships exist among the P³TQ subobjectives. Relationships, as revealed in data, are what data mining tools excel at revealing.

The unique P³TQ system of any company is constructed from the corporate resources available to it formed into business processes, as illustrated in Figure 6.17. Some processes are dedicated to determining the appropriate product, place, price, time, or quantity, whereas other processes attempt to get products to the right place, create products for the right time, have the

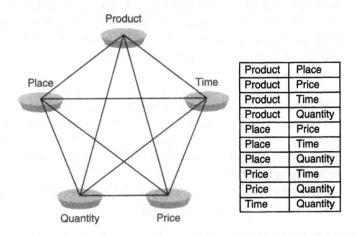

Product	Place
Product	Price
Product	Time
Product	Quantity
Place	Price
Place	Time
Place	Quantity
Price	Time
Price	Quantity
Time	Quantity

Figure 6.16   P³TQ system.

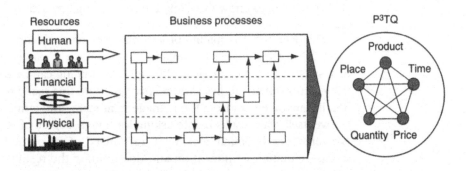

Figure 6.17   Structuring the P³TQ system.

right quantity at the right time, and so on. Considered pairwise, there are 10 crucial relationships that are of vital concern to any company, which are shown graphically in Figure 6.16. It is in these relationships that the first project is likely to be found. (Naturally, this whole section assumes that there isn't an already identified problem, and that the "problem" has to be found so as to create a successful data mining project.)

The key, of course, is timely, accurate, and available data. When starting a mining project with data, the first step is to audit the data using P³TQ relationships. For which relationships is the data most timely, accurate, and available? Probably, the data collected will already be used to understand the relationship that it was addressed to. Surprisingly, making a comprehensive audit of all data sets on the criteria of timeliness, accuracy, and availability often reveals data that could be used (but hasn't yet) to understand one or more of these core relationships. Sometimes one or more of the core relationships itself hasn't been explored. In one major industrial company, despite having a major corporate data warehousing initiative and a Six Sigma program, no structured evaluation of these core relationships had been made, and the place/price and place/time relationships had never been explored, even though the data was available in the system.

Every manager's core responsibilities map onto one of three areas: the P³TQ relationships, maintenance of the business processes, or management of corporate resources. However, many senior management responsibilities, and most high visibility projects, all map onto the P³TQ relationships, and this is where to seek a business situation that, when improved, produces a result that gets attention.

The results of the project have to be delivered to managers. Managers need three key clues in determining how to apply their managerial skills:

■ They need to recognize situations that have to be managed.

■ They need to know what actions are available to be taken in those situations.

■ They need to know the likely effect of taking any action.

The data-first data mining project has to deliver value in one of these areas. Discovering actions that managers could take in particular situations is not suitable for a first project. Although data mining can help discover possible actions that can be taken in any situation, this really requires a great deal of involvement from the management team, and a first project has to prove itself with results before asking for a high degree of management involvement and commitment (read "resources"). One of the two remaining areas—situation identification and determining the results of actions—is where the first project should seek to deliver value.

Many management decisions are made based on "forecasts." Within the framework discussed here, forecasts are used by managers as a situation recognition tool. Forecasts are not predictions; they are possible future outcomes based on some set of assumptions. The question that a forecast attempts to answer is: "What is the most likely outcome for x under conditions y." The symbol x could be sales and the symbol y could be current economic circumstances and corporate policies. Or x could be production in units this month and y could be the current level of labor and staffing. Whatever else a forecast does, it provides a linkage between one circumstance (x) and another circumstance (y). What links x and y is an (assumed) connecting relationship. Where there is accurate, relevant, and available data, data mining is a good candidate for producing accurate and timely forecasts. The forecasts that will get the most attention are those that address the P^3TQ relationships.

If the available data doesn't support forecasts that directly address the P^3TQ relationships, look for projects that are as close to these core relationships as possible. For example, the supply chain of a company focuses on four of the five core relationships: primarily product, time, and quantity, with a secondary focus on price. Since this touches on so many of the core P^3TQ relationships, this is a good secondary place to look for a valuable first project. Or again, Customer Relationship Management (CRM) touches all five core P^3TQ relationships, and again offers excellent opportunities.

6.5.3   Initial Project Size

The final question to address is the scale of the initial project. Your objective is to have a successful project. Success requires that the results are noticeable, that the project uses data already available, that it is of a suitable scale, and that it isn't too innovative. Why are these important?

Success requires noticeability so that the results can be used as a reference within the company to garner further support. It also has to be noticeable so that other managers not initially involved become aware that the project has produced useful results. This will, hopefully, motivate them to discover how business modeling and data mining can help them, too.

That the data has to be available is actually an assumption of this project. The whole project described in this section is based on the question "What can data mining do that is of value with our current data?" However, historical data stored in a warehouse may not serve the purpose. Such data describes history, and there is no guarantee that the present is now similar to the past represented in the collected data. *The best place to look is in current data streams,* because these are often more easily diverted for the project than attempting to modify the existing procedures for maintaining a large corporate warehouse.

The scale of the project is crucial. It has to be large enough to make a difference, but not too much of a difference. Deployment is going to require changing a business process in the company. This means, ultimately, that people will have to behave differently somewhere in the company. Since this is a first project of (what is to the company) an untried technology, the least change that the project requires for deployment, the better. The less change is required, the more likely it is to be implemented—and without implementation, and cooperative implementation at that, there will be no success.

The reasoning for the level of innovation is similar to the reason for keeping the scale manageable. People are willing to do more of the same, and often to try something slightly different, but if the project requires something really innovative, again, it's not likely to generate the necessary support among the beneficiary stakeholders.

6.6 Summary

Discovering the right model to fit a business situation is neither straightforward nor easy. It is a difficult process that requires experience, insight, and judgment. This chapter has provided many pointers to the issues that are involved. Discovering the problem to address involves talking to the right people (the stakeholders), in the right way (by asking open-ended questions). Using an appropriate metaphor, one that seems intuitive and relevant to the modeler and the stakeholders, create a cognitive map, and perhaps a cognitive model of the situation. Look for the key relationships, perhaps using cognitive model simulation as a tool to illuminate the situation. With the problem defined, create a business case for the project that appeals to the business managers whose support for any project is vital.

This is an appropriate process for discovering the right model when business modeling and data mining are used as tools for solving a problem, for improving a business process, or for supporting decision making in a corporate setting. Unfortunately, it's no help if the business problem starts with data already collected. Then the business problem is to find an opportunity to successfully apply business modeling and, most particularly, data mining in an effective way. Finding the initial problem that the data addresses requires a close focus on the core P3TQ relationships and how the data represents them, especially those relationships that are represented in the data but that have not been explored as deeply as the data suggests they might be.

The guidelines in this chapter will allow any business modeler, or data miner, to successfully discover the right model. But before modeling begins, it's equally important to be sure that the process used will get the model right—and that is the subject of the next chapter.

Chapter 7
Getting the Model Right

Discovering the structure and requirements that determine the right model forms only half the battle—the half that was fought in the last chapter (and to some extent in Chapter 5). Once that is discovered, there still remains the business of determining how to create the model so that it accurately represents the business situation—in other words, how to get the model right. That is the purpose of this chapter: to provide a modeler with the necessary guidelines to make sure that whatever model has been designed actually addresses the identified problem.

The material covered in this chapter forms a bridge between the business issues that were the focus of the last chapter and the technical issues of mining, which are covered in Part III. The business and technical issues first start to come together in this chapter. Some of these topics are fairly technical and seem highly data-related. However, the book is designed to, in the main, include business issues and modeling issues in Part II, and technical and mining issues in Part III. Technical as this chapter may seem to be in parts, these topics are covered here because every one of them requires information from the business problem in order to resolve the modeling, mining, or data issues.

7.1 Finding Data to Mine

There are only three sources of data:

1. Data obtained from outside the organization
2. Data on hand
3. Data developed specifically for the project

These three types of data differ from each other in many ways, but they share a number of common characteristics. This section looks, in part, at how data, regardless of its source, can be used in data mining to support the business model.

Clearly it is possible to create business models only from indirect data (i.e., the opinions of various stakeholders). Such models may be invaluable as expressions of opinion, but without empirical data to support them they remain exactly that, opinion. The ancient Greeks had many opinions about the nature of the world, but they much preferred logical thinking as opposed to evaluating what actually happened around them. It took Roger Bacon and his *New Organon* to displace this notion. The essential message that he delivered was, "Look at the evidence!" Evidence is, of course, data, and the valid evaluation of data is the only way to confirm (or deny) opinion as a representation of the world. But data is dangerous stuff! The facts may not lie, but they may not be either complete or relevant, and it's not always obvious that this is so. This section also looks at the various issues that are involved in finding data to mine (but see also Chapter 9 in Part III for more technical details for checking the value and suitability of data for mining).

7.1.1 External Data

Numerous companies offer many kinds of data for purchase. Axciom, for instance, offers a large data set containing geographic and demographic information, consisting of many hundreds of variables that include all kinds of lifestyle attributes. Credit agencies offer data on personal credit status and credit usage. Census information is available from the federal government. And this covers only the type of data that describes individual consumers. Data sets are also available about corporations and their activities—not just financial market information, but everything from environmental pollution records to advertising and marketing practices. Almost all of the financial markets produce reams of data, and there is also available meteorological data, sun spot data, oceanic condition data, agricultural data, economic data, manufacturing data, and a bewildering array of government data. For a price, it seems almost everything can be known and data found to describe it. However, this isn't quite so.

Although such data is publicly available, the fact that it is publicly available makes it of limited competitive value. After all, data that is available to everyone is, at least in principle, knowable by everyone, and common knowledge doesn't lead to competitive advantage. Where it is of immense value is for specific, although noncompetitive, purposes—identifying telemarketing or direct mail prospects, for instance, or screening bad credit risks, both personal and corporate.

It is possible to develop competitively advantageous data from public sources, but this requires care and insight. The "barriers to entry" are mainly financial. In other words, a company has to be willing to keep buying data well over and above the generally available data that is available to its competitors. It's possible, but expensive, and requires particular selection and insight into what is useful before beginning such a project. The keys here seem to be "possible" and "expensive."

However, nonpublic data developed by a company from its own resources is its most valuable resource. Adding external data to, and combining it with, internally generated data may well make both far more valuable for mining purposes. For instance, a company usually knows its customers. When this is the case, that data, augmented by (in the case of consumers) their socio- and demographic information, contributes to a much better understanding of the customers and, in principle, a better determination of their motivations.

Sometimes external data, particularly survey data, is incomplete. In this case, the corporate data and the external data may overlap more or less, but not entirely. Fusing these data sets together so that they combine to form a single mineable data set is a tricky problem. But this problem of fusing data sets can happen with internally created data sets, too. The issues and possible solutions are discussed later in Section 7.2.2.

7.1.2 Existing Data

Company-generated data can be a blessing and a curse. It has almost certainly been collected at great expense, and was collected to address particular business needs. However, whether those business needs are relevant to the model that now has to be built is a different issue. Yet there is often some pressure on a miner to use the data that is available. So far as the miner is concerned, this data should be evaluated exactly as if it were external data— that is, it needs to be assessed for relevance, not simply used because it is available. (Guidelines for determining relevance are described throughout the chapter, but see Section 7.2.)

Internal data can be enormously important since it is data that, very largely, is available only to that company. This data contains at least the seeds of the relationships needed for a company to gain a competitive advantage. However, much data may be collected, but not all of it is usefully maintained. Data warehouses sometimes maintain the current state, for instance, but don't maintain the changes that occur over time, which is necessary for some models. This is particularly true when the model outlined through the process described in this book addresses a new area of interest, a new problem, a new strategic situation, a new market, a new product, or the introduction of new tactics. Then the existing data simply doesn't bear on the issue at hand.

Alternatively, the data may appear to bear on the issue, but in fact turn out to be historical data. "Surely," the astute reader may ask at this point, "since all data is necessarily from the past, isn't it all historical?" In that sense, yes. However, the term *historical* as applied to data has a slightly different connotation. Imagine, for instance, an assembly line that is producing hard disk drives. Suppose that the disk drives for some reason have a higher failure rate than is expected or acceptable. Data from the manufacturing process—from the assembly line—can be used to determine whether there is a problem. But having discovered the problem, the assembly line is then modified to correct the problem. What of the state of the data? Any data that describes the process before the process changed is now historical data—it is no longer relevant to the current (changed) process.

In this case, the generating process for data has been deliberately altered in the real world. The old data doesn't describe the current process and is thus of limited value. Changes do occur in data-generating processes. When the generating process changes, it is highly likely that the nature of the data that the process generates changes, too. (Strictly speaking, if the process changes the data has to change as well since that is the only way to recognize that the process has changed. However, just because a process changes doesn't necessarily imply that the collected data changes; perhaps the changes occur only in data that isn't collected.)

The nature of any data is reflected in its distribution—literally a description of the way that the values occur. The so-called normal distribution with its well-known bell curve is one such description. Changing data-generating processes that produce changing distributions of the values that they generate are said to have *nonstationary distributions*. Processes generating nonstationary distributions are one reason that current data turns into historical data over time. For several reasons, the miner must determine the "shelf life" of data—how long it remains a viable resource for model creation. In other words, when does "current" data become "history"? Examining data distributions from different periods will reveal when the distribution changes or, in other words, point to when data becomes "historical."

7.1.3 Purpose-Developed Data

Data developed to specifically support model creation is far and away the most useful. On the other hand, it's always the most expensive to produce, since procedures and processes to create and capture the data have to be created, often from scratch. Also, there's an inevitable delay in creating the model since sufficient data first has to be accumulated. If timing is important—perhaps to capture a business opportunity before it disappears—purpose-developed data, however welcome it might be if it were available, simply isn't an option. But with foresight, data can be developed ahead of time. However, such data needs to be collected to address unknown future needs, and because they are unknown, what is needed is a method for determining what—in principle—will be useful information in future business situations. And that is a task that can be attempted.

Two very useful tools can be used to help determine what data needs to be collected for specific modeling purposes: *business process mapping* and *cause and effect mapping*. The next several sections discuss business processes and business process mapping in some detail since this is a very important topic for the modeler. Cause and effect mapping is discussed in Section 7.1.3.6 and is introduced there.

Everything that a business does can be represented as a business process—everything. Some processes, such as recruiting a new CEO, are executed infrequently by a company, and generate relatively little data; thus, they are unsuitable candidates as processes to generate business data for mining. Most business processes, and certainly a company's core activity processes, execute frequently and are a great place to look for purpose-developed data. Furthermore, all business processes have similar general features in common, just as systems diagrams have. In fact, of course, a business process map is just a special type of systems diagram.

Understanding the business processes in terms of their role in the system that forms the company very often leads to insights about what data will be useful to have for future modeling. The next section dives into a quick look at business processes. The objective is to look at business process mapping as a method of identifying which data to collect. This requires a brief look not only at process mapping as an activity, but also at the way that management interacts with business processes. Remember that the purpose of collecting data, mining it, and characterizing the model's relationships is to provide managers with insight, control, and the information to make appropriate business decisions. So this brief look has to connect what managers want to do in order to manage business processes with the nature of the processes themselves, since what managers want to do and to know are the purpose for creating the models. The intent of the next section is to provide enough understanding of management needs, as mapped into process maps, to understand what data is required and what needs to be modeled to meet management needs.

7.1.3.1 Mapping Business Processes

Business processes are what a company is built from, and everything that a company does can be represented as a business process. Finding new markets is a business process, as are developing new products, servicing customer complaints, acquiring other companies, opening a new division, managing the supply chain, creating marketing support materials, creating corporate communications, performing market research, and every other activity that any company engages in. Even the task for which data mining is often used—as a low-level, tactical tool for customer segmentation—is part of a business process. Far better data and models result from looking at the process as a whole rather than considering it as a task isolated from the processes of the company.

The architecture of a business process is built out of the same components familiar from the earlier systems discussion, but here the system elements are made more specific to business. They are:

- Inputs and outputs
- Flows (in flow units)
- Networks of interconnected activities
- Resources
- Information flow structure

The accepted technique for mapping business processes starts with developing a high-level structure and working down toward the details. It is important to maintain a fairly uniform level of detail at each stage of the map so that, at any stage, the map doesn't have far more details in some areas than others.

Figure 7.1 shows the initial and highest possible level of a business process diagram. To view a business organization in terms of its processes, first identify the inputs, the outputs, and the entry and exit points that define the process boundaries.

Any business process is intended to represent work, and work is only done (in business process terms) by individuals or groups of people. Consider as an example the corporate recruiting process illustrated in Figure 7.2. This shows the flow of a hiring request (from the time some other process determined the need and approved the request) through a number of subprocesses, and value is added at each stage until this process delivers qualified candidates as its output. The subprocesses here might be defined (in the subprocess boxes from left to right, or top to bottom, in each functional division) as:

- *Administrative assistant:* 1) log hiring request, 2) identify relevant recruiter specialty and send request, 3) pass qualified candidate résumés to requesting department.

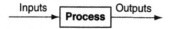

Figure 7.1   Simplest possible process map.

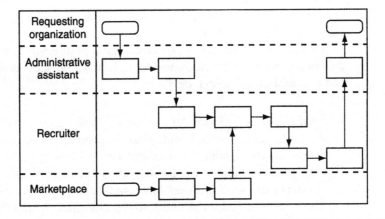

Figure 7.2   Process map sketching a recruiting process.

- *Recruiter:* 1) receive and log hiring request, 2) search database of applicants for suitable candidates, 3) manually screen résumés, 4) conduct initial phone interview, 5) select candidate short list.
- *Marketplace:* Candidate 1) notices vacancy, 2) submits résumé.

Perhaps the most important feature of process diagrams is that the processes' customers are clearly identified. Indeed, in many ways it is the customers of a process—those who get the value from it—who define the boundaries of the process.

The process map illustrated in Figure 7.2 is not yet complete. So far it has identified only the inputs and outputs, and begun to sketch the activity network. The most notable feature missing is the information flow structure. One set of information flows through the process; indeed, it is integral with the process. In the example shown, the process-integral information, for instance, indicates which position is to be filled, the range of salary offered, and so on. But these are inputs to the process, and an integral part of the process in this example. The information flow structure referred to earlier is the information that is separate from the process itself, but is required to manage it. Often the information flow structure is in the opposite direction to the process flow. So, for instance, information has to flow "backwards" or "upstream" from the recruiters to the administrative assistant about the recruiter's particular areas of expertise so the administrative assistant can direct the hiring request to the appropriate recruiter. There are also other significant information flows here. Perhaps the recruiters pass information to each other about the state of the marketplace. In addition, there are managerial information flows that are, at least formally, responsible for organizing, maintaining, and directing the process. Although not shown in the figure, all of these flows are important. In analyzing and understanding the process, they are crucial. However, in finding data to mine, the process map as shown provides a good place to start.

Business processes serve their customers, and the result of a process is to deliver a product to the customer. A product is a business object, of course, and has attributes that include:

- *Product value:* Includes the product cost and comprises the total cost to the customer for owning and using the product. In the example shown, the product is "qualified job candidates," and every part of the corporation has to contribute to maintaining the recruiting process. However, cost also includes losses incurred if the candidate should prove inappropriate. The benefit includes the return to the customers from filling empty job positions with qualified candidates.

- *Product delivery response time:* The time it takes to deliver a product from the initiation of the process. In the example, it is the time to recruit.

- *Product variety:* The range and limits to the product that the process can deliver. In the example, the recruiters may recruit all staff except temporary help and senior management positions.

- *Product quality:* Definitions of this are subject to much debate. In fact, R. M. Pirsig in *Zen and the Art of Motorcycle Maintenance* expressed the opinion that, "Quality is recognized by a non-thinking process, and therefore cannot be defined." However, in this case, "quality" indicates the fitness for purpose of the product. In the example, some qualified candidates suit the available employment opening better than others. High quality products in this example would be defined as all of the candidates who were highly suitable for the openings available.

Just as with the produced product, the process itself has attributes, including process cost, flow time, flexibility, and quality. Determining how well the business process meets its needs requires measuring the process customer's perceptions of the appropriate attributes.

The key places to collect data about a business process are where the information flow crosses functional boundaries. Figure 7.3 shows a process map for restaurant service. In this diagram, the measurement points are indicated as the places where the subprocesses pass the flow from one functional area to another. These are the important points to measure because they represent the important transition stages in the process, and it is their performance that reveals and characterizes the important relationships in the process.

The business process sketched for restaurant service in the figure illustrates several features of a business process map. Horizontal bands across the map indicate functional areas of business activity. Solid boxes show required

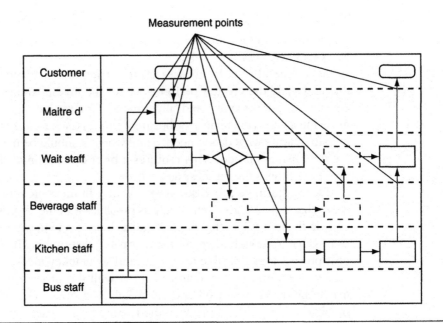

Figure 7.3   Process map suggesting data collection points.

subprocesses (each of which could itself be fully characterized as a business process). Dashed boxes show optional subprocesses. Generally, the process flows from top to bottom and left to right, but in business process maps, clearly marked flow arrows often flow in the opposite direction. Different information flows are not shown here, but could be distinguished by different colors or styles.

All business process maps tell a story. For the sketch in Figure 7.3, it starts with the bus staff preparing the table and telling the maitre d' of table availability. A customer arrives (the left-hand oval shows flow units coming from outside the process map), which prompts the maitre d' to seat the customer. Wait staff take a food order and determine whether the customer wants to place a drinks order (the diamond symbol). If so, the beverage order is taken, the beverage prepared, and the beverage delivered (the three dashed boxes). The wait staff take the food order and pass it to the kitchen staff. The kitchen staff take the order, prepare the food, and assemble the serving (three boxes). The serving is delivered by the wait staff to the customer.

Naturally, this is a sketch, but it serves to show the main features of a business process map. The important events in this map occur where the flow units pass from subprocess to subprocess. In this sketch, for instance, some of the events include when customers arrive, number and type of customers seated, type of food ordered, and so on. Note that each event includes a date and timestamp (to determine response time, flow rates, and so on), as well as context information measuring the product's value, variety, and quality at each transition.

As a general rule, businesses try to design and manage processes so that they yield the greatest performance for the investment. However, what constitutes "performance" and "investment" for a business process is not always the same. This review of business processes is to discover how they help to indicate what data is needed and where it should be measured to create the business model. This requires a brief discussion of how business processes fit into the business as a whole.

Ideally, business processes are tailored to fit their circumstances so that they achieve their ends as efficiently as possible—in other words, so that they convert the inputs into the outputs with as little loss to unwanted side effects as possible. Although there are many ways of determining how well a business process uses available resources (and several key measures will be discussed shortly), one key feature is how well the process is organized to match the demands placed upon it. Ideally, a process should be exactly as flexible as is needed to produce the required responses, and no more so. Figure 7.4 illustrates how process flexibility and product variety need to match. The dark diagonal band shows where the process flexibility matches the required product variety. The light areas at top left and bottom right show where there is a mismatch.

The lower left portion of Figure 7.4 shows where a low variety/low flexibility process is needed. Imagine a process for making sausages, a continuous flow process with constant inputs and constant outputs. No great variety is required in the product (sausages) and additional flexibility is never demanded

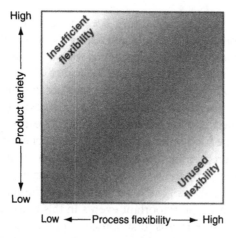

Figure 7.4   Process flexibility versus product variety.

of this process. The top right shows where high variety/high flexibility processes are required; for example, a custom printer who has to be able to produce very small quantities of very different printed products. This diagonal represents processes that are well suited to the demands placed on them.

The top left and bottom right, on the other hand, represent processes that are not well matched to the need. The top left shows a situation in which the process has insufficient flexibility. Perhaps, in addition to plain paper printing, which it can perform, a printer is required to print business cards and cardboard boxes, but has no presses that can do so. Meeting these needs requires additional resources and costs. The lower right shows a situation in which the process has surplus flexibility. The sausage maker, perhaps, has ice cream makers and cake mixers that are never used—the customers require only sausages. This represents unused resources, or lost opportunities.

7.1.3.2   Data from Process Flows

Processes use the flow metaphor; and since the type of data captured needs to characterize the process flows, this calls for a slightly more detailed look at exactly how such a metaphor is used. This detailed look is also important because the actions that managers take are actions that deliberately start, stop, or modify business processes. The managerial levers, knobs, dials, and switches connect to the process flows, and managerial control is a part of the information flow structure. Managerial actions are intended to have specific effects on corporate behaviors, and this is where understanding the precise nature of the relationships involved, and the confidence in the effects of specific interventions, becomes very important. This is close to the heart of what managers want out of business modeling—and mining data can only deliver if it's the right data that's mined.

There are three crucial pieces of data to capture: *time, event,* and *context*. These associated items of data are the molecules or droplets that form the process flows. Since management attempts to manage process flows, it's important to measure appropriate flow attributes. The first measurement definition needed is to determine what it is that flows, and to establish appropriate units. This could be number of cars, tons of steel, emails received, customers served, complaints closed, calls made, candidates delivered, prospects converted, or whatever is the appropriate unit of interest. But flow happens in time—cars per minute, tons per hour, emails per second, and so on.

Measures start with what is flowing, and the time at which one unit flowed. Remember that these flow units do not exist in isolation, not even at the point of flow, and the context has to be captured, too. The context is represented by the relevant information flow structure attributes. So, to return to Figure 7.3 for a moment, the maitre d' seats a customer at a particular time (an event), and passes the customer on to the wait staff (an event). However, the type of event and the time aren't enough data here. It's necessary to know at least at which table the customer is seated, and perhaps which waiter is assigned. Notice that the maitre d' needs to have the "upstream" information flow (i.e., which tables are empty) in order to make an appropriate selection.

Capturing this data leads to quickly discovering the basic relationships for this flow point:

- Average, maximum, and minimum number of units per unit of time
- Average, maximum, and minimum dwell period (how long a unit spends in a subprocess)
- Average, maximum, and minimum inventory per period (how many units are within the process boundaries at any one time)

This basic data of a time-stamped, identified flow unit event, along with the necessary contextual information, is the crucial business process information to collect. From this can be inferred stimulus, context, and event relationships. With this data in hand, a miner can conquer the world! Well, perhaps not—but the miner at least can create powerful and relevant business models. However, there is one other crucial item of data to collect. As Figure 7.5 shows, each function consumes resources—financial, human, and physical. These also flow into the process and are consumed as "energy" that drives the process to produce its flow. These process drivers can also be characterized as just described, and their flows recorded.

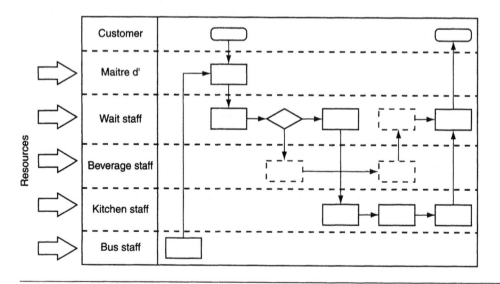

Figure 7.5   Business processes convert resources into process products.

The basic questions that need answering to characterize a business process are:

- Who are the customers for the process?
- What is the value that the customers receive from the process?
- What is the input to the process?
- What is the output from the process?
- What are the subprocesses?
- What starts each subprocess?
- What flows into each subprocess?
- Where does the flow to a subprocess originate?
- Where does the flow from a subprocess go?
- What information does the subprocess need to operate?
- Where does the needed information for the subprocess originate?
- What information does the subprocess generate?
- Where does the subprocess send its information?
- What resources does the subprocess consume?

Answering these questions characterizes the nature of the important flows: the product flow, the information flow, and the resource flow.

7.1.3.3 Data About What?

(See MII:TB.14) Managing a company requires managers to use five different types of process manipulation. They aren't necessarily all used at the same time, but they represent between them all of the knobs, levers, and switches that managers use. For convenience, call them all "levers." The five types of levers are for managing:

- Flow time
- Flow capacity
- Waiting time
- Process variability
- Process efficiency

Every business activity can be characterized as a business process, so managing these five process attributes is common to all business endeavors. A business process map shows where to get relevant data, but not exactly what process topics the data should address. Table 7.1 is a modified summary of these basic process management techniques, the first four levers of which are adapted from *Managing Business Process Flows*. (See the "Resources" section at the end of the book for details.) Naturally, the precise details of the data to be collected change depending on the nature of the process, but the table shows the management levers used to control all processes, and where data mined models offer great value.

TABLE 7.1 Business Process Management Levers

Business Process Levers	Applicable Data Mining Technique(s)	Note
Management Levers for Flow Time		
1. Reduce or eliminate work on the critical path.		
▪ Remove elements that add no value to the process (work smarter).	Context model	1
▪ Reduce the time for completion of each activity (work faster). ◆ Use faster automation. ◆ Use multiple machines for parallel flow. ◆ Provide or increase incentives for faster completion.	Context model Forecast model Check model	2
▪ Redesign or streamline processes and sub-processes to remove repetitive activities.		
▪ Redesign the product mix to reduce the total amount of work content for the specific activity required.		
2. Remove tasks from the critical path.		
▪ Restructure processes and subprocesses so that work is removed from the critical path and performed on a non-critical path.		
▪ Remove work from the critical path so that it is done outside the process (in pre- or post-processing activities).		
Management Levers for Flow Capacity		
1. Decrease the unit load on a bottleneck resource.		

TABLE 7.1   Continued

Business Process Levers	Applicable Data Mining Technique(s)	Note
■ Reduce the amount of work needed by a limited process resource (a bottleneck resource) by: ◆ Working harder. ◆ Working faster. ◆ Reducing error rate and rework (variability). ◆ Redesigning the produce mix to reduce the work required.		
■ Reassign some tasks to a less limited process resource.		
■ Increase the availability of flexible resources to share the workload.		
2. Add processing capacity at the bottleneck resource (increase scale of resource).	Relationship model	3
3. Lengthen the time the bottleneck resource is available (work longer).		
4. Add subprocesses that perform the bottleneck resource activity (increase scale of process).		
Management Levers for Waiting Time		
1. Decrease number of units in cycle inventory.		
■ Decrease batch setup or batch order costs.	Context model	4
■ Decrease number of units bought in anticipation of need (forward buying).	Forecast model	5
2. Decrease number of units in safety inventory.		
■ Anticipate actual demand and reduce demand variability using better forecasts.	Forecast model Check model	6
■ Decrease supply lead-time (get closer to just-in-time deliveries).		
■ Decrease variability in supply lead-time.	Context model Relationship model	7
■ Improve logistics: ◆ Consolidate safety inventory so that one store location serves multiple locations or products. ◆ Centralize inventory storage.	Context model Forecast model Check model	8

continued

TABLE 7.1 Continued

Business Process Levers	Applicable Data Mining Technique(s)	Note
◆ Specialize inventory storage. ◆ Optimize delivery schedules/distances/routes.		
■ Substitute one product for another where possible to reduce the overall product diversity.		
■ Redesign to use common components.		
■ Move product differentiation nearer to the point of demand.		
3. Control and adjust safety capacity.		
■ Add safety capacity.	Forecast model	9
■ Reduce and control variability of arrivals and service.	Context model Relationship model	10
■ Create a common safety capacity resource for shared use.		
4. Manage and adjust flows to match supply and demand.		
■ Synchronize capacity with demand.	Context model Forecast model	11
■ Synchronize demand with available capacity.	Context model Forecast model	12
■ Synchronize inter- and intra-process flows.	Context model Relationship model Check model	13
5. Manage customer perceptions to reduce waiting costs.	Context model	14
Management Levers for Process Variability		
1. Identify key performance variables and characterize their variability.	Context model Check model	15
2. Create and establish variability controls for the key performance variables.		

TABLE 7.1 Continued

Business Process Levers	Applicable Data Mining Technique(s)	Note
■ Determine acceptable variability for key process variables. (Use a rational structured process such as, for instance, a Six Sigma program.)	Relationship model	16
■ Control key process variable variability.	Check model	17
3. Reduce existing process variability.		
■ Simplify processes to have fewest "moving parts". ■ Standardize processes, subprocesses and product components. ■ Create control barriers to prevent known modes of failure and variance (make fool- and mistake-proof in so far as possible).	Context model Forecast model	18
4. Establish, standardize, and use best practices to minimize the impact of unavoidable process and product variability.	Context model Relationship model Forecast model	19
Management Levers for Process Efficiency		
1. Decrease human resource requirements.		
■ Reduce number of people required to complete a process or subprocess.	Context model Forecast model	20
■ Reduce the skills needed.	Relationship model	21
■ Reduce training required.	Forecast model Context model	22
■ Increase use of individual flexibility and skills.		
■ Select personnel most fitted to the task required.	Forecast model	23
■ Select tasks most fitted to the personnel available.	Forecast model	24
■ Reduce required maintenance (non-process-related) staff activities.		
■ Increase motivational feedback.	Context model Relationship model Check model	25

continued

TABLE 7.1   Continued

Business Process Levers	Applicable Data Mining Technique(s)	Note
▪ Reduce burnout factors.	Context model	26
▪ Facilitate information flows.		
2. Decrease financial resource requirements.	Context model Relationship model Forecast model	27
3. Decrease physical resource requirements.	Relationship model	28
4. Adjust the process flow rate to the most cost effective flow rate for the process.	Relationship model	29
5. Adjust the process size to most cost effectively match the flow rate.	Relationship model	30
6. Reconfigure processes to reduce the cost of inter-process flow unit transportation.	Context model Forecast model	31
7. Reconfigure subprocesses to reduce the cost of intra-process flow unit transportation.	Context model Forecast model	32
8. Reduce variability of incoming flow units.		
9. Reduce and remove process failure modes.		
▪ Create and monitor control barriers.	Check model	33
▪ Develop and monitor adaptive action process modifications and triggers.	Check model	34
▪ Develop and monitor corrective action process modifications and triggers.	Check model	35
10. Decrease variability of response to management levers.	Context model Relationship model	36
11. Align the available process flexibility with required product variety.		
▪ Remove or add flexibility in the process to the level required by product variety.		
▪ Remove or add variety to the product produced by the process to best use the flexibility in the process.		

Table 7.1 identifies 26 principal management levers for managing processes in the column titled "Business Process Levers." The needed data has to address these specific issues. The column titled "Applicable Data Mining Technique(s)" contains one or more of four types of data mining models that may be useful for characterizing the specific lever. Table 7.2 gives a brief description of each of these four types of models, along with notes about use and construction. (Full details and a comprehensive methodology for actually mining such models is provided in Parts III and IV.) Table 7.3 contains brief notes about what issues each type of model might address for each lever.

TABLE 7.2   Description, Use, and Construction of Business Lever Model Types

Model	Description, Use, and Construction	Notes
Context model	■ An inferential or explanatory model that discovers the features in the environmental context that are important. ■ Used to discover what factors (variables) are important and what features (single values or ranges of values) are important. ■ Constructed using supervised and unsupervised techniques such as SOMs (self-organizing maps) and CHAID (chi squared automatic interaction detection) trees. (See Chapter 10.)	1, 2, 4, 7, 8 10, 11, 12, 13, 14, 15, 18, 19, 20, 22, 25, 26, 27, 31, 32, 36
Check model	■ A predictive (classification) model producing outputs from as near to real-time data as possible. ■ Used to compare the actual current situation to the expected situation to check that business processes have not drifted out of their expected range of performance (that is, they remain calibrated). ■ Constructed using linear and nonlinear predictive (classification) modeling techniques, such as decision trees, neural networks, and linear and nonlinear regression. (See Chapter 10.)	2, 6, 8, 13, 15, 17, 25, 33, 34, 35
Forestcast model	■ A predictive (classification) model. ■ Used to indicate potential outcomes and confidence limits of the outcomes in hypothetical business scenarios that imply changed circumstances for the business process. ■ Constructed using linear and nonlinear predictive (classification) modeling techniques, such as decision trees, neural networks, and linear and nonlinear regression. (See Chapter 10.)	2, 5, 6, 8, 9, 11, 12, 18, 19, 20, 22, 23, 24, 27, 31, 32

continued

TABLE 7.2 Continued

Model	Description, Use, and Construction	Notes
Relationship model	■ A predictive (classification) model. ■ Used to explicate the relationship between one or more input variables and one or more output variables. Explication requires characterizing both the output value(s) associated with a particular input pattern(s) and the confidence with which the output value(s) is expected to occur, as well as the confidence with which any alternative value(s) is expected to occur. ■ Constructed using linear and nonlinear predictive (classification) modeling techniques, such as decision trees, neural networks, and linear and nonlinear regression. (See Chapter 10.)	3, 7, 10, 13, 16, 19, 21, 25, 27, 28, 29, 30, 36

TABLE 7.3 Notes on Use of the Four Model Types

Note	Sketch Description of Use
	Data mined models aren't equally applicable to all business process levers. Where there is no note and no model type shown, data mining techniques have not yet had much application.
1	Use a context model to discover which variables and features contribute most to value, and which have negative value.
2	Use a context model to discover which variables and features are the most motivating. Use a forecast model to project the most effective incentive structure. Use a check model to monitor that the incentive structure continues to operate as expected.
3	Use a relationship model to characterize the relationship between batch size and performance of the bottleneck resource.
4	Use a context model to discover variables and features affecting batch setup and order costs. Using data mining tools to audit purchasing data for inconsistencies can provide a firm basis for rationalizing corporate purchasing, leading to very significant cost savings.
5	Use a forecast model to create projections for forward buying that are closer to actual need. Forward buying attempts to ensure sufficient flow-unit supply to cover forecast error variability. Reducing forecast error variability reduces the quantity of forward purchasing needed.
6	Use a forecast model—same rationale as in note 5. Use a check model to monitor forecast performance. Adequate safety inventory is very important not only to the efficiency of the process, but also possibly to accomplish primary business objectives. A check model provides early warning to managers that additional management actions may be needed.
7	Use a context model to discover variables and features affecting replenishment lead time. Use a relationship model to characterize the relationship between the controllable environmental variables and features and replenishment time.

TABLE 7.3 Continued

Note	Sketch Description of Use
8	Use a context model to discover variables and features affecting logistical issues.
	Use a forecast model to explore different distribution scenarios.
	Use a check model to monitor performance and as an early warning tool.
	Context and relationship models also can be used in this lever as a discovery mechanism to support other modeling techniques such as linear programming. (This technique is highly applicable in this lever, but is not a data mining technique, and so is not covered in this book.)
9	Use a forecast model to create projections to estimate the required safety capacity.
10	Use a context model to discover environmental variables and features affecting scheduled arrivals and service.
	Use a relationship model to characterize the relationship between the environmental variables and features and actual arrivals and service.
11	(This lever presupposes that actual demand is known in advance.)
	Use a context model to discover environmental variables and features affecting capacity.
	Use a forecast model to forecast the needed capacity for the anticipated demand.
12	(This lever presupposes that demand is a manageable variable, but that process capacity is variable.)
	Use a context model to discover environmental variables and features affecting demand.
	Use a forecast model to forecast the needed level of demand for the anticipated capacity available.
13	Use a context model to discover variables and features affecting all process flows.
	Use many relationship models to characterize the inter- and intra-process flows. Use the characterized relationships in a process model to optimize process flows.
	Use check models to monitor process flow synchronization and performance. Deviation outside expected variability limits is an early warning flag that management intervention is needed.
14	Use a context model to discover important psychological variables and features affecting customer perceptions.
	(Such models are typically the result of market surveys, focus groups, and other instruments that yield data about only a fraction of the customer base. Different surveys may yield important data about different parts of the customer base. Producing models from such data often requires extensive and careful data fusion before valid results can be achieved.)
15	Use a context model to discover the key performance variables.
	Use one or more check models, as appropriate, to provide early warning of significant changes in overall process performance.
16	Use a relationship model to characterize the relationships over their normal range of performance. (This coordinates with note 17.)
17	Use a check model to monitor process behavior and give early warning that abnormal variability may be imminent, or is actually happening.
18	Use a context model to discover variables and features indicating potential process failure modes.

continued

TABLE 7.3 Continued

Note	Sketch Description of Use
	Use a context model to discover environmental variables and features affecting the effectiveness of extant control barriers.
	Use a forecast model to estimate the effect and outcome of different scenarios of potential failure conditions.
19	Use a context model to discover variables and features that have an important impact on process performance.
	Use a relationship model to characterize the relationships that have a significant impact on performance.
	Use a forecast model to evaluate a variety of scenarios and discover potential failure modes.
20	Use a context model to discover variables and features that characterize the relationship between staffing levels and process performance for all processes.
	Use a forecast model to explore process performance under various staffing levels and distributions.
	(This is also an excellent application for system simulation, in the form of process simulation in this case, to use the results of a relationship model.)
21	Use a relationship model to characterize the relationship between specific skills and process performance. (It may be possible to dispense with skills that have little or no impact. Unused available skills represent unused flexibility in the process. See Figure 7.4.)
22	Use a forecast model to explore process performance under different training regimens.
	Use a context model to discover which training features have the most significant impact on process performance.
23	Use a forecast model to discover a suitable employment scenario for an employee.
24	Use a forecast model to discover which task(s) should be assigned to which employees.
25	Use a context model to discover motivational variables and features that have the highest levels of impact on employee performance and satisfaction.
	Use a relationship model to characterize the relationship between the incentive profiles and employee performance.
	Use a check model to monitor continuing effectiveness of incentive package configurations on employee performance.
	(These approaches can be applied successfully at the individual level, thus allowing incentives to be tailored to individuals rather than groups of employees. Individual tailoring of motivational packages can produce significantly improved employee response compared to motivational inducements offered to groups of employees.)
26	Use a context model to discover variables and factors that most significantly contribute to employee burnout.
27	Use a context model to discover variables and factors that are indicative of return on investment for each type of investment opportunity.
	Use a relationship model to characterize the relationship between the indicative factors and the return for each investment opportunity. (Note that the variables and factors might vary from opportunity to opportunity.)

TABLE 7.3 Continued

Note	Sketch Description of Use
	Use a forecast model to explore the returns from different investment scenarios.
	(Note that system simulation [process simulation] is also an excellent technique in which to use the discovered relationships.)
	Use context and forecast models to discover which investments have little impact on process performance.
	(Note that there may be some ranges of investment values that have a large impact on process performance, and other ranges that have a very small impact, so the process is one of tuning the financial investment so that it has optimal positive impact on process performance while minimizing negative impact. Also, system simulation may reveal that increasing investment in some areas actually inhibits performance in other areas, so reducing investment in specific patterns may have the effect of increasing process performance and efficiency.)
28	Use a relationship model to characterize the relationship between availability of physical resources and process performance.
29	Use a relationship model to characterize the relationship between process size and inter- and intra-process flows. Adjust the flow rates to achieve most efficient process value-add to the flow units.
	(Optimizing the flows to the resources is an application where system simulation shines, but the simulation needs accurate relationship characterization.)
	(This lever assumes that the process flow rates are controllable and process sizes are relatively fixed.)
30	Use a relationship model to characterize the relationship between process size and inter- and intra-process flows. Adjust the process sizes to achieve most efficient process value-add to the flow units.
	(Optimizing the flows to the resources is an application where system simulation shines, but the simulation needs accurate relationship characterization.)
	(This lever assumes that the process sizes are controllable and the process flow rates are relatively fixed.)
31	Use a context model to discover the most influential variables and factors in reorganizing processes. (These may already be known. For instance, physical distance between processes and associated logistical delays and costs.)
	Use a forecast model to explore various process realignment and reorganization scenarios.
32	Similar notes to note 31, except for subprocesses within a process.
33	Use a check model to monitor control barrier effectiveness and performance and as a management early warning flag of needed management intervention.
	(There are physical and administrative control barriers, which are deliberate barriers to process failure. As an example, physical control barriers for automobile driving are roadside crash barriers and seat belts. Administrative barriers are driver licensing requirements and speed limits.)
34	Use a check model to monitor adaptive action effectiveness and performance and as a management early warning flag of needed management intervention.
	(Adaptive actions are nonroutine changes that are implemented in a business process to temporarily deal with a process failure. As an example, when driving, a flat tire causes the adaptive action of slowing, stopping, and replacing the tire with a temporary replacement.)

continued

TABLE 7.3   Continued

Note	Sketch Description of Use
35	Use a check model to monitor corrective action effectiveness and performance and as a management early warning flag of needed management intervention.
	(Corrective actions are nonroutine actions of a business process that are implemented to correct a process failure. For example, when driving, having the punctured tire repaired corrects the process failure.)
36	Use a context model to discover the variables and features that affect real-world response to management interventions—the levers. (Note that context models should also be used to discover the features that confound the effectiveness of the management levers.)
	Use a relationship model to characterize the relationship between management levers and process response.
	(These models are used to create more effective feedback loops, to use the appropriate context in the appropriate range of effect, and so on.)

To use Table 7.1 and its associated comments in Tables 7.2 and 7.3, consider the business problem and the actions that management wants to or can take to modify the process, and look at the type of model that can fruitfully be mined if the data is available. If there is no data available, refer back to the process map for the project and identify, at the inter-function boundaries, which data will characterize the relationship represented by the management lever.

For instance, the restaurant mentioned earlier may need more customers. It has business processes for attracting customers (such as sales, marketing, and advertising), which are not performing as desired. This might be a problem related to process efficiency—not converting enough of the resources used into customers. Say that the main resource used for generating customers is cash. Check the levers for managing process efficiency. Lever 2 applies to "decrease financial resource requirements." How can this be done? A context model will discover the various factors that are important in that they have a strong relationship with financial efficiency. A relationship model will characterize the relationship of input (cash) and output (customers) for all of the various customer conversion mechanisms (perhaps Yellow Pages, fliers, newspapers, etc.). A forecast model will point to the optimum mix of investments. However, perhaps this still does not have sufficient effect because the customer/noncustomer conversion ratio remains too low. Then perhaps the techniques of process efficiency lever 10, "decrease variability of response to management levers," might be applicable. This might result in making the levers pulled to increase prospect-to-customer conversion rate more effective.

Of course, these techniques cannot achieve improvements beyond what the highest possible business process efficiency allows. There is some maximum conversion rate for turning prospects into customers that the process can accomplish. Then if more customers are still needed, the process needs to be enlarged, or some alternative process developed. However, the tools for mining shown in the table are the tools to make any business process as efficient and effective as it can be.

It is important to note that the information in these tables is not intended to represent all of the techniques that can be used to create, characterize, improve, and operate these levers. The tables are intended to show only where data mining techniques are applicable to establish the management levers shown, in some cases as the primary tool to use, in other cases as a secondary tool. Thus, these tables do not represent all that can be done, but only areas in which data mining has a contribution to make in improving business processes. However, even a quick glance at Table 7.1 should show that data mining has a very broad role to play in improving business processes and in contributing to efficient corporate performance—even though the focus of this section is not how to make these models, but on where to find data and what data to find to create useful mined models.

7.1.3.4 Characterizing Business Processes

(See MII:TB.15) This has been a whirlwind tour of business processes: how they map a business to reveal where to collect time and event data, and what data is important in the business process (time, event, and context). Before examining context data and how to find it, it's important to note that not all business processes are created equal. Some processes are of primary importance to the company; taken together, these can be characterized as the primary process flow of a company. These processes that form the primary process flow of a company, typically, are related to the P^3TQ relationships described in Chapter 6, Section 6.5.2. There are many other processes and flows in a company, but they are all of secondary importance and can be characterized as the secondary process flows. The difference is fairly simple to see in practice. The primary process flow is the one that all other flows support. This is where a company's attention is focused. Secondary process flows are just as important, but far less the continuing focus of attention.

As an example of secondary flows, consider that all companies need to maintain the continuing supply of electricity and have a business process in place to ensure that this is so, even if it amounts to no more than paying the electricity bill. Or as another example, consider telephone service and water supply, not to mention such processes as payroll, training, and vacation management. These are secondary processes, and thus their flows are secondary process flows. It's notable that they all certainly affect the main process flow, especially if they fail.

Significantly, all data collection, aggregation, and storage processes, as well as analysis and business information processes, are secondary processes, not primary processes. In the main, the data that a company collects focuses on its primary process flow. But any data already collected is collected not just to reveal things. All data is collected in a way that, by design, hides important problems. It's worth reiterating the last part of that sentence again. All data is collected in a way that, by design, hides important problems. It has significant implications for mining any already existing data.

Any collected and stored data is structured. Any such structure imposes a predetermined view on the world that is defined by that structure. This predetermined structure is designed to make some things visible, and to make other things invisible. That is its purpose. The most significant problems, however, originate in the invisible areas, for they are unexpected and unwatched. Moreover, even those areas that are thought to be watched frequently are not.

All data originates with people. Even, say, a remote and fully instrumented weather station with not a person anywhere nearby was planned, designed, manufactured, assembled, and placed by people and for the use of people. Yet, as we know only too well, people are fallible and very often, in order to make the system do what they need rather than what the system wants, they do what works for them, not what the system expected or intended them to do—and the system can't tell the difference, and often nor can the data collected say what is wrong. As a single example, one company had equipment maintenance categories such as "planned," "unplanned," "routine," "emergency," "scheduled," and so on. Many of these required specific work orders authorizing the work; "planned routine maintenance" was permanently authorized. It turned out that in the data, almost all of the work was categorized as planned routine maintenance. Why? Because all of the other categories were for emergency work of some sort, and no one felt in an emergency situation that they could wait for authorization of the proper category. As a routine practice, the field staff of this company used whatever category allowed the system to serve their needs—in this case, getting the equipment working as soon as possible. (Some managers in this company had been very pleased with its equipment reliability record until this phenomenon was discovered when preparing to mine the data.)

Warning! Business processes don't always do what the designers intended, don't always work as expected, and don't always generate data that means what it says! In mapping the business processes, get all of the people in the process involved. For data generation, it's important to map reality as closely as possible, not some theoretical vision of what should happen. This requires the involvement of all stakeholders—and may deliver some surprises.

7.1.3.5 Context

Context changes everything. As pointed out early in this section, the crucial pieces of data to capture are time, event, and context. Time is a fairly straightforward piece of information to identify—there's a pretty good operational definition of what time means. Although we don't understand the nature of time very well at all, how to record, measure, and use those recorded measurements is very well understood and established through well over 100 years of usage in technical and cultural settings. This section has fairly much covered how to find appropriate events—transitions between subprocesses in process flows that impact, and are impacted by, the management levers. But context is equally important, because it is context that gives any event its meaning. Colloquially, to "put an event into context" means to explain its relevance and import, in fact, to explain the meaning of the event. How can this be applied to collecting contextual data?

Context affects data about an event in four ways. These are illustrated in Table 7.4.

Table 7.4 illustrates that event data falls into two broad groupings. Some data is sensitive to the context in which it is generated; some is insensitive. This breaks further into four categories of interest here:

- *Context-specific data* has meaning only within a restricted contextual range, and any change in the context can totally invalidate the data. A conductor's baton movements mean something in the context of an orchestral performance, but nothing in the context of repairing a car. The meaning of transfers of funds differs very significantly if it is in the context of making payroll or of collecting on defaulted accounts.

- *Context-general data* is implicitly sensitive to the context in which it occurs. In the context of medical diagnosis for males, pregnancy is not a valid option. In the context of eating a vegetarian meal, ordering steak is not a valid option.

- *Context-generic data* is independent of any context. The number of customers a company has, or the capacity of a shipping container, is generic data.

- *Context-free data* simply ignores context sensitivity. Frequently, forecasts such as market growth or sales projections are made context-free: "If things continue as before, then . . ." About the only thing that humans can be completely certain about, excluding perhaps death and taxes, is that things will definitely not continue as before, and that later will be different than now.

It's important to note the effect of context. Where context makes a difference—in other words, in context-sensitive data—two important features

TABLE 7.4 Event Context

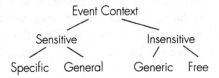

about the situation can change: *options* and *probabilities*. For instance, tactically the contextual concerns of price sensitivity and urgency can make a huge difference in choosing a shipping method. Overnight shipping may not be an option if price sensitivity is paramount. Or suppose that a customer is considering a wine purchase. The context makes a huge difference as to a suitable selection. Does the customer prefer red or white? Is geographic region a preference? Is it for entertaining or personal consumption? And there are many other contextual variables that might make a huge difference in selection. At a strategic level, suppose management contemplates expansion into a new corporate facility, or a new market, or a new product area. Context has to include the economic climate, availability of funds, competitive position, management objectives, and so on.

Capturing the context of a business event is just as important as capturing the time and event itself. Cause and effect maps (discussed in the next section) are a good way to discover contextually important data that has to be captured about an event. The questions to ask about any situation are:

- What are the actions possible in a situation?
- What causes the available options to change? (This can be determined using a cause and effect map that points to important contextual variables to capture.)
- What outcomes can result for a situation?
- What causes the outcome probabilities to change? (Again, this can be mapped and the indicated data captured.)

7.1.3.6 Mapping Cause and Effect

Context models, discussed in the previous section, are used to discover relevant variables and features that help to more fully characterize events. This is all well and good if the miner happens to have a selection of candidate variables and features for the context model to explore. But what if there aren't any? How does the miner discover appropriate context data to include in the business process model? The answer to that calls for another useful tool, *cause and effect mapping*.

There are several useful ways of mapping cause and effect, but the one that has proved to be most useful is what is known as a "fishbone" or an "Ishikawa diagram" (named after its inventor, Kaoru Ishikawa). The map is useful because the process of creating it promotes a structured exploration of possible causes and effects, and points directly to the data that needs to be collected to determine the relationships that the map proposes. Figure 7.6 shows a fishbone cause and effect map for part of the business process of producing a mined model.

A cause and effect map starts with the "head" on the right (conventionally) that labels the outcome—in this case, model quality. Each branch rep-

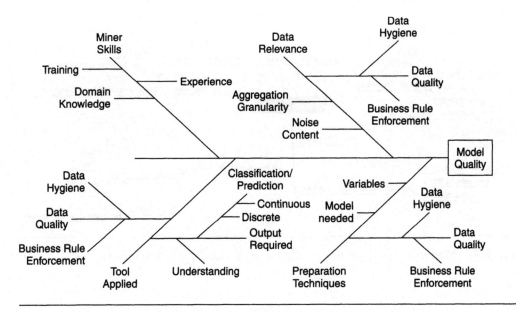

Figure 7.6   Cause and effect map for discovering what affects model quality in a data mined model.

resents a feature of a major causal factor; sub-branches represent features that contribute to it. To take a specific example, the first branch from the head leads down to "preparation techniques," indicating that these are a primary causal factor for model quality. Looking at that branch, notice that "data quality" affects the prep-aration techniques, and both "data hygiene" and "business rule enforcement" affect data quality. Figure 7.7 shows a similar, but more detailed, causal map for the same process; however, it uses a mind map instead of a fishbone map.

As another example, Figure 7.8 shows a cause and effect map for customer satisfaction in a restaurant. Notice that the primary drivers are "ambience," "food," and "beverage." Clearly, it seems from this diagram, customers want pleasant surroundings and good food and drink. But where is service? Initially, this might seem to be an independent causal factor. However, the service, it turned out in making this map, is related to the food, beverage, and ambience, rather than being an independent factor. Notice on the cause "ambience," "attentiveness" affects "service." In other words, the level of service affects at least part of the customer's impression of ambience, and the attentiveness of the staff affects the customer's impression of service. Notice in "food" and "beverage" that the factor "service" is italicized. The italicization indicates that this is a duplicate of service shown elsewhere, and although "attentiveness" still has an impact, the full "service" branch isn't shown.

In making cause and effect diagrams, it's important to keep representing more detailed causes until you reach something that can be measured. For

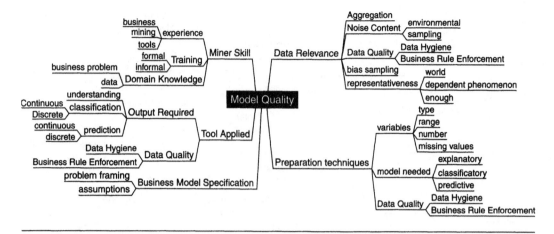

Figure 7.7 Mind map showing cause and effect for model quality in a data mined model.

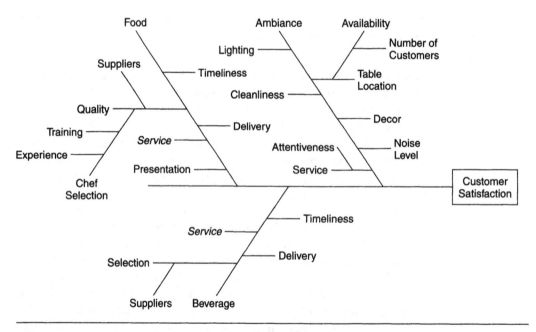

Figure 7.8 Cause and effect map for customer satisfaction in a restaurant.

instance, both training and experience drive the chef's selection of good quality foods. However, these can be measured—years experience, courses
taken, and so on. The undivided branches (using a tree metaphor) are leaves,
and it is the leaves that point directly and unambiguously to the data that has
to be measured.

Thus, process maps point to where data can be captured, and causal maps point to what data needs to be captured. Of course, process maps also point back to other important data that needs to be captured too, the data that describes process flows.

Taken together, process maps and cause and effect maps are powerful tools to use in discovering data for mining that addresses business problems.

7.2 Using Data

How data is actually used greatly impacts the quality and performance of any model—not just which data is gathered, but how it is characterized and incorporated into a model or used to reveal relationships. This section introduces two important issues in the way that any available data is actually used:

1. The types of variables available
2. Effectively fusing data sets of different domain coverage to create a single, common, domain-mineable representation

The data that is used in data mining, as applied to business models anyway, is always intended to have an impact. The outcome of the mining is expected to make a difference to a business situation. However, in this respect, not all data is equal. The data, in the form of a variety of variables, needs to be carefully considered, and different types of variables are of different use and significance in the model. Understanding the role and use of these different types of variables is very important in determining the way that they are incorporated into different models.

Perhaps more important than any other feature of data mining, at least in a business modeling environment, is determining that the models are validly constructed and that they model the range of behaviors important to the business. It is, thus, very important to make the best possible use of available data, and in the case where purpose-constructed data is assembled, it's equally important to make sure that the full range of system behaviors is covered. Without this being so, it is impossible to get the model right—except perhaps by pure luck.

Very often, the data that is available for modeling comes from disparate sources. These various data sets have to be assembled into one single data set for modeling—but this is not always either easy or straightforward. Take a company that has, say, a million customers. If they decide to conduct a detailed market survey of a thousand customers, how is this detailed information about one tenth of one percent of the total number of customers to be meaningfully fused with the original customer data set so that the result can be mined? Can it even be done? (Actually, yes, but only very carefully!) Anyone who has worked with data sets in databases or data warehouses is familiar with the problems inherent in joining data sets together. But those are types of problems that are well understood by the database community and will not be reiterated here. However, the two issues cited at the beginning of this section are problems that are specific to data mining—or at least to data analysis—that do need to be addressed.

7.2.1 Types of Variables

There are, of course, numerous ways to characterize variables. However, in getting the model right, one characterization is particularly important: the way that the variables will be used.

First, there are the variables that go into a model and variables that come out of a model. In Part III, such variables are described as clusters called *batteries,* and they are labeled as the input battery, and the output battery, as appropriate. Statistically inclined readers may think of them as the independent and dependent variable batteries. Some models don't use data sets with explicit output batteries, although all modelable data sets have at least an implicit output battery (more on this in Part III). Whether the variables are in input or output batteries, however, there is another important way of looking at them: as control, environmental, or intermediate variables.

Control variables represent objects, or features of objects, that can be controlled, or controlled for, directly by the organization. They appear, for instance, as the leaves in cause-and-effect diagrams. They often appear as variables in the output battery, too. Product price is a control variable, as are marketing budget, sales channel, incentive offered, product code, and so on.

Environmental variables represent features of the environment that are beyond any form of control by the organization, such as hours of sunshine, gross domestic product, inflation rate, and unemployment rate. For any given customer, age, gender, marital status, life stage, and the like are also environmental variables. These are sometimes called *nuisance variables* by statisticians, although they are absolutely essential in most business models, and are anything but a nuisance. They very often represent much of the contextual information that is crucial in making a decision. Statisticians call them nuisance variables because they find them to be a nuisance that they can't control, or even affect, but these variables most definitely have an impact on the outcome—a nuisance indeed! It may very well be a business modeler's task to discover what can be done to adjust the business processes when they are disturbed by events represented by these environmental variables. They are called environmental variables because they represent what is essentially the uncontrollable environment in which the model works, and to which it may have to react.

Intermediate variables lie between control variables and environmental variables. They are, therefore, influenceable to some greater or lesser degree.

These are often found in the output battery, and there they are no problem; but sometimes when they are in the input battery they can cause problems (as will be seen in the next section). The problem comes when they look like, and are treated like, environmental variables that are independent of each other. If, for instance, the model tries to explore the effect of different prices for different quantities of some commodity, it might prove to be impossible to change the one without the other since market forces simply connect the two in (perhaps) nonobvious ways. As noted, more on this later.

As a final note, it's often important to make sure that the model has control variables in the input battery. When the question deals with what managers can do to modify a situation, the question is really one of which control variables they can adjust. A sales forecast is used not simply for information—a sales manager may well want to know how to adjust the balance between products. It would be of no value to present a forecast based on environmental variables alone, however accurate it might be. The sales manager has no control over the mortgage rate or discount rate, for example, even if they are material to the forecast. The question is really one of how to affect business processes and, through them, the world.

7.2.2 Fusing Data Sets

Business data comes from a wide variety of sources, and often with great differences in data domain coverage. For instance, basic customer information may be fairly complete for all customers. A market research survey may be very comprehensive in its coverage for a minute fraction of the total number of customers, since it may cover many prospects who aren't customers as well as some that are. How can the two data sets be combined in such a way as to support modeling and mining? Another example: so-called "fundamental" financial data is available about many companies in more or less complete form. So, too, is market trend data for broad markets, using only a few companies in an industry group as exemplars. How are these two data sets to be combined for modeling and mining? Sometimes the data sets are even more disparate, such as market research questionnaire results, advertising placement-and-spend reports from competing companies, news feeds, and internally generated data. How are data sets derived from such disparate sources to be used for modeling and mining? The answer is through the use of a process called *data set fusion*.

This discussion assumes that the data sets to be fused are individually in the form of tables containing numerical or categorical variables. (Coding textual, graphical, audio-visual, or other highly qualitative data into such tables is outside the scope of this discussion.) The problem is how to combine these data sets that have some (usually small) overlap. Consider the situation shown in Figure 7.9. The table on the left represents a customer table. It contains some information about the customer, but not in anything like the depth

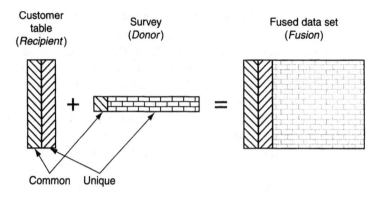

Customer
table
(*Recipient*)   Survey
(*Donor*)   Fused data set
(*Fusion*)

Common   Unique

Figure 7.9   Fusing two data sets of different data domain.

shown in the central table, which represents results from a market survey. This was very much the situation that existed for one company that had well over 1 million customers and had conducted a comprehensive survey of 8,000 people (customers as well as prospective customers) in very considerable detail. The customer table contained 35 fields of information about the customer; the survey over 2,000. Since this company had about a 48% market share, the actual survey covered more like 0.384% (48% of 0.8%) of their market. (Note the italicized terms in the figure that indicate what the various component data sets are called in data set fusion terms.)

One way to start the data set fusion is by creating a model on only the variables that the two data sets have in common; that is, it models which records in the donor data set are most similar to each record in the recipient data set. (Nearest neighbor methods are well suited to this, although any other algorithm of choice can be used. See Chapter 10 for a discussion of algorithms and algorithm selection.) No testing, training, and evaluation sets are needed in this type of modeling; the objective is to achieve the best possible match with the data sets on hand. It's a straightforward process to apply the model to score the recipient and then append the appropriate (best matching) record's unique variables from the donor. Figure 7.10 illustrates this process, showing that the nearest neighbor model finds in the donor the neighbor nearest to a recipient, based on the common variables, and inserts the appropriate values from donor to recipient in the fused variables.

A more complex approach initially models only the donor. This model uses the common variables as input, and is trained to predict the content of each of the unique variable values based on the content of the common variables. This model is then applied to the recipient, providing estimates for unique variable values for the entire recipient data set, as illustrated in Figure 7.11.

The first approach duplicates the content of the unique variables from the best matching donor record. The second approach makes the best estimate of values for the unique variables based on the common variables. Needless

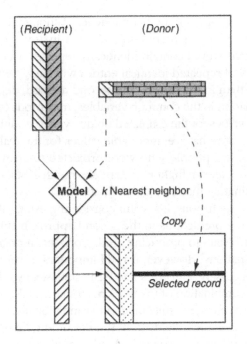

Figure 7.10   *k* nearest neighbor model selects donor records based on similarity of common values and the appropriate donor variables are copied.

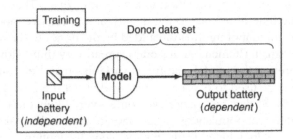

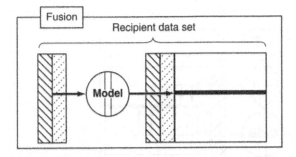

Figure 7.11   Predictive fusion where the model is trained to predict donor variable values based on the common variable values.

to say, there are problems with both approaches. Although the first approach finds the nearest match, it's highly unlikely that in any actual population many of the records would contain identically repeated values, and if they did, the frequency of repeated identical entries will likely be very much less in the real world than in the fusion. The second method, depending on the density of information in the common variables, may produce a more realistic distribution of values for the estimated unique variable values, but this can also produce estimates that are impossible values for the real world. For instance, in one survey, people who were projected to answer "No" to the question "Have you taken a flight in the last six months?" still had a projected entry for the destination that they didn't fly to.

In making data set fusions, it's worth considering using rule extraction as a way of generating predictions in the second approach suggested. These tend to be more resistant to producing predictions that represent impossible real-world combinations. However, it's still important to vet the fusion possibilities and, if necessary, enforce some basic consistency rules.

In practice, a combination of the two approaches, as illustrated in Figure 7.12, often produces better results than either individually. Use the first approach to select the context fields from the donor and insert them into the fusion. With this partial fusion completed, use a predictive model to fill in the remaining variables.

There still remains a tricky problem. The purpose of fusing data sets often isn't to add any information in a technical sense. That is to say, fusion may make little difference to the quality of a predictive model. This is because the amount of information added by the donor to the recipient is usually quite small. (Remember, it's often spread very thin.) However, in terms of interpreting the model, the fused variables may be of immense value. These may be used to explain a great deal about the model characteristics. The two fused data sets may have come—very likely did come—from extremely different populations. What "should" the resulting distribution of the fused data set look like? Clearly, the recipient distribution is unchanged in its original variables, but very likely the distribution of the donor data set isn't

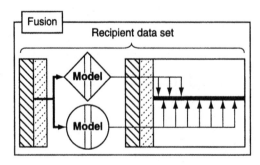

Figure 7.12   Using combined models to improve fusion quality.

duplicated in the donated variables in the fusion. The problem with fusion is that there is no way to definitively answer the question of what the distribution should look like, except by comparing it to real-world data—and if that had been available the fusion wouldn't have been needed. It's a Catch-22.

One way to attempt to address this problem is to extract from the donor data set a data subset that does match the distribution of the recipient data set in its common variables. In the example earlier, this would mean extracting a subset that not only included actual customers, but also contained mainly "typical" customers so that the overall distributions of common variables were similar in both data sets. This data subset might then be supposed to have a more representative distribution of the customer population in its donor variables than the whole donor data set.

Here's the method:

1. Locate all the records in the donor where the common variables match records in the recipient. (So, for instance, if the records refer to people, select records for those people in the donor data set that also have records in the recipient data set.)

2. Select a subset of these records that have a similar distribution in their common variables to the distribution in all of the recipient records in their common variables.

3. From this second subset, determine the distribution (measure the first four moments) of the distribution of the noncommon donor variables.

4. Compare the distribution just found to the distribution of the noncommon donors in the whole fused data set. (Look at the differences between the first four moments of both data sets.)

The *moments* of a data set are more fully the "moments about the mean." The moments use the sum of the powers of the difference between the mean and each number, divided by the total number of records. The mean, of course, is just the average found by summing all the values and dividing by the number of records. So:

- First moment $= \Sigma(x - \text{mean})^1/n$
- Second moment $= \Sigma(x - \text{mean})^2/n$
- Third moment $= \Sigma(x - \text{mean})^3/n$
- Fourth moment $= \Sigma(x - \text{mean})^4/n$

This comparison, if it's possible to make it, gives a fair idea of the similarity of the distributions, at least on a variable-by-variable basis, which is usually sufficient.(Of course, interactions [see Chapter 12, Section 12.2.17] could be included to give a better idea of the similarity of the distributions, but that's a lot more work and usually not needed. The idea is to check whether the distributions are roughly similar or very different.) If the distributions are very different, it's a strong indication that the fusion should not be relied on without further testing against the world. If no distribution checking is possible, testing is all that is left.

It's worth noting that there are standard measures that are based on the first four moments; these are the variance, standard deviation, skew, and kurtosis. Using these measures is usually a lot easier than using the "raw" moments as defined here because there are many software packages that calculate these standard measures. As a practical measure, checking the mean, standard deviation, skew, and kurtosis for the two samples works well.

It may seem that data set fusion is a very nonexact business—and that is indeed the truth! There is a lot more art than science here. The benefit is that such fusion can make a meaningful explanation of what is going on in a data set possible where it wasn't before. Fusing data sets that are comparable in size for record count may improve the models enormously. If two or more disjointed data sets have to be mined, fusing them is the only option, and results are very often worthwhile.

7.3 Summary

Most of this chapter explained how to find, use, and assemble the right data to "feed" the model outlined using the principles discussed in the chapters of Part II. Data comes from one of three sources: internal, external, or purpose-developed. The most useful is purpose-developed data enriched with external data, if it's possible to do so. The first part of the chapter described the hunt for appropriate data with a close look at the business processes that generate most of it, and which ultimately consume the results of modeling by means of managers pulling controlling "levers" to modify business processes. Although the tour of business processes started with a look at how, where, and why they generate useful data, it included a large detour to see how the results of modeling affect them.

The second main topic of the chapter looked at characterizations of variables that are important to modelers: control, intermediate, and environmental. These characterizations are important to recognize so that the models appropriately address the business process changes needed. Finally, the chapter took a brief look at the issue of fusing data sets.

The title topic, getting the model right, requires no more nor less than calibrating an appropriately constructed model with appropriate data. Finding the appropriate model, and the right data, has been the topic of all of Part II, and there remain only the issues of deploying the constructed business model, which is the subject of the next chapter, the last in Part II.

■ ■ ■

Chapter 8
Deploying the Model

This is a very short chapter, but the issues that it covers are utterly crucial to the modeling effort. Regardless of how much effort the modeler puts into the modeling project, and equally regardless of how technically successful the project turns out to be, unless the model is successfully deployed and remains productively engaged with the necessary business processes, the project must fail and deliver no return for the investment made. The one unambiguous fact that has to be faced by every modeler is that a less than perfect model that is deployed is of infinitely more value to a company than any better model that isn't deployed. It turns out that "better" is often the enemy of "good," in the sense of, "I've got a good model, but with just a little more time I can get a much better model!"

Many of the considerations in this chapter have to be addressed at the very beginning of any project, and many of the considerations have to be carried through from the project's start to its finish. However, it seemed intuitively unreasonable to begin Part II, which deals with modeling issues, with a chapter on deploying the model, in spite of the fact that many of the deployment considerations have to be made at the start of the project. Short though it is, this chapter looks at the business issues involved in deploying a model. The technical issues involved in deployment are discussed in Chapter 13 (Part III). Thus, this chapter looks at deployment from the modeler's perspective, and Chapter 13 looks at deployment from the miner's perspective. Although discussed separately as much as possible, there is much crossover between these two chapters, since it is during deployment more than in any other phase of the modeling/mining project that modeling and mining issues weave together. Thus, neither of these chapters can be freestanding, but rely on each other to cover all of the issues of deployment.

8.1 Modifying Business Processes

What does it mean to deploy a model? In detail, the answer to that question depends a great deal on what type of model is to be deployed. However, in general, the answer to the question is very straightforward. Deployment requires using the results of the modeling project to modify existing business processes. It really is as simple as that—and as complex, for modifying existing business processes is no simple matter.

The practice of any business process is always maintained by people. It is reinforced by written procedures, corporate culture, tradition, explicit incentives, emotional motivation, implicit and explicit expectation, and familiarity and is enmeshed in a formal and informal web of internal interactions that serve to maintain and modify it. In fact, any business process or set of business processes continually in existence has become an embedded system exactly as discussed in Chapter 6. As a result, it has an "inertia" that results from the influences just mentioned, which is to say that changing any system takes effort. The existing system will, if left to itself, tend to react so as to perpetuate itself unchanged. Successful model deployment has to recognize this from the outset; recruiting and maintaining support from all of the stakeholders from the beginning of the project through deployment is key to success.

The modeler, in the role of modeler, is responsible for delivering the model in an appropriate form for implementation. By some considerations, the role of modeler ends when delivery of the model is complete, although in practice the person in the role of modeler may at that moment "switch hats" as it were, and take on another role. However, the project is not complete until the deployed model has actually changed corporate behaviors and the changes have been monitored to determine if the actual outcomes matched expectations.

The delivered form of the model has to be defined near the beginning of the project. The form of the deliverable varies according to the type of model, who is going to use it, and how it is going to be used. For instance, for an inferential model, the explanations have to be presented at the level of understanding of the stakeholders who will use the insights. For business managers, this may well mean leaving out all of the technical details of modeling, and almost certainly all of the technical details of mining, and presenting the results in business terms. Automation engineers, industrial scientists, financial controllers, research analysts, and other groups require different perspectives, but few of them will be interested in the technical details of mining and modeling as such, only in the results as they apply to their particular domain.

Ultimately, the delivered and deployed model has to make a difference. It's not enough to propose and try to implement a new process simply because it is "self-evidently" a better way to achieve some end—and this is true even if it really is a better process. The way has to be carefully prepared first. This means keeping the stakeholders, all of them, as involved as possible. Depending on the size of the project this can be done by something as formal as a regular newsletter to all the stakeholders discussing progress and—this is very important—soliciting feedback, insight, and participation that is publicly appreciated and acknowledged. Involvement can also be maintained far more informally, but formal or informal, the connection between modeler and all the stakeholders needs to be structured, and two-way information flow and engagement maintained.

Recognizing that the data preparation portion of the project will take by far the longest time, this is the ideal phase in which to encourage active participation. In fact, having full stakeholder participation in the data preparation stage may well yield more benefit and drive more change than the actual modeling project was expected to have when initially proposed. The effects typically reach far beyond the areas initially expected. As an example of both the problems to be expected in a real-world project and how dealing with the problems created more positive change than expected, consider some of the early stage problems discovered during the data discovery and assembly part of data preparation in one large project:

- Initial expectations from the need and kudos stakeholders were unrealistic.
- Different individual stakeholders each had different, and some had conflicting, expectations for what the project would deliver.
- As the project proceeded, several nonobvious and previously unknown stakeholders emerged who turned out to have yet a different set of expectations.
- The data thought to be available came from multiple sources, which had no common piece to serve as a key to combine them.
- Many of the data sources provided data in different formats and on different media.
- When the necessary keys were generated (invented) it turned out that the data had huge and totally unexpected "holes" in it where data that was "known" to be present turned out to have been lost or, perhaps, never collected at all.
- Several completely identical requests for test data sets for the same data for the same period from the source data set owners resulted in delivery of totally different data sets.
- Many of the data sets being combined had been copied from legacy systems and, in the copying process, many nulls had been replaced with defaults for dates, values, and categories.
- Some of the data sets contained deliberate "fudges" that represented several "buried skeletons," which initial data preparation revealed. This led to some rather uncomfortable problems for some individuals—in one case, it led to dismissal from the company.

- Much of the data had already been used to create reports to management; yet when the reports were compared to the data to verify the two, there was no match at all in some cases—the reports often seemed to be totally at variance with what the data actually contained.

- Much of the data was collected for purposes totally unrelated to the project and although thought to be useful, was so distorted as to be utterly useless.

- Several data streams turned out to measure different things at different times—summary information at some times and actual figures at other times—with no indication of when the changes occurred.

- Several business processes designed to be universal across the company, and to therefore produce uniform measurements, were still open enough to interpretation that people in different groups used different categories and accounts to record identical events.

- Much of the assembled data, when "cleaned" of garbage, left nothing at all behind to analyze.

- The modeling project required a focus on causes, yet all of the data measured only effects (or even more distant, only symptoms).

- One clean, well-structured, relevant data set that was on the corporate server remained unavailable for over 6 months because no one knew who could give permission to use it in the project.

And yes, these are indeed all problems that occurred on a single large data mining/modeling project, and these are typical problems that could well apply, and should be expected, in any large project. Unfortunately, this list is by no means exhaustive! The point about these issues is that the modeler, at least as a modeler, can do nothing about any of these problems unless the appropriate stakeholders are informed, engaged, and committed.

The project discussed, although not complete as a modeling project as this is being written, has already led to reorganization of some parts of the company; far better data collection and management reporting procedures; removal, addition, and changes to corporate procedures; and perhaps most importantly, a significant increase in profitability for the company in a down market even as the restructuring remains a cost. Yet none of these effects, including the increase in profitability, was the direct intended consequence of the project, at least, not in the areas affected. It was the active participation of the stakeholders that made the difference. The fact that this project is still moving ahead, and with the active encouragement and support of the stakeholders, is entirely due to open communication and because the stakeholders have taken each potential setback as an opportunity to improve or fix existing processes. In fact, the project has acted as a focus for change, at least in a small way, for this company.

8.2 **Motivation for Success**

(See MII:TB.4, MII:TB.10) Regardless of which type of model is being deployed, there are several basic issues that form the framework for all deployment:

- Who will use the model?
- How will the users be motivated to gain the most benefit from the model?
- How will they actually use it in operation?
- What skill level will be needed to use the model?
- What training will be provided to the users?
- How will the effect of the model be measured?
- What will determine when the model is no longer valid?
- What are the model's maintenance requirements?

A model is a component of a business process and must itself have input, outputs, flow rates, and all of the concomitant parts discussed in the last chapter. At least one way to judge the effectiveness of any model is by the way that it impacts the business process into which it is embedded. However, since almost all business processes incorporate people, ultimately the deployed model has to change people's behaviors—or at least, enable them to change their behaviors in ways that are intended to affect a business process and effect an improvement in some way.

As Steven Landsburg notes right at the beginning of his book *The Armchair Economist,* in the first line of the first paragraph of the first chapter:

"Most of economics can be summarized in four words: 'People respond to incentives.' The rest is commentary."

This is a very profound statement indeed, and the implications have enormous consequences for us all in every area of life. It's equally important in deploying the model, and the most important consideration is making sure that the users of the model are indeed motivated to use it. Regardless of how much easier it might be for them, or how much improvement the company might glean, the users have to invest time and effort in changing a behavior that they already know works into a different behavior that uses the results of the model. Failing to provide the necessary motivation is the single largest cause of failure to change a system's behaviors because without an incentive to change—well, there's no incentive to change, so why make the effort? Successful deployment lies in large part on having a good answer to the question, "What's in it for me?" And the answer to that question is not necessarily financial.

Commenting on the relationship of money to motivation, an employee at one of the author's clients noted, "Well, the money is good and good money is what lets me sleep at night, but it's not what gets me up in the morning." There are many motivations for job satisfaction other than money, and they all need to be used as part of the model deployment strategy.

8.3 Impact of Model Types

Chapter 4 discussed the types of models in terms of five dimensions: inferential/predictive, associative/systemic, static/dynamic, qualitative/quantitative, and comparative/interactive. All data-based business models will fall somewhere on at least each of these five dimensions, and the precise characterization of these dimensions makes a difference to how the models are deployed. However, by far the biggest practical implications for deployment come with the distinction of the inferential/predictive dimension, and that's where this section focuses.

As in the discussion in Chapter 4, recall that in practice, any model will very likely fall somewhere along the dimension, rather than at the extremes. For instance, any modeler who has ever been asked why a purely predictive model produces the estimates that it does has discovered that regardless of the apparent initial criterion under which the model was created, inferential demands are now being made of it—and the modeler is expected to deliver. In turn, an inferential model is expected to deliver explanatory insights that allow the users of the model to go and do something differently and more effectively as a result of the explanation—in other words, to make better predictions about the outcomes of their actions.

8.3.1 Inferential Models: Delivering Explanations

Almost all models have to deliver explanations. Even if the model isn't used to explain relationships in the world, the modeler will at least have to explain what the model is doing. If the developed model is primarily an inferential model, then in this case, model deployment is actually delivering an explanation about relationships in the world. Whatever has been discovered, deployment requires a justified (by the data) and convincing narrative. This section takes a look at the components that make a justifiably convincing narrative.

A clear distinction must be drawn between explaining the modeling process, which is not a part of the inferential model at all, and explaining the relationships among the business objects in the real world, which is what an explanatory model is all about. The stakeholders may be more or less interested in the modeling process, and that may form part of the story that the modeler develops, but it is not any part of the explanatory model. The explanatory model only describes the world (at least as revealed by the data), quite regardless of how the relationships were discovered and explicated.

The key to any explanatory model is to tell a story—the story that the data reveals. The story is told in business terms: explicitly not in terms of the data, nor in terms of the modeling tools used, but entirely in terms that the stakeholders will understand. This is the purpose of framing the model (see Chapter 5) in which the crucial question is very simply, "In what terms is the answer needed?" In the appropriate terms for the audience, the model is a story with a beginning, a middle, and an end. The beginning opens the scene and hooks the interest of the audience. It answers the audience's unspoken question, "What's in this for me?" The middle presents the discovered relationships in narrative form, directly addressing the relevant business objects of interest to the audience and supported by charts, graphs, pictures, audiovisual images, slides, equations, algorithms, stochastic procedures, or whatever is appropriate and relevant to the audience. The middle, in other words, presents the evidence—the justifiable conclusions and the justifiable degree of confidence in those conclusions—based on the data available, along with all necessary caveats. The end summarizes the story, and lays out what difference it makes—why this explanation is important and relevant, the so-called "bottom line."

The key is to remember that it's a story. Any reader who has been present when the author has delivered an explanatory model will know that the author uses the metaphor fairly extensively, introducing the story's "heroes" (usually the relationships producing positive and wanted change), "villains" (usually the confounding, confusing factors, the levels of uncertainty, the negative evidence, the outliers, etc.), and main "themes" (different principal relationships). The story metaphor also includes "plot twists" (when unexpected relationships or surprises turn up) and other narrative devices as appropriate. The point is to be engaging, interesting, and (as far as possible) entertaining. (For more information on the use of business storytelling, see *The Story Factor,* by Annette Simmons, listed in the "Resources section.")

It is usually best to start with a summary of the conclusions, a sort of "executive summary" of the results. If the opening lines of the story don't grab attention and interest, the deployment fails right there. However, once attention is captured, the true narrative has to begin unfolding, and always it's the story of a voyage of discovery. Indeed, exploratory modeling takes place in two stages—discovery and verification—and the modeler performs different activities in each stage. This also needs to be a part of the deployment narrative. To be sure, the deployment narrative does not need to—indeed should not—cover everything that the modeler did. Narrating all of the mistaken paths and recovering all of the paths taken doesn't make for a compelling narrative. What's needed is a purposeful summary of the salient points, grouped thematically and presented with compelling evidence. Start with the tale of discovery.

8.3.1.1 Discovery

Discovery comprises 11 basic themes. Approximately in the order that they are used to explore the data, they are:

- Noting patterns and themes
- Discovering plausible explanations
- Clustering
- Counting
- Contrasting and comparing
- Partitioning variables
- Deriving generalities from particularities
- Proposing plausible explicit and implicit (latent) factors
- Identifying and explicating relationships among variables (or variable groups)
- Creating a logical explanatory chain
- Creating conceptual coherence

This is the story that needs to be summarized and compellingly recapitulated. Start, for instance, with identifying the patterns and themes that were apparent in the data. Describe all of the relevant plausible explanations that were examined, even those that were later discredited by the data. Describe apparently interesting clusters in the data. Count, and then contrast and compare the events of interest and how the data set characterizes them differently—or not. Continue through all of the stages until the logical explanatory chain has been recapitulated, including alternative explanations. Keep the narrative closely linked to the business objectives of the model. Conceptual coherence comes from carefully fitting the explanatory chain into the existing body of knowledge, pointing out where the narrative agrees or disagrees with existing knowledge and expectations.

Chapter 11 in Part III discusses some of the mining approaches for creating explanatory models. That chapter discusses the technical approach to exploring data in different terms than presented here, but nothing said there should be seen to conflict with the description here. These 11 stages are what a modeler does in the discovery stage of exploratory modeling, and they need to be convincingly summarized and recapitulated at model deployment. Chapter 11 describes how the miner goes about working with the data while exploring and discovering through the 11 stages described here.

Of course, in any one model, not all stages will be equally interesting or relevant. Only those for which a compelling case can be made should be presented, but keep in mind that the voyage of discovery sets the scene, and is the key to being persuasive in the conclusions presented.

8.3.1.2 Verification

Verification comes at the point that discovery stops. Then it's time to try to confirm, or deny, the various explanations that were discovered. In model deployment, it's only necessary to discuss how the final explanatory model(s) stood up to the verification process. The discovery process was summarized in 11 stages; verification can be summarized in 8:

- Checking for representativeness
- Checking for bias
- Triangulation
  - ◆ Using different data sources
  - ◆ Using different modeling methods
  - ◆ Using different theories
- Accounting for outliers
- Explaining surprises
- Incorporating negative evidence
- Incorporating external empirical and experiential evidence
- Corroboration of discovered insights, objects, and relationships from feedback

Here is where the story that has been developed during the discovery process is put to the test, as it were. It's easy to look at a data set with mining tools and accept whatever turns up, but if what is discovered is to be convincing, more than discovery is needed. The rational grounds for not dismissing the explanation as an aberration, or noise, are also needed.

Part III on mining discusses several ways of checking for representativeness, including the use of several data sets as cross checks (training, test, and evaluation data sets). This also appears on this list under the heading of triangulation; however, triangulation implies rather more than just representativeness checking. More on that in a moment.

Bias is always a problem—always. Bias in a data set often arrives hidden and unnoticed. It's there whenever the data is in some way selected from the whole population of data that the world has to offer. Since it's impossible to record everything that could possibly be recorded, some criterion always has to be used in data selection. However, this in itself is usually not a particular problem. Sometimes data sets are deliberately biased—if the object is to explain motivating factors for purchases of industrial catering equipment, it only makes sense to select data that represents those people and companies that are likely to buy such equipment in the first place. What's important is to ensure that the data set used to create the inferential model does indeed accurately represent the behaviors of all the entities likely to purchase—hotels, restaurants, catering companies, certainly, but also pet food manufacturers, churches, hospitals, retirement homes, cruise lines, and so on. For an explanatory model, the justification for considering the data set to be representative needs to be firmly established.

Triangulation can be a very powerful justification for accepting the results as valid. Using different data sources goes beyond the training, test, and validation sets discussed in Chapter 11 (see Section 11.2.3). It even goes beyond getting more data from the same source as before. So far as using different data is concerned, triangulation calls for seeking totally different data, from a different source, and using different variables, to see if the same phenomenon can be explained in agreement, or at least not in disagreement, with the original explanation. For relatively unimportant models, this may not be necessary, but if major strategic decisions hang on the results of the modeling, or human life on the outcome, or the commitment of billions of dollars, aggressively seek this sort of triangulation.

Similarly, seek similar results using different tools or different types of algorithm, although for a miner this is quite easy, and almost certainly part of standard mining procedure. Explanatory models require strong theoretical underpinnings—that's their purpose after all. Triangulation calls for the development of multiple theoretical underpinnings that all go to support the explanation. Why do people buy certain snack foods, for instance? There are many plausible theoretical explanations—hunger, mood, time of day, peer pressure, advertising, availability, impulse, taste, brand loyalty, packaging, convenience, and many, many more possible explanatory theories. A convincing explanation links as many of these as possible.

Validation of an explanatory model *always* has to account for outliers. Explanatory models positively cannot ignore any of the data or evidence. Perhaps the outliers are errors; perhaps they represent different circumstances that need to be modeled separately; perhaps they can be discounted; perhaps they can be incorporated into the model—but whatever they are, ignored is not among the options. Outliers may well represent crucial phenomena to include, perhaps even the most important phenomena to include. For instance, in the daily weather patterns, tornadoes and hurricanes are outliers, but crucial to include. Huge insurance claims occur very infrequently, are outliers, but are a focus of interest. Fraud is outlying behavior most of the time, but of primary interest. The list of outlying phenomena that are of primary concern is almost endless, but not a problem because those outlying events are already recognized as important. One purpose of an explanatory model is to make discoveries, and the discovery of meaningful outliers may be the most important result of modeling. If they can't be explained, they must be noted as inexplicable within the framework of the presented model.

In the same way that outliers need to be explicitly noted, so too must surprises be noted. These are by definition unexpected findings. But more important, all of the evidence available that refutes the explanation has to be included. No modeler should accept any of the inferences discovered without taking pains to actively seek negative evidence. Humans are more rationalizing animals than rational ones. It is only too easy to make up plausible explanations after the fact. More problematic is the human tendency to "anchoring," which in this context can be interpreted as a tendency to hang on to any likely sounding explanation, even in the face of evidence to the contrary. Anyone's "pet theory" on almost any topic probably falls into this category. When deploying an explanatory theory, it must be the modeler's position to accept the discovered explanation with only the greatest reluctance, and only after it turns out that the evidence cannot convincingly discredit it. And always keep in mind that however well buttressed the explanation is by the available evidence, new evidence may happen along at any time. A skeptical attitude is well taken here, because whatever explanation is produced and however valid it may in fact be, it's almost certainly only one of several equally good explanations for the same phenomenon.

Finally, any explanation should plausibly fit with what's already known. No explanation is freestanding; it has to fit into the world of which it is a part, and should also corroborate at least some existing suspicions or notions. An explanatory model that discovers and explains the obvious gains credibility, if it doesn't, there is something suspicious going on somewhere—bias, lack of representativeness . . . something.

8.3.2 Predictive Models

There are several types of predictive models. At one extreme, the model will deliver one, or no more than a few, predictions and never be used again. Such models are used, for instance, in scenario evaluation in which the object is to determine possible future outcomes. Perhaps a company, in planning future strategies, needs to project economic conditions with high, medium, and low inflation assumptions. Or again, city planners may need to predict service needs and traffic congestion under several different hypothetical emergency scenarios. These predictive models, although truly predictive, can be treated more like explanatory models in their deployment phase.

At the other extreme are fully automated predictive models that are embedded in dynamic systems and are intended to modify system behavior and response in real time. An example familiar to many millions of people is embedded in the amazon.com and bn.com Web sites. Their "recommendation engines" are predictive models that are designed to provide unique recommendations based on predictions of which products will be most likely to elicit additional purchases from browsers on the site. Such models are also common in many other applications, such as in industrial process control where the predictive models are used to predict the system's most likely future response to changes in conditions, allowing process correction and optimization.

Those predictive models that can be deployed as explanatory models present no additional business issues for a modeler. However, any of the more active model types do present issues that need to be addressed. Many of the issues are technical in nature and are discussed in Chapter 13. However, there is one clearly technical issue that will require major business support if it turns out to be an issue for deployment, and that's the issue of data modification.

8.3.2.1 Dynamic Data Modification

The important point is that during modeling, the data has necessarily been adjusted in many ways. It may have been cleaned, had missing values replaced, been recoded, had features added in the form of additional variables, and had any number of transformations and modifications made to it before actually constructing the model. (Part III discusses many of these transformations and adjustments in detail.) However, the model won't work on raw data, only on data that has been transformed and adjusted—so all of the transformations and adjustments that are made at modeling time have to be re-created and duplicated at predict time. That may be anything from easy to impossible to accomplish.

For instance, suppose that the feature "total purchases this year" turns out to be an important variable for the model. Is this available at predict time? The answer depends. It's certainly feasible to create this feature as a variable at modeling time, but if the main database is updated only monthly, then any purchases in the current month will not be included in that database. Are purchases this month available in any currently accessible data set? If so, is it a running total or a series of individual transactions that will have to be totaled dynamically? Perhaps; however useful this variable might be if it were available, it will turn out to be impossible to create at predict time, in which case, useful or not, it will have to be left out of the model.

The general issue, of course, is to make sure that whatever modifications are made to the data set at modeling time can also be made at predict time from live data. This is not always easy and may involve not using features that cannot be dynamically created at execution time. However, time turns up in more than one guise in predictive models, and in data sets the existence of "now" is always ambiguous, and may need special representation.

8.3.2.2   Missing "Now": Skip Windows

(See MII:AB.13, MII:TB.8) Data about "now" always presents an issue that needs to be thought about for models. The issue, at least for predictive models, is that data describing "now" is very likely not present in the execution time data stream. The duration of "now" depends very much on the system involved and may stretch from micro- or milliseconds to days, weeks, or years. For the U.S. census, for instance, "now" takes 10 years since that is the sampling rate for the U.S. population.

All systems that a modeler deals with have a sampling rate that essentially determines how recent the latest possible data available can be. Frequently, different systems have different sampling rates that have to be merged into the data set to be modeled. Although challenging, this isn't usually a problem. The difficulty is that for some period, defined here as "now," the data isn't actually available at execution time because it has not yet been assembled. These "now" periods form modeling windows, as shown in Figure 8.1.

In the figure, each period is represented by a subscripted number. Subscript 0 represents now. Of course, in a modeling data set, the future is represented since outcomes have to be known. Thus, positive subscripts represent future periods and negative subscripts represent past periods. To make the discussion concrete, imagine that monthly sales is represented here. It's clear that in reality, monthly sales for this month can never be known until this month becomes last month. After all, until the month ends, there is no comprehensive total for the month. As soon as such a comprehensive total is available, it can only be because the month has ended. Thus in modeling monthly sales, since this month's sales are unknown, if a prediction (forecast) of next month's sales is required, the most recent data available turns out to be that from last month. Although it's present in the training data, this month's sales are not ever available in the execution data, so it's necessary to skip over a month.

In general, although *skip windows* (as the periods of unavailable data are known) may not be required in a model, depending on exactly what has to be predicted and when, a modeler has to pay close attention to what data will actually be available to create the needed prediction at execution time, and not rely on what is available in the training data sets. Although the length of the skip window is clearly a technical issue of concern to a data miner, it's

Figure 8.1   Skip windows.

also a material business issue, of direct concern to the modeler. Remember the well-worn aphorism "Prediction is hard, particularly when it's about the future."

8.4 **Summary**

Probably the single biggest failing for data-based business models when they are deployed is a failure to close the loop, or in other words to put in place a mechanism to determine exactly what the effect and impact of the deployed model turns out to be. Success or failure should be determined by measuring the actual results and comparing them with the expected results, or as described in Chapter 5, comparing expectations and outcomes so that expectations can be better set (see Section 5.3.1). Without such feedback and correction, if necessary, deployment is not complete. The processes for measuring actual outcomes, like so much else about the deployment issues, have to be thought through at the beginning of the project, supported by the stakeholders, and incorporated into the project from the start.

But the loop closes here in a larger sense, too. This chapter closes Part II, which has looked at the business issues involved in creating a data modeling and mining project. What remains is the practice of actually mining data, and that is the part of the tale that is taken up in Part III.

Part III
Data Mining

Part III covers the techniques used to mine data. There is little reference here to finding, framing, and directing the mining to solve a business problem. All of those issues are thoroughly discussed in Part II and, although absolutely essential in any business situation, are not covered again here.

Various techniques and many workable methodologies (no one of which is "the" methodology) are available to an experienced data miner. This part of the book is not aimed at experienced data miners, but rather at business analysts and others unfamiliar with data mining who want or need to use data mining tools to analyze data. These chapters assume that the reader knows about data, at least in the form of spreadsheets, and where to find suitable data that addresses the identified business problem. It also assumes that the reader can access, and knows how to use, basic data manipulation tools. The mechanics of data manipulation aren't covered here. From there, and based on these assumptions, this part of the book describes a methodology the reader can follow, including basic "best practices" in data mining.

This methodology is presented as an integrated whole, as if there were only one path to follow. As an introduction, following such a path will not lead the miner far astray. If you follow these steps, you'll end up with reasonable, valid, and useable models, if such are to be had from the data at hand. If good models are not to be had, you will at least know why. However, as you gain skill and experience, and with this basic mining strategy as a starting point, you will want to experiment, take shortcuts, or develop additional techniques of your own. The chapters of Part III are your starting point.

A note about the references to the methodology. Part III describes how to mine data to create models. There are many references in Part III that point to the place in the methodology that deals with the topic being discussed. References to the methodology look like this: (MIII:AB.11.6). This reference (MIII.AB.11.6) points to the methodology for Part III, Action Box 11.6 which is the 6th action box associated with the material covered in Chapter 11. The methodology will be found in Part IV, along with Chapter 14, which fully explains how the methodology is constructed and how to use it.

Chapter 9
Getting Started

The path that leads from raw data to a deployable, mined model looks straightforward enough, but is in fact replete with many backtracks and detours. Developing mined models requires a lot of working with the data—making changes and taking actions that depend entirely on the needs of the business problem and what the miner discovers in the data. It will be quite easy to read through the next chapters and, for anyone unfamiliar with data mining, to assume that the miner's progress will be similar to the order in which the material is presented. However, you must expect that your path will not be so straightforward. Do not be at all surprised if you return to a previous stage several times!

Mining data is not magic, and it is not something that computer software will do for you. Essentially, data mining is a structured way of playing with data, of finding out what potential information it contains and how it applies to solving the business problem. The tools used to mine data aren't magic, either. Most of those currently in use were developed from three main areas: statistics, artificial intelligence, and machine learning. Despite apparently different roots, these tools essentially do only one thing: discover a relationship that more or less maps measurements in one part of a data set to measurements in another, linked part of the data set. That's it. Nothing startling, nothing fancy. Just an expression of the relationship between two linked parts of a data set.

When brought down to such basics, it's pretty obvious that the wonderful tools of data mining aren't going to solve problems, especially business problems, by themselves. Data mining is a human activity, and it is the miner that produces the results of data mining, not the tools. Yet data mining can produce powerful, startling, insightful, surprising, and highly profitable results—but never forget that the results come from the insight and understanding applied by human intelligence.

Most of a miner's time in any data mining project is devoted to preparing data sets, and such preparation is the place where a miner begins the work of mining. You can expect to invest between 60 and 90% of your time simply preparing the data for mining. Data preparation for data mining is a complex subject, and this chapter can provide only the basic foundations of this activity. (For a more extensive description of data preparation techniques, see the author's book *Data Preparation for Data Mining,* also from Morgan Kaufmann Publishers.) Nonetheless, this chapter is not an abbreviated recapitulation of that book. Instead, it lays out a basic method for preparing data that results in useable data sets.

The first three stages of mining data—the assay, feature extraction, and the data survey—are discussed in this chapter. These three stages taken together comprise most of what constitutes data preparation.

9.1 Looking at Data

The sort of data used in mining can be imagined to be very similar to data as displayed in a spreadsheet program, that is to say, in rows and columns (see Figure 9.1). The columns are usually referred to as *variables* and represent different values that the variable can assume. As a concrete example, the variable "Name" might, in a spreadsheet, be represented by a spreadsheet column headed "Name" to indicate the label for the variable, and the cells under the label would then contain some measured values such as "Dorian" and "Pat." Some of the cells might also be blank—that is, without any label. Or,

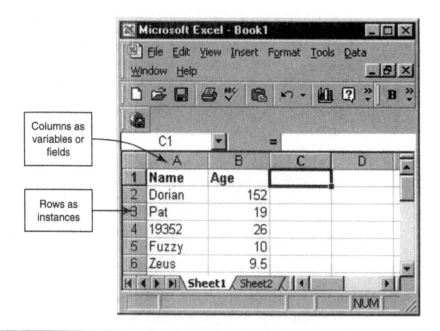

Figure 9.1   Spreadsheet representation of data.

perhaps one cell might contain "19352". Such an entry is almost certainly not a name and is most probably an erroneous entry.

If the data set contains more than one column, then in addition to characterizing the data in columns, it is also characterized in rows. Each row represents a collection of measured values that are associated together in some way. If, for instance, the column next to "Name" was labeled "Age," then we could fairly assume that an entry on any row was associated with the name on the same row.

This column/row representation of data is a fairly common representation, but by no means the only one. Databases are created to hold data in other types of representations. One quite common representation, for instance, is called a *star schema*. A number of column/row tables of the type just described are related to each other in a way that can be represented as a sort of star-like "hub and spoke" relationship. Figure 9.2 shows this conceptually.

Almost all databases are arranged in some way other than as a single column/row table. Databases are constructed almost exclusively to be efficient in storing, finding, and retrieving entries from table rows. They are, in general, from poor to disastrous when heavy-duty, column-oriented operations are demanded of them—yet column-oriented operations are exactly what data mining demands. Thus, although there are a growing number of "mining in place" tools (which means that they do not need to extract the

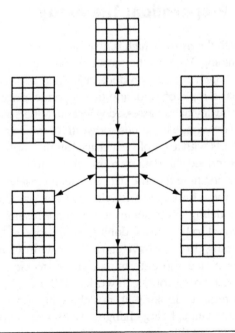

Figure 9.2   Several tables related to each other that form a star schema.

data from a database in order to mine it), in general, whether the miner has to explicitly extract the data before mining or the tool extracts data "invisibly," it is still true at this writing that most mining tools require access to data in the form of a single table. Even if the tool can mine in place, a miner may still want to extract the data into a single table to work on during the data preparation stage. The work of even basic data preparation such as that described in this chapter can pretty much overload any database not specifically designed to be mineable. In any case, both this chapter and the whole of Part III, will assume use of a single column/row format table—usually called a *flat file*—if only for descriptive and discussion purposes. *Columns* are synonymous with the term *variable* and *rows* with the term *instances,* in the sense that, in a given row for the variable "Name," the value could be described as "In this instance, the value of the variable 'Name' is 'Dorian.'"

Sometimes columns (or variables) are also called *fields*. Rows (or instances) are also known as *vectors*. This variety of terms for the same concept derives from the multiplicity of backgrounds that data miners come from—database, statistical, mathematical, and machine learning backgrounds all have their own terminology (jargon) for similar concepts, and in data mining these terms have all become common. For now, we just have to live with the situation.

9.2 First Steps in Preparation: The Assay

Preparation starts with the *assay,* which is no more than assessing the data's fitness or worth for mining. Perhaps the most common use of the term *assay* is associated with gold. Such an assay produces a justified assessment of the quality of some particular sample of gold, and thus its value, since a specific mass of gold of a specific quality has an assessed valuation. Miners assay data for very similar purposes: to determine the fitness or worth of the data for mining.

Assaying data starts with a simple but crucial step: simply look at the data and check that it is indeed the data as represented. It may well be that this close scrutiny is the first time that the data has been closely inspected. Don't be surprised at what you find! (See MIII:AB.9.3) Data, particularly of the sort used in business modeling, often seems to bear little resemblance to what it was at first represented to be. Please don't give up hope at this point. Many successful data mining projects have started out with what seemed to be hopeless data. Persistence and determination (not to mention a little constructive panic on some occasions) can work wonders.

The data assay requires looking at, not changing, data at this stage. In later stages when the data is being changed, work with a copy of the original, not the original file. At this stage it's looking and understanding that's important, so take notes if necessary.

The best plan of action to use when assaying data is to start with the variables as individuals and progress to considering the data set as a whole. The assay section of this chapter adopts this approach.

9.2.1   "Eyeballing" Variables

(See MIII:AB.9.2, MIII:AB.11.10) One very fundamental characteristic of data is that there are different types of variables. In mining business data, three qualitatively different types usually jump right out: numbers, dates, and some that are neither dates nor numbers. Variables that contain numbers are called *numeric variables,* those containing dates are called (unsurprisingly) *date variables,* and the others are usually known as *categorical variables.* Categorical variables contain labels such as "red" and "sausages," or perhaps names and addresses, or other labels that can be thought of as indicating a category of some kind.

(See MIII:AB.9.9) Start by checking the basic statistics for each of the variables. Confirm that the variable values actually contain what is expected and that they don't contain more than is meant to be there. Be aware that each of the three different types of variables needs to be checked in different ways. The next three sections describe the process for checking each variable type.

9.2.1.1   Basic Checks on Numeric Variables

The most basic check to perform on a numeric variable is its *range*—in other words, identify the maximum and minimum values in the data set. Compare these against the expected maximum and minimum that the data set is supposed to contain. This simple check often reveals some unexpected surprises.

In addition, and if relevant, there are several other criteria that are worth comparing against what should be expected. (Figures 9.3 and 9.4 illustrate several of the following points.)

- *Averages:* Look at the mean, median, and mode. The *mean* is what is colloquially called the "average value," and is calculated by summing all of the entries and dividing by the number of entries. The *median* is the value to be found in the middle of an ordered list of all the variable's values. The *mode* is the value that occurs most frequently. Collectively, these are called *measures of central tendency,* since they all in some way indicate the location of the middle of the distribution. Again, as with maximum and minimum values, discover if these are reasonable or expected values.
- *Missing values:* What constitutes a missing value in each numeric field? Many databases deliver *null* values (meaning "no entry made here"),

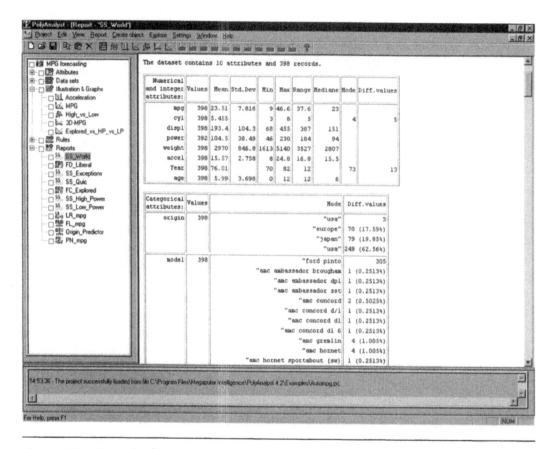

Figure 9.3 Screenshot from a data mining tool showing numeric and categorical basic statistics.

where there is no numeric value. Count the number of nulls present. Also check carefully for surrogate nulls. A *surrogate null,* at least in a numeric field, is a value that is actually numeric but is somehow entered when there is no known numeric value. Sometimes, zero is entered when no number is known. Some systems enter default values when no actual entry is known. (Consider, as an example, a field "Month," with numbers 0–12. Months 1 through 12 are expected, but what of month 0? It is a legitimate number but—presumably—entered when no month is known, not when the month is "Decembuary." Thus, the zero entry is, in fact, a surrogate null.) If surrogate nulls are present, they will cause a problem when mining the data. Any mining tool will, quite naturally, use any value entered as if it were a valid entry. Removing surrogate nulls, if you can find them, can improve a model tremendously. Replace them with nulls, or treat them as missing values (discussed a little later in this chapter).

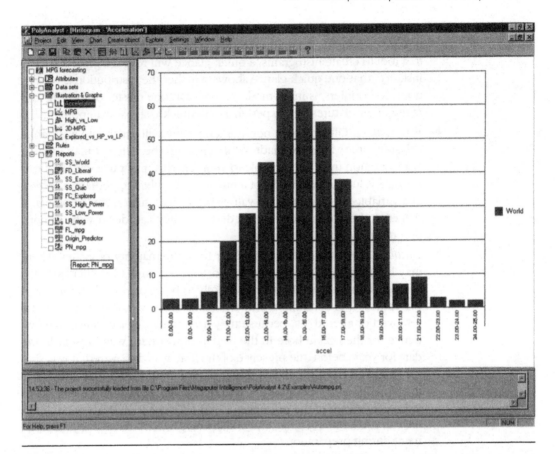

Figure 9.4 Screenshot from a mining tool showing the histogram for one variable.

- *Distribution estimates:* Measures of variance—the way that the values distribute themselves within the range—are very useful for understanding a "snapshot" view of a variable. Variance may be reported directly, or it may be expressed in terms of standard deviation. Useful distribution measures also include skew and kurtosis. Gaining an understanding of what these two measures mean can be very useful in assaying data. Briefly, *skew* measures whether the bulk of the instances have values that are above or below the midpoint of the range—literally, if the distribution is skewed. Roughly speaking, *kurtosis* measures whether the values tend to be at the extremes of the range, or to clump about the middle. These may seem like rather technical measures, particularly if you investigate their statistical definitions. However, by routinely looking at skew and kurtosis during the assay, you will discover that they help you build a quick picture of the nature of the variable.

- *Distribution histogram:* A *histogram* is a graph that depicts how many values are present in each part of the range of a variable. If you have access to a tool to create histograms, a quick glance will reveal a great deal. For instance, that one quick glance shows whether the distribution is continuous, has outliers, is multi-modal (more than one cluster of values), and many other features that experience will quickly show as important.

- *Error values:* Oftentimes, a non-numeric value will sneak into a variable. Or, sometimes an error made while creating the data set may move a whole section from one variable to another. This may put a chunk of categorical values in the middle of a numeric variable. Or, perhaps a section of a variable will have a set of values highly dissimilar from the others. If detected, these errors can be fixed; if not, they can destroy the miner's best efforts.

- *Outliers:* These values are located far from the majority of values. There may be nothing amiss when single or value-groups of outliers are discovered, but they are at least more likely to be erroneous than nonoutlying values. It is certainly worth checking. However, they shouldn't be removed or altered just because they are outliers. For instance, the evidence for the ozone hole in the upper atmosphere was present in the data for years before the presence of the hole was discovered. It was simply removed from the data set before modeling for all that time—and therefore ignored—because it was outlying data. However, a miner needs to be very aware of the presence of outliers since it makes a great difference to some mining tools, and outliers may have to receive special treatment during preparation.

9.2.1.2 Basic Checks on Date Variables

The main problem with time and date variables is that they appear in a wide variety of formats. Some mining tools can handle date variables, or at least recognize them as dates, if they are in the appropriate format; others can't recognize dates at all. That does not mean that such tools cannot be used to mine the information from date-type data; it only means that the date information has to be re-coded, (see Section 9.3). You can still perform some basic checks: Is the range of dates reasonable? Are any expected date ranges missing? Are there missing values, outliers, error values, and—most particularly for dates—surrogate nulls? The number of people reportedly born on 1/1/1901 is really quite remarkable in many data sets, for instance. As with numeric variables, a histogram for dates may be very revealing. In fact, all of the basic checks described above for numeric variables essentially apply to date variables too since these are, in a sense, only a particular type of numeric variable.

9.2.1.3   Basic Checks on Categorical Variables

Categorical variables may have few values (such as gender) or many (such as ZIP codes or personal names) in a variable. For a categorical variable with few values, it is usually quite easy to list all of them to determine whether they are reasonable. When there are many values, it's usually impossible to check them all individually.

When it is impossible to inspect all of the values, use a histogram type of graphical check. One difficulty with categorical values is that there is very often no rationale for ordering the categories, so there is no metric by which to determine how to arrange the category labels on the histogram's axis. Even so, much can be learned by quickly inspecting such a chart. Look for patterns such as the following:

- *Modal distribution:* Some categorical variables have a very high proportion of instances fall into relatively few categories, and only relatively few instances fall into very many categories. Retail grocery items purchased are a good example of this. In any single shopping basket, many people include selections from relatively few staples (bread, milk) in their purchases and relatively few people include any one of the nonstaple items (toothpaste, organic cereal). Recall that in numeric distributions, modal values occur the most frequently—it's the same for categorical values. Of course, at this stage in the assay for any variable, the miner only needs to see if the variable includes values and distributions that are at least not a surprise.

- *Uniform distribution:* Some categorical variables show their categories fairly evenly represented by count in a data set. A histogram-type display (in which the height of a bar represents the number of instances in a data set with a particular value) will show each category with relatively uniform height.

- *Monotonic distribution:* In this case, every categorical value is unique, so every category has exactly one entry. For instance, serial numbers, personal names, and Social Security numbers are all monotonic and categorical in spite of the term "number" in the categorical description. Although composed of digits, and although there may be very complex and useful information encoded in the way that each label is structured, there is no numerically meaningful structure in these variables. (What would it mean to add, subtract, multiply, or express the ratio of two Social Security or serial numbers, for instance?) Again, in the assay, ask yourself whether such a structure is expected, and what needs to be done if, as often happens in practice, some supposedly monotonic categories do have multiple entries. (The Social Security numbers "000-00-0000" and "999-99-9999" are very popular, for instance, but should almost certainly be recognized as surrogate nulls.)

9.2.2 Repairing Basic Problems with Variables

(See MIII:AB.9.6, MIII:TB.9.1) It is conceivable that one day a data miner somewhere will have a data set to model that has no problems and in which nothing needs to be repaired. But the author very strongly suspects that it hasn't happened yet, and isn't likely to any time soon! Strictly speaking, the assay is only a look at a data set, not adjustment to and modeling of data. As a description of the process, this works fine. The problem is that as the assay proceeds from examining variables individually to looking at the data set as a whole, it is best practice to fix at least the worst problems with each variable before proceeding to work with the entire data set. Correcting these problems is really the first step in preparing the data for mining rather than just assaying since from here on, after the problems have been fixed to at least some degree, the data is no longer in its "raw" state. So fixing problems requires making changes to data. But before starting work on the data, a few thoughts about process.

So far, the basic data that has been discovered, and which is expected to be used for mining, is untouched. (Just looking at it didn't change anything.) As a best practice, the miner should keep a copy of this untouched data set, at least as a reference. After every set of changes you make to the data, you should make and keep a backup copy. If disaster strikes, or in the event that some transform produces unwanted consequences, it's easy to take a step back and not lose too much time and effort. This can be very important when working with large data sets. The author uses a system considered big and fast at the time of this writing (1.2 Ghz processor with 1GB of memory and 100GB of high speed disk), although with the speed of computer development, such a system will probably be considered quite tame when you are reading this. Nonetheless, with large data sets and large transforms, a run that modifies data sets can still take hours. (A couple of thousand variables with several million records can take significant "crunching.") For this reason, and if the data set to be modified is large, it is well worth experimenting with a small sample of the whole data set and exploring and checking the results before committing to modifying the whole data set. (Sampling data sets for mining—why it's needed and how to do it—is covered in Chapter 11.)

Even more important than backing up the data set is to document and "carry" the transformations forward from stage to stage. Raw data sets almost always have to be modified before modeling. In fact, data preparation is a process of modifying data so that it "works" better for mining. Often, the model that a miner constructs has to be applied to fresh data from the real world. In this case, the raw data that is available at the beginning of the process is at least representative of the data that the mined model will ultimately have to run on—except that the mined model won't actually be created using raw data, but using the data as transformed and modified during data preparation. So, if the mined model is expected to run on new, run-time data making predictions, for example, then whatever transformations are ultimately made to modify the raw data set used for creating a mined model will also have to be made again to new raw data at run-time. Many modern mining tools automatically note and "remember" all transformations that a miner makes to variables—at least those made within the environment provided by the tool. Such tools can then automatically deploy the necessary data modifications at run-time. However, not all useful and powerful tools will do this. Tools that do not make or carry transformations assume that any data transformation is carried out separately from the mining tool environment.

Pros and cons of selected commercial mining tools are discussed in Chapter 11. However, it's worth briefly noting here that at present no commercial mining tool is capable of making many of even the basic transformations that a miner will want or need to make to adjust a data set, so there will almost always be sets of transformations that require tools outside of the commercial tool's environment. With experience, the number of useful transformations that the miner wants to make that a mining tool can't manage only increases. At present, and for at least the foreseeable future, the miner will find it necessary to make transformations outside the environment of even the most complete and sophisticated of the current crop of mining tools.

With this as preamble, there are some very basic transformations to variables that should be made before continuing with the assay. There are only a few of them at this stage, but they are important.

9.2.2.1 Basic Adjustments to Numeric Variables

There are essentially three basic adjustments to make at this stage to numeric variables:

1. *Constant values:* Checking the basic statistics for a variable may show that although the variable has a numeric value, it has only a single value and no variance. It's quite easy for such values to sneak into a data set, especially if they have been extracted from a larger data set. The variable may vary in the larger data set, but not in the sample. For instance, if the sample is being used to model credit card data of the most creditworthy individuals, the variable "Credit Limit" may have some uniform value since all highly creditworthy customers get the maximum. Whatever the reason, and if, after checking, the constant value is one that is expected, then this variable should be removed. With no change at all in its value, it at least carries no information. However, another reason for removing constant value variables at this stage is that some of the tools that will be used in the next stage of the assay may not be able to handle constant values. Some mining tools

really don't care about constant values, but others "blow up." It's easier just to remove the variable at this stage.

2. *Empty variables:* Sometimes variables turn up that are totally without any values—all nulls. ("Null" is not a value. In fact, null is explicitly not a value. That is the purpose of the null designation.) Naturally, these too carry no information since, as with all nulls, this is identical to not having the variable in the data set at all.

3. *Sparsely populated variables:* These are variables that are mostly populated with nulls—say 80% to 99.999% nulls—but that do have a few values present. These can be very tricky indeed, because it is possible that, in the limited number of instances where these variables do have values, the values may be quite important. Unfortunately, with so few values, many mining tools may have severe indigestion when mining such sparse data. What to do with sparse variables must depend to some extent on the capabilities and sensitivities of the mining tool to be used. There are advanced preparation techniques for handling such variables, but an easy way to deal with them is to try to model what happens with them in the data set, and then try modeling again without them in the data set. If they cause a problem, remove them. However, a beginning miner who isn't exactly sure how to recognize problems caused by sparsely populated variables is better off removing them. (If in doubt, throw 'em out!) With such a low general information content, removing them won't degrade the overall performance of the model much, whereas including them may significantly degrade overall model performance.

9.2.2.2 Basic Adjustments to Date Variables

As noted before, date variables can be considered as a special type of numeric variable. In a later section on feature extraction (Section 9.3), you will see how it becomes very important to make particular types of transformations to date and time variables. However, at this basic stage, and for purposes of continuing the assay, it is enough to think of date variables in a way similar to the numeric variables just discussed:

- *Constant dates:* These are not often encountered, but if a date variable does in fact contain only one date, remove the variable.
- *Empty dates:* As before, entirely empty variables are of no value as far as mining goes. Remove the variable.
- *Sparsely populated dates:* Use the same method as for sparsely populated numeric variables.

9.2.2.3   Basic Adjustments to Categorical Variables

(See MIII:AB.9.7) To quite a large degree, considerations for categorical variables are similar to those already mentioned. Constant, empty, and sparsely populated categoricals can be treated in the same way as numeric and date variables. However, even at this basic stage of adjustment, categorical variables begin to warrant additional consideration:

- *Pseudo-numeric categorical variables:* Remember that some categorical variables, such as ZIP codes, may masquerade as numeric variables. Most data mining tools that handle categorical variables (which is almost all of them) have some specific mechanism for flagging a variable as categorical, regardless of the fact that it appears to be numeric. It's important to identify and flag such variables at this point.

- *High category count variables:* Categorical variables that have very high numbers of categories are going to cause any mining tool some form of indigestion. One problem here is that many tools have some form of internal transformation that will allow the tool to cope with the problems that these variables would otherwise cause. The problem for the miner is that although whatever adjustment the tool suggests or adopts will allow modeling to continue, the adjustment almost certainly will not be the one that best suits the business problem. Since the assay is intended to determine the worth of the data set for mining, it's important to assay the variables as they will be mined, and high category count variables are certainly going to need more than automated adjustment. At this point, if the miner is not a domain expert and is unable to decide what adjustment should be made, it is worth getting a domain expert involved to determine what to do. Strictly speaking, this is more akin to feature extraction from variables (see Section 9.3), but this point in the assay is not too early to find out how to adjust these variables.

- *Ordinal categorical variables:* (See MIII:AB.9.8) Some categoricals have a natural ordering or ranking—at least within some domain. Whenever something is ordered but expressed as a categorical—say, "order of importance" or "sales rank"—it may be worth *numerating the categorical.* This consists of simply assigning a number to a category based on its rank position or ordering.

- *Monotonic categorical variables:* Recall that these are variables in which every category is unique. There are a huge number of such variables: account numbers, serial numbers, order numbers—their variety is endless. What they have in common is that each is intended to identify a unique instance of some event. It may well be possible to transform them in some useful way—Social Security numbers contain information about date and place of birth or naturalization, for instance; car license plates provide information about state, county, and date of registration. However, as they stand, monotonic categoricals can't be usefully mined. If they can't be transformed in useful ways, by far the safest thing to do is discard them.

9.2.3 Basic Checks on the Data Set

So far, the assay process has involved evaluating only one variable at a time. Next, the miner uses the assay to examine the data as part of an integrated whole using a basic data mining tool—a form of decision tree. The tree used here is a CHAID tree (an acronym for CHi squared Automatic Interaction Detection). Any form of tree will serve so long as the miner can make single variable splits with it. The next step in the assay is single variable analysis (comparing each variable against another); these examples will use single variable CHAID analysis.

Decision trees, along with other modeling tool algorithms, are discussed in Chapter 10. It is enough at this point to know that this mining tool, when given a single variable from a data set as a target, can automatically find the variable most associated with it from the others in the data set, and can characterize the association. It can also be given a target variable and specifically pointed at some other variable (or group of variables) and instructed to characterize whatever relationship exists. Using the tool this way allows the miner to determine if the data set "makes sense."

For instance, in one case, the author discovered that for some claims, 93% of employable males were not deceased. Not a particularly amazing discovery—but it confirmed that, at least in this regard, most of the data did indeed "make sense" since this is what might be expected. However, although this is the sort of common sense information that the assay is after, in part, there is a "rest of the story" here, too. Stated the other way around, the result is more surprising: 7% of the time, claims were from employable males who were dead! The data set contained 100,000 records, so there were apparently 7,000 claims from dead working men. Actually, at least 60% of this turned out—as you might expect—to be data entry errors. However, after careful checking, that still left about 2,800 unaccounted for (40% of 7,000), which in this case actually turned out to warrant investigation as potential fraud. Although this occurred only in a small part of the data set, the fraud turned out to be sizeable in value and ultimately significant to the business.

9.2.3.1 Single Variable CHAID Analysis

(See MIII:TB.9.2) As a data miner involved in a data assay, expect to spend some time looking at data with single variable CHAID (or similar) analysis.

Only a single, brief example is shown here to explain the principle, but the only way to gain familiarity is through practice—lots of it. It is a terrific way to extend familiarity with the data.

The example data set used to produce Figure 9.5 contains many variables. The variable PRD1 is a specially created predictor variable that reports on the future performance of the business object of interest—in this case, the stock market. Figure 9.5 shows that selecting the predictor as the variable of interest, single variable CHAID analysis finds that the variable SPRD (spread) is the one most associated with future market performance in this data set. It's an easy step from there to discover, for instance, which variables associate with spread. As shown in Figure 9.6, it turns out to be a variable SP, which isn't surprising as this is a different way of expressing spread—a slightly different feature in this case, and one that should associate well with spread. However, from this analysis, it seems to carry identical information, since the one perfectly predicts the other. Perhaps one is redundant?

As a matter of fact, it turns out that it's not redundant in this case, and interaction effects from the two variables are different, but discovering that requires more investigation than shown here. The relationships in this data set are highly discontinuous and much masked by noise, but this single variable CHAID analysis is a very good way of exploring and getting familiar with the data.

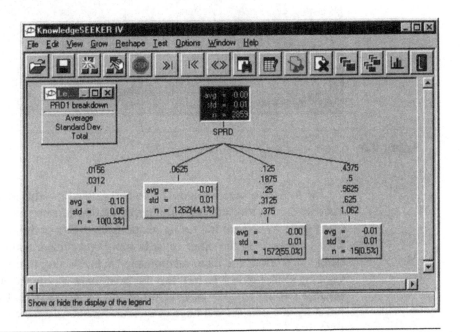

Figure 9.5   Single variable CHAID analysis on variable PRD1 which associates with SPRD.

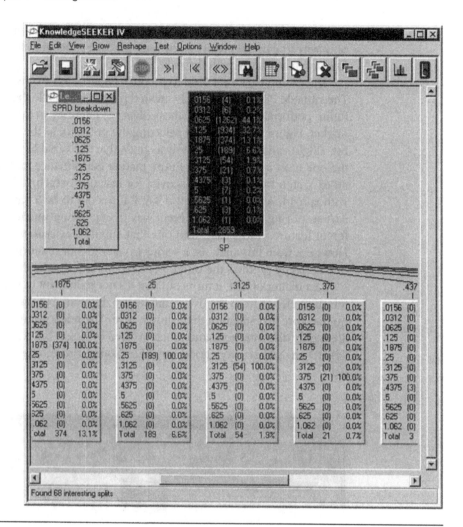

Figure 9.6 Single variable CHAID investigating SPRD.

The tool used here—Angoss KnowledgeSEEKER—also features a graphical display that reveals much about the relationship between SPRD and SP (see Figure 9.7). There is a strong relationship in part of the range. However, what's going on in the other cells? Is some other relationship masked here by the strength of the main relationship? Actually, yes, there is—and an interesting exploration it is, too. But the point here is only to introduce single variable CHAID analysis as an approach to exploring data. Uncovering the full story in a data set will have to be a useful exercise for you to do in your own time.

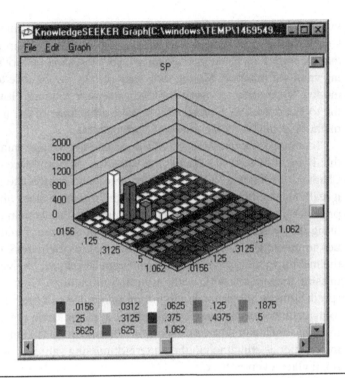

Figure 9.7   Graphical depiction of variable interaction between SPRD and SP.

9.2.3.2   Basic Adjustments to Missing Values

Missing values in any type of variable present special, and very tricky, problems due to the fact that values missing in a data set are very likely not missing at random. There is almost invariably some pattern to the way in which the values are missing. These missing values may be associated with each other, so that when "age" is missing, for instance, perhaps "date of birth" has a far higher chance of being missing than when "age" is present. Missing values may also associate with values that are present, so that when, say, "age" is present, "rental status" is missing more frequently than when "age" is missing. There may be conditional patterns as well, so that when "age" is filled in for some part of its range, other variable values may have a higher probability of being missing than when "age" is present, but in some other part of its range.

Discovering and understanding these missing value patterns may be an important part of the discoveries that a miner makes. However, at this stage, that isn't the main consideration. Focus on the fact that some values are missing or not missing, and the patterns with which they are or are not missing may themselves carry useful predictive or inferential information. The problem the miner now faces is that missing values may contain useful patterns that are important to keep in a data set, yet most tools cannot mine this missing value information. Mining tools may or may not be able to create useful models when some or many variable values are missing. However, none of the tools are (at this writing) able to take advantage of the information that might be available in the missing value patterns.

To simplify the explanation of this problem, consider mining tools as either being able to deal with missing variables, or not. (More on this topic in Chapter 10.) When a tool is said to be able to accommodate missing values, it really means that the tool will ignore the missing values and use only the present values in its calculations. It also means that its mining calculations using the present values are not distorted when some of the variables' values are missing (that is, having nulls). The first problem here is that, because the missing values are missing in some regular pattern, the values that aren't missing are present with some nonrandom pattern. Therefore, outcomes (predictions or inferences) depend on particular patterns of present values to make their conclusions. This is in itself a distortion in a mined model that the tools don't take into consideration. The second problem is that whatever information is contained in the pattern of missing values is not discovered—not, in fact, even noticed.

Whereas some mining tools are described as being able to handle missing values, other mining tools cannot handle these null values at all. When nulls are present, they will in some way "crash" the algorithm on which the tool is based. For such tools, some non-null value has to be found for the tool to work—but using inappropriate values actually introduces patterns into the data that simply are not justified, and almost certainly not present in the real world. A mining tool will "discover" these miner-introduced patterns in the data, and the miner may well think the relationships to be real, applicable, and useable. Even most of the validity checks on models (discussed in Chapter 11) won't reveal them. However, the expected results will not hold up in the real world. This is a troubling problem for a less experienced miner, particularly when a mining tool obligingly "fills in" the missing values with an automated routine that chooses fill-in values inappropriately.

It's a pernicious problem. There are good methods of finding replacement values, even good fully automated methods, but by and large, they are not incorporated into mining tools available today. A major problem is that whatever method is used has to be applied to run-time data, not just the data that a miner is using to make a model. Worse, the most commonly recommended methods of replacing missing values—using the mean, median, or mode as replacement values—are damaging choices.

What can a miner do at this stage? At this point, not very much. Remember, at this point, your objective is to evaluate what is in the data, not to model it.

The purpose of this preamble is to raise awareness of this as an issue, and to point out that there may be useful patterns and information from the fact that there are missing values. The assay needs, in part, to establish if this is the case. At this stage in the assay, none of the missing values are actually replaced with anything. Instead, one of the miner's tasks is to discover whether values are missing, and if so, to discover clues suggesting what to do about it.

One way to discover whether the missing value information is important starts with making a temporary copy of the whole data set. For this exploration, use the temporary copy instead of the original data set. Except for the target or output variable, replace all of the values that are present with, say, "1" and all of the values that are missing with, say, "0." The modified data set now contains no null, or missing, values. Use the tree tool to find which, if any, of the modified variables in this data set has a relationship with the target. If you find such a variable, exclude it and try again. Keep going until there is no strong association between the target and any individual remaining variable. Having done that, apply the tree, using all of the associated variables to predict the output. It's worth then trying to build a similar model using all of the variables. If it's possible to make any sort of prediction of the output, the missing values must be suspected of containing useful information. It's merely a suspicion at this stage because any information in the missing value patterns may be duplicated in some other way by the data in the unmodified data set. Thus, it isn't certain that any discovered relationship in the patterns of occurrence of missing values will turn out to be important. But it is important to have discovered that there may be additional and useful information in the pattern with which values are present or missing. This is the assay, so nothing more will be done at this stage. But whether missing values do, or do not, carry information, you've learned something important about the data. (Chapter 11 discusses how to use and incorporate any information from missing values into a mined model.)

9.2.3.3   Anachronistic Variables

(See MIII:TB.9.3) These are nasty wee beasties! An anachronism is something that is out of place in time. In this case, *anachronistic variables* carry information that is displaced in time. Specifically, the variable tells of something that cannot be known at prediction or inferencing time. Relative to some "now" in the data set, it tells of some future outcome, and is embedded in the "input" variable side of the data set. Such variables carry information that is useless to the miner in building a predictive model since, if used, the model will need information that cannot be known at the time that the prediction is needed. (It's easy to predict the overall stock market movement if the model includes tomorrow's closing price for the Dow. It's just that such a model can't be deployed.)

Sometimes these anachronistic variables can be very sneaky. In one case, a wireless company wanted a churn model—that is, they wanted a model that would calculate/predict the risk that a customer was going to leave the company. The model, obviously, could use only data that was available and could be known some time before a customer churned. In this case, this included call usage patterns, bill payment patterns, billing plan, geographic areas visited, and a lot of other criteria. It specifically did not include on the input side any information that indicated that the customer had definitely churned or definitely had not churned. Of course, the output side—that is, the predictor variable—had to be a did/did-not churn flag of some sort.

However, in many (perhaps most) real world data sets, it's not always easy to spot anachronistic variables. In this case, one of the variables included in the data set was a categorical variable that encoded the salesperson responsible for the account. The salesperson indicated was allegedly the person responsible for servicing the account during its lifetime. This looked like a harmless enough variable—until it turned out that the model was able to predict a proclivity to churn with 90% accuracy. This (in any real world churn model) is simply too good to be true! And it really was too good to be true. Further investigation showed that some salespeople had customers with a huge churn rate, whereas other salesfolk had a far more reasonable churn rate among their customers. In fact, it was possible to get a really good idea of who was going to churn simply by identifying their assigned account salesperson. Does this mean bad news for salespeople? Were some of the salespeople so repulsive that they were positively driving customers away?

Actually, no. What happened was that, after the fact, some of the sales team were assigned to call on customers who had given notice that they were canceling service in order to discover the reasons for the cancellation. After the fact, the name of the original salesperson for the account was changed and the name of the new salesperson assigned to call on terminating customers was substituted. So having one of these salespeople assigned to the account was not a cause of churn, but a result. However, since these salespeople couldn't have been assigned until after the fact, this field was worse than useless in building any churn model—it was positively damaging.

There are really only two ways to look for anachronistic variables. One is to look at and think about what is in the data. The other is to build single variable and simple, multiple variable models and look for results that are too good to be true. "Too good to be true" very often is exactly that. When faced with known or suspected anachronistic variables, remove them from the model.

The good news with anachronistic variables is that they won't do much harm in the real world since the model can't be deployed if it depends on having information from the future available at run time. The bad news is that any model built to be deployed on current data that actually calls for future data is a waste of time and resources, and can never return the results expected.

9.2.3.4   Basic Data Adequacy Assessment 1: How Much Is Enough?

At this point in the assay, the miner begins to have a feel for the data. However, the miner still does not know yet whether the data is sufficient for its intended purpose. Essentially, the miner needs some assessment of whether there is enough information about the real world reflected in the data to make a model that will actually "work"—that is, whether it will make decent predictions if a predictive model is needed, or allow decent inferences if an inferential model is needed, and so on. Unfortunately, there is no rigorous way to absolutely determine from the data alone whether this is so. However, there are various ways to estimate, given the data on hand, if the data is insufficient. In other words, although it's hard to determine if there is enough data, by turning the problem around, it's easier to determine if there is not enough.

A little more formally, having data describing all instances that have or could occur in the real world is the only way to know for sure that the data does in fact represent the world completely—or at least, the part of the world that the data purports to be about. This usually impossible to collect, comprehensive data set represents what is called the *population.* Roughly speaking, the population consists of all of the things that exist to be measured in the real world. Since it is almost always impossible to collect data that represents the population, a miner usually works with some lesser collection, called a *sample.* Intuitively, the larger a sample, the better it will reflect the population at large, so long as the sample instances are drawn at random from the population. True random selection means that data instances from every member of the population are equally likely to be included in the sample. So, instances that occur more frequently in the population will turn up more frequently in the sample. In fact, if the sample is big enough, the relative frequencies in a random sample will be very close indeed to the relative frequencies that occur in the population—so close, for all practical purposes, as to be identical. To assay data adequacy, the miner needs to determine whether there is enough data in the sample that it does indeed accurately reflect the relative frequencies in the population. This presents a fundamental problem: the miner has no access to the population as a whole to verify this, only to a sample.

To briefly illustrate the problem, consider trying to determine the mean height of the human population of the world. It's impossible, as a simple practical matter, to measure the height of everyone on the planet. Every minute some people are born, and some die. Some people are growing, while some are shrinking with age. Nonetheless, it's possible to obtain measurements for several million people—perhaps from driving license records—and work out an average reported height from that data. This would be a large enough sample that, if drawn from as many different countries as possible, the calculated average adult height at least could fairly confidently be expected to be close to whatever the actual, and continually varying, adult height "really" is at any instant for the whole human population. Not perfect for any number of reasons, but probably pretty close.

It's worth noting here that there are many more advanced techniques for determining data adequacy than those discussed next, some of which are highly computationally intensive. As a miner gains more experience, it's worth building (or perhaps, finding) tools that can make these more accurate assessments. Unfortunately, no commercially available mining tools at this writing incorporate components that will rigorously assess data adequacy, leaving it to the miner to devise some way of making the assessment. The description provided here is indeed a basic check, rough and ready, but far better than not knowing anything about data adequacy. But be warned—passing this test doesn't guarantee data adequacy. Failing this basic test, however, means that more or better data is needed. In other words, passing the test means that the data might be sufficient; failing means it probably isn't.

The technique involves using the modeling tool of choice to build a few models. (As already mentioned, the modeling tool discussion is coming up in Chapter 10.) Start by splitting the data set into two parts—one part with 80% of the data and one part with 20%. If possible, select the instances (records) for each data set at random from the initial data set. One way to do this is to add a numeric variable to the initial data set and fill it with random numbers having values between 0 and 1. Copy all records with, say, values in this random variable of >0.8 to the 20% data set, and copy the rest to the 80% data set. Call the 80% data set the "training" data, and call the 20% data set the "test" data.

Select 11 variables at random from the training data set. Use 10 of them to build a predictive model of the 11th variable. Repeat this process up to 10 times, not reusing any already used variables. Save each model with a different name. This process creates up to 10 predictive models, depending on the number of variables in the original data set. Note how well each model performs in the training data set. Turn now to the test data set. Use each of the saved models to make predictions in the test data set, and note how well each model performs. (Don't create new models in the test data set. Just use the models created in the training data set to make predictions in the test data set.)

The essential idea next is to compare how successfully each model predicts in the two data sets. If all of the models perform essentially identically in both data sets, then—at least by this basic test—the data set seems adequate. If results vary wildly, then the data set is very likely inadequate. It is, however, difficult to give precise instructions for how to make the comparison. Different data mining tools do not give similar measures of model performance. In any case, some of the models will probably perform quite similarly in the two data sets, and others quite differently. Note carefully that the actual quality of each model is completely unimportant in this comparison. It is only important that the same model be equally good or bad in both training and test data sets.

There are two measures of model quality that are common enough to be mentioned. One is a statistically based measure called *R*, sometimes also called *correlation*. Another is called a *confusion matrix*. R will appear as a number between 1 and −1. For comparison purposes, if you use the R measure, note the number generated for each model in the training set, sum them, and then divide by the number of models actually made. (In other words, determine the average R for all of the models in the training data set.) Repeat in the test data set. The two average R numbers should be within at least 10% of each other. Also, when comparing the performance of individual models in each data set, at least 60% of the models (6 of them if all 10 were made) should have R numbers from the training and test data sets well within 10% of each other.

A confusion matrix often appears as a square with four numbers in the square. Again, all of these four numbers should fall within 10% of each other, comparing each model with its own performance in training and test data sets across all 10 models. Again, at least 60% of the models individually should be within 10% of each other. (Confusion matrices are covered in more detail in Chapter 11.)

Remember that this is a rough and ready measure, but one that is very useful. Essentially, if the relationships learned by the modeling tool in the training data set represent the relationships in the population, then those relationships will also exist in the test data set (which is another data set that is representative of the same population). Since it takes less data to confirm a relationship than to learn one in a data set, most of the data goes into the training set, with a smaller portion going into the test data set. (See MIII:TB.9.4)

9.2.3.5 Basic Data Adequacy Assessment 2: Negative Examples

An industrial controls manufacturing company wanted to use data mining to run an acquisition program. They had plenty of existing customers and decided that the approach to use was to build a model of their best customers, buy a data set, and market to those people who, although not their customers, most resembled them. In order to do this, they carefully prepared a data set that represented their best customers. Using a quite advanced and powerful data mining tool, they extracted what they felt was a good model of their best customers. With this model in hand, and an expensively acquired data set, they applied the model to the data set and were amazed to discover that it seemed that everyone in the purchased data set was an excellent candidate to be one of their best customers. Very impressed with the quality of the purchased list, and confident in the quality of the purchased mining tool, they launched, on the basis of this model, a very expensive marketing campaign—that totally bombed. Panic, frustration, and recrimination set in, and data mining got the blame. Heave that out as an over-hyped marketing tool that was all sizzle and no steak! What went wrong?

The truth is that the tool never had a chance to mine data. The data set so carefully culled from their best sources, carefully prepared, and carefully modeled contained only characteristics of their best customers. What the mining tool learned was that regardless of the input data, everyone was a good customer. Some were slightly better than others to be sure, but essentially everyone in the universe was a great customer, and that was the relationship that the mining tool modeled. Given another data set, all that it could possibly predict was that everyone in it would be a good customer, since the tool had only been exposed to that kind of data. It simply had no way of characterizing anything other than a good customer. The problem wasn't in the tool, the marketing program, or anywhere else—except in the data.

If what's needed is to discriminate between good customers and bad customers, the tool needs to see examples of both. If the training data set contains 50% good and 50% bad customers, don't be surprised if that's what it predicts in some other data set, even if the real world proportions are different. A mining tool will learn what is present in the data set used for mining—it won't learn anything about the nature of the world at all, only about the data. If the model is to reflect the world, so too must the data used for mining reflect the world. And most specifically, the data must contain both examples of the phenomena of interest and counterexamples.

As a modeling technique (discussed in more detail in Chapter 11), it is sometimes necessary to structure the data so that it is easier to model. Imposing such structure means that the data doesn't any longer accurately represent the world. However, if deliberately and carefully distorted by the miner, the distortion can equally carefully be allowed for in the actual predictions. But however much distortion is introduced, it is still essential to include the full range of whatever is to be mined in the data, even if the proportions of occurrence don't match the proportions of occurrence in the real world. A mining tool won't—can't—learn about what it can't see in the data.

Be sure that you have answered these two assay questions:

1. Does this data represent the full range of outcomes of interest, or the full range of behaviors of interest?
2. How do the frequencies of occurrence of the outcomes/behaviors of interest in the data set compare to the outcome/behavior frequencies in the real world?

9.2.3.6   Sampling Bias

Data is always said to be "sampled," and a data set is usually called, in statistical terms, a *sample*. It's a sample because it usually represents only a small portion of all the data that could possibly be collected. All the possible data is called the *population,* and it's from this that the sample comes. Sometimes, though very rarely, all of the data—the population—is actually available; for mining this is still called a sample, but in this rare case it would be a 100% sample.

In all cases except for a 100% sample, the data that goes into the data set is only a part of the population, and very often only an infinitesimally small part. Sampling bias turns up when the method of selecting instances of data from the population results in the sample distribution not representing the population distribution. The key here is that it's the way that the instances are selected, the sampling method itself, that introduces bias.

Taking a sample of the American population, for instance, is often done by random selection from home telephone numbers in the United States. What's wrong with this as a sampling method? It depends. If the sample is to be used, say, to estimate what percentage of the population has telephone service, it's immediately obvious that this sampling method is a complete bust! The sample is biased in favor of instances (people) who have phones. Well, yes, this is obvious. What's less obvious, perhaps, is that not all homes have a single phone. It may well turn out that higher income homes have more phones per home than lower income homes. A random sample of phone numbers will be preferentially biased in this case to contact people with higher incomes simply because homes with multiple phones are more likely to be called than homes with single phones. Thus, a random sample of this sort uses a method that is inherently biased, or in other words, the method itself predisposes the data to reflect a different state of the world than actually exists in the population.

Whether a biased sample affects the results of modeling, of course, depends entirely on what is to be modeled, or, in other words, on the business problem. However, sampling bias can very often creep into a data set unnoticed, which is why sampling, and the design of sampling plans, requires such careful attention, and is a sort of subspecialty of it's own. (See the Resources section at the end of the book for some further pointers.)

However, a data miner usually has little or nothing to do with designing a sampling strategy, and little to do with designing even a data collection strategy. For a miner, the data set is usually pretty much a fait accompli, and has to be accepted as is, although modified for modeling as described in most of the chapters in Part II of this book. Going back to the source for better data is usually not an option. The miner's job is to work with what's available and do the best job possible.

As far as sampling bias is concerned, the miner's job is to infer, detect, and correct for it if it exists, and if it's possible at all. And there lies the rub! Theoretically, it's impossible to detect sampling bias in any data set considering only the content of the data set itself. However, there may be clues. If they are present, they will still only be clues, but they are the best hint that a miner can get from the data itself.

9.2.3.6.1 *Bias and Distribution*

Fairly obviously, as the value of the output battery variable(s) changes its value across its range, so too the input battery variables change in values across their ranges. The actual relationship between input battery variables and output battery variable(s) may not be obvious, indeed it may be tenuous, tortuous, or nebulous, but if it doesn't exist at all then the input battery has nothing to say about the output battery, and the miner should pack up and move on.

However, although the values may change, very often the distributions of values in the variables at different points in their ranges don't change. Here is where a clue to sampling bias may lie. It's by no means conclusive, but if the distributions among the variables change as the value of the output battery variable(s) changes, it's a hint that sampling bias may lurk in the data set. Why?

The essence of the idea is that if values are related to each other in however intricate and nonobvious a way, they are expected to change. Distributions are not, so if they do there must be some unaccounted phenomenon going on somewhere to account for it—and the somewhere that it is going on is outside of the variables collected in the data set. So, for instance, it might happen that variables possibly collected in the telephone sampling method mentioned earlier might be own/rent flag, house square footage, income level, occupation, and many other possible measurements that would change in distribution, not merely in value, with the changes in opinion collected. Here would be a clue that sampling bias was at work—but at best it's no more than a clue.

The best that a miner can do is to compare distributions for the input variables with subranges of values of the output variables, and be suspicious! Even with such clues in hand, if sampling bias exists, it will still have to be justified based on external evidence. Changes in distribution are no more than hints, but at least hint enough to raise suspicions.

9.2.3.7 Completing the Basic Assay

Although the assay is intended to help a miner discover the important parameters and limitations of a data set, finding out this information alone isn't enough. Of course, this is information that will be used in later stages, or used to justify a decision to go forward or change the direction of the mining project. Keep notes about what is happening in the data and how it was discovered. This section on the assay, even though it is a most basic assay, reveals a tremendous amount of useful information. Very often a written report of the assay information from the miner to the relevant stakeholders is one of the most useful results from mining. As noted earlier, it is always possible that this assay for mining is the first time that the data has been so carefully scrutinized.

Also, this is basic guidance. It is highly likely that other basic questions of interest will pop into the miner's head as the assay goes along. Fine—include them. These notes in this section are included as guidance, not as a comprehensive structure to be rigorously followed. Be inventive! Be creative! (Be careful!)

9.3 Basic Feature Extraction

A *feature,* in this case, means no more than "something notable in the data." Now, of course, something notable must depend on the defined mining purpose of the data set. It might or might not be notable, for instance, that some particular data set includes more men than women. (Although it's always pretty notable if a data set contains deceased men still working and making insurance claims!) Also, sometimes the variables of a data set are called *features* of a data set. In data mining, the term *feature* has a context-dependent usage, which isn't hard to understand, once you get the hang of it. As in the previous section, there is much more to feature extraction than this section covers, but there is enough explained here to get you started.

The term *extraction* is used here because the features discussed will originate from the data already assayed, but also will add to that data. This isn't getting more out of data than is already there; it's really a matter of re-expressing the information in the data so that it becomes useable. There can very well be a huge amount of information contained in a data set in a way that is completely inaccessible to any mining tool. As a brief example of how this occurs, suppose that a data set had latitude and longitude information for the home locations of customers. Suppose that it also contained latitude and longitude information for store locations. It makes no difference which mining tool is used, it won't discover that "distance to store" is important (supposing that it is important in this example) from raw latitude and longitude information. Some transformation is needed to make distance information accessible to the mining tool. One method involves creating, in the data set, a new variable for each store so that every customer's home location has a distance measure to that store. This might work if it was a local neighbor-hood with a few stores; for a national chain with (perhaps) hundreds of stores, this almost certainly wouldn't be too useful and some other approach would have to be devised depending on the exact circumstances. Each customer, for instance, could have a variable added that included "distance to nearest store," which would be gleaned by "extracting" this information from the latitude and longitude information in the data set.

At this basic level of feature extraction, the extracted features are manifested as extra variables. However, as the previous example shows, what is extracted must depend on the nature of the problem and the nature of the data. There are no hard-and-fast rules for how to extract features. However, the following sections offer useful, basic guidelines for what to think about.

9.3.1 Representing Time, Distance, and Differential Relationships

Remembering that the object of the exercise is to provide a transformation of data into the most accessible form for a mining tool, a very good first question to ask yourself is, "Could I easily use the data the way it's expressed now to make good analyses?" If the answer is "no," then ask, "How could I more easily understand this data if I could change the way it was expressed?" These are not trivial questions. For a start, they may very well require a lot of work to dig up the meanings of arcane variable labels. Or perhaps the variable's intention may be clear from its label, but the content of the variable's values may be very cryptic.

Another way to think about variables is as absolute, linear, or cyclic. An intuitive place to start is with variables that express time. Often, time is expressed in a data set as some sort of date/time label such as "July 4th 2001 at 17:27:45," which expresses a specific date and time to the nearest second. This is an absolute expression of time. There is only one specific instant that this label uniquely represents. But often in mining, absolute time is not much help. *Relative time* expresses the relation of that label to some other label of the same type. For example, with two customer purchases for the same customer at different times, it may be more useful for some mining purposes to extract a relative feature that expresses "length of time since last purchase," which might be abbreviated LOTSLP. In this case, the data set will have a variable added called LOTSLP to hold the extracted feature, and for every customer purchase, a suitable LOTSLP value will be calculated by comparing "this" date/time with the last purchase date/time and noting the difference. Or perhaps the latest purchase date and time will be compared with "now." In this example, LOTSLP is an extracted relative feature and allows a mining tool to learn relationships based on time between purchases.

Many time events turn out to be cyclic, very often based on an annual cycle. In the United States, peaks and troughs in various types of business and commercial activity are very regular, influenced by annual events such as Thanksgiving and Christmas. When such cyclicities are already known, or at least suspected, it is fairly easy to extract a relative feature such as "days to Christmas." But this doesn't help a mining tool to discover a cyclic relationship that is not even suspected. For such discoveries, some generic representation of the annual, or some other cycle, is needed. An unknown regularity is most easily understood and recognized when discovered if it is expressed as a relationship to some known regularity, such as, in this case, the annual cycle. With a generic representation of a cycle present in the data set, the mining tool can "notice" that some phenomenon relates to the cycle in some way. Without any representation of the cycle, no tool could make such an inference.

An apparently easy way to attempt this cyclic representation might seem to be to truncate the date indicator so that it only represents the day, week, or month of the year. The problem with this method, particularly when using day or week numbers, is that although it is intuitively obvious to us that week 52 in one year is right next to week 1 in the next year, it's not obvious to a mining tool. In fact, to a mining tool, it's a plain fact that, numerically, week 52 is as far away from week 1 as this variable ever gets! Not exactly what was intended. Figure 9.8 illustrates the problem, and it's important to note that there are no values that go between week 52 and week 1, so there is no plotted connection shown in this figure. The break is discontinuous. One apparent possible solution would be to represent the weeks or months as categories, but then the mining tool loses all idea of the order in which the

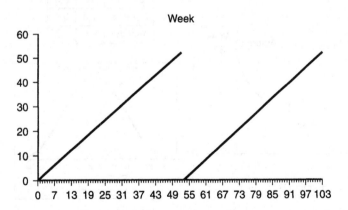

Figure 9.8   Week 52 is as far from week 1 as it can get—whereas for a cycle it should be adjacent. Note that there is a discontinuous transition from week 52 to week 1.

days, weeks, or months occur, and it is this ordering that is important to represent in the data.

The clue to what to do about this problem of letting a mining tool discover cycles lies in the fact that cycles, almost by definition, go around in circles, and circles can't be represented by only one variable or dimension—it takes two. This is illustrated in Figure 9.9. By using two variables, it's possible to extract a feature that has, taking both extracted variables together, a pair of values that uniquely identify any time during a year (or other cyclic period), and which continue to go around and around. This two-variable feature has values for any period that are right next to values for the next period, even when the adjacent periods are the end of one year and the beginning of the next.

So far, this section has discussed representing time in three different ways: in absolute, in linear, and in cyclic representations. The same three representations also apply to spatial variables, as the example of latitude and longitude in the last section showed. In that example, two variables, latitude and longitude, were represented by a single variable—distance to store. But it's not only spatio-temporal variables that can be represented in data in these three ways. Essentially, any variable—especially numerical variables, but also any categorical variable that can be ordered—can be represented in this manner. *Differential representation* expresses the difference between two measurements from here and there, or from now and then, which is what was occur-

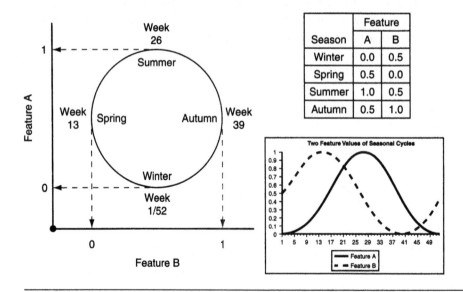

Season	Feature A	Feature B
Winter	0.0	0.5
Spring	0.5	0.0
Summer	1.0	0.5
Autumn	0.5	1.0

Figure 9.9 A two-feature recoding of time has a unique pair of values for every instant and no discontinuities.

ring in the change from absolute to linear feature extraction. So comparing the difference in admission rates between surgical and medical admissions, between household claims and auto claims in insurance, between millinery and hosiery in sales conversion rates, are all differential representations that extend the notion of absolute, linear, and cyclic representations into other domains.

In summary, a miner needs to ask how the data can be best presented to make it most understandable.

9.3.2 Recoding

Coding is the term applied to the results of the process of categorizing information. A simple example is using city names. In an address, the name of a city is simply a category. However, the label alone isn't enough to express the full richness of what the city address implies. A New York address carries very different implications than an address of San Francisco, Atlanta, or Fargo, all of which are North American cities. It may well be possible to discover differences associated with different cities in a data set, depending, of course, on exactly what the data set contains. But very often, a miner doesn't want to discover these associations, but instead wants to use them, in which case the associations have to be explicitly inserted in the data set.

If, to continue this example, the population in the local metropolitan area is thought likely to be an important feature to use in modeling, then add a feature to the data set that includes the population for each city. In one sense, this adds no new information to the data set since the density of the population influences the behavior of the other variables relevant to any specific city anyway. Every instance of "New York" implies an entry of "20 million," every entry of San Francisco, "4 million," and so on. However, if population information is important to the model, this is explicitly added to the data set, and it does add information about the appropriate ranking of cities by population. Perhaps economic activity, population density, geographical spread, and so on are all important. If so, adding all of these pieces of information as fields or variables would be valuable and lead to better models.

However, strictly speaking, adding this information is not really recoding, it's simply adding more data codes that are thought to be relevant to the data set. One example of recoding turned up in the previous section in which the date was recoded as a cyclic expression in two variables. For the date, making this recoding presented the modeling tool with access to a different phenomenon considered possibly important: temporal location in the annual cycle. How might information about cities be usefully recoded? There are a couple of ways. One is called *1-of-n recoding,* the other is called *m-of-n recoding*. It will turn out that 1-of-*n* is really a special case of *m*-of-*n*, but 1-of-*n* is the easier place to begin the explanation.

9.3.2.1   1-of-*n* and *m*-of-*n* Recoding

Some modeling tools may have difficulty in using city names in a single list. In such a form, the algorithm on which the tool is based cannot correctly characterize the information that the city name implies. One fairly common practice is to break out the individual categories, each represented as a separate variable, and then represent category membership by a binary indication (1–0) in the variable (illustrated in Figure 9.10). So for the 50 U.S. states, there would be 50 variables—one for each state—only one of which is coded "1" to indicate a state, all of the other 49 variables being coded "0." With this recoding, there is some maximum number of possible categories, and only one of the categories has the category flag set that indicates that this instance is included in the flagged category. The maximum number of possible categories is represented by *n*. Since only one category is flagged out of the *n* possible categories, this method of recoding is called 1-of-*n*.

This can work fairly well, but only if the number of categories is small. In the case of cities in the United States, as in Figure 9.10, even if the categories were limited to the 5,000 largest cities, this is a very considerable number of variables to add to a data set. In any case, almost all of the variables (4,999) will be flagged as "not-this-category" for any instance, and most of the category fields will be almost empty. In any case, for technical reasons that are touched on in the next chapter, increasing the number of variables in a data set is generally undesirable as it makes modeling the data more difficult. However, note that it's only a poor practice in general. In specific cases, adding a few more carefully chosen variables makes the task much easier. Nonetheless, the objective is to add as few additional variables as possible and in a way that adds useful representations of information into the data set. This is where *m*-of-*n* recoding comes in.

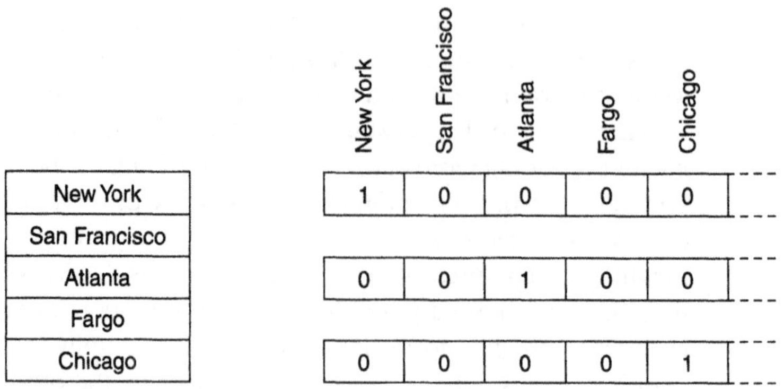

Figure 9.10   Recoding cities as 1-of-*n*.

By using an *m*-of-*n* recoding, the number of category variables can be significantly reduced. Instead of having only one category membership flag on in any instance, *m*-of-*n* has *m* flags on, where *m* is a number 1 or higher, but not more than *n*. Depending entirely on the model's purpose, of course, some additional category variables might be "Metropolitan Area," "Urban Area," "Rural Area," "North East," "North Central," North West," and so on. As shown in Figure 9.11, any specific city would have itself recoded to have several category flags on at the same time. One caveat here is that for an *m*-of-*n* recoding, it is quite possible to have different categories share an encoding. For example, both New York and Boston are major metropolitan cities in the northeastern United States. It is entirely up to the modeler and domain expert, not the miner, to decide if it is important to use a similar code combination, or a different code combination, in such cases. The one important caveat for the miner when making an *m*-of-*n* recoding is if you're unsure of exactly how to make the recoding, look it up or dig it up—don't make it up!

9.3.3 Representing Objects

Data, at least for business modeling, is always about objects. They may be customers, branches, departments, divisions, chart of accounts categories, fraudulent transactions, salespeople, profits, promotions, and a vast number of other similar objects. Data may represent the relationships between object features, such as promotional activity and customer spending, but still the data represents something about these objects. Indeed, for business modeling, these objects all represent real world phenomena. Ultimately, the objective of the mining is to understand what can be done to influence the

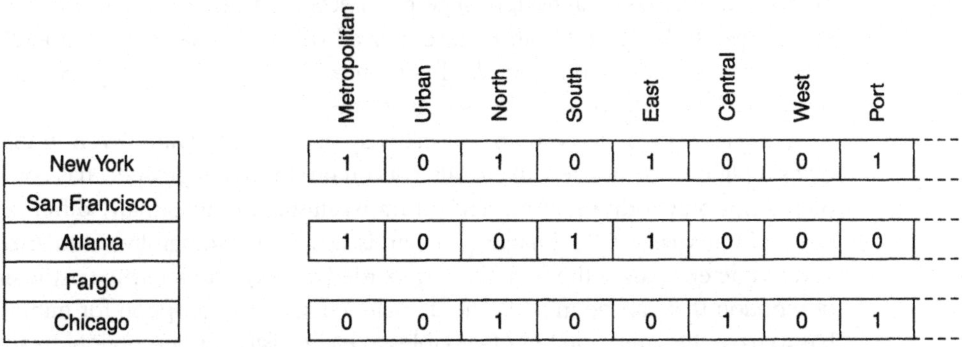

	Metropolitan	Urban	North	South	East	Central	West	Port	
New York	1	0	1	0	1	0	0	1	---
San Francisco									
Atlanta	1	0	0	1	1	0	0	0	---
Fargo									
Chicago	0	0	1	0	0	1	0	1	---

Figure 9.11 Recoding cities as *m*-of-*n*.

undifferentiated course of worldly—specifically business-relevant—events. Thus, in business modeling, it is always the case that the data is being asked to answer questions about business-relevant objects. So it's very important that the data adequately represents the objects of interest in order for the mining tool to infer the appropriate relationships between the features of the objects.

As a more concrete example of a simplified tactical mining problem, say a business wants to influence prospect behavior on a Web site. There are two different identified actions (say, Web pages representing different promotional offers) that it can present at some point in a prospect interaction. What are the objects in this problem, and what are the relationships that need to be characterized? Some of the objects here include the customer (specifically, the customer behaviors that have led to this point in the interaction), the outcomes, and the outcome likelihoods for the possible actions. There are many assumptions here, too. One assumption is that customer behaviors up to this point have some relevance in determining which of the actions to take; another is that taking different actions has some influence on the ultimate outcome. At least these objects and relationships need to be characterized explicitly in the data.

It's important to make sure that the data actually supports the problem to be modeled—if it doesn't, then it's important to reconfigure the whole data set, if necessary, to make sure that it does. Much of the reconfiguration may be in the form of extracting the necessary features as discussed so far, although it may simply build on those techniques and end with a wholesale reconfiguration of the data set.

One very common problem for miners is that the available data to begin with is transaction data, which represents a transaction as its primary object. In the Web site example mentioned previously, the transaction may include a prospect identifier, a date and time stamp, and an action code—say that some particular link was clicked. The data set available may include an almost limitless stream of such transactions. But none of these represents a prospect as an object, although since prospects are uniquely identified, it is at least possible in principle to discover all of the transactions that each prospect has made and assemble them into a description of the prospect's behavior. That indeed is what has to be done.

This can be a huge task, and it isn't easy or straightforward. Even in this oversimplified case, it's very likely (almost certain) that each prospect has completed not only a different number of transactions, but also many different types of transactions. So a major problem is how to meaningfully summarize and characterize all of the transaction-recorded activity into a useful customer description that can be mined. The ultimate customer description for mining has to have the same number of variables in each customer description. In addition, the outcomes of the actions have to be represented, otherwise it won't be possible to discover if customer behavior does indeed have a relationship that can be used to discover which action to take to influence the outcome.

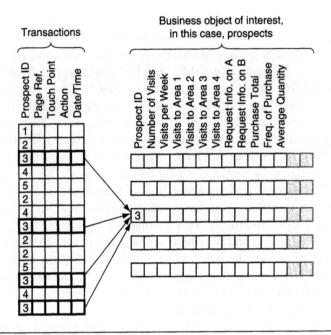

Figure 9.12 Reconfiguring a whole data set to represent the business object of interest, in this case prospects.

Fortunately with mining tools, the problem is only to think of as many different features as possible that might be useful in characterizing the relationship. Modern mining tools will happily discard, and not be much confused by, irrelevant features—as long as the miner supports them with good mining practice. But the crucial point for the miner is to determine and ensure that all of the relevant objects in the problem are indeed represented in the final data set to be mined.

Figure 9.12 illustrates the basic idea that is involved in turning a data set that describes one set of objects into a data set that describes another set of objects. In the Web site example, some of the features that might be of interest are how often the prospect has visited the site, how many visits were made per week, how often specific areas of the site were visited, if any previous information requests were made, and a host of other features—all of which require transformation and recoding to extract from the source data.

9.4 Surveying Data

The assay starts with raw data and ends with an assembled data set that addresses the business problem. Although presented as a continuous process, in fact, any miner will have to loop back through the various parts of the assay many times. Each new feature extracted will need a return to an earlier part of the assay. Nonetheless, the assay has almost entirely focused on the data as a collection of variables, and has looked at the variables as individuals. The data survey can begin only when the "final" data set is ready for modeling. ("Final" is a relative term since something discovered in the survey—or later, something discovered during mining—may always indicate that a change or addition is needed, which means returning to earlier parts of the process. As noted earlier, data preparation is the most time consuming part of mining, and it's not a linear process.)

The survey looks to answer questions about the data set as a whole, and about expectations for modeling based on that data. Surveying data is an advanced topic, and the tools for making a comprehensive data survey are not readily available and require advanced mining knowledge. Although a detailed survey is of incredible value in understanding the information content, as well as the applicability and reliability of any data set in making a model, at this writing there are no survey tools as such included in any commercially available data mining package.

To some extent, the data survey is accomplished by using mining tools and then carefully exploring the limits of the mined model. In advanced mining, the survey can yield a tremendous amount of pre-mining information that guides an experienced miner during additional data preparation and mining. However, because the survey is an advanced topic, it isn't addressed here, since this is intended as a primer on basic modeling. The topic is mentioned here only because it is an integral part of more advanced mining, and was mentioned as part of the full mining process at the opening of the chapter.

The parts of the survey that can be included in the basic mining process are covered mainly in Chapter 11 as a part of mining, not as a separate topic here. The basic approach to mining described here most usefully incorporates elements of the survey as a part of activities that a miner will use while working to improve, verify, and validate a mined model. A more detailed discussion of the data survey, with case studies, is included in the book *Data Preparation for Data Mining*.

9.5 **Summary**

By far the most difficult task, and one that will take the data miner the greatest amount of time, is actually preparing and getting comfortable and familiar with the data. For what it's worth, the author, when mining, spends a lot of time simply "slopping" data about—cutting off samples, building small models, trying different features, and looking for insight and understanding.

The essential idea for a miner is to get comfortable with the data. Feel that you intuitively know what's in it, what models it will support, what its limitations are. It is absolutely essential to connect the data back to the business problem, and to make quite sure that the data addresses that problem in the needed terms of reference.

This chapter has presented *an* approach—by no means *the* approach, just one of many that would work—to getting raw data into a state for mining. These are basic techniques that any miner will have to do to almost any data set, and use for addressing almost any business problem. It's probably worth noting that miners need other preparation techniques when mining data in other domains, such as biomedical data, industrial automation data, telemetry data, geophysical data, time domain data, and so on. This book is about business modeling and business mining, and these are the basic data preparation techniques needed in such environments. As noted at the beginning of the chapter, although not fully comprehensive, follow this path and you won't go far wrong!

With data prepared and assayed, it's time to look at building the needed model or models. However, before launching into modeling practices, it's time to introduce mining tools themselves and the principles on which they work. That is a subject for the next chapter.

Chapter 10
What Mining Tools Do

Many texts on data mining focus on algorithms. The truth is that in practical data mining, the algorithm isn't very important. So, be warned, don't get hung up on algorithms. But how can this be? "Surely," the reader is now commenting, "since algorithms figure so large in all of the books I've read on data mining and in all of the data mining courses I've taken, they must be important!" (The less charitable reader might even be thinking, "What? Does this guy really know what he's talking about?")

Algorithms are important—for researchers in data mining who are attempting to develop new ways of mining data, and who are attempting to mine data that hasn't yet been mineable. Much leading edge work is going into developing techniques (including new algorithms and variations of existing algorithms) for mining Web data, pictures, text, spoken words, and many other types of data. Also, there are enormous challenges involved in developing algorithms that are even theoretically capable of mining huge data streams, such as that generated by switches of large telephone networks. For such folk, algorithms are indeed crucial.

However, for an analyst who needs to use the techniques of data mining to solve business problems, reasonably good algorithms have already been developed, taken out of the laboratory, wrapped in robust and reliable commercial packaging, tested for usability, and delivered with help screens, training manuals, tutorials, and instruction. When so wrapped, these are tools, not algorithms. Buried inside the tool are one or more algorithms, but the miner is (or at least, should be) interested more in the usability and relevance of the tool for the business problem than in the details of what algorithms it contains. So, I repeat, please don't get hung up on algorithms! In general, all of the tools for mining business data that have survived in the marketplace are worthy of consideration since they have all proven that they can indeed extract business value from data—in the right hands.

The skill of the practitioner is far and away more important than the algorithm used. It is perfectly possible, feasible, and reasonable to get high value, meaningful results with a data-mining tool that leaves much to be desired from some technical criteria about its core algorithm. In skilled and experienced hands, it is usual to get good results, regardless of the technical merits of the underlying algorithm. Skill, experience, practice, and familiarity with the data and the domain are the keys to success, not the algorithms involved.

Nonetheless, and to take absolutely nothing away from the previous statements, the underlying algorithms that form the core technology, or technologies, of a particular tool do have different capabilities and features. Data mining *algorithms* are the core mathematical and logical structures that direct and determine a specific computational approach to examining data. Data mining *tools* are the commercially wrapped data mining algorithms ready for use in a business setting. This chapter first takes a look at data mining algorithms, but only enough to reveal where the strengths and weaknesses lie and why. After the brief tour through algorithms, the rest of the chapter looks at a few tools that exemplify specific algorithms, and briefly contrasts the tools' similarities and differences, and examines their range of application.

10.1 Data Mining Algorithms

A truth about data mining that's not widely discussed is that the relationships in data the miner seeks are either very easy to characterize or very, very hard. Most of the relationships in mining for business models consist of the very easy to characterize type. However, just because they are easy to characterize doesn't mean that they will be easy to discover, or obvious when discovered. What it does mean for the miner is that tools wrapping even the simplest algorithms can deliver great results. In mining, start simply and proceed from there.

Essentially, this tour through algorithms does exactly that: it starts with the simple algorithms, and works up from there. When evaluating tools, don't spurn the simple algorithms that they support and dive straight into the most complex ones! The tour starts with a quick overview of variable types and how different types of variables affect different algorithms.

10.1.1 Variable Types and Their Impact on Algorithms

Variables come in a variety of types that can be distinguished by the amount of information that they encode. They are briefly reviewed here starting with the "simplest" (those that carry the least information) to those that carry the most information.

- *Nominal variables:* Essentially, these are no more than labels identifying unique entities. Personal names are nominal labels identifying unique individuals. So too are order numbers, serial numbers, tracking codes, and many other similar labels.

- *Categorical variables:* These are group labels identifying groups of entities sharing some set of characteristics implied by the category. In addition to personal names, all readers of this book belong to the category of humans. (Apologies to any nonhuman readers for making unwarranted assumptions!)

- *Ordinal variables:* These are categories that can be rationally listed in some order. Examples of such categories might include small, medium, and large or hot, warm, tepid, cool, and cold. Notice that neither nominal nor categorical variables can be ordered; they are simply unordered labels for single entities and groups of entities, respectively.

- *Interval variables:* These are ordinal variables in which it is possible to determine a distance between the ordered categories. However, their intervals may well be arbitrary, as in a temperature scale. Additive distances between equidistant points are meaningful, but ratios aren't. For instance, there are 10 degrees between 20 and 30 degrees, and between 110 and 120 degrees. However, 50 degrees isn't twice as hot as 25 degrees on either Celsius or Fahrenheit scales.

- *Ratio variables:* These are interval variables in which ratios are valid, and which have a true zero point. An example is a bank account. The zero point is an empty account. The ratio between $10 and $20 is 1 to 2, and $20 is twice $10. The ratio between $100 and $200 is also 1 to 2, and $200 is twice $100. Same ratio—same relationship.

As far as mining algorithms are concerned, they don't distinguish between nominal and categorical variable types, although the miner may well have to. Mining algorithms are also insensitive to the interval/ratio distinction, although once again a miner may need to be sensitive to the distinction. Thus, as far as mining algorithms are concerned, variables are either unordered labels, ordered labels, or continuous numbers. This means that algorithm sensitivity can be described as nominal, ordinal, or numeric, respectively. Algorithms described as having nominal sensitivity are not sensitive to any ordering, only to the joint frequency of occurrence between labels. The labels may actually be continuous numbers, but the algorithm regards them, or more likely bins of them, as nominal labels. Ordinally sensitive algorithms are sensitive to the order in which values occur, but extract no meaning from the distances between values. Thus, for such an algorithm, the fact that there is a gap between 1 and 2 is neither more nor less significant than the fact that there is a gap between 10 and 100. The size of the gap is quite irrelevant. Algorithms described as having a numeric sensitivity are sensitive to the distance between values, and for them the difference in distance between 1 and 2, and 10 and 100 makes a difference even if no values fall in between.

These shorthand descriptions—nominal, ordinal, and numeric—are used here to indicate which algorithms are sensitive to which features of variables, and what difference it makes in mining.

10.1.2 Characterizing Neighborhoods: Nearest Neighbors

The term *nearest neighbors* is suggestive, but before addressing what it means for data mining, some preamble is needed. As already noted, the instances in a data set can be imagined to be rows, as in a spreadsheet. Just as a spreadsheet row has several values in it, so too must a set of instance values, since they are equivalent and are only different ways of referring to the same thing. If, as in Figure 10.1, only two variables are included, each row or instance has two instance values. Assuming, for the sake of this explanation, that the values are numeric as shown, then it is perfectly possible to regard each of the variables, or columns, as a dimension and create a two-dimensional graph to plot where every pair of instance values falls on the graph. This is illustrated in the figure.

For any point, the row that defines where it is to be plotted is usually called a *vector.* (Row and vector are more terminology for the same thing. These multiple terms used here, as already noted, come from the multifarious roots that contribute to data mining technologies. The terms are used interchangeably here since the miner is likely to come across all of them from

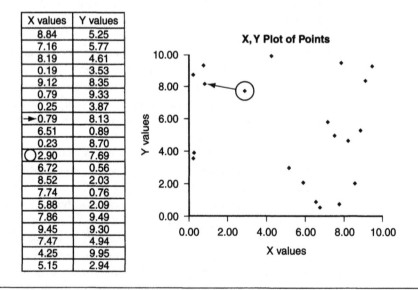

X values	Y values
8.84	5.25
7.16	5.77
8.19	4.61
0.19	3.53
9.12	8.35
0.79	9.33
0.25	3.87
➔0.79	8.13
6.51	0.89
0.23	8.70
◯2.90	7.69
6.72	0.56
8.52	2.03
7.74	0.76
5.88	2.09
7.86	9.49
9.45	9.30
7.47	4.94
4.25	9.95
5.15	2.94

Figure 10.1 Plotting vectors and identifying near neighbors.

time to time, and so needs to be familiar with them.) A glance at the graph in the figure intuitively reveals that each of the points shown is closest to some other point. In fact, using a ruler, it's quite possible, if a little tedious, to measure the distance from every point to every other point. It's also quite possible to calculate the distances using Pythagoras' Theorem. The circled point's nearest neighbor is the one pointed at by the arrow. This arrowed point, of course, has neighbors nearer than the circled point. These circled and arrowed neighbors' vectors (also known as *instances* or *rows*) are indicated in the figure's table.

Using this straightforward measure, for any particular point, any number of other closest points can be discovered. In this sense, for any vector, the nearest neighbor algorithm simply locates the nearest neighboring vector. But so what? What does this achieve?

The algorithm assumes that close proximity in this "space" works as a definition of similarity for the two vectors. This is quite reasonable. Assume that two vectors have identical values—the corresponding points would fall on top of each other if plotted on a graph. It seems quite reasonable to say that if two vectors have identical values then they are similar, even identical. So if two vectors are minutely different, and don't fall exactly on top of each other, but are close by each other, then intuition tells us that they are still more similar than vectors with very different values. Thus, this intuition suggests, similarity can be determined by the closeness of the nearest neighbor.

Data mined models, regardless of which of the types of business situation models they will be applied to, are usually used for inference or prediction. To be sure, the inferences or predictions are often incorporated into some other type of business situation model, but as far as mining alone goes, inferential and predictive models are desired. *Inferences* are essentially descriptions of what is going on in the variables in particular neighborhoods. *Predictions* answer the question, "Given one or more, but not all, of the values in a vector, what are the most reasonable values for the missing entry(s)?" Prediction with nearest neighbor requires only finding the nearest neighbor for the vectoral values that are present, and using the nearest neighbor's values as a reasonable estimate for the values that are missing.

A slight modification, at least as far as prediction goes, is to use more than one neighbor along with some weighting mechanism to average the values to be predicted across several neighbors. This is called *k-nearest neighbor,* where *k* stands for the number of neighbors to use.

In the real world, this nearest neighbor in data actually translates into really good inferences and predictions. At the limit, every vector would be represented in the space, and making a prediction or inference would be as simple as looking for the vector in plotted space that matched the vector produced by the world. The limit described here isn't ever reached, but still, with enough representative data points plotted, it works really well. It's quite easy (for a computer) to extend the number of dimensions to any amount desired and still determine proximity. So why isn't this a practical method?

The problem is twofold. First, in order to work well, the computer must hold a lot of vectors—a big to potentially enormous data set, especially when using a large number of variables. However, it's the second problem that's the downfall for a pure nearest neighbor algorithm. Notice that every point has to measure its distance from every other point. With as few as 1000 points, the only way to find a neighbor for a specific vector is to find the distance to all 1000 points. As the number of points increases—consider the roughly 25 million households in the United States for instance—the look-up problem becomes horrendous.

So although it can be shown that theoretically, and with sufficient representative data, a pure nearest neighbor approach can't be beaten, practically it certainly can be—not on quality of performance, but certainly in practical application. Nonetheless, note that any tool that provides memory based reasoning (MBR) is providing nearest neighbor. It's great if enough representative data can actually fit in memory, and if fast response isn't crucial. Also note that the algorithm works where distances can be determined, as with numerical values, but not with raw categorical values. So where the raw algorithm does apply, all is well. Otherwise, some alternative has to be found.

The alternative is to find some shorthand way to characterize neighborhoods that doesn't involve retaining all of the data for comparison, and doesn't need so many look-ups and comparisons to characterize an instance. There are several ways to achieve this, and some of them are briefly reviewed in the next subsection: decision trees, rule extraction, clustering, self-organizing maps (SOMs), and support vector machines. However, characterizing areas of state space by putting boundaries around selected areas isn't the only route to characterizing relationships in data. The following subsection examines continuous representations, including regressions, neural networks, and probabilistic representation. The regressions and neural networks rely on representing data as a *function* (a mathematical expression that translates a unique input value, or set of values, into a unique output value). However, some data set relationships cannot be represented by functions (particularly the very difficult relationships mentioned in the introduction to this chapter). The final subsection has only a single entry on evolution programs, which can be constructed to discover, if necessary, nonfunctional representations.

Nearest Neighbor Summary

Sensitivity: Numeric.

Features:

1. Cannot handle large data sets or high variable counts. (Exactly what "large" and "high" mean changes as computer power increases.

However, compared to other algorithms, these limits will remain true whatever their absolute capability.)

2. Requires a large model (since it carries the whole training data set as the model) that is slow to produce a prediction relative to other algorithms.

3. May require significant, possibly not straightforward, variable transformations to work effectively.

10.1.2.1   Decision Trees

Nearest neighbor methods do indeed characterize neighborhoods, but really only the immediate point, or area closely around a point, demarked by a vector—so it takes a lot of points to do a good job of characterizing the whole space. (This space, by the way, is technically called *state space,* and is a type of mathematical analog of real space.) A different way of characterizing the space is to chop out areas that are to some degree similar to each other; this is what a decision tree tries to do.

Continuing with a two-dimensional representation of the state space, Figure 10.2 shows how a decision tree might set the boundaries around different parts of the space that have something in common. In this case, and for sake of example, the figure plots points that are represented by vectors of three dimensions. Two of the dimensions are numeric and account for the position of the point, and the third dimension is a categorical variable that takes two values, "Square" and "Circle." It's important to note that the tree has to be directed to attend to variable 3 as the one of interest in characterizing state space. There are also techniques that don't need to be so directed. In the United States, these techniques are called, respectively, *supervised* and

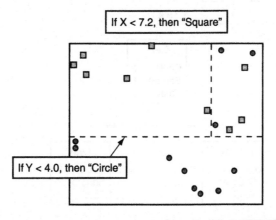

Figure 10.2   Finding areas that characterize the space as box containing or circle containing.

unsupervised learning techniques because the learning algorithm has, or not as the case may be, to be supervised in the sense that it's told the right answer. In Europe among English speakers, these are referred to, respectively, as *directed* and *undirected* techniques. Different names, same meaning.

A glance at the figure shows that the separators are all parallel to one of the axes, and that's not accidental. Most decision trees do slice up state space this way because for each variable (or dimension), the decision tree finds a point to make each split that best separates the areas. With each additional split, the separation in state space improves. Each separator line on the graph in the figure corresponds to one of the rules.

Figure 10.3 shows a tree that corresponds to the "cuts" made to separate squares and circles. The rules, and the tree that made them, don't perfectly separate the two classes, and some are misclassified. Each of the separate areas shown is called a *leaf,* perhaps because trees have leaves, and perhaps because the rule boxes each dangle like leaves. Maybe both. However, because of the way that a tree cuts up state space, the leaves can all be described as a series of rules. So long as there aren't too many rules, or the number of splits from the top of the tree down to a final leaf is not too many, these rules are, relatively speaking, intuitively understandable.

Since decision trees can easily accommodate categorical variables (indeed, many tree algorithms have to turn numerical variables into categories by a process called *binning*), trees easily handle most types of data found in business mining. However, something is lost in the variable translation from

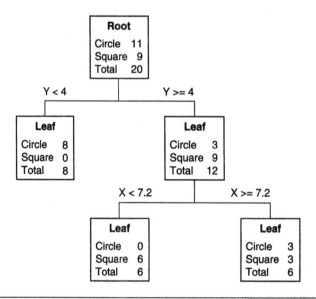

Figure 10.3   A tree illustrating the cuts made in Figure 10.2.

numerical to categorical. Numerical variables carry information in the distance relationships between values (their distribution), some of which is certainly lost in binning since there are fewer bins than values. If the relationship is truly complex and highly nonlinear, it's possible that a tree might not be able to characterize it.

Moreover, very often data sets have no unique tree characterization, and minute differences in the data can lead to what are apparently totally different tree structures.

The situation illustrated in Figure 10.4 shows a data set in which, when plotted, the lower left quadrant of the data has a and b values with one characteristic, and the remaining data with another. The tree algorithm has to decide which of the a or b variables to make the first split on. In the upper case it's the a variable; in the lower case it's the b variable. Every tree algorithm, and there are many, has some metric to determine which is the "best" variable and value (according to that metric) to begin with. However, different tree algorithms will very likely differ in the initial choice, and from there lead on to apparently totally different trees. Very small differences in the data set can also make apparently large differences in the "best" tree that any algorithm decides on. Thus the training and testing data sets (discussed later, but

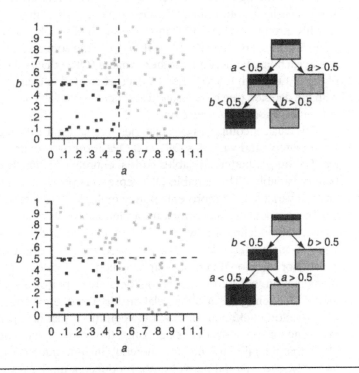

Figure 10.4   Same data, different trees.

they are two separate data sets that are extremely similar to each other) may both produce apparently very different trees.

The result is that there is no one "best" tree for any data set in more than narrowly drawn technical terms. As far as interpretation and prediction are concerned, there may be several trees, all equally valid. Thus the decision tree algorithm cannot provide the "one correct tree," just one or more of many equally valid trees.

Many different valid explanations in the same data set? Yes indeed. Since decision trees decide one variable at a time, any "explanation" has to depend entirely on what is "explained" first for what is "explained" later. Start with a different variable, or even a different splitting value for the same variable, in two identical data sets, and everything is different from there on.

However, note that decision trees decide how to split a data set one variable at a time. It's the "one variable at a time" part that is significant here. The tree algorithms pay no attention to interaction between variables, and modeling interaction between variables can be utterly crucial in crafting the needed model. However, if interactions are important, and a decision tree is the modeling tool chosen, then interactions have to be explicitly included in the input battery.

Demonstrating a decision tree's insensitivity to interactions between variables is easily accomplished. Create a data set that comprises five variables (say IP1 through IP5) and 1000 instances, each of which is a number between 0 and 1. Create another variable (OP1) that is the sum of the five random values in each incidence, and another variable (OP2) that is the result of multiplying IP1 through IP5 together. (A data set created in exactly this way, along with the decision tree models discussed here, is available on the author's Web site—*www.modelandmine.com.*)

This data set comprises two batteries—variables IP1 through IP5 form the input battery, and variables OP1 and OP2 form two separate output batteries. The output battery variables consist entirely of interactions of the input battery variables. The variable OP1 represents purely additive interactions, and the variable OP2 represents purely multiplicative interactions.

This is about as straightforward an interactive data set as it's possible to create, yet modeling the two output batteries with a decision tree produces a very poor model indeed. (The tree used for this demonstration is one of the author's personal favorites, an excellent professional decision tree implementation, not a tool chosen deliberately to perform poorly on this example.) Modeling the additive relationship, the tree produced a model with a correlation coefficient of 0.87 between the actual and predicted values. Modeling the multiplicative relationship, the correlation coefficient was 0.76. (Note that neural networks do inherently include interactions if configured correctly, and a neural network tool produced a model with correlation coefficients of 1.00 and 1.00 respectively, a perfect result.)

Note that a decision tree is a tool designed to characterize interactions between the input battery variables, considered one by one, and the output battery variable. A decision tree does not model the interactions between the input variables, nor does it characterize how any between-input-variable interaction relates to the output battery variable. When creating models using decision trees, it's very important to discover if between-input-battery-variable interactions are important. That is discussed in detail in Chapter 12 (see Section 12.2.17).

In general, trees do remarkably well, mainly because neighborhoods can be usefully characterized, and also because very often between-input-variable interactions are not, in fact, important. Remember, the secret is that the relationships are either very simple or very complex, so trees can be very useful indeed.

The decision tree needs only to store the rules that were discovered to be able to characterize any future data vector—that is to say, to identify the area of state space it falls into, and the properties of that area. This is a great saving over having to store all of the training data and making an extensive comparison, as MBR requires. (As a comparison, one of the data mining suites of tools looked at later in this chapter offers individual MBR and decision tree tools. Exploring one rather small data set with MBR produces the best model and takes 4 minutes and 52 seconds to complete the exploration. The decision tree exploration of the same data set takes less than half a second, although the model produced is very slightly less accurately predictive.)

Decision Tree Summary

Sensitivity: Some trees nominal, some trees ordinal. (The explanation presented here described an ordinally sensitive tree. The cuts are made between values, but the tree only cares that there is a gap, not how large it is. The tree used for single variable CHAID in Chapter 9 has nominal sensitivity only.)

Features:

1. Trees usually require numerical input to be binned, and binning always removes some information. All of the values in a bin are considered to be equivalent. Sometimes binning is invisible to the miner, but the quality of any tree is dependent on the quality of its binning strategy.

2. The tree model generated can be very sensitive to minute fluctuations in a data set. Choosing a different first-split variable, or even a different split point, can lead to totally different trees. If the variables or split points are almost equivalent, no tree is the "correct" one, and all may effectively be equivalent. A tree doesn't generate *the* explanation of a data set, only *an* explanation.

3. Trees can become very large and "bushy." Even with pruning, large data sets with high variable counts can lead to inexplicable and complex trees.

4. Trees cut state space so that every part is characterized, even if there is no data in some parts to justify the characterization imposed. Trees will predict or explain in areas where there was no training set data in order to justify the explanation or prediction.

5. Trees do not inherently include between-input-variable interactions, which can be crucial in creating the highest quality model. The importance of interactions between the input battery variables has to be discovered by the miner using nondecision-tree tools. If such between-input-variable interactions are important for model quality, they have to be explicitly created and added to the data set by the miner.

10.1.2.2   Rule Extraction

Decision trees work by dividing the whole of state space into chunks, so that the data in each chunk characterizes the whole chunk in some particular way. Rule extractors typically are not concerned with state space as such but search for common features among the vectors. Rule extraction works by generating *covering rules*. Not much mystery here: these rules cover a certain number of instances.

Most rule extraction algorithms begin by finding the most general covering rule—the one that covers the most instances. Then it removes all of the covered instances from further consideration and starts again with what's left by finding the most general rule covering the remaining instances, and so on.

The rules produced, if illustrated in the same way as the decision tree, would also seem to divide state space into areas with separators that are parallel to the axes. However, advanced rule extraction algorithms go further.

The basic form of an extracted rule is "If *condition,* then *outcome.*" Just as with a decision tree's division, the condition part of the rule can become quite lengthy and complex with multiple conditions joined by "and," so "If *condition* and *condition* and . . . then *outcome.*" Up to this point, there is not really much difference in the explanation between trees and rule extractors except for the precise details of the algorithm and the way the result is represented (no tree diagram for rule extractors). However, advanced rule extraction algorithms can take an interesting step further.

Rules of the form "If *condition,* then *outcome,*" only stipulate that the outcome, given some specific condition, turns up with some degree of probability. For example, in many data sets, "age" and "income" are very highly associated, so that a rule such as "If age > 35, then income > $35,000" will indicate approximate, but not perfect, correspondence. Such a rule, in some particular data set, may be true only 70% of the time, so that 30% of the time, income is equal to or less than the amount stated. However, a far more powerful rule would be "If, and only if, age > 35, then income > $35,000." This says that it is necessary for age to be > 35 for income to be > $35,000. This rule does not mean that everyone over 35 has an income of $35,000 or more, but it does say that no one less than age 35 has such an income. So, in other words, to have an income greater than $35,000 it is necessary to be older than 35.

Discovering a necessary condition yields a very powerful statement, and offers a more powerful insight into the data than the previous "If . . . then . . ." rule. However, this rule is more powerful than simply stating a necessary condition—notice it implies that if age < 35, then income is not greater than $35,000. So, in this example, this rule states a necessary and sufficient condition. To restate the rule in a way that makes the sufficiency clearer, consider "If age < 35, then income is *not* ≥ $35,000." Here it can be seen that if age is less than 35, no other check need be made to determine if income is more or less than $35,000. Knowing that age is less than 35 is sufficient to determine that income is less than $35,000. This ability to discover necessary and sufficient conditions allows extremely powerful statements about relationships discovered in a data set!

Powerful rules with this form are by no means as common as regular "If . . . then . . ." rules. This is a strong advantage. Real world data sets are often characterized by up to thousands of rules that are very hard to understand, although they are fine for automated execution to make a prediction. But the additional power of "If, and only if, . . ." rules makes them a much rarer discovery, and highly explanatory when they do occur.

Rule Extraction Summary

Sensitivity: Nominal, some algorithms ordinal.

Features:

1. Numerical input usually has to be binned, and binning always removes some information. All of the values in a bin are considered to be equivalent. Sometimes binning is invisible to the miner, but the quality of the rules is dependent on the quality of the binning strategy.

2. Rule extraction is generally limited to producing rules about binary splits of the output variable. (That is, rules in the form of "If . . . then result is equal to some category, or is greater than or less than some value, or is not equal to some category.")

3. Rules do not necessarily cover the whole of state space, so it is possible to have run time data to which no rule applies. (This usually produces an output equivalent to "no prediction.")

4. Rule extraction is insensitive to interactions between the input battery variables for reasons similar to those discussed in the decision tree

section, and the same precautions need to be taken by the miner as recommended there.

10.1.2.3 Clusters

Clustering is another method of characterizing areas of state space. It also is an algorithm that doesn't necessarily characterize the whole of state space. However, a major difference from the previous two algorithms is that the boundaries of the clusters are definitely not parallel to the axes. A glance at Figure 10.5 shows this.

It is also important to note that clustering can be implemented as either a supervised or an unsupervised algorithm, and is the most popular of the unsupervised data mining algorithms. As an unsupervised algorithm, it simply tries to find ways of segregating the data, based on distance, with all of the variables in a vector equally weighted. When used as a supervised method, the clustering is made (as the figure illustrates) based on the values of one, or more, nominated variables—usually those about which a prediction is wanted. (In the example, the prediction variable is again the categorical with squares and circles.)

The usual course with unsupervised clustering is to ask, after the clusters have been discovered, how well these clusters made on all the variables actually turn out to group the variable(s) of interest—usually the prediction variable(s). Continuing, for example, with income level as a variable of interest, a miner would perform an unsupervised clustering on all the variables and see if income levels are then conveniently grouped together in some way. Supervised clustering is usually more useful and relevant to most mining situations since at least the clusters are directed to be about something of interest. A supervised clustering of income would make the algorithm at least cluster income as well as possible and then determine what could be said

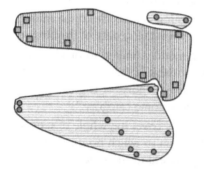

Figure 10.5 Finding clusters that characterize areas of squares and areas of circles.

about the way that the other variables distribute their values into the income-segregated clusters.

There are quite a number of clustering algorithms. However, what they all have in common is the idea of distance in state space, finding neighbors, and then characterizing the boundary points. One interesting method of clustering is the self-organizing map (SOM), discussed in the next subsection. SOMs will serve as a simplified example of how clustering can work.

Clustering Summary

Sensitivity: Numeric; some algorithms will digest ordinal.

Features:

1. Clusters tend to give equal weight to all variables unless manually adjusted by the miner—which takes domain knowledge that may be unavailable.

2. Clusters don't cover the whole of state space. Some algorithms obligingly give predictions or inferences in areas without any training data.

3. Many algorithms require the miner to select a number of clusters. This can produce an arbitrary number of clusters with no relevance to features in the data.

4. Clustering doesn't work for nominal data, and the transformations needed for effective categorical clustering have to be performed externally by the miner.

5. Although clustering with some algorithms may be sensitive to between-input-battery interactions, it turns out that for both supervised and unsupervised clustering, they make insufficient use of the information for the clusters to be useful when such interactions are important.

10.1.2.4 Self-Organizing Maps

A self-organizing map (SOM) is created from elements that are called neurons, since a SOM is usually regarded as a type of neural network. Figure 10.6 illustrates part of a SOM network where each of the neurons is connected to its neighbors, and each neuron has a set of weights, indicated in the figure by the small cylinders below each neuron.

Each neuron has one weight for every variable in the data set. Initially the SOM algorithm sets the weights for all neurons to random values so that every neuron has a different set of starting weights from every other neuron.

Training a SOM, illustrated in Figure 10.7, occurs when an instance of data is presented to the SOM. One of the neurons will have weights that are the closest match to the instance, although at first they may not be very similar; nonetheless, one of the neurons will still be closest. This closest neuron raises

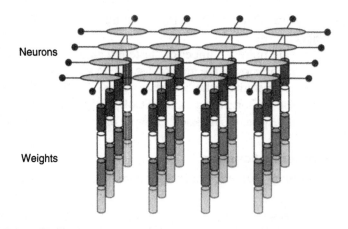

Figure 10.6 SOM neurons.

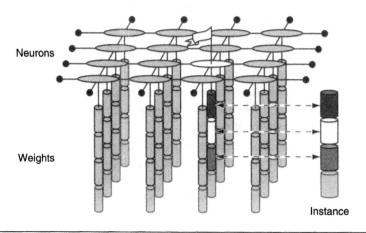

Figure 10.7 SOM instance recognition.

a flag and "captures" the instance. Having captured the instance by already being the closest neuron, it then adjusts its weights to be even closer to the actual values of the instance. However, the neuron only goes part way with the adjustment, so although it is closer, it isn't identical in values to the instance (unless by chance it was identical to begin with).

Finally, the SOM algorithm adjusts the neighbors of the capturing neuron, as Figure 10.8 illustrates, so that they are more similar to the capturing neuron, although they too are adjusted only part way, not to become identical to the capturing neuron. At this point the SOM is ready for another instance, and the training continues. As training continues, neighborhoods are adjusted to become more similar, and different instances are "attracted" to different neighborhoods.

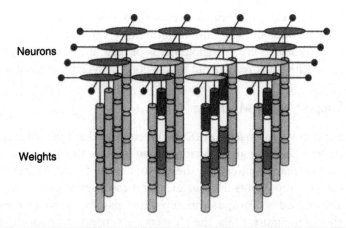

Neurons

Weights

Figure 10.8 SOM weight adjustment during training.

The idea is that whatever the "natural" neighborhoods are in the data set, they impose themselves on the map that self-organizes the neurons to reveal the organization in the data.

Self Organizing Map Summary

Sensitivity: Numeric only.

Features:

1. SOMs are very sensitive to miner weighting of the variables, as the un-modified map equally weights all variables. It requires the use of other exploration techniques, such as those discussed in other places in this chapter, to discover appropriate variable weightings. Discovering appropriate weightings requires art, not science, in the form of miner intuition.

2. Effective use of SOMs is *very* miner intensive. SOMs only make a map—the entire relationship discovery comes from the miner. On the other hand, the human eye backed by an experienced mind is the most formidable feature extraction and pattern recognition device we know of.

3. The algorithms require numeric variables; rationally translating nominal and categorical variables into a suitable format is an advanced mining topic.

4. Discoveries made by the miner using a SOM to investigate data require the miner to translate the insights into some other form for further use. In essence, the SOM doesn't make either an inferential or a predictive model. What it does is make a map that shows the practiced miner how to make a better inferential or predictive model than without the map.

5. As with other forms of clustering, a SOM is fairly insensitive to interactions between the input battery variables. However, when using SOMs to create visible maps of data, it is sometimes possible to see clues that result from interactions between the variables.

10.1.2.5   Support Vector Machines

Support vector machines (SVMs) recognize that the vast majority of the instances play no part in deciding how to place the separators in state space. All that really matters are the vectors at the "edge" of the "cloud" of vectors that represents the cluster. It is these edge vectors that support a separator, and so long as the separator passes between these vectors, as shown in Figure 10.9a, the clusters are separated. In this figure, the "problematic" circles have been removed from the XY plot for ease of explanation; otherwise, it is a plot similar to that discussed in clustering. Recall that the point positions shown represent vectors in the data. The dotted lines rest on the two outermost vectors in each cloud so that a separator constructed to fall between the dotted lines, as the solid line does, separates the classes.

The situation can be a little less clear, as in Figure 10.9b, where the problematic circle vector points are again shown so that the clouds overlap each other. This is a far more realistic situation with real world data, but it's easy enough (in principle) to "shrink" the boundaries of the clouds from the actual data points. Figure 10.9c shows the clouds shrunk by ignoring (in this case) the two most problematic circle points and the single most problematic square point. The separator can pass between the two clouds and misclassifies only the three ignored points or vectors.

SVMs result in clusters that are delineated by separators that, again, aren't necessarily parallel to the axes of state space, and may indeed wiggle about a fair amount. It's a relatively easy matter to store the vectors and use them to discover where any other instance vector falls when the model is to be used. Explanations are not always intuitively accessible.

Support Vector Machine Summary

Sensitivity: Numeric and ordinal.

Features:

1. The main limitation here is that the algorithms still reside in the laboratory! At this writing, SVMs don't handle large data sets well, nor do they handle high categorical counts well. However, there is promise here, and although as of this writing no good commercial tools yet take advantage of SVM technology, they promise to soon be available.

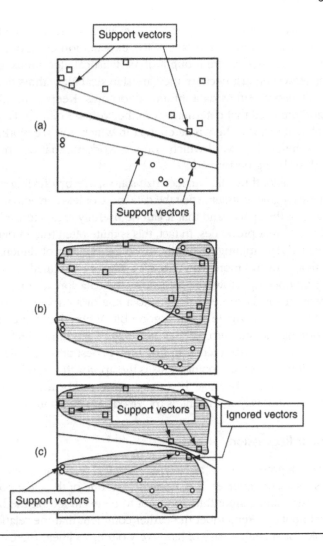

Figure 10.9 Support vector machines.

10.1.3 **Smooth Representations**

The previous subsection described various ways of chopping state space into discrete areas. There may be many different areas generated by any one of the mentioned techniques, but each area has its own distinct value and characterization. Crossing one of the separators results in stepping from one characterization to another—no gradual change, just a discontinuous step. This isn't the only way to characterize state space; a number of techniques result in smoothly changing output values rather than the step changes in values so far generated.

Many of these techniques are a result of what are called *regressions* for reasons that aren't important to the explanation of algorithms here. Many types of regression are thought of as statistical algorithms, and indeed they are. However, just because they are statistical algorithms doesn't mean they aren't also useful as data mining algorithms. Keep in mind that it isn't the algorithm used that determines whether you are mining data or doing statistical analysis, it is the whole context in which you are working, and specifically the goals toward which you are working, that determine the type of analysis being performed.

The algorithms that characterize state space by dividing it up into discontinuous segments assume that the data more or less spreads out through at least much of the space, and that it can be usefully characterized as patches that have different properties. In fact, this is quite often true in practical, business-oriented data mining. Naturally, since the number of dimensions (variables) is almost always more than two, it's a higher order analog of space that's being chopped up. However, sometimes the data spreads through state space in a way that is far more analogous to a line or a curve in two dimensions, although it may wiggle about a good bit. When this is the case, rather than chopping the line into patches as a way of grouping similar points, another way to characterize them is to find how to best draw the higher order analog of a line through the points. This is the approach taken by *smooth representations,* so called because the value represented by the line changes smoothly and continuously as the line is traversed between state space areas.

10.1.3.1 Linear Regression

Linear regression is an archetypal statistical technique, one that is taught in basic statistics courses. It is, nonetheless, one of the most powerful and useful data mining algorithms, and not to be excluded on the basis of its statistical heritage. Remember the earlier comment that the relationships a miner looks for are either easy or hard. Very often, it's linear regression that enables the miner to make valuable and insightful discoveries in data, as well as easy explanations of what's happening inside the discovered relationship.

Essentially, linear regression is a tried and tested way of fitting a single straight line through state space so that the line is as close as possible to all of the points in the space. Now, to be sure, when state space has more than two dimensions, it isn't exactly a line. In three dimensions it would be a plane, and in more dimensions it would be a higher-dimensional analog of what in two dimensions is a line. However, those are mathematical and computational details not needed to understand the essence of what regression does to represent the discovered relationship.

Fitting a straight line to a data set this way works well as far as explanation and prediction are concerned, so long as the data does bunch up in state space in at least a rough approximation to a line, as shown in Figure 10.10. Since the line is fitted to be as close to all the points as possible, if a prediction were needed (and one variable's value is known), the value of the other variable has to be nearby in state space. So returning the value of the line's position for that variable is a good estimate of a reasonable value—also shown in the figure. Thus, at the points shown, 55 year olds are predicted to be earning around $70,000.

As far as inferences go, linear regression offers clear insights. In the example shown, it's easy to see graphically that for every year's increase in age, income increases about $1,200 on average. (That is to say, the line rises by about $1,200 for every 1-year increase in age.) This is also pretty clear from the regression equation for a straight line, also shown at the top of the figure, which can be seen to have an actual beta weight (the second number) of 1.189. It shows how much effect there is in one variable (income) for a change in the other (age).

It's pretty clear that linear regression doesn't actually capture the true relationship very well. In this data, income increases until about age 65, when it takes a sharp drop. However, as a first pass at getting some idea that there is a relationship, and determining roughly what it is and its general direction, this linear regression is a quick and easy way to begin.

The example shows only a single variable regressed onto another variable. Invariably in data mining, there is more than one input variable involved—often hugely more. Nonetheless, the linear regression method can be easily extended to deal with multiple input variables—often called *independent*

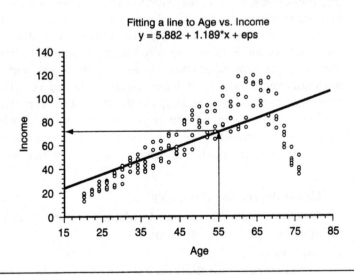

Figure 10.10 Fitting a straight line to continuous data with linear regression.

variables in regression analysis—so long as there is only one output (dependent) variable to predict. This extension is called *multiple linear regression*. Still, each of the input variables is assessed separately and each has its own weight (like the weight on income in the example). Checking these weights indicates the direction in which the relationship moves with changes in one variable. Negative numbers mean the variables' values move in different directions; positive weights mean they move together. Also, so long as allowance is made for the total range of a variable, a rule of thumb for interpreting weights is that large (relative to the range) changes in weights are more important than small (relative to the range) changes in weights. So linear regression can not only make good predictive models, but also point to the most important relationship variables and indicate the nature of the relationship.

Since linear regression is quick and easy, and since interpreting the results, once learned, yields a lot of useful information, it is an invaluable data mining algorithm when incorporated into a mining tool or tool set. A linear regression equation is indeed a succinct and compact encapsulation of the relationships in data.

Before leaving this brief discussion of linear regression, it's worth briefly returning to the point about how most relationships searched out with data mining are simple. It may well turn out to be true that the vast majority of relationships in the world are, in fact, anything but linear. Not only are there nonlinear and discontinuous relationships, but also recently discovered are chaotic relationships (a bad name since there is a pattern in chaotic relationships, not chaos, but we're stuck with the name now), complex relationships, fractal relationships, and a growing series of other very interesting ways of characterizing relationships. None of these are linear. However, in spite of the apparent inherent nonlinearity of most real-world phenomena, it is well worth noting that the vast majority of relationships that a miner encounters in business data turn out to be either linear, partially linear, semi-linear, or linearizable. That means that they are either linear already; are linear over parts of their range; are linear over different parts of their range but the degree of linearity changes from place to place over the range; or that the relationship isn't actually linear but can be re-expressed with an easy transformation so that it becomes linear. Because of this, no data miner should underestimate the importance and utility of linear and multiple-linear regression as a data mining tool.

Linear Regression Summary

Sensitivity: Numeric. Advanced variable transformations allow the algorithm to regress all variable types.

Features:

1. Linear regression finds only linear relationships, which may be all that's needed; a good place to start, but not to finish.

2. Linear regression is widely perceived not to be a data mining technique.

3. This technique is very sensitive to anomalous fluctuations in the data, such as outliers, although robust versions of the algorithm are available that are less sensitive to such fluctuations.

4. This algorithm struggles with co-linearity in the input variables—to the point of "blowing up" if the problems are severe.

5. It cannot deal with missing data, and many of the standard "default" methods of replacing missing values do more harm than good to the resulting model.

6. As with decision trees, linear regression only produces *an* explanation, and one that may be highly sensitive to small changes in the structure of the data set.

7. Linear regression is sensitive to additive interactions when fitting straight lines.

10.1.3.2 Curvilinear Regression

But what if the relationship isn't linear? Figure 10.11 shows the same age/income relationship as before, and it's obvious that it isn't really linear, it's curved. It's also obvious that the straight line fitted as closely as possible to all of the points isn't really very close to most of them. However, it's also intuitively obvious that fixing the problem here means fitting a curved line of some sort.

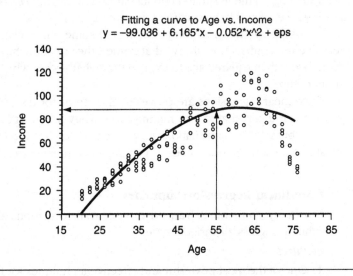

Fitting a curve to Age vs. Income
$y = -99.036 + 6.165*x - 0.052*x^2 + eps$

Figure 10.11   Fitting a curved line to continuous data with curvilinear regression.

Without going into the details of how it's done, the method ranges from quite easy (read "quick") to algorithmically easy but computationally intensive (read "slow") to discover almost any curve that's needed to fit what's called *curvilinear data*. When curvilinear relationships exist in data, generally speaking, it's not hard for data mining tools to discover them. Very often, what is hard is to explain them. The weights don't have straightforward interpretations since the relationships that they express are not constant—that is indeed a pretty good description of what nonlinearity in a relationship means. Even more difficult for intuitive interpretation is that different variables may be differently important to the explanation, depending entirely on what other variables are needed to explain what's going on and the precise value of the output. So for instance, the most important variables for explaining income level for a 22-year-old male may be education level, grade point average, and area of qualification, whereas in the same data set, for a 50-year-old male those variables may be all but irrelevant—previous income over 2 years and position held may be the most explanatory and predictive variables.

The curve fitted in the figure is a much better fit to the data than the straight line. The lines in the figure show that this curve would predict an average income of about $83,000 for 55 year olds—apparently, a better estimate than the linear regression produced. However, explaining what this curve means is difficult even though there is only a single curvilinear term in this regression. With a single term, a meaningful explanation can be attempted—at the beginning, income increases about $6,000 per year, but the amount of increase reduces by about $52 times the square of the age per year. This is *what* is happening on the illustrated curvilinear fit. Explaining *why* is much harder. For instance, why is it the square of the age that's involved? And is it really the square of the age that's important, or would some other relationship fit better? The next subsection shows that some other relationship actually does work better than squared age to explain the "what"—the "why" only becomes more obtuse.

Curvilinear regressions are powerful algorithms for discovering relationships when incorporated into mining tools. They are great for making predictions, but intuitive explanations may have to be discovered elsewhere since what nonlinear techniques reveal is generally not intuitively easy to represent.

Curvilinear Regression Summary

Sensitivity: Numeric. Advanced variable transformations allow the algorithm to regress all variable types.

Features:

1. One of the most powerful and effective techniques for finding and fitting functions mapping input to output data sets.

2. A powerful predictive tool, but almost invariably not interpretable as an explanation.

3. Curvilinear regression suffers from indigestion with co-linearity in the input variables—sometimes fatal indigestion.

4. It can't handle missing values—same caveats for missing values as with linear regression.

5. The algorithm itself cannot detect the degree of nonlinearity present in a data set. It relies on the miner's intuition to determine how much nonlinearity to include in the model.

6. Curvilinear regression is sensitive to all types of interaction between the input battery variables so long as enough flexibility is included in the input battery. (See Section 12.2.17 for details of how to include enough flexibility.)

10.1.3.3 Neural Networks

There is one class of algorithm that has become so closely associated with data mining that it needs to be addressed separately, even in this brief tour. In fact, after nearly 6 months of work at one client, after generating good insights that produced several millions of dollars in return with data mining tools that didn't use neural networks, they commented, "But we thought you were going to be using data mining. When are you going to do that?" Puzzled, further inquiries revealed that they didn't regard anything that had been done as data mining since neural networks weren't involved. Apparently their perception was that data mining and application of neural networks to data were synonymous! And this is not an isolated example by any means.

This position is not true at all. It is very often the case that a neural network is not the most appropriate algorithm in a tool to apply, and there are almost always other algorithms to use that are just as effective, even when neural networks are appropriate.

Neural networks are no more and no less than algorithms for building nonlinear regressions. They don't actually perform regressions in the same way that statistically developed regression techniques work, and they do have the potential, when properly configured, to characterize highly complex and convoluted nonlinear relationships that are really tough to discover with other nonlinear regression techniques. The bugaboo is in the expression "correctly configured." Correctly configuring a neural network is a very difficult art, and art it is, not science. Neural networks are highly complex algorithms, and the tools that encapsulate them have good rules of thumb, in general, for setting them up. But, unfortunately, at the current state-of-the-art, good rules of thumb don't guarantee success.

It's very hard to learn to tune a neural network, and there's no practical way to determine if more tuning would work better except to keep trying. It is possible to create good predictive models with neural networks in training and test data sets that are not stable on other data sets, specifically the run time data. And it ranges from hard to impossible to explain much from examining the network.

Nonetheless, there most positively is a place for neural networks in data mining. It needs considerable experience to get good results with them, but with that experience they can offer the quickest way to discover a complex relationship in a data set. However, the best way to gain experience is to build models using a variety of tools—say trees, rules, and neural networks—and carefully study differences in performance and results. It's also worthwhile to consider using some other technique that is easier to explain in terms of characterizing a relationship discovered with a neural network.

Figure 10.12 shows a curved line that intuitively seems to be a good fit to the data. Predicted income for 55 year-olds is now about $84,000. Although the neural network required to fit this data is relatively simple, explaining its internal workings in any way that explains what's going on in this relationship is effectively impossible. While this certainly appears to be a good predictive relationship to use, it's not much help as an explanation. Yet this data set is actually quite easy to explain—income increases from $20,000 by about $2,500 per year starting at age 20 and continues to increase at this rate until age 65, when it drops by about $6,000 per year. The amount of variability in income is directly proportional to the age from age 20 to age 65 and runs

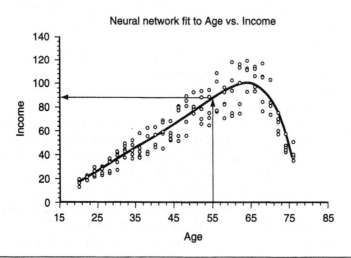

Figure 10.12   Fitting a curved line to continuous data with a neural network.

about 20% of income level. However, curvilinear regressions are tough ways to get to such an explanation!

Neural Network Summary

Sensitivity: Numeric. Advanced variable transformations allow the algorithm to regress all variable types.

Features:

1. Everything said in the limitations section of multiple curvilinear regression applies to neural networks with one major exception. (In fact, to all intents and purposes, neural networks are only a nontraditional method of nonlinear multiple regression.) The exception is that neural networks can determine the amount of nonlinearity present in a data set.

2. Although the algorithm can determine nonlinearity, the miner has to select the level of complexity the network can use, usually in terms of numbers of nodes (neurons) and network architecture. (Some tools hide all this complexity, but in turn take control out of the miner's hands.)

3. This is one of a few algorithms that can inherently predict multiple outputs simultaneously; that is, predict values for more than one output variable. However, this is not good practice in general since the joint predictions tend to be of lower quality than two separate networks each predicting a single output variable.

4. Neural networks are fully sensitive to interactions between the input battery variables. The only caveat is that the complexity of the network has to be sufficient. (See Section 12.2.4.9 for details of determining network complexity, and Section 12.2.17 for details of discovering interactions.)

10.1.3.4   Bayes and Probability

All of statistical analysis is based on probabilities. In general, it is based on a particular type of probability—that represented by a simple frequency of occurrence of events. There are essentially only two ways of statistically determining a probability. One way counts all of the possible outcomes (as, for instance, with the six faces of a die), and assesses the probability of each outcome simply by dividing each outcome by the total number of possible outcomes. So, for a fair die, the chance of throwing any particular number, say a 3, is the number of ways that a 3 can be thrown (1) divided by the total number of possible outcomes (6). Using this method, the chance of throwing a 3 on a die is $1/6 = 0.167$, or about 16.7%.

Another way to determine probabilities that is especially useful when it's impossible to determine all the outcomes—as, for instance, with counting all of the ways that it's possible to convert a prospect to a customer—is to look at lots of times when the event(s) of interest could have happened, and count the number of times it actually did happen. The ratio of occurrence of the event of interest to the total number of times it could have occurred represents the probability of occurrence. So if, in response to a marketing program, 1000 people are contacted and 10 become customers, then 10/1000 = 1%, so the observed chance, or probability, of converting someone to a customer using that marketing program is said to be 1%.

Bayesian methods are a way of starting with one set of evidence (in the form of multi-variable data) and arriving at an assessment of a justifiable estimate of the outcome probabilities given the evidence. More than just how to weigh the initial evidence, Bayes' formula also specifies how the probabilities should be revised in the light of new evidence. If, intuitively, such a method sounds obvious, that is because it is. But it took considerable insight to discover how to justifiably make the necessary calculations, and strictly speaking, they can only be made then under a very restricted range of circumstances. Theoretically, for instance, in order to discover the actual probability of an outcome given some multivariate evidence, a Bayesian method called *naïve Bayes* requires all of the variables to be "independent" of each other. That means that, theoretically, "age" and "income" can't be used together since as age increases, income also tends to increase in most data sets. Thus, age and income aren't independent since they are somehow connected. Figure 10.13a shows a conceptual diagram of naïve Bayesian variable

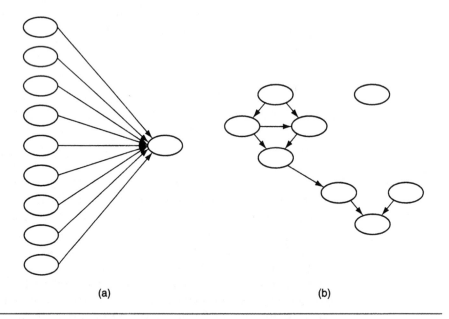

(a)   (b)

Figure 10.13   a) Naïve Bayes in b) Bayesian interdependent network.

interconnections. The ovals represent each variable, with all of the input variables connecting to the output variable.

There are other Bayesian methods that do not require independence of the input variables, but these become enormously computationally intensive for large data sets in their full form. Figure 10.13b shows a Bayesian network where the ovals again represent variables, but in this illustration, the interdependence of variables is shown in the interconnected clusters. This figure shows a couple of interdependent clusters and one variable that is completely independent of the others. There are computational shortcuts that make it practical to perform the computations allowing for nonindependence of the variables, although not as rigorously as the full computations would allow. On the other hand, they make the techniques useable in practice.

Regardless of theoretical constraints, Bayesian-based probability models very often work remarkably well in practice, even when many of the theoretical constraints are obviously breached.

Using the most probable chains of variable interaction and given a large set of multivariate evidence (data), various types of Bayesian networks can be constructed either manually or automatically. The automatic construction of Bayesian networks produces models that can be used for either explanation or prediction. Ultimately, all such networks are based on multivariate joint frequencies of occurrence in data sets combined using Bayes' Theorem, and are useful tools in mining data.

Bayesian Summary

Sensitivity: Nominal. (Can deal with all variable types, but only through binning.)

Features:

1. The naïve Bayes algorithm makes a lot of assumptions about the data that almost certainly don't hold up in the real world—but somehow this doesn't seem to matter in the results, which very often work well.
2. Bayesian networks can present insights as well as make predictions.
3. In practice, the real world performance of Bayesian networks seems to approximate the performance of multiple regression and neural networks.
4. Anything other than a naïve Bayes network can be very difficult to set up.
5. Bayesian networks offer the possibility of incorporating domain knowledge into a model other than just that present in a data set. A domain expert can add nodes not based on the data in the form of occurrence probabilities of inputs to, and outputs from, the added node.
6. Interactions are represented, but not well, since numeric variables have to be binned, which removes most of the granularity in numeric variables. This means that in practice, numeric interactions between

the input battery variables are very poorly represented except for interactions between categories. (Bayesian networks perform very poorly on the example discussed in Section 10.1.2.1.)

10.1.4 Discontinuous and Nonfunctional Representations

The truth is that in almost all cases in data mining where the discovered relationships are not linear, they are either curvilinear or clusters. This state of affairs is summarized in Figure 10.14a, which shows a linear relationship;

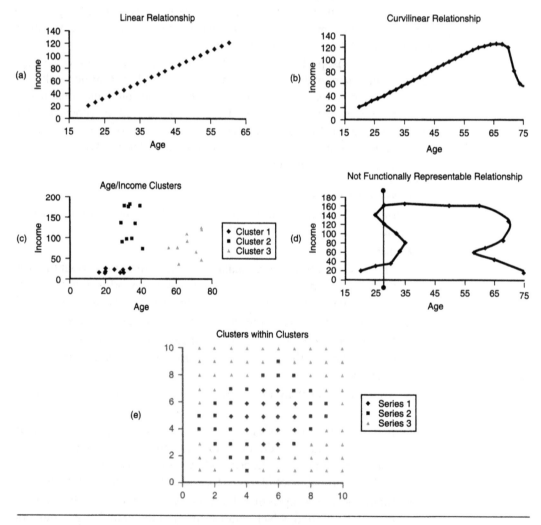

Figure 10.14 Summary of relationships addressed by mining algorithms.

10.14b, which shows a curvilinear relationship; and 10.14c, which shows a case with neither a linear relationship nor a curvilinear relationship, but clustering or some other method of neighborhood characterization. These characterizations account for well over 90% of the simple relationships that a data miner works with most of the time. What of the rest?

Figure 10.14d shows a relationship that none of the algorithms so far mentioned can touch. What is so intractable about it? And what of the situation in illustration 10.14e? These two relationships present big problems for at least some mining algorithms—and even bigger problems for the miner who discovers them.

Figure 10.14d shows a relationship that cannot be expressed as a mathematical function. A function is a mathematical construction that produces a single unique output value for every input value. A glance at the figure where the vertical line appears shows that this relationship has places where there are three values that the output can take for a given input value. All of the linear and nonlinear methods, including neural networks, are essentially methods for discovering a function that relates inputs to outputs. The problem here is that no function can adequately relate input to output under the circumstances shown—so no data mining tool that is based on discovering functions, however powerful, is going to do a good job. So for this situation, the miner needs a tool that uses an algorithm not dependent on characterizing relationships as functions.

The situation in Figure 10.14e also is clearly not a functional relationship. This is a very simplified representation of what can become a very intricate situation. Finding clusters in clusters, particularly with penetration of the cluster members, is a tricky and time-consuming task. Of course, a decision tree or other neighborhood-characterizing algorithm should be able to demark these boundaries since they aren't limited to functional representation. But a tree is limited to making straight cuts, and the curve is continuous, so approximating it is hard for a linear tool. Yet, in principle, in this case all the miner needs to characterize the central cluster is to discover an expression for a circle.

There are indeed algorithms that can deal with this situation. This subsection looks at one algorithm, and the next section looks at a couple of tools that support discovery of such relationships.

10.1.4.1 Evolution Programming

Evolution programming is potentially the most powerful relationship-discovering algorithm in the data miner's toolkit. There is a lot of rather misleading commentary in the data mining community about some algorithm or other being a "universal function-approximating tool." Well, the truth is that such a comment can be applied to many algorithms, and it's not a particularly powerful or relevant claim. What it intends to convey is that the algorithm noted (whichever one is being discussed at the time) can theoretically discover and represent any possible mathematical function. First, as observed in the previous discussion, mathematical functions only represent a subset of relationships that exist in data—and only the simple ones at that. And second, just because it's theoretically possible for an algorithm to get even that far doesn't mean that it actually will in practice. This is only mentioned here because such comments seem prevalent, and may well serve to mislead anyone who comes across them unless they are aware of the implications of the statement.

Evolution programming is not, even theoretically, a universal function-approximating tool. It may find a functional representation if it's there to be found, but this tool is perfectly happy to find any other relationship that can be characterized. It is quite capable of discovering "If . . . then . . ." types of rules, and then of characterizing what's going on in the neighborhood with a function, if appropriate—or, in fact, of discovering any other type of relationship. So, how does it work?

Essentially, *evolution programming* evolves computer programs that computationally represent the interrelationship between the two data sets, input and output. This means that, in theory anyway, if the relationship is computable, evolution programming will get there. This is a stronger claim than universal function approximation. The practice turns out to be not so very different most—but not all—of the time.

The evolution programming algorithm has some similarities to an area that is sometimes confused with it, genetic algorithms. Evolution programming is not the same as using genetic algorithms—it is, in fact, totally different in its application and result, although they do happen to share some features. Be careful not to confuse the one with the other. There is no discussion or explanation here of genetic algorithms. (Genetic algorithms are not really data mining tools. They're mainly used for optimizing functions and as such can be applied to many data mining algorithms. They can also be applied in many non-data mining related areas, too. But since they're not data mining algorithms they are not discussed here. They are only mentioned at all to point out a possible confusion between evolution programming and genetic algorithms, which may appear similar at first glance, but are actually completely different.)

Essentially, evolution programming works on the individual symbols and groups of symbols that form components of simple computer programs. These are typically the mathematical parts, like "+" and "−" and other mathematical operators such as "sine" and "logarithm," logical operators like "and" and "or," program flow statements like "If, then, else," and program variables, plus many others. What are going to be evolved are not whole programs, but program fragments that represent the relationship of interest between input and output batteries, and to be complete they have to be embedded into a larger programmatic framework. Since constants like π and e are available, as well as functions like sine, cosine, and the like, generating expressions for circles and other relationships isn't hard.

These programmatic expressions are assembled into groups using rules that ensure that all the expressions are well formed (meaning that they make sense within the program's framework as valid expressions) and assembles them into program fragments (initially at random) that are then executed and the result compared with the data to see how well they characterize the relationship. Of course, at first, not much is to be expected from this approach. However, there are many of these program fragments assembled into a "population," as shown in Figure 10.15. Each member, depending on how well it actually performs, is regarded as more or less "fit" (which here means only "good at estimating the relationship"). From time to time, the members of the population "breed" (exchange programmatic fragments, as illustrated in the figure's lower box) and "mutate" (have random changes made to the fragments) according to their level of fitness. The less fit die off, the more fit continue, and the population gets better and better at characterizing the relationship in the data with each succeeding generation. It may sound wonderful—and indeed, it is wonderful. However, it's not without problems!

For a start, it's not a fast method, although as implemented in modern data mining tools it is certainly not impossibly slow. The major problems involve deciding how complex to allow the programmatic expressions to grow. If they grow too complex, then they will characterize the relationship too well, including details that exist in the training data but not in the execution

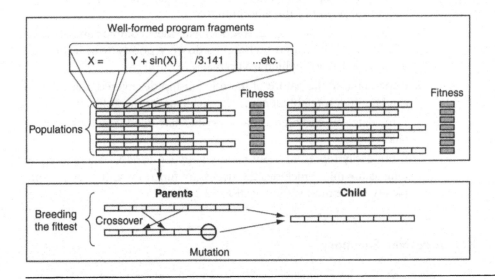

Figure 10.15 Evolution programming evolves program fragments.

data. (For a discussion of how this can happen see Chapter 12, where problems with noise are discussed.) Also, as the expressions become more complex, learning time increases dramatically. In addition, the more symbols that are available for use, the slower things go as there are simply more choices and combinations to try.

The discovery of relationships using these methods is called *symbolic regression*. Of course, it's a computational regression rather than a mathematical one, and what is produced is often a combination of continuous functions and discontinuous rules, but may include other forms, such as characterization of a circle as is needed in Figure 10.14e. It is, nonetheless, by these and methods similar to these that the "very hard" relationships in data mining may be discovered.

Evolution Programming Summary

Sensitivity: Inherently all variable types. However, in practice, the realization of the algorithm may limit the variable types in some way.

Features:

1. This is potentially one of the most powerful algorithms for discovering relationships between inputs and outputs.

2. In practice, the algorithm usually performs on a par with multiple nonlinear regression, neural networks, and similar techniques for two reasons. One is that the data is very often best characterized in ways that are easily accomplished by regression and the other algorithms mentioned. The other is that practical limits to prevent overtraining, unreasonable computation times, and so on limit, often very severely, the theoretical power of the algorithm.

3. Evolution programming can discover extremely complex and abstruse relationships that other techniques do very poorly with if they are there to be found—which isn't often.

4. Depending on the nature of the relationship discovered, this method can be uninterpretably incomprehensible as far as explanation goes.

5. Large data sets and high variable counts may need very long computation times.

6. It can easily represent input battery between variable interactions so long as the miner includes the necessary functions and enough complexity in the model. (See Section 12.2.4.11.)

10.1.5 Algorithm Summary

This hasn't been an exhaustive look at data mining algorithms by any means. Any reader even passingly familiar with data mining may have some favorite algorithm that has been left out of this very brief survey. But it's not important. In fact, as the chapter opening pointed out, specific algorithms aren't important to the practicing data miner, except inasmuch as each miner gets a feeling for those algorithms (and tools) that they commonly use. From a practitioner's standpoint, the results from one algorithm are usually pretty much like the results from another. There are occasions in which the data is characterized by some particular algorithm better than other algorithms, but that is almost certainly only a fortuitous combination of circumstances for that case. It's important to have some general idea of how the algorithm actually works (and it may be fascinating, although not important to their practical application, to understand the details of these algorithms). But the practical application of algorithms to data requires using several algorithms—preferably wrapped in a data mining suite of tools—and becoming familiar with their capabilities, performance, and applicability. Of course, if you have some experience with specific algorithms already and a good feeling for their applicability, you will need to find a tool or toolset that implements some version of your favorite. In general, try several, go with what works for you, and don't worry too much about what is going on "under the hood."

The relationships discussed and illustrated in Figure 10.14 are, in fact, the miner's "bread and butter" relationships. Naturally, these relationships are nowhere near as obvious when extended to far more variables. Algorithms are available that deal handily with linear, curvilinear, and cluster relationships as illustrated in Figures 10.14a, b, and c. Rarely do miners discover and use relationships such as those illustrated in Figures 10.14d and e. However, the lack of discovery of such relationships may be compounded by a chicken-and-egg type situation. Since current mining algorithms can't discover such relationships except by dint of particular and time-consuming effort, and perhaps not even then, it's not likely that such relationships will be discovered, even if they are there to be found. However, the author has developed algorithms to particularly seek such relationships. Even with those, discovery of such relationships in business data is still the exception, so perhaps business data really does have few of them that are of business value. Of these relatively rare relationships, the most common are those illustrated in Figure 10.14e, the clusters within clusters. Since these are of business interest when discovered, this artificial cluster within cluster data set is revisited after the next section to see what the tools described can make of it.

10.2 Tools and Toolsets

The opening section of this chapter offered a "once over lightly," and slightly theoretical, look at data mining algorithms. This part of the book aims to give you a practical introduction to mining data, not with algorithms in the raw, but with commercial data mining tools. (There is absolutely no reason to have to write a data mining algorithm from scratch these days, whatever the application, unless you really have the time and enjoy debugging some of the most complex algorithms ever implemented on computer systems. Buy an off-the-shelf toolset. Most of them are robust implementations of powerful algorithms that usually have been modified to perform better and more consistently than the raw algorithm.)

This section introduces a few commercially available tools and toolsets. Their appearance here does not particularly represent any endorsement by the author of these tools over other tools, although they are all excellent tools. These are chosen for one of two reasons: they are either available for downloading and evaluation without charge for some period of time, or they represent a particularly clear exposition of the underlying algorithm. Generally, these tools are introduced because you, the reader, can immediately begin to explore the tools of data mining with those discussed here. In the resources section of this book, and more particularly on the author's Web site *(www.modelandmine.com),* there are additional sources to explore, plus pointers and links to many other excellent data mining tools. The length of each tool discussion here owes more to the number of algorithms and features in each tool, and are not related to the author's preference.

The data set used to illustrate the tools in this section is a real world data set, taken from a credit card new customer acquisition program. The data set used is available for download from the author's Web site, or on a CD accompanying *Data Preparation for Data Mining.* This data set was used to determine who would respond to a credit card acquisition solicitation, and who would then remain as a profitable customer. There's no commentary accompanying the actual analysis since the purpose of this section is to introduce tools and toolsets. However, the illustrations shown were generated when modeling who would respond favorably to an acquisition solicitation. In some cases, so that the illustrations could be seen when printed in the book, the analysis is a very simplified version of a real analysis, since the purpose here isn't to analyze this data but to illustrate the tools, their interfaces, and their appearance.

10.2.1 Megaputer Intelligence *(www.megaputer.com)*

PolyAnalyst, the data mining tool kit from Megaputer Intelligence, comprises a well-integrated array of mining tools that can all be accessed from a common interface. (There are several versions of this product. The illustration is for the Pro version.) The interface is project-oriented, but organized around a data set referred to as "world." The suite includes tools for manipulating data sets, splitting data sets, and creating a limited number of extracted features. It also provides a very convenient hierarchical method of navigating the data sets, extracted features, and exploration results and rules that is reminiscent of Windows Explorer.

This tool's interface presents a three-paned window containing the project navigating pane; the general display pane where results, charts, and graphs appear; and a lower pane that reports progress. This is a client/server tool in which the server mines the data based on requests initiated by the client. Results are also returned to the client. There is no problem in running both components on a single machine.

The user manual for this product suite, which is available for download, is comprehensive, well written, and well worth the time invested in studying it. The manual and the suite itself come with a well-thought-out set of tutorials, and an inexperienced miner can learn a lot simply by reading through the manual and tutorials. With some minor restrictions, the tool suite can be used for evaluation for 60 days, which is plenty of time to work through the tutorials and evaluate the power and performance of this toolset. Screen shots from this toolset are shown in the last chapter (see Figures 9.3 and 9.4).

Figure 10.16 shows the PolyAnalyst main screen with the exploration tool selection opened (which is done here by pulling down the Explore menu.)

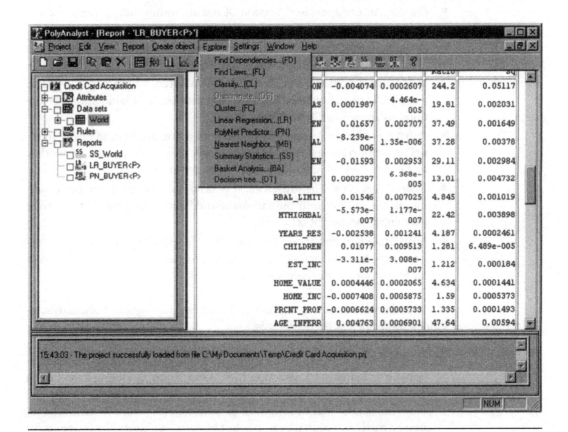

Figure 10.16   The main screen of Megaputer Intelligence's PolyAnalyst showing the exploration tools available.

The menu shows 11 different exploration tools, each of which embodies a different algorithm for exploring data sets. This is a very brief description of these tools. They are discussed roughly in the order that a miner might want to use them during an exploration project.

- *Summary Statistics:* Shown in the last chapter (see Figure 9.3), and definitely the place to start with a data assay.

- *Find Dependencies:* Similar to the single variable CHAID analysis discussed in the last chapter. The algorithm used isn't CHAID, but the intent and purpose are the same—given a variable, quickly discover what associates with it in the data set. This is an exploration tool rather than a modeling tool.

- *Linear Regression:* Explained in the last section. This is a very useful tool. This implementation is more useful than straightforward linear regression in that it automatically selects the most important variables for the regression. Plenty of graphical and text reporting from this tool make it a great place to start an exploration of a data set.

- *Cluster:* An unsupervised version of the algorithm that is useful for exploring a data set.

- *Decision Tree:* Offers a fast and visual way to examine data. The tree is presented as a sort of hierarchical structure from left to right, rather than as the more traditional tree. It is a binary split tree, which is to say, unlike the CHAID tree shown earlier, this tree splits each variable into two sections, as shown earlier in Figure 10.3.

- *PolyNet Predictor:* A neural network with automatic setting of the internal network parameters. This version will only build predictive models and doesn't reveal anything explanatory about the data.

- *Nearest Neighbor:* The MBR tool. It is slow and powerful, but the resulting model can be used only to make predictions, as there is no way of examining the neighborhoods.

- *Find Laws:* Somewhat similar to symbolic regression. This produces expressions that can include "If . . . then" structures, as well as more familiar function-type mathematical expressions.

In addition to these exploratory and modeling algorithms, PolyAnalyst includes some special purpose tools:

- *Basket Analysis:* Pretty much a free-standing tool that looks for associations in voluminous transaction files. Association modeling hasn't been mentioned before, as it is a limited and special purpose algorithm. The essential idea is that in long lists of transactions where items occur together, such as purchases in market baskets, it's useful to characterize which items are frequently purchased together. (If you have heard of the apocryphal association of beer and diapers being purchased together, that's market basket analysis. If you haven't heard of it, it's probably a good thing!)

- *Classify:* Used to separate a data set into two classes based on relationships discovered using the tools mentioned previously. When, for instance, a modeler has a good characterization of who will respond to a solicitation and who won't, or who is likely to make a fraudulent transaction and who isn't, and so on, Classify finds the optimum way to actually separate the data set.

- *Discriminate:* Uses two data sets. One data set is the "world" data set that is modeled. The other data set is compared to it and is essentially assessed instance by instance to determine if the new data set is similar to the data set modeled, or different from it. How and why this is a particularly powerful and useful capability is covered in more detail in Section 13.2.4. However, in essence, if the data set that was used for modeling and the run-time data set don't resemble each other, you can't expect to get worthwhile results in the run-time data set with the models or inferences made in the training (world) data set.

In addition to the exploration algorithms, PolyAnalyst has useful visualization techniques that deliver helpful insight into various aspects and relationships in the data set. Good visualization of exploration results is almost more important than the exploration method used. Only communication and application of the results is more important than understanding the exploration, and PolyAnalyst has a useful array of visualizations to support its exploratory tools.

In summary, this is a comprehensive collection of tools that is certainly an enterprise class data mining suite. Robust and reliable, it hides almost all of the complexity that lies behind the highly sophisticated algorithms and leaves the miner to concentrate on the analysis at hand. Its strengths are in predictive modeling rather than data exploration and understanding, although it is certainly more than adequate as an exploration tool. Data preparation and deployment into a production environment for real-time deployed models is difficult, although possible, with this suite.

It should also be noted that Megaputer Intelligence has two other tools: TextAnalyst, which is used for analyzing text, and WebAnalyst, a custom tool set for Web data analysis.

10.2.2 **Angoss Knowledge Studio** *(www.angoss.com)*

KnowledgeSEEKER and KnowledgeSTUDIO, are the flagship products of Angoss and have an emphasis on gleaning knowledge from, or discovery of knowledge in, data. In fact, its aim with the original tools was to facilitate data exploration rather than to produce predictive modeling. That philosophical underpinning is still present in its current suite; the tools and products mainly focus on discovering knowledge in data.

KnowledgeSTUDIO incorporates KnowledgeSEEKER as a main exploration tool. (KnowledgeSEEKER is a tree tool that was illustrated during discussion of single variable CHAID analysis in Chapter 9. See Figures 9.5, 9.6, and 9.7.) In addition, this suite incorporates tools for unsupervised clustering and for building neural networks. There are also facilities for connecting the suite to data sets and for visualizing the results of modeling. The visual interface for gaining insight into data is patterned after a decision tree presentation, with extensions where necessary to incorporate additional information. The strength of this approach is that when the miner has become familiar enough with understanding the data through the decision tree to feel it is an intuitive approach, the presentation of insights into data using the other algorithm-based tools will feel comfortable, too.

The suite, which is built with client and server components, as was PolyAnalyst, has very little support for data preparation and manipulation, so those operations will have to be carried out with some separate data manipulation tool. Also, deployment options are somewhat limited, a weakness with many data mining tools, particularly those not closely coupled into an enterprise data management system of some kind. Lack of deployment support in a tool is not a severe defect in any way, it simply means that deployment issues have to be considered separately, as with data preparation issues.

Figure 10.17 shows the main project interface, with all components integrated into a multi-window view. A project is organized through the metaphor of creating and manipulating a variety of objects including data objects, decision tree objects, cluster objects, and so on.

10.2.3 WizWhy (www.wizsoft.com)

WizWhy is a single algorithm-based rule extraction tool. The actual rule induction algorithm is proprietary but contrives to finesse the combinatorial explosion handily. (The combinatorial explosion occurs when the number of options that have to be compared with each other grows increasingly large. The number of combinations grows much faster than the number of objects to compare and can defeat any possible computational strategy in short order.) This rule extraction tool is capable of extracting necessary and sufficient rules, as described in the previous section.

The interface is quite straightforward and provides a limited number of options for connecting to data sets, but certainly covers all of the common

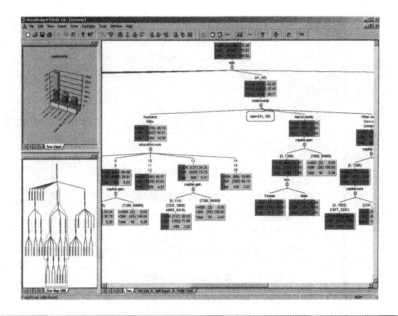

Figure 10.17   KnowledgeSTUDIO.

options, and connecting this tool to any data set should present no problem. Some of the terminology is a little idiosyncratic, but the interface is not highly complex and it doesn't take long to grow familiar with the conventions.

The number of rules produced—sometimes several thousand—can seem somewhat intimidating. However, this wealth of rules can be a very useful source of insight into the data, and the author's Web site contains a paper titled "Auditing Data with WizRule and WizWhy—What Do I Do with All These Rules?" describing the author's approach to using the rules.

The screen shown in Figure 10.18 displays part of the "Rule Report," which is a list of the discovered rules.

10.2.4   Bayesware Discoverer (www.bayesware.com)

Bayesware Discoverer is a tool for both building and discovering Bayesian nets. As shown in Figure 10.19, Bayesian nets consist of networks of nodes that are connected together. All of the nodes interact with each other in accordance with the principles of Bayesian probability calculations. The network shown was discovered in the CREDIT data set; some parts of the network are connected, through the intermediate nodes, to other parts of the network. However, there are two discrete clusters of interconnected nodes, and in the top right of the network window, one disconnected variable. The left-hand

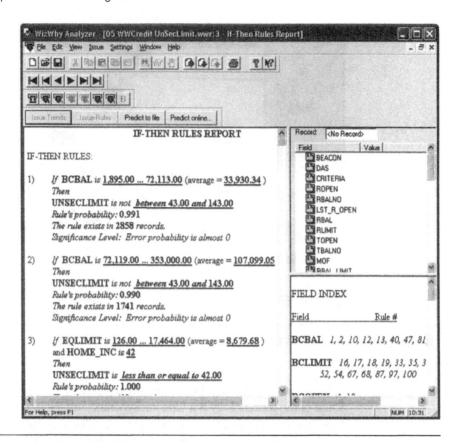

Figure 10.18   WizWhy displaying rules.

pane shows a list of the variable names. These names can be opened to show the frequency plots for the values they can take, as, for example, with the variable Married.

One of the features of this kind of network is that it can easily incorporate domain knowledge as nodes. Nodes either can be created, and their probabilities learned, from data, or can be created and the internal probability values set from domain knowledge. Exploring this form of Bayesian network can lead to insight and understanding of the relationships among nodes. This tool will actually discover the relationships in a data set and express them in the form of a network as shown.

Not only is the interconnecting pattern of nodes (variables) suggestive of the internal structure of the data set, it's possible to further explore the interactions among nodes by specifying a value for one or several nodes, and checking on the effect of such changes in other nodes of interest. Bayesware Discoverer offers a selection of visualizations, including fre-

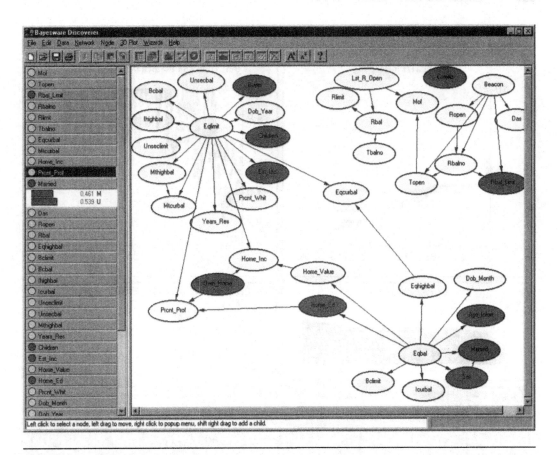

Figure 10.19 Bayesware Discoverer.

quency histograms and three-dimensional graphing. This system requires converting continuous variables into categorical values, a process called *binning,* and there are various options for creating the bins. Tuning these parameters can lead to changed networks, and different results. The networks aren't usually wildly different with different binning settings, but vary enough so that a lot of careful tuning may well be needed with high variable count data sets.

10.2.5 **e** *(www.sdi-inc.com)*

The tool "e" performs symbolic regression using evolution programming. Figure 10.20 shows the Windows interface. This screen shows this single algorithm tool in the process of evolving a representation of the data set shown in Figure 10.14e. The window consists of four panes, as well as several controls.

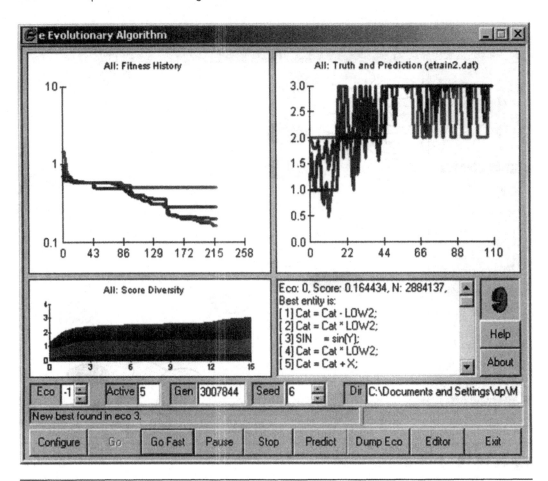

Figure 10.20 "e" evolving a solution to a difficult data set.

The top left pane shows the fitness (actually the error level) of each of (in this case) five populations that are evolving to solve the problem. As each population improves its errors diminish, thus the downward trend from left to right. At the top right, the actual current errors are shown for all of the five populations. Each of the three levels corresponds to each cluster in the data, and 110 vectors or instances. Each population produces different errors, which are shown as actual vs. predicted.

The bottom left pane shows diversity in the populations (not important in this explanation), and the lower right pane shows part of the pseudo code for the evolved program fragment to make the prediction. This pane scrolls to view all of the current best program fragment. The lower row of text displays various parameters and states, including "Gen" showing that so far, just over 3 million generations have evolved.

This is a very simple tool to use once the data is set up in the required format. However, it is very finicky indeed about the data format, and has no ability to connect to any data set through ODBC or other method. It loads the entire training data into memory, so maximum data set size is limited.

10.2.6 Microsoft SQL Server 2000 (www.microsoft.com)

Although it isn't illustrated here, SQL Server 2000 from Microsoft is a strong enough entrant that it needs to be mentioned. As a significant database management system, it is gaining strength, features, and market share, and is becoming ever more widely used as a business solution. This version has embedded data mining capabilities in the database, and so places data mining as a no-cost capability into any database or data warehouse built on the platform. This approach has both strong flaws and enormous strengths.

Technically, the product offers two algorithms, a decision tree and a neural network. Both are easy to use, and have been constructed to elegantly (although not optimally) handle problem data. So it is fairly easy to load data into this system and to build a model, being fairly assured that the model will be reasonable, and bad data won't crash the system.

One of the great strengths of this approach is that the mining suite is integrated into the data management system along with the data itself. This encourages data exploration and modeling as an easy activity. If the data that resides in the database, or data warehouse, is complete enough, has the necessary features extracted, is already optimally prepared, and has appropriate levels of aggregation for the level of detail of inference/prediction needed, this is an enormous benefit. One of Microsoft's gifts to all users of personal computers is a standard way of using and accessing the PC's power. This gift is embodied in the operating system known generically as Windows. To be sure, Microsoft didn't invent or create the ideas, and it wasn't first to market with them, but by having market dominance, its implementation of a windowing interface is now regarded as intuitive by the millions of users who are familiar with it and (relatively) comfortable using it. If its market presence can have even a shadow of this same familiarity with a data mining interface, that too will be an enormous benefit since, as is obvious in this section, there is no such thing at the moment as a standard way of presenting mining insights and results.

One weakness of this approach is that it might appear to end users that the tools included, and the capabilities of in-place mining, are all that are needed to have all the benefits of data mining. In Parts I and II of this book, much emphasis—although it might have sometimes been in the background—is placed on the idea that mining data is a technique that should support both strategic- and tactical-level business goals. The attitude might then arise, "Well, we bought SQL Server 2000 so we can do all the mining we need with that."

A data warehouse, and even most comprehensive databases, are created for some particular purpose. Data is summarized and aggregated to address specific needs, assumptions are incorporated in the construction of warehouse dimensions, business rules are enforced, dirty data is cleaned in ways that support reporting (not mining), and the data and the underlying business philosophy that supports warehouse construction are generally enforced and imposed on the data that is stored in the warehouse or database. Mining such a data set very often discovers only the enforced distortions imposed on such data—and delivers them as insights. Miners need to exercise enormous care when mining such data since, in more technical terms, this data is not a random sample, and is almost invariably biased—sometimes enormously. Although not a business example, keep in mind that the data revealing the ozone hole over the Antarctic was present in the collected data set, but was removed during preparation for modeling since it didn't fit with the modelers' perceptions of what should have been there. This is very often the case in warehouses, too. Perhaps it is always the case. Mining such data can very happily lead you "up the garden path."

Again, mining data is a skilled task that requires experience and expertise. A major department of one multi-billion dollar company bought a neural network package and applied it to their data. A "data mining analyst" was promoted from their help desk (where this person had been advising on network problems and therefore was seen as an obvious candidate to learn about neural networks). Given access to marketing data and a $200 neural network (from Brainmaker—not reviewed here) the analyst was expected, in 6 weeks, to produce the marvelous insights into marketing promised by data mining. When those insights didn't materialize, the company concluded, "Well, we tried data mining, and it doesn't work in our industry." It takes time and experience, plus commitment and training, to glean good results from mining data, as well as a commitment to apply any discoveries. In the right hands, Microsoft's tool can deliver high value and high return results; however, being readily available, it can also promote disillusion if casually applied inappropriately. Inasmuch as it promotes exploration and learning, it's a terrific benefit. Inasmuch as early poor results contribute to an assumption that continued experience will also bring no benefit, it's a flaw.

Another problem is that SQL—even the powerful version available in this product—is not capable of making the necessary transformations and feature extractions that experienced data miners need in order to fully prepare a data set. Full preparation may not always need transformations beyond the capabilities of database management systems, but certainly does at the moment. So full mining still requires extraction of data, if only for preparation. (And preparation for warehousing and database storage can actually destroy information that is useful for mining.)

Generally, inasmuch as mining tools should be available and integrated into the data warehouse, this is a great benefit and will help to deliver insight into, and value from, business data. Wherever these tools deliver business value, there is a tremendous strength in this product. However, inasmuch as it misleads, distorts results, and encourages managers to think that data mining is only to be used as a tactical tool on tactical data sets, it does at best a disservice and denies powerful tools for corporate strategic decision making. At worst, it promotes delivery of spurious and trivial results that get the tools a poor reputation, whereas it is the inappropriate use of the tools or inexperience in their use that should be blamed.

Only time will tell if this development encourages or delays the growth of the benefits of skilled data analysis. In summary, there is still a need for tools—data preparation, manipulation, and exploration tools—that are entirely separate from those embedded in a data management tool.

10.3 **Summary**

Algorithms are theoretical and mathematical constructions that outline methods for exploring data. When the algorithms are wrapped in a user interface, and tried and tested against the vagaries of the real world and still found to perform—when supported with documentation, technical support, bug fixes, training, help screens, and all the other facets that go to make a robust product—they are tools. No tool supports an algorithm in its raw form—there wouldn't be any point since it can't be used in that way. However, when suitably modified, algorithms do form the core of all mining tools. Different algorithms imply different capabilities and different constraints, and it's the capabilities and constraints that underlying algorithms imply that become important to a miner when constructing mined models, which is addressed in the next chapter.

Tools and software suites come in a variety of guises. Some support multiple tools within integrated suites; others support single algorithms. All have their place, and this chapter reviewed briefly the fundamental characteristics of algorithms that are important and looked at some tools and tool sets. The tools reviewed were chosen because they offer a good demonstration of commercial implementation of the various algorithms discussed. Nonetheless, all of the tools here have stood the test of time, and offer reliable, robust, and useful implementations that deliver good value.

The next chapter puts these tools into practice by introducing the techniques—the practices—of mining data.

Chapter 11

Getting the Initial Model

Basic Practices of Data Mining

Data mining, as should be very plain to any reader by now, is not simply concerned with applying either algorithms or mining tools to a data set, and then standing back and waiting for magic to happen. First and foremost, data mining helps to solve those types of business problems that require insight and action based on collected data. Acquiring the required insight and taking action does require applying algorithms to data in the form of mining tools. But crucial to the whole endeavor is that it takes the intelligent and knowledgeable application of those tools to data to achieve meaningful results. This chapter delves into how to decide which tools to use, how to handle the data with those tools, and what precautions to take to make sure that the model will work so that it provides the needed real-world insight, classification, or prediction.

In this chapter, practical examples focus mainly on one data set, which is explored in some detail using a number of methods. An interested reader can duplicate most of the example explorations. The data set used here is available on the author's Web site *www.modelandmine.com,* and no-charge evaluation versions of the tools used (available from the individual vendors) are sufficient to duplicate many of the explorations and models. In addition, the Web site includes various worksheets in an Excel workbook that contains some of the results demonstrated. Also, some of the actual models created to get the results shown and discussed in this chapter are available for download. Thus, this chapter offers the opportunity for an interested reader to duplicate and extend on the explorations presented. Even without active participation, the reader should find that the continued focus on exploring a single data set leads to some degree of familiarity with its contents. The repeated variety of explorations will present similar information in different formats, hopefully showing the strengths and weaknesses of each tool and technique in more contrast than if different data sets were used in each example.

At this point, it's assumed that the data for mining is assembled and prepared. Although it's crucial that the data set represents the business questions of interest (see Part II and Chapter 9 in Part III), that is assumed here. This chapter addresses the question, "So I have the business problem clear and got my data together. Now what?"

11.1 Preparing to Stay Honest

One of the biggest problems in mining data, particularly for an inexperienced miner, is that it's all too easy to inadvertently lead yourself astray. To avoid this pitfall, take precautions to make sure that the results achieved from mining are actually worth having. This means that the results, in whatever form they appear, should be applicable to the business problem, which in turn generally means that they should apply to the world at large.

It might seem, at first blush, that since the data comes from the world, there shouldn't be any problem with the model applying to the world. However, there are three separate "gotchas" to contend with: *bias, garbage* (also called *noise*), and *oversearching*.

- *Bias:* Data might not actually represent the part of the world that the model (through the business problem) is meant to address. For instance, a store selling maternity merchandise shouldn't expect that its customer data will be applicable to deciding on any course of action should they decide to launch a new line of products aimed at grandparents as a new market segment. Expectant or new mothers are likely to represent a different part of the population than grandparents, and expectant and new mother interests, motivations, and reactions are likely to be different than grandparents' interests, motivations, and reactions. At the very least, there is no particular reason to assume that they will be the same. This first gotcha is technically called *bias,* meaning only that the data is somehow skewed away from addressing the issue expected, or that the relationships in the data on hand will be different from those in a data set collected about the actual population to whom the results are to be applied.

- *Garbage:* The second gotcha is that every real-world data set contains more information than just the information about the relationships of interest. Some of the information is truly meaningful, but for any number of reasons, all real-world data sets that a miner in a business situation will see also will contain what is best characterized as *garbage*. No matter how carefully the data was collected and prepared, there always will be spurious relationships—they are simply unavoidable. Data mining tools are some of the most powerful technological tools for discovering and characterizing relationships in data that we know how to invent. Indeed, although the world really isn't waiting for a better data mining algorithm, if a truly better algorithm than those available today is discovered, it will be speedily co-opted for use. So we can deploy against any data set an array of the most powerful relationship-discovering tools we know how to build—and discover relationships they will. But the mining tools have no way to discriminate between meaningful and garbage relationships. The job of the tools lies in discovering patterns. It's up to the miner to make sure that the discovered relationships are meaningful. That's part of the good practices approach to data mining.

■ *Oversearching:* If you look long enough and hard enough for any particular pattern in a data set, the more you look, the more likely you are to find it—whether it's meaningful or not. It's the multiple looking that makes a big difference. To get a sense for how much difference multiple looking can make, suppose that we play a game. Toss a fair coin. If it comes up heads, I pay you a dollar; if it comes up tails, you pay me 50 cents. That probably sounds like a good deal for you at this point. However, if multiple looks make no difference, you won't mind if I get 10 tosses for each one you get, now will you? But I am sure that you will feel that this arrangement—one in which I get 10 looks, or tosses of the coin, for every one you get—makes a huge difference. Even if you don't know exactly how it will skew the odds, it's at least intuitively obvious that the more I look (toss the coin) on any one turn, the greater my chances of discovering a tail. (Actually, in 10 tosses, my chance of tossing at least one tail is 99.9023%.) So it is with data mining, which essentially looks and looks and looks again for patterns in the data, so the fact that any particular pattern is discovered isn't necessarily as meaningful as it might at first appear. Essentially, the old adage "no smoke without fire" may or may not be true—but if I keep looking long enough and hard enough, I can almost always turn up at least a whiff of something that might be smoke.

So these are three gotchas—bias, garbage, and oversearching. Fortunately, so long as the miner keeps these three problems in mind, one procedure serves as the foundation for keeping these beasts on a short leash. The key to taming these problems is to use at least three data sets, not one. Three is the minimum. This chapter in part looks at dealing with, or allowing for, noise and oversearching. A look at some possible ways of discovering bias waits until Chapter 12.

How do you get the three needed data sets? Very simple. Take the original data set developed through the assay and chop it into three parts. Call one the training data set, one the test data set, and the other the evaluation data set.

(See MIII:AB.11.2) Ideally, each of these three data sets needs to be large enough to pass the tests for having enough data that are described in Section 9.2.3.4, which means that each of the three data sets must be large enough to be representative of the pool from which it was drawn. However, it turns out that it takes more data for a mining tool to learn a relationship than it does to confirm a discovered relationship. This can be seen intuitively by realizing that it takes several to many examples or repetitions for us to learn a relationship, but it takes only one brief error to show if we didn't learn it. That's why in school it takes a semester to learn a topic, but that learning can be assessed in a test that lasts only about an hour. So the test and evaluation data sets can have relaxed representativeness requirements. In other words, the training data set must be as representative as possible of the full range of variations that the world is likely to show, whereas if data is not plentiful, it's possible to get away with less representative test and evaluation data sets.

(See MIII:AB.11.3) As a rule of thumb, and it is only a rule of thumb, with plenty of data on hand, divide the data into 60/20/20% for train, test, and evaluation, respectively. With less data on hand, try 70/20/10% or 70/15/15%. But don't squeeze below 75/15/10%, however sparse the data. If you don't have enough data to make the 75/15/10% division, you don't have enough data to reliably mine for good models. Eliminating the test and evaluation data sets in order to increase the amount of data in the training data set just isn't an option. If you don't have enough data, recognize that the applicability, generality, and accuracy of any mined model may be far less than ideal— but try to get the best model possible anyway. It's often the case that a poor model is better than no model, so even with a paucity of data, go ahead and make the best possible model. Just be careful to clearly note the limits of any model—particularly when the model is not as well founded as it might be. (More on this in Chapter 13.)

Having said this, there are other options for testing the reliability of mined models that are described in the literature. Terms such as *ten-fold cross validation, leave-one-out validation, bootstrap,* and *resampling* may appear. These are ingenious ways to try to get around a shortage of data and yet still get a representative model. When carefully applied by experienced modelers, they can deliver useable results. In any case, these are usually implemented as internal checks applied, probably invisibly, to the mining algorithm within the tool. These are helpful—maybe very helpful—but they don't replace the verification and validation (done in part with the test and evaluation data sets) that the miner needs to use when mining data. In any case, they are valid methods for compensating for a shortage of data. The real answer, though, is to have enough data. These are models on which millions of dollars may ride, on which strategic business decisions may be made, and on which competitive advantage may be gained or lost. The best practice is to have enough representative data—or to at least know that enough data for reliable modeling isn't currently available.

11.2 **Addressing the Data**

Actual data mining activities address data sets, and although the whole mining endeavor is set up to solve a business problem, at some point the miner must address the data directly. At this "directly addressing the data" level, the actual process of data mining becomes remarkably simple. In essence, as already mentioned, all that data mining tools do is to discover a relationship between two parts of a data set—the input variables and the output variable(s)—such that specific configurations of values in the input variables map, more or less well, to specific configurations in the output variable(s). The map is in the form of rules or expressions of some sort that make the linkage as described in the discussion of algorithms in the last chapter.

Apart from data preparation issues, a data miner addresses data directly by building a purposeful model. In general, there are only three types of purposes for constructing a model: for understanding, for classification, and for prediction. (Modeling for classification and for prediction are often mistakenly assumed to be the same. The differences will be explained later in this chapter.) These three ways of modeling data are partly related to the nature of the business problem, partly to the nature of the input and output data sets, and partly to the nature of the relationship sought. The remainder of this chapter focuses on these key issues related to modeling for understanding, classification, and prediction.

11.2.1 **Input and Output Data Set Configurations**

All business data sets for mining consist of many variables—usually tens, often hundreds, and sometimes thousands. In rare cases, some data sets may have tens of thousands of variables. The variables are grouped into what are called *batteries,* so the group of input variables is often called the *input battery,* and the group of output variable(s) is called the *output battery.* However high the number of variables in a data set, they are grouped into batteries. It is not at all unusual for the output data battery to be entirely composed of a single variable. Far from being unusual, it is generally the case that the output, however complex a phenomenon it references in the world at large, is expressed in the form of a single variable (see Figure 11.1a.) In the CREDIT data set used in the last chapter, and used again as the example to explore in this one, the exploratory models built use only a single variable in the output battery. One single prediction variable, for instance, is a binary variable (taking values of only 1 and 0) that indicates if someone did (1) or did not (0) respond to a credit card solicitation.

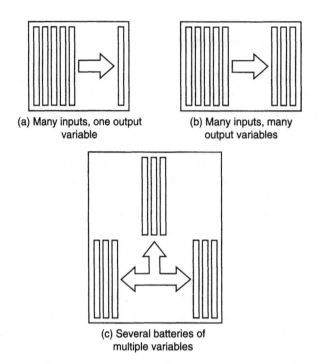

(a) Many inputs, one output
variable

(b) Many inputs, many
output variables

(c) Several batteries of
multiple variables

Figure 11.1   Batteries of variables in a data set.

However, the prediction variable doesn't have to be binary. It can easily be a categorical or continuous variable. To move away from a credit example, the prediction variable might have been a category indicating if someone was predominantly a beer, wine, or spirits drinker. Or again, it could have been a continuous variable, say a measure of average beer consumption over some period. Each of these three cases—single binary, categorical, and continuous prediction variables—are illustrated in Figure 11.2, where the shading indicates the nature of the values. Each calls for different modeling techniques, which will be explored in a moment. In addition, of course, the input variables could also be binary, categorical, or continuous, or indeed some mixture of all three types, and their type also has an impact on mining. For instance, if the output variable were average beer consumption and the input variables were mainly categorical (such as occupational and other demographic information about individuals), but the input variables also included a continuous variable (say, income), the objective might be to understand how beer consumption varied in occupational and demographic segments after allowing for the different income levels.

However, multiple-input, single-output variable data sets are not the only variety of data set encountered. Although the single-output variable types of

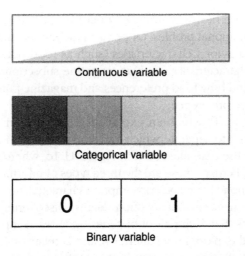

Figure 11.2 Types of variables.

Beer	Wine	Spirits	Description
0	0	0	Teetotal
1	0	0	Beer only
0	1	0	Wine only
1	1	0	Beer & Wine, no Spirits
0	0	1	Spirits only
1	0	1	Beer & Spirits, no Wine
0	1	1	Wine & Spirits, no Beer
1	1	1	Beer, Wine & Spirits

Figure 11.3 Categorical binary coding.

investigation form perhaps 90% or more of all business data mining, other combinations turn up, too. As Figure 11.1b shows, another possibility is having two sets of variables in the same data set so that there are multiple-input variables and also multiple-output variables. Again, inputs and outputs may be any of the three types mentioned—binary, categorical, or continuous. The example shows three output variables, which might indicate (categorically) a person's drinking preferences: beer, wine, spirits, beer and wine, beer and spirits, wine and spirits, beer and wine and spirits, or teetotal. Categorical binary codings for these are shown in Figure 11.3. If the input variables were similar to the previous single variable output case, the objective this time might be to find the best way to classify people according to their demographic and occupational profiles. Or perhaps the inputs might be a mixture of continuous behavioral characteristics (such as food purchase amounts) and categorical characteristics (such as magazine subscriptions), the object being to understand how food preferences and magazine purchases relate to alcoholic beverage preference.

In this last case (in which an explanation rather than a prediction is needed), it's harder to separate which variables constitute input and which output. Consider the case illustrated in Figure 11.1c, where there are three variable batteries. Perhaps these are the three types of information mentioned previously—alcoholic beverage consumption characteristics, food purchase information, and magazine subscription details. Discovering how these are interrelated means that each pair of batteries operates as inputs to the third. So a miner would explore how batteries A and B relate to C, A and C to B, and B and C to A. What's important in this case is understanding the relationships, not classification or prediction. This type of investigation usually focuses on discovering and characterizing the associations, and how strongly they relate to each other.

There is an assumption in the descriptions of these three modeling situations. The assumption made so far has been that the models needed will produce an explanation, classification, or prediction by relating the patterns in the variables to each other, and that is indeed one way of modeling. However, it's not the only way to model data. Instead of considering how the variables interact, it is equally possible and valid to consider how the instances (also called *vectors* or *records*) interact. Implicit in any discussion of group clustering is that similarity of instances is most interesting. In the alcoholic beverage preference example, each instance represents an individual consumer. So the question of interest might be to discover how many common consumption patterns these consumers show and to characterize the discovered common patterns of overall alcoholic beverage consumption. The focus is on similarity (and difference) among the instances (or customers), rather than among the variables. Another and more common example of this type of modeling that groups instances rather than variables is *market basket analysis,* which typically looks at large numbers of purchase transactions to find which types of products associate together, or in other words, are purchased together.

As a brief summary, variables, whether input or output, can individually be binary, categorical, or continuous. Variables in a data set are grouped into batteries and each battery may contain a mixture of variable types. One way of modeling a data set relates the variables to each other; for instance, determining how beer consumption varies with income and occupation. Another way of modeling data relates instances to each other; perhaps determining the number of typical types of beer drinkers. Basic ways of modeling data include modeling for understanding, modeling to classify, and modeling to predict.

(See MIII:AB.11.4, MIII:AB.11.5, MII:TB.11.1) Table 11.1 summarizes the situation described so far in this subsection. It's a fairly self-explanatory tabular depiction, but note that the column headed "Modeling For:" hasn't been explained yet. The two subcolumns under "Modeling For:" are labeled with

TABLE 11.1 Tool Selection Matrix

Input Variable Type(s)	Output Battery Variable Count	Output Variable Type(s)	Modeling For: (Keys to Table 11.2 Abbreviations)	
			Understanding	Classifying
Binary	1	Binary	T, s, I	R, B, T
Categorical	1	Binary	T, s, I	R, B, T
Continuous	1	Binary	T, S, I	R, b, T, n, e
Bin & Cat	1	Binary	T, s, I	R, B, T, e
Bin & Cont	1	Binary	T, s, I	R, B, T, n
Cat & Cont	1	Binary	T, S, I	R, B, T, n
Bin, Cat, & Cont	1	Binary	T, S, I	R, B, T, n
Binary	1	Categorical	T, s, I	r, B, T, n
Categorical	1	Categorical	T, s, I	r, B, T, n
Continuous	1	Categorical	T, S, I	r, B, T, n, e
Bin & Cat	1	Categorical	T, s, I	r, B, T, n, e
Bin & Cont	1	Categorical	T, S, I	r, B, T, N, e
Cat & Cont	1	Categorical	T, S, I	r, B, T, N, e
Bin, Cat, & Cont	1	Categorical	T, S, I	r, B, T, N, e
Binary	1	Continuous	T, s, I	r, B, T, n, e
Categorical	1	Continuous	T, s, I	r, B, T, N, e
Continuous	1	Continuous	T, S, L	r, b, T, N, e
Bin & Cat	1	Continuous	T, s, L	r, b, T, n, e
Bin & Cont	1	Continuous	T, S, L	r, b, T, N, e
Cat & Cont	1	Continuous	T, S, L	r, b, T, N, e
Bin, Cat, & Cont	1	Continuous	T, S, L	r, b, T, N, e
Binary	Many	Binary	TT, S, II	RR, BB, b, TT
Categorical	Many	Binary	TT, S, II	RR, BB, b, TT
Continuous	Many	Binary	TT, S, II	RR, BB, b, TT, n, ee
Bin & Cat	Many	Binary	TT, S, II	RR, BB, b, TT, ee
Bin & Cont	Many	Binary	TT, S, II	RR, BB, b, TT, nn
Cat & Cont	Many	Binary	TT, S, II	RR, BB, b, TT, nn
Bin, Cat, & Cont	Many	Binary	TT, S, II	RR, BB, b, TT, nn

continued

TABLE 11.1 Continued

Input Variable Type(s)	Output Battery Variable Count	Output Variable Type(s)	Modeling For: (Keys to Table 11.2 Abbreviations)	
			Understanding	Classifying
Binary	Many	Categorical	TT, S, ll	rr, BB, b, TT, nn
Categorical	Many	Categorical	TT, S, ll	rr, BB, b, TT, nn
Continuous	Many	Categorical	TT, S, ll	rr, BB, b, TT, nn, ee
Bin & Cat	Many	Categorical	TT, S, ll	rr, BB, b, TT, nn, ee
Bin & Cont	Many	Categorical	TT, S, ll	rr, BB, b, TT, NN, ee
Cat & Cont	Many	Categorical	TT, S, ll	rr, BB, b, TT, NN, ee
Bin, Cat, & Cont	Many	Categorical	TT, S, ll	rr, BB, b, TT, NN, n, ee
Binary	Many	Continuous	TT, S, ll	rr, BB, b, TT, nn, n, ee
Categorical	Many	Continuous	TT, S, ll	rr, BB, b, TT, NN, n, ee
Continuous	Many	Continuous	TT, S, LL	rr, bb, b, TT, NN, n, ee
Bin & Cat	Many	Continuous	TT, S, LL	rr, bb, b, TT, nn, n, ee
Bin & Cont	Many	Continuous	TT, S, LL	rr, bb, b, TT, NN, n, ee
Cat & Cont	Many	Continuous	TT, S, LL	rr, bb, b, TT, NN, n, ee
Bin, Cat, & Cont	Many	Continuous	TT, S, LL	rr, bb, b, TT, NN, n, ee

two generic types of modeling activity that a miner can undertake: modeling to understand and modeling to classify. (Why there is no entry for modeling to predict will become apparent later in this chapter.)

Tables 11.1 and 11.2 taken together provide a guide that a modeler can use to start to decide which tool is most appropriate for which job. To use the tables:

1. Inspect the data (which should have been done in the assay anyway).
2. Decide which type or types of variables are predominantly important.
3. Determine the input/output configuration required.
4. Determine which sort of model is needed.
5. Find the appropriate row in Table 11.1.
6. Look up the recommended tool choices in Table 11.2.

However, selecting a mining tool is not quite as easy as that. For one thing, over time, every miner develops individual techniques and preferences for particular tools. For another, tools are expensive, and a miner may well

TABLE 11.2 Algorithm Selection

Abbreviation	Algorithm	Notes
T, t	Decision tree	Trees come in a variety of guises. All are worth using. The basic types are those that can produce only two leaves per split and those that can produce several leaves per split (like CHAID). Most tools wrap robust, well-tried, and well-tested algorithms. However, the miner needs to remain aware that any tree is just one of many that any data set supports. A minute change in the data set (such as a different division between training, testing, and evaluation data sets) can result in apparently completely different trees. Similarly, starting with a different variable for the initial split will result in a very different tree—possibly one more interesting than the initial model. So what a tree produces is *a* model of a data set, not *the* model. It's worth exploring several of the possible trees that explain or classify a data set. In a representative data set, regardless that a variety of trees are possible, in general their classification performance is quite similar.
S, s	Self-organizing map	SOMs are powerful data visualizers; however, there are a couple of important caveats in using them. First, the results are not always immediately obvious to anyone not familiar with them, although familiarity comes quickly with practice. This means that they aren't always ideal for reporting results to, say, management. Secondly, all input needs to be numerical and properly scaled. Appropriately transforming data in this way is a nonobvious, nontrivial problem that is a more advanced topic than is covered in this book. (However, a software toolkit that does this is included with *Data Preparation for Data Mining*, which covers the issues and practices in detail. The download is available from *www.modelandmine.com*.) Also note that it is up to the miner to determine the relative importance and weight that should be given to each variable in the SOM. Appropriate weightings, as well as variable transformations, can make a huge difference to the resulting map, but what the appropriate weights and transformations are is not always easy to determine.
L, l	Linear regression	Linear regression is a simple and quick algorithm implemented in many tools. It works best with continuous input and output variables and misses all nonlinearities, which are certain to be present—but are not always important—in any real-world data set.
R, r	Rule extraction	Rule extraction tools can be very powerful at characterizing nonlinear relationships. Many commercial tools produce discrete classifications rather than continuous estimates. In complex data sets, rule counts can become quite large, making understanding difficult.

continued

TABLE 11.2   Continued

Abbreviation	Algorithm	Note
B, b	Bayesian network	The type of Bayesian network referred to here is primarily a naïve Bayesian network. Commercially available tools that induce other types of Bayesian networks may be useful in understanding data, and possibly also in classificatory modeling. But at this writing it is the experience of the author that the tools are not yet perfected, and are unreliable. Most of the naïve Bayesian commercial tool implementations seem robust.
N, n	Neural network	Neural network tools are fairly common and quite popular. Robust commercial implementations are available in a very wide range of prices, making them among the most affordable mining tools. However, whereas it is almost always possible to get some sort of model quite easily, tuning a network—indeed, even setting one up in the first place—requires considerable experience. Most tools wrap the complexity in a shell so it's not exposed to the miner. This can be very helpful—but it can also prevent a more experienced miner from being able to optimize the network.
E, e	Evolution programming	Evolution programming is one of the potentially more powerful tools available for classificatory modeling. Sometimes the symbolic regression produced can also be usefully interpreted as an explanation, but by no means is this always true. If the tool exposes the complexity of its underlying algorithm, tuning the tool to deliver best results is not a straightforward process. If the tool shields the user from algorithm complexity it may be impossible to get access to the full power offered. In addition to these caveats, some tools require data to be held in computer memory for modeling. This may or may not be a problem, depending on the size of the data set to be modeled.

not have access to one the table recommends. And for a third, comfort with whatever user interface the tool offers may be more important than the particular algorithm it implements when dealing with a complex data set. But these tables are offered as a summary guide, a place to start, for beginning an exploration of which tools work under which circumstances. It's the author's answer to the oft-asked question, "Which is the best mining tool?" There isn't one—it depends on the circumstances. Look up the circumstances in the table, and there's the recommendation for a place to start. Practices for successfully applying selected tools to data follow in later sections in this chapter.

> **Keys Used in Tables 11.1 and 11.2**
>
> Note in the "Modeling For:" column the two subcolumns, "Understanding" and "Classifying". The uppercase and lowercase letter keys in both subcolumns cross-reference to Table 11.2. These keys indicate the various modeling techniques that should be considered with each of the circumstances listed. The type of technique indicated by both upper- and lowercase keys is the same, so both "L" and "l" refer to the row containing "L" under the heading "Abbreviation" in Table 11.2 (where "L" symbolizes "linear regression").
>
> *Uppercase letter key:* Indicates that this technique is a good candidate for creating the model under the circumstances indicated, and should be considered.
>
> *Lower case letter key:* Indicates that the technique might help, but isn't the preferred method of modeling in this situation.
>
> *Double-letter key:* Relates to models that will predict several output variables simultaneously. (Most tools can't do this. More on this topic later in the chapter.) In such a case, one technique to use is to create a separate predictive model for each output variable, indicated by a doubled letter, say "LL," which would mean "using the preferred method for this situation, build a separate linear regression model for each output variable." The same applies to the secondary technique indicated.

11.2.2 Missing Value Check Model

(See MIII:AB.11.7, MIII:AB.11.8, MIII:AB.11.9, MIII:AB.11.10) Chapter 9 covered the basic assay and made some introductory remarks about missing values. With the data set assembled and partitioned (into training, test, and evaluation data sets), the very first model to build should be a missing value check model (MVCM).

Start by making a copy of all three data sets. In each data set copy, replace all of the values in the variables of the input battery that are *not* missing with a "1" and all of the values of the input battery variables that *are* missing with a "0." Notice that only the input battery variables are modified, not those of the output battery. You end up with an all-binary input battery of variables, and the output battery remains untouched. Now, regardless of what type of model the business problem ultimately calls for, create a predictive model that attempts to predict the value of the output variable(s).

Now the only information that remains in the input data set is whether or not there is something entered for a variable's values. If after this transformation any of these variables show any pattern that relates to the output variable, then it has to be a pattern based entirely on the presence or absence of data. How does this help?

The unmodified credit data set shows a very interesting pattern with the MVCM. First, glance at Figure 11.4. This figure shows the result of single variable CHAID (SVCHAID) analysis on the whole data set, not on the modified data set. The predictor variable is who responded to the solicitation (BUYER). The left-hand image shows the most associated variable as BEACON (a type of credit rating). This variable contains the Beacon score for each person. On the right-hand side of the figure is a list of the variables ordered by the significance of their interaction with BUYER. It only shows the variables worth splitting on, which is not all of the variables in the data set. Thus, this figure shows that of all the variables in the unmodified data set, 27 have a significant relationship with BUYER, BEACON (heading the

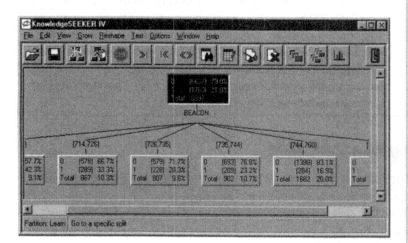
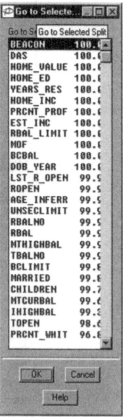

Figure 11.4   Single variable CHAID on unmodified data set.

list) being the most significant and PRCNT_WHIT (at the bottom of the list) being the least significant.

Compare this with the same situation for the MVCM on the modified data set shown in Figure 11.5—what a telling difference! There are far fewer variables of any interest at all—but the leading candidate is DOB_MONTH. Look carefully at the right-hand leaf. For clarity, its content is duplicated here:

0	(0)	0.0%
1	(656)	100%
Total	656	7.8%

This split comes down from DOB_MONTH = 1. The "1" in "DOB_MONTH = 1" indicates that there is a value for month of birth—no more nor less than that since all values that are present were replaced with the value "1." However, note that the "0" and "1" shown inside the leaf refer to the state of "BUYER," which is the output variable. Its values have not been replaced, so "0" means that there was no response to the solicitation, and "1" indicates that there was a response. This leaf indicates that everyone who had an entry in the DOB_MONTH field (all 656 entries in the training data set) were all buyers—every one. (The count of 656 is discovered on the bottom line of the leaf, which says, "Total 656 7.8%"). This is a variable that doesn't even show up in the partition list in the single variable CHAID on the unmodified data set (Figure 11.4), yet every single person who has an entry for birth month

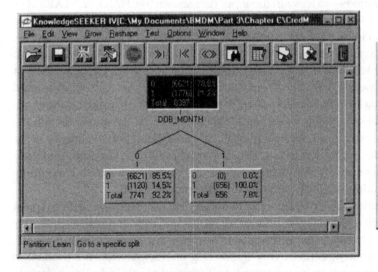
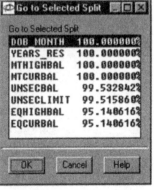

Figure 11.5 Single variable CHAID creating MVCM.

in the data set responded to the solicitation. What is going on here—and what does it mean?

It turns out that most of the entries that have anything entered at all in the DOB_MONTH field are, in fact, entered as "00." Not a month at all. Very few have any value that indicates a month, that is to say a number between 01 and 12. When the single variable CHAID looks at this variable (which is mostly empty anyway) and partitions the values that are there, there really isn't much in the partitions of any significance—both colloquially and, more importantly for the algorithm, statistically. So in the unmodified data set, this variable appears to carry little information that CHAID notices.

However, although not all responders have a DOB_MONTH entry, it is *only* responders who get any entry at all, whatever the value is—even if it's only "00." Thus, any entry in DOB_MONTH is, in fact, a partial surrogate for someone who responded—it's only entered if the customer did respond—so it can't be used to predict who responded because the entry is only made after the fact.

Thus, the MVCM has pointed straight to a problem in this data set. And although the SVCHAID model of the original data set ignored this variable anyway, other modeling tools and algorithms may very well not. They might notice that it is a seemingly significant variable, and try to use it. But since it's only filled in after the fact, any model that placed reliance on the content of this variable would be doomed to fail in the real world. It would, however, seem to work in the training, test, and evaluation data sets because they would all contain the same entered-after-the-fact data in this variable.

Interestingly, YEARS_RES, the next most significant split in the MVCM, is present both for responders and for nonresponders, and so is fine—at least on those grounds—to leave in the input data set. An SVCHAID for YEARS_RES in both data sets (original and MCVM) is shown in Figures 11.6 and 11.7. The left leaf in Figure 11.6 shows the MVCM in which no value is entered for YEARS_RES, and this leaf shows a quite high response rate—far higher than that of any leaf in the original unmodified data set shown in Figure 11.7. It seems that people who do not reveal (or at least, who have no value entered into the data for) the number of years they have resided at their current address are far more likely to respond than those who do have such an entry!

This is certainly an interesting observation, although what it means as far as the business problem is concerned is hard to tell without further investigation. However, for the purpose of modeling this data set, it is certainly worth including a YEARS_RES missing/present value flag.

This section has looked at only two variables, yet this has revealed a great deal. The first discovery is that DOB_MONTH can't be used because it's *anachronistic*—it leaks information from the future back into the past. Second, YEARS_RES has a very interesting interaction with the prediction variable that needs to be explained, and it's well worth including a derived missing/present binary variable in the training, test, and evaluation data sets if this proves to be a valid phenomenon. The MVCM often reveals a lot of

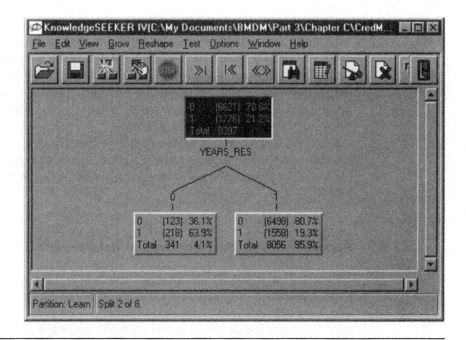

Figure 11.6 SVCHAID in MVCM data set.

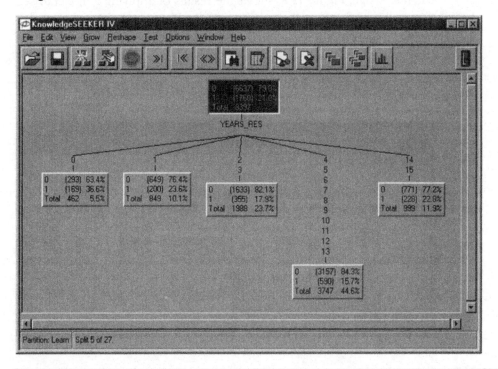

Figure 11.7 SVCHAID for YEARS_RES in unmodified data set.

interesting and applicable information exactly of the type discussed here. Working with the MVCM is always worthwhile, and each variable of significance can usefully be examined in the same way as discussed here. This data set has eight variables from the MVCM input battery that SVCHAID shows to have a relationship with the prediction variable, and all of them need to be investigated. Unfortunately, examining all of the variables in the CREDIT data set would take too much space to complete here. However, before leaving the MVCM data set, it's worth using it to illustrate how the training and test data sets work as a check to help confirm that what is discovered is actually a real phenomenon rather than simply a meaningless aberration. (See MIII:TB.11.2)

11.2.3 Applied Honesty: Using Training and Test Data Sets

Before getting to the MVCM, look at Figures 11.8, 11.9, and 11.10, which show a sequence of model performances on a data set that's full of noise. The three data sets—train, test, and evaluation—are used for different purposes. The training data set is used to actually create the model, and so any model tested on this data set ought to be as good as a model is going to get! The first image, Figure 11.8, shows the results of applying a model to see how well it performs on the training data set. It's a tough data set to model, and the accuracy is about 65.15%, which is shown on the last line of the image.

How does this model do on the test data set? Figure 11.9 shows that the results aren't good. The accuracy is down to a little over 36%. Why? Well,

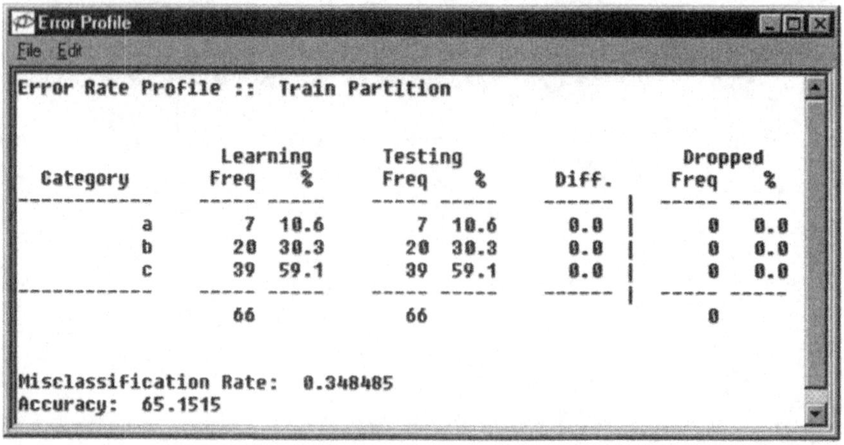

```
Error Profile                                                    _□×
File Edit

Error Rate Profile ::  Train Partition

                 Learning        Testing                  Dropped
     Category     Freq   %         Freq   %      Diff.      Freq   %
    ----------   ----- -----      ----- -----   -------    ----- -----
            a       7  18.6          7  18.6      0.0    |      0   0.0
            b      20  30.3         20  30.3      0.0    |      0   0.0
            c      39  59.1         39  59.1      0.0    |      0   0.0
    ----------   ----- -----      ----- -----   -------    ----- -----
                   66                66                         0

Misclassification Rate:   0.348485
Accuracy:   65.1515
```

Figure 11.8 Noisy data set training partition performance.

```
Error Profile                                          [_][□][X]
File  Edit

Error Rate Profile ::  Test Partition

                    Learning      Testing                  Dropped
     Category      Freq    %      Freq    %     Diff.      Freq    %
    ------------   ----  -----    ----  -----   ------     ----  -----
            a        7   10.6      10   22.7    12.1  |       0    0.0
            b       20   30.3       9   20.5    -9.8  |       0    0.0
            c       39   59.1      25   56.8    -2.3  |       0    0.0
    ------------   ----  -----    ----  -----   ------ |     ----  -----
                    66              44                 |       0

Misclassification Rate:   0.636364
Accuracy:   36.3636
```

Figure 11.9   Noisy data set test partition performance.

```
Error Profile                                          [_][□]
File  Edit

Error Rate Profile ::  Evaluation File

                    Learning      Testing                  Dropped
     Category      Freq    %      Freq    %     Diff.      Freq    %
    ------------   ----  -----    ----  -----   ------     ----  -----
            a        7   10.6      17   15.5     4.8  |       0    0.0
            b       20   30.3      29   26.4    -3.9  |       0    0.0
            c       39   59.1      64   58.2    -0.9  |       0    0.0
    ------------   ----  -----    ----  -----   ------ |     ----  -----
                    66             110                         0

Misclassification Rate:   0.445455
Accuracy:   55.4545
```

Figure 11.10   Noisy data set evaluation partition performance.

there's a lot of noise (read "garbage") in this data set, and what the model learned as predictive patterns were only present in part of the data set. That's the whole point of using multiple data sets. Intuitively, any real underlying relationship will exist in all of the data sets, but spurious noise won't remain constant, and will differ from data set to data set. So these two data sets reveal that most likely there isn't enough data here to make a reliable model, and at any rate, this model isn't to be relied on since its accuracy in any new data set may vary wildly.

Figure 11.10 shows the same model applied to the evaluation data set. Here there is a different result again—a little over 55% accuracy. Quite a swing in the range of performance in this model. There's a good chance here that the relationships discovered are highly unreliable and probably not consistently applicable to the real world. Discovering this, and dealing with this as well as possible, is the whole purpose of having these three data sets.

The training data set is used continuously in creating the model. A miner will almost certainly make several, perhaps many models over the course of a project. Each will be checked against the test data set to determine the model's level of calibration accuracy—in other words, how well it fits the world. The whole objective is to build a model exclusively in the training data set that fits the test data set as well as possible. But there's a major problem here—it's the flipping a fair coin 10 times problem. The miner is looking again and again and again using the same data sets. This is fine, but how well is the model really likely to perform? The answer is: use the evaluation data set. This is only used once—really only one time and one time only—at the end of modeling. This is a single-use data set, one that hasn't been involved in the model construction process. It's the results in this data set, and only the one-time results in this data set, that are used to indicate how applicable or reliable the model is likely to be when used with real world data. Don't cheat—it's only yourself that you are cheating!

How does this apply to the MVCM? Well, we're not going to use the evaluation data set for the MVCM. The CREDIT data set is a fairly large, real-world data set. Figure 11.11 shows the results for the training partition in the upper screenshot, and the results for the test partition in the lower screenshot. A quick glance reveals that the data sets are different sizes since there are 8397 instances in the training (called "Learning" by this tool) data set and 5599 in the testing data set. The accuracy rates, however, are almost identical in both data sets, which suggests that the relationship is almost certainly real and not based on garbage. In this case, the relationship shown is for the DOB_MONTH MVCM, but the results for YEARS_RES, although not shown, are similar in that the model performs about equally in both data sets.

These checks mean that a miner can move forward from here with some confidence. In the two example cases in the MVCM, the relationships discovered in the training data set do seem to hold up—at least as indicated in the test data set reserved for exactly that purpose.

11.3 **Modeling to Understand**

Whenever the underlying question about a data set is "Why?", the miner needs to provide answers that will help explain what's happening in the world. Of course, a data set is limited, and any answer can be determined only in terms of the data contained in the data set. A particular explanation may be expanded by specialist domain knowledge and by reasonable assumptions

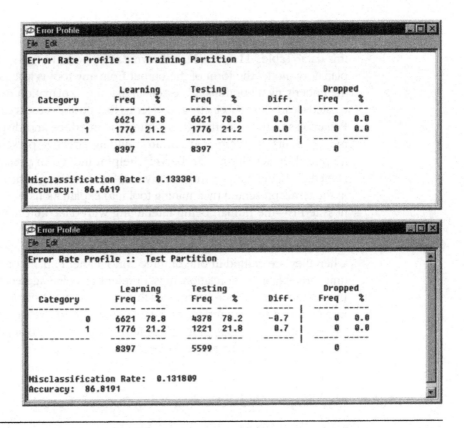

Figure 11.11 DOB_MONTH MVCM train and test partition performance comparison.

about the way the world works, but as far as the miner is concerned, explanations can be produced only in terms of the data actually available.

However, variable transformation can be particularly important for explanatory models. Very often, transforming the way the information is presented can be of enormous help to comprehension, even as simple a matter as using familiar units that refer to the business objects of interest. If, for instance, an explanation turns up in terms of different ZIP codes, it may be of far more explanatory interest to convert the ZIP code into its PRIZM description, or perhaps into the distance the center of the ZIP area is located from, say, a store or branch office. (PRIZM is an acronym for Potential Rating Index for ZIP Markets; it categorizes ZIP codes by demographic types with suggestive names such as Money & Brains, Fur & Station Wagons, Black Enterprise, Grey Power, and about 35 other categories.) The point here is that although the model may use a ZIP category as an explanatory variable, the question for the miner is how to explain the relevance of different ZIP codes in humanly accessible terms.

The very first question a miner must address is: can the data be transformed into more meaningful features? Next, what tools are appropriate for this data? Tables 11.1 and 11.2 shown earlier point to tools, but for an explanatory model the form of the output from any tool is just as important as the underlying algorithms. It's essential that the explanation can be communicated clearly and succinctly and in terms that business users can understand. Regardless of the underlying algorithm, the interface and display format of mined results go a long way toward building effective presentations—and graphical presentations can be very helpful indeed in presenting results. Nonetheless, the miner is the primary tool for converting explanations of data in the terms presented by a mining tool into explanations presented in business terms—the human being interacting with data, automated tools, and business users.

It's also worth keeping in mind that explanations of a data set work best when they are crafted in one of three ways: either explain one variable at a time, or explain linear relationships, or refer to labeled aggregates as wholes. In addition, the author recommends three tools as good starting points to use in gaining an understanding of data—decision trees, self-organizing maps (SOMs), and linear regression. These tools are used to explain the data in the CREDIT data set in the following sections.

11.3.1   Modeling for Understanding Using Decision Trees

Explanatory models communicate relationships of business relevance in a data set in easily understood words and illustrations. The explanatory model built here uses the same tree tool introduced for SVCHAID—in fact, the tree explanation is partly built on SVCHAID examinations. However, the tool that you choose or have available may work slightly differently than the one illustrated. Some types of trees split each leaf only into two subleaves rather than into the multiple leaves shown in Figures 11.12 on p. 384 and 11.13 on p. 385. The tree tool in PolyAnalyst, for instance, makes binary splits, which follow the format of the simplified explanation of a tree given in the last chapter. Such trees are neither better nor worse than the multiple-split option, only different. As a personal preference, the author finds the multiple-splits-per-leaf version often provides good explanations at only one level of splitting. However, the binary-split versions get to essentially the same place, although the actual tree construction may be quite different, and the trees are often larger and with more elements (leaves and branches) for the same degree of explanation.

A more important consideration than the number of splits in selecting a tree tool for exploring and explaining data is that the tree should be highly controllable. For instance, it's important to be able to easily split the root node, or any selected leaf node, on a variable that the miner chooses—not just on whatever the tree picks as the best split. For instance, four widely available and commercially popular tree tools all choose BEACON as the variable to make the first split when explaining BUYER in the example data set. However, only one tool allows the user to easily choose another variable instead. And only one allows the user to see a ranked list of all split possibilities. So, in explaining data, it is very important that the tree tool does not steer the miner, but allows the miner to steer the tool! This is very important: without steerability, the miner is limited to explaining what the tree algorithm wants to explain, not what the miner wants to explain. It often turns out that, as far as explanation goes, it's not the "best" split that is the most interesting, but the second, third, or fourth best. For explanatory modeling purposes, it is crucial to be able to step through the split variables and examine the relationships.

A second important criterion for tool selection is that it is valuable to be able to look at both absolute and relative weights among the leaves at each split. For instance, glance at Figure 11.12. The pies shown illustrate the relative proportions of responders and nonresponders in each leaf. The relationship is intuitively and immediately obvious since the size of the pie wedge representing responders associated with each leaf increases fairly uniformly from leaf to leaf. The graphical representation of the same situation shown in the bar graph below the pies shows exactly the same information and relationships, but this part of the relationship is anything but obvious. That's because it shows the absolute numbers in each leaf, not the relative proportions. But the pie charts do not show how large the effect is in each segment, whereas in the bar graph it's immediately obvious that the leaf with the highest proportion of responders accounts for only a minute number of them. So any explanatory tree tool must make it easy for the miner to look at the relationships presented in as many different ways as possible, but certainly in both relative and absolute representations.

Once you are comfortable with the decision tree tool you have chosen, turn now to using it for explaining data in the three ways mentioned: one variable at a time, linear relationships, and labeled aggregates.

- *Explaining one variable at a time:* This was illustrated in the previous section when observing that people with nothing entered for "years of residence" tend to respond to the solicitation more strongly than people who do have an entry for a length of residence. This describes one relationship in the data in terms of a single feature of a single variable.
- *Explaining linear relationships:* Depicting a linear relationship also works well, as shown in Figure 11.12. This figure shows parts of the tree exploration of the relationship between BUYER and RBAL_LIMIT, which is the existing revolving balance limit, or the credit limit for a revolving balance. To some extent, it indicates how much credit a customer is already using. The tree finds five interesting splits, but it's the pie charts, one for each

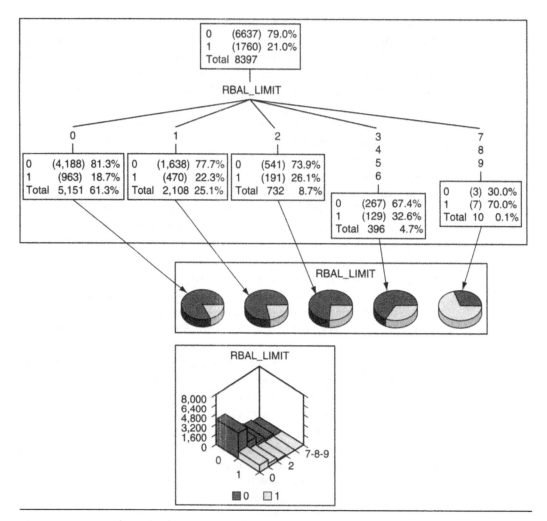

Figure 11.12 Relationship between BUYER and RBAL_LIMIT.

of the resulting leaves, that tell an interesting part of the story. The limit amount is categorized into 10 categories labeled 0–9. Although the tree treats them as unordered categories, not as numbers, it's interesting to notice that the higher the limit number, the more likely the person will respond to the solicitation. This is shown by the increasing size of the pie segment that represents buyers versus nonbuyers. The numbers in the leaves tell the tale—the pies show it. This observation reflects the well-known insight (at least in the financial world) that people who already have credit cards are those most likely to take new ones. However, note the very small number of people in the higher-numbered segments compared to the large number of people in the lower segments.

- *Explaining labeled aggregates:* First, glance at the left image in Figure 11.13, which shows a SVCHAID tree predicting SEX using MARRIED. (The inset box with title "SEX breakdown" indicates the predictor variable and its values. The root node shows the actual counts for each value, and their proportions as a percentage.) It turns out that in this data set, there are no married females, only married males. To see this, notice that the left-hand leaf takes the split value "M" for married, and there are no "F" or "U" instances shown in the left-hand lower leaf—thus no females or unknowns. The data set has variables for age and a variable that indicates gender, but explaining both age and gender together requires creating a new variable that aggregates information about both. AGE_INFERR takes

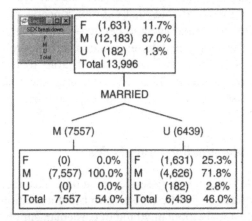

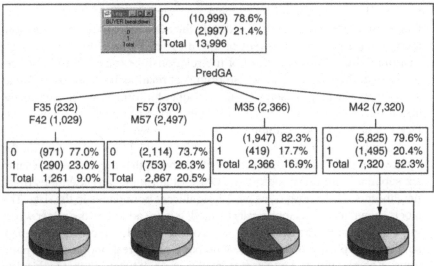

Figure 11.13 Relationship of age and gender to BUYER.

three values—35, 42, and 57. SEX, the gender variable, takes two values, M and F (ignoring in this example the small number of gender "U" or unknown). Combining inferred age with gender gives six categories; for convenience, these categories are labeled F35, F42, F57, M35, M42, and M57 for females and males of the appropriate inferred ages. Using this aggregated variable to predict buyers shows the interesting pattern seen at the bottom of Figure 11.13. The left-hand leaf comprises the younger women (F35, F42) who have a slightly higher response rate than average, and the next leaf is the older men and women (F57, M57) who have the highest response rate. Thus women (at least unmarried ones) and the older people in general have a higher response rate than younger males.

The last example also illustrates the point made at the beginning of this subsection: creating new variables that express concepts meaningful to humans—in this case, combined age and gender—helps to explain what relationships exist in the data. The data set contains variables for age and a variable for gender, but those two alone are unable to easily reveal the relationship that was just explained. This recoding hasn't added any information to the data set, but it certainly helps explain what's happening.

11.3.2 Modeling for Understanding Using SOMs

Inherently, a SOM is not a supervised learning tool. This means that, unlike a tree, which requires a specific objective to build a relationship, the SOM tool doesn't create a map about anything in particular, simply about the data in general. So whereas the tree reveals specific relationships about, for example, BUYER in terms of AGE_INFERR, the SOM reveals the same relationship only insomuch as it is part of the integrated whole. Essentially, after mapping, the SOM presents all of the relationships together and at once, rather than through sequential "prodding" at relationships one at a time as with a tree. The map presents a huge amount of information very succinctly, and it's up to the miner to work through and explore the map and all its facets in order to add meaning to the revealed relationships.

But what does a map actually reveal? Figure 11.14 shows a SOM for the by now familiar CREDIT data set. The map shows that the data resolves into six separate neighborhoods. The SOM tool automatically identifies these neighborhoods, or clusters, as having significant boundaries in the data. The labels shown are not automatically created, but are added by the miner working with the map. The SOM looks at all of the variables in creating the map, so it is not explicitly about people who have or will respond; it simply partitions or divides the data into representative areas. It turns out that in this data set, the upper right area of the SOM main map is labeled "Buyers" because

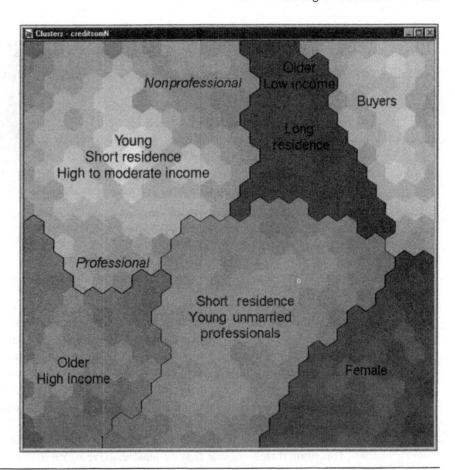

Figure 11.14   Self-organizing map (SOM) of CREDIT data set.

the people who did respond are all grouped into this area. Those who are female are grouped in the area below labeled "Female," and so on.

To see how the labels were created, look at Figure 11.15. The SOM tool creates not only an overall map of the data, but also a series of other maps that includes one map for each of the variables in the data set. This figure shows three of the variable maps used in the SOM. Figure 11.14 shows the composite map for the whole data set, whereas Figure 11.15 shows a map for each of three individual variables, but with the main SOM cluster boundaries imposed over each variable map. Color plays a large part in interpreting SOMs since almost all SOM tools use color variations and shades to indicate features of the data. The multicolored maps are difficult to meaningfully reproduce in black-and-white since reproduction loses the important color differentiation. However, since these particular variables are binary, the map

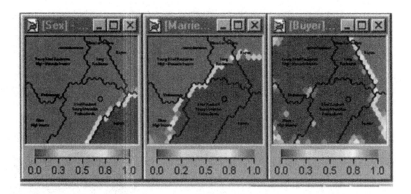

Figure 11.15   Individual variable maps in the CREDIT SOM.

can choose only two colors. This two-color partition shows up reasonably well in the black-and-white illustration used here. (Colored versions of these maps and this model can be downloaded from the author's Web site.)

The left-hand map shown represents the variable SEX, and it is immediately apparent that the lower right-hand boundary in the main map simply cuts out men from women. (See how the boundary line runs exactly along the separation between males and females.) Similarly, a glance at the right-hand map shows that the upper right boundary mainly cuts out buyers from nonbuyers—except that a careful look will notice that actually the boundary only cuts out male buyers; female buyers are inside the female boundary. This immediately signals that all females have more in common with each other than with all buyers. Conclusion? Female buyers behave differently (respond differently in this case) than male buyers. Why this is true has still to be discovered from looking at other areas and variables in the map.

The central map illustrates the variable MARRIED. Obviously, the borders from the main map don't cut married out from unmarried particularly, so presumably being married is not of primary importance in interactions in this data set. However, the lower right area—females—is entirely inside the area of those who are not married, so this again shows that there aren't any married females in this data set. But the lower center and lower right areas do, in fact, seem to be influenced by the state of MARRIED and, roughly, follow the borders.

Looking at the other variables and considering their impact leads to labeling the lower central area "short residence, young, unmarried professionals." What is the significance of this group of short residence, young, unmarried professionals? In terms of the interest of this data set—who will respond to a credit card solicitation—they won't! Not one of them intersects with the area of the map that indicates people who did respond. In any solicitation, this is a clearly identifiable group that is not worth soliciting. (At least, not with the offer used in the test marketing that generated this data set.) This is an important, highly nonlinear, multivariable relationship that pretty much jumps out of this map.

As a whole, this map repays much scrutiny. There is an enormous wealth of explanatory information to be had here, and this brief look has barely touched the surface. Figure 11.16 shows several more variable maps included in the overall tool interface. However, since the other variables are continuous, and therefore multi-colored, a black-and-white rendition makes explanation here more difficult.

As a project, a comprehensive study of this map takes several to many hours. For instance, the area of each color in any variable map is proportional to the number of people with the characteristic represented by the color. The map in the middle row of the left column in Figure 11.16 is the variable map for estimated income. Most of the high-income instances are in two patches on the left and lower center parts of the map—about as far from BUYER as the map can place them. So, in general, responders come from the lower estimated income groups. Except that there are two small—and they are small—

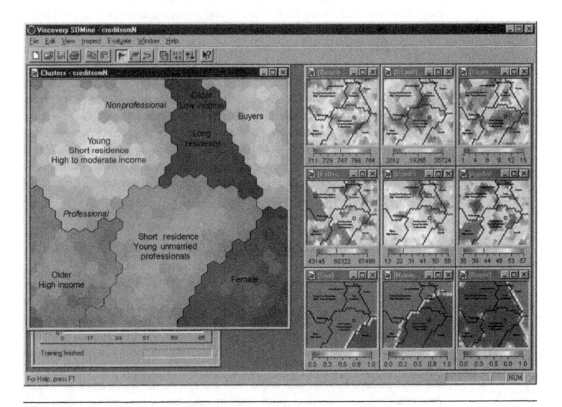

Figure 11.16 SOM map with nine variable maps for the CREDIT data set.

patches of higher income groups to be seen inside the group of people who did respond. These turn out to be from the longer residence and older age groups. We don't know how age was estimated in this data set, and length of residence may have been part of the estimation method. (Only estimated age is included here. Actual age can't legitimately be used since it is entered only after a response.) However, if it was not used to create the estimated age, it appears that older males who have resided at their current address for a longer time tend to respond. On the other hand, the older females who respond have very short residence periods. Indeed, older females who have long residence periods are about as far away from buyer on the map as they can get and still remain in the female group! How is this to be explained? That requires domain knowledge beyond the bounds of this data set—but it is an interesting and potentially valuable relationship.

Exploration of a SOM results in what is very much a qualitative understanding of the data and the relationships that it enfolds. The relationships themselves are clear enough, although it may take persistence to find all that are relevant. The strength of each relationship can be easily seen by the congruence of colors and patterns across and between the variables and the main map. The size of effect of each variable and feature is also clear since it is related to the size of the areas involved. This is a very powerful explanatory tool.

However, most often, explanations have to be turned into action—what can be done with this new understanding? Recall that the ultimate project here required making a solicitation to those most likely to respond, and, although not explicitly stated, also to avoid soliciting those least likely to respond. The understanding of this data set in this project can be best expressed in terms of discovered features. The last example relationship discovered in this data set seems to imply that, when any predictive model is built, it might be worth including a feature that identifies older males who have resided in the same place for a longer time, and another for older females who have a less stable residence history.

11.3.3 Modeling for Understanding Using Linear Regression

Table 11.1 shows the linear regression symbol in lowercase as a tool for understanding most of the combinations of variables; however, it appears last for each situation. Why? Because tree and SOM exploration, although more time consuming, are far more rewarding in terms of the information revealed. It is, as the name implies, not going to find any nonlinear relationships—although, as already noted, that may not be all that important since many of the relationships a miner will work with are essentially linear anyway, or approximately linear. So, as a quick look at data, linear regression works very well. However, not as much can be expected from this approach as from the two techniques previously discussed.

Figure 11.17 shows how well the linear regression tool in PolyAnalyst manages to fit the CREDIT data to BUYER—not at all well. The diagonal line from bottom left to top right represents the estimate, and the two vertical lines of dots represent the actual values—one column for "0," the other column for "1." Not as good a fit as a predictive model, but it's not as a predictive model that it's needed. How does it do for providing an explanation?

Figure 11.18 shows the parameters produced for this data set. There are two items of interest. One is the size of the "F-Ratio"; the other is the sign,

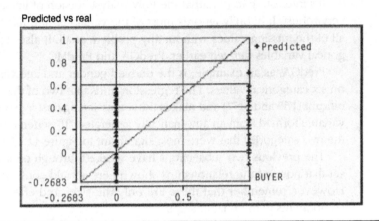

Predicted vs real

Figure 11.17   PolyAnalyst linear regression predicting BUYER in CREDIT data set.

Terms:

name	coef.	std. dev.	F-Ratio	part sum of sq
BEACON	−0.004098	0.000262	244.6	0.05073
DAS	0.0002045	4.514e−005	20.53	0.002153
ROPEN	0.01712	0.002727	39.44	0.001748
RBAL	−8.527e−006	1.355e−006	39.59	0.004027
TOPEN	−0.01597	0.002965	29.02	0.002929
MOF	0.0002268	6.476e−005	12.26	0.005181
RBAL_LIMIT	0.01477	0.007052	4.385	0.0009507
MTHIGHBAL	−5.474e−007	1.178e−007	21.59	0.003903
YEARS_RES	−0.002572	0.001238	4.317	0.0002513
EST_INC	−4.257e−007	3.017e−007	1.991	0.0002725
HOME_VALUE	0.0003888	0.0002083	3.483	9.175e−005
HOME_INC	−0.0006363	0.0005905	1.161	0.0004414
PRCNT_PROF	−0.0006387	0.0005769	1.226	0.0001669
AGE_INFERR	0.006784	0.001653	16.84	0.006
if (PredGA = 'PredGA: f57',1,0)	−0.09025	0.04407	4.194	0.0003071
if (PredGA = 'PredGA: m57',1,0)	−0.03233	0.02927	1.22	0.0001896
if (PredMC = 'PredMC: m0',1,0)	−0.01317	0.009349	1.985	0.0002507

Figure 11.18   PolyAnalyst linear regression parameters when predicting BUYER in CREDIT data set.

plus or minus, in the "coef" column. Essentially, the F-ratio can be interpreted to indicate the importance of each variable to the regression equation. (A p-ratio might be a better choice to use if it's available, but it's not used in this tool.) The coef's sign indicates whether the input variable and output variable move in the same or opposite directions. For instance, BEACON has the highest F-ratio by far and is the most important variable in this equation. It also has a minus coefficient value, which means that as the value of BEACON decreases, the value of BUYER increases (i.e., they move in opposite directions). Figure 11.19 shows the F-ratio information graphically.

It's interesting to note that the PolyAnalyst version of linear regression is very robust. It happily ignores most of the variables, and handily deals with all of the missing values without any problem at all. It also digests the categorical variables derived earlier, PredGA and PredMC.

PredGA, as an example, is the derived gender and age variable. It takes on six categorical values. The regression finds that two of the values are significant (F57 and M57) and makes the regression against a psuedo or dummy variable formed from an automatically generated "If" statement. (These were the two categories that were most significant in Figure 11.13.)

The previous two subsections have worked through enough of the data set that none of the relationships shown here should come as any surprise. However, remember that these are only the sizes and effects of the linear components in the relationships.

Linear regression is very much affected by which variables turn out to be the most significant—it can have a dramatic effect of the weightings of the

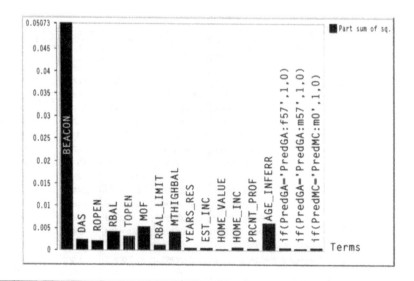

Figure 11.19 PolyAnalyst linear regression F-ratios when predicting BUYER in the CREDIT data set.

other variables. It's always worthwhile removing the most important variable
or two from consideration and rebuilding the regression to look for other relationships that the strongly interacting variables may mask. Figure 11.20
compares the F-ratio graphs for the regression with and without the presence
of the variable BEACON. The relative importance of the variables does

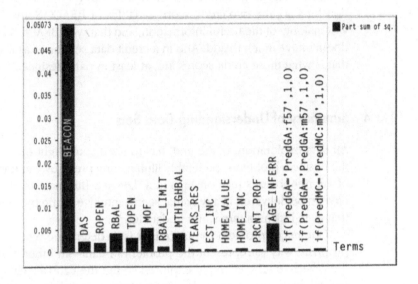

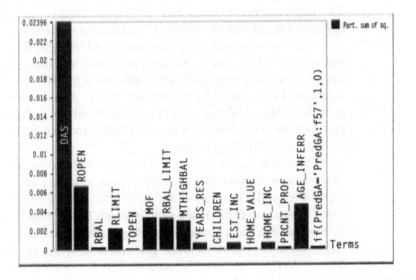

Figure 11.20 PolyAnalyst linear regression F-ratios when predicting BUYER in the CREDIT data set,
with and without the variable BEACON.

change. Without BEACON, for instance, the variable CHILDREN is included in the regression, whereas two of the categorical dummy variables that were used have disappeared. This certainly comments on what information BEACON carries in the data set, and it is interesting that without BEACON, fewer variables are included. AGE_INFERR and MTHIGHBAL have approximately the same importance in both cases.

However, the general conclusion seems to be that as far as linear relationships go, the two credit score variables of BEACON and DAS carry the vast majority of the useful information, and that with BEACON included, DAS doesn't have much to add. And in a credit data set, this is as it should be, for that is what these credit scores are, at least in part, designed to do!

11.3.4 Summary of Understanding Data Sets

All data exploration, in the end, has to shed some light on how to address the business problem—preferably illuminating previously unknown and, best of all, nonobvious relationships in a data set. But most of all, explanations have to be delivered in a way that seems intuitive to the business manager— that is, in business terms, not in data terms.

One major problem for any miner is to determine what is the most appropriate way to represent the problem in data—in other words, to define the objective. The example explored so far, the CREDIT data set, rather finessed that problem since the objective was to explain who responded and who didn't respond to a solicitation. Even though this was indicated by a binary variable, BUYER, explanation still required the development of several derived features so that an explanation could be more fully developed. In this example, for instance, one derived feature was the gender/age combination. Some of the insights developed were nonobvious. Why does the mere absence of a value for YEARS_RES indicate a tendency for a higher than normal likelihood of response? When YEARS_RES is not missing, what is it about length of residence that has older males and females behaving in ways totally different from each other?

Explanation started by simply looking at the patterns of values that were entered in the data set, and comparing them with the patterns of values that weren't entered. This pointed not only to the odd YEARS_RES relationship, but also to a potential mining problem with DOB_MONTH. It would have been a problem had it not been discovered. Also, as with residence and birthdays, some explanations were presented in terms of single variables. RBAL_LIMIT, a single variable surrogate here for existing credit usage, points out a well-known phenomenon: people who have credit take credit. But discovering the already known—even the blatantly obvious—is a useful confirmation that the explanation is valid. If it works, and the data set is indeed representative of the world, the known and obvious ought indeed to be discovered. Confirmation is never a bad, nor a wasted discovery.

Linear relationships, such as that between BEACON, DAS, and BUYER, are useful—confirmatory in this case. Both credit scores indicate creditworthiness, and since those with credit take credit, these scores should have a linear relationship with those who will take more credit.

It's the nonlinear relationships that are usually the least obvious, and frequently the most interesting too; they are also the most difficult to discover and, particularly, to explain. It was segmenting multiple variables—age, gender, and residence period into a single grouping, for instance—that developed these relationships to show an interesting and nonobvious interaction in a part of their joint range.

These are the basic techniques of explanation—single variables, linear relationships, and identified segments. Presenting the results, however, requires both qualitative explanation and quantitative explication of the size of the result to be expected. Here, too, is where a miner needs to be creative—and always remember that a picture is worth the proverbial thousand words. Illustrations—relevant and simple illustrations—present powerful results. Illustrations that need more than a thousand words to explain them are probably of little help! The key to explaining data is practice and familiarity. (See MIII:TB.11.3)

11.4 Modeling to Classify

Statistical classification is a knotty problem, and it's a subject that is well represented in the literature. It is a very difficult problem indeed to decide how a data set should best be divided into classes (or classified). The technical issues are formidable, but fortunately the data mining practice is much easier than the statistical theory.

Classification, to a data miner, looks very much like a special case of what is colloquially called "prediction." In other words, classification is often expressed as a problem in trying to predict to which class an instance belongs. In the case of the CREDIT data set, for instance, the problem looks very much like trying to predict who will respond to the solicitation, and who won't respond. A predictive model will produce a score of some sort that can be applied to the run-time data set and used to determine who will and who won't respond. Easy.

However, it is highly unlikely that the score will be straightforward to interpret. For instance, responders in the training, test, and evaluation data sets are all indicated by BUYER = 1, and nonresponders by BUYER = 0. But the chances are that the predictive or classification model will produce a score that is a continuous number between 0 and 1, rather than a binary score equal to either 0 or 1. This score is a number that needs to be interpreted. And even if the miner uses a tool that does produce a model yielding a binary classification of exactly a "1" or a "0," there is a real chance that the model will not be valid.

One big problem with the CREDIT data set as modeled is that it contains roughly 20% responders (BUYER = 1) and 80% nonresponders (BUYER = 0). But this is a very heavily adjusted data set. Nonetheless, any mined model will immediately assume that on average, with no other data available, about 20% of solicitations will result in a response, and may well thus arrange its predictions so that it predicts BUYER = 1 about 20% of the time. But this is simply not right. In fact, the data set had to be heavily adjusted in order to make this model, and now is the time to look at why and how this was done, and how to allow for it in classification. (See MIII:TB.11.10)

11.4.1 Balancing Data Sets

The essential difficulty in modeling to classify is that the world often does not cooperate in helping solve the miner's problems. In the case of the CREDIT data set, the actual response rate was about 1%, not 20%. For many tools, a 1% response rate simply isn't good enough to build a decent model. All that a mined model has to do to get a 99% hit rate in such a data set is to predict "0" all the time. After all, 99 times out of 100, with a 1% response rate, the model will be spot on. This is what is sometimes called the *naïve prediction rate* (or *naïve error rate*), and in order to be effective, any model has to do better than this. So, for a start, in classification and predictive models, to have a 99% accuracy rate (or any other number other than exactly 0% or 100%) doesn't mean much at all. What is important is the *lift,* or how much better a model does than the naïve prediction rate.

Put colloquially, with very low effect rates such as the 1% response rate, many mining tools simply don't have enough examples of the data that's needed to model. The amount of other data simply swamps the relatively low level of information that is present. In order to get the needed information exposed to the tool, the data set has to be adjusted, as with CREDIT, to appear to have more of the desired effect than actually turns up in the real world. But it has to be done very carefully so as not to distort the data more than is absolutely necessary in order to build a model. Then it has to be equally carefully undone again, although in a completely different way, in order to use the output for either classification or prediction.

Since there are a relatively low number of instances with the desired effect, BUYER = 1 in the case of CREDIT, it is important to keep all of those instances that do show a responder. Reduction in this case was in the number of instances without the effect of interest to the miner (BUYER = 0). However, such a wholesale reduction in the amount of data could remove important relationships that are needed if the adjusted data set is to be as representative of the real world as possible.

Succinctly put, to create an effective model we need to have a higher ratio of buyers to nonbuyers in the training, test, and evaluation data sets than the real world produces. Yet it is imperative that, apart from this single adjustment, the data set otherwise be as uninfluenced by adjusting the buyer ratios as possible. The key constraint in the final size of the data set available for mining is the number of buyers, since we have to keep all of the buyers that are available while removing nonbuyers, and at the same time making as sure as possible that no other relationships are changed. (For more details on deciding when to balance a data set, see Chapter 12.)

To make this adjustment, first construct the data representation models described in Chapter 9. These models, constructed on the whole data set, are used to verify that there is sufficient data to represent the whole population so long as it was appropriately sampled in the first place. With these models already constructed, remove noneffect data at random, that is to say, in this case, every BUYER = 0 instance has an equal chance of being removed until the desired balance arrives, in this case 80/20. At this point, use the data representation models to check that they still apply to the adjusted data set. The adjusted data set should (by the performance of the check models) still represent the population—at least, insofar as it's possible to confirm this. Therefore, this means that the check models all performed roughly as well (or badly) in the adjusted data set as they did in the unadjusted data set. If it had turned out that the data set was not representative, perhaps another try at random reduction of noneffect instances might work. However, if that fails, the only answer is to try for a lower level of effect, say, to aim for a 10% level of BUYER = 1. (See MIII:AB.11.23)

As a point of interest, reducing the CREDIT data set much below a 70/30 ratio did make it very difficult to find a data set that passed the rule of thumb tests for representativeness mentioned earlier. So, to have some margin of safety, the ratio ended up here as 80/20. (The data set has to be able to be further divided into train, test, and evaluation sets, and they too need to be as representative as possible. Squeezing to 70/30 leaves the test and evaluation data sets dangerously nonrepresentative when tested.) This 80/20 ratio is a useable ratio, although the data set would have been balanced to 50/50 had it been possible to get a data set that was representative in all respects other than BUYER. Having a representative data set is important; getting some exact ratio of balance isn't.

11.4.2 Building a Dichotomous Classification Model

The idea of a classification is to put each instance in a data set unambiguously into the relevant class. However many classes there are that apply to the data set as a whole, each individual instance can belong only to one class. As far as a model trying to classify it goes, either it is correctly classified, or it isn't. In a way, as far as any individual instance is concerned, there are only two classes that are relevant—the right one, and all the other classes lumped together which make a wrong one. This becomes important when measuring how well a classification model works, and in deciding how to adjust the model to improve the classification.

It's often the case that one single model is not the optimum way to model classes. The problem is that a model that may be quite good at separating, say, class "A" from all other classes isn't necessarily so good at separating class "B" or "C" from the other classes. In the case of CREDIT, when the classification task is about only two classes of interest, BUYER = 0 and BUYER = 1, this issue doesn't arise. The same model that is good at separating BUYER = 1 from BUYER = 0 must also be good at separating BUYER = 0 from BUYER = 1.

One of the difficulties in even a two-class classification is that the purpose of the classification can make a big difference. Let's say the objective is to solicit buyers using a promotional mailing. A common approach involves appending a continuous classification score to a data set and using the score as a ranking mechanism in order to mail to some selected number of the top scores. Fine as far as it goes. But if the question "What's the expected return from this promotion?" is asked, the score cannot be used to give an answer. One way to determine expected return is to multiply the amount of the return by the probability of getting it. But the score is not—most emphatically not—a probability of response, so it's not the probability of getting a return. In the example CREDIT data set, any score has at least to be offset by the 20/80 distortion that was deliberately introduced to make modeling possible. There is no easy way to make that adjustment. If the model reports that the instance belongs to the class BUYER = 1, how does the miner interpret this?

The problem is that the ability of the model to separate classes is not necessarily related in any simple way to the balancing introduced into the training data set. If the model really can separate classes perfectly, regardless of what data set is used to train it, then it can separate classes—and it will separate classes in the real-world data set just as well as in the training data set. However, the case probably will turn out to be that the model makes errors. Looking at the 80/20 adjustment of data from its original 99/1 ratio does not help in trying to estimate how well a classification model will actually classify real world data. Nonetheless, it's easy to determine the performance of a classification model, but only by analyzing the model's performance in detail.

11.4.3   **Classification Errors**

A two-class classification model can produce two classifications leading to four results. Taking "1" to indicate class membership and "0" to indicate class nonmembership, Table 11.3a shows the possibilities. The model can classify as 1 (Class 1) when the actual result is 1 (Is 1), or it can classify as 1 (Class 1) when the actual result is 0 (Is 0). Similarly, it can indicate 0 (Class 0) when the actual result is 0 (Is 0), or indicate 0 (Class 0) when the actual result is 1 (Is 1). This table forms the basis of what is called a *confusion matrix* because it allows an easy indication of where the model is confused (classifies 1 for 0 and 0 for 1) and where it isn't confused.

The easiest way to show the use of a confusion matrix is with a practical example. For this example, WizWhy was used because the model it builds produces a classification of BUYER as 0 or 1 rather than a continuous number score. The CREDIT data set was divided at random into train, test, and evaluation data sets as 60/20/20. The evaluation data set isn't used in this example. The model was built in the training data set, and the results discussed here are derived from applying the model to the test data set. (The data sets used, and the model produced, are available on the author's Web site.)

Table 11.3a summarizes the performance of the model. The row labeled "Class 1" contains a count of the number of times the model predicted 1 as the class. Similarly, row "Class 0" contains counts of the number of times the model predicted 0. The column headed "Is 1" contains counts for the number of instances that actually are 1, and similarly column "Is 0" contains counts for the number of instances that actually are 0. At the bottom in row "Tot" is the column total, and to the right is the row total.

Interpretation is very straightforward. The 203 at the intersection of "Class 1" and "Is 1" indicates that 203 of the instances that the model predicted to be in Class 1 actually were in that class. The cell at the intersection of "Class 0" and "Is 1" shows that 444 instances were predicted to be 0, but actually were 1. Similarly, the "Is 0" column shows the appropriate counts for instances that actually are 0. Column totals add up to the actual counts of 0's and 1's, row totals sum the totals for the number of predictions made in each class.

TABLE 11.3a   Confusion Matrix

Model	Is 1	Is 0	Tot
Class 1	203	186	389
Class 0	444	1966	2410
Tot	647	2152	2799

The test data set has a total of 2799 records, of which 647 are BUYER = 1 and 2152 are BUYER = 0, which are shown in the column totals. Table 11.3b shows the totals for the number of correct and incorrect classifications. The total for correct classifications is simply the sum of the top left and bottom right count cells. The total of incorrect classifications comes from bottom left and top right. The table also shows percentages, so this model classifies about 77% of the instances correctly and 23% incorrectly. This leads to a correct/incorrect ratio of 2169/630 = 3.44. In other words, the model gets about 3.44 predictions correct for every error it makes. However, as already explained, this by itself is a meaningless assessment of how well this classifier actually performed. The question that needs answering is how much better this is (or, perhaps, isn't) than the naïve prediction rate.

The naïve prediction rate for this data set is found by determining what a confusion matrix would look like if classes (1's and 0's in this case) were generated at random in proportion to their frequency of occurrence in the training data set. This naïve classification rate confusion matrix is shown in Tables 11.4a and 11.4b. (Details of how this confusion matrix was generated

TABLE 11.3b   Correct and Incorrect Classifications

Model	Count	%
Correct	2169	77
Wrong	630	23

TABLE 11.4a   Naïve Classification Rate Confusion Matrix

Naïve	Is 1	Is 0	Tot
Class 1	150	497	647
Class 0	497	1655	2152
Tot	647	2152	2799

TABLE 11.4b   Naïve Correct and Incorrect Classifications

Naïve	Count	%
Correct	1804	64
Wrong	995	36

are in the supplemental material to this chapter, but are not needed to understand how the model performed.) Interpreting this matrix leads to the conclusion that random assignment (the naïve classification) returns a correct/incorrect classification ratio of 1804/995 = 1.81.

The model's classification does considerably better than the naïve classification. Comparing the classification ratios gives 3.44/1.81 = 1.90, so overall the model performs about 90% better than random classification. However, this is an overall, or average, sort of model performance. Table 11.5 shows that in each of the four classification tasks, the model performs with different facility. It's much better, as a percentage, at classifying Class 1 than it is at classifying Class 0. It also does best at avoiding misclassifying Class 1, and worst at misclassifying Class 0, even allowing for the difference in frequency.

To put this into a different perspective, if the business problem gave equal weighting to all outcomes, then this model can be expected to do almost twice as well as previous models. However, it is almost certain that the business problem doesn't give equal weighting to all outcomes. In this example, the only outcome of interest is probably how well the model allows responders to be selected. Assuming this is the case, the probable strategy would be to solicit only those people that the model categorized as likely to respond (BUYER = 1). Of the 389 instances in Class 1, 203 actually were correctly assigned, so the success rate here is 203/389 = 52.19%, as against the naïve rate of 150/647 = 23.18%. So, for correctly categorizing responders who actually do respond, this model achieves a 52.19/23.18 = 2.25 improvement ratio over previous efforts.

If the previous response rate was 1%, this model can be expected to produce a response rate of 1% × 2.25 = 2.25%. (Note that this is a rate discovered against the test data set. Final checking against the evaluation data set is made only after development of the ultimate model to deploy, which may well not be this one. Additional adjustments to data and model may be indicated before moving to a deployable model. How to choose and make those adjustments is discussed in Chapter 12.) (See MIII:TB.11.5, MIII:TB.11.6)

TABLE 11.5 Model Performance According to Classification

	Class 1, Is 1	Class 1, Is 0	Class 0, Is 1	Class 0, Is 0
Naïve Chance of:	5.43%	17.77%	17.77%	59.11%
Model Chance of:	7.25%	15.86%	6.65%	70.24%
Lift (% better than chance)	35.73%	12.04%	167.44%	18.82%

11.4.4 **Classification by Score**

The previous example used a tool designed for binary classification. Often, the nature of the data, or even the limitations of the tools available to a miner, requires a tool that produces a continuous numeric output—in other words, a number. This number is a score, indicating the proper class to assign to a given instance. This continuous variable output can offer more power and flexibility than a binary categorical assignment, depending on the actual business problem, but the problem for the miner is in deciding exactly how to use a continuous score.

Consider the problem in the previous subsection: to decide what response rate in the real world the model will generate. With a continuous score, the model response rate will clearly depend on where the score cutoff is set for assigning instances to the different classes. For instance, if the 10 highest scored instances were all in one class, say "1," and the 11th wasn't, if the miner set the cutoff value between instances 10 and 11, the model may produce a perfect predictive result—but identify so few responders as to be of little practical use. Sliding the cutoff to some lower value allows in more instances, but also reduces the discriminatory power of the model.

Intuitively, as the cutoff value slides along its range, it changes the numbers of instances in each of the four cells of the confusion matrix. The miner's problem involves finding the optimal place to make the cutoff, or, in other words, how to adjust the cutoff value to get the best possible confusion matrix given the needs of the business problem. A seemingly small change in the way the problem is stated can have a large impact on the classification cutoff adjustment.

11.4.5 **Building a Continuous Classification Model**

Using the same CREDIT training and test data sets as before, the neural network tool in PolyAnalyst created the model that will be used in this example. The neural network was trained on the training data set, and only after training was complete and the model created was it applied to the test data set. This is mentioned here specifically since neural network algorithms are often described as needing training and test data sets. In this case, the PolyAnalyst tool automatically, and invisibly to the miner, created the network and performed its own internal testing. Thus it only used what in this example is called the training data set. The test data set was not used at all in constructing the network, only for applying the resulting model.

When applied to the test data set, the model created a score in the form of a number that ranged from about 0.87 as a maximum to about 0.10 as a minimum. Using this score, the instances in the test data set can be ranked in order from "most likely to be in Class 1" to "least likely to be in Class 1." Depending on the quality of the model, most of the actual Class 1 instances should be at one end of the ranked list and most of the Class 0 instances at the other end.

Recall that this is the identical test data set already used, so it contains the same 2799 instances, of which 647 are Class 1 and those remaining are Class 0. The chance of selecting an instance at random that is in Class 1 has to be $647/2799 = 0.2311$, or 23.11%. In fact, if the model is successful at classifying the instances, the actual chance of discovering a Class 1 instance will be higher than this in the highly scored sections, and lower than this in the lower-scored sections. The actual frequency of Class 1 instances discovered in the data set when it is ordered by the value of the prediction can be plotted against the accumulated average expectation, which is shown in Figure 11.21. This is what is known as a *cumulative response curve*, since it literally shows the accumulated response on the data set ordered by the score.

The scale along the bottom shows the number of instances to that point. The diagonal straight line running from lower left to upper right shows how many Class 1 instances would be expected up to that point if the data set were actually ordered randomly. The curve that rises above the line is the actual cumulative response curve, showing how many Class 1 instances have actually been discovered up to that point. If the number of instances is more than the random ordering expectation, the cumulative response curve appears above the random expectation. Of course, if the number were less, the

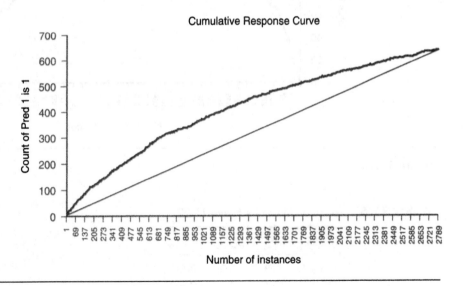

Figure 11.21 Cumulative response curve.

cumulative response curve would appear below the random expectation. Since the curve is above the line here, the model is to some extent at least successfully ordering the data set.

This cumulative response curve (often erroneously called a *lift curve*) is a very common way of displaying the quality of a continuous classification model. The problem is that it isn't apparent how to use this curve to decide the location of the best cutoff point. The answer is to plot the actual lift—that is, the amount by which the cumulative response is greater than the random expectation. This is shown in Figure 11.22.

In Figure 11.22, the height of the curve indicates the amount of lift. While the curve rises, the number of correct classifications increases. At the highest point, separation is at a maximum, for as it falls, it is Class 0 that is being grouped. Thus, the highest point on this curve shows immediately where the optimum separation of classes occurs. It turns out to be at instance 733. At this point, it is possible to divide the data set and create the confusion matrix shown in Table 11.6 to compare with the previous classification.

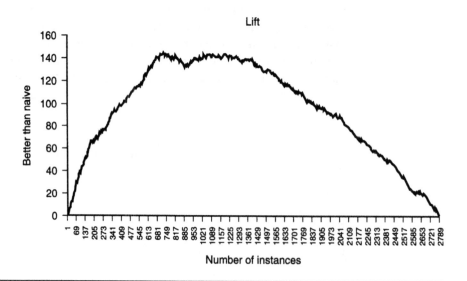

Figure 11.22 Lift.

TABLE 11.6 Confusion Matrix for Figure 11.22

Model	Is 1	Is 0	Tot
Class 1	313	420	733
Class 0	334	1732	2066
Tot	647	2152	2799

The total number of instances classified as Class 1 is 733, of which 313 are correctly classified, so the success rate of this classification is approximately 313/733 = 42.70%. Recall from the earlier discussion that the naïve rate is 23.18%, so the performance of this model produces a 42.7/23.18 = 1.84 improvement ratio.

So which is the best classifier? The dichotomous classification model previously discussed has an improvement ratio of 2.25; the continuous classification model has a ratio of 1.84. Does this make the first model better? Well (and with luck, this refrain will now be expected!), that depends on the business problem.

If the business objective is to earn the greatest return for marketing dollars invested, for instance, the dichotomous classification model is expected to return, assuming a 1% base response rate, 1% × 2.25 = 2.25%. The continuous classification model will return only 1% × 1.84 = 1.84%.

But perhaps the objective is to obtain as many responders as possible for a given investment. The best model now depends on whether the number of prospective customers who can be solicited is limited in some way, or effectively unlimited. If the marketing department can afford to purchase however much data it takes to solicit enough people to get the required number of new customers, for instance, the number of prospects and the needed data are not the limiting factors. Although the number of responders per unit is lower in the first model, the return is higher, and the low conversion rate is of no moment since it simply means that more data is needed to get any selected absolute number of responses.

However, perhaps the amount of data available is limited. This would, for instance, be the case if a company were soliciting its existing customers for a cross-sell or up-sell program, or if the company were geographically limited and had only a large but finite number of prospects it could approach. The objective then might be to get the maximum number of responses from a fixed data set for the highest return on investment (ROI). In this scenario, the conversion rate is crucial. The rate of responders in the dichotomous model (the first one discussed) is the 203 correctly classified as a proportion of the whole data set of 2799, thus 203/2799 = 7.25%. The second model correctly classifies 313 for a conversion rate of 313/2799 = 11.18%.

Which is the best model? That depends. The dichotomous model has a higher performance ratio, but the continuous model has a higher conversion ratio. In these examples, the quality of the dichotomous classification model seems better, but the continuous classifier offers more flexibility. (See MIII:TB.11.7)

11.4.6 Building a Multiple Classification Model

Thus far, the techniques developed to create classification models have focused on the situation in which the data set should be partitioned into only two classes. Very many workaday data mining models do, in fact, require no more than a single, two-class model. However, many problems crop up that require the classification of far more classes. Every time the problem entails selecting one action from several choices, one product from many products, one offer from several possibilities, one page from several pages, or a single selection from several choices, the miner faces a multiple classification problem. As already noted earlier in this section, this calls for building several classification models since a model separating, say, Class A from Class B and C may well not do a very good job separating Class B from A and C. However, the basic techniques covered so far—developing a naïve confusion matrix, a model confusion matrix, a cumulative response curve, and the lift plot—form the basis of modeling multiple classes.

A classification problem never calls for using two models. With two classes, as covered previously, one model is enough. With three classes, however, three models are needed, one per class. Another example from the CREDIT data set will keep the discussion concrete. This time, however, the object will be to create the AGE_INFERR classification.

The technique used is to build one model that predicts each class. In this case, the PolyAnalyst neural network tool is applied to produce one separate model each for Age35, Age42, and Age57. Each model is trained on a separate dummy variable, and each model produces a separate estimate for its particular class. The Age35 model, for instance, is trained in a data set with a pseudo- or dummy-variable set to the value 1 for all instances with an estimated age of 35, and 0 otherwise. For the purposes of comparison in this explanation, a single neural network model was also trained that tries to estimate all three classes in the same model. However, the place to start the explanation is with what a perfect classification model looks like.

11.4.6.1 The Perfect Classification Model

If it were possible to create a perfect classification model for estimating age, all of the instances of each category would be aligned next to each other in a data set that was ordered by the score. Looking at the lift curve for the perfect age estimation model shows, in Figure 11.23, three separate lift curves, one for each category.

The lift for category Age35 (shown by a curve labeled Lift35) starts at 0 on the left of the graph in the figure and rises sharply while the other two curves fall. This occurs because all of the instances with age estimates of 35 are grouped together, so the model performance exceeds the expected average performance by the maximum amount. However, once it climbs to its peak, there being no more instances of an estimated age of 35 in the data set, it falls away to 0 across the span of the rest of the graph. This is the perfect lift curve for this category.

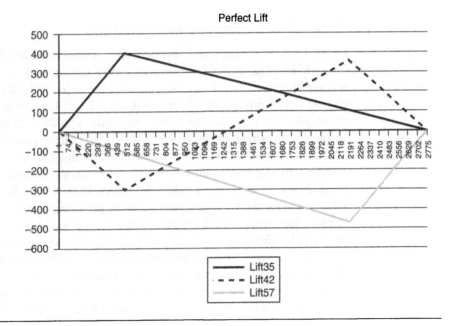

Figure 11.23 Perfect lift curves in a three-class classification.

The curve for category Age42 (shown by the curve labeled Lift42) also starts at 0. However, moving left to right this falls, there being no instances with the appropriate value, until the curve for Age35 peaks. At exactly the point at which Lift35 peaks and begins its descent, Lift42 begins its ascent. This is the point at which all of the instances with an estimated age of 42 begin, and the curve climbs to its peak. Notice that in every case, the length of the rising part of the curve is directly proportional to the number of instances of the appropriate category in the data set. The curve continues to rise until all of the instances of Age42 are covered, when it peaks.

The curve for Age57, which has been falling until Lift42 peaked since there were no instances in category Age57, begins its rise immediately as Lift42 passes its peak, since it is from this point that all of the instances of Age57 are clustered.

This is the lift chart for a perfect model when the age classifications are perfectly ordered. Looking at the chart in this figure, it is intuitive that the optimal way to use the continuous prediction is to make the category cutoffs at the point immediately following a peak. The category with the rising curve is the category into which instance assignments should be made. This would be fine with a perfect model on hand. Unfortunately, perfect models are rare, and often suspect when they do turn up because of possible leakage from anachronistic variables and the like. What does a real-world model produce?

11.4.6.2 Using a Single Multiple-Classification Model

Figure 11.24 shows the actual lift curve for a single model for classifying the three classes. The model was trained on estimated ages in the training data set, and then was used to create a single score in the test data set. The test data set is then ranked from lowest rank to highest. Actual scores range from about 37.26 up to 51.16. (An Excel workbook with data, calculations, and graphs for this single multi-classification, and the three separate binary classification models, are available for download on the author's Web site.)

The actual lift curves are at best only a very rough approximation of anything shown by the perfect model lift curves. However, as far as using this information for classification goes, the same principle applies. One difficulty in using the curves in their raw state is that they are very jagged. To make the optimal classification, select the curve that has the steepest upward trend, moving from left to right, as the class in which to make the assignment. Why? Because the curves only rise when the ranking has produced an above average grouping of the instances in the class indicated by the curve. The best answer is to smooth the curves, and the smoothed lift curves are also shown

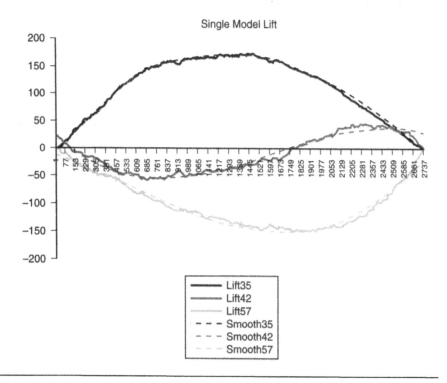

Figure 11.24   Actual and smoothed lift curves from a single model in a three-class classification.

in the same figure. (Details of how to produce the smoothing are contained in the supplemental material to this chapter.)

Just as with the perfect classification, using the most steeply rising smoothed curve as indicating the assigned class divides the data set into its three classes at points that are optimal for this ranking. It's not as good as the perfect ranking, of course, but it is the best possible for this single model ranking. So how good is this model?

Exactly as before, the only way to determine the performance of this model is to compare it with the naïve model. The three-way confusion matrix for the naïve model is shown in Table 11.7a. To briefly illustrate how a three-way confusion matrix for the naïve model is created, recall that in the naïve model, classes are assigned in direct proportion to their prevalence in the data set. So, for instance, there are 494 instances of Class Age35. Thus, 494 instances of Class Age35 are assigned at random to the actual instances. In the case of Age35, there is 494/2799 = 17.65% of the test data set in this class. Since the naïve model also generates 17.65% of its assignments as Class Age35, there is a 17.65% × 17.65% = 3.11% chance that Class Age35 will actually be assigned to an instance that is Class Age35. With 2799 instances, 3.11% of them come to a total of 87, to the nearest whole number. Thus, cell "Class 35/Is 35" shows that the naïve model would, purely by chance, get 87 "predictions" correctly assigned.

As another example, consider cell "Class Age57 Is 42." This is the naïve model's prediction that the instance belongs to Class Age57 when in fact the Class is Age42. The percentage of instances that actually are age 42 is the actual number of such instances (1708) divided by the total number of instances, which is 2799. In this case, 1708/2799 = 61.02%, so this is the proportion of Age42 instances present in this data set. The number of predictions of Age57 is the same number as the number of instances in the data set, so as a proportion, this is 597/2799 = 21.33%. The chance of naïvely assigning a "prediction" of Age57 to an instance of Age42 is therefore 61.02% × 21.33% = 13.02%, which translates into 13.02% × 2799 = 364 instances, as shown in the naïve confusion matrix. Every cell is completed using similar reasoning—probability of occurrence times the percentage of times it actually occurred.

TABLE 11.7a Three-Way Confusion Matrix for the Naïve Model

Naïve Model	Is 35	Is 42	Is 57	Total	Efficiency	Performance
Class Age35	87	301	105	494	17.65%	0%
Class Age42	301	1042	364	1708	61.02%	0%
Class Age57	105	364	127	597	21.33%	0%
Total	494	1708	597	2799	44.90%	0%

The same reasoning is applied to the single model data set shown in Table 11.7b. In this case, there are 494 cases that are actually Class Age35 (as before since it's the same data set) and this model predicts 1060 to be in Class Age35, whereas the actual number of instances is 353. Since 353/1060 = 0.3330, the actual prediction efficiency here is about 33.30%, which in turn is 33.30/17.65 (in the naïve model) = 1.887 times better than the naïve model at predicting Class Age35. This ratio is shown in the column headed "Performance," which compares the model performance by class of prediction with naïve model. (In the naïve model, the "Performance" is 0% since the naïve model is 0% better or worse than itself.)

It is a very interesting phenomenon that although the model is classifying Class Age35 nearly 89% better than chance, Class Age42 nearly 12% better than chance, and Class Age57 about 88% better than chance, nonetheless the model, overall, is only nearly 6% better than chance. This is because the naïve model classifies 1257 instances correctly and 1542 incorrectly (see Table 11.8a) for a classification accuracy of approximately 44.91%. The single model improves on this with 1328 correctly classified for 1471 incorrect and an overall accuracy of 47.45% (Table 11.8b.). Comparison shows 47.45/44.91 = 1.06 times better than the naïve model or about 6%. Thus overall, this results in only a small improvement, although each class has a much larger improvement. (See MIII:TB.11.8)

TABLE 11.7b   Single Model Confusion Matrix

One Model	Is 35	Is 42	Is 57	Total	Efficiency	Performance
Class Age35	353	595	122	1060	33.30%	1.887
Class Age42	131	672	182	985	68.22%	1.118
Class Age57	10	441	303	754	40.19%	1.884
Total	494	1708	597	2799	47.45%	1.057

TABLE 11.8a   Naïve Model Classification Accuracy

# right	1257
# wrong	1542

TABLE 11.8b   Single Model Classification Accuracy

# right	1328
# wrong	1471

11.4.6.3 Combining Multiple Classification Models

An alternative approach to the single model classification approach is to create several separate models, one predicting each class. In this example with three classes, this requires three separate models. How are these three models going to be used?

The combined outputs of these three models can be assembled into a three-variable intermediate data set with one variable for each separate model's predictions, as illustrated in Figure 11.25. The prediction variable is the actual AGE_INFERR value, and a fourth neural network model combining the predictions of the three individual models is built to thereby combine them into a single score that can be used for ranking the test data set exactly as before with the single model. Does this make any difference? Figure 11.26 shows the lift curves and smoothed versions of the curves for the combined models. They appear barely different from the curves in Figure 11.24, although on careful comparison some small difference is apparent. Table 11.9 shows the confusion matrix for the combined models.

By comparing the tables for naïve, single, and combined models with each other, it's easy to see that the combined model does produce better predictions than either the single model or the naïve model. The ranking produced by combining multiple models, and discovering the associated cutoffs by inspecting the smoothed lift curves, does improve performance in two categories, Age35 and Age57. Nonetheless, the apparent anomaly still persists that overall model performance is far less than individual category performance over the naïve model! This is a warning to a miner that no single

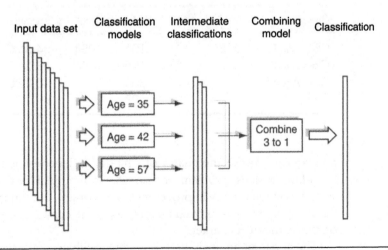

Figure 11.25 Combining multiple models into a single classification model.

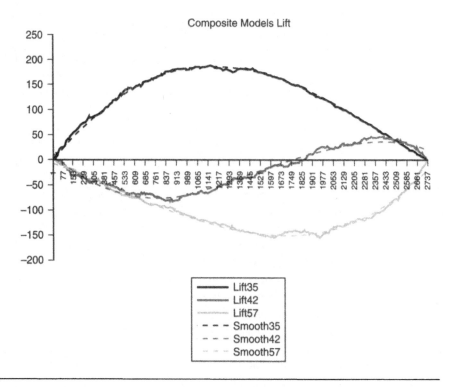

Figure 11.26 Actual and smoothed lift curves from a three-model combination in a three-class classification.

TABLE 11.9 Confusion Matrix for Combined Models

Comb Model	Is 35	Is 42	Is 57	Total	Efficiency	Performance
Class Age35	338	545	101	984	34.35%	1.946
Class Age42	147	737	196	1080	68.24%	1.118
Class Age57	9	426	300	753	40.82%	1.914
Total	494	1708	597	2799	49.12%	1.094

number can express the quality of a model. It depends, as ever, on the nature of the business problem, and on what is important for the model to classify. If individual class improvement is important, is it improved accuracy that's important, or improved quantity, or some combination of both? (More on this in the next chapter.)

The apparent anomaly here is that although accuracy has improved per class, it's at the expense of quantity. (Something has to give in any model!) Each class expresses its own efficiency in terms of the instances that it actually classifies, and classification efficiency can always increase even if the quantity of instances classified goes down—even dramatically. Yet, the overall quality of the model reflects an accuracy weighted by the quantity of instances classified per class. Notice that although the actual class classifications improve, overall the total number of correct versus incorrect classifications doesn't increase all that much from model to model.

This apparent anomaly gets close to a phenomenon known as *Simpson's Paradox*. By adjusting the class boundaries slightly, it's possible to get into the truly paradoxical situation that each class is better predicted than the same class in the naïve model, yet the model has *worse* overall predictive performance than the naïve model. Better in every class, worse overall. It certainly seems both counterintuitive and paradoxical, but the actual models produced in these examples to classify estimated age are very nearly paradoxical in exactly this way.

The only answer to how "good" these models are can only—and that is *only*—be given in terms of the business objective. (See MIII:TB.11.9)

11.4.7 Summary of Modeling to Classify

Very often, a miner works with classification models when the required business result is described in colloquial business terms as a "prediction." Scoring a data set is a classification problem, not a prediction problem. Selecting one object or action from a choice based on data is a classification problem. Even the colloquially archetypal nonbusiness prediction problems of trying to "predict" which politician will win an election, or which horse will win a race, are really classification problems. (Splitting the apparent hair that is the difference between classification and prediction problems comes in the next section.)

Splitting data sets into classes in these examples—who will respond to a solicitation and who won't, and who is in one age group rather than another—is the bread-and-butter work of data mining. Even the previous section on modeling to understand leads to classification because much of the purpose behind understanding data sets is to build better classification models.

Sometimes the number of classes is small—very often, only two. Responders either do or do not respond, and those are the only two classes of interest. As the number of classes increases, the problem looks more and more like a continuous estimation rather than a classification problem. However, the principles of classification introduced here still hold true, however many classes there are to be distinguished. After a point, of course, the problem of discovering optimal classification boundaries requires automated assistance—but that's the job intended for computers.

Data miners do very little in the way of true predictive modeling at the time of this writing. It's the area that provides the most interesting problems, and it certainly offers an as yet untapped realm for deriving business value. But if you were to stop at this point and master the arts of modeling to understand and modeling to classify, and then skip the next section, you would be able to address almost all of the problems that data mining is applied to in the business world. However, you would miss out on the techniques with the most promise to actually impact a company's strategy, and to address areas in which business managers have not yet, in the main, applied the power of these techniques.

11.5 **Modeling to Predict**

There seems to be an impression that prediction is just like classification, except about the future. It's not. Prediction is about intelligently forecasting states that have not yet been encountered in existing data.

Prediction is entirely the wrong word to use for any data mining activity. In both the *Shorter Oxford English Dictionary* and in Webster's *New World Dictionary of the American Language* the word *prediction* is defined entirely in terms synonymous with prophecy, prognostication, and foreknowledge of the future. (A sort of high-class "fortune telling.") That, most emphatically and categorically, is not what data miners do when engaged in what is commonly called "prediction"—and it is equally emphatically not the purpose of predictive models. Misappropriation of the term *prediction* has created a lot of misapprehension and misunderstanding about the nature of the activity in data mining. However, we're stuck with it now, and the best that can be done is to clarify the actual purpose and rational expectation for predictive modeling in a business setting.

The last section closed by observing that classification is not prediction, and it's time to take a look at the difference between classification and prediction as far as mining data for models is concerned. The last section already showed classification as a technique, supported by tools, for dividing a data set into two or more parts based on characteristic features in the data: dividing the credit data set into the two classes of buyers and nonbuyers, for instance. Prediction is concerned with causes and effects, with dynamic relationships that interconnect the objects represented in the data. Prediction explores rational expectations of what will be encountered in situations that haven't happened before.

The essence of the difference is this: *classification* characterizes and associates patterns in input and output batteries; *prediction* characterizes system behaviors and uses the characterization to estimate outcomes under novel circumstances where no outcome pattern is known.

Some expansion of this brief description will help clarify the differences. Data represents measurements about a selected system that exists in the world. *Classification* addresses the problem of how to use some of the features of that system, as represented in the data, to determine other features of the same system. In other words, classification uses data that describes both the patterns and the outcome from those patterns and characterizes which outcomes belong to which patterns. From there on, it's essentially a "look-up" problem—get some data, look up the appropriate pattern, look up the associated outcome, and report it as the outcome class.

Prediction addresses the problem of how changes in one set of features in a system will affect other features of the same system. Again, data represents measurements about a selected system taken to exist in the world. This time, however, it is the relationships among the objects in the system that are important. The available data cannot contain any patterns describing how the system will behave under the circumstances of interest since the unique combination of circumstances of interest hasn't happened yet. In prediction, there is no outcome pattern available in data anywhere to associate with the input battery patterns.

For example, a manager may want to know how changes in commission rates will affect the level of sales. Or what changes in the level of research investment will have on a competitive position. Or how introducing a new product will affect sales of existing products. Or which skill sets are least impacting to profitability and market position, and thus most dispensable in a required downsizing. Or what products should be placed on order now to meet anticipated future need. Or any of an almost infinite number of questions about how changes in one part of an organization, or distribution of resources, will affect other parts of the system as a whole. This is the task of prediction.

Essentially, businesses use prediction for a couple of purposes. One is to discover which possible business scenarios are most likely to occur based on the present circumstances. The other main purpose is to examine different possible business scenarios, however the scenarios are devised, and to explore the likely outcomes in each scenario.

Another view is that classification is about modeling the state of stocks in a system, whereas prediction is about modeling the information connections and flows. The answer to the question "Where do we need to most effectively invest resources to reduce backlog?" is not a classification problem. It's a predictive problem.

As yet, there are no commercially available tools that specifically address prediction problems (except, of course, for the type of modeling colloquially called "prediction," but that is actually classification). Some of the same classification tools can be turned to predictive investigation and modeling with great success, but doing that relies entirely on data mining technique. In other words, at the moment, predictive modeling requires the miner to use inferential and classification modeling tools plus particular methods and skills in applying those tools. The key lies entirely in miner skill sets, not in automated tools or technologies. There are new algorithms that are just now being developed that specifically support predictive and causal modeling of the type described here. These, however, call for advanced data mining techniques, not the basic modeling techniques that are the subject of this book. These tools will require collecting and assembling data that is not currently stored in forms immediately suitable for predictive mining. In building predictive models, one major task that a miner faces is simply building the minable data set.

Since specific intra-systemic predictive mining tools aren't commercially available, the rest of this section takes an introductory look at the problems that require development of particular data mining techniques (methods, knowledge, and skill) that are needed to apply the current tools to create predictive models. The three main problems that face a miner (that is, after defining both the business problem and the system that needs modeling) are:

1. Gathering data
2. Looking for causes
3. Reporting outcomes

The rest of this section briefly introduces the issues in gathering data and looking for causes, and why they are different from classification issues. (Reporting outcomes is similar for all models and is covered in Chapter 13.)

11.5.1 Gathering Data for Prediction

Data used for building classification models is different from that used for building predictive models. A glance at the data in two data sets, one designed for classification and the other for prediction, might not show any apparent differences—both would have variables containing dates, categorical values, numerical values, and so on. The input batteries would still consist of several to many variables and the output batteries few or, most likely, one variable only. Even someone who made a full assay of each data set without otherwise knowing whether the data was destined for classificatory or predictive modeling might not immediately notice the difference between the two. The difference is real nonetheless, and it is indeed a marked one. Understanding the types of data needed for each model goes a long way to explaining the difference between classificatory and predictive models.

Classification models look for structure in data sets. In the credit card acquisition data set used earlier to look at explanatory and classification models, part of the structure was related to features of age, gender, length of residence, and the like. The exploration in this chapter only scratched the surface of the complexity and intricacy of the patterns that the data set contains, and there are many more relationships to be discovered than there was room to discuss. Both the explanatory and particularly the classification models use these structures in relating patterns in the input battery to the state of the single variable output battery predictor.

In a sense, the classification model discovers the input battery structures and, it can be imagined, takes "snapshots" of each pattern, including the outcome associated with each. The snapshot represents a sort of average behavior of all the instances that are most similar to the basic pattern in a particular snapshot. When it's time to make a classification of a new instance of data, the classification model can be imagined as looking through these snapshots to find the one most like the instance to be classified. The classification model compares the instance's input variables to all of the snapshots' input variables until it finds a snapshot that is the closest match to the new instance, and whatever class the snapshot has as its class is assigned to the new instance as the most likely class for that instance. The sophistication is greater, but that is what the rules that map input to output actually encapsulate in a structured way in the algorithms described in Chapter 10. All the algorithms seek to match the pattern in a to-be-classified instance and assign the most likely outcome as its class.

Thus, the ideal data for classification is rich in easily distinguishable data structures covering the full range of input and output values that the variables in each battery can take. The full range needs to be covered as well as possible since the model needs to find the best matching snapshot to make good classifications. If at run time instances turn up with values for which there are no well-matched snapshots (since that part of the range wasn't in the input data), the classification model won't be able to make a good or accurate classification. (Remember, colloquially, that is usually called a prediction.)

Predictive models, as distinct from classificatory models, are inherently asked to estimate system behavior for states of the system that have not previously been seen, and thus, that cannot be represented in data. "But," you may object, "If there is no data, how can it be possible to make a model of it?" If you ask that question, you immediately understand the difference—and the difference in challenge—between creating and using classification models and creating and using predictive models.

Classification models recognize situations portrayed in data and associate particular outcomes with each situation. Where there is no data representing the situations of interest, what is to be done?

What is to be done is to try to create a representation of the behaviors of important parts of the system using data describing individual system component interactions. The system model to be created describes how each component relates to the other components. The data available will not describe the output behavior of the system under the circumstances of interest, but it may well describe more or less completely the full range of behaviors and interactions of each subsystem. Using the models created from the data that is available may allow a modeler to estimate how the system as a whole would behave in the new configuration of interest.

This is all a more detailed way of saying that predictive models play the "What if . . ." game. So the question would be posed as, "What if everything stayed the same except that we changed thus-and-so?" It's the change to thus-and-so that makes the prediction necessary. The way forward is to construct a model of the system in which thus-and-so exists that is as complete as possible and duplicates known results. With such a model in hand, change thus-and-so and see what the system produces. Whatever it does produce, along with the necessary caveats of confidence and probable variance, is the prediction. In fact, of course, the model will produce data describing the outcome of interest, and this data will have to be explained in terms of the business problem. However, this explanation draws only on techniques already discussed, as the data produced can be used as an output battery, with the original data simulating the system as an input battery, and the whole explained exactly as described earlier in this chapter in Section 11.3.

Inherently, predictive modeling calls for extrapolating—or going beyond—current, known, and recognized system behaviors and using well-founded and rational extrapolations to make best estimates of how a system will behave under changed circumstances. Usually, at least in the case of data mining approaches to this problem, there is plenty of data. It's just that the data doesn't describe system behaviors and responses under the circumstances of interest.

To make this more concrete, and to continue with credit card acquisition as a theme, one classification model explored earlier seeks only to answer the question of who will respond to a solicitation used in the marketing test. A predictive approach might ask who would respond to some different offer, one that has never been tried before. Or a predictive approach might ask what should be put into a new offer so that it would both appeal to the largest number of target market prospects and return the highest ROI to the company making the offer. The first question posed asks how the existing system would behave under changed circumstances (i.e., the different offer). The second question asks how to change operating values in the system (the various components of the offer) to create a specified desired change (most new customers for highest ROI).

Note that neither question asks how the system might be changed in its structure—that is a task for system modeling, not data mining. These questions ask either how the existing system will perform under changed external circumstances or which circumstances internal to the system should be changed to modify system behavior. These are questions about which there is inherently no data available. In the first case, there is no data about how people would respond to the different offer since this particular offer has never been made. In the second case, there is no data since the components of the offer—interest rate, payoff conditions, length of time to pay, associated benefits, and so on—have not only never been tried, but they also haven't ever been thought of since it is the discovery of some optimal set of components that is the object of the prediction.

So how is any data to be assembled that bears on the needs of building a predictive model?

It should be apparent that the miner needs data that covers the behavior of the individual subsystems, and the interactions between subsystems, as fully as possible. The intuition is that data representing the fullest possible range of system component behaviors can be modeled to represent the interacting relationships. Prediction poses questions about how a system will behave when as a whole it is in some novel condition. However, it is most likely that, although the total configuration is novel, none of the subsystems is actually far outside—or even outside at all—of a configuration about which there is data.

In the case of the first question—who will respond to a newly created credit card solicitation—the specific components of the offer as a whole have never been assembled and offered to prospects, but it is very likely that the individual components of terms and conditions, interest rates, introductory offers, features, and benefits have all been individually made in previous offers. If so, the problem is to construct a model that tries to use the existing data, allow for all of the changed conditions, and extrapolate a response to the hypothetical offer. Thus, the data needed for this model needs to cover the widest possible range of behaviors for the individual parts of the system.

The second question also requires similar data describing the relationships among all of the system components. In this case, the required model attempts to find where an optimum point turns up in the mix of components. That optimum may well turn out to be a precise mix of components that has never been tried. But the system components are exactly the same as in the previous question. These include the components that are available to be included in the offer (payoff period, interest rate, and so on), plus data describing the reactions and interactions among components (how different payoff periods affect willingness to accept different interest rates, for instance), as well as how different groups of customers responded to different components of the offer. However, note that in this second case, although the components of the system remain the same, the question is about what set of values should be assigned to the various components to achieve a selected response, and the values required to get the desired response may never have, as a whole, been assigned to the system's components.

These models can become quite complex, although each stage builds on the same techniques used in building classification models. Collecting the necessary data is usually the most difficult task. However, the key objective is to identify the relevant system components and to ensure that as much data as possible is found, created, or collected that describes the subsystem interactions as fully as possible.

11.5.2 Causality

The predictions from a predictive model do not foretell the future. Predictions are estimates of how a system might behave under specified circumstances that the system has not previously experienced. Only sometimes does the circumstance specify that the time is somewhere in the future. Predictions of the future are very hard indeed because they depend not only on understanding the system to be modeled, but also on understanding changes in the world at large that could materially affect the system of interest. However, not all predictions are really about the future. Many predictions are concerned more with how the system of interest will perform under conditions that, to all intents and purposes, are in the present. That is to say, the business managers asking the questions are happy to accept that the predictions are only relevant for the state of the world as it is right now, since the decision on which the model bears has to be taken under what may as well be the present time. So predictions are not about foretelling the future, but about rationally exploring various business scenarios under a range of circumstances, only some of which involve displacement into the future.

The essential problem that a miner faces in creating predictive models is that most situations are looked at from the "outside" rather than the "inside." Classification models, for instance, are models about a situation, circumstance, or system. The system that is presumed to influence whether someone accepts or rejects the solicitation in the CREDIT data set exists intact, and the classification model doesn't presume it changes—it simply observes it. In other words, the classification model is attempting to create a model that can be looked at as saying, "Given these inputs, the observed system will produce this output." What goes on inside the system, whether simple or complex, is quite irrelevant to the classification. Prediction looks at a situation totally differently.

Predictive models always, to some extent, have to be explanatory models. In every case, along with a depiction of likely outcomes and the confidence and limits associated with each, it is very important to be able to explain why the outcomes are likely, and what the limits are and why. But most importantly, the model must provide a type of explanation known as a *causal explanation* that is different from the explanatory models described earlier in the chapter.

The explanatory models described previously present their explanations in terms of associations. In the CREDIT data set, for instance, one association is higher than average response with higher than average estimated age. This is the way that explanatory and classificatory models work, by finding and characterizing associations. Predictive models require explanations in the rather different terms of causality.

Consider the example of a sales manager wanting to know the likely effect on sales of a new commission plan. It is very likely that there is not a straightforward relationship between the two objects "sales" and "commission plan." In fact, there may be very little in the way of direct causal connection. If the commission plan terms and conditions were too complex for most of the sales force to understand, there may be no noticeable impact attributable to the plan itself. Or it may actually demotivate the sales force if it is incomprehensible. Or identical plans may have totally different impacts if other circumstances are different. For instance, if the economy is booming and the company doing well, a plan that calls for sharing some of the company's profits could work as a motivation. At a different time when the company is suffering in the marketplace, an identical plan may be seen by the sales force as nothing but a cheap tactic to try to force additional sales in a declining market and designed to further penalize an already suffering sales force. (Both of the above "potted" descriptions are based on real situations.) In fact, it's quite possible that the actual terms and conditions in the commission plan don't matter much, but just the fact of introducing a new plan produces positive or negative consequences.

The key point here is that the same, even identical, "inputs" to the system can produce wildly different system behavior depending entirely on what other parts of the system are doing. This makes it crucially important in any predictive modeling task to carefully use the techniques discussed in Part II to discover the important system components.

Typically, if the predictive model produces welcome predictions, no further questions are asked about how results might be improved still further—and that's true even if the improved results are still far from the best. However, given less than welcome predictive estimates, the sales manager would almost certainly immediately ask, "What would make the sales force behave like that?" Followed almost immediately by, "What can we do about it?" The first question could be rephrased as, "What would cause the sales force to behave like that?" The second question can be rephrased as, "What can we modify that will cause sales to be positively impacted?"

Causality is a tough concept and is fraught with a vast array of philosophical problems. One way or another it looks very much as if every event or action that is the cause of some phenomenon always itself has a cause. This leads to the philosophical notion of the necessity of a "prime mover" that is the original uncaused cause of everything that follows. Today, the notion arrives at the "big bang" before which, nothing of causes can be known.

This, however, is not the everyday way that causality is discussed. In everyday usage, such as the sales manager's questions, what's needed is a sort of leverage point. The leverage point, also called a *causal nexus,* is where a small intervention yields a very large result. What ultimately causes lung cancer is a very large question and depends on human physiology, biochemistry, environmental factors, and a vast array of interacting events. However, in everyday terms, it's enough to explain smoking as a cause since the single action of smoking or not smoking has a huge impact on the result. Similarly, what causes thunderstorms? The brief answer is cold fronts, although the long answer includes a host of atmospheric physics. What causes global warming? Carbon dioxide. What causes the Antarctic ozone hole? Fluorocarbons. And so, in everyday usage, it's not ultimate causes that are needed, but the leverage points that get the maximum effect for the minimum intervention. Predictive models, especially ones well calibrated against real-world data so that the actual quality of the predictions is well established, do very well at pointing out causes in the sense described here.

11.5.3 Summary of Modeling to Predict

Predictive modeling is an essentially different mining task from classification modeling. However, the tools used are similar—even sometimes the same. It is the use to which they are put that is different. Predictive modeling requires constructing a network of interacting models, each expressing the relationships that exist among components of some system of interest. The key question to be answered is how the system will behave under some set of conditions that has not previously occurred, and for which there is no descriptive data.

A predictive model is the most difficult of the three model types to set up, but potentially the most valuable in the insights it delivers and the power that it offers. It is, nonetheless, an advanced data mining technique at the present state of the art, which a miner will approach only when thoroughly familiar with the basic modeling techniques of explanatory and classificatory modeling. (Obviously, a predictive model is an extension of a system model since it produces predictions of how a system will behave outside of its so-far-observed range of behaviors. For more information on and help in creating simple system models, something not discussed in this section, see Part II.)

Earlier in the chapter, the introduction to Table 11.1 noted that there was no column for predictive modeling. It should be apparent now that in the practice of modeling data to create a predictive model, at the actual addressing-the-data level, what the miner produces is actually a set of interlocking associative models that emulate the system for which predictions are needed. Also as already noted, at this writing there are no commercially available tools that directly support predictive modeling—thus no column entry in Table 11.1.

Despite the potential power of predictive data mining to directly address significant business problems, particularly important strategic business issues such as scenario exploration, the bread-and-butter work of data mining today is explanatory and classificatory modeling.

11.6 **Summary**

The central message of this chapter is very simple. First, explore the data set with whatever tools you favor or simply have on hand. Generate the best explanation of the data in business terms that you can get. Second, use the explanation to reconfigure the data and to generate business relevant features. Third, build the best model you can get.

Of course, the detail of actually performing those steps may be quite complex and will very likely be time consuming, but the outline is straightforward. However, even with the model in hand, the process of modeling is only just begun. The next stage is to "tune" the model, and that, in essence, is the subject of the next chapter.

▩ ▩ ▩   **Supplemental Material**

Generating the Random Confusion Matrix for CREDIT Classifying BUYER

The naïve model is one in which classes are assigned at random to each instance in proportion to their frequency of occurrence in the base data set. In practice, the frequency used for the assignment should be that found in the training data set. So as to make this explanation clearer, rather than using the frequency in the training data set, the frequency in the test data set is used. The actual difference in frequency is very small, but the explanation is a little more accessible when the total counts are exact. However, note that in a practical application, it is the training set frequencies that should be used in order to stay honest.

In this data set, there are 647 responders (1) and 2152 nonresponders (0), for a total of 2799 instances. This gives ratios of 647/2799 = 23% responders, and 2152/2799 = 77% nonresponders. (All percentages are approximate due to rounding.)

Answers to four questions are needed to create the naïve confusion matrix:

1. What is the chance that an instance of Class 1 will be randomly assigned Class 1?
2. What is the chance that an instance of Class 1 will be randomly assigned Class 0?
3. What is the chance that an instance of Class 0 will be randomly assigned Class 1?
4. What is the chance that an instance of Class 0 will be randomly assigned Class 0?

In case 1 (what is the chance that an instance of Class 1 will be randomly assigned to Class 1), note that Class 1 forms 23% of the population used here, and also has a 23% chance of being randomly assigned to any instance. The chance of randomly selecting an instance of Class 1 is therefore 23%, and the chance of randomly assigning Class 1 to it is also 23%; thus, the chance of randomly assigning Class 1 to an instance of Class 1 is 23% × 23%, or 23% squared. The 23% is an approximation, so the calculation in this data set comes out to approximately 5.34%. Since there are a total of 2799 instances, 5.34%, or 150 instances of Class 1, to the nearest whole number, will be correctly assigned as Class 1 by the naïve model.

In case 2 (what is the chance that an instance of Class 1 will be randomly assigned Class 0), Class 1 still forms 23% of the instances. But since there is a 77% chance of selecting an instance of Class 0, there is a 77% chance that it will be assigned to Class 0. Since 23% of 77% is approximately 17.77%, this is the chance that an instance of Class 1 will be randomly assigned to Class 0. Thus, 17.77% of 2799 instances, or 497 to the nearest whole number, of Class 1 will be assigned to Class 0.

In case 3 (what is the chance that an instance of Class 0 will be randomly assigned to Class 1), this time there are approximately 77% of Class 0 and 23% of Class 1 to be assigned. The calculation is 77% of 23%, which gives 17.77%. This is the same percentage as in case 2, and 497 instances, to the nearest whole number, of Class 0 will be assigned to Class 1.

In case 4 (what is the chance that an instance of Class 0 will be randomly assigned to Class 0), there are approximately 77% of the instances in Class 0 and 77% of the random assignments will be to Class 0, so 77% of 77%, or about 59.11%—1655 instances to the nearest whole number—of Class 0 will be assigned at random to Class 0.

This reasoning generates the entries for the confusion matrix shown in Table 11.4a.

Smoothing Lift Curves

Fitting a smooth curve to any lift curve begins with creating a dummy variable that sequentially numbers the ordered instances from 1 and continues up to the total number of instances. Thus, every lift curve can be paired with this dummy to create a two-variable series—the dummy and the height of the lift.

Perfect lift curves will all have one or two "corners" or inflexion angles. The lift curves at the extreme values have one inflexion angle; all of the others will have two. Real lift curves are approximations to perfect lift curves and are regarded as having a similar number of inflexion points as their perfect counterparts. It turns out that a smooth curve requires one "power" for each corner. (A "power" as used here is shorthand for raising a number to a power. When the power is 2, the number is squared; when the power is 3, the number is cubed.) Thus, using y to indicate a variable representing the height of the lift curve, and using x to represent the dummy index variable, two corners require a representation including both x^2 and x^3 in addition to x.

The smooth curves shown were generated by creating a multiple linear regression to predict the value of y using three input variables, x, x^2, and x^3.

Note that any data miner has available a formidable array of tools for estimating nonlinear functions that will produce a better fit than this smoothing. The point in this smoothing is *not* to get the best possible fit, but to get a smoothed approximation to the actual lift curves.

Chapter 12
Improving the Model

This chapter looks at improving a model, which presupposes that at least a model exists. Chapter 11 covered the process of mining the initial model. However, just because a model exists doesn't mean that it has no problems, or that it is the best or most appropriate model that the data permits. This chapter looks at the process of turning the initially created model into one that better fits the data and the business problem. Although most of the processes apply as much to improving an explanatory model as to improving a classificatory model, most of the issues here are addressed as if the model to be improved is classificatory—except, of course, where the issues discussed are specific to one type of model or the other.

The process of improving a model can, for discussion purposes, be broken into two broad categories: discovering where the model has problems, and fixing the discovered problems.

This chapter is divided into two major, but very connected, sections that align with these two categories and their associated activities:

- The first major section discusses how to determine model performance by performing a number of checks. (The methodology section of Part IV notes these as *discoveries*.)
- The second major section covers what to do about the results of the checks, or, essentially, how to fix the model.

These two activities—diagnosing model problems and applying remedies—are both applied in order to refine the initial model. This chapter presents the second step in the mining/refining process, the first step of which was covered in Chapter 11.

Regardless of where it occurs, the ultimate purpose underlying all of the issues and processes discussed in this chapter is to deliver a model that represents the business-relevant, meaningful relationships in the data set as perfectly as the data permits, and as simply as possible. (In fact, this can serve as a good definition of business data mining!)

It is in this stage of refining the initial mined model that a data miner must expect to start revisiting earlier parts at least of the mining process, and perhaps of the whole modeling process. None of the processes is carried out in isolation from any other part. Mining is an interactive whole, and all of the processes interact—hopefully to improve the model. It is here, too, that the main use of training and test data sets comes into its own. As shown in Figure 12.1, mining involves many loops through an iterative cycle in order to create the best possible model in the training data set that performs as well as possible in the test data set. That bears repeating—models are created on the data in the training data set, but all of the checking for problems and improvements happens in the test data set. During the following discussion, it is very important to remain aware of which data set is being used for which purpose. In every case in this chapter, whenever there's a change to the data—to the variables included in a model, to the individual variables, or to any other feature or parameter of the model, or if there is any adjustment to the data—the cycle works as follows: rebuild the model in the *training* data set, and look for any change in results when applying the new model in the *test* data set.

If the data needs adjusting, remember to make the necessary adjustments in all three data sets, but don't change the instances (records) that are included in the data sets. That is to say, for any individual model or integrated group of models, it's important that the same records stay in each data set throughout. If the data sets were rebuilt from scratch on each modification, as modeling progressed the model would be tested on data that in earlier iterations had been used for training. This mixing of training and test data would pretty much invalidate the purpose of the separate data sets, and wholly undermine the purpose of the evaluation data set altogether.

Throughout most of this book, except in Chapter 11, the terms *predict* and *predictive* are used with their usual colloquial meaning. Chapter 11 made

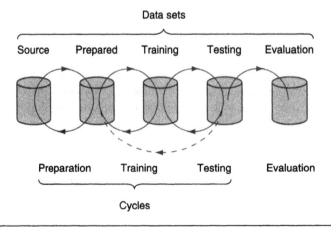

Figure 12.1 Interaction between mining activities and data sets.

an exception so that a clear distinction could be drawn between classification and prediction. As that chapter showed, at the present state-of-the-art, a miner builds predictive models only by combining particular system modeling skills and techniques with classificatory and explanatory modeling. However, it is normal usage to speak of a classificatory model "predicting" an output value when it is actually making a class assignment, and for the remainder of this book it is the colloquial use of prediction that is intended. Where predictive is used other than in its meaning of "most likely class assignment," the context will make that clear. (See MIII:AB.12.1)

12.1 **Learning from Errors**

We are all encouraged to learn from our mistakes, and it's no different when mined models make the mistakes. There is a lot to be learned from a close examination of the errors made by a classification model. These errors represent the difference between what the model predicts and what the actual outcome turns out to be in the real world. Whenever a model turns out to be worth considering for application, the next step is to look at the errors that it makes in the test data set—and very often, actually looking is a useful thing to do, not merely a metaphorical looking. However, the first modeling example in the last chapter showed a binary outcome, BUYER, taking values of either 1 or 0. The initial classification model made (with WizWhy) predicted either 1 or 0. Graphical error plots aren't very helpful in this case. The absolute value of the error can only be either 0 or 1, and the best way to look at binary outcome model performance is to use the confusion matrix. The last chapter already introduced confusion matrices and discussed them for all of the models built. There is little to add here. For a binary classification model predicting a binary outcome, the confusion matrix reveals the most about the model's performance. (See MIII:DB.12.1)

The next model created in the last chapter produced a continuous score that was turned into a binary classification. The *residual value,* or simply the *residual,* is the name given to the difference between the predicted and the actual values. In this case, actually looking at the residuals from the continuous score as well as looking at the confusion matrix begins to be helpful. Residual values are determined by subtracting the predicted value from the actual value. Symbolically, this might be represented as $r = a - p,$ where r represents the residual value, a represents the actual value, and p represents the predicted value. In the case of the continuous score classification model, the actual values are all between 0 and 1, so the predictions should also be (and actually are in this example) between 0 and 1—thus all predicted values are positive numbers. Obviously, when using the model created earlier, in the case when the actual value is 0, all of the residual values have to be negative, since 0 minus any positive number has to give a negative result, and the predictions are all positive numbers. Similarly, when the actual value is 1, all the residuals will be positive since 1 (the actual value) minus any positive number between 0 and 1 (the prediction) has to return a positive result.

It's worth remarking that many tools do not limit the range of their predictions to the range found in the training data set, and using such a tool in this example could result in predicted values that lie outside the range of 0–1. This would make a difference in the appearance of the plotted graph, but no material difference to the interpretation of the plots.

12.1.1 Looking at Errors

The first graphical display (illustrated in Figure 12.2) shows the predicted values versus the residual value. This is the place to start because at run-time— that is, when the model is applied in the real world to real-world data—nothing is known about the actual value except for the prediction made by the model. The prediction is intended to be the best possible estimate of the actual value given the data available. (Usually, if the real-world, run-time data includes the value to be predicted, there isn't any need to make the prediction.) It is important to get a feel for (and later to quantify) the differences between the model's predictions of the values and the actual values. In the training (and test and evaluation) data sets, the actual value is known, since that is what is being used to train (test or evaluate) the model. So it is quite possible to check the residuals made by the model. It is always possible to characterize the pattern made by the residuals across the range of the prediction. Very often, the pattern is one that has nothing to offer toward improving the model. However, sometimes the pattern of the residuals can be used to improve the model, and it is this sort of pattern that a miner must seek.

12.1.1.1 Predicted versus Residual Diagnostic Plot

(See MIII:DB.12.2) The points shown in Figure 12.2 form what is known as an *XY plot*. Each point is plotted in a position on the graph to represent its values on two measurements, the predicted value and the residual value. For example, the extreme left point shown is at a value of about 0.75 on the prediction scale and about −0.75 on the residual scale. The coincidence of these two values isn't accidental. The residual value indicates, being negative, that the actual value was 0 and, as shown, the predicted value was 0.75. With an actual value of 0, using $r = a - p$ to create the residual, this has to produce a residual value equal in magnitude, but opposite in sign, to the predicted

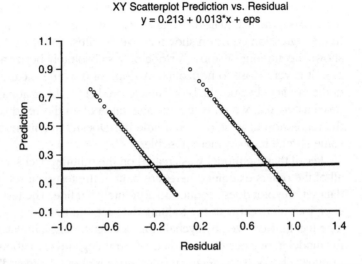

Figure 12.2   Prediction versus residual scatterplot in CREDIT estimating BUYER with continuous prediction and binary actual values.

value. Thus with an actual value of 0, and a predicted value of 0.75, the residual has to be $r = 0 - 0.75 = -0.75$. Since this is the case for all the residuals when the actual value is 0, they have to line up in a 45-degree slope because in every case, the magnitude of the residual is identical to the magnitude of the prediction. When the actual value is 1, the magnitude of the residual is not identical to the predicted value, but an analogous situation arises, and these residuals too arrange themselves in a 45-degree sloping line. The two lines are displaced only by whether the actual value was 0 or 1. (Since the graph is not reproduced exactly square, the appearance of the angle of slope may not seem to be 45 degrees. A simple algebraic calculation of line slope, however, will indicate the slope as 45 degrees, and it is this algebraic sense of slope that is intended in this discussion.)

Pay close attention to the almost horizontal line that crosses the plot at a value of approximately 0.2 on the prediction (*y*) axis. This is a linear regression line fitted to the residual values. Linear regression is often thought of as producing a prediction and, although there is no interest in its predictive role here, if it were to be used predictively, it would be estimating the predicted values using only the information in the residuals. Clearly, if the model has done a good job, the residuals won't be useful for predicting the model's predictions; if the residuals did carry any information about how to make a better prediction, the prediction could be improved—and that is precisely the point that the plot in Figure 12.2 is used to check.

The almost horizontal regression line shown in Figure 12.2 indicates that in this case, the residuals do, in fact, carry almost no additional information. In the regression equation shown above the illustration, the number "0.013" shows the amount of slope. A slope of 0 is absolutely horizontal, and in this plot, it is very close to horizontal. A slope of 0 would mean that regardless of the predicted value, the best value to predict for the residual would be approximately 0.2, which is the average value of all the residuals. But why is the regression line tilted even a little bit? Doesn't this indicate that there is some minute improvement possible?

Recall that the model was created on the training data set. This plot, and all of the others examined here, are built in the test data set. In the training data set, the plot does produce an absolutely flat line. The test data set, however, isn't identical with the training data set and thus, the model isn't quite a perfect fit. However, by eyeball, this line is near enough flat to indicate that the model in practice fits both data sets (training and test) about equally well, or equally badly. The average residual error is about 0.2 regardless of the predicted value or the actual value.

For the more technically inclined reader, it is possible to determine if this slope is statistically significantly different from one that is absolutely horizontal. However, beware of such measures. With the very high numbers of instances prevalent in data mining, every difference can become statistically significant, but statistical significance, although important in context, isn't a good measure in this case. For a miner, by far the best practice is to eyeball the residuals and to become familiar with the look and feel of these plots.

12.1.1.2 Predicted versus Actual Diagnostic Plot

(See MIII:DB.12.3) The other useful XY plot that a miner needs to become familiar with shows predicted versus actual values. Figure 12.3 shows a predicted/actual plot for the same model as in Figure 12.2. This is similar to the previous plot except that the values form vertical columns. Since BUYER takes only two values, the predictions are constrained to line up at one of those two values on this graph. The fitted regression line shown here crosses the column at BUYER = 0 with a prediction value of about 0.19. At BUYER = 1, the prediction value is about 0.29. These two values represent the mean of the predicted values in each column, and therefore the mean of the prediction values for each class. In other words, when the actual value of BUYER is 0, the average value of all of the predicted values is about 0.19; when the actual value of BUYER is 1, the average value of all of the predicted values is about 0.29. The slope of the line, in some sense, represents the quality of the model—not very good as you will recall from the confusion matrix, but a considerable improvement over chance.

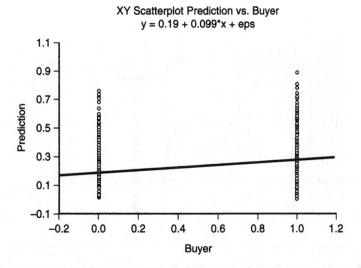

Figure 12.3 Prediction versus actual scatterplot in CREDIT estimating BUYER with continuous prediction and binary actual BUYER values.

12.1.2 **Predicting Errors**

(See MIII:DB.12.4) Looking at the errors in the form of residuals provides a fair amount of information. However, if the original data set could somehow be used to predict what the errors were going to be, that prediction of the errors could be used to improve the prediction. In a sense, that is what the linear regression tried to do with the results shown in Figure 12.2.

Data mining tools are, or should be, very good at characterizing relationships, whether linear or non-linear. The resulting relationship between the actual and predicted values, however rough and imprecise, should at least be linear, so a linear comparison is quite a reasonable way to check on the actual relationship. However, as a sort of "sanity check," it's worth building a model that attempts to predict the value of the residual. Again, this model will be built using the training data set input battery and predicting the residual value in the training data set as the output battery. This process of creating the residual test model is illustrated in Figures 12.4, 12.5, and 12.6.

To make the initial model and residual model:

1. Build an initial model (Figure 12.4).
2. Apply the initial model to the training data set, creating a set of predictions (Figure 12.4).
3. Calculate the residuals using the predicted values in the training data set (Figure 12.4).

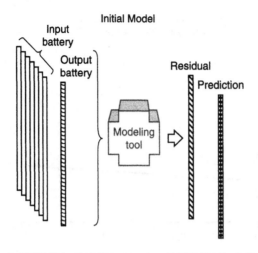

Figure 12.4   Initial model predicts the output battery.

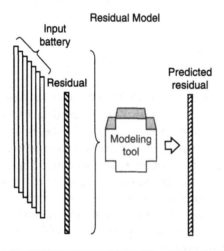

Figure 12.5   Residual model uses original input battery and residual as output battery.

4. Add a variable to the training data set input battery containing the value of the residual (Figure 12.5).

5. Build a second model to predict residuals using all of the training data *except* the original output variable and the predicted values (Figure 12.5).

Thus, the residual test model must not include any actual values or predicted values from the original model. If using a multiple-algorithm mining

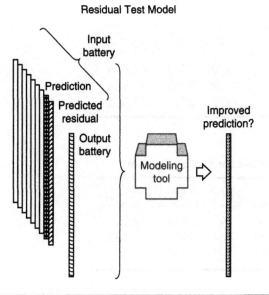

Figure 12.6 Residual test model adds prediction and predicted residual to original input battery to model the original output battery.

tool, it's worth building the second model with a different algorithm than the original model.

Next, build the residual test model (see Figure 12.6):

1. Include the prediction and predicted residuals in the input battery.
2. Build a model to predict the original output battery.

In doing this for the binary classification of BUYER, it turns out that the residual model isn't all that good. The original model shows a correlation co-efficient (one way of estimating how well a model makes its predictions) of about 0.06. The model predicting the residuals has a correlation with the residuals of about 0.02. However, the test is what happens if the output from the two models—the original prediction and the residual models—are combined to predict BUYER, as shown in Figure 12.5. Is there any improvement?

Actually, applying the combined model to the training data set does, in this case, produce an apparent improvement—in the training data set. However, when the combined model is applied to the test data set, the situation changes. Tables 12.1a and 12.1b show the story. Table 12.1a duplicates the confusion matrix for the original model shown in the last chapter in Table 11.7. Recall that this is the confusion matrix for the best classification model for classifying BUYER. If the residual test model does in fact improve

TABLE 12.1a Original Model

Model	Is 1	Is 0	Tot	Efficiency
Class 1	313	420	733	42.70%
Class 0	334	1732	2066	83.83%
Tot	647	2152	2799	73.06%

TABLE 12.1b Residuals Test Model Result in Test Data Set

Model	Is 1	Is 0	Tot	Efficiency
Class 1	357	491	848	42.10%
Class 0	290	1661	1951	85.14%
Tot	647	2152	2799	72.10%

performance, then the confusion matrix will show it. However, as Table 12.1b shows, although model performance in the training data set may have been improved, it certainly hasn't happened in the test data set.

What has happened here is that the combined model has learned some of the noise—relationships that exist in the training data but not in the test data. However, do notice that whereas overall performance is down and performance classifying BUYER = 1 is also down (both marginally), performance on classifying BUYER = 0 seems somewhat improved. In truth, these small changes are almost certainly due to nothing more than noise and instability in the model and, to all intents and purposes, information from the residuals in this case makes no meaningful difference. That is to say that minute fluctuations in performance of this magnitude (or larger) should be expected simply by applying the model to different, fully representative data sets. The conclusion? In this case, the residuals contain no additional useable relationship in predicting the actual value. (See MIII:TB.12.25)

12.1.3 **Continuous Classifier Residuals**

With only two classes, the residual plot and predicted/actual plot can produce only limited additional insight over that offered by the confusion matrix. In fact, for a two-class output classification, the confusion matrix pretty much offers the best insight into the workings of the model. When the output variable is to all intents and purposes a continuous variable, confusion matrices become totally impractical, and the only way to understand model performance is by using these plots.

As in the previous example, start with an XY plot of the residual values versus the predicted values. When the output variable is continuous, it is necessary to order the residuals by the prediction value. It doesn't really matter whether the order is from least to greatest or greatest to least, just so long as the miner knows which end represents which values.

Figure 12.7 shows the residuals plot for a real-world data set. A couple of features jump out from this image, even at a quick glance. One feature is that the mean value of the errors is about 0. In fact, with the exception of a couple of distortions (to be mentioned in a moment), the mean of the residual values is specifically set by the model to be 0, and this point is significant enough to be worth additional discussion.

Most algorithms that fit functions, curves, and other characterizations to data use one of a relatively few methods to determine how good the fit is, and the algorithms adjust their parameters until the fit, according to the criterion chosen, is as good as possible. There are, in fact, relatively few metrics for determining the level of fitness, but the most popular for continuous variables is Mean Least Squares (MLS). This involves minimizing the sum of the weighted squares of the residuals. It is a feature of MLS, and of most of the other goodness of fit metrics, that the mean of the residuals is 0—at least in the training data set. There are other metrics that do not require the best fit to produce residuals with a mean of 0, but their popularity, at least in

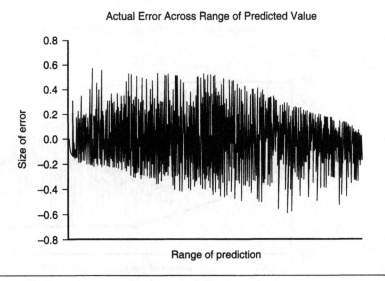

Figure 12.7   Ordered residuals from a model predicting a continuous predictor variable.

general purpose mining tools, is vanishingly small compared to MLS. In fact, at this writing, all of the commercial tools known to the author use goodness-of-fit tests that should produce mean-of-zero residuals.

The point here is that when the miner looks at the residuals in the test data set, they may not have a mean of 0. Generally speaking, the divergence from 0 represents a problem of some sort—insufficient data, poor model, problems with the data, inappropriate modeling tool, or some other problem. However, if the divergence from 0 in the test data set is large, it may be worth checking the mean of the residuals in the training data set. If it isn't 0 there, either the tool or algorithm is somehow "broken" or the tool is using some other best-fit metric. As noted, at this writing, all of the commercially available tools should produce residuals averaging 0, and will very likely continue to do so. But there are alternatives. Just because the residuals do not have a mean of 0, it does not *necessarily* follow that there is a problem, but it does bear investigation.

In general then (and as of this writing), the mean of residuals in the test data set should be 0. In addition, a straight line fitted across the range of the prediction with linear regression should fit through the center of the residual distribution, and should be flat along the zero point. Thus, ideally, not only should the mean of the residuals be 0, but across the range of the prediction the residuals also should fit around the zero line. The mean of the residual distribution in Figure 12.7 does fall along the zero point, but it doesn't fit the zero line. At the left-hand end of the plot, the mean seems to be above the zero point, and at the right-hand end below it. Is this a problem?

The "shoulders" are illustrated in Figure 12.8 along with a zero line. In fact, this is a fairly common appearance of residuals, and in this case, it doesn't

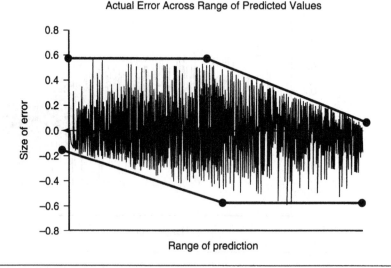

Figure 12.8 Ordered residuals highlighting features of the distribution.

represent any problem with the model at all. This is a case where the actual values of the output range vary between 0 and 1. What is happening here is that the model is limiting its predicted output to remain within the range of the actual values seen when training. The residuals appear to be fairly random in size except where the limiting clips them.

The underlying model in this case may attempt to make predictions that vary outside the limits of 0 and 1. However, the limit on the output says, in effect, "If the prediction attempted is less than 0, make it 0. If the prediction attempted is greater than 1, make it 1. If it's between 0 and 1, use the value as it is." Thus, as the range of the prediction approaches 0 (at the left-hand end) and 1 (at the right-hand end), the possible range of the error is clipped, resulting in the regular "shoulders" shown.

Even with these clipped shoulders, the distribution of the residuals is fairly close to a normal distribution, as Figure 12.9 shows. This is a histogram of the residuals, along with a normal curve for comparison. This is another diagnostic test that the model has fit the data well. Recall that whatever the distribution of the input data, and however nonlinear the relationships between input battery and output battery, a mining tool should, if effective, characterize the fit between input and output to include any peculiarities of distribution and to accommodate any nonlinearity present. What remains should pretty much be random noise, which is very typically (although not absolutely always) characterized by being normally distributed. Almost all—from the author's experience, more than 99%—of all business mining situations produce residuals that are at least approximately normal or distorted

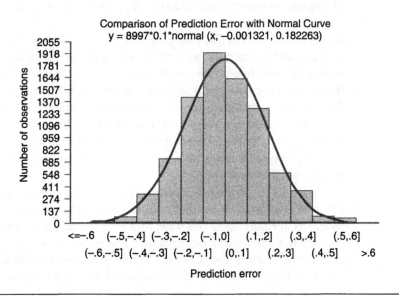

Figure 12.9   Histogram of residual distribution.

from normal. However, dealing with other types of residual distribution when modeling with continuous input and output battery variables is an advanced modeling topic not covered here. In effect, if the residuals' distribution is far from normal, it almost certainly indicates a potential problem with the model. (See MIII:DB.12.5)

If the histogram of residuals in the test data set is far from normal, compare it with the histogram of residuals in the training data set. If the distributions are dissimilar between training and test data sets, the problem is most likely with the data. If the distributions are similar and both are far from normal, the culprit may well be the modeling tool. If possible, try a different algorithm and check again. However, it's possible that the input battery, while being generally representative, isn't representative over particular ranges. In other words, the input data may be clustered so that some parts of the range are relatively sparsely described by the data available. The answer, of course, may be more, or better, or more balanced data.

12.1.4   Continuous Classifier Residuals versus Actual Values Plot

(See MIII:DB.12.6) Figures 12.7 and 12.8 showed the residual values plotted against the predicted values in an XY plot. Recall that at run time, the best available estimate of the actual value is the prediction produced by the model. We know for sure that there will be errors, and using training and test data sets (which have actual values for the output variable available to train the model), it's possible to know the actual residual error. Looking at plots of residuals versus predicted values graphically shows what can be expected when the model is actually deployed. Figures 12.7 and 12.8 show that the model constructed in this data produces unbiased errors. This doesn't mean that the model is as good as it can be—it might be possible, for instance, to reduce the variance of the residuals, which will result in a model that produces more accurate predictions. However, what these figures do show is that there is no systematic error in the model at run time. If, for instance, all of the predictions were high when the predict value was near the top of its range, and low when the predict value was near the bottom of its range, that would be a type of systematic error, and it could be corrected. However, no such systematic error appears.

Figure 12.10, on the other hand, seems to show exactly such a systematic error. This shows the residuals, in the same data set, and uses the same model as in Figure 12.8. This time, however, the residuals are plotted against the ordered actual value rather than the ordered predicted value. The mean of these residuals is also 0, but the linear regression line fitted shows a clear rise from left to right. Does this represent a systematic error?

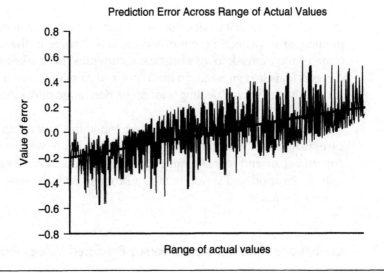

Figure 12.10 Actual versus residual plot.

No, actually it doesn't. At least, not a systematic error in the model nor in the raw prediction. There is a systematic bias here, but with the data available, there isn't anything that can be done about it as far as the predictions produced by the model are concerned. So what does it represent?

Actually, it's no more than the result of the limit function. Consider the effect of the limit function on the left-hand end of the range. The raw model would make errors by predicting values that are outside the output variable's actual range. These values are "trimmed" off by the limit function. On the left-hand side where the actual value is approaching 0 (due to trimming), all of the positive errors that the unlimited model would have made have been truncated, leaving only the negative errors, thus pulling down the average values. On the right-hand side, the reverse is true—the negative errors have been removed, leaving only the positive errors. Thus, the limit function has produced this bias. So there is indeed a bias in the estimates or predictions of the output value, but this bias has been deliberately and knowingly introduced to ensure that the predictions stay in the original range of the output.

Beware when evaluating residual plots since, although bias is very evident here, it isn't unanticipated and shouldn't be unexpected. The algorithm embedded in the tool that produced these models is of a type that doesn't inherently limit itself to making predictions that remain in the original range of the output. The algorithm in the tool, then, is occasionally trying to predict values of more than 1 and less than 0. Some algorithms do indeed behave this way, whereas others inherently will not make predictions that are outside the range present in the training data. The tools that implement algorithms that can make out-of-range predictions often do indeed "adjust" the predictions to maintain them inside the actual range in the output battery. (One of the better-known statistical techniques that makes similar adjustments is logistic regression, so this is not a "data mining algorithm problem." It's simply one way of dealing with prediction range difficulties in any quantitative model.)

So, although there is bias here, there is nothing "wrong" in this particular case. However, the miner needs to take careful note whenever this type of pattern occurs and to make quite sure that the source of any bias like this is fully understood and is not, in fact, a problem with the data, the modeling tool, or the model.

12.1.5   **Continuous Classifier Actual versus Predicted Values Plot**

(See MIII:DB.12.7) Another plot that a miner should routinely examine is an XY plot of actual values versus predicted values, as is shown in Figure 12.11. In addition to the data points, shown by small circles, the line running from lower left to upper right is a linear regression line fitted to the points. The equation for the line is shown below the title of the plot.

A glance at this figure shows clearly that the actual values range from 0 to 1, and that the predicted values range only from 0 to 0.9. At first glance,

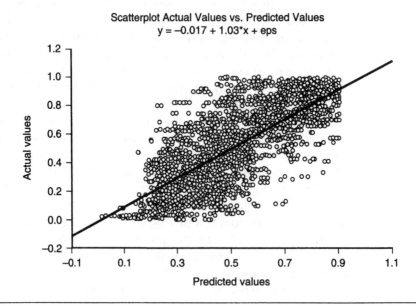

Figure 12.11   Actual versus Predicted values plot.

this seems to be strange, and it's worth investigating why the tool produced predictions with this pattern. Perhaps there is some error in the settings for the tool, or perhaps the training data was somehow missing any values above 0.9. Whatever the reason, this needs to be checked since it is an unexpected finding. (In this case, it turned out to be a "bug" in the limit code.)

The problem here is that the distributions of predicted values and actual values differ. Different distributions mean that the predictions are biased since, in an ideal model, the distributions of predicted and actual values will be identical. A quite reasonable way to check would be to compare histograms of the two distributions. However, the model checking techniques later in this section reveal distribution problems as well as other very useful information.

(See MIII:DB.12.8) It's also well worth the time to try to fit a curve to this type of plot, as shown in Figure 12.12. (The supplemental material in Chapter 11 describes a simple method of curve fitting.) The relationship should be linear, however much the points vary about the diagonal. The curve fitted should be very close to a straight line, although it almost certainly won't be perfect. Data mining tools should model nonlinearity very well, so the predicted/actual values relationship should be pretty much linear, with all of the nonlinearity accounted for in the model. If there is an evident curve that clearly fits the data better than the diagonal, it is an indication that the model is *underspecified,* which means not complex enough to capture the nonlinearity present. (An *overspecified* model captures too much complexity, so it

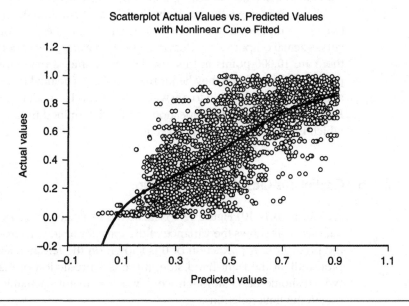

Figure 12.12   Actual versus Predicted values plot with fitted curve.

characterizes noise. For more detail about model specification see Section 12.2.4.) Remember that the fit may not be a perfect straight line not only because of random variation, but also because the model was fitted to the training data and all of these evaluations have to be made in the test data set. In Figure 12.12, the curve shown potentially had a great deal of flexibility and could have been very curved indeed—if the data warranted it. Except for the lower left portion, which is essentially out of the range of the plot, the curve appears to be quite close to a straight line; this shows that the model has done a good job of modeling any nonlinearity present in the input battery to output battery relationship. (As it turns out, in the data set used for this illustration, there happened to be a highly nonlinear relationship between the batteries, so the model has in fact done a good job of characterizing it.)

(See MIII:DB.12.9) Returning now to Figure 12.11, regardless of why the prediction range is truncated, the diagonal regression line shows that this model has characterized the relationships well. The ideal result would show that all of the predicted values were identical to the actual values. If that were the case, the XY plotted points would all fall exactly on the diagonal running from (predicted value, actual value) 0,0 to 1,1. The points themselves by no means fit this ideal, but the regression fitted to this predicted/actual plot line does fall almost exactly on this ideal. On the left of the plot, it passes almost exactly through the 0,0 point, and on the right, almost equally exactly through the 1,1 point. In addition, the slope of the linear regression line is very close to perfect, which would be a slope of 1:1. The number "1.03" in the regression equation below the plot title in Figure 12.11 indicates that for every change of 1 unit in Y, this line changes by 1.03 in X, which is indeed very close to 1:1.

Thus, on average, the model has pretty well captured the relationship between the input data set, as expressed in the plot here, of predicted value versus actual output value. But pretty well on average isn't perfect. Although there are 10,000 points in this test data set, some of them are very poor as predicted values since they lie far from the line. The final basic question that a miner needs to be able to answer is: how good a model can be expected? Part of the answer to that question can be determined from a variance plot, which is addressed in the next section.

12.1.6   Continuous Classifier Variance Plot

(See MIII:DB.12.10) Figure 12.13 shows the variance plot associated with this data set. This shows the variance of the error, or residual, across the range of the prediction. A prediction of 0 is shown on the left increasing across the plot until, at the right-hand side, there is a prediction of maximum value (which should be 1) although we now know that it's actually 0.9 due to the bug in the limit function).

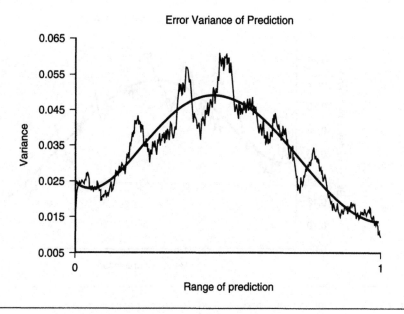

Figure 12.13   Actual and smoothed variance in residual across the range of the prediction.

Variance is a very straightforward measurement. It simply expresses how much the value of a group of values varies from the mean value of the group. In this case, the measurement is of how much the residual, or error, varies from the predicted value. In this case, it indicates the limits of confidence for any particular value of the prediction. (Showing confidence bands above and below the predicted value is another way of showing the same information, but is more difficult for a miner to generate. A spreadsheet program such as Excel can be easily used to create a variance plot—or almost any of the plots shown if they aren't available elsewhere—and can therefore be used as a basic mining technique.)

The curve shown fairly much speaks for itself. The variance is highest around the middle values of the prediction, and is lowest when the prediction is nearest to 1. Variance can be extremely useful in understanding the model's performance. However, Figure 12.14 shows what, on a cursory glance, may seem to be an almost identical plot. However, although the differences are small, for explaining model performance this plot may serve better than the previous one. This figure shows the standard deviation of the error over the range of the prediction.

Since we know (from Figure 12.9) that the distribution of the error term is very nearly normal, it is relatively easy to explain the "reliability" of the prediction from the properties of the standard deviation. For instance (and these figures can easily be found in a table describing the area under the standard

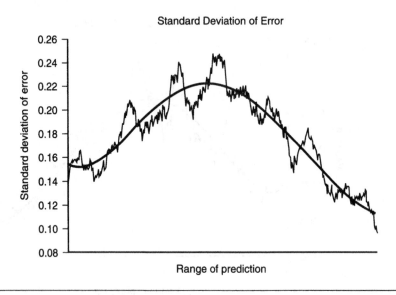

Figure 12.14   Actual and smoothed standard deviation of error in residual across the range of the prediction.

normal curve in any basic statistical text), since approximately 68% of the instances fall within ± one standard deviation of the mean, then in the worst case prediction (which seems to be a prediction of about 0.5), we know that 68% of the actual values will fall between about ±0.22 from the prediction value, so between $0.5 - 0.22 = 0.28$ and $0.5 + 0.22 = 0.72$. (The value of 0.22 is derived from the maximum height of the fitted curve in Figure 12.14.) Thus, it's fairly easy to determine that about 70% of the time, when this model predicts the value to be 0.5, the true value will lie between 0.28 and 0.72.

Similarly, for any point on the curve, the reliability of the prediction can be easily described in terms of how many of the actual values (as a percentage) can be expected to be within what distance of the predicted value.

12.1.7 Perfect Models

(See MIII:DB.12.11) Perfect models rarely, if ever, occur. Even very good models that are close to perfect are highly suspicious. Genuinely, justifiably perfect models are only likely when either the problem is utterly trivial and the relationship and predictions are obvious, or when leakage from anachronistic variables feeds information back from future to past. (See Chapters 9 and 10.) If any suspiciously good model turns up (that is, one that is far better than expected), it is worth checking very, very carefully to discover the nature and source of the error.

12.1.8 Summary of Classification Model Residual Checking

Looking at residuals and comparing them with actual and predicted values in the structured way described here are important. This is a diagnostic technique used to determine if there are problems with the data, and either with the modeling tool, with the model, or both. Although working through the explanations here may be time-consuming, and obtaining experience from many models may take time, with practice and experience, performing the diagnostic checks shown here is a quick and easy way to discover potential problems.

The miner uses residual error versus prediction plots to look for possible problems with the data, the model, or the modeling tool. Figure 12.15 illustrates an ideal distribution of residuals. The fitted regression line is nearly flat and fits at the zero point as well as possible. The residuals are uniform in amplitude and density across the whole plot. Figure 12.16 shows one result from an underspecified model. In this case, the model hasn't captured all of the nonlinearity present in the data set. Figure 12.17 shows a different underspecification problem. In this case, the amplitude of the residual increases as the prediction value increases. (It could also have decreased as the prediction value increased, or had some other identifiable pattern.) In this case, it is most likely that the model has insufficient flexibility to transform the nonlinearity in one or more of the input variables.

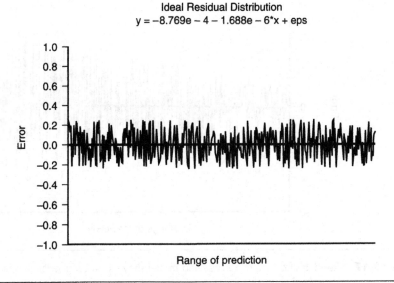

Figure 12.15   Example of ideal residual distribution.

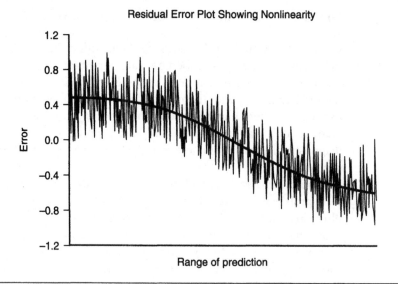

Figure 12.16 Residuals from an underspecified model showing nonlinearity.

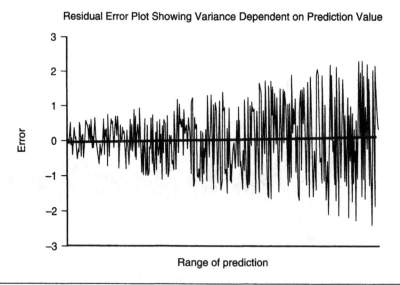

Figure 12.17 Residuals from an underspecified model showing residual error dependent on pre-dicted value.

In the example discussed in this section (an example which is taken from an actual engagement), it was quick and easy to discover a problem with the modeling tool used (Figure 12.11). It was also quick and easy to discover that an apparent bias between actual and predicted values was in fact introduced by the modeling tool and not, as had been suspected by the client, the result of a problem with the model itself (Figure 12.10). In addition, using Figures 12.13 or 12.14, the modeler is in a good position to begin to build an explanation of the performance of the model. Figures 12.7, 12.8 (which expands the explanation of 12.7), and 12.9 quickly demonstrated that the tool had built a robust model once the "shoulders" in Figure 12.7 had been explained.

In brief, looking at plots of residual values across the range of the prediction can be very illuminating to a miner, and are very helpful in getting the model right.

12.1.9 Improving Explanatory Models

Diagnosing problems with an explanatory model is, in a sense, much easier and less technically exact than with classification models. Essentially, either an explanatory model does provide a convincing, relevant, applicable explanation that serves to address the business problem, or it doesn't! If it does, no further diagnosis is needed—the model works. If it doesn't, that in itself is pretty much the diagnosis.

Given a diagnosis that the model performance needs improving, and that it is because the model is at fault and not the miner's ability to explain, several actions may well serve to improve the model's quality. (If it's the miner's inability to explain the problem, the techniques described in the next chapter on deployment should help.)

One major problem arises when the data doesn't seem to represent relationships of interest. Perhaps it actually doesn't. That's not a problem with the model, of course, but an indication that better data is needed. However, it often turns out that reformatting the data will reveal relationships that seemed hidden. (See Section 12.2.3.) Tools that display relationships, such as the SOM, are quite sensitive to distributional changes. (See Section 12.2.3.3) Other tools, such as SVCHAID, improve their explanatory power when business-relevant features are extracted from the data set. (See Section 11.2.1)

Sometimes the model seems to reveal nothing of interest. The possible conclusions derived from a model may be nothing but broad generalities that are hard to practically apply to the problem. On other occasions, a model might seem to deliver a host of trivial detail, but that very detail seems to obscure the interesting relationships as if in a froth of trivia. Either of these circumstances may be caused by having the model complexity, and its power to extract detail from the data, set either too low (in the case of overly general models) or too high (in the case of extremely detailed models). This ability of a model to capture detail is called its *specificity,* and when the model does not capture enough detail, it is called *underspecified.* When it captures only the froth of detail, the model is *overspecified.* Setting an appropriate level of specification is as important in an explanatory model as it is in a classificatory model. (See Section 12.2.4)

For explanatory models, it is very important that any important relationships be presented as clearly as possible. All that has to be done to completely obfuscate an explanation based on ordinal or categorical variable relationships is to assign inappropriate numbers to those categories. Inappropriate numeration of categorical values is a real problem when using explanatory tools that can only model numeric variables, like a SOM. However, the appropriate numeration of categories can retain clear explanations—a very important consideration when explaining categorical variable relationships. (See Section 12.2.3.2)

Sometimes it is convenient, or easier to understand, if categories are used to explain a relationship, even when the underlying variable is a continuous number. A process called *binning* turns continuous variables into categories. The important trick for explanatory models is to use meaningful categories rather than arbitrary ones that may hide meaningful structure. Sometimes the implicit structure of the data reveals meaningful bin structures in a numeric variable, although it is always preferable to use expert knowledge, if it's available, to create and label the bins. When relevant labels are applied to the bins, they can help clarify a relationship more than trying to describe the relationship numerically. (See Section 12.2.3.1) (See MIII:DB.12.14, MIII:TB.12.26, MIII:TB.12.27, MIII:TB.12.28)

12.2 Improving Model Quality, Solving Problems

Most of the rest of this chapter looks at how to address the problems that became apparent from the diagnostic tests described in Section 12.1. This section focuses on what changes might be made to improve the quality of the model given one or more problems revealed by the model diagnostics. Unless the model is justifiably perfect, one or more of the diagnostic checks will point to areas where the initial model can be improved. Even if the initial model seems not to have any particularly egregious problem revealed during diagnosis, it's probable that the model can still be improved by applying the techniques in this section. In fact, although these are presented as "solutions" to particular discovered problems, this section really introduces techniques for improving a model's quality. Thus, the techniques described in this section shouldn't be viewed as only a set of solutions to problems; these techniques should be employed in the pursuit of general good practices in basic data mining.

Improving the quality of a model means understanding what "quality" means in terms of a model. There are lots of different ways to characterize the quality of a model. Partly, of course, it depends on the type of model. As far as evaluating the quality of explanatory models goes, it's the quality of the explanation that counts. Based on the needs of the business problem, of course, judging the quality of an explanatory model is pretty much a subjective exercise. There are some useful guidelines for delivering the results of explanatory models to their greatest advantage, which allow a miner to make the most of what any explanatory model has to offer (these are discussed in Chapter 13). But the actual performance of the explanatory model is a qualitative, rather than a quantitative, assessment. If it works, it works. If not, it doesn't work.

However, the ability of classificatory models to address the business problem, which is still pretty much a qualitative issue, can be judged against each other on technical criteria. In addition to the diagnostic tests described in the previous section, it's useful to become familiar with understanding and interpreting any other quality measures provided by a mining tool. The fundamental diagnostic tests of a model's quality were discussed in Section 12.1—interpreting confusion matrices, XY plots of residuals, predicted values, actual values, and residual histograms. These are the fundamental and crucial determinants of model quality. If the quality measures provided by a mining tool leave any doubt about the nature of the problem, the real answer is to return to the diagnostic tests described in this chapter. These are powerful and useful precisely because they not only reveal problems, but also can be easily interpreted to reveal what needs to be done to improve the model. Many model quality measures provided by mining tools are useful, but only indicate model quality on some selected scale, giving no indication of what might be done to improve the model. The key to successful modeling is to use measures that both indicate quality and direct attention to what needs to be adjusted.

The remainder of this section expands on and explains the Catalyst methodology MIII for improving model quality. The Methodology sections of Part IV, through the use of the various discovery and action boxes, MIII explicitly links specific discoveries, or diagnoses, to specific possible problems, and the possible problems to specific actions and techniques for dealing with those problems. This section is intended to stand on its own, but its full richness and power can be appreciated only when it is used to supplement the methodology.

12.2.1 Problem: The Data Doesn't Support the Model

A miner might find that the input battery doesn't relate to the output battery—in other words, the data doesn't support the model needed. (See MIII:AB.12.2) This might be indicated when:

- There is no significant difference in naïve and mined model performance. (See MIII:DB.12.1)
- There is an almost flat regression line in predicted versus actual XY plot. (See MIII:DB.12.3)
- There are significant clusters present in the input battery with a high degree of separation between them. (See MIII:DB.12.13)

This is a perennial data mining problem. The data available to fill the input battery simply doesn't have any very useful relationship to the output battery. Given the input and output batteries, no data miner is going to get a very useful model if this is genuinely the situation. However, all is certainly not lost!

For one very important point, "No" is very often a good answer. For some reason, we have been trained to think of "no" as a bad answer. However, justified knowledge of the limits of a data set—to answer a question, to enable a decision, or to guide an action—is useful, not useless, to know. Discovering that a data set does not allow an answer, at least as presently posed, is useful information that can be used constructively to guide action, decisions, insight, and future activities. This mining-justified discovery of the limits to knowledge available in a data set is every bit as useful, in context, as would have been the justified representations of relevant relationships in data expressed as a mined model, had one been possible. It's useful in a different way, of course. The actions, decisions, insights, or activities are different than if a useful model had been generated. At the very least, such an answer may save the use of resources committed to a project on the basis of faulty or unfounded decisions not supported by the data. At best, it may provoke, or justify, collecting data that relates to the business problem of interest.

The best approach is to find more or different data—that is, data that hopefully holds the relationships of interest. (Chapter 7 in Part II discusses the issues of discovering data to mine, and that discussion is not reiterated here.) However, discovering that a data set does not contain any very useful relationships to the object of interest is a useful contribution of knowledge to the search for appropriate data. Part of the process of discovering data to mine requires creating a pool of candidate measurements. Discovering that a data set doesn't support the model of interest can contribute a great deal to the search for appropriate candidate measurements since it clearly shows measurements that need not be further considered. It may indeed show whole related areas that need not be pursued.

The "useless" data set may also provide clues as to what other data set may be worth investigating. The presence of such clues depends on the source of the supplied data set. The question is: was the mining data set generated from original source data, or from some secondary source? If from a secondary source, and the original data is available, it's not at all unlikely that going back to the original data and beginning again will turn up different, possibly better results. The problem is that secondary data, such as that from a data warehouse or from a standardized database, may well have had many of the interesting relationships removed inadvertently. This happens because data for, say, warehousing is cleaned, summarized, and prepared to suit the needs of the warehouse. As far as the warehouse is concerned, this is a necessary and useful contribution. However, preparing the data for the warehouse imposes business and other rules, normalizes data, and performs other adjustments needed from the viewpoint of what the warehouse is intended to support. Cleaned and prepared in this way, the data may no longer have its original relationships to the mining output battery intact. Although it may well be a lot of work, it is always possible that the original data may be of more value than the secondary source data.

As a final consideration, although by technical measures a model may seem of little use, "it ain't necessarily so!" The truth is that the credit card solicitation model is, by most technical criteria, pretty useless. The data set hardly supports a predictive model of any technical merit whatever. Nonetheless, for solving a business problem, it is a very good model. Even in its raw form, it seems to hold the promise of doubling the response rate, and it is no shabby model that can double a response rate! So however little improvement there seems to be, and however poor a model seems to be, technical criteria are not the only—and may not even be the most important—criteria by which to judge a model.

12.2.2 Problem: The Data Partially Doesn't Support the Model

Another possible problem is that the input battery doesn't sufficiently define the relationship to the output battery over all or part of the output range—in other words, the data doesn't support the model needed. (See MIII:AB.12.3) This might be indicated when the value of the smoothed residual variance estimate is so great over some or all of the plot as to make the predictions unsatisfactory. (See MIII:DB.12.10)

The issue here is that over some part of the output battery's range, the prediction is simply not accurate enough to provide the necessary level of confidence to use the model—at least, not when it makes predictions in the problematic part of the range. Depending on how much of the range is problematic, it is possible that some of the suggested remedies in the previous subsection (Section 12.2.1) might help. However, and more to the point, since most of the output range of the model is working sufficiently well, what is really needed is to improve the accuracy over the problematic part of the range.

Rather than rebuild the entire data set from scratch, it is worthwhile to work to discover additional data that better defines the relationship over the problematic part of its range. First, look in the existing data set itself. Careful explanatory modeling may reveal features in the input battery that, when introduced into the data set as dummy variables, do elucidate the relationship more clearly. (See Section 11.3 for explanatory modeling and feature extraction.)

Whether extracting features helps depends to some degree on which underlying algorithm the modeling tool uses. Different algorithms are sensitive to different types of patterns. Because this is the case, it's often helpful to combine the outputs of two different models, each generated by a different underlying algorithm. The way to do this is very straightforward. Build the best model with one tool supporting, say, a decision tree. Build the best model with identical input and output batteries with another tool supporting, say, a neural network. Take the two separate predictions, form them into a new input battery and, using the original output battery as the new output battery, build a third model that combines the predictions of the two original models. This method, illustrated in Figure 12.18, often results in a model with less variance than either of the original models. (See MIII:TB.12.1)

Another variant of the same technique may also help, even when using the same underlying algorithm in this case. Good practice may have excluded a large number of the variables in the input battery as redundant. (See, for example, Section 12.2.16) If this is the case, try constructing a separate model on the original output battery, but form the input battery entirely from the discarded variables from the original model's input battery. With the second model in hand, combine the two models as just described. These two models, even if constructed with the same tool, may show less variance than a single model constructed with all of the variables now in use.

12.2.3 Problem: Reformatting Data

A miner might find that the tool (algorithm) selected to make the model cannot deal with the data in the format provided. (See MIII:AB.12.4) This might be indicated when:

- There is no significant difference in naïve and mined model performance. (See MIII:DB.12.1)
- There is an almost flat regression line in predicted versus actual XY plot. (See MIII:DB.12.3)

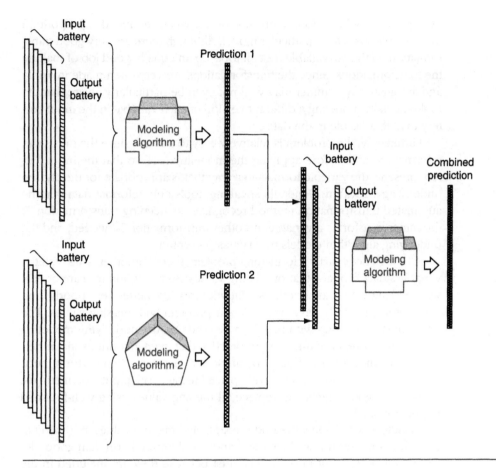

Figure 12.18 Combining two models.

- The "tails" (outer edges) of the distribution are smaller than the comparison normal curve shows should be expected. (See MIII:DB.12.5)
- The fitted curve differs markedly from a straight line where it passes through the data. (See MIII:DB.12.8)
- The value of the smoothed residual variance estimate is so great over some or all of the plot as to make the predictions unsatisfactory. (See MIII:DB.12.10)
- You discover that an explanation is not convincing, relevant, or applicable to the business problem. (See MIII:DB.12.14)

This is a problem that turns up more frequently than it should, given that most tools implement automated methods of transforming the variables of the input battery into a form more suitable for whatever underlying algorithm the miner chooses for a particular model. Although there are very good transformation methods available, not all tools do an equally good job of making the transformations. Since the transformations are very often made invisibly and automatically, a miner may well not even be particularly aware that the tool is actually modeling a different version of each variable in the input battery than that visible in the data set.

Fortunately, the problem is relatively easy to address since the miner can reformat the data before applying the modeling tool, so that the input battery presents the variable formats in a way that is appropriate for the chosen underlying algorithm. Generally speaking, tools only reformat data that the automated transformation method recognizes as needing transformation. If the miner transforms a variable, no other transformation is needed, and the underlying algorithm models the data as presented.

Although not exactly a formatting problem, there is another issue with the variable's data format—that of missing values. Some algorithms cannot deal with missing values at all; others deal with missing values very poorly; and yet others apparently have no particular problem with missing values. The importance of dealing with the issue depends on the underlying modeling algorithm. However, it turns out in practice that even algorithms that inherently aren't meant to be affected by missing values very often perform much better when the missing values are replaced using good imputation methods. Thus, it is a good practice to replace all missing values using well-founded imputation methods.

Most tools offer some method for replacing missing values, but many of these methods are not well-founded and can do more harm than good, despite their being built into the tool. Just because they are included in the tool does not mean that they work well! There are good methods of replacing missing values, but unless the tool actually incorporates well-founded methods, missing value imputation methods have to be applied to data sets outside the tool's environment, just as, in general, with the reformatting methods.

There are three basic techniques for reformatting data, plus the not-exactly-reformatting technique of replacing missing values:

- Binning
- Normalizing range
- Normalizing distribution

Apply these techniques with care, as they are not all equally applicable under all circumstances. This section looks at each technique in turn with guidelines for when each is most likely to be applicable.

12.2.3.1 Reformatting Data: Binning

(See MIII:TB.11.12) Mainly, binning is a very simple and straightforward technique for turning continuous variables into ordinal or categorical variables. It should be noted that ordinal and categorical variables could also sometimes be usefully binned. However, binning ordinal or categorical variables requires advanced binning tools and techniques, such as information-based binning, discussed later in this section. Numeric variables often have to be binned because tools often use underlying algorithms—decision trees and naïve Bayesian networks, for instance—that require the variables to be categorical or ordinal rather than numeric.

Binning is so called, perhaps, because when binning a variable, various subranges of values of the variable are all put together into a bin. Figure 12.19 illustrates the concept, using as an example a numeric variable measuring the temperature of coffee (in degrees Celsius.). The temperature of coffee ranges, say, from just below the freezing point of water to close to boiling. In daily conversation, we don't often discuss the temperature of coffee in terms of degrees of any temperature scale. Instead, we characterize the temperature in terms of classifications—such as iced, cold, warm, and hot—which have a generally accepted colloquial meaning and an understood subjective range of experience associated with each label. In the terms used here, this is a form of binning in which each of the categories is the bin label, and the upper and lower limits of the range of temperatures associated with each bin form what are called the *bin boundaries*. Of course, a mining tool doesn't care if the bin labels are arbitrary or meaningful, but it is good practice to make the labels as meaningful as possible.

The principle of binning is very straightforward, even intuitive. However, whenever any continuous variable is binned, it's very important to keep in mind that information is unavoidably lost in the binning process. All of the

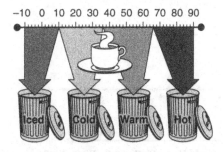

Figure 12.19 Binning numerical values.

separate values in any bin are treated as if they were identical. All information about the distribution of values across the range of the bin is lost. On the other hand, the lost information may be a worthwhile sacrifice in order to make the variable useable to a mining tool. And on some occasions, binning can actually remove more noise than useful information, especially if the binning is optimally done. This can sometimes result in better models, even for algorithms that could use the variables in their unbinned form. The problem is in the expression "if the binning is optimally done." Optimal binning is not necessarily straightforward.

The problem of deciding how to bin a variable is twofold: 1) discover how many bins to use, and 2) determine how best to assign values to each bin.

12.2.3.1.1   *Assigning Bin Boundaries*

(See MIII:TB.12.3, MIII:TB.12.31) One simple way to assign bin boundaries is to divide the range of the variable into a number of bins, and let each bin cover its appropriate fraction of the range. In Figure 12.20, there are 10 bins in total. Eight bins cover the range of the variable across its expected range, so each bin covers one-eighth (12.5%) of the entire expected range of the variable. At each extreme of the range is a bin that takes any values that fall outside the expected range of the variable. The too-large and too-small values often turn up in real-world data sets, and it's quite easy to put in a couple of catchall bins to hold any that are found. Although not shown in the figure, another bin is sometimes used for instances with missing values.

The bins in Figure 12.20 are shown across the ordered range of the variable with, say, least values on the left and greatest on the right. Each bin covers the same amount of the range of values of the variable as any other bin, and this binning arrangement is called *equal range binning*. This arrange-

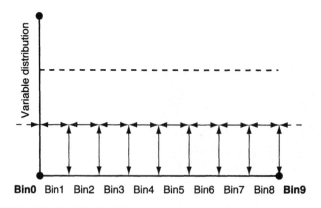

Figure 12.20   Equal range bins.

ment might work if the variables' values were distributed fairly evenly across the range of the variable, as indicated by the dashed horizontal line representing the distribution. However, most variables don't have particularly uniform distributions.

Figure 12.21 illustrates a nonuniform distribution that approximates a normal distribution. Here it's easy to see that most of the values cluster around the mean value, which is indicated by the peak of the dashed line. If equal range binning were used in this circumstance, it's easy to see that the bins around the mean would contain most of the instances, and the bins at the extremes would have very few. In the absence of any specific reason to use some other arrangement, it's been found most generally useful to have bins with fairly equal numbers of instances in each, so the bin boundaries illustrated in Figure 12.21 are adjusted to evenly balance the bin contents. This arrangement, not surprisingly, is called *equal frequency binning* since the bin boundaries are arranged so that, as much as possible, all the bins have a similar number of instances in them.

However, it's hard to know how many bins to have under either of these arrangements. Exactly where the optimum number lies is very hard to determine. Starting with 20–30 usually seems to work well. The key is to have enough bin categories so that the mining tool can develop a sufficient complexity of patterns in the input battery to map to the output battery. Experimenting with adjusting the bin count and boundaries often helps with these simple binning strategies.

These are basic and fairly common methods of binning. Given a number of bins, it's fairly easy to arrange the boundaries automatically, and equal frequency is the binning method to try first. The number of bins in the input battery needs to be partly determined by the desired resolution of the output battery—more resolution calls for more bins. Binning the output battery,

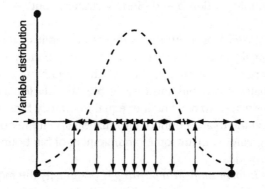

Figure 12.21   Equal frequency bins.

if needed, has to be driven by the needs of the business problem determined by the desired degree of resolution. In general, with the simple binning methods, the input battery variables should start with approximately as many bins as the output battery if the output battery is itself binned. If the output battery is left as a continuous variable, try 20 or 30 equal-frequency bins.

These are two common, simple binning methods, and although they are not optimal, mining tools usually offer at least these methods and sometimes only these methods. Or, more appropriately put, there is no justification to think that any particular arrangement of equal range, or equal frequency, bins will turn out to be optimal. Many mining tools that offer alternative binning methods often implement binning strategies that, although more complex and far less straightforward than these simple methods, are also not necessarily optimal. However, there are methods of achieving binning strategies that are nearer to optimal.

12.2.3.1.2 *Information-Based Binning*

The simple binning strategies just discussed are unsupervised strategies. That is to say, any binning of a variable is made without any reference to any other variables at all, including those in the output battery. Since a classificatory model has an output battery, it is possible to use the output battery to direct the binning of the input battery so that the binning reveals the maximum amount of information about the output battery. This, of course, would be a supervised binning strategy. Potentially, it can do a better job than the simple binning strategies since it uses information from both the input battery variable and the output battery.

Information content in variables can be measured according to the underlying theory called *information theory*. It is possible to create a binning strategy using information theory that retains in one variable the maximum amount of information about another variable. There are several ways of implementing an information-based binning strategy, but two are particularly useful.

Least information loss binning, as the name implies, creates bin boundaries that optimally retain information in the input battery variable that describes the output battery variable. This method retains any ordering present in the input battery variable and creates bin boundaries accordingly. The boundaries are placed to have neither equal frequency bins nor equal range bins, but so that the total amount of information about the output variable in all the bins is greater than any other arrangement of bin boundaries, or number of bins, provides.

Maximum information gain binning is potentially the most powerful information-based binning strategy. This is another supervised binning strategy, but in this case, the ordering of the input variable is not necessarily maintained, and input battery variable values are mapped into bins so that maximum information is gained about the output battery. For maximum information gain binning to work, it is crucial to have a data set that is fully representative of the actual distribution to be modeled. Without it, this binning strategy will produce garbage. Surprisingly, it is not always possible to represent the distribution of a population, however large the sample size. For an explanation of this, see Section 13.2.

These are very powerful binning strategies, but their practical implementation requires a high degree of complexity and calculation. This is easy for a computer, but totally impractical as a humanly applied technique. Optimal binning can be crucial in deriving a good model from a data set. Unfortunately, very few mining tools offer any very sophisticated binning strategies, let alone optimal ones. Because binning is so important to building good models, on the author's Web site there is available a binning tool that will address a data set and determine the appropriate bin boundaries using several binning strategies, including those described here. Once the binning tool has discovered the bin boundaries, it's easy to set them in any mining tool that allows custom bins to be created. For readers who do not have easy access to adjust manual bin boundaries, the binning tool will also write out a binned version of any variable, or set of variables, so the miner can incorporate them into the input battery. This should allow any reader of this book with access to the Internet to experiment with different binning strategies and to discover the power, importance, and effectiveness of optimal binning. (See MIII:TB.12.32, MIII:TB.12.33)

12.2.3.2 Reformatting Data: Normalizing Ranges

Some algorithms, most notably neural networks, are highly restricted in the range of values to which they are sensitive. Many of the most popular types of neural networks require a numeric input range, including values either from -1 to $+1$ or from 0 to 1. For any tool implementing one of these algorithms, there's no problem whatsoever in modifying the input range of a numeric variable to match the needs of the algorithm. The tool simply scans the input battery, determines the maximum and minimum values present for all numeric variables, and rescales the input values appropriately. However, any algorithm that requires all numeric input has to deal somewhat differently with categorical or ordinal variables.

As an example, consider days of the week. Chapter 9 discussed recoding cyclic variables, so a reader who has already read that chapter will realize that a weekly cycle requires coding into two variables with values; Figure 12.22 shows them as V1 and V2. However, days of the week actually occur sequentially, one after the other from, say, Sunday through Saturday. This naturally occurring sequence of days can be numbered as, for the sake of this example, 1–7, and shown in the column headed "Seq."

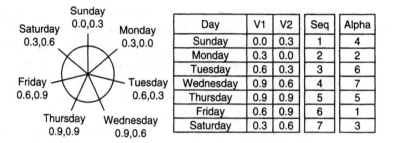

Figure 12.22 Coding days of the week.

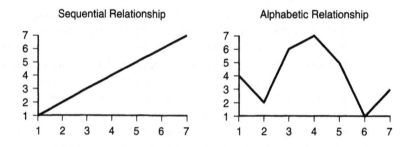

Figure 12.23 Different relationships for different day of week codings.

(See MIII:AB.9.8) When the underlying algorithm of a mining tool can take variables only in the form of numbers, it is necessary to recode any categorical or ordinal values numerically to represent either a sequence or a cycle as needed. (Miner-executed recoding is discussed in Chapter 9.) One common practice, and one that some mining tools adopt in automated conversion of categorical variables into a numeric representation, is to simply assign numbers to categories as they are encountered in a data set. For the sake of this example, the figure shows such a numeric assignment to the categories of day values based on their alphabetical order. This numeric assignment is shown in the column headed "Alpha" in Figure 12.22. But note that this assignment imposes an implied order on the categories. In this case, the implied order imposed doesn't match the naturally occurring sequence. (There is no reason to suppose that assigning numbers to categories in the order that they are encountered in a data set will match any naturally occurring sequence either.) Figure 12.23 shows that if the natural sequence were appropriately matched, the relationship between natural sequence and assigned order would be as shown in the graph on the left. However, the arbitrary alphabetic assignment results in a relationship between the natural sequence and the assigned sequence shown in the graph on the right. This assignment produces what seems to be a complex, and certainly a nonlinear, relationship between the natural sequence and the assigned values. Since the natural sequence is the one that occurs in the real world, it is important to represent that sequential information to the model—and as simply as possible.

For the few categories used in this example, the relationship is not terribly complex, and it would be quite easy for any mining tool to discover and characterize it. However, when the number of categories rises, say when using SKUs (stock keeping units) or ZIP codes, any natural ordering that exists in the real world can be made so inaccessible to a mining tool that it becomes impossible to discover any useable relationship.

The first point for any miner to note is that whenever there is a need to convert categorical and ordinal—particularly ordinal—variables to numerical representations, it is very important to discover if there is a naturally occurring order or sequence for the categories, and to distribute the categories in their appropriate locations in the range of the numeric representation. As is often the case when dealing with data, the rule is: "wherever possible, look it up or dig it up rather than make it up."

This issue of discovering an appropriate ordering is obviously pretty important to the quality of the resulting model. Yet what is to be done for categorical and ordinal variables when there is no apparent rationale for assigning numerical values?

A data set as a whole incorporates many patterns and relationships among its variables. If a categorical variable actually does have a naturally occurring order, as is always the case for an ordinal variable, this relationship is incorporated into the structure of the relationships embodied in the data set. It may be complex and nonobvious on inspection, but it will nonetheless still be present. Although hard for a miner, it is relatively easy for an automated tool to discover any ordinal relationship for any categorical variable in a data set, and to derive appropriate numerical labels for each category.

Assigning appropriate numerical labels, if this can be done, is far better than using an automated discovery of numerical labels. Adding appropriate numerical labels actually adds information to a data set. When this can't be done, the automated assignment, although it doesn't actually add any information to the data set, at least doesn't add erroneous information, which arbitrary assignment of numbers to labels almost certainly does. The arbitrary assignment simply adds noise to a data set and may well hamper a tool's ability to discover and characterize the important and meaningful relationships that do exist. Automated discovery of appropriate numerical labels at least avoids the possibility of actively adding garbage!

Replacing arbitrary numeric assignment of category values with those reflected out of a data set can considerably improve a model created by an algorithm requiring all numeric representation. However, although easily accomplished, very few tools are capable of discovering, let alone assigning, appropriate numeration to categories. Thus, as with binning, and for all the same reasons, the author has made a category numerating tool available on the author's Web site. (See MIII:TB.12.4)

12.2.3.3 Reformatting Data: Normalizing Distribution

The distribution of a variable describes the way that the variable's values spread themselves through the range of the variable. Some distributions are fairly familiar, such as what is known as the *normal distribution,* shown earlier in Figure 12.21. In a normal distribution, the greatest number of values occurs clustered around the mean (or average) of the distribution, with far fewer values falling at the extremes. However, it's not only numeric variables that have a distribution. Ordinal and categorical variables also have values, although they aren't numeric values, and the values usually occur with frequencies different from each other. An easy way to represent such a distribution is with a histogram, each column representing the number of instances in each class.

In spite of the similarity in name, normalizing a distribution isn't necessarily the process of making the distribution more like a normal distribution. Rather, the term means regularizing or standardizing a distribution in some way. It is possible, although very unusual, to normalize categorical or ordinal distributions, although to some extent that is what is going on if one of the more advanced binning techniques is applied to such variables. Usually, it's only numerical variables that have their distributions normalized, and in this discussion, distribution normalization is confined to numeric variables.

Equal frequency binning works as well as it does in part because it is a distribution normalizing technique. Consider that any algorithm regards each of the bins as just as significant as any other bin. However, in equal frequency binning, each bin is arranged so that it contains the same number of instances as any other bin, at least insofar as it's possible to do so. This has redistributed the values in the variable so that they are uniformly spread across the range of the variable. To be sure, there are fewer values, only one value for each bin, but each bin value occurs as often as any other bin value, so the distribution is as close to uniform as this binning metric can get it. Thus, one strategy for normalizing a distribution that can work quite well is to use equal frequency binning with a high bin count (say 101 bins), and assign each bin a value a uniform increment apart. If the chosen bin value ranges from 0 to 1, the bins would be assigned values of 0, 0.01, 0,02, 0.03 . . . 0.98, 0.99, 1.00. This strategy normalizes both the range and the distribution, of course. To normalize just the distribution, assign each bin the mean value of the instances in the bin.

Note that it is also possible to continuously remap any numeric distribution so that it is uniformly distributed across its range. "Continuous" means that there are no bins and each value is uniquely mapped to some other unique value, rather than mapped to a bin value shared by several adjoining values. Such a continuous remapping allows every different value in a distribution to participate in contributing to the model, and retains all of the information that a variable has to offer. Binning always necessitates loss of information since, as already noted, all of the values in a bin, no matter how different they are from each other, are all assigned the same bin value. Few, if any, mining tools incorporate continuous distribution normalization, so the author has included a tool that will perform continuous remapping of numeric variables with the binning tool mentioned earlier in this section.

12.2.3.3.1   *Why Does Distribution Normalization Work?*

Consider an extreme case of skew in a distribution. Think of the series of numbers 1, 2, 3, 4, 5, 6, 7, 8, 9, 1000. This series ranges from 1 to 1000. However, almost all of the values fall in only 1% of this range. The value 1000 is called an *outlier* since it lies far from the bulk of other values in the series. For this example, it is a rather extreme outlier, but it may be quite impossible to say that it is an error of any sort or even an erroneous value. Quite justifiably, this might be a perfectly valid entry. For an example of a real-world situation in which such extremes occur, consider insurance claims, where most are for very small amounts but a few are huge. Or think of legal settlements. Now consider the problem for a numerical mining algorithm. In order to span the range, it has to encompass values from 1 to 1000, yet almost all of the values are to all intents and purposes indistinguishable from each other. If these values were binned using a 101-bin equal-range strategy, one bin at one end of the range would contain all but one of the values in it, 99 of the bins would be totally empty, and one bin at the other extreme of the range would contain one instance. The mining algorithm would see only two values! (This, of course, is why equal frequency binning is preferred since it wouldn't have this problem.)

Without binning or some other redistribution strategy, almost all numerically sensitive algorithms, when presented with this range of values, would have to scale their inputs such that this actual distribution would be indistinguishable from a data set containing only two values. This means that any information carried by the values 1 through 9 would be effectively lost.

Intuitively, the problem is similar, although by no means as severe, whenever a distribution has some values that group together, even when the grouping is fairly benign, such as that of the normal distribution. It takes at least a great deal more complexity in any model to deal with clumping in distributions, and more complex models are far more prone to learn noise rather than the desired relationships, take longer to train, and are more difficult to understand than simpler models. So although it may be theoretically possible for a mining tool to deal with almost any distribution problem, in practice, in order to make the tool sufficiently noise-resistant, the complexity has to be limited—and so is its ability to deal with clumps and bumps in a distribution.

For such distributions as the example used here, either high-bin count, equal-frequency unsupervised binning, continuous remapping, or supervised binning handily finesses the problem by producing a variable with a distribution from which any mining tool can extract the maximum information.

12.2.3.3.2 Distribution Normalization in Explanatory Models

Distribution normalization can play a very important role in improving the performance of classificatory models. However, it can play an even more important role in building explanatory models, particularly when using clustering, and especially when using visually based clustering tools, such as the SOM tool illustrated in the previous chapter.

The problem is that when the range is broad, but most of the values are packed into some small part of the range, a couple of things seem to happen on a map. First, since color represents value, almost all of the values are represented by a single hue. Second, since at least one of the extremes has very few values, the map seems to show an almost uniform hue, as if the variable had only a single value for the vast majority of the instances. Thus, meaningful patterns that might well actually exist are effectively invisible.

Figure 12.24 illustrates a variable that has a highly concentrated cluster of values with an extreme outlier. The linear, or unmodified, distribution can be seen in the left-hand histogram, showing that almost all of the 30,000 instances have values of less than 50 but at least 1, although certainly very few, instances have a value of over 12,000. When mapped or clustered, this appears to show a binary variable with, as far as can be determined visually, all of the instances having a single value. Redistributing the values as shown in the right-hand histogram spreads the values that are present across the displayable range, and makes any patterns present far easier to see. (See MIII:TB.12.5)

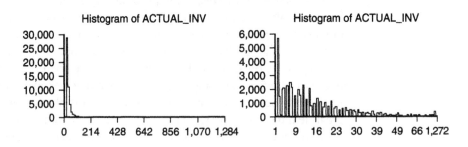

Figure 12.24 Redistributing variable values.

12.2.3.4 Reformatting Data: Replacing Missing Values

Replacing missing values doesn't change the format of the data. However, it's necessary in some cases, and always worthwhile, for a number of reasons. For those algorithms that cannot deal with missing values, something has to be done—the miner has no choice. Some tools automatically ignore the whole instance, and all of the values it contains, if one of them is missing. In many real-world data sets, this can make some otherwise perfectly useable data sets totally unmineable as almost every instance has one value or another missing. Even for those mining algorithms that can inherently deal with missing values, empirical evidence suggests that replacing missing values with well-founded imputed values turns out to improve the quality of the resulting model. The problem, of course, is in the phrase "well-founded imputed values." It turns out that many of the missing value replacement options offered by many mining tools are actually damaging to a data set in that they add spurious relationships, obscure existing relationships, and generally reduce model quality, sometimes quite severely. How does this happen?

In almost all data sets, values are not missing at random. To see that this is so in at least one real-world data set, think back to the Missing Value Check Model created at the beginning of the last chapter (see Section 11.2.2). This is a model that is built on a data set that within the input battery, contains only and exclusively within the input battery a characterization of which values are missing and which values are present. The fact that many of the input battery variables had interesting relationships with the output battery with only a missing/present flag indicates that the values weren't simply missing at random. Random occurrences do not form consistent patterns, and these are consistent patterns. Of course, the fact that it holds true in this one data set is merely anecdotal evidence that missing values are not missing at random, and is only evidence that this is true in this case. However, experience shows that in far and away the majority of cases, values turn out not to be missing at random in most data sets with missing values.

Note that if it is indeed true that values are not missing at random, they must be missing with some regularity, or pattern. Replacing missing values with any constant value, exactly as was done in the MVCM, will reveal that pattern. Now this isn't in itself a bad thing since it may very well be that those patterns need to be explicated, which is why the MVCM technique calls for adding a variable describing any useful discovered relationship. The problem is how replacing missing values affects the other patterns in the data set.

Notice that all the talk about patterns in data sets comes down to this: there is a relationship between the values that any one variable takes in any particular instance, and the values that the other variables in the same instance take. Some of these relationships might be "tighter" than others in the sense that for some variables, when one takes on certain values in an instance, it pretty much constrains another variable in the same instance to have values in a narrow range. Some relationships might be "looser" in the sense that, when one variable takes on certain values, another might have values that still tend to range around a fair amount. But whatever the constraints on the ranges of values, a model describes no more than what the ranges are and how tight the coupling is among all of the variables in the input battery, and how those relate to similar relationships in the output battery. The key here is that, to a greater or lesser extent, all of the variables change their values together and in lockstep. Whatever the patterns are, a good model needs to characterize them as clearly and accurately as possible.

It is, regrettably, a very common practice to replace missing values with some constant value, such as the mean of a numeric variable or the most frequent category of a categorical. Many tools offer this as the only missing value replacement method. What happens to the data set's relationships if some constant value is used as a replacement for a missing value?

Since there is a pattern to the way that variables' values occur in an instance, it's obvious that the pattern implies that any one variable's value is related at least somewhat to the values in the other variables. Given that such a relationship between variable values—a pattern—exists, when one value is missing any replacement value has to take account of the other nonmissing values and find a replacement value that best fits the existing pattern so as not to add to, modify, distort, or damage it. There can be no generally good, single value that will serve in all cases. The ideal value to plug in when one is missing has to be whatever value turns out to best match the values that are present, given the relationships that exist between them. However, if some inappropriate value is used instead, the modeling tool has no choice but to incorporate that inappropriate value as a true part of the actual pattern.

Note what occurs as a result of replacing any single value. The missing value pattern discovered with the MVCM in a given variable is not a part of the interrelated pattern of that variable to the other variables. The MVCM type of relationship is a separate relationship that needs to be described separately, which is why good practices call for it to be added as a separate variable. But the first thing that any constant value replacement does is to co-mingle two patterns in one variable—one is the pattern defined by the interrelationships with other variable values, and the other is the MVCP-type pattern.

The second effect of using a constant value replacement is to confuse any modeling tool into thinking that a variable actually takes on specific values in relationship to all the other values when, in fact, no such relationship can possibly be justified. There is actually no reason to suppose that the replacement value is the one that would have existed had the value not been missing, and, in fact, based on the other variables' values, most of the time there's good reason to think that whatever fixed value is used is wrong!

In summary—and just considering these two effects alone, which are quite bad enough—adding any constant value as a replacement for missing values overlays the actual pattern that exists with another pattern that exists, and then additionally distorts the first pattern by specifying that the variable's relationship behaves in ways that it actually doesn't. In short, missing value replacement with a constant value can utterly destroy some relationships that do exist, hide others, and make yet others inaccessible.

It should hardly be a surprise that inappropriate missing value replacement very often does more harm than good, and always—*always*—reduces the quality of the best possible model. The best possible model from the damaged data set simply isn't as good as the best possible model from the same data set with well-founded and appropriately imputed missing value replacements.

So what should the miner do? Well, part of the answer, of course, is already accomplished, since the best practice of creating a separate variable where necessary with the MVCM retains one pattern in the data set without co-mingling, and consequent obfuscation, of the two patterns just mentioned.

The other part of the answer is not to use any constant value as a replacement for missing values. The answer—the only answer that does not damage data for mining—is to use a value that takes account of all the values that are present in a given instance. In fact, there are a number of methods that work well, some more complex and theoretically well-founded than others. These go by such grandiose names as "maximum likelihood missing value estimation" and "covariate imputation." However, in practice, which one is used seems to make little difference to the final result. The difficulty, of course, is that once again, replacement of missing values is most easily accomplished by automated tools as it is impractical to manually make the necessary calculations to build the replacement algorithm. Therefore, the author has made available a missing value replacement tool on the supporting Web site so that the reader can explore the benefits from a good practice (that is, well-founded missing value imputation when the reader's tool of choice doesn't support it), or simply view the effect of different imputation strategies. The tool will replace missing values and provide a dynamic missing value algorithm developed from the training data for use at run-time. (See MIII:TB.12.6)

12.2.4   Problem: Respecifying the Algorithm

One of the possible problems a miner might face is that the model wasn't able to characterize the relationships from the input battery to the output battery adequately. (See MIII:AB.12.5) This might be indicated when:

- There is no significant difference in naïve and mined model performance. (See MIII:DB.12.1)

- The residuals appear to contain information that could be used to improve the prediction. (See MIII:DB.12.2)

- The regression line fitted to the actual value versus residual XY plot is not horizontal. (See MIII:DB.12.6)

- The value of the smoothed residual variance estimate is so great over some or all of the plot as to make the predictions unsatisfactory. (See MIII:DB.12.10)

- You discover that an explanation is not convincing, relevant, or applicable to the business problem. (See MIII:DB.12.14)

The viewpoint here is that the difficulty in improving model performance may not necessarily lie with the data, but in the capabilities of the mining algorithm and the way it has been specified. Recall that an underspecified model is one in which the constraints on the algorithm were such that it didn't have enough flexibility to properly characterize the relationships in the data. An overspecified model is one that has so much flexibility that it captured not only the underlying relationships, but a lot of junk too. As with the tale of Goldilocks and the three bears, the amount of specification that's needed is "j-u-s-t r-i-g-h-t!" How is just right to be determined? The answer lies with the training and test data sets.

As a reminder, the object of modeling is to create the best model possible in the training data set that works best in the test data set: build in training, apply in test. If the model performs about equally in both training and test data sets, then it may—*may*—be underspecified since it's possible that it hasn't yet fully characterized the noise-free relationships. If the model performs far better in the training data set than in the test data set, then the model is overspecified since, so long as the data sets are properly representative, it has obviously learned noise that exists in the training data set but not in the test data set.

The answer to determining when the model is well-specified—not too much, not too little, but "j-u-s-t r-i-g-h-t"—is to keep improving the model until it is just overspecified, and use the immediately previous iteration just before overspecification set in. In other words, keep building more specific models in the training data set all the time the improved models do better in the test data set. Regardless of performance in the training data set, as soon as a model returns worse results in the test data set than a previous iteration of the model, use the previous iteration as the final specification level for the model.

It's well worth noting that the iterations are needed for each diagnostic test. The problem is that, strictly speaking, the diagnostic symptoms are not independent. For instance, however appropriately specified a model is under one set of circumstances, any change in, say, the data set required to improve performance on another diagnostic test will affect the model's specificity. This implies that any change in any of the model parameters requires a total re-calibration of all the others, thus leading to an almost endless improvement process. The practice is not so tough. Improving model performance in any one of the diagnostic areas does not usually have any dramatically detrimental impact on the other areas. (See MIII:DB.12.12)

Each mining tool features a different set of knobs to twiddle to adjust the algorithm in use, even when the different mining tools employ the same basic algorithm. So although the particulars of what has to be done varies from tool to tool (and even sometimes from release to release of the same tool), what can be done with each mining algorithm incorporated in each tool is, in general, fairly easy to describe. In some tool sets, the knobs that a miner could twiddle to tune the algorithm are completely removed, in which case there's nothing to be done to adjust the algorithm. There are still some options to try. You could use a different algorithm, in the case of a multi-algorithm tool set, or you could try a different tool. As a general good practice, it is always worth having more than one algorithm to try on a data set. Just as there is no one right answer to most problems, there is no one right mining tool, nor one right mining algorithm, for all data sets and all problems.

This section next looks at the knobs that are available to generically adjust each algorithm, and presents them algorithm by algorithm. Note that the discussion here assumes that the algorithms are wrapped in tools that have eliminated most of the complexity that is involved in applying the raw algorithm to any data set. The techniques discussed here cover only those adjustments that tool vendors often provide to allow for tuning of different algorithms. But this discussion covers only algorithms as they are embedded in tools. This section does not cover tuning and adjusting the various raw algorithms, which is a far more complex process than covered here.

Just as a reminder, don't necessarily expect to find controls in each tool that allow a miner to make these adjustments. On the other hand, this discussion does not cover all of the possible adjustments that could possibly be made to each algorithm, just the more popular ones. Some vendors offer more knobs, some vendors less, some none at all. The vendors' problem is how much complexity to expose; the miners' is how much flexibility is available. To discover what any individual tool offers, it's important to read the documentation and work with the help screens for each tool. Each algorithm is discussed here in the same order that they were introduced in Chapter 10. (See MIII:AB.12.17)

12.2.4.1 Algorithm Adjustment: Nearest Neighbor or Memory-Based Reasoning

Nearest neighbor algorithms offer only two types of basic adjustment: the number of neighbors to be considered, and the method of determining the estimated value.

Adjusting the number of neighbors is fairly straightforward. The algorithm is sometimes known as k-nearest neighbor, where k stands for the number of neighbors. So one of the controls offered is sometimes simply called "k," assuming that the miner knows what it means.

Increasing k tends to make the model more resistant to noise, and therefore less sensitive to learning nuance. If the model seems underspecified, try reducing k so that the model is more sensitive. If the model seems overspecified, try increasing k. All that is happening here is that with more neighbors in consideration, the estimated result is being averaged over a larger group; with fewer neighbors, it's averaged over a smaller group.

Ignoring for the moment the effect of the size of the group, the estimated value is determined by looking at the output battery values for each of the k neighbors and taking an average of them all as the estimate. In this basic method, all neighbors contribute equally to the final result. Alternatively, weight the value of each neighbor according to its distance from the instance to be estimated. With such a weighting mechanism, more distant neighbors have less effect on the estimated value than nearer ones. In general, with all neighbors equally weighted—using a simple mean—the algorithm is less sensitive than when using distance weighting. Thus, as far as neighbor weighting is concerned, if the model is underspecified, try using a distance-weighted estimate. If the model is overspecified, use equally weighted (or unweighted) estimates. (See MIII:TB.12.7)

12.2.4.2 Algorithm Adjustment: Decision Trees

Decision trees split individual variables into leaves. At each leaf, the decision tree selects the best variable to split that leaf from all of the available variables. The root covers the whole data set. At the first split, the smallest leaf cannot cover more than 50% of the instances in a data set, and may cover less than 50%. (Consider that if the tree makes binary splits, an equal split between the leaves would be 50/50, and it probably would not be equally balanced. A nonbinary split tree [like the SVCHAID] would have the smallest leaf cover considerably less than 50%.) At the split on the first-level leaf, the smallest next leaf can cover no more than 25% of the instances. Thus at each level of splitting, each leaf covers a smaller and smaller amount of the data set. Eventually the number of instances covered by any leaf becomes so small that it isn't representative of the population, and the leaves at that point are only characterizing noise.

It's an odd difference between real trees and decision trees: whereas real trees have their roots in the ground and their leaves in the air, a decision tree has its root in the air (or at least, at the top) and its leaves in the ground (or at least, at the bottom). In general, the higher up a decision tree that a leaf is located—that is, the nearer to the root—the more general it is. The further from the root that a leaf is located, the more specific (i.e., nongeneral) it is. Thus, one way to prevent trees from learning noise is to set some minimum amount of instances that a leaf must contain. If that limit is set too high, the tree will be underspecified. If the limit is set too low, the tree will be overspecified.

There are other metrics that stop trees growing in some algorithms, such as how significant each split is, with a tree not splitting below some chosen level of significance. However, all of the methods prevent the tree from growing trivial leaves that only represent noise. Some tree tools allow the miner to select leaves to merge. This allows a miner to not only steer tree growth, but also to some extent incorporate domain knowledge into the tree structure through this type of guidance. Tree tools offering this feature should be looked on more favorably than those that don't.

Whatever technique is used to adjust the specificity of decision trees, it amounts in the end to having as many leaves as possible that contain enough instances to be representative of the underlying relationships in a data set. Too few leaves, or in other words, leaves with large numbers of instances, and the tree is underspecified since it can only represent at best the main trends and no detail of the relationships. Too many leaves, or in other words, leaves with few instances, and the tree is overspecified since it then represents too great a level of detail. The key here is to have as many representative leaves as possible so that all of the detail is captured, and to ensure that they are all truly representative to make certain that they represent real relationships, not noise.

12.2.4.2.1   *Selecting Root Splits*

Decision trees choose to split each leaf on the variable that the tree algorithm determines as providing the best split. This applies to the root just as much as to the other leaves. The SVCHAID tree algorithm used earlier can show a list of variables ranked by the order in which the tree algorithm would choose each variable to split the root (or any other leaf if desired). (See, for instance, Figure 12.4 or 12.5.) It is sometimes the case that a better-specified tree results if the second or third choice variable is chosen to split the root. It's important not to remove any variables from consideration for the other leaves, so the first or second choice candidate variables have to remain in the data set for other leaves to be split on those variables. Thus, simply removing the variable on which the initial tree split the root from the input battery is not suggested here—just change the variable that is allowed to split the root. (Not all tree tools implement this important feature, so when using some tools, the miner may not be able to steer the tree growth in this way. Trees without this feature are of extremely limited value to a miner, and should, if possible, be avoided.)

Empirically, the reason that better-specified trees result from not using the "best" split of the root is that it rearranges the tree so that the later leaves are more appropriately split and are more resistant to learning noise. Do note that a totally different tree is very likely to result from using a different variable to split the root. Recall that there is no one "proper" explanation of a data set, and there is no "correct" model of a data set. Left to its own devices, a tree will produce an explanation or model, but this is not to be regarded as the only one, nor even necessarily the best one. The best one is the one that most appropriately meets the modeler's/miner's needs—and that may not be what the tree algorithm wants to produce when left to itself.

In this case, what's needed is the best specified tree, and the controls that need twiddling are leaf size and root split. (See MIII:TB.12.8)

12.2.4.3 Algorithm Adjustment: Rule Extraction

Among the features of rules, there are three that are important to specification:

1. They cover some number of instances.
2. They have some probability of being true.
3. Each rule has a level of complexity depending on how many conditions can be included in each rule.

All three of these features can be adjusted to change the specificity of the model.

Rules are required to cover some minimum number of instances in the data set. If the rules are required to cover more instances, then this will result in generating less specific rules. Contra wise, the fewer instances required as a minimum for a rule to apply to (cover), the more specific the rule.

Rules will almost certainly not be perfect. In almost all cases, there will be exceptions and counter-examples to any general rule. (These exceptions also can be very interesting in explaining a data set.) The number of instances in which the rule is correct, divided by the number of instances to which the rule applies, correct or not, gives the accuracy (also sometimes called *probability level* or *confidence level*) of a rule. Requiring a higher minimum level of accuracy produces more general models; lowering the required minimum accuracy increases specificity.

Rules can be constructed from multiple conditions. The conditions are the "if" part of the rule. Each additional condition can be joined by logical connections such as "If . . . and . . . and . . . then . . ." This rule has three conditions. Some rule extractors—by no means all—can incorporate other logical connectors such as "or" and "not." The more conditions allowed in a rule, the more specific the rule becomes; the fewer conditions permitted, the more general the rule. Similarly, allowing more variety of logical connectors enables the resulting rules to be more specific; less variety restricts the specificity. (See MIII:TB.12.9)

12.2.4.4 Algorithm Adjustment: Clustering

There are many different algorithms that perform unsupervised clustering; there are also many that perform supervised clustering. They do not work in the same manner, and so each particular algorithm will almost certainly produce a very different set of clusters from the other clustering algorithms. However, and very usefully for the miner, regardless of the very considerable technical differences, the "knobs" appear much the same for all clustering techniques.

Clustering algorithms offer essentially two adjustments. One is the number of clusters specified by the miner. It's very common that the algorithm requires the miner to select some number of clusters for the algorithm to use to cluster the data. A "good" number of clusters may not be apparent from any well-founded basis, even to a highly experienced miner. It's rather like simple binning—work with clustering, and discover what seems to work with the type of data on hand. Not a very theoretically satisfactory state of affairs, but there it is. Obviously, the more clusters selected, the more specific the resulting model; the less clusters selected, the more general the model. This scenario is sometimes called *k-means clustering*. The *"k"* is the number of clusters (rather like *k*-nearest neighbor—data miners are apparently not a very imaginative lot at naming algorithms!). The "means" part of the name is derived from the fact that clustering algorithms of this basic type work with the means (average values) of various clusters to decide which instances are included in which clusters.

The second adjustment works with a set of slightly different clustering algorithms that try to find some appropriate number of clusters, rather than having the miner choose some arbitrary number. If left to themselves, these clustering methods have a rather unfortunate habit of ending up with every instance in a separate cluster. Thus, analogously to the instance count in decision tree leaves and the instance count in extracted rules, in clustering algorithms that try to discover an appropriate number of clusters, as well as to which cluster to assign a particular instance, it's important to limit the algorithm's enthusiasm and require some minimum number of instances in each cluster discovered. Just as before, the higher the minimum, the more general the model; the lower the minimum, the more specific the model. (See MIII:TB.12.10)

12.2.4.5 Algorithm Adjustment: Self-Organizing Maps

The specificity of a SOM requires a fairly straightforward adjustment. More neurons, more specificity; fewer neurons, more generality. With very few neurons, the map will be extremely general. Imagine a 10-neuron × 10-neuron map. Then compare that map to one with 500 × 500 neurons. Obviously, with more neurons, more detail shows. Adding neurons makes the map more specific in that it reveals more detailed relationships.

An overspecified SOM (too many neurons) tends to show all of the fine detail—the relationships that exist between small numbers of instances that are very likely mainly noise. An underspecified SOM (too few neurons) tends to show only very broad, sweeping generalities.

Note that creating a map in the training data set and applying it to the test data set to see if it produces similar maps (the diagnostic test for over/ underspecification) works for SOMs just as well as for any other mining algorithm. However, the key is to make sure that the explanations revealed by the map are similar, not that the appearance of the two maps is approximately identical. The physical layout will almost certainly be different, but the relationships should be the same.

There is an additional way to judge the specificity of a SOM. If a SOM develops very few clusters (say, two or three), so long as the data is reasonably complex, the chances are that the SOM is underspecified. With more than 20 clusters, unless the data set is huge, the map may well be overspecified—but even if it isn't, it may be too complex to explain (which is the whole purpose of a SOM). If the complexity is genuine, it's worth breaking the data set into overlapping sets of variables in multiple input batteries and explaining the whole data set, section by section. The overlapping variables in input batteries help to connect the explanations in one battery to the explanations in the next.

Although not directly related to appropriate specification of the SOM, a very useful technique for improving the explanatory insight from a SOM can be normalizing distributions. (See Section 12.2.3.3.) SOMs sometimes appear to be underspecified—that is, they don't show much detail in the nature of the relationships—when the difficulty actually is that the ranges of values in a variable are not presented to the SOM conveniently. Normalizing distributions often produces more insight than trying for more specification. (See MIII:TB.12.11)

12.2.4.6 Algorithm Adjustment: Support Vector Machines

Support vector machines are another form of clustering (See Section 12.2.4.4) and have many similar issues. The main specificity issues that are particular to support vector machines concern how the overlapping clusters are to be separated—and almost all clusters in real-world data sets overlap. In addition to the same "knobs" that clustering algorithms have, there is usually one that determines the "tightness" or "stiffness" of the cluster boundary. The tension really determines the curvature of the boundary between the clusters. More flexibility, more specification; less flexibility, less specification.

Essentially, the more flexible the boundary, the more easily it is able to modify each boundary to surround each cluster; but too much flexibility, and it will be cutting out relationships that do exist in the training data, but not in the test data. (See MIII:TB.12.12)

12.2.4.7 Algorithm Adjustment: Linear Regression

The basic linear regression algorithm is a masterpiece of mathematical simplicity and elegance. In its basic form, it has no "knobs" at all. However, no tool applies linear regression in its basic form—usually multiple linear regression at the very least. Modifications, all of them needed, deal with all kinds of problems—the need for all numerical input, its inability to deal with missing values, and many similar problems. Most of these problems, and how to deal with them, were discussed earlier.

Linear regression inherently resists overspecification. After all, it can only represent linear relationships, and in this sense is the ultimately "stiff " fit to any data set. It's a linear relationship or nothing. However, although the data mining interpretations of the linear regression theme still adhere to the basic premise of a linear fit, there is one control that impacts specification in some data sets.

The linear regression algorithms in mining tools are usually one of a variety of "robust" regressions. This means that they are modified to accommodate many of the problems that beset nonrobust regression. The main one that concerns specification is the presence of outliers. The problem is that data points that lie a long way from the regression plane, and are at the extremes of the range, disproportionately effect the results. Imagine it as a seesaw problem. The effect that any rider has on the seesaw depends on how near to the ends each sits—the further out, the more effect. Riders in linear regression also get bigger (same as heavier) the farther they are from the regression line. So imagine 20 children all sitting near the pivot point of the seesaw. Moving one doesn't make any huge effect. However, sit an elephant on one end, and the elephant has more effect than all the children you care to pile on the middle of the seesaw. Same thing with linear regression. The outliers can move the regression plane out of all proportion to their actual importance. This over-sensitivity to a few, possibly only one, data points is an example of overspecification. The more robust a linear regression, the more general it is; the less robust the regression, the more specific.

However, an astute reader will note that normalizing the distribution (see Section 12.2.3.3) in part removes the inordinate effect of outliers in any case. Robust regressions are really only needed for data sets that are not prepared as described here. When the data is prepared in accordance with good practice procedures for data mining, the robustness of the regression makes little difference. Thus, this "knob" and any others intended to affect specificity of linear regressions have very little impact in adequately prepared data sets. (See MIII:TB.12.13)

12.2.4.8 Algorithm Adjustment: Curvilinear Regression

The real difference between linear regression and curvilinear regression is that the seesaw referred to in the previous section is more like a piece of rope—not much good for riding. But suppose that the children, fed up with an elephant sitting on their seesaw, go off to play in the sandbox. They are scattered across the sandbox in no particular order. A stiff plank of wood, no matter how it is arranged to lie across the edges of the sandbox, probably won't come very close to many of the denizens. A piece of rope, however, is flexible enough to be passed from hand to hand so that all of them can, without moving their position, hang on to it.

So much for children in sandboxes. When it comes to data points, the purpose is to find a flexible line that best characterizes any curvature that exists in the data set. To do that, it has to pass as close as possible to all the points that represent the true curvature present in the data without being too flexible. Too much flexibility and the curve starts to represent the fluctuations that are present in the training data set but that aren't in the test data set—or elsewhere in the world. Too much flexibility and the curve represents noise.

The "knob" in nonlinear regression is the amount of curvature allowed in the regression curve. It may be called "degrees of freedom" or "magnitude of exponent" or "stiffness" or quite a lot of other things according to the toolmaker's whim. However, the knob simply adjusts the algorithm to allow more (or less) kinks, twists, bends, and curves. The more flexible the curve is allowed to be, the more specific the model; the less flexible the curvature, the less specific or more general the model. (See MIII:TB.12.14)

12.2.4.9 Algorithm Adjustment: Neural Networks

Neural networks offer the ultimate in flexibility of fitting a regression curve to a data set. Unlike curvilinear regression, if properly set, they can induce greater stiffness on some parts of the curve than other parts. Curvilinear regression is limited to having the same degree of stiffness, or flexibility, over the whole of the curve. Exactly as with curvilinear regressions, specificity of the models produced using neural networks is accomplished by controlling the amount of flexibility allowed the curve. However, along with the additional power of neural networks goes a good deal more complexity.

Neural networks are built from artificial neurons. Conceptually, each of the input battery variables is assigned to an input neuron, and each output battery variable is assigned to an output neuron. Between the input and output neurons there may be—and almost always are—what are called *hidden neurons*. They are hidden in the sense that they are sandwiched between the input and output neurons, and like the cheese in a cheese sandwich where the slices of bread hide the cheese, so the input and output neurons hide the hidden neurons.

Hidden neurons are often arrayed in layers. A network containing one hidden layer connects all of the input neurons to one side, and all of the output neurons are connected to the other side. With more hidden layers, one layer connects to the next—so you'd have input, hidden, hidden, and output in a four-layer network. Several things contribute to the allowed flexibility of the fitted curve, but in general they all boil down to more neurons, more flexibility. The number of input and output neurons is fixed—one per variable—and can't be altered without changing the data set. What varies is the number of hidden neurons. The number of hidden layers can alter too, of course, but that has less effect on curve flexibility and more on learning speed.

Rule of thumb: Start with three layers (so one must be a hidden layer). Usually, the output is a single neuron corresponding to the single-variable output battery. Structure the hidden layer so that it has half the number of neurons as the input layer. It's a rule of thumb, and a starting point only, but in manually set networks, it often proves to be a good place to start. Many tools use automated procedures to estimate an appropriate beginning network architecture.

In general, more neurons make for a more specific model; less neurons make for a less specific model. (See MIII:TB.12.15)

12.2.4.10 Algorithm Adjustment: Bayesian Nets

Naïve Bayesian networks look, if their architecture is drawn out, rather like neural networks. However, these networks are built of nodes, not neurons. The internal complexity of each node is very different from that of neurons, but the architecture in which the nodes are arranged appears similar. Naïve Bayesian networks may have no hidden layer, so the inputs connect straight to the output. More complex Bayesian networks still may not have layers, but separate clusters of nodes cross-connected in complex ways.

As a rule of thumb, the complexity in Bayesian networks derives from both the number of nodes and the number of interconnections between the nodes. It's more the complexity of interconnections that is important; but complexity of interconnection is roughly proportional to the number of interconnections, and it is easier to count interconnections than to try more involved methods of determining complexity. Sometimes, especially when a Bayesian network is induced from a data set, the network can be extremely complex indeed. Even there, counting nodes and interconnections seems to work well as a complexity estimate in practice.

Rule of thumb: More complex networks are more likely to be overspecified than less complex networks. So, more nodes, more connections, or both means more specificity. Less nodes, connections, or both means less specificity, thus more generality. (See MIII:TB.12.16)

12.2.4.11   Algorithm Adjustment: Evolution Programming

Evolution programming produces program fragments that can be embedded into complete programs for execution. The fragments are usually more or less complex logical and/or mathematical statements that express the relationship between input battery and output battery. Internally, the algorithm uses populations of candidate programs that evolve using techniques analogous to mating and mutating. Most of the knobs that control the evolution process have more influence on speed of convergence (how quickly the best program fragment is discovered) than on specification of the resulting model. Of course, if the population sizes, breeding rates, mutation rates, and so on aren't appropriately set, the model might appear to be underspecified, but that is really a result of a poor learning process, not inherently in the way the model is specified. It's worth noting, though, that of the algorithms mentioned here, it is really only this one that separates the learning process from model specification. It's true that neural network algorithms also separate the learning process from model specification, but not as presented in mining tools, only in the raw algorithm. The commercially available tools implementing evolution programming, however (at least those known to the author), do expose knobs for adjusting model specification and, quite separately, controls for adjusting the learning process. Commercial tools generally don't expose controls for adjusting the learning process for other algorithms.

The model resulting from an evolution programming tool is itself a program. It has a degree of complexity that depends on how long it can be (that is, how many lines of program code it can include) and what mathematical and logical functions can be included. The longer the program, or the more the variety of functions, the greater the complexity and the higher the degree of specification. The shorter the program, or the fewer the variety of functions, the less the degree of specification. In fact, program length has far more effect on level of specification than variety of functions permitted. Program length, because it limits how many discrete program steps can be included in the final program, seems to have far more impact on specification than allowing or not allowing complex mathematical or logical structures as part of the evolved program such as sine, exclusive, or hyperbolic tangent, for instance. (See MIII:TB.12.17)

12.2.4.12   Algorithm Adjustment: Some Other Algorithm

The listing of algorithms included in this book is certainly not comprehensive. There are other algorithms included in some tools that are not covered here. The author has tried to include the most popular algorithms, and those that seem to be gaining in popularity even if not yet included in commercially available tools as of this writing. However, new algorithms are continually being invented, and even were that not the case, there are still several commercial mining tools that implement algorithms not mentioned here. Those not mentioned here are usually only implemented by a single vendor in their tool. However, there are at least a couple of dozen mining algorithms that are commercially available at this writing that are not included here. Many of them are sufficiently similar to one of the algorithms mentioned here that they are, as far as tuning specification goes, simply different flavors of those that are already discussed. Others may seem to be sufficiently different to justify being labeled as different algorithms. However, so far, all the mining algorithms have certain broad features in common, at least as far as model specification goes.

First, all algorithms pretty much separate the learning process from the specification process. There are almost always some controls on raw algorithms—and certainly on any of the more complex raw algorithms—that tune the training or learning process, and a pretty much separate set of knobs that tune the specification process. It is generally the case that when wrapped in tools, the tool vendor hides most or all of the complexity involved in the training or learning process. When complexity is exposed, it is usually for knobs to tune the specification process. This is because it turns out, in general, to be much harder to find a good automatic specification tuning process than to find a good automatic training tuning process.

All mining algorithms available in tools today can be viewed as working in one of two fundamental ways. Either they chop instances up into discrete chunks, as in decision tree leaves or clustering algorithm clusters, or they find continuous estimates, as with regressions or neural networks.

With any algorithm that chops instances into discrete chunks, adjusting a knob that decreases the minimum permitted size of the chunks always increases specificity of the resulting model. Increasing the minimum permitted chunk size decreases model specificity.

Algorithms that assemble a continuous estimate always seem to require a number of internal structures. For neural networks, it's neurons; for Bayesian networks, it's nodes and interconnections; for self-organizing maps, it's neurons; for evolution programs, it's program steps; for nonlinear regression, it's degrees of freedom, and so the list goes on. Whatever the exact nature of the internal structure, the rule of thumb is that more of it increases specificity, and less of it decreases specificity of the resulting model.

These two generalizations about chunk size and internal complexity seem to have held true so far, and there are also good theoretical grounds to support these conclusions. Thus, whatever mining algorithm is embedded in a tool, if adjustments affecting specificity are available, they will almost certainly influence, as appropriate, either chunk size or internal structural complexity. Once a miner has identified what these knobs are, adjusting them should tune the specificity of any mining algorithm in any modeling tool. (See MIII:TB.12.18)

12.2.5 Problem: Insufficient Data

One of the possible problems a miner might find is that the test data set isn't representative of the same relationships that are in the training data set. (See MIII:AB.12.6) This might be indicated when:

- The regression line fitted to the predicted value versus residual value XY plot isn't effectively flat. (See MIII:DB.12.2)
- The model's predicted values are all systematically skewed to be either higher than the actual values, or lower than the actual values. (See MIII:DB.12.5)
- The regression line fitted to the actual value versus predicted value XY plot is far from laying on the lower-left, upper-right diagonal. (See MIII:DB.12.9)
- The value of the smoothed residual variance estimate is so great over some part of or all of the plot as to make the predictions unsatisfactory. (See MIII:DB.12.10)

Having different underlying relationships in different data sets is normally a problem with shortage of data. Without sufficient data, it often happens that noise predominates since, when split into the three required data sets, there isn't enough data to truly represent the underlying relationships adequately in the separate data sets. Because it's hard to build accurate and reliable models without representative data, the earlier chapters have already covered important rule-of-thumb checks to help a miner make sure that there is sufficient data, and that the training, test, and evaluation data sets are all also representative of the underlying structures and patterns in the data to produce accurate and reliable models. Chapter 9 (See Section 9.2.3.4) discussed how to check for data adequacy by building several check models. Chapter 11 (See Section 11.1) discussed applying the check models to assure that the training, test, and evaluation data sets are all relatively representative of the same relationships as each other. This discussion assumes that these checks have been done, and that the data set as a whole, and the separate training, test, and evaluation data sets, passed those tests for consistency. If those tests have not been done, or the data set did not pass the tests, then the problem is almost certainly insufficient data—and considerably insufficient data, too. To arrive at this diagnosis almost certainly means that there simply isn't enough data available for a reliable model to be discovered, the rest of this discussion notwithstanding.

If you are reading this section during model diagnosis, if the tests have not yet been done, or if the tests indicated insufficient data, stop reading and go and find more data, or accept the model as the best that can be had under the circumstances. The remainder of this section applies *only* if the earlier tests were applied and successfully passed.

Anyone who is still reading this section as a diagnostic aid rather than for general information almost certainly has a sampling problem—but it's also probably exacerbated by a variable representation problem. Dividing a source data set into training, test, and evaluation data sets requires that each instance in the source has a proportional chance of being assigned to one of the data sets. Thus, with a 60/20/20 division, any instance has to have a 60% chance of being assigned to the training data set, a 20% chance of being assigned to the test data set, and a 20% chance of being assigned to the evaluation data set. Simply taking the first 60% of a data set as the training data set, the next 20% as a test data set, and the remainder as an evaluation data set is a dangerous practice, and is fraught with problems—even if the data sets produced this way pass the rule of thumb tests for representativeness. The potential problem comes from the fact that very often, and frequently unbeknownst to the miner, the data in a source data set is in some sort of order. The CREDIT data set, for instance, has all the BUYER = 1 instances first, and all the BUYER = 0 instances following. This is because of the way that the data set was balanced (See Section 11.4.1) in that all the BUYER = 1 records were selected first and the appropriate BUYER = 0 records were later appended to the file to achieve the needed balance. If the first 60% of this data set were used for training, the test and evaluation data sets would have no BUYER = 1 responders at all.

The rule-of-thumb checks for representativeness do not check all of the variables in a data set. They only work at all so long as the instances in the three data sets are indeed chosen at random from the source data. So, if the three data sets were not built using random selection, rebuild them.

However, the possible problem that introduced this section—where training and test data sets are not representative of the same relationships—may be an indication that the data set needs balancing. (For a discussion of balancing a data set, see Section 11.4.1.) The fact that the relationships don't represent the same patterns in the test and training data sets only applies between input and output batteries. It's quite possible to have all of the three data set input batteries representative of the same patterns in all data sets, but find that the output battery isn't representative—which is exactly the case in the unmodified CREDIT data set with BUYER = 1 occurring for about 1% of the instances. Even testing input and output batteries separately to ensure that each is representative doesn't solve the problem, since it is quite possible to have the input battery representative in all three data sets, the output battery representative in all three data sets, but have dissimilar relationships between input and output batteries in all three data sets. How?

In the CREDIT example, assume the input battery in all three data sets actually is fully representative of the same patterns. Testing the output battery in all three data sets would reveal only that, for the binary variable that comprises the whole output battery, about 1% had the value 1, 99% had the value 0, and that this was true in all three data sets. As far as possible, testing the input and output battery separately would reveal each as being representative. However, with such a low density of responders in the output battery, it is quite possible that the few instances that did occur would have different relationships between input and output battery in each data set.

The only real answer is to check that the relationship between input and output batteries is similar in all three data sets—but that isn't accomplished by a rule of thumb. That calls for full-scale modeling of any relationships, which is what the miner is trying to do in constructing the model in the first place. There is no shortcut, only good modeling practice.

Thus, the possible problem that introduced the section may well be a sign that the data set needs balancing in order to build a robust model.

Failing that, rule-of-thumb checks notwithstanding, there simply may not be enough data. The rule-of-thumb is a guide, not a certainty, and only modeling finally discovers whether the data is in fact sufficient to define a satisfactory model. If, despite all efforts, this turns out to be the case, the only answer is to get more, or better, or more and better data. (See Part II, Chapter 7.)

12.2.6 Problem: Uneven Data

Another problem a miner might find is that the training and test data represent some relationships better than others. (See MIII:AB.12.7) This may be indicated by some residual values that are more common than others. (See MIII:DB.12.13.)

An input battery of any complexity contains a huge number of relationships. The only ones of interest to a modeler are, in a classification model, those that relate to the output battery, and in an explanatory model, those that relate to the business problem. Naturally, some of the patterns in the input battery will be more indicative of output battery states than other patterns ("better correlated," to use a more technical term). One problem is that the correlation of the patterns in the input battery may change depending on various factors, such as the actual value of the input battery variable(s).

Imagine a data set containing a single-variable input battery and a single-variable output battery. Suppose that when the values of the input battery are low in their range, the correlation is very good, but as they increase the correlation becomes less in proportion to the magnitude of the input. What would the residuals look like? A glance back at Figure 12.17 shows what might be expected.

The correlation between two variables, which is traditionally measured over the whole of the range of both variables, usually does vary from one part of the range to another. It is possible for multivariate data sets, as the input battery almost always is, to behave this way, too. However, the impact is usually more "blurred" when many variables are involved. As the patterns in one set of input battery variables lose their relevance, other patterns, perhaps in other variables, assume higher relevance. In many data sets, the correlation between input battery and output battery turns out to be pretty even. It's still true nonetheless that some parts of the multivariate range will be more correlated with the output battery than other parts. It is possible for the correlation between input battery and output battery to change in "steps" rather than smoothly. When this happens (not often in practice) the residuals also tend to change in steps and to show "clumps" of common residual values.

Far more common is the situation shown in Figure 12.25, or some variant of it with more variables. In some parts of the range of data, the relationship is reasonably well defined. The problem is that in other parts there is no data to define the relationship—if there is any. The dashed line indicating the relationship between about 0.50 and 0.62 on the Y axis, and 0.31 and 0.52 on the X axis, simply has no data defining what it might be. The mining algorithm can make a "best fit" through this area based only on the influence of the distant points where data occurs more densely. It's not that the mining algorithm made any errors in discovering how to make the best fit. The problem is that there aren't many data points around in important parts of the relationship to give much clue as to the true relationship in that area. If the test data set contains any data points in that area, the model is not very likely to have estimated the actual underlying relationship.

Now, to be sure, Figure 12.25 is an exaggeration to illustrate a point. The sorts of data sets modeled in data mining will have far more data points than those illustrated—and far more variables. However, the concept still applies. Where input battery data in its multivariate distribution clusters together, the relationships will be much better defined than in areas where the density of points is less dense. If, as often happens, the data does have such clusters, variance of the residuals will tend to increase and decrease with the density of the data in the input battery. The "patches" or clusters in the input battery will tend to be reflected as patches, or clusters, in the residuals.

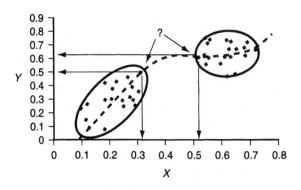

Figure 12.25   Ill-defined portions of a relationship.

There may be nothing to be done about the problem. Some things in life come in patches or clusters, and the data simply reflects this as a fact of life. Data miners don't always accept this as a valid excuse and do things like balancing data sets to account for it, which will work in this case, too. However, before balancing a data set, it's worth ensuring that the data as collected for mining does, in fact, reflect the full range of behaviors that the world offers, and that the data set hasn't been selectively truncated in some way. Selectively including, or not including, some instances introduces bias into a data set, something that needs to be very carefully monitored. (See Section 12.2.7 for a fuller description of bias.) (See MIII:TB.12.30)

12.2.7   Problem: Estimation Bias When Mining a Model

A miner might find that the model is "biased" into preferentially producing certain predicted values (see MIII:AB.12.8). (Also see Section 12.2.13 about variance bias.) This may be indicated by:

- Patches, clumps, or clusters of residuals in the residual lines. (See MIII:DB.12.2)
- The regression line fitted to the actual value versus predicted value XY plot is far from laying on the lower-left, upper-right diagonal. (See MIII:DB.12.9)

Bias here is used in exactly its colloquial meaning—to lean toward, to be predisposed toward, or to favor something. In mining, therefore, a mined model is said to be *biased* when it has a tendency to produce one, or several, particular classifications. A mined model is also biased when it produces estimates that are all offset by a fixed amount, or by an amount that varies in fixed relationship to the magnitude or class of the estimate. As an example, a model choosing which of several cross-sell products to offer that predominantly chooses the same product from the selection available is biased in favor of that product. Similarly, a model to estimate the ROI from a project that consistently underestimates the actual return by some fixed amount, or by some fixed percentage, is also biased. Bias in the estimates of mined models are relatively easy to address, and may be produced by underspecification (see Section 12.2.4).

Although an appropriately specified model should not have any bias in its residuals (see Sections 12.1 and 12.2.4), sometimes a mining algorithm may have trouble if some of the relationships are not well represented in the data. When this is the case for the output battery, it calls for balancing the data set (see Section 11.4.1); this may also work to help the model learn relationships that are important but not well represented in the source data set.

It's worth noting that bias is a crucial issue when constructing data sets (see Part II, Chapter 7) and during deployment (see Chapter 8), but these issues don't arise during mining and refining a model and are not covered here.

12.2.8 Problem: Noise Reduction

A miner might discover that in order to avoid learning noise, the tool was too restricted in the flexibility it was allowed when learning the relationships. (See MIII:AB.12.9) This may be indicated when:

- There is no significant difference in naïve and mined model performance. (See MIII:DB.12.1)
- The mean of the residuals is not 0. (See MIII:DB.12.5)
- The curve fitted to the actual value versus predicted value XY plot differs markedly from a straight line where it passes through the data. (See MIII:DB.12.8)
- The value of the smoothed residual variance estimate is so great over some or all of the plot as to make the predictions unsatisfactory. (See MIII:DB.12.10).= (See also Section 12.2.16 on noisy and irrelevant variables.)

Noise is a problem, and using an underspecified model is one of the techniques that makes the model more noise resistant. However, finding an appropriate specification level is better than underspecifying a model just to enable it to resist learning noise. (Section 12.2.4 describes in detail how to appropriately specify a mining algorithm regardless of the level of noise in a data set.) Nonetheless, it may be possible to increase the specificity of the mining algorithm if some of the noise present in a data set can be reduced.

The intuition here is that if some of the noise can be removed from a data set, the model can better learn the underlying relationships without having to be as noise resistant. Naturally, any noise-removing techniques that are applied to the source data set have to be duplicated on any run-time data during deployment, so the transformations to reduce noise have to be carried forward.

One important noise reduction technique is missing value replacement. (See Section 12.2.3.4.) Replacing missing values may allow a more specific model to be created on a data set than before they were replaced. Replacement tends to have this noise-reducing effect even on algorithms that can handle missing values without replacement. This action also tends to reduce the variance of the residuals, or, in other words, to produce more precise (or more confident) estimates, even if the specification level of the model isn't changed.

Another noise reduction technique is binning; the supervised binning techniques for input battery variables are particularly useful. (See Section 12.2.3.1.) Another, perhaps preferable, alternative to binning is normalizing the distribution of the input battery. (See Section 12.2.3.3.) If the noise is in the output battery, equal frequency binning is a good practice, although redistribution of the output battery distribution is again a better alternative.

Manual aggregation of variable detail also sometimes works well, especially if a data set has several aggregation levels. It's often beneficial to have variable aggregations along some common metric. For instance, aggregating hourly sales to daily, daily to weekly, or weekly to monthly (depending on the needs of the business problem) may produce better estimates. If most of the aggregation periods are monthly and sales are aggregated daily, for instance, a common aggregation period could very well reduce noise. Either convert the aggregation period to daily by taking 1/29th, 1/30th, or 1/31st of the monthly amounts as appropriate to the month, or roll up daily to monthly sales amounts. Common aggregation periods tend to introduce less noise and produce less residual variance. However, rolling up isn't a choice if the estimates needed are for short periods, say daily. The choice then is to try a "roll down" of monthly to daily.

Another noise reduction technique that works when there are a fair number of variables in the input battery is to "bundle" groups of variables together. (This is a data miner's version of what statisticians think of as *principal curves and surfaces analysis*.) Many mining tools provide information about how well the variables correlate with each other. If the tool available doesn't provide such information, Excel will do the job, although it's more time consuming. Take bundles of variables that correlate well with each other, create a model using one bundle at a time as the input battery, and use the original output battery to build the bundle model. When all of the commonly correlated variables have been grouped into bundles, replace the bundles in a new input battery with the bundle predictions. Bring any unbundled variables forward into the combining model. This creates a composite model built from several models, with input variables feeding into bundling models, the output from which becomes the input to later combining models. Figure 12.26 illustrates this concept. (See MIII:AB.12.9, MIII:TB.12.19, MIII:TB.12.20, MIII:TB.12.21, MIII:EB.12.1)

Even when well specified, it is always tough to create a model that learns the underlying relationships (called *signal*) and at the same time resists learning the spurious relationships (called *noise*) that exist in any data set. The ideal would be to determine some sort of signal-to-noise ratio and use it to calibrate the model. Unfortunately, that is an advanced mining topic not covered here. However, one technique is to create an initial model that is as good as possible, then add the output from that model to the original input battery as another variable, and remodel the newly created input battery. The idea is that the initial model will have learned some of the signal at least. The second model can use this as a starting point and, with the initial model's output as an added feature, may be able to improve on the final output.

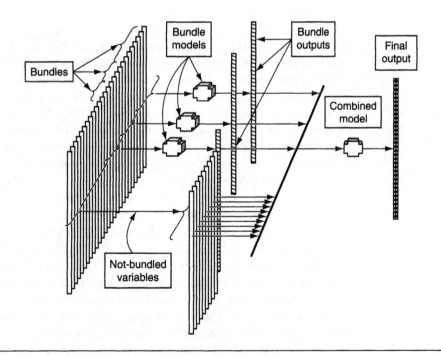

Figure 12.26   Combining bundles of variables to reduce noise.

12.2.9 **Problem: Categorical Correlation**

A miner might find that there are many categorical values in the input battery that all represent a similar phenomenon or phenomena. (See MIII:AB.12.10) This may be indicated when:

- The residuals histogram (and, therefore, the residuals distribution) is obviously not normal. (See MIII:DB.12.5)
- The apparent ranges of actual and predicted values are different or the density of points is not uniform, and not symmetrical about a diagonal line from lower left to upper right in the actual value versus predicted value XY plot. (See MIII:DB.12.7)
- The curve fitted to the actual value versus predicted value XY plot differs markedly from a straight line where it passes through the data. (See MIII:DB.12.8)

Categorical variables, just as with other types of variables, can carry information that is sufficiently similar to each other so that the variables seem effectively identical to the modeling tool. Age and income are typical examples of this phenomenon in many data sets. Age and income can be represented as categories, and if this were done, both age and income, on average, might very well increase together.

Sometimes there are several to many variables carrying essentially similar relationships. Many mining algorithms make what is called an *assumption of independence*. Independent variables do not have similar relationships to each other. Similarity of information content makes variables "dependent" on each other in the sense that what value one variable takes on depends on the value taken by another variable. When many variables carry similar information, some mining algorithms give undue weight to the evidence that they provide—rather as a human may be persuaded by the behavior of a crowd, even if everyone is making a mistake. For instance, if everyone read the *New York Times* and was very much influenced by the film critic, asking 100 people who all agreed that a film was excellent doesn't mean any more than the single critic's opinion if the 100 all reflect the critic's opinion. Thus, the views of the readers would be dependent on the views of the critic. It's similar with variables. In the same way that you might think that you had 100 independent reviews of a film, so the mining algorithm "thinks" it has multiple sets of evidence leaning in a particular direction. If all of the variables actually represent different expressions of the same underlying phenomenon (technically called a *latent* phenomenon), the mining algorithm may be unduly influenced by the apparent predominance of the evidence. Bundling highly correlated variables serves, in part, to overcome this tendency toward bias. (See Sections 12.2.7 and 12.2.8.)

Regardless of the desired resolution of the output, the output can't have any finer resolution than the granularity of the input battery allows. When many variables carry few categories, and particularly when the input battery variables are all highly dependent, the predicted values may be clumped into discrete groups. Perhaps, after bundling, the categories in the input battery are still too few to provide sufficient resolution for the prediction (or understanding, if the model is an explanatory one). If the input battery does have many categories, it may be that most of the categories are only sparsely represented, many of them represented by relatively few instances as a proportion of the data set. In this case, it might be worth trying to balance the data set carefully to better represent categories of interest. (See Section 11.4.1.)

In the end, it may simply be that the data available doesn't contain relationships sufficient to provide the resolution or continuity of output needed. Then the only choice is to find data with more variability. (See Part II, Chapter 7.)

12.2.10 Problem: Partial Colinearities

Another possible problem is that a large number of variables in the input battery may carry similar information over parts of their range. (See MIII:AB.12.11) This may be indicated when:

- The residuals histogram (and, therefore, the residuals distribution) is obviously not normal. (See MIII:DB.12.5)
- The apparent ranges of actual and predicted values are different, or the density of points is not uniform, and not symmetrical about a diagonal line from lower left to upper right in an actual value versus predicted value XY plot. (See MIII:DB.12.7)
- The curve fitted to the actual value versus predicted value XY plot differs markedly from a straight line where it passes through the data. (See MIII:DB.12.8)

Variables, quite naturally, vary their values over their range. However, the variance is usually not uniform over the range of the variable. This nonuniformity shows up in the variable's distribution, which in at least some sense is a description of the nonuniformity of variance of a variable. The central "hump" of the normal distribution, for instance, represents a clustering of values about the variable's mean. Glance back, for instance, at Figure 12.9. It's also possible for variables to have actual, or relative, gaps in their distributions, as shown earlier in Figure 12.25.

When individual variables exhibit such behaviors, it usually doesn't cause a problem. Even when many variables show such behaviors, it still causes little problem—unless the variables are partially dependent on each other. Perhaps for some parts of their range, the variables are somehow linked, whereas over the rest they aren't. Apart from common missing value ranges this situation is rare. However, when it does happen, it can affect the output quite severely. The correlated subranges can bias the output values so that the residuals have a far higher variance in some parts of their range than in other parts, or the residuals seem patchy in some areas as the model makes systematic errors.

Distribution normalization, or possibly binning, may ameliorate this problem.

12.2.11 Problem: Data Not Representative of the Business Problem

A miner might face the problem of an input battery that, although it checks as representative of the population, has some parts of the output battery range represented by very few instances (records) and other parts represented by very many instances. (See MIII:AB.12.12) This may be indicated when:

- The residuals histogram (and, therefore, the residuals distribution) is obviously not normal. (See MIII:DB.12.5)

- The apparent ranges of actual and predicted values are different, or the density of points is not uniform, and not symmetrical about a diagonal line from lower left to upper right in an actual value versus predicted value XY plot. (See MIII:DB.12.7)

- The curve fitted to the actual value versus predicted value XY plot differs markedly from a straight line where it passes through the data. (See MIII:DB.12.8)

- The value of the smoothed residual variance estimate is so great over some or all of the plot as to make the predictions unsatisfactory. (See MIII:DB.12.10)

This is exactly the problem encountered in Chapter 11 with the CREDIT data set. In the original data set only 1% of the instances were BUYER = 1. These relatively few records were insufficient for many mining tools to adequately model. ("Adequately" only means "well enough to impact the business problem.") The answer already discussed is to balance the data set. (See Section 11.4.1.) The reason for the rebalancing is quite fundamental to the process of modeling and mining. Initially, it is important to both modeler and miner that the data set be as unbiased as possible. Thus, the data set should represent as true a state of the world as is possible. It is only from this beginning that the data set can be carefully adjusted to least distort any other relationships, save those specifically balanced. This ideally results in a data set that is still as representative of the world as possible, but that is more amenable to the needs of the mining tool. The reason for the balancing adjustment is that although the initial data set may be as representative of the world as possible, it isn't necessarily representative of the business problem. Adjustment is needed to make the data set representative of the business problem as well as of the world.

12.2.12   Problem: Output Limiting

A miner might discover that the tool may be clipping the output predictions. (See MIII:AB.12.13) This may be indicated when the regression line fitted to the actual value versus residual XY plot is not horizontal. (See MIII:DB.12.6)

Some tools limit the range of the output predictions to the range discovered during mining; some don't. The idea is, for instance, that if the minimum value in the training data set range was 0, it makes little sense to have a predicted value of, say, -0.4. However, assuming that the model is not perfect, it will make errors, and these will naturally tend to range both above and below the actual value—including at the top and bottom of the range.

Whether or not the output limiting is important to the business problem, it will produce apparent distortion in the residuals similar to that shown earlier in Figures 12.7 and 12.8. As far as checking the residuals for systematic error is concerned, output limiting is not a problem.

12.2.13   Problem: Variance Bias

One of the problems a miner might find is that there may be a bias that affects all of the input battery variables. (See MIII:AB.12.14) This may be indicated when the regression line fitted to the actual value versus residual XY plot is not horizontal. (See MIII:DB.12.6)

The discussion of sampling bias (see Sections 8.3.1.2, 9.2.3.6, and 11.1) looked at a possible way of seeing the effects of bias on a data set. As patterns in the input value change, it is to be expected that, with some degree of confidence, the output battery will change its value, too. However, in general, regardless of the change in magnitude of either input or output battery, the distribution remains fairly constant over the whole range. Sometimes when bias is present, it may leave traces of its presence by changing distribution as magnitude changes.

Another possible result of bias that affects the output variance is that, while retaining a mean of 0, the variance is nonetheless correlated to prediction magnitude. Figure 12.17 illustrated this effect where the residual variance was low when the predicted value was at one end of its range, and larger when the predicted value was at the other end, and the variance at any point was proportional to the magnitude of the prediction.

Whatever is going on in the real world to produce such a change in residual variance is outside the system of variables that form the input battery. Something else changes that is biasing all of the input variables. This is a firm clue not only that better data would improve the model, but also that the data might be available—or at least, a clue that the phenomenon might be measurable. If it affects all, or a very significant fraction, of the input battery variables so significantly, it should be possible to discover what is actually producing this effect.

12.2.14 Problem: The Modeling Tool Is Broken

A broken mining tool or algorithm (see MIII:AB.12.15, MIII:AB.11.25) may be indicated by almost any untoward situation or circumstance.

Mining tools or algorithms do break—but not very often! Data mining tools are computer programs—pieces of software—and as with all other software, they are subject to the normal array of "features" (also known as bugs and glitches). As a miner, if you discover one of these features, just shrug your shoulders—such are the vagaries of fate. It's worth contacting the vendor with bugs and with usability feedback. As with any vendor, what they choose to do about helpful feedback (and unsolicited advice from data miners) lies in the lap of the gods.

However, software bugs are not the main subject of this section. Occasionally—very, very occasionally—the tool or algorithm is fundamentally flawed. The example in this chapter illustrated in Figure 12.11, in which the tool actually fails to make predictions in part of the range where it obviously should, is certainly a flaw. Whether it is a bug or a fundamental problem greatly depends on the definition of each term, and is irrelevant for the purposes of this discussion. It is a failure in algorithm or program logic that is permanently embedded in this version of the mining tool's code. A workaround won't fix it, it isn't an intermittent or transient problem, and it isn't dependent on the data that a miner chooses to model. In this case, the tool is broken and requires repair before it is again useable.

This situation really doesn't happen very often. Almost all data mining tools, and certainly all of those that have been in the marketplace for some time, are not likely to be broken in the sense discussed here. Naturally, they will all have their idiosyncrasies and their unintended "features"; that is only to be expected. However, nothing is perfect, and the example discussed in this chapter is not a contrived example to prove a point. This example is drawn from a real business modeling and data mining project, and this is an example of a real broken mining tool.

The corrective action here is simply to use another tool. Do, of course, report the problem to the tool vendor. The point to note is that sometimes—not often for sure, and only after conscientious checking, but sometimes—a good workman really is constrained to blame the tools!

12.2.15 Problem: Anachronistic Variables

Leakage from anachronistic variables (see MIII:AB.12.16) may be indicated by a model making perfect, or near perfect, classifications that are not explicable as either trivial or obvious. (See MIII:DB.12.11)

Anachronistic variables are a pernicious mining problem. However, they aren't any problem at all at deployment time—unless someone expects the model to work! Anachronistic variables are out of place in time. Specifically, at data modeling time, they carry information back from the future to the past. Many, perhaps even most, business classification models are outcome models—that is, they are modeling outcomes that occur later in time. For the purposes of mining, the data has an arbitrary "now" point so that the model can learn to classify the future outcomes that have, in fact, already occurred. The modeled outcomes are, of course, only in the future relative to the arbitrary "now" point. Since the data set necessarily contains information about events that occur later than the "now" point, it's crucial to take scrupulous care that no later information leaks back.

Any future information that does leak back will be present in all three data sets, and so it won't be detected until the model is deployed; performance is far from the anticipated model performance because the needed information about the future outcome will be missing. A clue that there's temporal leakage is that the model turns out to be too good to be true. Too good to be true usually is, and perfect models are a "dead giveaway." (See Section 9.2.3.3.)

If any outcome classification model seems far better than reasonably expected, check carefully for anachronistic variables. Build single variable models to discover any variables that individually seem too good to be true. Think carefully about how or why they might be anachronistic. Eventually, deployment will certainly prove whether any temporal leakage occurred, but that is not the best time to discover the problem.

12.2.16 Problem: Noisy or Irrelevant Variables

Another possible problem is that the input battery contains one or more very noisy or completely irrelevant variables. (See MIII:AB.12.18) This may be indicated when:

- There is no significant difference in naïve and mined model performance. (See MIII:DB.12.1)

- The residuals appear to contain information that could be used to improve the prediction. (See MIII:DB.12.2)
- The value of the smoothed residual variance estimate is so great over some or all of the plot as to make the predictions unsatisfactory. (See MIII:DB.12.10)
- There are significant clusters present in the input battery with a high degree of separation between them. (See MIII:DB.12.13)

Noisy or totally irrelevant variables may be a problem, and certainly are for some algorithms. The problem is not with the noise, nor the irrelevancy, but with the fact that they interfere with the algorithm's ability to discover relationships from the other variables. This may seem to be odd at first glance. If there are variables in the input battery that have some specific degree of relationship with the output battery, how is it that adding irrelevant or highly noisy variables to the input data set prevents the mining algorithm from learning the best relationships that are present?

Consider this. If noisy or irrelevant variables do have an adverse impact, the noisiest and most irrelevant certainly should have such an impact. A variable that is all noise has to be totally irrelevant. Such a variable is one that is constructed to be purely random. If it's a binary variable, the toss of a fair coin to determine its value would produce a random variable of this sort. Other analogous techniques produce random variables of all types.

The interesting thing about random variables is that they don't look random—at least, not to human intuition. In fact, random variables are, perhaps surprisingly, guaranteed to contain patterns. The longer the random sequence, the more patterns the random variable will contain. If you have the patience, flip a fair coin 100 or more times and look at the result. What turns up has runs and sequences in it that at first sight don't look random at all. (See Section 3.5.1.1.) Nonetheless, random it is. However, if there are patterns, they will correlate more or less with the output battery. Algorithms that chop the data set into smaller and smaller pieces, such as decision trees or rule extractors, will eventually come to a piece in which the apparently most suitable variable on which to split is the random variable—and from there on it's all downhill as this causes random fragmentation of the data set.

Even some continuous estimators, such as neural networks, are distracted by the apparent, but actually spurious, patterns. In those parts of the data set where the random variable appears to have a correlated pattern, the continuous estimator will incorporate the apparently useful pattern. Naturally, the test data set won't have the same pattern, but learning will be halted before the model is specific enough to extract the entire pattern that is actually available. (See Section 12.2.4.)

As an aside, there are tools that are quite impervious to noisy or irrelevant variables, such as naïve Bayes. However, these algorithms pay a very heavy price since they assume independence of variables, and where the variables carry redundant information they are sorely swayed. That's why one of the earlier techniques advises removing correlated variables by bundling. (See Section 12.2.8.)

Many mining tools list the variables by "importance." Be careful with this term. Variables are ranked only as they are important for a specific model. Different models of the same data set, sometimes even with the same mining algorithm, can rate the importance of variables differently for the separate specific models. This is not to say that some variables don't carry more information than others, and it's not to say that several different models created using different algorithms won't commonly select a similar set of variables. But the importance of variables is not really something to be reported or counted on, except as they are important for a specific model in a specific data set. At this writing, there is no generally accepted measure of importance for variables, no generally accepted method of determining importance, and no sign of one on the horizon. However, as an advanced data mining technique, it is possible to measure how much information any variable or set of variables carries about any output battery, and to define, before building any model, how good it could be at its best. But this is not a measure of importance. Importance is relative only to specific models, not to data sets.

Nonetheless, and given the caveats in the last paragraph, many mining tools do rate variable importance for the created model. After trying several iterations of refining a model, if it turns out that some selection of variables are consistently rated as unimportant, remove them. Recall that it is good practice to create the simplest model, and one facet of "simple" is as few variables as possible.

If an importance measure isn't available, try building several models with small but different selections of variables. Discard any variables that are commonly present in the worst models. (See MIII:TB.12.22, MIII:TB.12.23)

12.2.17 Problem: Interaction Effects

One of the possible problems a miner might find is that the tool (algorithm) selected does not inherently explore interaction effects when important interaction effects are present. (See MIII:AB.12.19) This may be indicated when:

- The curve fitted to the actual value versus predicted value XY plot differs markedly from a straight line where it passes through the data. (See MIII:DB.12.8)
- The value of the smoothed residual variance estimate is so great over some or all of the plot as to make the predictions unsatisfactory. (See MIII:DB.12.10)

- Discovering that an explanation is not convincing, relevant, or applicable to the business problem. (See MIII:DB.12.14)

Interaction effects can be crucial, and they are very easy to understand. If you want to carpet a room, it's not enough to know just the length of the room, nor is it enough to know just the width of the room. Interaction between length and width gives the number of square feet of a room, and that is what is needed to buy carpet. In this example, multiplication produces the interaction effect.

Several data mining algorithms do not incorporate interaction effects into their modeling. Several other algorithms do. (See Chapter 10 for more details.) However, whether any algorithm does or does not incorporate interaction effects, it is very useful to explicitly incorporate them where they are known. Even when an algorithm can learn interaction effects, it speeds learning and better resists noise if the interaction effect is explicitly included. (In this example, it would save the mining tool having to learn how to multiply, which is easy, but why force it to learn something already known to the modeler/miner?)

For those algorithms that don't incorporate interaction effects, explicitly representing them in a data set can make a crucial difference to the quality and power of the model. An easy way of representing interacting variables is to multiply them and add another variable to the input battery with the result. On the other hand, it's always worth at least checking performance using a tool with an algorithm that does incorporate interaction effects, such as neural networks. Even if the main model is, say, a decision tree, and it performs well, it's still worth checking the models against each other as a sort of "sanity check."

Better still, if the tools are available, is to explicitly check for interactions. In order to do that, it's worth taking a quick look at what interactions are, how they affect data and mining tools, and how to actually discover and characterize interactions in a data set.

12.2.17.1 Variable Interactions

Interactions between variables very simply means that the effect that one input variable has on the output variable changes depending on the value of some other variable. So, as an example, with "Y" as the output variable and "A" and "B" as input variables, the effect that "A" has on "Y" depends on the value of "B."

All of the multitude of data mining algorithms available have different signature behaviors, capabilities, and performance. In Section 10.1.2.1, discussing decision trees, an example shows that decision trees don't inherently include interactions and that neural networks do. Does this mean that networks are inherently better than decision trees? No! It does mean that if interactions are important, they have to be explicitly included in the input battery for any algorithm that doesn't inherently discover them. However, other algorithms that do discover such interactions still benefit from having them included. It requires greater complexity in the algorithm to discover such interactions, and without sufficient complexity, it still won't discover the interactions. Additional complexity can itself be a problem, mainly because of three things:

■ The increase in complexity might simply lead to the algorithm learning noise instead of the desired relationship.

■ The complexity will slow the learning, sometimes to a crawl, making discovering meaningful models a far slower process, and possibly slowing learning so much that the project becomes impractical.

■ There is no easy way to determine how much complexity is enough.

However, an easy way to determine whether the data contains important interactions, and a good rules-of-thumb to indicate how to characterize the interactions, is through the use of interaction indicator plots (IIPs).

12.2.17.2 Interaction Indicator Plots

Using IIPs allows the miner to put the important interactions into the input data set instead of into model complexity, even for those algorithms that could, if so configured, characterize the interactions. Understanding the interactions can make an enormous difference in explaining relationships in a data set. For predictive models with those algorithms that don't inherently characterize such interactions, it can improve the model enormously. It might at first glance seem easy to include all of the interactions as a matter of course. However, this direction leads to a variable explosion! For a data set with 10 variables in the input battery, and including only two interactions, say x^2 and x^3, this adds $10 \times 9 \times 2 = 180$ additional interaction variables to the original 10. For each of the 10 variables, every one can interact with one of the other 9 (thus 10×9), and there are two possible interactions proposed (x^2 and x^3). Try it with a 20-variable input battery, and it requires 760 extra interaction variables. Not only is this variable bloat damaging to the data set, but it's also almost certainly unnecessary since many of these interactions won't carry any useful information. The answer is to pick and choose, and use only the interactions that are useful and appropriate. Understanding the use of IIPs is a place to start.

The principle underlying IIPs is straightforward. It requires all the variables to be numeric, or recoded numerically using a principled recoding method if they are categorical (see Section 12.2.3.2). It's convenient to normalize the range of the input variables; 0–1 is usual. In essence, an IIP plots the values of the output variable for every input variable, as influenced by every one of the other input variables in turn. Thus, for an output variable, say *y*, it's discovering the interaction, if any, between two input variables, say *a* and *b*, that is important.

To understand how this is done, start by considering the plot of how output varies with a single variable. When a single variable is used, the result is called a *main effects plot,* one of which is illustrated in Figure 12.27. It simply shows the values for the output variable *y* over its range for the values of the input variable, shown here as *a*, over its range.

Notice that in this figure variable *b* is shaded out since in a main effects plot it's only the relationship between *y* and *a* over the range of both variables that shows up. To discover if there are interactions between *a* and *b* when *y* is the output variable, the data is (at least conceptually) ordered on the variable *b* and then split into two parts with equal numbers of instances in each part, as shown in Figure 12.28.

One part of the divided data set contains all instances of above average values of *b*, and the other part contains all of the instances of average or less value for *b*. A separate effects plot for each part of the data set shows two plotted curves. Each curve shows the relationship between *y* and *a*. However, since the variables have been ordered and separated into two parts based on the values of *b*, if there are any differences in the relationship between *y* and *a* in the two plots, it can only be because of the change in the value of *b*, since that is all that has changed. Any differences in the relation-

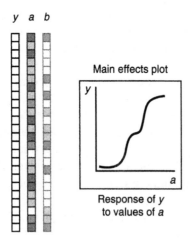

Figure 12.27   Main effects plot.

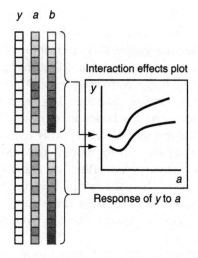

Figure 12.28 Interaction effects plot.

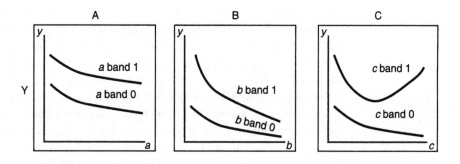

Figure 12.29 Typical IIPs.

ship will show up as differences in the height or shape of the two curves. Or to put it another way, if the relationship between *y* and *a* in the two partitions is identical, the two curves will lie one on top of the other, and it would appear to be a single curve. If two curves appear, something changes in the relationship between *y* and *a* at different values of *b*. The differences can only be because *a* interacts with *b*.

The differences in shape between the two curves indicate the nature of the interaction between the two variables. Interpreting IIPs is quite straightforward after only a little familiarity. Some typical interactions are shown in Figure 12.29.

Figure 12.29 shows IIPs for three variables; *a, b* and *c*. In the left-hand IIP showing interactions of *a* with *y*, the response curves are similarly shaped and essentially parallel to each other. The interaction that is present is clearly additive since the plotted curves are at different heights. Since they are the same distance apart and the same shape, it's clear that the only difference in response for the two bands of values is that band 1 has had a constant value added to it compared to band 0. (Or conversely, band 0 has had some constant value subtracted from it compared to band 1.) In any case, the response is identical except for the addition (or subtraction) of some value. It's usually not necessary to include additive interaction explicitly in a data set, but see Chapter 10 and all parts of Section 10.1 for more details. (Also, note that in statistical terms an additive interaction is called "no interaction" and is not distinguished from the situation where the two plotted curves lie one on top of another. As far as data miners are concerned, these purely additive effects can be important and are most easily characterized as "additive interactions," statistical use notwithstanding.)

The central IIP showing interactions of b with y shows that the slope of the interactions in the two bands changes, although the direction of curvature remains the same. An IIP such as this suggests that a multiplicative relationship exists in the output response between b and x. Thus, including an interaction variable created from bx in the input battery is indicated.

The right-hand IIP showing interactions of c with y shows two phenomena. Not only does the slope change, but so does the direction of curvature. The slope change again suggests a multiplicative interaction, as in the interaction with b. However, the change in the direction in curvature suggests that higher degree interaction is needed too: cx^2. (Notice that on the left of this image both curves are falling. However, about the middle of the image the upper curve begins to rise while the lower curve keeps falling.)

In general, a change in slope suggests the interaction term x^1 (usually shown simply as x), and every additional curvature divergence suggests the need for an additional degree of interaction, x^2, x^3, x^4, and so on.

Figure 12.30 shows a set of IIPs for five variables, a through d in the input battery with variable Y as output. Inspection of these IIPs suggest that interaction effects ba (perhaps b^2a), da, d^2a, a^2b, and cd should be included in the input battery.

Why these particular interactions? Take them individually:

- The plot in row A, column B has curves that are pretty much the same shape, but diverge, or separate, in appearance from left to right. Recall that plot lines that are essentially the same shape but at different distances apart at different points in the plot show a multiplicative relationship, thus indicating that the interaction can be represented as $b \times a$, which is usually represented as ba or "b times a."

- In the same plot, row A and column B, it's possible that at the right-hand side of the plot the curvature direction of the two plot lines are moving

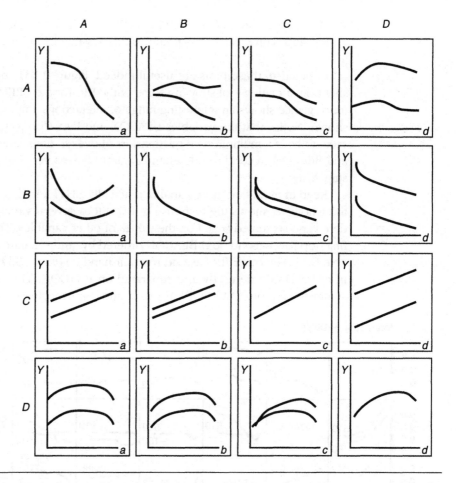

Figure 12.30   IIPs for five variables a through d interacting with output variable Y.

in different directions. Recall that a change in the direction of curvature indicates the possibility of a higher order interaction (square, cube, and so on) with one additional power possibly needed for each change in direction. The change in direction here isn't much, if it's there at all, so it's just a hint that one additional order might be useful, so this would be b^2a. But it's just a hint and probably not needed here.

- Consider the IIP in column D, row A. Notice that there is some divergence between the two plot lines. Recall that divergence points to a multiplicative interaction, so this points to *da,* as well as a possible change in direction of slope. If so, d^2a. (That is, the square of *d* multiplied by *a*.)

- Column A, Row B. Is there some divergence here? Perhaps. Enough for a^2b? Perhaps.

- How about column C, row D? Looks like a multiplicative interaction since the slopes diverge, so this points to the possible need for *cd*.

In practice, these plots are useful indeed. Figure 12.31 shows a screen shot from a mining tool showing some of the IIPs for the CREDIT data set. A quick glance shows an interesting range of interactions among the variables shown. Notice that the variables BEACON and DAS (top row, second box) seem to have a multiplicative relationship. However, note carefully that DAS and BEACON (second row, left-hand column) have a very different relationship. Why?

Keep in mind that the Y variable is actually BUYER in this set of IIPs. So the whole set shows the response of BUYER to several variables when ordered and separated based on the values of other variables. The plots show first (top row, second box) BEACON ordered by, and separated on, the variable DAS. The other IIP (second row, left-hand column) shows the interactions for DAS ordered by and separated on BEACON. Thus these are not symmetrical plots. DAS by BEACON cannot be expected to look anything

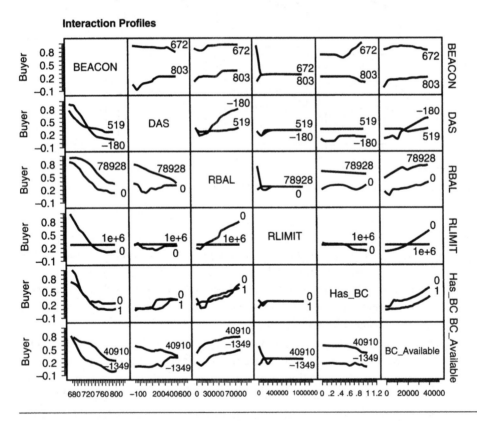

Figure 12.31 Interaction plots from the CREDIT data set.

like BEACON by DAS. Mind you, although different, if there is an interaction one way, then expect an interaction of some type the other way too.

So far, so good (as Wiley Coyote so often noted when pursuing the Roadrunner). This works fine with five or six variables. It might even be tractable with 10 input variables and 1 output variable so long as the modeler/ miner has access to automated IIP tools. But with many more than 10 input variables, and certainly when dealing with the many tens or hundreds of variables of most mineable data sets, this is not any sort of practical solution.

Note that it is, in principle, fairly easy to automate input variable interaction detection and variable creation, including detecting the necessary degree of interaction, although few, if any, commercial data mining tools available at this writing offer such an option. Alternatively, it's also fairly simple in principle to add the necessary interaction variables to a data set using a data preparation tool separate from the mining tool, but this too at this writing is not currently available as an option in data mining or separate data preparation tools at this writing. It's also worth noting that to do the job properly, the interaction variables created should themselves be checked for interactions. But to do all this by hand is to all intents and purposes impossible. Tough for people, although computationally not much of a problem— *if* it were automated.

There are noncommercial tools available that help (see the "Resources" section at the end of the book for the author's Web site address), but short of such aid a miner has to fall back on other methods. First, go back to the business problem frame (see Chapter 5), the problem map (described in Chapter 5), the cognitive map (Chapter 6), the business process map (described in Chapter 7), and the cause and effect map (described in Chapter 7). In all these places, there are clues as to where variables are expected to interact, and which variables they are. At least create IIPs for these variables. If there is one, use the system simulation or a process simulation and look at where the interactions occur in these simulations (discussed in Chapter 6). Simulations allow a priori (or before the fact) determination of probable interactions.

In addition, use mining tools to discover which variables are collinear. Data sets with many variables almost certainly have large numbers of variables that are collinear or in other words, are effectively carrying the same information as each other. Create "bundles" of collinear variables (see Section 12.2.8). Use one variable from the bundle, or a composite surrogate variable created from the bundle, to represent the bundle. This will very often reduce the number of variables in a data set to a manageable number to create IIPs, especially if an automated IIP tool is available. (It's harder if they are built "by hand" using, say, Excel, but perhaps still possible.)

The main point here is that incorporating interaction variables is essential in creating the best quality models for some algorithms, and extremely useful for others. Including necessary interactions almost always improves a model, and never harms it. Conversely, not including them can be very damaging. Use any means available to determine and incorporate the relevant interaction variables. (See MIII:TB.12.24)

12.2.18 Problem: Insufficient Data

Sometimes the data available is very limited in quantity, or instances describing specific outcomes of particular business interest represent a very low proportion of the total number of instances and are insufficient to build a useful model, even with a balanced data set, and no further data is to be had. (See MIII:AB.12.12) This is indicated when no further data is available and:

- The total number of instances (records) available are too few for modeling and it is known that the data represents the full range of behaviors of interest in the business problem.
- Balancing the data set to increase the relative prevalence of specific outcomes requires reducing the total size of the data set so that it is no longer representative of the population.

The essence of this problem is that the existing instances somehow have to be increased in number to a total number large enough for modeling. The data has to somehow be increased in quantity in such a way that the expanded sample remains at least as representative of the population as the original sample. There are a couple of approaches to expanding, or multiplying, the quantity of data, one far less technically complex than the other. Both have their benefits and problems, and neither should be used as a substitute for getting more data if possible. These are both last resort methods for use when no further data can possibly be had.

12.2.18.1 Expanding the Data

The most straightforward method of increasing the apparent amount of data is simply to duplicate the instances. Copy the original data set and append the copy to the original. Do this several times and the result appears to be a sizeable data set. It's just the original data set in multiple copies of course, but this certainly increases the amount of data without introducing any changes in any of the data's other characteristics.

One problem here is that some algorithms won't really notice this as more data, simply multiple runs through the same data set—which is true since that's what it is. In this case, this sort of expansion will not benefit the situation. Some tools are actually sensitive to the order that the instances are presented and since this expansion hasn't reordered the records, it's possible that randomly ordering the expanded records will make a difference.

However, whether reordered or not, expanding the data in this way only results in creating duplicates of the existing instances. Some mining algorithms are sensitive only to differences in the instances. (Imagine clustering—all of the duplicated instances fall on top of each other changing nothing about the state space at all. See Figures 10.1, 10.2, and 10.4, for instance, and note that duplicating the data points as described so far would change nothing about these figures.) Nonetheless, data expansion as described so far does help model quality with some tools. Sometimes additional benefit can be had by adding a small amount of random noise to each value. The noise has to be constructed so that, if numeric, the noise component itself has a mean of 0, or if categories, so that the modal category is still the original category. This noise added to the duplicate instances in total amounts to no change, but makes each instance appear unique.

12.2.18.2 Multiplying the Data

A second approach to increasing the apparent amount of data, data multiplication, requires the availability of appropriate and technically more complex tools than those used for data expansion. The idea here is to determine the joint distribution of the data set, and to create random values that have the same joint distribution characteristics as the original data set. This technique does not work if only the univariate distributions are considered, and determining a multivariate distribution requires tools specifically designed for the task.

To understand why using multivariate distributions is essential, glance ahead to Figure 13.4. This shows the univariate distributions for two variables, imaginatively labeled "Y" and "X" in two data sets "Set 1" and "Set 2." A quick glance reveals that variables X and Y in both data sets are approximately normally distributed. If univariate distributions were sufficient to duplicate the data sets, both Set 1 and Set 2 should be identical. In both data sets X and Y have the same range, 0–1, and the same distribution, normal.

However, a glance at Figures 13.5 and 13.6 will quickly show that the joint ranges of these variables are totally different. Of course, the data set used to illustrate this point was specifically put together so that the individual variables had the same range and distribution in both data sets, yet none of the XY points in Set 1 fall into the same space as those in Set 2. This issue is precisely the same in any real world data set—it's the joint distribution, the multivariate distribution, that is crucial to duplicate, not the univariate distributions.

There is no substitute for having sufficient data. However, if sufficient data is positively not to be had, multiplying the data that is available by adding random instances that are similar in their total multivariate distribution to the original data set is usually far more effective than expanding the data in the way described in the previous section. (See MIII:TB.12.29)

12.3 **Summary**

Refining the model is a crucial piece of the data mining process. Refining requires methods for checking a model's performance, insight for understanding what the checks reveal, knowledge of what applicable techniques are relevant to improve model performance, and methods for applying the techniques to modeling data, or business problems, as appropriate. This chapter walks through the methods of diagnosis to discover problems with examples, and presents methods for applying the techniques. Insight and understanding come only with practice and repetition.

No matter how technically effective the model appears, and no matter how well tested, the model has no value unless effectively deployed. Deployment is where the technical effort blends into meeting the business needs. Deployment is the final, utterly crucial step in effective data mining, and that is the topic for Chapter 13.

Chapter 13
Deploying the Mined Model

The road that leads from raw data to deployed mined model is not a straight one, but this chapter is the home stretch. After considerable effort to create a simple, reliable, and robust model—or one as simple, reliable, and robust as the business problem and data permit—it's time to take the result of the hard work and use it to get some business value from all the effort. It is, in other words, time to deploy it.

This chapter looks at the technical issues concerned with deploying a mined model. Chapter 8 in Part II has already looked at the business issues. However, the technical deployment of a mined model and the business deployment of a data-based business model are two parts of a single whole. The two deployment chapters, while discussing many deployment issues that are separate, also intertwine several themes because, in the end, these are not separate issues. The mined model must solve, or at least address, business issues, and the business issues have to be so framed that they lead to a solution through mining data. In this sense, these two chapters fit together like two pieces of a jigsaw puzzle.

13.1 Deploying Explanatory Models

An explanatory model has to tell a story. Plain and simple, deploying an explanatory model is no more than delivering a narrative explanation of the world supported by the facts (data). It's a special sort of story, and it has to tell about particular features, but it is a story nonetheless. Don't be confused by any business manager or stakeholder who tells you that they "just want the facts!" They don't. If they just wanted the facts, they could have looked at the raw data—raw data is "just the facts." Recall that an explanation summarizes the data with some purpose. A summary—an explanation—has to interpret the facts. "Just the facts" is no good to anyone. It is the thread of explanation—the narration of interconnections and relationships—that is important. What they really want is a story that provides "just the meaningful summary of the facts." Of course, this particular type of story has to be justifiable; that is to say, the objects and relationships in data have to be exposed so that the narrative is demonstrably connected to the data. And here is where a story is worth a thousand pictures. However, many of the deployment issues for explanatory models are business issues—telling the business story: for that see Section 8.3.1.

13.2 Novelty, and Keeping the Model Working

The world constantly creates new events, circumstances, ideas, and experiences. Always there is something new under the sun. For no two instants is the world ever the same. Yet in the way that we experience the world it seems that much stays the same. The same tree grows from year to year. The same political parties contest for office. The same fruits are offered in the local supermarket. The romance of attraction between human beings has been with us probably as long as there have been human beings.

Yet the tree that grows is not the same. It grows so that it is ever larger with new twigs and branches. The political parties are not the same, as their positions and opinions fluctuate with the struggle to remain in, or to gain, power. Fruit availability not only varies with the season, but new and exotic varieties previously not seen in the greengrocery section appear from time to time. Even the current notion of romantic love was a Victorian English invention to a large extent, and certainly postdates the industrial revolution. So although some things remain broadly the same over even quite long periods of time, everything is also simultaneously in a constant flux, and that makes problems of many sorts for reliably deploying models.

13.2.1 Regression to the Mean

(See MIII:AB.13.1) The constant novelty of the world is not without patterns. To be sure, nothing, not even the patterns, remain quite the same; yet still the pattern is there, and one of the patterns that is of great importance for many models is labeled with the formidable title of *regression to the mean*. The *mean* intended is simply an average value. The term *regression* was originally used in a sense of "return," so the pattern that this label applies to could be, perhaps, a little more intuitively termed "return to the average." The essential idea is really quite straightforward and fairly obvious on reflection. It's simply a label for the insight that when something performs extraordinarily, or reaches a size or effect that is unusually large or small, over time it tends to return to the average value.

To take a concrete example, see Figure 13.1. The idea illustrated here is that sometimes someone is born who is for some reason exceptionally large

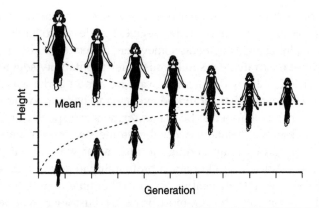

Figure 13.1   Regression to the mean.

(or small). It is usual that men and women who marry choose mates who are approximately their own size, thus tall men tend to marry tall women, and short men tend to marry short women. (And vice versa, naturally.) Yet it turns out that the children of tall couples, while still remaining taller than the average height of the population, are still generally shorter than their parents. Similarly, the children of short couples, while still remaining shorter than the average height of the population, are generally still taller than their parents. Thus, over time, the average height of the population remains fairly stable since children overall tend to be more nearly average in height than their parents. The same sort of phenomenon applies to dogs, where through the careful selection of breeding pairs, some full-grown dogs weigh over 100 pounds, and other full-grown dogs weigh 5 or less pounds. Nonetheless, left to themselves, "crossbreeds" or "mutts" over time resume the natural 35–40 pound animal that is the basic dog. It takes the constant input of effort and energy by the breeder to maintain the various breed characteristics that are far from the average or mean. The essential idea is simple: anything that is at some point extreme tends later to be less extreme.

Actually, this relationship is true for any two or more less than perfectly related phenomena. As an example, age and income are related, but not perfectly so. Since the relationship is not perfect, regression to the mean implies, for instance, that even though extremes of income will tend to be related with extremes of age, nonetheless extreme incomes will generally relate to less extreme ages. It also means that extreme ages will be associated with less extreme incomes. What does all this have to do with model deployment? A great deal.

Consider, for instance, that it is quite possible to segment customers by their performance on some criteria, say profitability, into perhaps 10 segments of 10% each of the customer base. Clearly, one segment contains the most profitable customers and another segment the least profitable customers, with the remaining eight segments somewhere in between. Also, it is equally clear that it's easy to make a similar customer profitability segmentation at any time. There will, by definition, always be a most and a least profitable segment. However, what should be expected to happen to the most profitable customers who happen to be in that segment at a specific time? Suppose that you tracked the profitability of all customers who were most profitable in, say, June through succeeding months. What would their expected profitability profiles look like? Since profitability in any one time period is imperfectly related to profitability in any other time period, the answer should be that profitability for the most profitable customers will decline—regress to the mean. Similarly, profitability for the least profitable customers will increase—again, regress to the mean.

Any deployed model, or at least, monitoring the results of any deployed model, will be impacted in various ways by this regression-to-the-mean phenomenon.

Just as the constituent companies in the Dow Jones Industrial Average change over time, yet the average is still the "same" average, so too the constituent companies of "the most profitable segment" will change over time. It is appropriate to track the performance of the segment; it's also appropriate to track the performance of the "companies forming the most profitable segment in June 2000" (just as its appropriate and interesting to track the performance of the companies forming the DJIA in January 1900)—but discriminate carefully between the two!

One client launched a program to improve the profitability of its underperforming customers—and tracked the performance of those customers over time from the start to finish of the campaign. In general, the profitability of those customers improved remarkably—and far more than the "control" group of customers who didn't receive the benefit of the promotional campaign. The company concluded that the promotion was a great success and were prepared to extend it further, and at much greater expense. What they had completely overlooked was how much improvement should have been expected for this group due to regression-to-the-mean effects. It turned out in this case that the "successful" campaign had, in fact, no detectable effect on expected customer performance. Nonetheless, it was exceedingly hard to persuade management of this—until they spent a very considerable sum of money on a follow up promotional campaign that seemed to have no effect whatsoever on profitability, and simply cost many hundreds of thousands of dollars investment for no quantifiable return. (This was, for the company, a very expensive way for the modeler involved to gain credibility!) On the other hand, having had at least one warning—the modeler's—they were able to terminate the project early, at least not spending the intended several millions on the project.

It's important to explicitly determine what regression-to-the-mean effects are to be expected before deciding about any deployed model's effects on the otherwise uninfluenced course of events. More generally, of course, the point is to create a baseline estimate of the probable course of uninfluenced events to compare against the influenced (by the model) course of events. Far and away, the phenomenon that most frequently misleads miners, modelers, and business managers (stakeholders in general) is the effect of regression to the mean. It turns out that very often business models are trying to either:

- Move extreme events back toward the mean (say, under-performing customers).
- Move mean events out toward the extremes (say, reduce plant industrial accidents toward zero).
- Move the mean of the whole population of events (say, reduce overall energy consumption of the company).
- Change the shape of the distribution of events (say, increase the ratio of satisfied customers to dissatisfied customers).

or otherwise manipulate the shape and parameters of the distribution (likelihood of outcome) of uninfluenced events.

Whenever such changes are made, the world "pushes back." This pushing back has been a recurring theme in this book—systems try to maintain themselves against changes, for example. Regression to the mean is just another, although quantifiable, example of this same phenomenon.

13.2.1.1 Quantifying Regression to the Mean

The essential point is to get a grasp on the way that the world would have changed had the model not been employed. Regression to the mean (for this discussion this will be abbreviated "R2M" from here on) takes place between any two variables that are imperfectly correlated. This is true regardless of the nature of the relationship between the two variables, specifically it doesn't matter if the relationship is linear or nonlinear, nor whether the distribution of the two variables is normal or something else other than normal. However, for the sake of this discussion, assume that the population is normally distributed. (It often turns out in practice in business modeling that many outcome distributions are near normal.) To make the discussion concrete, consider the case of the company just mentioned who was trying to improve the profitability of the less profitable customers. The promotional campaign was aimed at improving the profitability of these customers, so the question to answer here is: "How is profitability of these customers expected to change if no promotion was offered to them?"

First, remember that these customers were selected because they were the worst performing ones. Customer performance literally can't get worse than this—but it can get better. And given a chance, it probably will since if it changes at all it will, on average, get better. Thus, following this far from formal but somewhat "common-sense" reasoning, since it is certain that customer performance will change from period to period, the chances are that this group will perform better in a later period even if left alone. How much turns out to depend roughly on how correlated the two variables are. (The two variables are performance in one period and performance in a later period.)

Figure 13.2 shows the actual plot of customer performance for all 3,169 customers of the company in two separate periods. Each point represents how one customer performed in the two periods. Had all customers behaved identically in both periods all the points would fall onto the dashed line. In fact, fitting a straight line to the customer performance plot results in the continuous straight line that is "rotated" slightly clockwise from the dashed line.

The lower left part of the figure shows the under-performing customers. The "rotation" of the continuous line fitted to all the customers from the dashed line position is due to the R2M effect. If a low-performing customer had performed exactly as before it would fall on the dashed line. If a low-performing customer does worse, the point representing the customer will fall on the right of the dashed line. If the customer performs better, the representative point will fall to the left of the dashed line. It turns out that most of the under-performing customers have "improved" their performance. On the other hand, most of the high-performing customers (hardly to be called

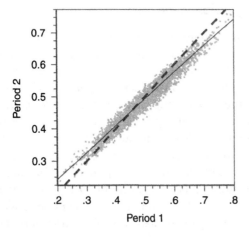

Figure 13.2 Customer performance in two periods.

"over-performing"!) have not maintained their high-performance status, so they are to the right of the dashed line. Overall, a clockwise rotation.

It turns out that the R2M effect is directly proportional to the correlation between the two variables, and can be determined (when nothing else changes and the distributions are normal) from the correlation coefficient. If the correlation coefficient r is known, the expected R2M effect can be approximated from the following expression:

$$R2M\% = 100 \times (1 - r)$$

This simple expression provides an approximation of the percentage change due to R2M effects.

In this example the correlation coefficient turns out to be approximately 0.9546. Thus:

$$R2M\% = 100 \times (1 - 0.9546) = 100 \times (0.0454) = 4.54\%$$

In this case the mean of the sample group is expected to move 4.54% of the distance from where it started toward the mean.

The lowest performing 10% of the customers in this example have a mean performance of 34.20 sales units in the first period. The mean for the period for all customers is 49.99 sales units. The distance from actual performance to mean performance is 49.99 − 34.20 = 15.79 sales units. The R2M% calculation leads to an expectation that, left alone, and subject only to R2M effects, the mean customer performance for this group of customers would increase by 4.54% of these 15.79 sales units, or about 0.72 sales units. Thus, the R2M expectation is for this group to increase sales performance to a performance of 34.92 sales units just from R2M effects. When actually measuring the change in sales performance for the periods immediately before the trial promotional campaign was launched it turned out that in fact the lowest performing 10% of customers had improved their performance by approximately 15%—three times the amount expected, on average, from R2M effects. These changes have to be taken into account when determining whether the promotion actually had any effect.

Similar reasoning applied to the highest performing group of customers leads to an expectation that they will reduce their sales performance.

Interesting and highly relevant as this calculation may be, this very brief introduction barely touches the surface of a truly important topic, and there is very much more that could be usefully said—a whole book's worth in fact. However, that will have to be left for the reader to dig into on another day. For pointers to a fascinating topic that actually turns out to explain much in life, and the understanding of which can enormously improve modeling predictions, look in the Resources section at the end of the book (See MIII: TB.13.2).

13.2.1.2   Explaining Regression to the Mean

R2M turns out to be difficult to convincingly explain to many stakeholders, so it's worth discussing the point a little more here since the miner's (and the modeler's) biggest problem, after working out the expected R2M effects, will certainly be to convincingly explain what's going on. The problem is that "common sense" does not lead to an expectation of R2M effects, so people, specifically stakeholders and corporate managers, don't understand it. Worse, although very simple and straightforward, it's perceived as nonintuitive. Interestingly, many R2M effects are, in fact, embedded in daily common-sense expressions. Any expression or expectation that "things will get back to normal" expresses R2M most explicitly, as does an expression or expectation that "things will even out over the long haul," and usually a colloquial appeal to the "law of averages" is also an appeal to R2M. Yet it turns out that parents expect their children to be as bright as they are, business managers expect that their best customers will remain so, and investors expect that above average performing investments will continue above average. In general, "it just ain't so!"

People who do begin to grasp R2M often fall into what's known as "the gambler's fallacy." Consider this argument: "After 10 flips of a fair coin, 7 turn out to be tails. Since, over the long haul, the law of averages says that these flips will average out at 50% heads and 50% tails, there is now a deficit of heads. The next few flips should have more heads than tails to balance the deficit. Therefore the chance of getting a head in the next few flips has to be more than 50%." How do you respond to this reasoning? And what, if anything, does R2M have to say about the issue?

Well first, note that the reasoning is fallacious. What the "law of averages" actually has to say on the issue is that over the long haul the *ratio* of heads to tails will approach 50%. However, as the number of tosses gets larger, it also says that you can expect that the absolute numbers of heads and tails will not only not be equal to each other, but will get farther apart. (And the "law of averages" also points to how far apart you might expect them to be based on how many tosses have been made.)

However, what R2M has to point out is that with the first 10 flips having 70% tails (which is not the mean expectation), the next 10 flips will be more likely to be closer to the mean—that is, closer to 50%. How much more likely? To know that (from the formula presented earlier) what's needed is the correlation between one set of 10 flips of a fair coin, and the next set. And that amounts to a correlation of "0." (Note that it's a fair coin, which by definition has a 50/50 chance on any toss of being either a head or a tail. By definition, no flip or set of flips has any influence on the state of the next flip or set of flips.) This leads to an expectation that:

$$R2M\% = 100 \times (1 - r) = 100 \times (1 - 0) = 100 \times 1 = 100\%$$

or in other words, that the mean head/tail ratio of the next 10 flips will move 100% of the way to the mean. To put the conclusion together, knowing the state of heads and tails of 10 flips of a fair coin says nothing about the average of the next 10 flips—and the best estimate is the mean expectation!

Nonetheless, people seem to expect that extreme events will be followed either by more events as extreme (child intelligence, corporate sales performance, or investment performance) or by extreme events offsetting or "balancing" the original extreme events (the gambler's paradox). The truth is that extreme events regress—return—to the mean. Randomness reigns supreme—and that's the way life works, like it or not!

The message from R2M is watch for it—or it will catch you out! (See MIII:TB.13.2.)

13.2.2   Distributions

(See MIII:AB.9.10) The most familiar distribution is the one known variously as "the bell curve," "the normal distribution," or "the Gaussian distribution." However, this is only one of a host of recognizable distributions, and one of an infinity of possible distributions. In practice, no real-world distributions actually duplicate any theoretical distribution, although they may show a marked resemblance to one or another.

The point about distributions is that they are really only a way of expressing the relative frequencies with which particular values turn up. For the normal distribution, for instance, values that are nearest to the mean of the distribution (the point in the center of the bell shape) are the most likely, whereas those far away (in the tails) are far less likely. The key point here is that all modeling techniques used in data mining are essentially frequency-based. Information about a distribution simply summarizes the characteristic frequency of occurrence of any value. However, it does mean that all models fit themselves to the distributions present in the data used to build them.

Several places in this book have discussed the need to make sure that the data used to create the model is representative of the data that exists in the world. Really, this is almost the same as making sure that the distributions in the model-creating data set are the same as the distributions in the world.

And the reason is because the models will only apply to the world so long as the distributions in training and run-time data are similar, or training set distributions are carefully adjusted to allow for any distortion (which is a topic covered in Chapter 11).

However, there is no guarantee that the distribution in the real world will not change. Very often distributions do change, if not so much in type as in form. In other words, although the distribution may remain normal, perhaps the mean or the standard deviation may change over time either quickly or slowly. (Mean and standard deviations are both measures of the exact shape and position of a normal distribution.) If the distribution of values for one or more variables changes over time, the model will become less relevant; the more the distribution changes, the less relevant the model becomes.

There are several things that can be done to deal with this. One apparently obvious solution would be to measure the distribution of the incoming data, and compare it with the distribution for the data that was used to create the model. This, however, is easier said than done. For a start, it is the joint distribution of the multiple variables that is important to determine, and high dimensionality multivariate distributions are quite hard to determine. However, difficulty of practical determination aside, a really significant issue is that determining any distribution requires a representative sample of data. Collecting the representative sample may take a significant amount of time, and in any case the assembled representative sample reports what the data was like when it was collected, not what it is like "now." Yet what is important to know in a deployed model is how reliable it is "now," not how it was performing yesterday, last week, last month, or last year. Thus, the apparently obvious approach of comparing the distribution between a current run-time data set sample and the training data set may be either not practical or too difficult to feasibly manage.

Usually, predictions are made only when the predicted value is unknown. However, sometimes the actual value is known shortly after the prediction has been made. If that's the case, then one way to check model performance for run-time data distributional nonstationarity (drift in the distribution) is to compare actual against predicted output. This goes immediately back to making all of the techniques covered in Section 12.1 applicable.

The key here is to compare distribution characteristics of the evaluation data set residuals (actual versus predicted) with the real-world data set residual distribution. This is fine if it can be done. Usually, of course, it can't. Actual outcomes may not be available until long after predict time, in which case these techniques only indicate how the model was working some time in the past. In that case, it's time to look at the techniques in Section 13.2.4 that deal with detecting novelty. However, first consider the case where there is no distribution at all. Is this possible?

13.2.3 **Distributions That Aren't**

Recall that distributions have a "shape," among other characteristics, that represents the relative frequency of occurrence of specific values (or categories) in specific parts of the variable's range. For numeric variables such distributions have various features that describe the distribution, such as the mean, median, or mode. Categorical distributions have analogous descriptive features of their distributions. Yet there are some collections of numbers or categories that have no known "shape," nor any other of the descriptive measures used for distributions, and these are collections of values that have no distribution. Unfortunately, they aren't at all rare, and even in business modeling, the data miner is very likely to have to model such apparently strange beasts as collections of data that have no distribution. Thus it's worth discussing what they are, where they are, how to recognize them, and what to do about them.

For example, consider a numerical variable with a normal distribution. A collection of data will reveal, with some degree of confidence, the mean and other features of its distribution. Since it is normally distributed, the only other parameter needed to fully specify everything about its distribution is its variance, or standard deviation. Now note that if this variable represents a phenomenon that continues through time, more data describing its behavior can be collected and added to the data set. Several things may happen. Perhaps its distributional characteristics don't change, in which case more data changes nothing; mean and standard deviation don't change. Or perhaps one or more of the distributional characteristics may change over time. For instance, during the 19th and 20th centuries, the mean height of the human population seems to have increased, as has the mean age of the population. The distribution has remained pretty much normal, the standard deviation has changed a little, and the mean has wandered a fair distance over the last 200 years or so. This represents a nonstationary distribution.

If a miner can identify a nonstationary distribution, and if the distribution is changing quickly enough to affect the performance of the model, it's perfectly possible and legitimate to try to create a predictive model that estimates the changed distributional parameters. With the adjusted parameter estimates, it may well be possible to make corrections to the original model to allow for the nonstationarity. But what of variables without a distribution?

Suppose that two players, Alice and Belinda, agree to play a fair game based on the flip of a coin. The idea is that both will put money into a pot, and they'll flip a coin. Alice will win if the coin comes up heads, Belinda if tails. The winner takes $1 out of the pot. How much should they each pay into the pot so overall it provides the winning amount? Well, this is easy—the mean frequency of winning for both players is 1 in 2 games, or 50%. Thus the winner gets $1 half the time, so the fair amount to pay to play this game is $0.50.

Notice that the fair value of this game depends on the mean of the distribution since that defines how much each player will receive, on average, over many games that are played.

After awhile they are pretty fed up with this game. To make it more interesting, they decide that the winner should get an amount that depends on how many consecutive times they toss the same side of the coin. Each player will flip the coin until their consecutive run stops. The first toss will be worth $0.01, and each succeeding toss in the run will double the winnings. So, for instance, Alice throws HHHT and wins 4 cents. (The three sequential heads yield $1 \times 2 \times 2 = 4$.) Belinda throws TTTTTH and wins 16 cents. (Five sequential tails yield $1 \times 2 \times 2 \times 2 \times 2 = 16$.) Alice throws TH and wins 1 cent.

What is the fair value of this game? That is, how much should they each pay into the pot before they take a turn? Or, the more fundamental question, what is the mean of this series? Notice that both Alice and Belinda have an equal chance of winning since this is a fair coin fairly tossed that makes the determination

If you try working this out, you are in for a surprise. It turns out that for any specific length of a specific game (in other words, for any specific and limited data set) there is a distribution. (It's not normal by any means, and Figure 13.3 shows the distribution of simulations for Alice's and Belinda's winnings after 65,536 turns.) However, what's the mean? Well, it depends on how long the game continues because it's constantly changing. It may *seem* to settle down for a while, but recall that in a long enough series, runs of any arbitrary length are guaranteed to happen. Those will perturb the mean in totally unpredictable ways, and thus propel winnings to completely unpredictable values. This series has *no* mean. And actually, it doesn't have any other characteristics of a usually accepted statistical distribution either.

Is this sort of series unlikely in everyday mining? Well, the Dow Jones Industrial Average index has a component of exactly this sort, and so do almost all of the other market indexes. Many of the economic series are of this type, or have components of this type. So too for many corporate series—even some sales forecasts. Despite the fact that these series have distributions for their historical series up to date, for many of these series, history has no implication at all for where they will head off to tomorrow. It makes for an interesting future!

(For a little further digging by anyone interested, many of these nondistributional series can be described using a phenomenon called *self-organized criticality [SOC]*. This is not a topic explored here, but check the Resources section at the end of the book for pointers to places to look for more information.)

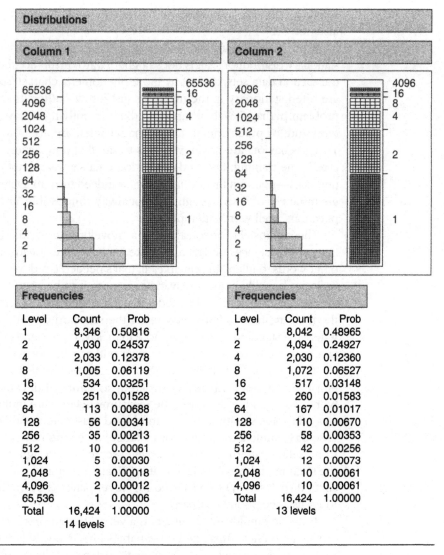

Figure 13.3 Outcome frequency for non-distributional series.

13.2.4 **Detecting Novelty**

(See MIII:AB.13.1) So far, the problem of keeping models working in the face of changing (nonstationary) distributions—and indeed series that have no theoretical distribution, stationary or otherwise—seem difficult to manage until the model has failed anyway, and that may be known only long after the fact. This is not a lot of help in trying to determine how well the model is working right now, and whether it's likely to work acceptably in any specific instance.

Even when running the models against data sets whose variables all have stationary distributions, all is not straightforward. Insurance, healthcare, credit transaction data sets, and many more phenomena characterized in data sets are often stationary in the main; it's just a few outliers that change. Not a problem perhaps? Well, it turns out that the outlying behaviors are very often fraud, or precursors to major changes that are about to hit the model. These behaviors are novel, which is to say that they haven't been seen before in the training, test, and evaluation data sets—and not even in the run time data—not seen that is, until they do indeed turn up. Detecting novel single instances of data is tough, but not always impossible, and for critical applications, well worth attempting.

The key insight for constructing a "novelty detector" is simply to realize that novel instances of data are unlike instances previously encountered—in other words, outliers. In principle, all that's needed is a device (or model) that indicates how likely the multivariate instance is to be an outlier compared to the data set used to train the model. For a normally distributed single variable, the measurement is fairly easy using the standard deviation. Any instance where the standard deviation is more than, say, three standard deviations distant from the mean may be declared an outlier, or a novel instance.

The difficulty is that first, much of the data that miners work with is most emphatically not normally distributed, so standard deviations of this sort won't work, and in any case, the measures needed are multivariate. What's more, in some situations, the method used must detect outliers on a case-by-case basis almost instantly. For instance, detecting fraudulent phone calls from calling patterns requires a novelty score fast enough to respond during the making of the call. In fact, that application required over 20,000 calls per second (per server) to be vetted for novel patterns of fraud for one major long-distance phone company.

Detecting multivariate outliers is a very different problem from detecting univariate outliers. Imagine two variables imaginatively labeled "X" and "Y" that are both normally distributed with a standard deviation of about 0.091 and a range of values from 0 to 1. These variables are present in two data sets called, say, "Set 1" and Set 2." Thus, there are two data sets, each with variables X and Y. In both data sets, the variables are normally distributed and have the same range and standard deviation.

This is the situation illustrated in Figure 13.4. The distribution histograms of each variable in the two data sets are shown with a normal curve fitted to them. From univariate considerations, it looks very much as if these two data sets are pretty much equivalent. Same variables, same range, same distribution. The problem is that these two data sets are actually totally different—about as different as it's possible for them to be.

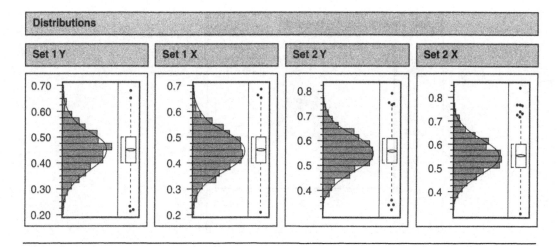

Figure 13.4   Distributions of two variables in two data sets.

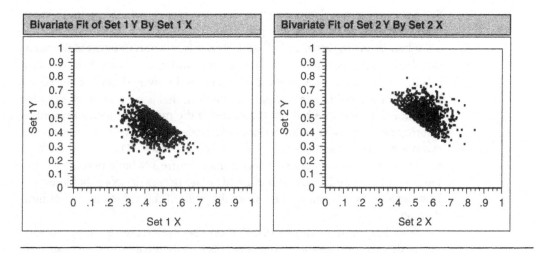

Figure 13.5   Joint distributions of two data sets.

A glance at Figure 13.5 shows the problem. Plotted in separate XY plots, none of the points in Set 1 fall into the same joint range as the points in Set 2. There is, in fact, no coincidence at all between the two data sets. Any model trained in Set 1 would find all the data in Set 2 to be entirely novel, and the model would almost certainly fail completely. Figure 13.6 shows the situation more explicitly, with both data sets plotted together in the same XY plot, but in different shades. It's apparent there that there is no overlap at all. Detecting that there is something very different about the two data sets—that

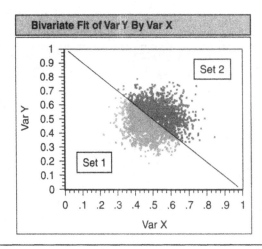

Figure 13.6   Combined two-data set XY plot.

Set 2 is entirely novel compared to Set 1—requires something much more than univariate distribution comparison.

When detecting how "novel" an instance is in a variable that is normally distributed, the measurement needed is some indication of just how unlikely it is for the instance value to turn up using the known "shape" of the distribution. For the univariate normal distribution, this is a measure of how far the value falls from the bulk of the values at the mean; the measure used as a surrogate for novelty was standard deviation, also known sometimes by its symbol z, which is why it's sometimes called a *z-score*. (One z measure represents 1 standard deviation in this nomenclature.) What's needed for the measure of novelty is some sort of multivariate pseudo z-score that indicates how far any given instance falls from the bulk of the values in the training data set.

Note that the multivariate distribution may well have several groups of values that cluster together—and cluster is exactly what they do. These clusters can be found by the technique called *clustering,* which is especially designed to find local clusters in multivariate distributions. Knowing where the centers of these clusters are in the data set will allow a determination of how far away from these centers any other point in the data is. The farther away any instance is from the cluster centers, the more likely it is to be a novel instance.

Using a technique called *k-means clustering* (one of the common clustering methods, and one that requires the miner to choose how many clusters to make) with three clusters and using data Set 1, the Cluster characteristics are shown in Figure 13.7. This has discovered, for instance, that Cluster 1 has a center at variable Y = 0.4014 and X = 0.5204. This can be seen in the fig-

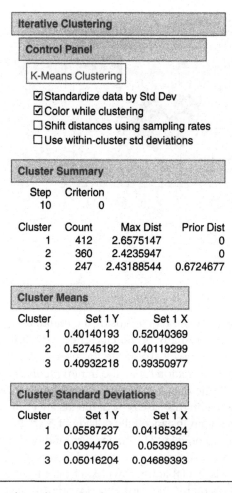

Figure 13.7   Three clusters details in Set 1.

ure at the line labeled "1" in the section labeled "Cluster Means." Figure 13.8 illustrates approximately where the cluster centers are discovered in this data set. Cluster 1 center falls at approximately where "Line 2" and "Line 4" meet; Cluster 2 center is approximately where "Line 1" and "Line 3" meet; and cluster 3 is approximately where "Line 2" and "Line 3" meet.

Remember that the idea here is not to get perfect separation—real world data sets are not usually as clearly demarked as the data set created to illustrate the point. The object is to measure how novel any particular instance is. The actual degree of novelty is impossible to measure, but the distance from cluster centers at least serves as one measure of how "likely" or "unlikely" any given instance is. Thus, distance from the cluster centers serves well as a surrogate for novelty.

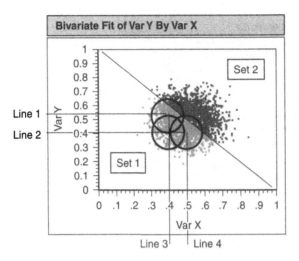

Figure 13.8   Three cluster's centers in Set 1.

Creating a novelty detector requires using the minimum distance that an instance is located away from any of the cluster centers. If it's close to one of them, it's not likely to be novel. To create the pseudo z-score, call it $_pz$, first determine the standard deviation for all the minimum distances to cluster centers for all the data in the data set. In this example with three clusters, $_pz =$ 0.03067. It turns out that in this case 88% of the instances in Set 1 fall within 3 $_pz$. Thus, in this case, if an instance falls outside of 3 $_pz$, then there is a good chance that it represents novelty. The circles surrounding the cluster centers in the figure show approximately the area covered by the $_pz = 3$. (All of the data used in this example is available for download from the author's Web site.)

The explanation actually takes longer to work through and understand than it takes to create the novelty detector. This is a quick and easy device to create to estimate novelty instance-by-instance (or, in other words, record-by-record).

There are many other uses for novelty detectors in advanced mining, and more sophisticated ways to create them. But this is quick, easy, intuitive, and works well in practice. What more could a miner want?

Well, rigor might be useful, but unfortunately this novelty detector depends on clustering, and most forms of clustering require the miner to select the appropriate number of clusters, and the best that can be done there is a rule-of-thumb estimate. (Read "guess.") However, a workable rule of thumb seems to be:

- Use no less than three clusters.
- Then: use the number of clusters equal to the square root of the number of variables.

- Adjust the number of clusters, if necessary, until a $_pz = 3$ captures about 90% of the instances.

Table 13.1 shows what this looks like.

Keep in mind that this is only a rule of thumb. However, this technique seems insensitive to the type of clustering used, and works fairly well.

13.2.5 Using the Novelty Detector

A novelty detector is simply a device that, on a case-by-case basis, produces a score that goes some way toward indicating whether an individual instance (record) is from a distribution that is similar to, or dissimilar from, the distribution of the data set used for training (and test and evaluation data sets too, of course). It's devised so that any $_pz \leq 3$ indicates that the instance is likely to come from a similar multivariate distribution, and any $_pz > 3$ points to a likelihood that the instance is novel.

The algorithm used to produce the $_pz$ estimate is very easy to implement and fast to execute. Any data set can be quickly scored as a whole, appending the $_pz$ score to each record, or, in a real-time setting where instances arrive asynchronously, it's still possible to make case-by-case judgments, keep moving averages, and so on. Far outlying instances can be almost instantly recognized and flagged for individual treatment, or large data sets can be split into sections—one that matches one model, and another section (of outliers) that requires a separate model.

More sophisticated uses can split incoming real-time data into streams based on which cluster center the instance is closest to, and model each stream of data separately. (Of course, this will require the original training data set to have been so split in the first place, and then require deploying multiple models, one for each stream.) This approach results in several $_pz$ scores, one per cluster, say $_pz_c$, where each c represents the cluster.

In short, $_pz$ and $_pz_c$ scores are quick and easy to generate, intuitive to understand, and easy to use and deploy: a powerful front-line check on current model relevance. Additionally, they can provide a powerful mechanism for

TABLE 13.1   Cluster Count for Different Numbers of Variables When Determining $_pz$

Variable Count		Clusters
From	To	
1	13	3
14	onward	sqrt(var count)

potentially improving overall model performance by splitting the data set for multiple models. Quite a lot of benefit from such a simple mechanism. However, deployment details are really advanced mining topics, and left for the reader to develop further. (See MIII:TB.13.3)

13.3 Deployed Model Form

The form of the delivered model has to be considered at some point in model creation. Some data mining tools require the modeler to deploy the model by calling some run-time version (or perhaps even the full version) of the modeling tool. This requirement is imposed by making a generic form of the model either hard or impossible to retrieve from the modeling environment.

It's all very well to have a neural network or decision tree or clusters as a model that works fine, but if a set of equations, rules, or whatever cannot be produced that express the model, it can't then be ported into a different environment. Some models are created in one environment (usually some form of MS Windows) and have to be deployed elsewhere—perhaps on a mainframe or running under some version of Unix, or as a distributed application on multiple systems. On the other hand, sometimes it is most convenient to have the model as a callable executable routine embedded in a library, a COM object, or some other form provided by the tool vendor.

Whatever the final needs for the form of the deployed model, checking how the tool allows the model to be deployed can save some nasty surprises when it comes time to put it into a production environment.

Keep in mind too that any form of the model that can be turned into source code suitable to the application's needs will usually execute a lot faster than making external calls to a run-time software implementation of the model external to the main application.

However, it has to be noted that at this point, deployment issues blend into the general application development and deployment issues; these need to be addressed by the miner, probably with the stakeholders and the IT folk responsible for getting the model into production.

13.4 Summary

If you have worked through this book sequentially, or at least dipped into all of the parts, you will now have followed through a comprehensive coverage of business modeling and data mining in a business environment. Congratulations! You have the knowledge—or will with practice—to go forth and make a real difference to data-based decision making, scenario planning, and process and performance improvement in any company that collects, or can collect, useful data.

However, there is much in this book, and the material is dense. Although there is clearly a methodology laid out, precisely how the parts connect may not be clear from just working through the material presented. Precisely encapsulating the techniques covered in the whole book, and explicitly laying out the fully detailed business modeling and data mining methodology covered here, is accomplished in Part IV.

Part IV
Methodology

Part IV provides a path to business modeling and data mining in the form of a detailed, step-by-step methodology. Chapter 14 provides a short introduction to the methodologies, which is available in printed form in this part of the book, and is also available for download from the authors Web site www. modelandmine.com.

Chapter 14
Methodology

Throughout the book, the narrative explanation has implied that all of the components should be able to be tied together into a methodology—a step-by-step series of instructions for what to do next depending on what has happened so far. Part IV of the book puts together just such a methodology. It's called "Catalyst"—something that does not itself change, and is not used up, but actively participates in enabling the process of change. This methodology, or more strictly these two methodologies, for there are two of them, should act as a catalyst for the modeler and miner.

One of the two methodologies corresponds to Part II of the book, and the other to Part III. The methodology that corresponds to Part II concerning modeling is referred to as "MII"; the other that corresponds to Part III concerning mining is referred to as "MIII." As far as possible, the form and format of the two methodologies is similar.

The structure of MII is illustrated in Figure 14.1. The top of the figure shows the starting point for a modeler—one of five initial situations:

1. "Explore this data set and find interesting and useful relationships."
2. "Here is a business opportunity we need to address—see what data mining can do to help."
3. "What can data mining do for us?"
4. "Use data mining to build a . . . model" (Fill in the blank.)
5. "In this strategic situation, can data mining help us to find out what's happening and what our options are?"

There are a number of techniques, shown in the center of the figure, that a modeler applies to any situation, and the objective of the whole exercise is to discover two key features:

1. The data needed for mining
2. The real requirements, including assumptions and considering all stakeholder needs

The techniques applied are shown in the center of the figure, and the outputs—needed data and real requirements—appear at the bottom.

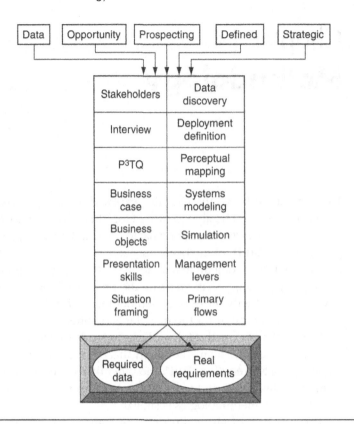

Figure 14.1 Methodology II themes.

As a figure, this is fairly straightforward. However, since all of the material is the content of Part II, it's clear that this diagram hides much of the complexity, and particularly doesn't give much help as to what to do when, and under what circumstances. That is what the methodology for Part II does cover in some detail.

The second methodology covers the material for Part III—a detailed, step-by-step guide to mining the data to produce the required model. The essential steps for MIII can be seen in Figure 14.2.

Once again, any reader who has even dipped into Part III will realize that although these are the main steps, the path from data preparation to deployment is not one continuous route. At any point, it may be necessary to return to an earlier stage—even to return to the modeling stage if the original situation was not adequately framed, or the data available proves inadequate.

Surrounding and covering both methodology figures should be a fine gray spider web-like mass of interconnections running from point to point within

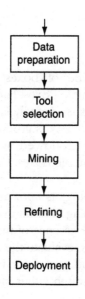

Figure 14.2   Essential steps in mining data.

the methodology, linking the parts and taking the miner from one point to any one of a multitude of others, depending on the exact circumstances.

During the process of modeling and mining, any modeler and miner has insights, which are part of the purpose for modeling and mining after all. But the insights will arrive unpredictably, perhaps as flashes of inspiration or just as just a slight inkling. Whatever and however they are manifested, when it means changes in the way the data is prepared, modeled, or presented, it means, perhaps, repreparing the data, creating a new model, or otherwise leaving one stage and going to another part of the methodology. These insight-driven modifications to what to do next during the project are not included in the methodology; it would be impossible to do so since inspiration can strike at any time, and at any stage. So these methodologies are not offered as *the* way to model and mine data, only *a* way. They are more a guide, a checklist, of possible actions and recommendations that, insofar as possible within the confines of the medium, have enough flexibility to offer relevant suggestions, recommendations, and pointers depending on the state of progress, and the circumstances, difficulties, and problems that face the modeler and miner.

However, not much more needs to be said about the content of the methodologies at this point. To describe the content of the methodologies themselves is simply to recapitulate the content of Parts II and III! What the methodologies offer in addition to the subject matter of the two parts is explicit directions for deciding when to do what, and how to discover what needs to be done next.

14.1 **Structure of the Methodologies**

The methodologies are constructed of four types of "boxes": Action Boxes, Discovery Boxes, Technique Boxes, and Example Boxes. Each box type has a different role in the methodology. Each box is uniquely labeled for reference and, as printed in the book, each type of box is grouped with similar boxes. Thus, all the Action Boxes come first followed by the Discovery Boxes, then Technique Boxes, and finally Example Boxes. However, neither methodology can be read sequentially.

This point bears repeating. The methodology is *not* a sequential document. Any attempt to read it sequentially is going to result in utter confusion. There is no one path through the boxes. The essence of these methodologies is for a modeler or miner to take actions, evaluate the results, and decide, based on the outcome, which box to read next. Some boxes have only one choice; some have many. The paths through either methodology are many and varied, particularly for MIII.

Each methodology is envisioned as a hypertext document, but also devised so that it can be structured in printed form. The book contains the printed version, but on the author's Web site *(www.modelandmine.com)* a hypertext version is available for download. At the time of this writing, the content of both versions is identical, but clearly it's much easier to make corrections, updates, and adjustments to the downloadable version. One important difference between the two versions is that the printed version has "Go to" and "See" connectors that indicate which box to visit next. The electronic version has no such pointers. Instead the text is hyperlinked to the appropriate next box, and clicking the link navigates the methodology. In this chapter, both the printed version and the electronic version are illustrated.

14.1.1 **Action Boxes**

Figure 14.3 illustrates a printed Action Box from MIII. All boxes have three common features: the top identifying bar, the central body, and a reference bar at the bottom.

The identifying bar at the top in the figure shows this to be Action Box 9.2. In MII, the boxes are numbered sequentially; however, in MIII, box numbers have two components. The first part, "9," refers to the chapter in Part III that the box can be associated with. The second part, "2," shows that this is the second Action Box associated with Chapter 9. The word "Preparation" indicates that this box contains actions to be taken during the data preparation stage of mining.

Action Box 9.2—Preparation: Inadequate or Insufficient Data

Situation:

- Errors and inadequacies in the original data collection process.
- Insufficient data.

Next Step:

- Mine the data as is, noting the deficiencies.
- Get better data.   ⇒ Go to MII:AB.13, p. 551

Return to data preparation actions list.   ⇒ Go to AB.9.1, p. 571

Reference: ibid 9.2.1

Figure 14.3   An Action Box (print version).

The reference line at the bottom contains, in this case, the word "ibid," which means approximately "this book," and the number 9, which points to Chapter 9 as containing relevant material. Most boxes point to one or more specific sections by their full reference; for instance, "14.1.1" refers to Chapter 14, Topic 1, Section 1—this section of this book. The "military" numbering system can become quite lengthy, but the purpose in this book is to provide cross-referencing with these methodologies. References, where relevant, are also made to specific sections in the author's previous book *Data Preparation for Data Mining*. Such references are prefixed with the identifier "DPDM." Thus, "DPDM 11.2" would refer to *Data Preparation for Data Mining*, Chapter 11, Topic 2.

The body of the box contains two headings, "Situation" and "Next Step." The Situation represents, or describes, one or more situations that are usually discovered as a result of taking discovery actions indicated in a Discovery Box. The Next Step or steps are the same for all indicated situations, so more than one path to any box may well exist. That is to say, more than one Discovery Box may result in a situation covered by this Action Box.

Action Boxes all indicate one or more Next Steps for the miner (in MIII) or the modeler (in MII) to take. Some of them are actions to take and move on. "Mine the data as is, noting the deficiencies" is one possible action to continue with in this example. To pursue this course, continue with the default action at the bottom of the box, "Return to data preparation actions list" in this case. This action has a pointer to the next appropriate action "⇒Go to AB.9.1." The symbol "⇒" is a visual clue to leave this Action Box and find Action Box 9.1. (That it is an Action Box is indicated by the "AB.")

Alternatively, the miner might choose to "Get better data," in which case the action continues "⟹Go to MII:AB.13," which is Action Box 13 in the methodology for Part II.

14.1.2 **Discovery Boxes**

The Discovery Box illustrated in Figure 14.4 comes from the section dealing with refining the model, and is the third Discovery Box associated with Chapter 12. The reference section points to a specific paragraph in that chapter for reference, which describes the discovery action in detail.

A Discovery Box always contains one "Discovery Action." This is an action that the miner needs to take to discover what to do next. Although specific, the Discovery Action is only a brief summary statement of what needs to be done. How to actually take the action is described, in this case, by Technique Box 12.26, which is indicated by the pointer "⟺See TB.12.26." The "⟺" symbol is a visual clue to visit the technique box and return to this Discovery Box. Technique Boxes have no pointers in them; they are always only visited.

Discovery Box 12.3—Refining: Check Predicted/Actual XY Plot

Discovery Action:

Create and inspect a predicted value versus actual value XY plot. Include a linear regression of the predicted values estimating the actual values.   ⟺ See TB.12.26, p. 652

Result:

Almost flat regression line in predicted versus actual XY plot.

Interpretation:

The model does a very poor job of predicting the output.

Possible Problems:

- The input battery doesn't relate to the output battery—in other words, the data doesn't support the model needed.   ⟹ Go to AB.12.2, p. 587

- The tool (algorithm) selected to make the model cannot deal with the data in the format provided.   ⟹ Go to AB.12.4, p. 588

Otherwise:

Continue refining the model.   ⟹ Go to AB.12.1, p. 586

Reference: ibid 12.1.1.2

Figure 14.4   A Discovery Box.

Every Discovery Box has one or more sections with the three headings "Result," "Interpretation," and "Possible Problems." The "Result" section indicates one possible outcome from the discovery action—in this case a "flat regression line." If this is the discovered result, the "Interpretation" section gives a brief explanation of what the result means. The "Possible Problems" section contains one or more possible problems that might give the discovered result, and pointers to other boxes that will indicate what can be done about the problem—Action Boxes 12.2 or 12.4 in this case.

If none of the one or more Results turns up, the next thing to do is pointed to by the "Otherwise" action, in this case, to "continue refining the model," as pointed to in Action Box 12.1.

14.1.3 Technique Boxes

Technique Boxes contain the common identifying and reference bars shown in Figure 14.5. The example shown is Technique Box 11.2 from the Mining

---

Technique Box 11.2—Mining: Missing Value Check Model

Technique:

- Create a copy of all three mining data sets.
- Replace all variables in the input battery that have a value with a "1."
- Replace all variables in the input battery that have no value (missing or null) with a "0."
- Use a mining tool to characterize the relationship between each input battery variable that has missing values and the output battery variable(s).
- Note the relationship and characterize it for any input battery variable that has a relationship with the output battery variable(s).

Why Apply This Technique:

To discover the presence of bias in the data set and to note and explain the effect that missing values have in the data set. The technique also discovers when, where, and how missing value information has to be explicitly included in a data set to improve the model.

Reference: ibid 11.2.2

Figure 14.5 A Technique Box.

stage, and outlines how to create the MVCM. The two sections "Technique" and "Why Apply This Technique" are summary encapsulations of the technique described more fully in the appropriate section (Chapter 11, Topic 2, Section 2 in this example).

14.1.4 Example Boxes

At this writing, there is only one Example Box, and that is in MIII. It's rather large, and not illustrated here. It has the same identifying and reference bars as the other boxes. The content points to a resource, in this case an Excel worksheet that is available for download, and a detailed explanation of the example in the worksheet.

14.1.5 Differences between the Printed and Downloadable Versions

The differences between the printed and downloadable versions of the methodologies are mainly in formatting, layout, and media. The same Discovery Box in both its formats are shown in Figures 14.6 and 14.7.

Discovery Box 9.4—Preparation: Leakage Check

Discovery Action:

Check for anachronistic variables.   ⇌ See TB.9.3, p. 630

Result:

The variable checked is unreasonably predictive.

Interpretation:

Any variable to be used to make a prediction that is too strongly predictive must be suspected of carrying information that won't be available at the time that the model is to be deployed. Using such a variable may result in excellent models during mining, but cannot actually be used in practice.

Possible Problem:

▪ The variable leaks anachronistic information.   ⇒ Go to AB.9.6, p. 573

Otherwise:

Continue with the next data preparation step.   ⇒ Go to AB.9.1, p. 571

Reference: ibid 9.2.3

Figure 14.6   A Printed Discovery Box.

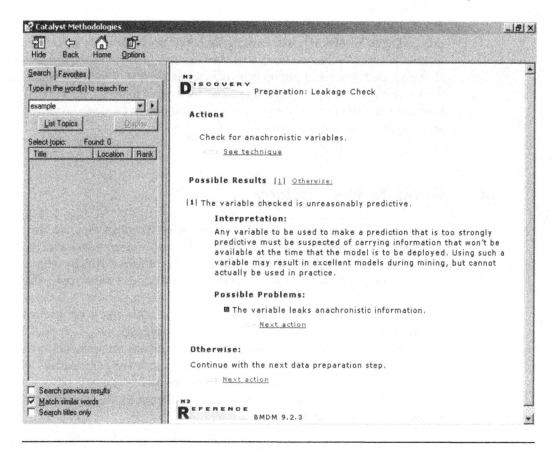

Figure 14.7 An Online Discovery Box.

In the downloadable version, the format of the methodology is changed due to the differing demands of the electronic medium. The electronic version, offered as a download from the author's website, is designed in the form of a Microsoft HTML Help application and includes Search and Favorites capabilities. (Since the methodology is not intended as a linear document, there is no Table of Contents.)

The major difference in terms of content is that the "Situation" section, which appears at the beginning of each Action Box in the printed version, does not appear in the electronic version. As you work your way through the electronic version, the situation is stated clearly before taking an action (i.e., on the link that you click on to reach the appropriate Action or Discovery Box). Therefore, the addition of the "Situation" text at the start of each Action box didn't seem necessary in the electronic version. Otherwise, the content is the same.

There are other more minor differences. In the print version, the "Go to" and "See" blocks provide the box and page numbers that indicate what is, and where to find, the next step in the process path. In the electronic version, those blocks are replaced by hypertext links labeled as "Next action" (when proceeding to an Action box), "Explore situation" (to a Discovery box), "See technique" (to a Technique box), and "See example" (to the Example box). However, each link has a popup box that carries the title of the next box in the process path. Also, wherever it seemed reasonable to do so, detailed explanations in the hypertext version appear in small popup windows (activated and closed by clicking on a link).

14.2 Using the Methodology

There are several ways to use these methodologies. Although separate, they are linked, so it is quite possible to simply start at the beginning, work all the way through to the end, and stop. The beginning is MII:AB.1, which presents the five entry point scenarios and a default action if none of them apply. The end is at MIII:AB.13.2. In between start and finish in version 1 of these methodologies are 179 boxes—36 in MII and 143 in MIII—that walk through the whole process of business modeling and data mining.

To use it this way, familiarize yourself with the layout and nomenclature, and then work through each box as you come to it, leaving bookmarks as appropriate and referring back to the chapters for more detail.

However, there are differences in character between the two methodologies, and other ways to use them.

14.2.1 Using MII: The Modeling Methodology

As the five different entry scenarios indicate, modeling depends very much on the business circumstances that prompted the modeling in the first place. "Build me a retention model" is a very different situation than "Take my data and look for gold." Different scenarios not only put different emphasis on various topics covered in Part II, but in some scenarios some topics covered in Part II need not be considered at all, whereas in other scenarios everything in the book needs to be used—and more, perhaps. Scanning through MII and noting which topics are referred to in which scenario points directly to which topics are important to which scenario (although reading through the whole of Part II is highly recommended for any modeler).

Each box in MII draws from themes in several parts of Part II, and the boxes do not associate with particular chapters. To a large degree, MII provides list of actions that have to be completed depending on the circumstances, and the decision points referred to in the Discovery Boxes are relatively few.

14.2.2 **Using MIII: The Mining Methodology**

Mining has a series of stages that have to be completed in order. No model can be built until the data is prepared. No model can be refined until it is initially created. Models not yet constructed cannot be deployed. Unlike MII in which, for instance, all of the situation framing tasks have to be completed, but several may be taking place at the same time, mining has to proceed from stage to stage. Very often, developments in a later stage—say, refining—will necessitate a return to an earlier stage, such as preparation. Nonetheless, the stages have to proceed from one to the next.

In Part III, one of the chapters covers each stage. Similarly, MIII also moves from stage to stage. Chapter 9 covers data preparation, and Boxes AB.9.*x*, DB.9.*x,* and TB.9.*x* all deal with data preparation issues. Similarly, Chapter 11 and Boxes *X*B.11.*x* deal with mining the initial model. Chapter 12 and Boxes *X*B.12.*x* deal with refining or improving the initial model—and dealing with many problems that a model is heir to. Chapter 13 and Boxes *X*B.13.*x* deal with deployment issues.

Every stage in MIII starts with a main Action Box: AB.9.1, AB.11.1, AB.12.1 and AB.13.1. Each of these presents a list of the main steps required for each stage, and the methodology returns to this main list several times until the miner has completed all tasks without problems—or at least has acknowledged and noted the problems as limits to the mined model's performance.

It's possible to dive into the middle of MIII and use it as a sort of "fault finding" or "diagnostic" tool in a mining project. Perhaps, without working through the whole methodology, a miner has a model, but its performance is odd or problematic in some way. Find AB.12.1 on refining the model and work through that section to discover ways of improving the model.

14.3 **Caveats!**

The presented methodologies are comprehensive in the sense that at every stage there is an explicit recommendation for what to do next. At no point do these methodologies leave either miner or modeler wondering what to do next, nor how to do it.

On the other hand, no methodology can possibly be complete in the sense that it lists every possible action that could conceivably be taken in every circumstance. Insofar as possible, the author has attempted to include a reasonably comprehensive list of suitable actions for a wide array of circumstances, and certainly the most common modeling and mining situations. In any case, humans are fallible, including the author, and that's where to lay the blame for any errors or omissions!

As a user of this book and the methodology, your opinion is valuable, and the author would be very pleased to receive suggestions for changes or improvements. The methodology, indeed the whole book, is intended to be accessible, useable, and helpful. If you find it so, or if you don't find it so, your comments will be very gratefully received. (To contact the author, check the Web site *www.modelandmine.com*.)

M II   *Modeling Methodology*

Note 1: This is *not* a linear document. Each Action Box and Discovery Box directs the flow to one or more next boxes according to the situation. Work from box to box as indicated. The linear, numerical ordering of the boxes is only to aid in locating the appropriate box.

Note 2: This methodology is intended to be used in conjunction with *Business Modeling and Data Mining* only. The directions are not, and are not intended to be, complete in themselves but to be encapsulations and "memory joggers" for topics discussed fully in the main text.

ACTION BOXES

Action Box 1—Beginning a Business Model for Data Mining

Situation:

You are responsible for, or have a lead role in, a data mining project in a corporate environment. Congratulations! This methodology will lead you step by step through the project, through the stages of developing a representation of the business opportunity or problem to be addressed, to actually mining the data and delivering a relevant data-mined model—and all steps in between.

Next Step:

- If your project starts with a data set and an injunction to "explore this data set and find interesting relationships"   ⇒ Go to DB.1, p. 554
- If your project starts with a business situation (problem or opportunity) that has to be explored   ⇒ Go to AB.6, p. 547
- If your project is designed to discover where data mining in general can offer value within your corporate environment   ⇒ Go to AB.11, p. 550
- If your projects starts with an injunction to create a specific data mined model for a specific purpose   ⇒ Go to AB.9, p. 549
- If your projects starts requiring a strategic analysis to support corporate scenario planning   ⇒ Go to AB.12, p. 550

Otherwise: ⇔ Go to AB.10, p. 549

Reference: ibid Part II

Action Box 2—Restart an Old Project

Situation:

The original project lost support because the stakeholders saw the problem or opportunity addressed as of diminishing interest.

Next Step:

- Create an outline business plan (management summary only!) for the original business case. ↤ See TB.4, p. 562
- Contact the original need stakeholders. ↤ See TB.1, p. 559
- Determine the status of the current interest in the original problem or opportunity.
- Propose to readdress the need. ↦ Go to DB.2, p. 555

Reference: ibid Part II

Action Box 3—Reevaluate Original Project

Situation:

- The original project failed to deliver results within a time and expense horizon sustainable by the stakeholders.
- The timeline for a single project is too long.

Next Step:

- Create an outline business plan (management summary only!) for the original business case. ↤ See TB.4, p. 562
- Contact the original need stakeholders. ↤ See TB.1, p. 559
- Determine the status of the current interest in the original problem or opportunity.
- Propose to readdress the need in manageable stages, each project accomplishing part of the goal, each stage designed to return value within 6–9 months. ↦ Go to DB.2, p. 555

Reference: ibid Part II

Action Box 4—P³TQ

Situation:

Need to discover a problem or opportunity that the data addresses and that is of sufficient business relevance and interest to accomplish what the company regards as a successful data mining project.

Next Step:

- Identify the core P³TQ relationships that either produce the data or which the data measures.
  ⇔ See TB.3, p. 561
- Identify potential need stakeholders.
  ⇔ See TB.1, p. 559
- Using stakeholder input, identify the business objects that the data represents.
  ⇔ See TB.5, p. 563
- Frame the opportunity.
  ⇔ See TB.7, p. 564
- Prepare an outline business case—keep it to the management summary only.
  ⇔ See TB.4, p. 562
- Propose the project(s) to the needs stakeholder(s).
  ⇒ Go to DB.3, p. 556

Reference: ibid 6.5.2

Action Box 5—Create a Business Case

Situation:

The stakeholders require a business case.

Next Step:

- Discuss the issues with the stakeholders.
  ⇔ See TB.2, p. 560
- Frame the business situation.
  ⇔ SeeT B.7, p. 564
- Create the business case.
  ⇔ See TB.4, p. 562
- Present the business case.
  ⇒ Go to DB.4, p. 556

Reference: ibid 6.4

Action Box 6—Explore Opportunity

Situation:

The project starts with a business situation (problem or opportunity) that has to be explored.

Next Step:

- Identify and characterize the relevant stakeholders.
  ⇔ See TB.1, p. 559
- Explore the business situation with the stakeholders.
  ⇔ See TB.2, p. 560
- Frame the business situation.
  ⇔ See TB.7, p. 564
- Define the relevant business objects for the project.
  ⇔ See TB.5, p. 563

- Find the data to mine.
- Create an outline business case.
- Present the outline business case to the stakeholders.

⟺ See TB.8, p. 565
⟺ See TB.4, p. 562
⟹ Go to DB.5, p. 557

Reference: ibid 5, 6, 7

Action Box 7—Insufficient Opportunity

Situation:

- The opportunity doesn't provide the level of ROI or resource investment opportunity needed.
- The business situation that prompted the original project exploration has changed.

Next Step:

- Not all projects are going to be worthwhile—which is what the investigation was intended to discover. Discovering that the effect needed can't be reasonably expected given the resources available is worthwhile, and saves pursuing wishful thinking for no likely return.
- No further action on this project. On to the next project!

Reference: ibid Part II, 6.4.4

Action Box 8—Seek Stakeholders

Situation:

- Need to discover stakeholders with resources who are interested in supporting a project that the data does address.

Next Step:

- Characterize the P³TQ relationships that the data does address.
- Map the business objects that the data addresses.
- Talk with potential stakeholders.
- Discover which of the 26 management levers is of most concern to each potential stakeholder.
- Match the management levers of concern to the business objects addressed by the data.

⟺ See TB.3, p. 561
⟺ See TB.5, p. 563
⟺ See TB.2, p. 560
⟺ See TB.14, p. 568

- Prepare an outline business case for each significant opportunity.

⟺ See TB.4, p. 568

- Present the outline business opportunity.

⟹ Go to DB.5, p. 557

Reference: ibid Part II, 6.1.1

Action Box 9—Specific Model

Situation:

- The project starts with an injunction to create a specific data-mined model for a specific purpose.

Next Step:

- Identify the stakeholders.

⟺ See TB.1, p. 559

- Discuss the requirements with stakeholders.

⟺ See TB.2, p. 560

- Frame the business situation.

⟺ See TB.7, p. 564

- Find the data to mine.

⟺ See TB.8, p. 565

- Define deployment requirements.

⟺ See TB.10, p. 566

- Mine the data.

⟹ Go to MIII:AB.9.1, p. 571

Reference: ibid Part II, 5.Intro

Action Box 10—Something New

Situation:

None of the initial business situations seems relevant to the situation that you face.

Next Step:

- One of these situations usually applies to pretty much all data mining projects in a business situation. If none of the listed situations are relevant, the author would be pleased to know for future reference!

⟺ See TB.9, p. 566

- Find the nearest and most relevant situation, and move into the project.

⟹ Go to AB.1, p. 545

Reference: ibid Part II

Action Box 11—Problem Hunt

Situation:

> The project is designed to discover where data mining in general can offer value within your corporate environment.

Next Step:

- Characterize your corporate key P³TQ relationships.   ⇔ See TB.3, p. 561
- Identify the corporate primary process flow.   ⇔ See TB.15, p. 569
- Identify potential stakeholders.   ⇔ See TB.1, p. 559
- Talk with potential stakeholders.   ⇔ See TB.2, p. 560
- Discover which of the 26 management levers is of most concern to each potential stakeholder.   ⇔ See TB.14, p. 568
- Characterize the most applicable business lever models.
- Explore data sources.   ⇔ See TB.8, p. 565
- Prepare an outline business case for each significant opportunity.   ⇔ See TB.4, p. 562
- Present the outline business case to the stakeholders.   ⇒ Go to DB.5, p. 557

Reference: ibid Part II 6, 7, 8

Action Box 12—Strategic Scenarios

Situation:

> The project starts requiring a strategic analysis to support corporate scenario planning.

Next Step:

- Identify potential stakeholders.   ⇔ See TB.1, p. 559
- Talk with potential stakeholders.   ⇔ See TB.2, p. 560
- Frame the business situation.   ⇔ See TB.7, p. 564
- If necessary, interactively work with the stakeholders to create a perceptual map of the strategic scenario.   ⇔ See TB.11, p. 567
- From the map, create a systems model of the strategic situation.   ⇔ See TB.12, p. 567
- Characterize your corporate key P³TQ relationships.   ⇔ See TB.3, p. 561
- Match the map to the corporate key P³TQ relationships.

- If necessary, simulate the strategic situation to discover uncertainties, ambiguities, or mismatches with intuitive understanding and discover crucial relationships (those not understood, well characterized, or for which small changes have potentially large effects).

↔ See TB.13, p. 568

- Characterize the key system relationships in terms of the 26 management levers.

↔ See TB.14, p. 568

- Discover which of the 26 management levers is of most concern to each potential stakeholder.

↔ See TB.14, p. 568

- Characterize the most applicable business lever models.
- Explore data sources.

↔ See TB.8, p. 565

- Frame each business problem or opportunity in the strategic model with particular attention to the strategies, strategy interactions, and risks including benchmarked risks and expectations.

↔ See TB.7, p. 564

- Mine the data to characterize the actual (rather than hypothetical) relationships to bring the system model and simulation into closer concordance with worldly behavior. "Deploy" the discovered relationships into the system map and simulation and exercise the simulation through the range of scenarios required.

⇒ Go to MIII:AB.9.1, p. 571

Reference: ibid 6, 6.3.3.2, 6.3.3.3, 7, 8

Action Box 13—Inadequate Data

Situation:

- Errors and inadequacies in the original data collection process.
- Insufficient data.
- Faulty data collection.
- The data stream represents data that has no determinable distribution, or for which the distribution is constantly changing.
- There is insufficient data to clearly enough define the explanatory relationships.
- The data is plentiful but the relationship variance produces a lack of definition in the important connections between input conditions and outcomes.

- The explanation is clear, but the variables and features used in the explanation are not business objects that the business managers or stakeholders can use to effect change.

- The useful variables available in the input battery turn out not to be able to provide an explanation in the terms required by the business managers or stakeholders when framing the problem.

- The data in the input battery may not relate to the output battery.

- The input battery doesn't relate to the output battery—in other words, the data doesn't support the model needed.

- The input battery doesn't sufficiently define the relationship to the output battery over all or part of the output range—in other words, the data doesn't support the model needed.

- The testing data set isn't representative of the same relationships that are in the training data set.

- The training and testing data represent some relationships better than others.

- There are many categorical values in the input battery that all represent a similar phenomenon or phenomena.

- There are a large number of variables in the input battery, many of which carry similar information over parts of their range.

- Although the input battery checks as representative of the population, it has some parts of the output battery range represented by very few instances (records) and other parts represented by very many instances.

- There may be a bias that affects all of the input battery variables.

- The data set represents only phenomena that can be known after the time that explanations, classifications, or predictions are needed.

- The amount of data available isn't enough to create representative training, testing, and evaluation data sets to support creating the data-mined model.

Next Step:

- Find more or better data.   ⇔ See TB.8, p. 565

- If necessary, discuss the situation with the relevant stakeholders (and in any case keep them all informed).

- If necessary, reframe the problem.   ⟺ See TB.7, p. 564
- Rebuild, prepare and mine the new data set.   ⟹ Go to MII:AB.9.1, p. 571

Reference: ibid 7, 6.2, 8.3.2.2

Action Box 14—Inadequate Frame

Situation:

- The business problem was not properly framed before modeling began.
- The relationships revealed by the model were not interpreted to address the stakeholder's needs.

Next Step:

- Identify the appropriate stakeholders, and remember that new stakeholders and new frame requirements can turn up at any time during modeling and mining.   ⟺ See TB.1, p. 559
- Clarify and outline the business situation with the stakeholders. Use any tools necessary to get a clear understanding of the situation and requirements. Use mind maps, cause-and-effect maps, system maps, any other techniques, so long as they are intuitive to the modeler and stakeholders.   ⟺ See TB.2, p. 560
- Reframe the situation.   ⟺ See TB.7, p. 564
    - Since this is reframing, pay particular attention to the following points:
        - Clarify the implications of the positioning on the nine level decision map—what is simplified, what is ignored, what it implies.
        - Clarify the implications of the strategies chosen.
        - Clarify the implications of the unadjusted and adjusted risks (BRAVE) and why it is important.
    - Framing is important regardless of whether an explanatory model, a classificatory model or a predictive model is required.
- If the revised frame requires:
    - more data   ⟹ Go to AB.13, p. 551
    - a different model in the existing data set   ⟹ Go to MII:AB.11.1, p. 575

- refinement of an existing model ⇒ Go to MIII:AB.12.1, p. 586
- changed deployment of a refined model ⇒ Go to MIII:AB.13.1, p. 595

Reference: ibid 5, 6

DISCOVERY BOXES

Discovery Box 1 — Project Starts with Data

Discovery Action:

- Determine the provenance of, and rationale for, collecting the data in the first place.
- Identify the project's original stakeholders. ⇔ See TB.1, p. 559
- Discuss the original project with the stakeholders. ⇔ See TB.2, p. 560
- Characterize the data set in terms of the P^3TQ relationships it was collected to address, or turns out to address. ⇔ See TB.3, p. 561
- Characterize the business motivation to collect and store the data in the first place.
- Discover who, or which department, funded the project and what return they expected.

Result:

The original business problem or opportunity addressed by the data was not fully addressed.

Interpretation:

There is an opportunity to return to the original business situation.

Possible Problem:

- The original project lost support because the stakeholders saw the problem or opportunity addressed as of diminishing interest. ⇒ Go to AB.2, p. 546
- The original project failed to deliver results within a time and expense horizon sustainable by the stakeholders. ⇒ Go to AB.3, p. 546

Result:

The data was collected to address a specific business situation, which it successfully did or continues to do. This project's motivation is to discover if there is any other corporate value to be had from the collected data.

Interpretation:

This is one of the classic data mining scenarios: "I heard that other companies found gold in their data, so we'll find some in ours. Get someone on it!"

Possible Problem:

- Discovering a problem that the data addresses that is of sufficient business relevance and interest to accomplish what the company regards as a successful data mining project. ⇒ Go to AB.4, p. 546
- Discovering stakeholders with resources who are interested in supporting a project that the data does address. ⇒ Go to AB.8, p. 548

Otherwise:

Discover a business situation that the data at least partially addresses, and for which additional data is available to add to the original data set. Treat this as primarily a search for a data-available business situation to address with data mining to which the original data set might contribute something. ⇒ Go to AB.11, p. 550

Reference: ibid 6.5

Discovery Box 2—Restart in Smaller Stages

Discovery Action:

Propose a project as a set of smaller incremental projects.

Result:

No interest.

Interpretation:

Time and circumstance have moved on. For whatever reason, the situation no longer attracts attention.

Possible Problem:

- Discover a business opportunity that the data does address. ⇒ Go to AB.4, p. 546
- Discover a business opportunity that the data partially supports and for which stakeholder support and other data may be available. ⇒ Go to AB.11, p. 550

Result:

Interest.

Interpretation:

The opportunity is still active.

Possible Problem:

- Creating a feasible and supported business case.

⇒ Go to AB.5, p. 547

Reference: ibid 6.1.2, 6.4.2

Discovery Box 3—Model Available Data

Discovery Action:

Propose a new project for which initial data is available.

Result:

The stakeholders are not interested in the project.

Interpretation:

Since the presentation of the outline business case (if created as suggested here) is aligned with business objectives, culture, and capabilities, the disinterest has to be for some other reason.

Possible Problem:

- The presentation wasn't convincing.
- The opportunity doesn't provide the level of ROI needed. Need to find another opportunity.
- The scale of the project is larger than the available resources can support.
- The timeline is too long.

⇔ See TB.6, p. 564

⇒ Go to AB.4, p. 546

⇒ Go to DB.2, p. 555

⇒ Go to DB.2, p. 555

Otherwise:

The stakeholders are interested in executing the project. Either:

- Create the business case if one is required.
- Frame the business situation.
- Define deployment requirements.
- Begin mining.

⇒ Go to AB.5, p. 547

⇔ See TB.7, p. 564

⇔ See TB.10, p. 566

⇒ Go to MIII:AB.9.1, p. 571

Reference: ibid 6

Discovery Box 4—Final Business Case

Discovery Action:

Present the requested final business case.

Result:

After consideration the required resources are not committed.

Interpretation:

> The time and resources required to gain the ROI as presented don't match those available, or perhaps the stakeholders hoped to use the business case to recruit support that wasn't forthcoming.

Possible Problem:

- The presentation wasn't convincing ⟷ See TB.6, p. 564
- The opportunity doesn't provide the level of ROI needed. Need to find another opportunity. ⟹ Go to AB.4, p. 546
- The scale of the project is larger than the available resources can support. ⟹ Go to DB.2, p. 555
- The timeline is too long. ⟹ Go to DB.2, p. 555

Otherwise:

- Frame the business situation for mining. ⟷ See TB.7, p. 564
- Define deployment requirements. ⟷ See TB.10, p. 566
- Begin mining. ⟹ Go to MIII:AB.9.1, p. 571

Reference: ibid 6.4.5

Discovery Box 5—Outline Business Case

Discovery Action:

> Present the requested outline business case.

Result:

> After consideration the required resources are not committed.

Interpretation:

> The time and resources required to gain the ROI as presented don't match those available, or perhaps the stakeholders hoped to use the business case to recruit support that wasn't forthcoming.

Possible Problem:

- The presentation wasn't convincing. ⟷ See TB.6, p. 564
- The opportunity doesn't provide the level of ROI or resource investment opportunity needed. ⟹ Go to AB.7, p. 548

- The business case is ambiguous. Without actually evaluating data projecting ROI, needed resources and timelines are too uncertain. Propose a data exploration data mining project that will result in supporting the development of better estimates in a full business case.

  ⇒ Go to DB.6, p. 558

- The scale of the project is larger than the available resources can support.

  ⇒ Go to DB.7, p. 559

- The timeline is too long.

  ⇒ Go to DB.7, p. 559

Otherwise:

- Frame the business situation for mining.

  ⇔ See TB.7, p. 564

- Define deployment requirements.

  ⇔ See TB.10, p. 566

- Begin mining.

  ⇒ Go to MIII:AB.9.1, p. 571

Reference: ibid 6.4.5

Discovery Box 6—Propose Exploratory Project

Discovery Action:

Propose a data exploration data mining project that will result in supporting the development of better estimates in a full business case.

Result:

After consideration, the required resources are not committed.

Interpretation:

The stakeholders aren't interested in even a discovery pilot.

Possible Problem:

- The business situation that prompted the original project exploration has changed.

  ⇒ Go to AB.7, p. 548

Otherwise:

- Frame the business situation for mining.

  ⇔ See TB.7, p. 564

- Define deployment requirements.

  ⇔ See TB.10, p. 566

- Begin exploratory mining. On completion, "deploy" the model into the business case.

  ⇒ Go to MIII:AB.9.1, p. 571

Reference: ibid 5, 6

Discovery Box 7—Reconfigure Business Case

Discovery Action:

Propose a project as a set of smaller incremental projects.

Result:

No interest.

Interpretation:

Time and circumstance have moved on. For whatever reason, the situation no longer attracts attention.

Possible Problem:

- The business situation that prompted the original project exploration has changed.

⇒ Go to AB.7, p. 548

Result:

Interest.

Interpretation:

The opportunity is still active.

Possible Problem:

- Reframing a feasible and supported business case.

⇒ Go to AB.5, p. 547

Otherwise:

- Frame the business situation for mining.
- Define deployment requirements.
- Begin mining.

⇔ See TB.7, p. 564
⇔ See TB.10, p. 566
⇒ Go to MIII:AB.9.1, p. 571

Reference: ibid 6

TECHNIQUE BOXES

Technique Box 1—Identify Stakeholders

Technique:

- Identify the stakeholders, who come in five categories important to a modeler:

    Need—Those who "feel the pain."

    Money—Keepers of the purse.

Decision—Those who can make the go/no-go project
decision.

Kudos—Those who get the "glory" or "blame" for project
success or failure.

Beneficiary—The grass-roots who "benefit" from the project's results.

Why Apply This Technique:

For a project to be properly framed it must meet the needs of
all its stakeholders, particularly when the data mining component is only a part of a larger project. Discovering and characterizing the people involved in the project is the first step in
meeting their needs.

Reference: ibid 6.1.1

Technique Box 2—Interview Stakeholders

Technique:

- Have a goal in mind for every project discussion and meeting. Realize that others have their own goals, too, but know
  what you need to get out of any meeting, whether it's one-
  on-one or with a group.

- Listen carefully to what other have to say, and the way that
  they say it.

- Reflect back your understanding of what they said: "What I
  hear you saying is . . ."

- Listen to clues to what is important—and equally for clues
  to what is not.

- Ask relevant open-ended questions to encourage information flow.

- Ask for help: "What should I be asking you now?"

- Do not be critical of any opinion.

- Do not point up inconsistencies during information gathering sessions.

- Develop an idea of the explicit purposes and intentions of
  the participants: "What are the goals of this project?"

- Develop an idea of the implicit purposes and intentions of
  the participants: "If the project is a success, what will you
  know that you don't know now? What will you be able to do
  that you can't do now?"

- Discover the caveats for the project: "What would have to change if this project is to be successful? Who will be affected by the project? What difference will it make, and where will the difference be felt?"
- Ensure that you can answer the three keys for every issue, situation, assumption, and action:

    What?

    So what?

    Now what?

Why Apply This Technique:

To encourage and elicit the maximum amount of relevant and useful information from the stakeholders, to understand the objectives and assumptions about what is required for success.

Reference: ibid 6.1.2

Technique Box 3—Identify P³TQ

Technique:

- Any data set or business situation, problem or opportunity affects, addresses, or bears on one or more of a company's core business concerns.
- Identifying which concerns are addressed provides a frame for the situation.
- The five core issues are:

    Product

    Place

    Price

    Time

    Quantity

    which can be represented by the acronym P³TQ.
- Restated, the core concerns of any company are having the right product, in the right place, at the right price, at the right time, and in the right quantity. All other systems of a company are secondary, aimed at facilitating this one primary system. This is true whether the products are goods or services, tangible or intangible.
- The most successful data mining projects bear directly on this core system, or on one of the secondary systems that have a major impact on the primary system.

- Discover and characterize exactly which, how, and how much the project affects each component of the core P^{3}TQ system, and what has to change to capture the opportunity or solve the problem presented.

Why Apply This Technique:

To discover, justify, and direct a data mining project to the core and management-visible issues that affect every business and develop a business case for the project to deliver the "gold."

Reference: ibid 6.5.2

Technique Box 4—Create a Business Case

Technique:

- The business case is the material that is presented to decision makers to persuade them that the idea proposed should be pursued.
- The two components of any business case are
  1. The written material
  2. The persuasive presentation
- The written material consists of a summary and six sections:
  1. *The Management Summary.* This is a *short* summary of the case as a whole, preferably one side of a sheet of paper—not more than two. Include six subheadings; each subheading is a one-sentence to one-paragraph summary of the corresponding section in the document.
  2. *The Opportunity.* Describe the situation as an opportunity, why it exists and the potential return.
  3. *Current Situation.* Describe the current situation, specifically what has to be changed and why to capture the identified opportunity's benefits.
  4. *Alternatives.* What else could the company do, and remember to address doing nothing as an alternative.
  5. *The Solution.* What do you propose to do? Why this choice? What is the anticipated result? Why does this fit with the corporate objectives?
  6. *Resources.* What it takes to get the job done. Who, what, and how much. Include a financial analysis in business terms. To be persuasive and convincing this section must be presented in terms that address management concerns, not the modeler's or miner's.

7. *Proposed Action*. This outlines the timetable, how the resources will be used, what deliverables can be expected, and when.

- Align the business case proposal with corporate culture, investment strategy, and process capabilities. Explicitly explain how the project aligns with each.

- Explicitly address ROI in business terms.

- In the Solution section, include the crucial deployment issues:

  - Which corporate systems will be modified?

  - How will they be modified?

  - Who will use the model?

  - How will the users be motivated to gain the most benefit from the model?

  - How will they actually use it in operation?

  - What skill level will be needed to use the model?

  - What training will be provided to the users?

  - How will the effect of the model be measured?

  - What will determine when the model is no longer valid?

  - What are the model's maintenance requirements?

Why Apply This Technique:

- To gain support from and engage stakeholders, senior management, and executives.

- To provide a "blueprint" for the overall structure of the business modeling and data mining project.

- To set and manage management, stakeholder, modeler, and miner expectations.

- To provide a "map" against which to gauge progress.

Reference: ibid 6.4, 8.2

Technique Box 5—Identify Business Objects

Technique:

- Create a business objectives goal map.

- At the top level of the map, represent the highest-level goals of the corporation.

- At each successive level identify specific subgoals that support the higher goal.

- Continue until the specific goals relate to measurable business processes.
- Measurable business processes will yield data that addresses the specific goals—and are justified, since each directly supports some higher goal, and ultimately the core business objectives.
- The objects from which data is measured are the business objects that the data addresses. (These business objects may be intangible or immaterial—they are nonetheless business objects.

Why Apply This Technique:

To discover existing data, generate new data, or recognize the value of previously collected data in supporting primary business objectives of a corporation.

Reference: ibid 6.4.2, 1.3.1

Technique Box 6—Presentation Skills

Technique:

- Improve presentation skills.
- These skills are not explicitly covered in BMDM. See the Resources section and the Web site for pointers to resources for developing presentation skills.

Why Apply This Technique:

To improve delivery of business cases, explanatory models, and all group corporate personally delivered communications.

Reference: ibid Resources

Technique Box 7—Frame the Opportunity

Technique:

- Identify the frame through which the stakeholders view the situation.
- Identify what features the stakeholders see as important.
- Discover in what terms the answer is to be provided.
- Locate the opportunity on the nine-level decision map.
- Articulate and clarify with the stakeholders the simplifying assumptions implied by the mapped level.

- If appropriate, determine or discover the action choices.
- If appropriate, characterize the strategies available.
- If appropriate, characterize the strategy interactions and pay-off interactions.
- If appropriate, characterize the benchmarked risks.

Why Apply This Technique:

To align the modeling and mining project goals and assumptions, particularly any unexpressed (hidden) assumptions, with all parties involved, including stakeholders, modeler, and miner, and to provide justified expectations for the delivered result.

Reference: ibid 5, 5.1.1

Technique Box 8—Find the Data to Mine

Technique:

- Seek data from existing sources:
  - Data from inside the organization.
  - Data from outside the organization.
  - Determine whether the available data addresses, or can be formatted or converted to address, the business objects in the project.
- Develop data specifically for the project from business processes:
  - Create business process maps for all relevant business processes.
  - Identify which of the 26 principal management levers the project has to provide control for.
  - Identify the subprocess transition points.
  - Create cause-and-effect maps (with stakeholder involvement and participation where necessary).
  - Capture business object data of time, event, and context from the relevant points.
- Develop data specifically for the project from system metaphor:
  - Conceive the situation in terms of physical (or other familiar) analogues.

- ◆ Represent the components as they interact in a system with feedback and feed-forward reinforcing and negating relationships.
- ◆ Use system diagramming, influence diagramming, or other familiar techniques.
- ◆ Within the metaphor, use analogues of across, through, and against variables.
- If necessary, merge or fuse several data sets into one integrated data set.
- Note the skip window required, if any.

Why Apply This Technique:

To discover or create the data necessary to support the project.

Reference: ibid 7, 6.2, 8.3.2.2

Technique Box 9—Support

Technique:

- Contact the author through his Web site, *www.modelandmine.com*. Direct email to the author is available on the site, or at dpyle@modelandmine.com.

Why Apply This Technique:

To expand the methodology to cover more business situations.

Reference: Web site *www.modelandmine.com*

Technique Box 10—Define Deployment Requirements

Technique:

- For each and every component of the model to be developed, define:
  - ◆ In what form is the model, or model results, to be delivered?
  - ◆ Who will use the model?
  - ◆ How will they actually use it in operation?
  - ◆ What user skills are needed to use the model?
  - ◆ What training is to be given to the users?
  - ◆ How will the effect of the model be measured?
  - ◆ What will determine when the model is no longer valid?

♦ How will the model be maintained?

♦ What documentation is required?

Why Apply This Technique:

To ensure that the model is developed to meet the user's needs and that the model as delivered can be deployed into the required application.

Reference: ibid 8.2

Technique Box 11—Perceptual Mapping

Technique:

- Create a visual and shared representation of the stakeholder's perceptions about the situation.
- Use any technique that is intuitive and interactive. One technique is mind mapping. Either:
  ♦ Use manual mind mapping with pencil and paper, or
  ♦ Use an automated mind mapping tool that can be used on a PC and projected for shared perception of a situation.
- Create a cognitive map using any tool or technique of choice:
  ♦ Define objects
  ♦ Define properties

Why Apply This Technique:

To generate an agreed and shared perception of the strategic situation and all important components.

Reference: ibid 6.3.1, 6.3.2

Technique Box 12—Systems Map

Technique:

- Extend an already created cognitive map into a system map.
- Define the relationships in the system with units of measure ranges of values, nature, and strength of the interaction.
- If convenient use a physical system metaphor:
  ♦ Conceive the situation in terms of physical (or other familiar) analogues.

- ◆ Represent the components as they interact in a system with feedback and feed-forward reinforcing and negating relationships.
- ◆ Use system diagramming, influence diagramming, or other familiar techniques.
- ◆ Within the metaphor, use analogues of across, through, and against variables.

Why Apply This Technique:

To characterize a system representation explicitly to point to the data required to validate the cognitive representation against real world behaviors.

Reference: ibid 6.3.3

Technique Box 13—Simulation

Technique:

Simulate the model to discover (often completely unexpected) behaviors.

For simulation tools, see the resource links at *www. modelandmine.com*.

Why Apply This Technique:

- ■ To discover important relationships to characterize with data.
- ■ To evaluate business scenarios for strategic planning.

Reference: ibid 6.3.3.1

Technique Box 14—26 Management Levers

Technique:

Use Tables 7.1, 7.2, and 7.3 (in Chapter 7) to characterize the 26 management actions that business managers can take to modify business processes and so manage the business.

Why Apply This Technique:

To identify management options.

Reference: ibid 7.1.3.3

Technique Box 15—Primary Process Flows

Technique:

- Identify flows form the main "pulse" of corporate activity. They usually relate to the company's core P^{3}TQ system. These are the primary process flows.

- Segregrate primary process flows from secondary flows, important as they may be, which support primary flows. Any failure in a secondary flow directly affects one of the primary flows, but usually not the other way round..

Why Apply This Technique:

To identify the relationships of primary concern to a company.

Reference: ibid 7.1.3.4

M III   **Mining Methodology**

Note 1: This is *not* a linear document. Each Action Box and Discovery Box directs the flow to one or more next boxes according to the situation. Work from box to box as indicated. The linear, numerical ordering of the boxes is only to aid in locating the appropriate box.

Note 2: This methodology is intended to be used in conjunction with *Business Modeling and Data Mining* only. The directions are not, and are not intended to be, complete in themselves but to be encapsulations and "memory joggers" for topics discussed fully in the main text.

ACTION BOXES

Action Box 9.1—Data Preparation: Main Steps

Situation:

Data needs to be prepared for mining.

Next Step:

- Check the variable characteristics matrix.   ⇒ Go to DB.9.1, p. 596
- Check for basic variable problems.   ⇒ Go to DB.9.2, p. 597
- Check for basic data set problems.   ⇒ Go to DB.9.3, p. 599
- Check for anachronistic variables.   ⇒ Go to DB.9.4, p. 600
- Check for sufficient data.   ⇒ Go to DB.9.5, p. 600
- Check outcome representation.   ⇒ Go to DB.9.6, p. 601
- Check basic feature representation.   ⇒ Go to DB.9.7, p. 602

If All Preparation Actions Are Complete:

Create the initial model.   ⇒ Go to AB.11.1, p. 575

Otherwise:

Continue with the next preparation step.   ⇒ Go to AB.9.1, p. 571

Reference: ibid 9

Action Box 9.2—Preparation: Inadequate or Insufficient Data

Situation:

- Errors and inadequacies in the original data collection process.
- Insufficient data.

M III
Action Boxes

Next Step:

- Mine the data as is, noting the deficiencies.
- Get better data.   ⇒ Go to MII:AB.13, p. 551

Return to data preparation actions list.   ⇒ Go to AB.9.1, p. 571

Reference: ibid 9.2.1

Action Box 9.3—Preparation: Incorrect Data Set

Situation:

The data set checked isn't the one that it was supposed to be.

Next Step:

- Find the right data set.

Return to data preparation actions list.   ⇒ Go to AB.9.1, p. 571

Reference: ibid 9.2

Action Box 9.4—Preparation: Faulty Data Collection

Situation:

Faulty data collection.

Next Step:

- Get better data.   ⇒ Go to MII:AB.13, p. 551

Reference: ibid 9

Action Box 9.5—Preparation: Faulty Data Selection

Situation:

Faulty selection of the mining data set from a source data set.

Next Step:

- Rebuild the mining data set from the source data set.

Return to data preparation actions list.   ⇒ Go to AB.9.1, p. 571

Reference: ibid 9

Action Box 9.6—Preparation: Problem Variable

Situation:

- The variable is no longer used in the source data set.
- No mining tool can make any use of this variable.
- Many mining algorithms cannot deal with mainly empty variables.
- When categories are unique, or nearly so, and there is no rational ordering to the categories, no mining tool can discover useable patterns.
- The variable leaks anachronistic information.

Next Step:

- Discard the variable from the mining data set.

Return to data preparation actions list.　　　　　⇒ Go to AB.9.1, p. 571

Reference: ibid 9.2.2

Action Box 9.7—Preparation: Categorical Variables

Situation:

Unless specifically flagged as a categorical value, or converted to non-numeric representation, many mining tools will assume the variable has numerical meaning.

Next Step:

- If the mining tool allows, flag the variable as categorical.
- Convert the categories to a non-numeric representation.

Return to data preparation actions list.　　　　　⇒ Go to AB.9.1, p. 571

Reference: ibid 9.2.2.3

Action Box 9.8—Preparation: Ordering Categories

Situation:

Mining tools that are sensitive to numerical and ordinal variables will be unable to access the ordering information that the variable could expose to the mining tool.

Next Step:

- Number the categories in an appropriate order.

M III
Action Boxes

Return to data preparation actions list.

⇒ Go to AB.9.1, p. 571

Reference: ibid 9.2.2.3, 12.2.3.2

Action Box 9.9—Preparation: Variable Performance

Situation:

- One of the variables isn't measuring the phenomenon that its label suggests it should.
- One of the variables has somehow picked up data about phenomena that it shouldn't be representing.

Next Step:

- Rebuild the mining data set from the source data set.
- Discard the variable from the mining data set.

Return to data preparation actions list.

⇒ Go to AB.9.1, p. 571

Reference: ibid 9.2.1

Action Box 9.10—Preparation: Distribution Problem

Situation:

The data stream represents data that has no determinable distribution, or for which the distribution is constantly changing.

Next Step:

- The data requires transformation, if possible, to represent a modelable phenomenon. This requires advanced data preparation and mining techniques not covered here, but refer to Section 13.2 for more information.
- Get better data.

⇒ Go to MII:AB.13, p. 551

Reference: ibid 9, 13.2.2

Action Box 9.11—Preparation: Absolute Measurement

Situation:

The variable as presented in the data set represents only an absolute measurement.

Next Step:

- Recode the variable as a relative measure.
- Recode the variable as a cyclic measure.

Return to data preparation actions list.

⇒ Go to AB.9.1, p. 571

Reference: ibid 9.3.1

Action Box 11.1—Mining the Initial Model: Main Steps

Situation:

The initial model needs to be created.

Next Steps:

Structure the data for mining.

⇒ Go to DB.11.1, p. 603

Characterize the input and output batteries.

⇒ Go to DB.11.2, p. 603

Choose the mining tool.

⇒ Go to DB.11.3, p. 605

Construct the MVCM.

⇒ Go to DB.11.4, p. 606

If mining to understand:

Create the initial explanatory model.

⇒ Go to DB.11.5, p. 607

If mining to classify:

Discover the appropriate type of initial classification model.

⇒ Go to DB.11.6, p. 608

If mining to predict:

Discover the appropriate type of predictive model.

⇒ Go to DB.11.7, p. 611

If all initial mining actions are complete:

Refine the model.

⇒ Go to AB.12.1, p. 586

Otherwise:

Complete the next initial mining step.

⇒ Go to AB.11.1, p. 575

Reference: ibid 11

Action Box 11.2—Mining: Insufficient Data

Situation:

There isn't enough data available to create fully representative, equally sized training, testing, and evaluation data sets.

Next Steps:

Restructure the data.

⇒ Go to DB.11.8, p. 582

Reference: ibid 11.1

M III
Action Boxes

Action Box 11.3—Mining: Unrepresentative Data Sets

Situation:

There isn't enough data available to create fully representative 60/20/20 training, testing, and evaluation data sets.

Next Steps:

Restructure the data.

⇒ Go to DB.11.9, p. 613

Reference: ibid 11.1

Action Box 11.4—Mining: Tool Selection

Situation:

An appropriate mining tool has to be selected, including:

- Selection of an appropriate unsupervised mining tool.
- Selection of an appropriate supervised mining tool.
- Selection of a mining technique capable of modeling several outputs simultaneously from the same input data.
- Selection of several mining techniques, each capable of modeling one of the outputs needed at a time.
- Selection of an advanced mining technique capable of modeling many inputs to many outputs simultaneously.
- Selection of various techniques, supervised or unsupervised, to characterize the various relationships needed.

Next Steps:

First, collect the information to select the mining tool

⇔ See TB.11.1, p. 631

Then, choose the appropriate mining tool.

⇒ Go to DB.11.3, p. 632

Reference: ibid 10, 11.2.1

Action Box 11.5—Mining: Algorithm Selection

Situation:

Mining tools are available, but not one that incorporates the suggested algorithms.

Next Steps:

- Either:
  - ◆ Use the most appropriate algorithm in the tool available.
  - ◆ Seek a tool that incorporates an appropriate algorithm.

⇔ See TB.11.4, p. 633

  - ◆ Reframe the problem to fit the tool available.

⇔ See MII:TB.7, p. 564

- Then:
  - ◆ Select the algorithm.   ⇒ Go to DB.11.3, p. 605

Reference: ibid 11.2.1

Action Box 11.6—Mining: Vendor Selection

Situation:

The miner has no mining tools currently available and needs
vendor sources to select from.   ⇒ See TB.11.4, p. 633

Next Steps:

- Seek a tool that incorporates an appropriate algorithm.   ⇒ Go to DB.11.3, p. 605

Reference: ibid 10

Action Box 11.7—Mining: MVCM Relationships

Situation:

The MVCM relationships have to be explained.

Next Steps:

- Interpret the relationships as for any explanatory model.   ⇒ See TB.11.3, p. 632
- Discuss the interpretation of MVCM relationships with the
  relevant domain experts and stakeholders.   ⇒ See TB.11.11, p. 637
- Determine the presence of bias and, if necessary, rebuild a
  less biased data set.
- Either:
  - ◆ Get better data, or   ⇒ Go to MII:AB.13, p. 551
  - ◆ Continue mining:
    an explanatory model   ⇒ Go to DB.11.5, p. 607
    a classificatory model   ⇒ Go to DB.11.6, p. 608
    a predictive model   ⇒ Go to DB.11.7, p. 611

Reference: ibid 11.2.2, 11.1, 9.2.3.6, 8.3.1.2

Action Box 11.8—Mining: Sampling Bias

Situation:

MVCM relationships indicate the possible presence of sampling
bias in the way that the modeling data was assembled.

M III
Action Boxes

Next Steps:

- Discuss the interpretation of MVCM relationships with the relevant domain experts and stakeholders.

  ⇔ See TB.11.11, p. 637

- Determine the presence of bias and, if necessary, rebuild a less biased data set.

- Either:
  - ◆ Get better data, or

    ⇒ Go to MII:AB.13, p. 551

  - ◆ Construct a model in the biased data set.

    Note the biasing conditions for inclusion as limits to applicability of the final model.

  - ◆ Continue mining:

    an explanatory model

    ⇒ Go to DB.11.5, p. 607

    a classificatory model

    ⇒ Go to DB.11.6, p. 608

    a predictive model

    ⇒ Go to DB.11.7, p. 611

Reference: ibid 11.2.2, 11.1, 9.2.3.6, 8.3.1.2

Action Box 11.9—Mining: External Bias

Situation:

MVCM relationships indicate the possible presence of external bias that affects the representativeness with which the data represents phenomena in the world.

Next Steps:

- Discuss the interpretation of MVCM relationships with the relevant domain experts and stakeholders.

  ⇔ See TB.11.11, p. 637

- Determine the presence of bias and, if necessary, rebuild a less biased data set.

- Either:
  - ◆ Get better data, or

    ⇒ Go to MII:AB.13, p. 551

  - ◆ Construct a model in the biased data set.

    Note the biasing conditions for inclusion as limits to applicability of the final model.

  - ◆ Continue mining:

    an explanatory model

    ⇒ Go to DB.11.5, p. 607

    a classificatory model

    ⇒ Go to DB.11.6, p. 608

    a predictive model

    ⇒ Go to DB.11.7, p. 611

Reference: ibid 11.2.2, 11.1, 9.2.3.6, 8.3.1.2

Action Box 11.10—Mining: Missing Values

Situation:

Values are missing and the selected mining tool's inherent algorithm does not handle missing values, which have to be replaced before creating the initial model.

Next Steps:

- When building the *initial* model (and only when building the initial model), use the tool's default missing value replacement method.
- Incorporate the MVCM binary flag version of the original variable in the data sets to be mined where the MVCM variable had a relevant relationship with the output battery.
- Continue mining:

  an explanatory model
  a classificatory model
  a predictive model

⇒ Go to DB.11.5, p. 607
⇒ Go to DB.11.6, p. 608
⇒ Go to DB.11.7, p. 611

Reference: ibid 11.2.2

Action Box 11.11—Mining: Insufficient Data

Situation:

There is insufficient data to clearly enough define the explanatory relationships.

Next Steps:

- Refine the model.
- Get better data.

⇒ Go to AB.12.1, ■1, p. 586
⇒ Go to MII:AB.13, p. 551

Reference: ibid 11.3

Action Box 11.12—Mining: Relationship Variance

Situation:

The data is plentiful but the relationship variance produces a lack of definition in the important connections between input conditions and outcomes.

Next Steps:

- Refine the model.
- Get better data.

⇨ Go to AB.12.1, ■1, p. 586
⇨ Go to MII:AB.13, p. 551

Reference: bid 11.3, 12.1.6

Action Box 11.13—Mining: Business Objects

Situation:

The explanation is clear, but the variables and features used in the explanation are not business objects that the business managers or stakeholders can use to effect change.

Next Steps:

- Reframe the problem.
- Then either or both:
  - ◆ Restructure the data set to include at least intermediate, and, if available, control variables.
  - ◆ Find better data.

⇔ See MII:TB.7, p. 564

⇨ Go to MII:AB.13, p. 551
⇨ Go to MII:AB.13, p. 551

Reference: ibid 11.3, 7.2.1, 6.2.1.2

Action Box 11.14—Mining: Lack of Explanation

Situation:

The useful variables available in the input battery turn out not to be able to provide an explanation in the terms required by the business managers or stakeholders when framing the problem.

Next Steps:

- Reframe the problem.
- Then either or both:
  - ◆ Restructure the data set to include at least intermediate, and, if available, control variables.
  - ◆ Find better data.

⇔ See MII:TB.7, p. 564

⇨ Go to MII:AB.13, p. 551
⇨ Go to MII:AB.13, p. 551

Reference: ibid 11.3, 4.3.3

Action Box 11.15—Mining: Binary Outcome, Binary Prediction

Situation:

The model required is a binary outcome classification model and the tool selected produces a binary prediction.

Next Steps:

- Apply the binary classification tool to the data.
- Create a binary confusion matrix.
- Determine initial model performance.
- Check model performance.

⇔ See TB.11.5, p. 633
⇔ See TB.11.6, p. 634
⇒ Go to DB.11.10, p. 614

Reference: ibid 11.4.2, 11.4.3

Action Box 11.16—Mining: Binary Outcome, Continuous Prediction

Situation:

The model required is a binary outcome classification and the tool selected produces a continuous score.

Next Steps:

- Apply the continuous classification tool to the data.
- Create a binary confusion matrix.
- Determine initial model performance.
- Check model performance.

⇔ See TB.11.7, p. 634
⇔ See TB.11.6, p. 634
⇒ Go to DB.11.11, p. 615

Reference: ibid 11.4.4, 11.4.5

Action Box 11.17—Mining: Multiple Outcome, Multiple Prediction

Situation:

The model required is a multiple outcome classification and the tool selected produces multiple classes.

Next Steps:

- Apply the multiclass classification tool to the data to create a single model—the mono-model.
- Create a mono-model multiclass confusion matrix.
- Determine mono-model performance.
- Create multiple models, one for each output battery class— the multi-model.
- Determine multi-model performance.
- Select either the mono-model or multi-model as the initial model based on the performance of each.
- Check model performance.

⇔ See TB.11.8, p. 635
⇔ See TB.11.6, p. 634

⇔ See TB.11.9, p. 635
⇔ See TB.11.6, p. 634

⇒ Go to DB.11.12, p. 616

Reference: ibid 11.4.6

Action Box 11.18—Mining: Continuous Outcome, Continuous Prediction

Situation:

The model required is a continuous outcome classification, and the tool selected produces a continuous score.

Next Steps:

- Apply the continuous classification tool to the data.
- Determine initial model performance.   ⇔ See TB.11.10, p. 636
- Refine the model.   ⇒ Go to AB.12.1, ▪5, p. 586

Reference: ibid 11.4.5

Action Box 11.19—Mining: Tool/Objective Incompatibility

Situation:

Either the business situation must be reformulated or some other tool used.

Next Steps:

- Choose or find a mining tool that produces the needed type of output.   ⇒ Go to DB.11.3, p. 605
- Reframe the problem in terms that the available tool can address.   ⇔ See MII:TB.7, p. 564
- Restart mining the data to fit the new business situation frame.   ⇒ Go to AB.11.1, p. 575

Reference: ibid 11.2, 5.2

Action Box 11.20—Mining: Systems Modeling

Situation:

Need to discover sources and system representations suitable to frame the business problem.

Next Steps:

- Locate system modeling tools.   ⇔ See TB.11.4, p. 633
- Create the systems model.   ⇔ See MII:TB.12, p. 567
- Identify key system relationships.   ⇔ See MII:TB.13, p. 568
- Obtain the relevant data indicated by the systems model and/or systems simulation.

- Prepare the data and mine it to characterize each of the key system relationships.

⇒ Go to AB.9.1, p. 571

Reference: ibid 11.2, 11.5

Action Box 11.21—Mining: System Characterization

Situation:

Characterize each relationship using a classification model of an appropriate type.

Next Steps:

- Choose or find a mining tool that produces the needed type of output.

⇒ Go to DB.11.3, p. 605

Reference: ibid 11.2

Action Box 11.22—Mining: Multiple Outcome, Continuous Prediction

Situation:

The model required is a multiple outcome classification model with the output estimated as a score.

Next Steps:

- Apply the continuous classification tool to the data.
- Bin the model's score into bins that best correspond to the multiple classes.
- Determine initial model performance.
- Refine the model.

⇔ See TB.11.8, p. 635
⇔ See TB.11.10, p. 636
⇒ Go to AB.12.1, ■5, p. 586

Reference: ibid 11.4

Action Box 11.23—Mining: Balance a Data Set

Situation:

The data set presents very few examples of a class, or several classes, of significance to the business situation. The low level of prevalence of such examples that are of business significance inhibits the algorithm incorporated in the mining tool of choice from characterizing them.

M III
Action Boxes

Next Steps:

- Enhance, "balance," or "oversample" the data set so that the categories or outcomes of interest are more prevalent in the training data than they are in the world. (This bias is deliberately introduced to enable the mining tool to characterize the relationships; the intentional bias introduced is counteracted during other stages of mining.)

- Create a set of check models in the unmodified data set (if these are not already available).

⟺ See TB.9.4, p. 631

- Create a new data set that includes all of the low frequency class(es) of business significance, and exclude these instances from further consideration.

- Of the classes still in consideration, select instances of these to add to the new data set by selecting them from the original data set at random so that any instance has a chance of being selected that is proportional to its prevalence.

- Initially, continue balancing until each class is represented in proportion to the number of classes. (For instance, if a business-significant class is one of 20 classes, and one such class accounts for 1% of the data, balance the data set so the class accounts for not less than $1/20 = 5\%$ of the instances in the modified data set.)

- Ultimately, continue rebalancing the data set (and rebuilding initial models) until the mining tool represents all of the business-significant classes in its estimates.

If the model is:

- a binary outcome classification model with a binary prediction

⟹ Go to DB.11.10, p. 614

- a binary outcome classification predicted as a continuous score

⟹ Go to DB.11.11, p. 615

- a multiple outcome classification predicted as classes

⟹ Go to DB.11.12, p. 616

- a continuous outcome classification, predicted as a continuous score

⟹ Go to AB.12.1, ▪5, p. 586

- a multiple outcome classification model with the output predicted as a score

⟹ Go to AB.12.1, ▪5, p. 586

Reference: ibid 11.4.1

Action Box 11.24—Mining: Confirmation Explanatory Model

Situation:

The data in the input battery may not relate to the output battery.

Next Steps:

- Use explanatory modeling techniques to explore the data set to confirm that the input battery does not relate to the output battery.

⟷ See TB.11.3, p. 632

- Create features from insights gained from the explanatory model.

⟷ See TB.11.3, p. 632

- If explanatory techniques indicate potential relationships, yet the initial model doesn't characterize them, the model may well be underspecified. Refine this model as it stands, but expect a poor model at best. (Note that a poor model may well be highly business significant, depending on the business situation.)

⟹ Go to AB.12.1, p. 586

- If explanatory techniques confirm that the input battery doesn't relate to the output battery, the only choice is to get data that does address the issue.

⟹ Go to MII:AB.13, p. 551

Reference: ibid 11.4.1, 12.2.4

Action Box 11.25—Mining: Check the Mining Tool

Situation:

The mining tool is suspect.

Next Steps:

- Create a model for the suspect tool using a previously characterized data set where the input battery did characterize the output battery. Check that the tool is still performing as it was.

- Create a model using the same data set and a different tool and using a different algorithm if possible. Check that both tools perform about as well as each other at creating a mined model, allowing for differences in algorithm.

- If the mining tool does not perform as previously in a known data set, and if it does not perform similarly to another tool, try to reinstall the tool.

- If this is a new release, version, or upgrade of an existing tool, try reverting to the previous release or version.
- If the tool has previously worked and now failed, or has never performed similarly to another tool or algorithm, report the tool as broken.

⇒ Go to AB.12.15, p. 592

- If reinstallation restores tool performance, report the circumstances to the vendor and resume modeling from the beginning, as any MVCM, initial model, and so on may be suspect.

⇒ Go to AB.11.1, p. 575

Reference: ibid 12.2.14

Action Box 12.1—Refining the Model: Main Steps

Situation:

Model needs refining.

Next Steps:

- If an inferential (explanatory) model:
  Diagnose explanation.

⇒ Go to DB.12.14, p. 627

- If Binary outcome classification with binary prediction:
  Diagnose confusion matrix.

⇒ Go to DB.12.1, p. 617

- If Binary outcome classification predicted as a continuous score:
  Diagnose confusion matrix.
  Diagnose predicted versus residual plot.
  Diagnose predicted versus actual plot.

⇒ Go to DB.12.1, p. 617
⇒ Go to DB.12.2, p. 617
⇒ Go to DB.12.3, p. 618

- If multiple outcome classification predicted as classes:
  Diagnose confusion matrix.
  Diagnose predicted versus residual plot.
  Diagnose predicted versus actual plot.
  Diagnose residual test model.

⇒ Go to DB.12.1, p. 617
⇒ Go to DB.12.2, p. 617
⇒ Go to DB.12.3, p. 618
⇒ Go to DB.12.4, p. 619

- If continuous outcome classification, predicted as a continuous score:
  Diagnose predicted versus residual plot.
  Diagnose predicted versus actual plot.
  Diagnose residual test model.
  Diagnose residuals histogram.
  Diagnose actual versus residual XY plot.

⇒ Go to DB.12.2, p. 617
⇒ Go to DB.12.3, p. 618
⇒ Go to DB.12.4, p. 619
⇒ Go to DB.12.5, p. 619
⇒ Go to DB.12.6, p. 621

Diagnose actual versus predicted range.	⇒ Go to DB.12.7, p. 621
Diagnose actual versus predicted curve.	⇒ Go to DB.12.8, p. 622
Diagnose actual versus predicted fit.	⇒ Go to DB.12.9, p. 623
Diagnose residual variance.	⇒ Go to DB.12.10, p. 624
Diagnose perfect model.	⇒ Go to DB.12.11, p. 625

If all steps completed:

Deploy model.   ⇒ Go to AB.13.1, p. 595

Otherwise:

Continue refining the model.   ⇒ Go to AB.12.1, p. 586

Reference: ibid 12

Action Box 12.2—Refining: No Relationship

Situation:

The input battery doesn't relate to the output battery—in other words, the data doesn't support the model needed.

Next Steps:

- If the input battery is drawn from secondary data sources and the primary sources are available, try using the primary data. Locate and use the primary sources. Reprepare the data including primary source variables.   ⇒ Go to AB.9.1, p. 571

- Develop measures to generate new input battery data about the business problem of interest.   ⇒ Go to MII:AB.13, p. 551

- Create and deliver a report outlining the limits of the available data to support the business issue and its implications for the business problem. Deploy the report as an explanatory model.   ⇒ Go to AB.13.1, p. 595

Reference: ibid 12.2.1

Action Box 12.3—Refining: Poor Relationship

Situation:

The input battery doesn't sufficiently define the relationship to the output battery over all or part of the output range—in other words, the data doesn't support the model needed.

M III
Action Boxes

Next Steps:

- Create multiple models using different underlying algorithms.   ⟺ See TB.12.1, p. 638
- Create multiple models using different variable subsets of the
  original input battery.   ⟺ See TB.12.2, p. 638
- Use explanatory modeling to uncover additional features in
  the input battery.   ⟺ See TB.11.3, p. 632
- Seek to discover or develop additional variables to add to
  the input battery that specifically relate to the range of the
  output that is poorly defined.   ⟹ Go to MII:AB.13, p. 551
- Continue refining the model.   ⟹ Go to AB.12.1, p. 586

Reference: ibid 12.2.2, 11.3

Action Box 12.4—Refining: Data Format

Situation:

The tool (algorithm) selected to make the model cannot deal
with the data in the format provided.

Next Steps:

- If using a category sensitive algorithm
  - ◆ Bin any numeric variables.
    - ▥ To use equal range bining   ⟺ See TB.12.3, p. 638
    - ▥ To use equal frequency binning   ⟺ See TB.12.31, p. 655
    - ▥ To use least information loss (LIL) binning   ⟺ See TB.12.32, p. 656
    - ▥ To use maximum information gain (MIG) binning   ⟺ See TB.12.33, p. 656
  - ◆ Bin any high category count categorical variables.
    - ▥ To use equal range bining   ⟺ See TB.12.3, p. 638
    - ▥ To use equal frequency binning   ⟺ See TB.12.31, p. 655
    - ▥ To use least information loss (LIL) binning   ⟺ See TB.12.32, p. 656
    - ▥ To use maximum information gain (MIG) binning   ⟺ See TB.12.33, p. 656
- If using a numerically sensitive algorithm
  - ◆ Recode categorical variables with appropriate numeric values.   ⟺ See TB.12.4, p. 640
  - ◆ Redistribute numerical and coded categorical values.   ⟺ See TB.12.5, p. 640
  - ◆ Replace missing values using value imputation.   ⟺ See TB.12.6, p. 641
- Continue refining the model.   ⟹ Go to AB.12.1, p. 586

Reference: ibid 12.2.3, 10.1

Action Box 12.5—Refining: Inadequate Relationship

Situation:

The model wasn't able to characterize the relationships from the input battery to the output battery adequately.

Next Steps:

- Check for model underspecification.
- Check for model overspecification.

⇒ Go to DB.12.12, p. 626
⇒ Go to DB.12.12, p. 626

Reference: ibid 12.2.4

Action Box 12.6—Refining: Unrepresentative Data

Situation:

The testing data set isn't representative of the same relationships that are in the training data set.

Next Steps:

- Check for source data set representativeness.
- Check for training, testing, and evaluation data set representativeness.
- Check that random sampling created the training, testing, and evaluation data sets from the source data set.
- Balance the data set.
- Get better data.

⇒ Go to DB.9.5, p. 600

⇒ Go to DB.11.1, p. 603

⇒ Go to DB.12.15, p. 628
⇒ Go to AB.11.23, p. 583
⇒ Go to MII:AB.13, p. 551

Reference: ibid 12.2.5

Action Box 12.7—Refining: Uneven Relationships

Situation:

The training and testing data represent some relationships better than others.

Next Steps:

- Remove input battery clusters.
- Get additional data that contains relationships addressing the parts of the input battery range with poor definition of the output battery.

⇒ Go to DB.12.13, p. 626

⇒ Go to MII:AB.13, p. 551

Reference: ibid 12.2.6

**M III
Action Boxes**

Action Box 12.8—Refining: Model Bias

Situation:

The model is "biased" into preferentially producing certain predicted values.

Next Steps:

- Respecify the model.   ⇒ Go to AB.12.17, p. 593
- Remove input battery clusters by balancing the data set.   ⇒ Go to AB.11.23, p. 583

Reference: ibid 12.2.7

Action Box 12.9—Refining: Underspecification

Situation:

In order to avoid learning noise the tool was too restricted in the flexibility it was allowed when learning the relationships.

Next Steps:

- Respecify the model.   ⇒ Go to AB.12.17, p. 593
- Replace missing values.   ⇔ See TB.12.6, p. 641
- Bin the variables.
    - To use equal range binning   ⇔ See TB.12.3, p. 638
    - To use equal frequency binning   ⇔ See TB.12.31, p. 655
    - To use least information loss (LIL) binning   ⇔ See TB.12.32, p. 656
    - To use maximum information gain (MIG) binning   ⇔ See TB.12.33, p. 656
- Aggregate the input battery.   ⇔ See TB.12.19, p. 648
- Bundle input battery.   ⇔ See TB.12.20, p. 648
- Use multiple models.   ⇔ See TB.12.21, p. 649
- Continue refining the model.   ⇒ Go to AB.12.1, p. 586

Reference: ibid 12.2.8, DPDM 3.1.1

Action Box 12.10—Refining: Categorical Colinearity

Situation:

There are many categorical values in the input battery that all represent a similar phenomenon or phenomena.

Next Steps:

- Bundle the input battery.   ⇔ See TB.12.20, p. 648
- Remove input battery clusters by balancing the data set.   ⇒ Go to AB.11.23, p. 583

- Seek data with more variability.
- Continue refining the model.

⇒ Go to MII.AB.13, p. 551
⇒ Go to AB.12.1, p. 586

Reference: ibid 12.2.9

Action Box 12.11 — Refining: Partial Colinearity

Situation:

There are a large number of variables in the input battery, many of which carry similar information over parts of their range.

Next Steps:

- Replace missing values.
- Redistribute numerical and coded categorical values.
- Bin the variables.
  - To use equal range binning
  - To use equal frequency binning
  - To use least information loss (LIL) binning
  - To use maximum information gain (MIG) binning
- Seek data with more variability
- Continue refining the model.

⇔ See TB.12.6, p. 641
⇔ See TB.12.5, p. 640

⇔ See TB.12.3, p. 638
⇔ See TB.12.31, p. 655
⇔ See TB.12.32, p. 656
⇔ See TB.12.33, p. 656
⇒ Go to MII.AB.13, p. 551
⇒ Go to AB.12.1, p. 586

Reference: ibid 12.2.10

Action Box 12.12 — Refining: Input Battery Clusters

Situation:

Although the input battery checks as representative of the population, it has some parts of the output battery range represented by very few instances (records) and other parts represented by very many instances.

Next Steps:

- Balance the data set.
- If insufficient data prevents data set balancing try:
  - Get more data.
- If more data isn't available try:
  - Expand or multiply the data.
- Continue refining the model.

⇒ Go to AB.11.23, p. 583

⇒ Go to MII.AB.13, p. 551

⇔ See TB.12.29, p. 653
⇒ Go to AB.12.1, p. 586

Reference: ibid 12.2.11, DPDM 10.6, DPDM 10.7

Action Box 12.13—Refining: Clipping

Situation:

The tool may be clipping the output predictions.

Next Steps:

- Note the limiting for the deployment report.
- No remedy needed.

⇒ Go to DB.12.6, p. 621

Reference: ibid 12.2.12

Action Box 12.14—Refining: Input Bias

Situation:

There may be a bias that affects all of the input battery variables.

Next Steps:

- Devise measures to record the biasing phenomenon. In other words, observe that the biasing phenomenon is an important factor that is missing from the data set. Use, for example, cause-and-effect mapping to determine the biasing factors. Add them to the data as additional variables.
- Get better data.

⇒ Go to MII:AB.13, p. 551
⇒ Go to MII:AB.13, p. 551

Reference: ibid 12.2.13

Action Box 12.15—Refining: Broken Tool

Situation:

Broken tool (or algorithm).

Next Steps:

- Report the problem to the vendor.
- Select another tool.

⇒ Go to DB.11.3, p. 605

Reference: ibid 12.2.14

Action Box 12.16—Refining: Leakage

Situation:

Leakage from anachronistic variables.

Next Steps:

- Create single variable models to discover any that have very strong correlations with the output battery.
- Think carefully about how temporal leakage could influence a variable.
- Remove any variables that leak "future" information back to the "past."
- Continue refining the model.

⇒ Go to AB.12.1, p. 586

Reference: ibid 12.2.15

Action Box 12.17—Refining: Specificity

Situation:

The algorithm requires more flexibility so that it can better characterize complex relationships in the training data set.

OR

The algorithm requires less flexibility so that it can better reject noise in the training data set.

Next Steps:

- Use the appropriate respecification technique:
  - If using nearest neighbor (MBR) ⇔ See TB.12.7, p. 642
  - If using decision trees ⇔ See TB.12.8, p. 642
  - If using rule extraction ⇔ See TB.12.9, p. 643
  - If using clustering ⇔ See TB.12.10, p. 643
  - If using self-organizing maps ⇔ See TB.12.11, p. 644
  - If using support vector machines ⇔ See TB.12.12, p. 644
  - If using linear regression ⇔ See TB.12.13, p. 645
  - If using curvilinear regression ⇔ See TB.12.14, p. 645
  - If using neural networks ⇔ See TB.12.15, p. 646
  - If using Bayesian nets ⇔ See TB.12.16, p. 646
  - If using evolution programming ⇔ See TB.12.17, p. 647
  - If using some other algorithm ⇔ See TB.12.18, p. 647
- Continue refining the model. ⇒ Go to AB.12.1, p. 586

Reference: ibid 12.2.4

Action Box 12.18—Refining: Noisy Variables

Situation:

The input battery contains one or more very noisy or completely irrelevant variables.

Next Steps:

- Remove "unimportant" variables:
    - ◆ If the mining tool supports a variable measure of importance   ⇔ See TB.12.22, p. 649
    - ◆ Otherwise   ⇔ See TB.12.23, p. 650
- Continue refining the model.   ⇒ Go to AB.12.1, p. 586

Reference: ibid 12.2.16

Action Box 12.19—Refining: Variable Interactions

Situation:

The tool (algorithm) selected does not inherently explore interaction effects and important interaction effects are present.

Next Steps:

- Add variables to the input battery representing the variable interactions.   ⇔ See TB.12.24, p. 650
- Use a mining tool that includes an algorithm (for example a neural network) that inherently incorporates interaction effects in its model.
- Continue refining the model.   ⇒ Go to AB.12.1, p. 586

Reference: ibid 12.2.17, DPDM 2.6.3

Action Box 12.20—Refining: Ordered Data

Situation:

The original source data is ordered in some way unknown to the miner and the ordering has been retained in the mining data set used to construct the training, testing, and evaluation data sets.

Next Steps:

- In any case, suspect sampling bias that may or may not affect the final quality of the model, but that has to be accounted for.

- Try to reorder the original data set using a random ordering of records and reconstruct the training, testing, and evaluation data sets from the reordered original.

⇒ Go to DB.11.8, p. 612

- If the training and testing data sets remains unrepresentative of the same phenomena, regardless of passing the rule-of-thumb representativeness checks, the data is insufficient. The only answer is to get more or better data.

- Afterward, prepare the new data set.

⇒ Go to MII:AB.13, p. 551

Reference: ibid 12.2.17, DPDM 2.6.3

Action Box 13.1—Deploying: Main Steps

Situation:

The model has to be deployed.

⇔ See TB.13.1, p. 657

Next Steps:

- If an explanatory model:
  - ◆ Review the requirements discovered during framing.

⇔ See MII:TB.7, p. 564

  - ◆ Create the discovery narrative, including:
    - Noting patterns and themes
    - Discovering plausible explanations
    - Clustering
    - Counting
    - Contrasting and comparing
    - Partitioning variables
    - Deriving generalities from particularities
    - Proposing plausible explicit and implicit (latent) factors
    - Identifying and explicating relationships between variables (or variable groups)
    - Creating a logical explanatory chain
    - Creating conceptual coherence
  - ◆ Create the verification narrative including:
    - Checking for representativeness
    - Checking for bias
    - Triangulation
      - ◦ Using different data sources
      - ◦ Using different modeling methods
      - ◦ Using different theories

M III
Action Boxes

> ■ Accounting for outliers
> ■ Explaining surprises
> ■ Incorporating negative evidence
> ■ Incorporating external empirical and experiential evidence
> ■ Corroborating from feedback

- ■ If a classification model:
  - ◆ Review the requirements for delivery developed before mining. ⇔ See MII:TB.10, p. 566
  - ◆ Review the requirements discovered during framing. ⇔ See MII:TB.7, p. 564
  - ◆ Prepare the supporting explanation. (See the notes above for an explanatory model. Remember that all classification models have to be explained, specifically in terms discovered during framing.)
  - ◆ Create regression-to-the-mean calibration. ⇔ See TB.13.2, p. 657
  - ◆ Review the required model delivery format. ⇔ See MII:TB.10, p. 566
- ■ If a run-time model, create a novelty detector. ⇔ See TB.13.3, p. 658
- ■ Deliver the model. ⇒ Go to AB.13.2, p. 596

Reference: ibid 13.2.1, 13.2.4, 8.2, 8.3.1, 8.3.2

Action Box 13.2—Deploying

Situation:

Model delivery.

Next Steps:

- ■ Hand the remaining parts of the project over to the implementers as appropriate.
- ■ Go and celebrate! This project is complete (at least as far as the miner and modeler are concerned) and there are no more actions to take. On to the next!?!

Reference: ibid 13.3

DISCOVERY BOXES

Discovery Box 9.1—Preparation: Characterize Variables

Discovery Action:

Create variable characteristics matrix. ⇔ See TB.9.1, p. 629

Result:

The actual variable characteristics don't match the expected variable characteristics.

Interpretation:

Data for mining is often anticipated by the business stakeholders, and even by the technical staff, to be better collected and more error free than turns out to be the case.

Possible Problem:

- Errors and inadequacies in the original data collection process.

⇒ Go to AB.9.2, p. 571

- The data set checked isn't the one that it was supposed to be.

⇒ Go to AB.9.3, p. 572

Otherwise:

Continue with the next data preparation step.

⇒ Go to AB.9.1, p. 571

Reference: ibid 9.1

Discovery Box 9.2—Preparation: Check Variables

Discovery Action:

Inspect each variable in the variable characteristics matrix.

⇔ See TB.9.1, p. 629

Result:

The variable has only a single value in all instances.

Interpretation:

Since the value changes not at all this variable carries no information.

Possible Problem:

- Faulty data collection.

⇒ Go to AB.9.4, p. 572

- Faulty selection of the mining data set from a source data set.

⇒ Go to AB.9.5, p. 572

- The variable is no longer used in the source data set.

⇒ Go to AB.9.6, p. 573

- No mining tool can make any use of this variable.

⇒ Go to AB.9.6, p. 573

Result:

The variable is entirely empty.

Interpretation:

This variable isn't used at all for anything.

Possible Problem:

- Faulty data collection.

⇒ Go to AB.9.4, p. 572

**M III
Discovery Boxes**

- ▪ Faulty selection of the mining data set from a source data set.   ⇒ Go to AB.9.5, p. 572
- ▪ The variable is no longer used in the source data set.   ⇒ Go to AB.9.6, p. 573
- ▪ No mining tool can make any use of this variable.   ⇒ Go to AB.9.6, p. 573

Result:

The variable has 80% or more of empty instances.

Interpretation:

Most of the values of the variable are empty.

Possible Problem:

- ▪ Faulty data collection.   ⇒ Go to AB.9.4, p. 572
- ▪ Faulty selection of the mining data set from a source data set.   ⇒ Go to AB.9.5, p. 572
- ▪ Many mining algorithms cannot deal with mainly empty variables.   ⇒ Go to AB.9.6, p. 573

Result:

The variable appears numeric but is actually a numeric representation of categories.

Interpretation:

This is one of the many categorical variables that use numeric digits instead of letters to represent categories.

Possible Problem:

Unless specifically flagged as a categorical value, or converted to non-numeric representation, many mining tools will assume the variable has numerical meaning.   ⇒ Go to AB.9.7, p. 573

Result:

The variable has very many (hundreds or more) unique categories.

Interpretation:

The variable records categorically almost unique measurements such as personal names.

Possible Problem:

When categories are unique, or nearly so, and there is no rational ordering to the categories, no mining tool can discover useable patterns.   ⇒ Go to AB.9.6, p. 573

Result:

Every instance value has a unique category label.

Interpretation:

This variable is probably a nominal variable that identifies unique items such as personal names. However, variables of this type appear in many guises: serial numbers, order numbers, shipment codes, ZIP or postal codes, Social Security numbers and many more.

Possible Problem:

When categories are unique, or nearly so, and there is no rational ordering to the categories, no mining tool can discover useable patterns.

⇒ Go to AB.9.6, p. 573

Result:

A categorical variable has a natural order by which the categories can be ranked.

Interpretation:

Although the variable uses non-numeric category labels, there is a justifiable way of ranking them.

Possible Problem:

Mining tools that are sensitive to numerical and ordinal variables will be unable to access the ordering information that the variable could expose to the mining tool.

⇒ Go to AB.9.8, p. 573

Otherwise:

Continue with the next data preparation step

⇒ Go to AB.9.1, p. 571

Reference: ibid 9.2.2

Discovery Box 9.3—Preparation: Perform SVCHAID

Discovery Action:

Single Variable CHAID analysis.

⇐ See TB.9.2, p. 630

Result:

The variable checked does not associate with a variable it was expected to, or associates with a variable that it was expected not to.

Interpretation:

The variable checked isn't behaving as domain knowledge suggests it should, indicating a possible problem with the data set.

Possible Problem:

- One of the variables isn't measuring the phenomenon that its label suggests it should.
⇒ Go to AB.9.9, p. 574

- One of the variables has somehow picked up data about phenomena that it shouldn't be representing.
⇒ Go to AB.9.9, p. 574

Otherwise:

Continue with the next data preparation step.
⇒ Go to AB.9.1, p. 571

Reference: ibid 9.2.3

Discovery Box 9.4—Preparation: Leakage Check

Discovery Action:

Check for anachronistic variables.
⟷ See TB.9.3, p. 630

Result:

The variable checked is unreasonably predictive.

Interpretation:

Any variable to be used to make a prediction that is too strongly predictive must be suspected of carrying information that won't be available at the time that the model is to be deployed. Using such a variable may result in excellent models during mining, but cannot actually be used in practice.

Possible Problem:

- The variable leaks anachronistic information.
⇒ Go to AB.9.6, p. 573

Otherwise:

Continue with the next data preparation step.
⇒ Go to AB.9.1, p. 571

Reference: ibid 9.2.3

Discovery Box 9.5—Preparation: Check Data Adequacy

Discovery Action:

Randomly split the source data set 80%/20% into two data sets, "A" and "B." Select each variable from the source data set so that it has an 80% chance of being placed into one data set, and a 20% chance of being placed in the other. Construct several 11 variable models on randomly selected variables in the 80% "A" data set and check their performance in the 20% "B" data set.
⟷ See TB.9.4, p. 631

Result:

> The models do not perform similarly in both data sets.

Interpretation:

> The relationships that exist in the 80% data set and the 20% data set are different. If they were similar the models would perform equivalently in both data sets. This suggests that there isn't enough data to model reliably.

Possible Problem:

> - Insufficient data.
>
> - The data stream represents data that has no determinable distribution, or for which the distribution is constantly changing.

⇒ Go to AB.9.2, p. 571

⇒ Go to AB.9.10, p. 574

Otherwise:

> Continue with the next data preparation step.

⇒ Go to AB.9.1, p. 571

Reference: ibid 9.2.3

Discovery Box 9.6—Preparation: Check Outcomes

Discovery Action:

> Check with a domain expert to verify that the data set contains the full range of outcome behaviors, even including those that may seem not to be of interest.

Result:

> The data set cannot be confirmed to have all of the outcome behaviors of interest.

Interpretation:

> A model can only classify, or predict, as outcomes events that are represented in the data. If all of the events of interest aren't represented in the data, the model, no matter how technically well constructed, may well not be able to produce the needed results.

Possible Problem:

> - Insufficient data.

⇒ Go to AB.9.2, p. 571

Otherwise:

> Continue with the next data preparation step.

⇒ Go to AB.9.1, p. 571

Reference: ibid 9.2.3.5

M III
Discovery Boxes

Discovery Box 9.7—Preparation: Check Basic Feature Representation

Discovery Action:

Determine, with a domain expert if necessary, if any variable would make more sense to a human explanation if it were re-expressed or recoded. (Ask the domain expert to explain the data and why and how each variable is important.)

Result:

The data set includes a variable recording absolute values (e.g., date/time stamps) when the model requires relative or cyclic representations.

Interpretation:

The absolute values of a variable are often not important to a model, but relative measures (e.g., how long ago from "now" an event occurred, or how distant from "here" a location is) or cyclic time (e.g., in what part of the season an event occurred) very often is important.

Possible Problem:

- The variable as presented in the data set represents only an absolute measurement.

⇒ Go to AB.9.11, p. 574

Result:

The data set includes a categorical variable that is better explained in terms of what the categories mean.

Interpretation:

When categories (or even numerical ranges) carry semantic significance it's important to expose that information to the model.

Possible Problem:

- The variable as presented in the data set represents only an absolute measurement.

⇒ Go to AB.9.11, p. 574

Otherwise:

Continue with the next data preparation step.

⇒ Go to AB.9.1, p. 571

Reference: ibid 9.3

Discovery Box 11.1—Mining: Structure Data

Discovery Action:

Split the original data set into three equal parts. Label one the training data set, one the testing data set, and one the evaluation data set. Cross-check the three data sets for representativeness:

- First, using the training data set as "A" and the testing data set as "B," perform the data sufficiency check.   ⇔ See TB.9.4, p. 631

- Then, using the testing data set as "A" and the evaluation data set as "B," perform the data sufficiency check.   ⇔ See TB.9.4, p. 631

- Finally, using the evaluation data set as "A" and the training data set as "B," perform the data sufficiency check.   ⇔ See TB.9.4, p. 631

This discovery action requires all three data sufficiency checks.

Result:

One or more of the data sets fails the test for representativeness.

Interpretation:

The amount of data available isn't enough to create three equal data sets to support creating the data mined model.

Possible Problem:

There isn't enough data available to create fully representative, equally sized training, testing, and evaluation data sets.   ⇒ Go to AB.11.2, p. 575

Result:

All data sets pass the test for representativeness.

Interpretation:

There is sufficient data to support creation of the initial mined model.

Next Action:

Characterize the input and output batteries for the needed initial model(s). Choose the appropriate mining tools.   ⇒ Go to DB.11. 2, p. 603

Reference: ibid 11.1

Discovery Box 11.2—Mining: Characterize Batteries

Discovery Action:

Characterize and record the characterization of the input and output battery(s) as a step in selecting an appropriate mining tool.

Result:

> Only one input battery of many variables.

Interpretation:

> The output battery is implicit in that although there are outcomes of interest they are not explicitly represented in the data set.

Next Action:

> ▪ Select an appropriate unsupervised mining tool.   ⇒ Go to DB.11.3, p. 605

Result:

> Only an output battery.

Interpretation:

> The data set represents only phenomena that can be known after the time that explanations, classifications, or predictions are needed.

Possible Problem:

> ▪ The available data can't be mined for the needed model.
>
> ▪ Get more, or better, data   ⇒ Go to MII:AB.13, p. 551

Result:

> Two batteries, input and output, with many variables in the input battery and one variable in the output battery.

Interpretation:

> The multiple variables in the input battery are to be used to explain, classify, or predict a phenomenon represented by a single variable's values.

Next Action:

> ▪ Select an appropriate supervised mining tool.   ⇒ Go to DB.11.3, p. 605

Result:

> Two batteries, input and output, with many variables in the input battery and many variables in the output battery.

Interpretation:

> The data set not only represents the state of several business objects to be used for characterizing the output, but also requires several different output phenomena to be explained either individually or together.

Next Action:

> ▪ Select a mining technique capable of modeling several outputs simultaneously from the same input data.   ⇒ Go to DB.11.3, p. 605

- Select several mining techniques, each capable of modeling one of the outputs needed at a time.

⇒ Go to DB.11.3, p. 605

- Select an advanced mining technique capable of modeling many inputs to many outputs simultaneously.

⇒ Go to DB.11.3, p. 605

Result:

Several batteries.

Interpretation:

The data set represents several phenomena, each of which is itself represented by several to many variables. The several phenomena are to be contrasted, compared, and characterized with some or all of the other phenomena.

Next Action:

- Selection of various techniques, supervised or unsupervised, to characterize the various relationships needed.

⇒ Go to DB.11.3, p. 605

Reference: ibid 11.2.1

Discovery Box 11.3—Mining: Select Tool

Discovery Action:

Choose the mining tool.

⇔ See TB.11.1, p. 631

Result:

The preferentially indicated type of algorithm is not available to the miner.

Interpretation:

The selection table indicates several types of algorithms embedded in mining tools the miner could consider in any mining situation. The indicated selection is not available to the miner.

Possible Problem:

- Mining tools are available, but not one incorporating any of the suggested algorithms.

⇒ Go to AB.11.5, p. 633

- The miner has no mining tools currently available and needs vendor sources to select from.

⇒ Go to AB.11.6, p. 634

Result:

The preferentially indicated type of algorithm is available to the miner.

Interpretation:

A tool incorporating one of the recommended algorithm types, or one similar, is already available.

M III
Discovery Boxes

Next Action:

- Construct the MVCM.

⇒ Go to DB.11.4, p. 606

Reference: ibid 11.2.1

Discovery Box 11.4—Mining: Create MVCM

Discovery Action:

Create and evaluate the missing value check model (MVCM).

⇔ See TB.11.2, p. 632

Result:

Some of the variables are predictive of, or associated with, the output values.

Interpretation:

The simple presence or absence of a value—whether or not a null or missing value is present in a variable in a particular instance—is in itself related to the values present in the output battery.

Possible Problem:

- The MVCM relationships have to be explained.

⇒ Go to AB.11.7, p. 577

- MVCM relationships indicate the possible presence of sampling bias in the way that the modeling data was assembled.

⇒ Go to AB.11.8, p. 577

- MVCM relationships indicate the possible presence of external bias that affects the representativeness with which the data represents phenomena in the world.

⇒ Go to AB.11.9, p. 578

- Values are missing and the selected mining tool's inherent algorithm does not handle missing values that have to be replaced before creating the initial model.

⇒ Go to AB.11.10, p. 579

Result:

Either none of the variables have any missing values or the MVCM discovers no associations of values between the input battery and the output battery.

Interpretation:

The simple presence or absence of a value in an instance is not meaningful, either because there are no missing values or because any relationship that does exist is completely unrelated to the output value.

Next Action:

- Create the initial model. To create:

    an explanatory model   ⇒ Go to DB.11.5, p. 607
    a classificatory model   ⇒ Go to DB.11.6, p. 608
    a predictive model   ⇒ Go to DB.11.7, p. 611

Reference: ibid 11.2.2, 11.2.3

Discovery Box 11.5—Mining: Build Explanatory Model

Discovery Action:

Create the initial explanatory model.   ⇔ See TB.11.3, p. 632

Result:

The quality or nature of the relationships discovered does not support the needed explanation.

Interpretation:

The model can explain the output in terms of the input, but the amount of uncertainty, the lack of precision, or features of the explanation do not lead to insights that the business managers, or other stakeholders, feel justifies taking any business action.

Possible Problem:

- There is insufficient data to clearly enough define the explanatory relationships.   ⇒ Go to AB.11.11, p. 579
- The data is plentiful but the relationship variance produces a lack of definition in the important connections between input conditions and outcomes.   ⇒ Go to AB.11.12, p. 579
- The explanation is clear, but the variables and features used in the explanation are not business objects that the business managers or stakeholders can use to effect change.   ⇒ Go to AB.11.13, p. 580
- The useful variables available in the input battery turn out not to be able to provide an explanation in the terms required by the business managers or stakeholders when framing the problem.   ⇒ Go to AB.11.14, p. 580

Result:

The explanation appears to address relevant business objects in the required terms and provides adequate insight into the nature of the business problem or opportunity.

Interpretation:

The model meets the business needs.

Next Action:

Deploy the explanatory model.

⇒ Go to AB.13.1, p. 595

Reference: ibid 11.3

Discovery Box 11.6—Mining: Build Classification Model

Discovery Action:

- To discover the appropriate type of initial classification model, characterized as binary (B), multiple classes (M), or continuous (C):

    1. The nature of the output battery variable(s)

    2. The output of the mining tool

- Note the type of model in use to select the appropriate options in the methodology. For example, (B:B) represents a binary output battery and a modeling tool that produces a binary output. Similarly, (M:C) represents a multiclass output battery and a modeling tool that produces a continuous estimated value.

Result:

(B:B) The output battery variable is binary (two values only) and the selected modeling tool produces a binary categorization as its category estimate.

Interpretation:

The prediction is required as one of only two values and the mining tool produces a prediction as one of two values.

Next Action:

- Create a binary outcome classification model with a binary prediction.

⇒ Go to AB.11.15, p. 580

Result:

(B:C) The output battery variable is binary (two values only) and the selected mining tool produces a continuous value as its category estimate.

Interpretation:

The prediction is required as one of only two values and the mining tool produces a prediction as a continuous value that has to be further translated into the binary value prediction that is required.

Next Action:

- Create a binary outcome classification model with output predicted as a continuous score.

⇒ Go to AB.11.16, p. 581

Result:

(M:B) The output battery variable has several classes and the selected mining tool produces a binary value as its category estimate.

Interpretation:

Either one of the output classes is to be segregated by the model from all other classes or, although there are multiple classes, they are binned into two groups only, and the model has to try to estimate group membership. This is to all intents and purposes a B:B model and should be treated as such.

Next Action:

- Create a binary outcome classification model with a binary prediction.

⇒ Go to AB.11.15, p. 580

Result:

(M:M) The output battery variable values fall into more than two, but a limited number of classes, and the selected mining tool produces a limited number of classes as its category estimate.

Interpretation:

The prediction is required as one of several categorical values and the mining tool produces an estimate of the most likely or most probable category based on the input battery values and limits its category predictions to the categories found in the output battery during modeling.

Next Action:

- Create a multiple outcome classification model with the output predicted as classes.

⇒ Go to AB.11.17, p. 581

Result:

(M:C) The output battery variable values fall into more than two, but a limited number of classes, and the selected mining tool produces a continuous value as its category estimate.

M III
Discovery Boxes

Interpretation:

The prediction is required as one of several categorical values and the mining tool produces a continuous value as a score.

Next Action:

- Create a multiple outcome classification model with the output predicted as a score.

⇒ Go to AB.11.22, p. 583

Result:

(C:B) The output battery variable is a continuous variable that can take on any value (presumably within its range) and the selected mining tool produces a binary value as a category estimate.

Interpretation:

The input is a continuous value but the model will produce only a two-class output, thus dividing the output variable's range into two bins. This can be considered a B:B model and should be treated as such.

Next Action:

- Create a binary outcome classification model with a binary prediction.

⇒ Go to AB.11.15, p. 580

Result:

(C:M) The output battery variable is a continuous variable that can take on any value (presumably within its range), and the selected mining tool produces multiple classes as a value estimate.

Interpretation:

This is a case known as binning where a continuous value is partitioned into bins, or categories. The binning is required in this case because the tool (or the algorithm in the tool) cannot produce continuous estimates. Usually such tools produce enough classes so that the multiclass output more or less emulates a continuous output. For the purpose of refining the model this can be considered a C:C and should be treated as such.

Next Action:

- Create a continuous outcome classification model with the outcome predicted as multiple classes emulating a score.

⇒ Go to AB.11.18, p. 582

Result:

> (C:C) The output battery variable is a continuous variable that can take on any value (presumably within its range) and the mining tool produces values that form a continuous estimate of the output value.

Interpretation:

> The prediction is required as a number and the mining tool produces a prediction that is a number.

Possible Problem:

> ■ Create a continuous outcome classification model with the outcome predicted as a continuous score.

⇒ Go to AB.11.18, p. 582

Result:

> The output battery characterization and mining tool output form some other combination.

Interpretation:

> The tool is not suited to producing the type of model required.

Possible Problem:

> ■ Either the problem must be reformulated, or some other tool used.

⇒ Go to AB.11.19, p. 582

Reference: ibid 11.4

Discovery Box 11.7—Mining: Characterize Predictive Model

Discovery Action:

> Discover the appropriate type of predictive model.

Result:

> System modeling tools need to be selected.

Interpretation:

> Predictive modeling requires extrapolation of system behaviors in states that have not previously been experienced. Data mining is a tool that can help characterize system behaviors, but is not itself a system characterization tool.

Next Action:

> ■ Discovering sources and system representations suitable to frame the business problem.

⇒ Go to AB.11.20, p. 582

Result:

> The system structure requires the essential relationships to be characterized.

Interpretation:

> Data mining has a role to play in characterizing systems models when data is available describing the relationships.

Next Action:

> Characterize each relationship using a classification model of an appropriate type.
⟹ Go to AB.11.21, p. 583

Reference: ibid 11.5

Discovery Box 11.8—Mining: Restructure Data

Discovery Action:

> Split the original data set into three unequal parts 60%, 20%, 20%. Label the 60% data set as the training data set, one of the 20% data sets as the testing data set, and the other 20% as the evaluation data set. Cross-check the three data sets for representativeness:
>
> - First, using the training data set as "A" and the testing data set as "B," perform the data sufficiency check. ⟺ See TB.9.4, p. 631
> - Then, using the testing data set as "A" and the evaluation data set as "B," perform the data sufficiency check. ⟺ See TB.9.4, p. 631
> - Finally, using the evaluation data set as "A" and the training data set as "B," perform the data sufficiency check. ⟺ See TB.9.4, p. 631
>
> This discovery action requires all three data sufficiency checks.

Result:

> One or more of the data sets fails the test for representativeness.

Interpretation:

> The amount of data available isn't enough to create the 60/20/20 data sets to support creating the data-mined model.

Possible Problem:

> - There isn't enough data available to create fully representative 60/20/20 training, testing, and evaluation data sets.
⟹ Go to AB.11.3, p. 576

Result:

> All data sets pass the test for representativeness.

Interpretation:

There is sufficient data to support creation of the initial mined model.

Next Action:

Characterize the input and output batteries for the needed initial model(s). Choose the appropriate mining tools.

⇒ Go to AB.11.1, ■2, p. 575

Reference: ibid 11.1

Discovery Box 11.9—Mining: Alternative Data Structure

Discovery Action:

Split the original data set into three unequal parts with training/testing/evaluation as 70%/20%/10%, 70%/15%/15%, or at minimum 75%/15%/10%. Cross-check the three data sets for representativeness:

- First, using the training data set as "A" and the testing data set as "B," perform the data sufficiency check.

⇔ See TB.9.4, p. 631

- Then, using the testing data set as "A" and the evaluation data set as "B," perform the data sufficiency check.

⇔ See TB.9.4, p. 631

- Finally, using the evaluation data set as "A" and the training data set as "B," perform the data sufficiency check.

⇔ See TB.9.4, p. 631

This discovery action requires all three data sufficiency checks.

Result:

One or more of the data sets fails the test for representativeness.

Interpretation:

The amount of data available isn't enough to create representative training, testing, and evaluation data sets to support creating the data-mined model.

Possible Problem:

- There isn't enough data available to create the initial model.
    - ◆ Get more or better data.

⇒ Go to MII:AB.13, p. 551

- A model can be created but stakeholder expectations may have to be adjusted as a result of the limits imposed by the data.
    - ◆ Get more or better data.

⇒ Go to MII:AB.13, p. 551

M III
Discovery Boxes

Result:

All data sets pass the test for representativeness.

Interpretation:

The data probably is sufficiently representative to create a mined model.

Next Action:

Characterize the input and output batteries for the needed initial model(s). Choose the appropriate mining tools.

⇒ Go to AB.11.1, ▪2, p. 575

Reference: ibid 11.1

Discovery Box 11.10—Mining: Check Binary Prediction

Discovery Action:

Check that the model actually predicts both output battery classes.

Result:

Only one output class is predicted.

Interpretation:

The model output is actually a constant value, one of the classes, regardless of the actual input and output values. The model has almost certainly picked the prevalent class that exists in the output battery as its constant prediction.

Possible Problem:

- The prevalence of the category that is not predicted in the output battery is so low that the model makes least mistakes by simply always predicting the most prevalent class.

⇒ Go to AB.11.23, p. 583

- The data in the input battery doesn't relate to the output battery.

⇒ Go to AB.11.24, p. 585

- The mining tool is suspect.

⇒ Go to AB.11.25, p. 585

Result:

Both classes are predicted.

Interpretation:

The model works. How well it works is indicated by the comparison of the confusion matrices of actual and naïve models. Refining the model may improve on the baseline performance already established.

Next Action:

- Refine the model.

⇒ Go to AB.12.1, ■2, p. 586

Reference: ibid 11.1

Discovery Box 11.11 — Mining: Check Binary Model

Discovery Action:

- Create a supervised binning of the score based on the actual binary outcome values.
- Check that the score can actually be binned into two classes that relate to the actual binary outcome.

⇔ See TB.11.12, p. 637

Result:

The score turns out not to associate with the actual classes in any meaningful way.

Interpretation:

The model can't actually discriminate between the two output classes. Although the score varies in value, the value of the score doesn't indicate anything about the actual class—it might as well be random noise.

Possible Problem:

- The prevalence of one category is so low that the model makes the fewest mistakes by simply always predicting the most prevalent class. The variance in value is pretty much random and the score represents only the prevalent actual class, ignoring the less prevalent class. To all intents and purposes the model is indicating only a single class as its estimate.

⇒ Go to AB.11.23, p. 583

- The data in the input battery doesn't relate to the output battery.
- The mining tool is suspect.

⇒ Go to AB.11.24, p. 585
⇒ Go to AB.11.25, p. 585

Result:

The binning does result in a meaningful association with the actual binary classes.

Interpretation:

The model works. How well it works is indicated by the comparison of the confusion matrices of actual and naïve models. Refining the model may improve on the baseline performance already established.

Next Action:

- Refine the model.   ⇒ Go to AB.12.1, ■3, p. 586

Reference: ibid 11.4

Discovery Box 11.12—Mining: Check Multiclass Model

Discovery Action:

Check that the model actually predicts all output battery classes.

Result:

Not all classes in the output battery are represented in the model's classification.

Interpretation:

The model cannot separate some classes from the others. This may or may not be important to the miner, modeler, and stake-holders, depending on the business significance of the classes that the model ignores. There is a problem here only if the missed classes have business significance.

Possible Problem:

- The prevalence of the missed categories is so low that the model makes the fewest mistakes by predicting the most prevalent classes.   ⇒ Go to AB.11.23, p. 583
- The data in the input battery doesn't relate to the output battery.   ⇒ Go to AB.11.24, p. 584
- The mining tool is suspect.   ⇒ Go to AB.11.25, p. 584

Result:

All classes in the output battery are present in the model's estimates.

Interpretation:

The model works. How well it works is indicated by the comparison of the confusion matrices of actual and naïve models. Refining the model may improve on the baseline performance already established.

Next Action:

- Refine the model.   ⇒ Go to AB.12.1, ■4, p. 586

Reference: ibid 11.4

Discovery Box 12.1—Refining: Check Confusion Matrix

Discovery Action:

Create and compare the naïve model confusion matrix and the model confusion matrix.

- For a binary outcome with binary prediction   ⇔ See TB.11.5, p. 633
- For a binary outcome estimated as a continuous score   ⇔ See TB.11.7, p. 634
- For a multiple outcome estimated as classes   ⇔ See TB.11.8, p. 635

Result:

There is no significant difference in naïve and mined model performance.

Interpretation:

The model does a very poor job of predicting the output.

Possible Problem:

- The input battery doesn't relate to the output battery—in other words, the data doesn't support the model needed.   ⇒ Go to AB.12.2, p. 587
- The tool (algorithm) selected to make the model cannot deal with the data in the format provided.   ⇒ Go to AB.12.4, p. 588
- The model wasn't able to characterize the relationships from the input battery to the output battery adequately.   ⇒ Go to AB.12.5, p. 589
- The input battery contains one or more very noisy or completely irrelevant variables.   ⇒ Go to AB.12.18, p. 594
- In order to avoid learning noise the tool was too restricted in the flexibility it was allowed when learning the relationships.   ⇒ Go to AB.12.9, p. 590

Otherwise:

Sanity check before deployment! Check with the modeler and stakeholders.   ⇒ Go to DB.12.14, p. 627

Reference: ibid 12.1

Discovery Box 12.2—Refining: Check Predicted/Residual XY Plot

Discovery Action:

Create and inspect a predicted value versus residual value XY plot. Include a linear regression of the residual values estimating the predicted values.   ⇔ See TB.12.26, p. 652

Result:

The regression line fitted isn't effectively flat.

Interpretation:

The residuals appear to contain information that could be used to improve the prediction.

Possible Problems:

- The model wasn't able to characterize the relationships from the input battery to the output battery adequately.   ⇒ Go to AB.12.5, p. 589
- The testing data set isn't representative of the same relationships that are in the training data set.   ⇒ Go to AB.12.6, p. 589
- The input battery contains one or more very noisy or completely irrelevant variables.   ⇒ Go to AB.12.18, p. 594

Result:

Patches, clumps, or clusters of residuals in the residual lines.

Interpretation:

Some residual values are more common than others.

Possible Problems:

- The training and testing data represent some relationships better than others.   ⇒ Go to AB.12.7, p. 589
- The model is "biased" into preferentially producing certain predicted values.   ⇒ Go to AB.12.8, p. 590

Otherwise:

Continue refining the model.   ⇒ Go to AB.12.1, p. 586

Reference: ibid 12.1.1.1

Discovery Box 12.3—Refining: Check Predicted/Actual XY Plot

Discovery Action:

Create and inspect a predicted value versus actual value XY plot. Include a linear regression of the predicted values estimating the actual values.   ⇔ See TB.12.26, p. 652

Result:

Almost flat regression line in predicted versus actual XY plot.

Interpretation:

The model does a very poor job of predicting the output.

Possible Problems:

- The input battery doesn't relate to the output battery—in other words, the data doesn't support the model needed.   ⇒ Go to AB.12.2, p. 587
- The tool (algorithm) selected to make the model cannot deal with the data in the format provided.   ⇒ Go to AB.12.4, p. 588

Otherwise:

Continue refining the model.   ⇒ Go to AB.12.1, p. 586

Reference: ibid 12.1.1.2

Discovery Box 12.4—Refining: Apply Residual Test Model

Discovery Action:

Create a residual test model. Apply the model. Compare the confusion matrices of the original model and the residual test model.   ⇔ See TB.12.25, p. 651

Result:

The residual test model markedly improves predictive performance over the initial model.

Interpretation:

There remain relationships in the input battery that the original model has not discovered.

Possible Problems:

- The tool (algorithm) selected to make the model cannot deal with the data in the format provided.   ⇒ Go to AB.12.4, p. 588
- In order to avoid learning noise the tool was too restricted in the flexibility it was allowed when learning the relationships.   ⇒ Go to AB.12.9, p. 590

Otherwise:

Continue refining the model.   ⇒ Go to AB.12.1, p. 586

Reference: ibid 12.1.2

Discovery Box 12.5—Refining: Check Residuals Histogram

Discovery Action:

In the testing data set, create a residuals histogram for models predicting continuous variables. Project a sample normal curve on the histogram for comparison.   ⇔ See TB.12.28, p. 653

M III
Discovery Boxes

Result:

The "tails" (outer edges) of the distribution are smaller than the comparison normal curve shows should be expected.

Interpretation:

There are not as many large residual values as might be expected.

Possible Problem:

- The model is clipping its output (which isn't actually a problem, but needs to be noted.)

⇒ Go to AB.12.13, p. 592

Result:

Mean of the distribution is not zero.

Interpretation:

The model's predicted values are all systematically skewed to be either higher than the actual values or lower than the actual values.

Possible Problem:

- In order to avoid learning noise the tool was too restricted in the flexibility it was allowed when learning the relationships.

⇒ Go to AB.12.9, p. 590

- The testing data set isn't representative of the same relationships that are in the training data set.

⇒ Go to AB.12.6, p. 589

Result:

The residuals histogram (and, therefore, the residuals distribution) is obviously not normal. (There are many ways that the histogram may deviate from normal, but they all need to be dealt with in a similar way.)

Interpretation:

Some predicted values are more likely than others and, even though the mean of the residuals distribution is zero, the model nonetheless makes systematic errors in its predictions.

Possible Problem:

- Many categorical values in the input battery that all represent a similar phenomenon or phenomena.

⇒ Go to AB.12.10, p. 590

- A large number of variables in the input battery, many of which carry similar information over parts of their range.

⇒ Go to AB.12.11, p. 591

- The input battery, although it checks as representative of the population, has some parts of the output battery range represented by very few instances (records) and other parts represented by very many instances.

⇒ Go to AB.12.12, p. 591

Otherwise:

Continue refining the model.

⇒ Go to AB.12.1, p. 586

Reference: ibid 12.1.3

Discovery Box 12.6—Refining: Check Actual/Residual XY Plot

Discovery Action:

Create an actual value versus residual XY plot. Fit a regression line estimating actual value given the residual value.

⇔ See TB.12.26, p. 652

Result:

The fitted regression line is not horizontal.

Interpretation:

The value of the residual depends on the actual value being predicted. This looks like, and may very well be, a systematic bias in the model.

Possible Problem:

- The tool may be clipping the output predictions.
- In order to avoid learning noise the tool was too restricted in the flexibility it was allowed when learning the relationships.

⇒ Go to AB.12.9, p. 590

- The model wasn't able to characterize the relationships from the input battery to the output battery adequately.

⇒ Go to AB.12.5, p. 589

- There may be a bias that affects all of the input battery variables.

⇒ Go to AB.12.14, p. 592

Otherwise:

Continue refining the model.

⇒ Go to AB.12.1, p. 586

Reference: ibid 12.1.4

Discovery Box 12.7—Refining: Check Actual/Predicted Ranges

Discovery Action:

While looking at the actual value versus predicted value XY plots, compare the range of the actual values to the predicted values. Also look for a uniform density of plotted points over the whole area.

⇔ See TB.12.26, p. 652

Result:

> The apparent ranges of actual and predicted values are different, or the density of points is not uniform, and not symmetrical about a diagonal line from lower left to upper right.

Interpretation:

> The model prediction range does not resemble the actual range so the pattern of predictions (more technically, their distribution) will not resemble the pattern of actual values that really occur.

Possible Problem:

> - Many categorical values in the input battery that all represent a similar phenomenon or phenomena.

⇒ Go to AB.12.10, p. 590

> - A large number of variables in the input battery, many of which carry similar information over parts of their range.

⇒ Go to AB.12.11, p. 591

> - The input battery, although it checks as representative of the population, has some parts of the output battery range represented by very few instances (records) and other parts represented by very many instances.

⇒ Go to AB.12.12, p. 591

> - "Broken" tool (or algorithm).

⇒ Go to AB.12.15, p. 592

Otherwise:

> Continue refining the model.

⇒ Go to AB.12.1, p. 586

Reference: ibid 12.1.5

Discovery Box 12.8—Refining: Check Relationship Curvature

Discovery Action:

> Create an actual value versus predicted value XY plot. Fit a curve estimating predicted value given the actual value.

⇔ See TB.12.26, p. 652

Result:

> The fitted curve differs markedly from a straight line where it passes through the data.

Interpretation:

> The model hasn't captured the nonlinear relationships that exist between the input battery and the output battery.

Possible Problem:

> - The tool (algorithm) selected to make the model cannot deal with the data in the format provided.

⇒ Go to AB.12.4, p. 588

- In order to avoid learning noise the tool was too restricted in the flexibility it was allowed when learning the relationships.

⇒ Go to AB.12.9, p. 590

- Many categorical values in the input battery that all represent a similar phenomenon or phenomena.

⇒ Go to AB.12.10, p. 590

- A large number of variables in the input battery, many of which carry similar information over parts of their range.

⇒ Go to AB.12.11, p. 591

- The input battery, although it checks as representative of the population, has some parts of the output battery range represented by very few instances (records) and other parts represented by very many instances.

⇒ Go to AB.12.12, p. 591

- The tool (algorithm) selected does not inherently explore interaction effects, and important interaction effects are present.

⇒ Go to AB.12.19, p. 594

Otherwise:

Continue refining the model.

⇒ Go to AB.12.1, p. 586

Reference: ibid 12.1.5

Discovery Box 12.9—Refining: Check Relationship Bias

Discovery Action:

Create an actual value versus predicted value XY plot. Fit a linear regression estimating predicted value given the actual value.

⇔ See TB.12.26, p. 652

Result:

The fitted regression line is far from laying on the lower-left, upper-right diagonal. Specifically, the regression line does not pass near the 0,0 point, does not pass near the 1,1 point, or both.

Interpretation:

The pattern of the way the predicted values are made doesn't match the pattern of the actual values. There is, therefore, some sort of systematic bias offsetting part, or all, of the predictions from where they should be. If the regression line is high (above both the 0,0 and 1,1 points), the predicted values all are predominantly higher than the actual values over their whole range. If the regression line is low (below both the 0,0 and 1,1 points), the predicted values all are predominantly lower than the actual values over their whole range. If the regression line is tilted (one end high, the other low), the amount of offset depends on the value being predicted.

Possible Problem:

- The testing data set isn't representative of the same relationships that are in the training data set.

⇒ Go to AB.12.6, p. 589

- The model is "biased" into preferentially producing certain predicted values.

⇒ Go to AB.12.8, p. 590

Otherwise:

Continue refining the model.

⇒ Go to AB.12.1, p. 586

Reference: ibid 12.1.5

Discovery Box 12.10—Refining: Check Prediction Variance

Discovery Action:

Create a plot of the standard deviation (or variance) of the residual ordered by the value of the prediction. Add a smoothed estimate of the standard deviation.

⇔ See TB.12.27, p. 652

Result:

The value of the smoothed residual variance estimate is so great over some or all of the plot as to make the predictions unsatisfactory.

Interpretation:

When variance is high over all or part of the range of the prediction, confidence in the accuracy of the predicted value has to be correspondingly low. But note that interpretation of this particular diagnostic test *must* depend on the requirements of the business problem. What is acceptable or unacceptable is a business decision, not a technical one.

Possible Problem:

- The input battery doesn't sufficiently define the relationship to the output battery over all or part of the output range—in other words, the data doesn't support the model needed.

⇒ Go to AB.12.3, p. 587

- The tool (algorithm) selected to make the model cannot deal with the data in the format provided.

⇒ Go to AB.12.4, p. 588

- The model wasn't able to characterize the relationships from the input battery to the output battery adequately.

⇒ Go to AB.12.5, p. 589

- The testing data set isn't representative of the same relationships that are in the training data set.

⇒ Go to AB.12.6, p. 589

- In order to avoid learning noise the tool was too restricted in the flexibility it was allowed when learning the relationships.

⇒ Go to AB.12.9, p. 590

- The input battery, although it checks as representative of the population, has some parts of the output battery range represented by very few instances (records) and other parts represented by very many instances.

⇒ Go to AB.12.12, p. 591

- The input battery contains one or more very noisy or completely irrelevant variables.

⇒ Go to AB.12.18, p. 594

- The tool (algorithm) selected does not inherently explore interaction effects, and important interaction effects are present.

⇒ Go to AB.12.19, p. 594

Otherwise:

Continue refining the model.

⇒ Go to AB.12.1, p. 586

Reference: ibid 12.1.6, DPDM 5.1.4, DPDM 5.1.5

Discovery Box 12.11—Refining: Check for Leakage

Discovery Action:

Discovering model too good to be reasonable.

Result:

A model making perfect, or near perfect, classifications that are not explicable as either trivial or obvious.

Interpretation:

A model that's too good to be true is very likely to be just that. There is a very high chance that the information that the model is using to make the too-good predictions won't be available to the model during deployment.

Possible Problem:

- Leakage from anachronistic variables.

⇒ Go to AB.12.16, p. 592

Otherwise:

Continue refining the model.

⇒ Go to AB.12.1, p. 586

Reference: ibid 12.1.7

Discovery Box 12.12—Refining: Check Specification Level

Action:

Compare model performance in training and testing data sets.

Result:

Model performs about equally well in both data sets.

Interpretation:

The model may be underspecified, which means that it may not have best characterized the input battery to output battery relationships common to both data sets.

Possible Problem:

- The algorithm requires more flexibility so that it can better characterize complex relationships in the training data set.   ⇒ Go to AB.12.17, p. 593

Result:

Model performs noticeably better in the training data set than in the testing data set.

Interpretation:

The model may be overspecified, which means that it may have learned relationships that exist in the training data set, but not in the testing data set. These relationships are almost certainly noise or garbage.

Possible Problem:

- The algorithm requires less flexibility so that it can better reject noise in the training data set.   ⇒ Go to AB.12.17, p. 593

Otherwise:

Continue refining the model.   ⇒ Go to AB.12.1, p. 586

Reference: ibid 12.2.4, DPDM 3.1.1

Discovery Box 12.13—Refining: Input Clusters

Action:

Cluster the input battery.   ⇔ See TB.12.30, p. 654

Result:

There are significant clusters present in the input battery with a high degree of separation between them.

Interpretation:

- The clusters indicate that there will be a possible problem with the quality of the estimates produced. Where data is plentiful, the relationship will be better defined than in the less well populated parts of the input battery.

Possible Problem:

- The source data set data doesn't represent the full range of behaviors that exist in the world. Thus, the data set is biased. ⇒ Go to MII:AB.13, p. 551
- The data set is unbalanced. ⇒ Go to AB.11.23, p. 583
- The input battery doesn't relate to the output battery—in other words, the data doesn't support the model needed. ⇒ Go to AB.12.2, p. 587
- The input battery contains one or more very noisy or completely irrelevant variables. ⇒ Go to AB.12.18, p. 594

Otherwise:

Continue refining the model. ⇒ Go to AB.12.1, p. 586

Reference: ibid 12.2.6

Discovery Box 12.14—Refining: Test Deploy Explanatory Model

Discovery Action:

Presenting an initial explanation of a business situation, problem, or issue based on insights gleaned from an explanatory model.

Result:

Discovering that an explanation is not convincing, relevant, or applicable to the business problem.

Interpretation:

Trouble!

Possible Problem:

- The business problem was not properly framed before modeling began. ⇒ Go to MII:AB.14, p. 553
- The relationships revealed by the model were not interpreted to address the stakeholder's needs. ⇒ Go to MII:AB.14, p. 553
- The data doesn't support the model needed. ⇒ Go to AB.12.2, p. 587
- The tool (algorithm) selected to make the model cannot deal with the data in the format provided. ⇒ Go to AB.12.4, p. 588

M III
Discovery Boxes

- The model is either too general or too detailed and does not present the needed descriptions of relationships in the data.

⟹ Go to AB.12.5, p. 589

- The tool (algorithm) selected does not inherently explore interaction effects, and important interaction effects are present.

⟹ Go to AB.12.19, p. 594

Otherwise:

Deploy the model.

⟹ Go to AB.13.1, p. 595

Reference: ibid 12.1.9

Discovery Box 12.15—Refining: Verify Source Data

Discovery Action:

Determine from the source data experts that random sampling created the training, testing, and evaluation data sets from the source data set.

Result:

The data set was not deliberately created to represent a random sample. (Ignorance of the record selection process does not constitute a random sample. A selection mechanism that does not deliberately introduce any particular order to the records is not a random selection method. Random selection often requires a very deliberate and carefully constructed selection mechanism.)

Interpretation:

Unless the selection mechanism is one deliberately constructed and verified to be random, many kinds of order may inadvertently creep unnoticed into a data set.

Possible Problem:

- The original source data is ordered in some way unknown to the miner and the ordering has been retained in the mining data set used to construct the training, testing, and evaluation data sets.

⟹ Go to AB.12.20, p. 594

Otherwise:

Regardless of the data sufficiency checks, there is insufficient data. The project requires more or better data.

⟹ Go to MII:AB.13, p. 551

Reference: ibid 9.2.3.4

TECHNIQUE BOXES

Technique Box 9.1—Preparation: Create Variable Characteristics Matrix

Technique:

- Use a data manipulation tool to look at each variable in the data set individually. Some mining tools provide all the basic assay information; otherwise, use any data manipulation tool of choice that has the needed functionality.
- Identify each variable as categorical, numeric, or date.
  - For each numeric variable:
    - Determine range.
    - Calculate mean, median, and mode.
    - Count any missing values.
    - Identify values used as surrogate missing values.
    - Calculate standard deviation, skew, and kurtosis.
    - Create a distribution histogram.
    - Determine if there are any non-numeric labels mixed in.
    - Identify outliers.
  - For each date variable:
    - Determine range.
    - Look for missing periods.
    - Count any missing values.
    - Identify values used as surrogate missing values.
    - Identify outliers.
    - Create a distribution histogram.
  - For each categorical variable:
    - Count any missing values.
    - Identify values used as surrogate missing values.
    - If there are many categories, create a distribution histogram.
    - Identify modal, uniform, or monotonic distribution.
  - For all variable types:
    - Determine what each variable was intended to measure.
    - Convert cryptic variable names into meaningful descriptions.
    - Confirm that the data set has all of the variables expected to be included.

- Confirm that the data set doesn't have extra variables not expected to be included.
- Confirm that the actual variable contents match the expected variable contents.

Why Apply This Technique:

To discover the true status of the data set and the variables it is constructed from, so as to diagnose any needed basic remedial actions.

Reference: ibid 9.2.2, DPDM 4.4, DPDM 4.5

Technique Box 9.2—Preparation: Single Variable CHAID Assay

Technique:

- Use a visual mining tool to explore the relationship between each variable in a data set, or a sample of the most significant ones in a data set with many variables, and the rest of the data set.
- Confirm that the strongest interactions for each variable are as expected, and that the data set "makes sense."
- Note any unexpected interactions, or interactions that were expected but weren't noted.

Why Apply This Technique:

To discover the true status of the data set and the variables it is constructed from, so as to diagnose any needed basic remedial actions.

Reference: ibid 9.2.3.1, DPDM 4.4, DPDM 4.5

Technique Box 9.3—Preparation: Anachronistic Variable Check

Technique:

- Use a visual mining tool to explore the relationship between each variable in a data set, or a sample of the most significant ones in a data set with many variables, and the output variable to be predicted.
- Note any unexpectedly strong interactions.
- Check carefully if there is any possibility that the variable carries information that cannot actually be known at the time the prediction has to be made.

Why Apply This Technique:

> To discover variables that leak information from the future that is not actually available when the model is deployed.

Reference: ibid 9.2.3.3, DPDM 2.6.2

Technique Box 9.4—Preparation: Data Sufficiency Check

Technique:

- Use the source data set split into two data sets, "A" and "B."
- Randomly select groups of 11 variables to form 10 groups.
- In each group select one variable as the output.
- For every group create a model to predict the output variable's values using the other 10 variables in the group.
- Check and note the performance of each group in the "A" data set.
- Without rebuilding the models, check and note the performance of each group in the "B" data set.
- Compare the performance of each model in the two data sets.
- Count how many models perform similarly to within 10% of each other in both data sets.
- If at least 60% (6 out of 10) models perform well within 10% of each other note this test as PASSED; otherwise, FAILED.

Why Apply This Technique:

> To check that there is enough data to consistently represent the relationships that need to be modeled.

Reference: ibid 9.2.3.4

Technique Box 11.1—Mining: Select Mining Tool

Technique:

- Inspect the data (which should have been done in the assay).
- Decide which type or types of variables are predominantly important.
- Determine the input/output configuration required.
- Recall which sort of model is needed.
- Find the appropriate row in Chapter 11, Table 11.1.

- Look up the recommended tool choices in Chapter 11, Table 11.2.

Why Apply This Technique:

To select the modeling tool appropriate to the situation.

Reference: ibid 11.2.1, Table 11.1, Table 11.2

Technique Box 11.2—Mining: Missing Value Check Model

Technique:

- Create a copy of all three mining data sets.
- Replace all variables in the input battery that have a value with a "1."
- Replace all variables in the input battery that have no value (missing or null) with a "0."
- Use a mining tool to characterize the relationship between each input battery variable that has missing values and the output battery variable(s).
- Note the relationship and characterize it for any input battery variable that has a relationship with the output battery variable(s).

Why Apply This Technique:

To discover the presence of bias in the data set and to note and explain the effect that missing values have in the data set. The technique also discovers when, where, and how missing value information has to be explicitly included in a data set to improve the model.

Reference: ibid 11.2.2

Technique Box 11.3—Mining: Initial Explanatory Model

Technique:

- Parse individual variables' values and/or subranges of values in intuitively meaningful ways.
- Use graphical displays where meaningful and possible.
- Explore and characterize relationships between individual input battery variables and individual output battery variables.
- Explore and characterize linear relationships.
- Explore and characterize relationships between aggregate wholes in the input battery and the output battery values.

- Using all of the above techniques, derive as many explanatory features as possible. (Note that "features" are usually qualitative, but can be quantitative expressions of noticeable similarities and differences between identifiable groups of instances. It is always possible to create a coded variable, or several coded variables, that express the presence, absence, or intensity of a feature.)

Why Apply This Technique:

To characterize the primary relationships that will be selected from and used in crafting the final explanatory model.

Reference: ibid 11.3

Technique Box 11.4—Mining: Sources

Technique:

- Visit the Web site *www.modelandmine.com* created in part to support the book *Business Modeling and Data Mining*.
- Navigate to the "Archive" page, which provides detailed reviews of several tools.
- Navigate to the "Data Mining Links" page, which provides current links to many tool vendors.
- Explore the site for updates to the book, support materials, and updates to the methodology.

Why Apply This Technique:

To find sources, articles, discussions, and help with business modeling and data mining issues.

Reference: ibid Resources

Technique Box 11.5—Mining: Create a Binary Confusion Matrix

Technique:

- A binary outcome has two states, say "1" and "0."
- A binary class estimate similarly has two states.
- Two outcome states and two estimates yield four possible outcomes.
- The binary confusion matrix represents the numerical counts of each state, or the percentage of each state.
- In one cell of the matrix, count the number of predicted state "1" that actually were state "1."

- In one cell of the matrix, count the number of predicted state "1" that actually were state "0."
- In one cell of the matrix, count the number of predicted state "0" that actually were state "1."
- In one cell of the matrix, count the number of predicted state "0" that actually were state "0."

Why Apply This Technique:

A binary confusion matrix enables assessing the performance of a model whose estimates can be represented as binary classes when assessing binary outcomes.

Reference: ibid 11.4.3

Technique Box 11.6—Mining: Initial Model Performance

Technique:

- Create a confusion matrix for the naïve model.
- Compare the mined model's classification rate with the naïve model's classification rate. The ratio of one to the other is a measure of performance—how much better or worse the mined model did than random expectation.

Why Apply This Technique:

To discover a performance measure for the mined model, to begin to assess the model's quality, and to note improvement (or worsening) in performance in the model refining process.

Reference: ibid 11.4.3, 11.Supp.1

Technique Box 11.7—Mining: Continuous Prediction Binary Confusion Matrix

Technique:

- A binary outcome has two states, say "1" and "0."
- The continuous estimator has a potentially infinite number of ordered outcomes.
- The task is to find an optimal point to divide the estimated values into two parts, thus collapsing one set to one binary value and the other set to the other binary value, such that the actual outcomes are optimally separated.

- Create a cumulative response curve (see Section 11.4.5).
- Derive a lift curve, which represents a cumulative expression of by how much the continuous estimator has done better (or worse) than the random expectation.
- Use the estimator value that is represented when the lift curve is at its greatest extent of lift.

Why Apply This Technique:

To discover the optimal value to use for converting a score into a binary estimate of output battery value.

Reference: ibid 11.4.5

Technique Box 11.8—Mining: Mono-model Multiclass Confusion Matrix

Technique:

- The output battery has more than two classes as output states.
- The number of output classes is limited.
- One single model (mono-model) can estimate class membership for the several classes.
- A multi-class confusion matrix has as many rows and columns as there are classes.
- The cells represent counts for all combinations of the actual class and the estimated class.

Why Apply This Technique:

To discover a performance measure for the mined model, to begin to assess the model's quality, and to note improvement (or worsening) in performance in the model refining process.

Reference: ibid 11.4.6.2, Table 11.8

Technique Box 11.9—Mining: Create A Multi-model

Technique:

- For every class in the output battery, create a binary model that estimates whether an instance is or is not in a particular class.

- Create a file that contains one variable for each binary estimate.
- Use the binary estimators as the input battery.
- Use the original multi-class output battery.
- Create a model (using a suitable mining algorithm) using the new input battery estimating the output battery. (This serves as a mechanism for combining the models.)

Why Apply This Technique:

Models that have to simultaneously make estimates of all classes of outputs often do not perform as well when estimating any specific class as a model dedicated to estimating that the output does, or does not, belong to a specific class. The combined output of multiple models, each optimized for estimating a particular class, often performs better than any single model.

Reference: ibid 11.4.6.3

Technique Box 11.10—Mining: Continuous Initial Model Performance

Technique:

- Model performance is important, but different tool vendors use different metrics for presenting the performance of the model. Comparing them with each other is problematic. However, noting the vendor's metric value for the initial model at least allows that metric to be compared during refinement.
- What vendors' metrics often (usually) do *not* provide is any comparison with the naïve model, which makes them useless for judging the improvement, or lift, of a model. (And this is true even in some cases where the vendor reports "improvement" or "lift" scores.)
- The refinement techniques used in this methodology when an initial model is developed do not depend on any vendor's performance metric.

Why Apply This Technique:

To provide a benchmark to compare during model refinement.

Reference: ibid 11.4

Technique Box 11.11—Mining: MVCM Relationship Discussion

Technique:

- Identify the appropriate stakeholders who are knowledgeable about the data, how it was developed, and what it means within the framework of the business situation.

- Present the MVCM relationships using all the techniques for explanatory models. (The MVCM relationships form an explanatory model. The difference here is that in this case the miner—and perhaps the modeler—see these relationships as unexpected anomalies and are seeking insight from the stakeholders.)

- Assume that the MVCM relationships are an indication that the data set is biased. Is the bias known? Expected? Does it limit the applicability of the model? (It must inasmuch as similar missing value patterns have to continue to be expected as a valid phenomenon if the model is to remain valid.)

Why Apply This Technique:

MVCM relationships are almost always unexpected. In fact, where missing values exist, they often have apparently meaningful relationships with the output battery values. Discovering the validity of missing value pattern relationships may form an important part of determining model validity and applicability, as well as being a "surprising" discovery.

Reference: ibid 6.1

Technique Box 11.12—Mining: Binning Continuous Estimates of Categories

Technique:

- If available, use a supervised binning tool to bin the score supervised by the output battery classes. Use the binning algorithm to assign scores to classes.

- If no supervised binning tool is available, collapsing scores to classes is straightforward but requires significant data manipulation by the miner:

  1. Determine the mean of the scores for each output category.

  2. For any score, assign the category whose mean value is closest to the score value. (This is not the optimal way of assigning categories to continuous scores, but it is by far the easiest and usually works reasonably well in practice.)

Why Apply This Technique:

To estimate a category for an output given only a continuous score.

Reference: ibid 12.2.3.1, DPDM 10.1.2, DPDM 11–DPDM 11.4

Technique Box 12.1—Refining: Multi-algorithm Model Combination

Technique:

- Build two or more models on identical input and output batteries with tools using different algorithms.
- Combine the outcomes from the multiple models using a separate model that uses the outputs from the multiple models to predict the original output battery.

Why Apply This Technique:

This technique often works to reduce the variability of the residual and thus increases the accuracy of a prediction.

Reference: ibid 12.2.2

Technique Box 12.2—Refining: Data Subset Model Combination

Technique:

- Build two or more models on different subsets of the variables in the input battery.
- Combine the outcomes from the multiple models using a separate model that uses the outputs from the multiple models to predict the original output battery.

Why Apply This Technique:

This technique often works to reduce the variability of the residual and thus increases the accuracy of a prediction.

Reference: ibid 12.2.2

Technique Box 12.3—Refining: Equal Range Binning

Technique:

Equal range binning.

- If you use an automated binning tool:
  - ◆ Select the variable to be binned in the training data set.
  - ◆ Select equal range binning.

- Either: Select 20–30 bins as an initial bin count.
- Or: Select the bin count to match the required resolution.
- ◆ Apply the tool.
- ◆ Apply the binning to the variable in all three data sets.
- ◆ Iterate varying bin count for best effect.
- ◆ Record the final bin structure (or binning algorithm) for use in deployment if the model is to be deployed to a run-time data set.
- ■ If you perform manual binning:
  - ◆ Select the variable to be binned in the training data set.
    - Either: Select 20–30 bins as an initial bin count.
    - Or: Select the bin count to match the required resolution.
  - ◆ Add one bin each for over-range and under-range values.
  - ◆ If needed, add one bin for missing values.
  - ◆ Assign every instance value of the variable to the appropriate bin according to its value.
    - Either: Assign the mean of all the instances that fall into a bin as the bin value.
    - Or: Assign bin values in uniform increments.
  - ◆ Create a copy of the variable to be binned in all three data sets.
  - ◆ Replace each actual value with the appropriate bin value in all three data sets.
  - ◆ Replace the original variable in the battery with the new variable in all three data sets.
  - ◆ Iterate varying bin count for best effect.
  - ◆ Record the final bin structure (or binning algorithm) for use in deployment if the model is to be deployed to a run-time data set.

Why Apply This Technique:

- ■ To allow algorithms sensitive only to categories to model numerical variable data.
- ■ To bin variables in the output battery while retaining some information about the original distribution.
- ■ To create an unsupervised binning of variables in the input battery that are fairly evenly distributed.

Reference: ibid 12.2.3.1.1, DPDM 10.1.2, DPDM 11–DPDM 11.4

M III
Technique Boxes

Technique Box 12.4—Refining: Normalizing Range

Technique:

- Numerical variables
  - ◆ Almost all tools automatically normalize numeric range without any user intervention.
- Ordinal variables
  - ◆ Use the known ordering to assign values that retain the appropriate order.
  - ◆ If the variable is known to be ordinal but there is ambiguity or uncertainty about the appropriate order of categories, treat the variable as categorical.
- Categorical variables
  - ◆ Either: Make every effort to discover appropriate values to assign to each category.
  - ◆ Or: (Only if category order information is unavailable) Use a category numeration tool in the training data set to discover best available category numeric labels from the training set data.
  - ◆ Apply the category numeration in all three data sets.
  - ◆ Record the final numeric labels (or labeling algorithm) for use in deployment if the model is to be deployed to a run-time data set.

Why Apply This Technique:

- To allow use of ordinal and categorical variables by tools that require all numeric variables.
- To avoid adding noise and spurious patterns to the input battery by inappropriate numeration.
- To reduce complexity in the relationships of input battery variables to the output battery so the mining tool can better use the relationships.
- To reduce the spurious patterns (noise) in the input battery.

Reference: ibid 12.2.3.2, DPDM 6.2.12–DPDM 6.3.3

Technique Box 12.5—Refining: Normalizing Distribution

Technique:

- Either: Use equal frequency binning with high bin count, say 100+ bins.

- Or: Use an automated distribution normalization tool.
    - ◆ Select the variable(s) to be redistributed in the training data set.
    - ◆ Apply the tool to the training data set to create the redistributed variable values.
    - ◆ Replace the original variable in the battery with the new variable in all three data sets.
    - ◆ Record the final bin values or redistribution algorithm for use in deployment if the model is to be deployed to a run-time data set.

Why Apply This Technique:

- To improve numerically sensitive mining algorithm model accuracy and performance.
- To reduce noise in the input battery.
- To clarify the relationship between an input battery variable and the output battery.
- To reduce or eliminate problems with outliers.

Reference: ibid 12.2.3.3, DPDM 7 (all)

Technique Box 12.6—Refining: Missing Value Replacement

Technique:

- Use an automated missing value tool (required).
- Select the training data set.
- Apply the tool to the training data set to create the missing value replacement algorithm.
- Replace the missing values in all three data sets.
- Save the final missing value replacement algorithm for use in deployment if the model is to be deployed to a run-time data set.

Why Apply This Technique:

- To allow full usage of a data set by an algorithm that cannot cope with missing values.
- To avoid damaging, perhaps severely, the relationships that exist in a data set.
- To improve model quality.
- To reduce noise and distortion in the input battery.

Reference: ibid 12.2.3.4, DPDM 8 (all)

Technique Box 12.7—Refining: Nearest Neighbor Model Specification

Technique:

Try one or more of:

- Underspecified model
  - ◆ Use less neighbors (smaller k).
  - ◆ Use distance weighted mean estimates.
- Overspecified model
  - ◆ Use more neighbors (larger k).
  - ◆ Use unweighted or equally weighted mean estimates.

Why Apply This Technique:

- To capture more (if underspecified) or less (if overspecified) characterization of the relationships between input and output batteries.

Reference: ibid 12.2.4.1

Technique Box 12.8—Refining: Decision Tree Model Specification

Technique:

Try one or more of:

- Underspecified model
  - ◆ Allow the tree to grow smaller leaves.
  - ◆ Try splitting the root on variables more distantly ranked.
- Overspecified model
  - ◆ Increase the minimum required number of instances per leaf.
  - ◆ Try splitting the root on variables more distantly ranked.

Why Apply This Technique:

- To capture more (if underspecified) or less (if overspecified) characterization of the relationships between input and output batteries.

Reference: ibid 12.2.4.2

Technique Box 12.9—Refining: Rule Extraction Model Specification

Technique:

Try one or more of:

- Underspecified model
  - Reduce the minimum number of instances to be covered by any rule.
  - Reduce the minimum required accuracy for any rule.
  - Increase the maximum number of conditions allowed in any rule.
  - Increase the maximum variety of conditions allowed in any rule.
- Overspecified model
  - Increase the minimum number of instances to be covered by any rule.
  - Increase the minimum required accuracy for any rule.
  - Reduce the maximum number of conditions allowed in any rule.
  - Reduce the maximum variety of conditions allowed in any rule.

Why Apply This Technique:

- To capture more (if underspecified) or less (if overspecified) characterization of the relationships between input and output batteries.

Reference: ibid 12.2.4.3

Technique Box 12.10—Refining: Clustering Model Specification

Technique:

Try one or more of:

- Underspecified model
  - Reduce the minimum number of instances required in any cluster.
  - Increase the number of clusters.
- Overspecified model
  - Increase the minimum number of instances required in any cluster.
  - Reduce the number of clusters.

Why Apply This Technique:

▪ To capture more (if underspecified) or less (if overspecified) characterization of the relationships between input and output batteries.

Reference: ibid 12.2.4.4

Technique Box 12.11—Refining: Self-Organizing Map Model Specification

Technique:

Try one or more of:

▪ Underspecified model

　◆ Increase the number of neurons.

　◆ Reduce the number of variables in the input battery.

　◆ Create multiple input batteries with variable overlap across the batteries. Create separate maps. Explain each map. Merge the explanations.

▪ Overspecified model

　◆ Reduce the number of neurons.

Why Apply This Technique:

▪ To capture more (if underspecified) or less (if overspecified) characterization of the relationships in the input batteries. (No output battery in an explanatory SOM.)

Reference: ibid 12.2.4.5

Technique Box 12.12—Refining: Support Vector Machine Model Specification

Technique:

Try one or more of:

▪ Underspecified model

　◆ Increase the number of clusters.

　◆ Increase the flexibility of the boundary membrane.

　◆ Reduce the minimum number of instances required in any cluster.

▪ Overspecified model

　◆ Increase the minimum number of instances required in any cluster.

- Reduce the flexibility of the boundary membrane.
- Reduce the number of clusters.

Why Apply This Technique:

- To capture more (if underspecified) or less (if overspecified) characterization of the relationships between input and output batteries.

Reference: ibid 12.2.4.6, 12.2.4.4

Technique Box 12.13—Refining: Linear Regression Model Specification

Technique:

Try one or more of:

- Underspecified model
  - Decrease the robustness of the regression.
- Overspecified model
  - Increase the robustness of the regression.

Why Apply This Technique:

- To capture more (if underspecified) or less (if overspecified) characterization of the relationships between input and output batteries.

Reference: ibid 12.2.4.7, ibid 10.1.3.1, DPDM 8.Supplement

Technique Box 12.14—Refining: Curvilinear Regression Model Specification

Technique:

Try one or more of:

- Underspecified model
  - Increase the flexibility of the regression curve.
- Overspecified model
  - Decrease the flexibility of the regression curve.

Why Apply This Technique:

- To capture more (if underspecified) or less (if overspecified) characterization of the relationships between input and output batteries.

Reference: ibid 12.2.4.8, DPDM 3.1.1

Technique Box 12.15—Refining: Neural Network Model Specification

Technique:

Try one or more of:

- Underspecified model
  - ◆ Increase the number of neurons in the hidden layer.
  - ◆ Increase the number of hidden layers.
- Overspecified model
  - ◆ Decrease the number of neurons in the hidden layer.
  - ◆ Decrease the number of hidden layers.

Why Apply This Technique:

- To capture more (if underspecified) or less (if overspecified) characterization of the relationships between input and output batteries.

Reference: ibid 12.2.4.9, DPDM 10.3

Technique Box 12.16—Refining: Bayesian Network Model Specification

Technique:

Try one or more of:

- Underspecified model
  - ◆ Increase the number of nodes in the intervening layer between input and output.
  - ◆ Increase the number of interconnections.
- Overspecified model
  - ◆ Decrease the number of nodes in the intervening layer between input and output.
  - ◆ Decrease the number of interconnections.

Why Apply This Technique:

- To capture more (if underspecified) or less (if overspecified) characterization of the relationships between input and output batteries.

Reference: ibid 12.2.4.10

Technique Box 12.17—Refining: Evolution Programming Model Specification

Technique:

Try one or more of:

- Underspecified model
  - ◆ Increase the limit on maximum program length.
  - ◆ Increase the variety of functions that can be selected from.
- Overspecified model
  - ◆ Decrease the limit on maximum program length.
  - ◆ Decrease the variety of functions that can be selected from.

Why Apply This Technique:

- To capture more (if underspecified) or less (if overspecified) characterization of the relationships between input and output batteries.

Reference: ibid 12.2.4.11

Technique Box 12.18—Refining: Other Mining Algorithm Model Specification

Technique:

Try one or more of:

- Underspecified model
  - ◆ Increase the internal complexity of a continuous value estimating mining algorithm.
  - ◆ Decrease the minimum permitted chunk size for a discrete value estimating mining algorithm.
- Overspecified model
  - ◆ Decrease the internal complexity of a continuous value estimating mining algorithm.
  - ◆ Increase the minimum permitted chunk size for a discrete value estimating mining algorithm.

Why Apply This Technique:

- To capture more (if underspecified) or less (if overspecified) characterization of the relationships between input and output batteries.

Reference: ibid 12.2.4.12

Technique Box 12.19—Refining: Aggregate the Input Battery

Technique:

- Determine the predominant aggregation unit in the input battery. (Example aggregation units might be: per day or week, per department or store, per product or manufacturer, per item or product line.)
- Determine the aggregation resolution required in the output battery by the constraints of the business problem.
  - ◆ If the predominant input battery aggregation level is in finer units than, or is equal to, the required output battery aggregation level, roll all the input battery aggregation units into terms of the predominant unit. (For example, input battery predominantly by department, output required by store, roll all input into a by-department aggregation.)
  - ◆ If the output aggregation resolution required is finer than the predominant input battery resolution, roll down to output aggregation. (For example, output required by department, predominant input is by store, roll down stores to department level estimates.)

Why Apply This Technique:

- To reduce the spurious relationships (noise) in the input battery so that the mining algorithm can better characterize the underlying relationships.

Reference: ibid 12.2.8

Technique Box 12.20—Refining: Bundle Input Battery Variables

Technique:

- Create a variable correlation matrix for the input battery. Either use the facilities in the mining tool, or use a statistical tool, or

  ⇔ See Example Box 12.1

- Identify correlated groups of variables. Select variables that have a correlation coefficient of, say 0.75 (or -0.75).

  ⇔ See Example Box 12.1

- Bundle each group with a bundling model. Use each group as input battery when modeling the output battery. Each bundle is represented by a bundle estimate of the output battery.

- Combine the bundle estimates along with any unbundled variables from the original input battery into a new input battery. Use the second input battery to create the final model.

Why Apply This Technique:

- To reduce the spurious relationships (noise) in the input battery so that the mining algorithm can better characterize the underlying relationships.

Reference: ibid 12.2.8

Technique Box 12.21—Refining: Combine Multiple Models

Technique:

- Create an initial model.
- Modify the original input battery to include the output from the initial model.
- Mine the modified input battery to create the final model.

Why Apply This Technique:

- To reduce the spurious relationships (noise) in the input battery so that the mining algorithm can better characterize the underlying relationships.

Reference: ibid 12.2.8

Technique Box 12.22—Refining: Noisy Variable Removal with Importance Measure

Technique:

- During the diagnostic refining cycle keep note of which variables are consistently identified as unimportant.
- Discard batches of the least important variables (those that are consistently least important first).
- Continue until the quality of the model deteriorates, then replace the last batch discarded in the input battery.

Why Apply This Technique:

This technique often works to reduce the variability of the residual and thus increases the accuracy of a prediction.

Reference: ibid 12.2.16, DPDM 10.5

M III
Technique Boxes

Technique Box 12.23—Refining: Noisy Variable Removal without Importance Measure

Technique:

Option 1

(Preferred, but potentially long!)

- Build a variety of models using small combinations of the input battery variables.
- Note model performance and variables used.
- Discard the variables common to the worst performing models.
- Continue until the quality of the model deteriorates, then replace the last batch discarded in the input battery.

Option 2

(Not preferred, it ignores potentially significant interaction effects.)

- Build a single variable model for each variable classifying the output battery.
- Discard the lowest performing variables until model performance is affected.
- Continue until the quality of the model deteriorates, then replace the last batch discarded in the input battery.

Why Apply This Technique:

This technique often works to reduce the variability of the residual and thus increases the accuracy of a prediction.

Reference: ibid 12.2.16, DPDM 10.5

Technique Box 12.24—Refining: Variable Interactions

Technique:

- Create variable interaction plots.
- Interpret the interaction plots to discover which variables have significant interactions.
- Characterize the significant interactions.
  - ◆ If the two plot lines overlay each other and appear almost as a single line there is no interaction.
  - ◆ If the two plot lines are roughly the same shape as each other and a fairly constant distance apart there is an additive interaction.

- ◆ If the two plot lines are roughly the same shape as each other and diverge so that they vary their distance apart across the plot there is a multiplicative interaction.
- ◆ If the two plot lines are a different shape so that in some parts of the plot they approach each other and in other parts they diverge there is a higher order interaction (square, cube and so on). The order of the interaction is approximately proportional to the number of changes in convergence/divergence between the two lines.

- ▪ Include the interaction characterization as a new variable in the input battery.
- ▪ (Note that some of these may be discarded through remaining diagnostic cycles so that only relevant and non correlated interaction variables will remain.)

Why Apply This Technique:

This technique can dramatically increase the classification performance of a model. It can also reveal explanations that were previously invisible. It often works to reduce the variability of the residual.

Reference: ibid 12.2.17

Technique Box 12.25—Refining: Residual Test Model

Technique:

Build an initial model.

- ▪ Apply the initial model to the training data set, creating a set of predictions.
- ▪ Using the predicted values in the training data set, calculate the residuals.
- ▪ Add a variable to the training data set input battery containing the value of the residual.
- ▪ Build a second model to predict residuals using all of the training data except the original output variable and the predicted values.

Build the Residual Test Model:

- ▪ Try a different mining algorithm from the one used for the initial model if one is available.
- ▪ Include the prediction and predicted residuals in the input battery.
- ▪ Build a model to predict the original output battery.

Why Apply This Technique:

The residual test model is one method used to determine if the mining tool has made best use of the information contained in the input battery. The results of this diagnostic model may directly indicate specific remedial measure needed to improve the model.

Reference: ibid 12.1.2

Technique Box 12.26—Refining: Creating Diagnostic XY Plots and Linear Regressions

Technique:

- Use any convenient tool to create and inspect the plots shown.
- An Excel spreadsheet can easily be used for constructing XY plots, and all linear regressions shown, using the basic functionality included in the spreadsheet program.
- Detailed instructions for adding data, creating graphs, and performing linear regressions are available in Excel documentation or most books about Excel.

Why Apply This Technique:

Diagnostic XY plots, some with fitted regression lines as necessary, are invaluable, indispensable and primary tools for diagnosing problems with models. Great insight and clues into problems with models are to be had by studying and understanding the significance of the residuals and errors from models through these plots.

Reference: ibid 12.1

Technique Box 12.27—Refining: Creating Diagnostic Variance and Standard Deviation Plots

Technique:

- Use any convenient tool to create and inspect the variance plots shown.
- An Excel spreadsheet can easily be used for constructing variance plots using the basic functionality included in the spreadsheet program.
- Smooth the variance or standard deviation plot.

- Detailed instructions for adding data and creating graphs are available in Excel documentation or most books about Excel.

Why Apply This Technique:

Diagnostic variance and standard deviation plots provide insight into the accuracy of models and a way to easily quantify the error range and confidence that can be placed in any classificatory model.

Reference: ibid 12.1

Technique Box 12.28—Refining: Creating Diagnostic Histogram Plots

Technique:

- The truth is that it's a real pain, and a lot of work, to make histograms in Excel, never mind adding normal curves for comparison!
- There are low-cost add-ins for Excel that make creating histograms a snap, as well plenty of non-Excel alternatives.
- See the following Resources section, as well as the Resources section of *www.modelandmine.com* for additional information.

Why Apply This Technique:

Histograms provide a quick, intuitive and easily created (with appropriate tools) method of understanding distributions. Understanding distributions of predictions, errors and other outputs from classificatory models provides quick insight into many problems and helps with explanations of results.

Reference: ibid 12.1

Technique Box 12.29—Refining: Expand or Multiply the Data

Technique:

- Expansion 1: Copy the original data set. Append the copy to the original. Continue until sufficient data exists for mining.
- Expansion 2: Copy the original data set. Add a small amount of random noise to the values in the copied data set. Ensure that the noise magnitude is small relative to the scale of the original values. Ensure that the mean value of the noise component is zero for each variable. Continue until sufficient data exists for mining.

- Multiplication: Characterize the multivariate distribution of the original data set using a tool designed for the purpose. (Check the links to "Simulation tools" at *www.modeland-mine.com* for pointers to vendors of such tools.) Create sufficient random instances that have the same multivariate distributional characteristics as the original data set until sufficient data exists for mining.

Why Apply This Technique:

To increase the size of a data set too small for reliable mining when no additional data is available.

Reference: ibid 12.2.18, DPDM 10.6, DPDM 10.7

Technique Box 12.30—Refining: Unsupervised Clustering

Technique:

- Select an unsupervised clustering tool, preferably one that uses an algorithm which itself determines the "natural" number of clusters present in a data set. For instance, try a SOM.
- If the selection is restricted to a clustering method that requires the miner to select the number of clusters, initially try 10–20.
- Using only the input battery, apply the tool and create clusters.
- Use whatever metrics and information the clustering tool chosen provides to determine if the clusters represent a relatively homogenous data set—that is, one where the clusters are not clearly distinguishable—or whether the data set has clearly separated clusters.
- Clearly distinguishable clusters imply that the density of the data points represented by the instances are more dense in some areas and less dense in other areas. Areas of low density, if they exist, represent multivariate values in the input that are relatively rare. If they are extensive, the relationship between input and output will be relatively less defined for those values.

Why Apply This Technique:

To identify ranges of the data where input to output relationships are poorly defined.

Reference: ibid 12.2.6, 10.1.2, 10.1.2.3, 10.1.2.4

Technique Box 12.31 — Refining: Equal Frequency Binning

Technique:

Equal frequency binning.

- If you use an automated binning tool:
  - ◆ Select equal frequency binning.
  - ◆ Select the variable to be binned in the training data set.
    - Either: Select 20–30 bins as an initial bin count.
    - Or: Select the bin count to match the required resolution.
  - ◆ Apply the tool.
  - ◆ Apply the binning to the variable in all three data sets.
  - ◆ Iterate varying bin count for best effect.
  - ◆ Record the final bin structure (or binning algorithm) for use in deployment if the model is to be deployed to a run-time data set.

- If you perform manual binning:
  - ◆ Select the variable to be binned.
  - ◆ Plot a histogram of the variable's distribution in the training data set.
  - ◆ Determine 20 to 30 split points that have approximately the same count of instances in each bin.
  - ◆ Add one bin each for over-range and under-range values.
  - ◆ If needed, add one bin for missing values.
  - ◆ Assign every instance value of the variable to the appropriate bin according to its value in all three data sets.
    - Either: assign the mean of all the instances that fall into a bin as the bin value in the training data set.
    - Or: assign bin values in uniform increments.
  - ◆ Create a copy of the variable to be binned.
  - ◆ Replace each actual value with the appropriate bin value in all three data sets.
  - ◆ Replace the original variable in the battery with the new variable in all three data sets.
  - ◆ Iterate varying bin count for best effect.
  - ◆ Record the final bin structure (or binning algorithm) for use in deployment if the model is to be deployed to a run-time data set.

Why Apply This Technique:

- To allow algorithms sensitive only to categories to mine numerical variable data.
- To bin variables in the output battery.
- To create an unsupervised binning of variables in the input battery.

Reference: ibid 12.2.3.1.1, DPDM 10.1.2, DPDM 11–DPDM 11.4

Technique Box 12.32—Refining: LIL Binning

Technique:

Least Information Loss Binning.

- Use an automated binning tool (required).
- Select the variable(s) to be binned in the training data set.
- Apply the tool to the training data set to create the bins.
- Replace the original variable in the battery with the new variable in all three data sets.
- Save the final bin structure (or binning algorithm) for use in deployment if the model is to be deployed to a run-time data set.

Why Apply This Technique:

- To allow algorithms sensitive only to categories to mine numerical variable data.
- To create an Information Theory based optimal supervised ordinal binning in the input battery.

Reference: ibid 12.2.3.1.2, DPDM 10.1.2, DPDM 11–DPDM 11.4

Technique Box 12.33—Refining: MIG Binning

Technique:

Maximum Information Gain Binning.

- Use an automated binning tool (required).
- Select the variable(s) to be binned in the training data set.
- Apply the tool to the training data set to create the bins.
- Replace the original variable in the battery with the new variable in all three data sets.
- Save the final bin structure (or binning algorithm) for use in deployment if the model is to be deployed to a run-time data set.

Why Apply This Technique:
- To allow algorithms sensitive only to categories to mine numerical variable data.
- To create an Information Theory based optimal supervised binning in the input battery regardless of the instance ordering.

Reference: ibid 12.2.3.1.2, DPDM 10.1.2, DPDM 11–DPDM 11.4

Technique Box 13.1—Deploying: Deployment

Technique:
- Congratulations! This is the final stage of the project, and if you have worked through the methodology all of the work has already been done! All of the earlier stages of the methodology are designed to make sure that the model has been constructed to meet business, stakeholder, and technical needs—and holds no surprises. Right now the model is almost fully deliverable, and additional miner actions are really only needed if the deployed model is going to be active in a run-time environment.
- Review the deployment criteria developed earlier in the methodology.
- Check that the model actually meets all the revealed needs.

Why Apply This Technique:
Final check before delivery.

Reference: ibid 13, 8

Technique Box 13.2—Deploying: Regression to the Mean Calibration

Technique:
- Determine the expected regression to the mean effects regardless of model application.
- Find the correlation coefficient between the time-separated states of the output battery.
- Note that regression to the mean effects do not only apply to time-separated states—this is simply the most common application in business modeling. If other less-than-totally-correlated relationships are key in the model, use them as appropriate.

- Determine the regression to the mean effects that are to be expected in the undifferentiated course of events.
- Use this as the baseline—even if you have a control group to compare against—for determination of any real effect in the world.
- Research further into regression to the mean effects than the space for a brief introduction here allows.

Why Apply This Technique:

To calibrate expectations prior to model deployment so that the "real" effects of the model on the world can be discovered.

Reference: ibid 13.2.1

Technique Box 13.3—Deploying: Novelty Detector

Technique:

- Use an unsupervised clustering tool of choice. (*k*-means works fine.)
- To determine the number of clusters, use the greater of three clusters or a number of clusters equal to the square root of the number of variables.
- Determine the distance for every instance to the closest cluster center.
- Create an initial pseudo z-score ($_pz$) as the standard deviation for all instance-to-closest-cluster-center distances.
- Adjust the number of clusters, if necessary, until a $_pz = 3$ captures about 90% of the instances.

Why Apply This Technique:

To create a tool that can be used on an instance-by-instance basis to estimate if the instance came from a similar population as the data set used to create the model. If the $_pz$ score of a run-time instance is >3, the instance may not have come from such a distribution, and the model's output is more or less suspect. If many novel instances turn up, particularly if there is an increase in their relative proportion over time, suspect that perhaps the current distribution of run-time data has changed—a situation known as a nonstationary distribution. (Note that a novelty detector has an array of other uses in data mining that are not covered here.)

Reference: ibid 13.2.4, 13.2.5, DPDM 11.8

EXAMPLE BOX

Example Box 12.1—Correlation Matrix

Resource:

Excel spreadsheet "Correlation Matrix." (downloadable from *www.modelandmine.com*)

This example shows how Excel (or any similar spreadsheet program) can be used to discover input battery variable bundles.

The Example Workbook contains the following worksheets:

- credit_DP1. (A fully prepared version of the CREDIT data set, including adjustments such as multivariate missing value imputation, range and distribution normalized, and categorical values appropriately numerated.)

- Correlation Matrix. (Shows the correlations between all variables and used in finding Bundle 1.)

- Finding Bundle 2

- Finding Bundle 3

- Finding Bundle 4

Using the Correlation Matrix

In this case, 0.5 has been chosen as the lower cutoff for correlation. Correlations of 1 are excluded since this usually only occurs on the diagonal where a variable correlates with itself.

When horizontally or vertically scrolling the worksheet to identify highlighted variables, it helps to prevent the top row and left column from scrolling. (Method: Select cell B2. Select from the pull-down menu "Window > Freeze Panes".)

Apply highlights to variables. (Method: Select the whole area of the correlations. Select from the pull-down menu "Format > Conditional Format". Enter cell colors for two conditions:

  i) cell value is between 0.5 and 0.999999

  ii) cell value is between −0.5 and −0.999999.)

- How to identify a bundle:
  - Create a list of all the variables in the data set
  - In the Correlation Matrix Worksheet, look for the first column with highlighted variables
  - In the variables list, tick or mark all highlighted variables
  - For each ticked or marked variable, find and check that variable's column for highlights

♦ Tick or mark all highlighted variables not already ticked or marked

♦ Continue for each marked variable until there are no more to add

- (Note that this may not, and probably will not, include all the highlighted variables. This identifies all of the variables to be bundled together.)

- Look for variables with highlights that have so far not been included in a bundle.

- Using the so far not included variable as a starting point, repeat the "How to identify a bundle" instructions.

- Repeat this process until there are no highlighted variables that are not included in a bundle.

Practical Example: Identifying Bundles

- Use the prepared data set CREDIT

- Create a correlation matrix for all variables with all other variables. (The example spreadsheet shows how to do this in the worksheet "Correlation Matrix".)

- Highlight the "highly correlated" variables' correlations. (The example worksheet "Correlation Matrix" uses a correlation of 0.5 to define "highly correlated" for this example as explained above.)

- Create a separate complete list of all of the variables in the data set. (You can do this in another worksheet, or even on a piece of paper.)

Discovering the First Bundle

- Use the complete list of all variables that you just created.

- Look in the "Correlation Matrix" worksheet for the first column with highlighted variables—it will turn out to be BEACON.

- In the variables list, tick BEACON.

- Look in the BEACON column for highlighted variables and tick those in the list. Discover as highlighted and add ticks for:

  ♦ DAS

  ♦ RBAL

  ♦ RBAL_LIMIT

  ♦ BCBAL

  ♦ UNSECBAL

- Check the columns for these ticked variables:

  ♦ The DAS column contains no highlighted variables not already included.

- ◆ The RBAL column has highlighted some not yet included variables. Tick:
  - ▪ RBALNO
  - ▪ RLIMIT
  - ▪ TOPEN
  - ▪ EQBAL
  - ▪ UNSECLIMIT
- ◆ The RBAL_LIMIT column contains no highlighted variables not already included.
- ◆ The BCBAL column contains no highlighted variables not already included.
- ◆ The UNSECBAL column contains no highlighted variables not already included.
- ■ Check the columns for the additionally ticked variables:
  - ◆ The RBALNO column has highlighted one not yet included variable. Tick:
    - ▪ ROPEN
  - ◆ The RLIMIT column has highlighted one not yet included variable. Tick:
    - ▪ BCLIMIT
  - ◆ The TOPEN column contains no highlighted variables not already included.
  - ◆ The EQBAL column has highlighted some not yet included variables. Tick:
    - ▪ TBALNO
    - ▪ EQLIMIT
  - ◆ The UNSECLIMIT column contains no highlighted variables not already included.
- ■ Check the columns for the additionally ticked variables:
  - ◆ The ROPEN column contains no highlighted variables not already included.
  - ◆ The BCLIMIT column contains no highlighted variables not already included.
  - ◆ The TBALNO column has highlighted some not yet included variables. Tick:
    - ▪ IHIBAL
    - ▪ ICURBAL
  - ◆ The EQLIMIT column contains no highlighted variables not already included.

- Check the columns for the additionally ticked variables:
  - ◆ The IHIBAL column contains no highlighted variables not already included.
  - ◆ The ICURBAL column contains no highlighted variables not already included.
- There are no more unchecked variables for this bundle.

These 17 variables form the first bundle.

The table below summarizes the progress of the discovery of highlighted variables for bundle 1. (This is not an illustration of the list you made, but of the variables checked and order of discovery of variables.)

- On your first check you discovered BEACON as shown in the column "Check 1".

- On your second check you looked in the BEACON column and discovered as highlighted the 5 variables listed in column "Check 2".

- On your third check you looked in the columns discovered on your second check and found: no new highlighted variables in the DAS column; four new highlighted variables in the RBAL column; none in RBAL_LIMIT; none in BCBAL; one in UNSECBAL, all of which are shown in column "Check 3".

- On your fourth check you looked in the columns discovered on your third check and found: one new variable in RBALNO; one new variable in RLIMIT; no new variables in TOPEN; two new variables in EQBAL, all of which are listed in column "Check 4".

- On your fifth check only variable column TBALNO had any new variables, and there were two as shown in column "Check 5".

- There were no more variables to be discovered for this bundle, so no more checks were needed.

	Check1	Check2	Check3	Check4	Check5
1)	BEACON				
2)		DAS			
3)		RBAL			
4)			RBALNO		
5)				ROPEN	
6)			RLIMIT		
7)				BCLIMIT	
8)			TOPEN		

9)		EQBAL		
10)			TBALNO	
11)				IHIBAL
12)				ICURBAL
13)			EQLIMIT	
14)	RBAL_LIMIT			
15)	BCBAL			
16)	UNSECBAL			
17)		UNSECLIMIT		

Remove the bundled variables from the "Correlation Matrix" worksheet. After the removal of the variables forming bundle 1, your correlation matrix worksheet will look like the worksheet "Finding Bundle 2". (The worksheet "Finding Bundle 2" is a copy of the correlation matrix worksheet with the bundle 1 variable columns deleted).

Discovering the Second Bundle

- Create a list of the variables in the data set. (Note that this is the same as before with the 17 variables for bundle 1 removed.)
- Look for the first column with highlighted variables—it will turn out to be EQHIBAL.
- In the variables list tick EQHIBAL.
- Look in the column for highlighted variables and tick those in the list. Add ticks for:
  - EQCURBAL
  - MVP_A
- Check the columns for the additionally ticked variables:
  - The EQCURBAL column contains no highlighted variables not already included.
  - The MVP_A column contains no highlighted variables not already included.

These 3 variables form a bundle as shown in the summary table:

	Check1	Check2
1)	EQHIBAL	
2)		EQCURBAL
3)		MVP_A

M III
Discovery Boxes

M III
Technique Boxes

M III
Example Box

Remove the bundled variables from your correlation matrix worksheet. Your worksheet will look like the worksheet "Finding Bundle 3". ("Finding Bundle 3" is a copy of the "Finding Bundle 2" worksheet with the bundled variable columns deleted.)

Discovering the Third Bundle

Proceed as before. Discover:

	Check1	Check2	Check3
1)	MTHIBAL		
2)		MTCURBAL	
3)		EST_INC	
4)		HOME_VALUE	
5)			HOME_ED
6)			PRCNT_PROF
7)		HOME_INC	

These 7 variables form a bundle.

Remove the bundled variables from the worksheet. See the worksheet "Finding Bundle 4" that is a copy of the "Finding Bundle 3" worksheet with the bundled variable columns deleted.

Discovering the Fourth Bundle

Proceed as before. Discover:

	Check1	Check2
1	DOB_YEAR	
2		AGE_INFERR

These 2 variables form a bundle.

There are no remaining highlighted variables when these are removed

Build 4 bundle models, one for each bundle.

Include all remaining variables in the final model unbundled.

Reference: ibid 12.2.8

Resources

This is a list of books for further reading, and other resources to look for on the author's Web site.

Chapter 1   The World, Knowledge, and Models

Peter L Berger & Thomas Luckmann, *The Social Construction of Reality*. Anchor Books, Doubleday. 1966. ISBN 0-385-05898-5.

What is reality? Whatever it is, part of it is created by our participation in society as individuals and in groups like companies. This book is seminal in the field and a classic, but readable, informative and interesting. It lays much groundwork for understanding how enormously cultural and social mores affect what constitutes reality. Since every company has its own social and cultural mores, understanding the implications of the content of this short book is very helpful in fitting a model to the preconceptions of any company.

Of background interest to anyone concerned with making models of reality—business or otherwise.

Edward de Bono, *I Am Right—You Are Wrong*. Penguin Books. 1990. ISBN 0-14-012678-3.

This is one of a large number of books by Edward de Bono, most of which deal with thinking, creativity, and many related topics, and all of which are useful to any modeler, let alone any business manager. This particular title is interesting because Dr. de Bono seems to have independently come up with the idea called a neural network. He certainly raises a number of interesting and relevant topics in this book, as in many of his others.

Of interest to modelers and miners.

Chapter 2   Translating Experience

Jack Foster & Larry Corby, *How to Get Ideas*. Berrett-Koehler Publishers, Inc. 1996. ISBN 1-57675-006-X.

What's the difference between data mining and getting ideas? "amn getes." (And that you'll have to work out for yourself!) Essentially there is no difference. Getting ideas involves looking for interesting, novel, and useful relationships in data inside our heads. Data mining involves looking for interesting, novel, and useful relationships in data outside our heads. Any good book on getting ideas helps a miner and probably a modeler, too. Data mining tools do some of the heavy lifting of sifting and characterizing data and relationships, but recognizing interesting, novel, and useful relationships is an essentially human activity—identical in practice to getting ideas. This is a great book on the topic.

Of interest to folk interested in getting ideas, including miners and modelers.

Chapter 3　Modeling and Mining: Putting It Together

Dashiell Hammett, *The Maltese Falcon*. Vintage Books. 1930. ISBN 0679722645.

This is a terrific detective story—one of the best of its type, and a great story. Even if you've seen and enjoyed the film, the book will still grip you.

Starring Humphrey Bogart & Mary Astor, *The Maltese Falcon*. Directed by John Huston. 1941.

Bogey at his best. He isn't Dashiell Hammett's vision of Sam Spade, but the film is terrific in its own right.

Chapter 4　What Is a Model?

Sorry—no further resources on constructing a model in here! Actually, I looked for books on business models and modeling in the sense discussed here, and in truth I couldn't find any—so I wrote one. This is it.

Marvin Harris, *Our Kind,* HarperPerennial, HarperCollins. 1989. ISBN 0-06-015776-3.

Interesting speculations as to how and why humans developed the skills, faculties and cultural blandishments that we turn out to have, including our mental capabilities. Non-technical and of general interest to all.

Chapter 5　Framing Business Models

William Poundstone, *Prisoner's Dilemma*. Anchor Books, Doubleday. 1992. ISBN 0-385-41580-X.

The prisoner's dilemma is mentioned in several places in this book as well as in this chapter. There are many, mostly fairly technical, treatments of this interesting structure. This book mixes historical, personal, and technical fact in an interesting blend that provides a nontrivial but nontechnical explanation set against a background of what was going on that prompted exploration of this particular situation.

Of general interest to all interested in modeling business situations.

Robert Axelrod, *The Evolution of Cooperation*. Basic Books. 1984. ISBN 0-456-02122-0.

A now classic book that includes details of the famous computer tournament of programs submitted by many different people to play each other in many repeated rounds of a prisoner's dilemma tournament. Dr. Axelrod's conclusions are relevant for anyone who has to decide what to do in any situation that has an outcome whose value varies depending on what decision is made. That pretty much defines business decisions!

Of interest to modelers, business analysts, and business managers.

Chapter 6   Getting the Right Model

Joseph O'Connor & Ian McDermott, *The Art of Systems Thinking: Essential Skills for Creativity and Problem Solving*. Thorsons. 1997. ISBN 0-7225-3442-6.

This is an accessible and easily read book that covers the principles of systems thinking. Moderately comprehensive, it is a "beginners guide," but a useful one for anyone not familiar with the general principles.

Of interest to business modelers.

John D. Sterman, *Business Dynamics: Systems Thinking and Modeling for a Complex World*. Irwin McGraw-Hill. 2000. ISBN 0-07-231135-5.

At the other extreme from the previously noted book, this is a complete, comprehensive, technical, thorough, and utterly outstanding book on systems thinking and systems simulation. Whatever you want to know about the latest state-of-the-art in this field is covered in this book. A must read for all serious advanced business modelers.

Of interest to advanced modelers.

Tim Hindle, *Essential Managers: Making Presentations*. DK Publishing Inc. 1999. ISBN 0-789-42449-5.

Tips and pointers to creating and making presentations. Aimed at managers, but of use to all who need to improve their presentation skills.

Chapter 7 Getting the Model Right

▨ George Lakoff & Mark Johnson, *Metaphors We Live By*. The University of Chicago Press. 1980. ISBN 0-226-46801-1.

Metaphor is not a casual adjunct to our lives. To some degree, metaphor is all that we have to interpret experience. Metaphor is, actually, absolutely fundamental to the way that we view and interpret the world—both as individuals and as groups, such as businesses. In fact, models *are* metaphors. A model is in some ways "like" some phenomenon in the world, and that "this is like that" assertion makes models metaphors. This book offers deep insight into just how fundamental to our perception of reality metaphor really is, and points to their care and feeding.

Of interest to all interested in translating experience into models.

▨ Ravi Anupindi, Sunil Chopra, Sudhakar D. Deshmukh, Jan A. Van Mieghem, Eitan Zemel, *Managing Business Process Flows*. Prentice Hall. 1999. ISBN 0-13-907775-8.

Excellent coverage of understanding business process flows. The table of business levers in BMDM is adapted and expanded from an appendix in this book.

Of interest to business modelers and business managers.

Chapter 8 Deploying the Model

▨ Annette Simmons, *The Story Factor: Inspiration, Influence, and Persuasion through the Art of Storytelling*. Perseus Publishing. 2001. ISBN 0-7382-0369-6.

Explanations are narratives, and the most compelling narratives are stories. Deploying an explanatory model requires telling stories—stories about the data to be sure, but all stories about data are really intended to be stories about the world. When deployed, the explanatory model has to be inspirational, influential, and persuasive. This book addresses the creation and use of stories for a variety of purposes in a business setting.

Of interest to all interested in delivering explanations of models—and in improving communications in general.

Chapter 9 Getting Started

▨ Dorian Pyle, *Data Preparation for Data Mining*. Morgan Kaufmann Publishers. 1999. ISBN 1-55860-529-0.

Preparing data is where mining starts. It's the stage in which any miner will spend 60–80% of the project, and no one had discussed the issue in any detail when I wrote this book. Amazingly, there still seems to be no other book on the topic. Data prep is a technical topic, but this was written to use no more than forgotten high-school math to understand what's needed and how to prepare data. BMDM takes a quick look at the topic, but for more depth dig in here.

Of interest to miners.

Steven K. Thompson. *Sampling.* John Wiley & Sons, 1992. ISBN 0-471-54045-5.

A mathematical and authoritative treatment of standard and modern sampling methods, but is very applicable to real life situations. It has a special focus on sampling inherently difficult to sample populations.

Of interest to modelers, miners and technical data collection designers of all types.

Chapter 10   What Mining Tools Do

Check the Web site *(www.modelandmine.com)* for the following support material for this chapter:

- Data set and decision tree illustrating the lack of interaction characterization in the input battery
- Pointers to a wealth of commercial, academic, shareware, and freeware data mining tools (plus a whole lot more)
- The "credit" data set prepared and explored in this chapter
- The white paper that extends the discussion of rules

Chapter 11   Getting the Initial Model: Basic Practices of Data Mining

Check the Web site *(www.modelandmine.com)* for the following support material for this chapter:

- Links to the vendors mentioned for evaluation versions of their tools
- Excel worksheets containing the data and modeling results shown in the figures of this chapter
- Color versions of the SOM images shown in the figures (the monochrome reproduction possible in the book doesn't show the detail in the colored maps)
- The "credit" data set and models produced using it in this chapter

Chapter 12 **Improving the Mined Model**

Check the Web site *(www.modelandmine.com)* for the following support material for this chapter:

- Binning tool referred to in this chapter
- Category numerating tool referred to in this chapter

Chapter 13 **Deploying the Mined Model**

▨ Donald T. Campbell & David A. Kenny, *A Primer on Regression Artifacts*. Guilford Publications. 1999. ISBN 1572304820.

The title notwithstanding, this is about the effect and workings of regression to the mean. The early chapters are nontechnical, and digging into this book reveals much about this fascinating, relevant (so relevant that its an "in-your-face" effect), and important topic. Every data miner needs to understand, and be able to explain the effects of, regression to the mean. Start digging here.

Of interest to miners and modelers.

▨ Per Bak, *How Nature Works*. Copernicus, Springer-Verlag. 1996. ISBN 0-387-98738-X.

Per Bak, a professor at the Niels Bohr Institute in Denmark, discovered (or created) the theory of self-organized criticality while working at Brookhaven National Laboratory. This book is his account of the discovery, use, and applicability of self-organized criticality. This is a fascinating theory that promises far deeper insight into the ways of the world than many currently popular notions if and when it is fully developed and deployed.

Dr. Bak's account is an enjoyable read, non-technical and accessible to all.

▨ Henrik Jeldtoft Jensen, Self-Organized Criticality. Cambridge University Press. 1998. ISBN 0-521-48371-9.

A technical presentation and discussion of self-organized criticality (SOC), including the discussion and analysis of SOC in computer models.

Of interest to miners interested in exploring SOC ideas.

Chapter 14 **Methodology**

Check the Web site *(www.modelandmine.com)* for the following support material for this chapter:

- MII, the Catalyst modeling methodology in an electronic, hyperlinked version
- MIII, the Catalyst mining methodology in an electronic, hyperlinked version

Further Resources

www.modelandmine.com
This is the author's Web site, created in part to support this book. It is as chock full as the author can make it of material on modeling and mining—stuff to help. There are white papers, tools to download, data sets to play with, links to all kinds of other sites on the Web, tips, techniques, FAQs, tool reviews, book recommendations, and a host of other stuff. There are also contributions from other people who are modeling and mining—and take this as a direct invitation to *you* to become one of the contributors! If what you're looking for isn't there, let the author know. The site is updated monthly at least, and it's also the primary contact point for getting in touch with the author. And I look forward to hearing from you! ☺

Index

About the Author

Dorian Pyle has 25 years of experience in the artificial intelligence and machine learning techniques that are used in data mining. He has applied this knowledge as a consultant with Data Miners, Naviant, Thinking Machines Corporation, and various companies directly involved in credit card marketing for banks and with manufacturing companies using industrial automation. In the 1970s he was involved in building artificially intelligent machine learning systems that pioneered neural computing and associative memory technologies. He is experienced in the most advanced data mining technologies such as information theory, chaotic and fractal decomposition, neural technologies, evolution and genetic optimization, algebra evolvers, case-based reasoning, concept induction, and other advanced statistical techniques. He is the author of *Data Preparation for Data Mining* (1999, Morgan Kaufmann Publishers).

CPSIA information can be obtained
at www.ICGtesting.com

9 781558 606531